BUILDING PHP APPLICATIONS WITH SYMFONY, CAKEPHP, AND ZEND® FRAMEWORK

Building PHP Applications with Symfony™, CakePHP, and Zend® Framework

Building PHP Applications with Symfony™, CakePHP, and Zend® Framework

Bartosz Porębski

Karol Przystalski

Leszek Nowak

Wiley Publishing, Inc.

Building PHP Applications with Symfony™, CakePHP, and Zend® Framework

Published by
Wiley Publishing, Inc.
10475 Crosspoint Boulevard
Indianapolis, IN 46256
www.wiley.com

Published by Wiley Publishing, Inc., Indianapolis, Indiana

Published simultaneously in Canada

ISBN: 978-0-470-88734-9
ISBN: 978-1-118-06792-5 (ebk)
ISBN: 978-1-118-06791-8 (ebk)
ISBN: 978-1-118-06790-1 (ebk)

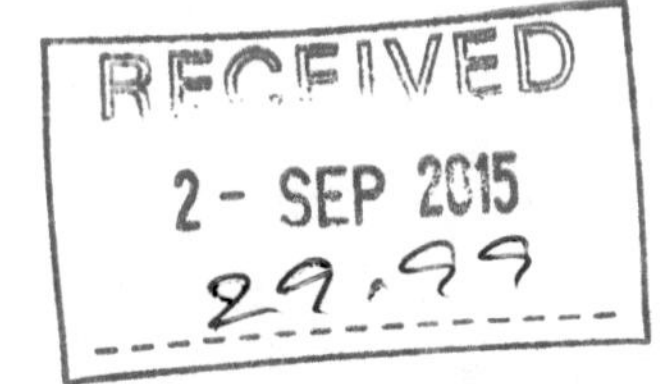

Manufactured in the United States of America

10 9 8 7 6 5 4 3 2 1

For general information on our other products and services please contact our Customer Care Department within the United States at (877) 762-2974, outside the United States at (317) 572-3993 or fax (317) 572-4002.

Wiley also publishes its books in a variety of electronic formats. Some content that appears in print may not be available in electronic books.

Library of Congress Control Number: 2010942182

For my beloved Olcia, who keeps inspiring me to achieve goals I could have never dreamed of. The way you are able to solve with your pure wisdom all the analytically unsolvable problems, your dedication, and your sense of humor still amaze me every day. And the sweet cakes (no PHP added) you baked for me while I was writing this book were simply delicious. I would also like to thank my parents for their continuing faith and support.

—Bartosz Porębski

For Agata.

—Karol Przystalski

I dedicate this book to my parents, for their constant love and support. They made this book possible. I also warn any readers of this book not to try and run the code examples backward! It may cause hellspawns to appear out of thin air.

—Leszek Nowak

CREDITS

EXECUTIVE EDITOR
Carol Long

PROJECT EDITOR
Tom Dinse

TECHNICAL EDITOR
Wim Mostrey

PRODUCTION EDITOR
Daniel Scribner

COPY EDITOR
Nancy Sixsmith

EDITORIAL DIRECTOR
Robyn B. Siesky

EDITORIAL MANAGER
Mary Beth Wakefield

FREELANCER EDITORIAL MANAGER
Rosemarie Graham

ASSOCIATE DIRECTOR OF MARKETING
Ashley Zurcher

PRODUCTION MANAGER
Tim Tate

VICE PRESIDENT AND EXECUTIVE GROUP PUBLISHER
Richard Swadley

VICE PRESIDENT AND EXECUTIVE PUBLISHER
Barry Pruett

ASSOCIATE PUBLISHER
Jim Minatel

PROJECT COORDINATOR, COVER
Katherine Crocker

PROOFREADER
Word One

INDEXER
Robert Swanson

COVER DESIGNER
Michael E. Trent

COVER IMAGE
© xiaoke ma/istockphoto.com

ABOUT THE AUTHORS

BARTOSZ PORĘBSKI is a video games, web applications, and C++ software developer. He works as Brain-Computer Interface researcher and lecturer at Jagiellonian University in Kraków.

KAROL PRZYSTALSKI is a Software Quality Engineer at Sabre Holdings and a PhD student at Jagiellonian University in Kraków. He has worked with Symfony since its earliest versions and wrote a book on the Symfony framework.

LESZEK NOWAK has years of experience in web development and graphics design with such frameworks as Django, CakePHP and CodeIgniter. He also works with 3D modelling, animation, image recognition, and artificial intelligence development. He says, "Science is fun, if used in games."

ACKNOWLEDGMENTS

NO BOOK IS THE SOLE effort of its authors, especially such a long book. It took long months and countless cups of coffee to keep us awake and writing and programming the code examples. We could not have made it through this if not for the help and patience of many kind souls.

First of all, we want to say a big THANK YOU! to the Wiley/Wrox team we had the pleasure of working with. Carol Long showed great patience and motivated us when we were down. Tom Dinse and Nancy Sixsmith worked hard to get our English right. Wim Mostrey made sure that all technical matters are 100% correct. Ashley Zurcher helped to successfully deliver the book to the market, and Helen Russo took care of our legal matters. It was really fun to work with you folks!

We also want to thank our superiors on the faculty of Physics, Astronomy, and Applied Computer Science of Jagiellonian University in Kraków: dr hab. Ewa Grabska, prof. dr hab. Maciej Ogorzałek, prof. dr hab. Maciej A. Nowak, and dr hab. Paweł Węgrzyn, who were really supportive and did their best not to swamp us with additional jobs while we were busy writing.

Finally, our thanks go also to all the developers who dedicated their precious time to write good documentation and share their knowledge.

CONTENTS

INTRODUCTION

Honest differences are often a healthy sign of progress.

— Mahatma Gandhi

For a long time, PHP was disregarded as a language not serious enough for rich web applications. Everyone knew it was popular and perhaps good for small one-shot projects, but all the praise was reserved for the aristocratic elite of frameworks such as Spring, Ruby on Rails, or Django. Only recently has the situation changed, and it changed dramatically. In 2007, it became clear that PHP has not just one, but three major web application frameworks extending capabilities of this language: **Symfony, CakePHP,** and **Zend Framework**. The pace of development was fast and steady. Object-oriented source code written in PHP5 was elegant and maintainable. More and more new projects began using them, and their successful completion made the PHP frameworks even more popular.

Nowadays, the popularity of PHP web development frameworks surpasses all others (the evidence is inside this book), and they have become a leading force in the industry. The aim of this book is to gather as much knowledge about this dynamic force as possible and portray all the features these frameworks provide to our fellow programmers.

WHO SHOULD READ THIS BOOK?

If you are actually looking for a vampire novel, put this book back on the shelf. Immediately. If you are a hard-core Assembler programmer who needs no web interfaces at all, you might not be interested, either. However, if you are involved in some kind of web development, you will probably find this book useful. It is thick and heavy enough to cover a wide range of topics and provide various perspectives for all kinds of readers:

- **Professional PHP web application developers** were the first people we thought of when we started writing this book, perhaps because we are PHP programmers, too. Frameworks offer multiple advanced features that can make our lives easier and more exciting. That's why we wanted to dig deeper and try out whole potentials of different frameworks and thoroughly compare them for your pleasure and convenience.
- **Experts in Ruby on Rails, Django, TurboGears, Struts, ASP.NET, or other non-PHP frameworks** who want to take a closer look at PHP. Instead of buying separate books for each framework or choosing one more or less at random, they can benefit from comparing examples hands-on. They can experience the differences between the frameworks, which sometimes are really subtle, and perhaps switch to PHP one day.

- **Students and PHP beginners** should not be afraid of the complexity of some more advanced topics. This book is a tutorial, but it is also much more! We have put a lot of effort into making it accessible. The first part of this book, "The Basics," covers everything to get the whole thing (or even three things) running. The second part, "Common Tasks," is more than adequate to serve the needs of most academic courses or a plan of individual education. The rest of the book will be very useful if you decide to continue your romance with any one of the frameworks.
- **Project managers, analysts or system administrators** who often decide on which technology to choose or who need a deeper understanding of existing computer systems and applications. We have prepared a whole part (Part 4, "Comparison") that is focused on comparing the three frameworks and discussing their capabilities.
- **Advanced non-web programmers,** such as C++ application engineers or database experts who want to explore the vast world of web development, will find that this book is also a good starting point for them. They might be delighted with the object-oriented approach of PHP5, the rapid building process made possible with the frameworks, and all the advanced features provided by them. Meanwhile, the comparative approach provides a broad view of web-specific problems, and the tutorial side of the book prevents being stuck simply with more trivial tasks.

COMPARATIVE APPROACH

There are many great tutorials and books on each of the frameworks covered in this book. What makes this book unique is the comparative approach we've adopted. We wanted to do more than just present three advanced technologies — we wanted to point out their advantages and disadvantages by comparing how each solves certain problems. This gives you a very practical tutorial-like experience and a solid base for more advanced discussion. It allows you to formulate your own views on PHP web frameworks and their suitability for your needs.

Flame wars are a hallmark of all discussions about web frameworks. Everyone has a favorite and tries to promote it against all others. The problem is that all web frameworks are used for the same purpose, but have different internal structures. Knowing one of them is generally enough to produce web applications, so there are few people interested in mastering multiple tools of this kind. This makes comparisons difficult. No wonder many discussions are based on stereotypes, personal opinions, and unverified data.

In this situation, many unanswered questions arise: Which framework is best suited for my particular purpose? Which one is the quickest to learn? Which one produces applications the fastest? Which one has the richest features? Which one will I like best? Is there one that surpasses all the others? We have asked these questions ourselves and found no reliable answers. However, because these questions are often asked by other developers, we decided to do our best to find the solution and then share it in this book. The results were often really surprising.

STRUCTURE OF THIS BOOK

The main principle of this book is to show how to do some tasks in each framework (in parallel wherever possible). To accomplish this, each example is repeated for each framework. Sometimes the solutions are really similar in order to make all subtle differences easily visible, but sometimes one framework provides a unique solution, in which case we are not afraid to use it. The book is divided into four parts that will gradually introduce you to the complexities of PHP frameworks. More experienced developers can freely skip the first part or read only the chapters they need.

Basics

Chapter 1: Introducing Symfony, CakePHP, and Zend Framework — One of the biggest hardships with most frameworks is how to get started. This chapter addresses that problem with a comprehensive tutorial starting with a general discussion of web application frameworks, their structure, and the underlying Model-View-Controller (MVC) pattern. We also briefly present all available frameworks and explain why we chose Symfony, CakePHP, and Zend Framework for detailed comparison.

Chapter 2: Getting Started — Next we move to installation and configuration. We provide instructions for Windows, Linux, and MacOS operating systems for every framework as well as the chosen database and web server. This is a stage in which many things can go wrong and discourage an inexperienced developer, so we are extra meticulous.

Chapter 3: Working with Databases — All frameworks are installed over a database engine, so Chapter 3 is dedicated to mitigating differences between relational databases and the world of object-oriented programming. Then you learn how to communicate with a database from the level of the frameworks, which encompasses constructing an object model with schema files and direct communication with databases through a command-line interface.

Chapter 4: My First Application in the Three Frameworks — Finally some programming. With all frameworks properly configured and running in your favorite environment, it is time you wrote your first application. The address book example presented in this chapter explains how to use tools to develop web applications quickly and efficiently.

Common Tasks

Chapter 5: Forms — This part of the book focuses on the standard elements used by every web developer in his everyday work. The first of these elements are user input forms. You'll start with a simple problem of validating fields and then move on to customizing forms for various application needs. Finally, we'll discuss protection against automated forms submission, namely Captcha.

Chapter 6: Mailing — Mailing is another common task required in nearly all web applications. We need it for user registration, sending announcements, and commercial advertising. In this chapter, several mailing engines will be presented and implemented: SwiftMailer, CakeMailer, ZendMailer, and PHPMailer.

Chapter 7: Searching — This chapter starts with in-depth theoretical descriptions of full-text searching, commonly used algorithms, and approaches. Then we move to practical solutions using the popular search engines Sphinx, Lucene, and Google Custom Search.

Chapter 8: Security — Security issues are always important for a professional web developer. After reading this chapter, you will know how to provide secure connections and defend against the two most dangerous kinds of attacks: server-side XSS injections and client-side cross-side request forgeries (CSRF). We discuss the various types of dangers and introduce security measures.

Chapter 9: Templates — The last thing covered in this part of the book is something everyone should know: how to make a web app visually appealing. In this chapter, we first show you how to create a simple image gallery and then we compare native template engines of the frameworks with add-ons such as the very popular Smarty engine.

Advanced Features

Chapter 10: AJAX — The first of more advanced topics discussed in this part is Asynchronous JavaScript and XML, or AJAX. It allows various features that are both useful and impressive. The first that we discuss is autocompletion of text fields with strings from a given database. The second example is dynamic popup windows for fun and profit, and the third is a simple chat room for multiple users.

Chapter 11: Making Plug-ins — Plug-ins provide advanced functionalities that you need. This chapter discusses creating your own plug-ins. For Symfony and CakePHP, you will write a PDF creation tool, but Zend Framework plug-ins work in a somewhat different manner, so they will be discussed with an appropriate example.

Chapter 12: Integrating Web Services — Web applications cannot live alone. They need integration with other web services and we discuss how to do it here. This chapter discusses the two most common standards, REST and SOAP, as well as providing examples of their use.

Chapter 13: Back end — Most web applications have a content management system (CMS). This chapter shows how to implement simple CMSs and how to use more advanced plug-ins. We also introduce the topic of content management frameworks.

Chapter 14: Internationalization — Internationalization doesn't end with the use of UTF8 character encoding. This chapter covers everything you need to know in order to make a website truly multilingual, including right-to-left languages, user input, collation for sorting algorithms, date formats, and other localization techniques.

Chapter 15: Testing — *Quality* is the word that best describes the emphasis of this chapter. Testing is a very important part of web application development. This chapter introduces basic testing, including manual and automatic functional tests using the Selenium testing suite; and also black box, grey box, and unit tests.

Chapter 16: User Management — Web 2.0 applications revolve around users, who log-in, socialize, and create content. This chapter discusses efficient and secure ways to authenticate users and grant them access to certain features, starting with Role-Based Access Control (RBAC) and access control lists (ACLs) provided by the frameworks, and then moving on to Lightweight Directory Access Protocol (LDAP), an enterprise-grade solution.

Comparison

Chapter 17: Performance — This last part has fewer chapters than the previous parts, but it starts with an important one. We show here how to use JMeter to run your own customized performance and load tests. We also present two benchmarks made by us: throughput of a simple CRUD application and something even more important: comparison of lines of code written to create this application.

Chapter 18: Summary — The last chapter summarizes everything we have learned in this book. It lists all the pros and cons of each framework, both from a programmer's point of view and the quality of applications that can be developed with their help. And we'll tell you which PHP framework is the best one.

Appendices

We feel really sorry for less-popular frameworks because some of them are really delicious, and we had to focus on three mainstream ones only. However, we added basic info on CodeIgniter, Lithium, and Agavi with some code examples. They are young but very promising, and have good chances to gain great popularity.

There are also a list of interesting web resources for download and further reading, and a glossary of acronyms and technical terms used in the book.

SOURCE CODE

The source code presented in this book is designed to illustrate technologies described in the chapters in which it appears. Consistent with the idea that you should be able to freely read the code, not figure it out, the snippets are as simple and informative as possible. We didn't aim to print full listings of all files in the book.

However, we wouldn't leave you without full working applications. They can be downloaded from the Wrox website at `www.wrox.com` or from a dedicated website maintained by us at `www.phpframeworks.org`. The advantages of this approach are that we can put all needed files in one convenient downloadable packet. What is even more important is that you can adapt the examples to newer versions of the rapidly evolving frameworks.

To find the source code at the Wrox website, simply locate the book's title (use the Search box or one of the title lists) and click the Download Code link on the book details page to obtain all the source code for the book. Code that is included on the website is highlighted in this book by the following icon:

You'll find the filename in a code note such as this:

Code snippet filename

Because many books have similar titles, you might find it easiest to search by ISBN; this book's ISBN is 978-0-470-88734-9.

Once you download the code, just decompress it with your favorite compression tool. Alternately, you can go to the main Wrox code download page at `www.wrox.com/dynamic/books/download.aspx` to see the code available for this book and all other Wrox books.

CONVENTIONS

Conventions used in this book are pretty intuitive and straightforward. In order to distinguish inline source code from normal text, we are using a `monospace font`. The same applies to filenames and directories. Names of variables are additionally *`italicized`* (unless they appear in code snippets or listings, where they are not italicized). Names of all methods and functions have parentheses at the end in order to make more visible that they are methods; however, their arguments are usually omitted and the parentheses are empty, as in this `ExampleMethod()`. URLs are `monospace_and_underlined`.

Snippets of code look like this:

```
$ zf create model AddressBook
```

Italic font is used in multiple contexts:

- When introducing new terms and important words.
- When joking and generally not being completely serious.

In the whole book, "Symfony" is always capitalized, like any other specific name, even when referring to 1.x versions, which were called "symfony." It not only appeals to our aesthetic sense but it is also *much* easier to find in dense text this way.

CONTACT US

We have worked hard to make this book approachable, informative, and bug-free. If you have any comments or suggestions, please let us know. Also, if you find an error, you would do us a favor by telling us about it. More general info about this book, the authors, and an up-to-date list of errata can be found on our website at `www.phpframeworks.org`.

Also, if you ever wish to buy us a drink for job well done or insult us for massive incompetence, feel free to write us at `web-frameworks-book@googlegroups.com`.

Contact info for individual authors for more intimate proposals:

Bartosz Porębski: bartosz.porebski@gmail.com

Karol Przystalski: kprzystalski@gmail.com

Leszek Nowak: dr.leszek.nowak@gmail.com

The authors (from left): Bartosz Porębski, Karol Przystalski and Leszek Nowak.

ERRATA

We make every effort to ensure that there are no errors in the text or in the code. However, no one is perfect, and mistakes do occur. If you find an error in one of our books, like a spelling mistake or faulty piece of code, we would be very grateful for your feedback. By sending in errata, you might save another reader hours of frustration, and at the same time, you will be helping us provide even higher-quality information.

To find the errata page for this book, go to http://www.wrox.com and locate the title using the Search box or one of the title lists. Then, on the book details page, click the Book Errata link. On this page, you can view all errata that have been submitted for this book and posted by Wrox editors. A complete book list, including links to each book's errata, is also available at www.wrox.com/misc-pages/booklist.shtml.

If you don't spot "your" error on the Book Errata page, go to www.wrox.com/contact/techsupport.shtml and complete the form there to send us the error you have found. We'll check the information and, if appropriate, post a message to the book's errata page and fix the problem in subsequent editions of the book.

P2P.WROX.COM

For author and peer discussion, join the P2P forums at p2p.wrox.com. The forums are a web-based system for you to post messages relating to Wrox books and related technologies and interact with other readers and technology users. The forums offer a subscription feature to e-mail you topics of interest of your choosing when new posts are made to the forums. Wrox authors, editors, other industry experts, and your fellow readers are present on these forums.

At `http://p2p.wrox.com`, you will find a number of different forums that will help you, not only as you read this book, but also as you develop your own applications. To join the forums, just follow these steps:

1. Go to `p2p.wrox.com` and click the Register link.
2. Read the terms of use and click Agree.
3. Complete the required information to join, as well as any optional information you wish to provide, and click Submit.
4. You will receive an e-mail with information describing how to verify your account and complete the joining process.

You can read messages in the forums without joining P2P, but in order to post your own messages, you must join.

Once you join, you can post new messages and respond to messages other users post. You can read messages at any time on the Web. If you would like to have new messages from a particular forum e-mailed to you, click the Subscribe to this Forum icon by the forum name in the forum listing.

For more information about how to use the Wrox P2P, be sure to read the P2P FAQs for answers to questions about how the forum software works, as well as many common questions specific to P2P and Wrox books. To read the FAQs, click the FAQ link on any P2P page.

Introducing Symfony, CakePHP, and Zend Framework

An invasion of armies can be resisted, but not an idea whose time has come.

— Victor Hugo

WHAT'S IN THIS CHAPTER?

- General discussion on frameworks.
- Introducing popular PHP frameworks.
- Design patterns.

Everyone knows that all web applications have some things in common. They have users who can register, log in, and interact. Interaction is carried out mostly through validated and secured forms, and results are stored in various databases. The databases are then searched, data is processed, and data is presented back to the user, often according to his locale. If only you could extract these patterns as some kind of abstractions and transport them into further applications, the development process would be much faster.

This task obviously can be done. Moreover, it can be done in many different ways and in almost any programming language. That's why there are so many brilliant solutions that make web development faster and easier. In this book, we present three of them: *Symfony*, *CakePHP*, and *Zend Framework*. They do not only push the development process to the extremes in terms of rapidity but also provide massive amounts of advanced features that have become a must in the world of Web 2.0 applications.

WHAT ARE WEB APPLICATION FRAMEWORKS AND HOW ARE THEY USED?

A web application framework is a bunch of source code organized into a certain architecture that can be used for rapid development of web applications. You can think of frameworks as half-produced applications that you can extend and form to make them take shape according to your needs. Well, that means half your work has already been done, but for some it is as much a blessing as a curse because this work was done in a particular way, without your supervision.

Thus all frameworks are either stained with a coding methodology and naming and structural conventions, or if they try to avoid these restrictions, they need to be heavily configured by you. This either reduces their flexibility or makes their learning curve significantly steeper. And if you really want to escape from these problems toward a more library-like approach, you have to sacrifice some development speed. You can see that frameworks are all about tradeoffs.

That's why it is really good to take a look at many frameworks and compare their differences. Perhaps one of them offers conventions that you would use as good practices, anyway? Perhaps you have nothing against some initial configuration that allows you to be rapid and flexible at the same time? And maybe you want just a library of powerful components to link together by yourself? The choice is yours, and if you find a way to mitigate their disadvantages, you can fully enjoy the greatest benefit of all frameworks: truly rapid development.

Further advantages of frameworks are elegance of code and minimizing the risk of programming errors. Frameworks conform to the Don't Repeat Yourself (DRY) principle, which means that they have all the pieces of logic coded only once in one place. This rule forbids duplication of code, especially *copypasting*. This facilitates maintenance of code and prevents nasty errors. Generally, frameworks promote code reusability and other good programming practices wherever they can, which is great for programmers who do not have enough knowledge or discipline to care for quality of code by themselves.

Another great feature is the clean organized look of links that can be done with URL rewriting, which is supported by most frameworks. Instead of `/animals.php?species=cats&breed=mainecoon`, type just `/animals/cats/mainecoon`. This is not only appealing to the eye but also very search engine optimization (SEO)–friendly.

Framework versus Library

The main difference between a library and a framework is that:

- *libraries* are called from your code
- *frameworks* call your code

In other words, a framework in your application is a skeleton that you fill with features or serves as a platform on which you build your modules. Whereas a library instead provides attachable modules on top of a platform made by yourself. Some people perceive a framework as something better or more complete than a library, so "framework" became a buzzword that is often overused. That's why people call some libraries *frameworks*, even though they do not invoke developers' code. There is nothing wrong with a piece of code being a library, as it is just a different entity. And there are also some bad frameworks that damage the reputation of the good ones — basically you can take any half-done application, release it, and call it a framework. These two software groups just behave differently and should not be confused.

The application architecture utilized by frameworks is called *inversion of control*, because the data flow is inverted compared to ordinary procedural programming. It is also referred to as *The Hollywood Principle*: "Don't call us, we'll call you." This corresponds to third-party code calling developer's code. The main reason behind it is to make the high-level components less dependent on their subsystems. High-level components pass the control to low-level components, who themselves decide how they should work and when to respond. A good example is the difference between a command-line program, which stops and then asks the user for input, and a program with a windowed user interface, in which the user can click any button and then the window manager calls the program instead.

Some frameworks, such as Zend Framework or CodeIgniter, follow *loosely coupled* architecture, which means that their components are less dependent on each other and may be used separately, more library-style. Loosely coupled frameworks do not provide development as rapidly as those following a tighter framework architecture and Model-View-Controller (MVC) pattern; however, such an approach allows more flexibility and control over code.

When You Should Use a Framework and When You Should Not

Frameworks are not the cure for all programming problems. Putting aside today's awesome state of development, you should always remember how frameworks were created a few years ago. Most of them were more or less unoptimized junk created by one guy to help him speed up *his* development process, without much care for documentation, elegance, ease of use, or even readability of his code. Then another group of guys took this code and bloated it with a patchwork of extra functionalities barely consistent with the original code. Then it became apparent that this whole lot needs a solid cleanup in order to be usable, but this would mean either rewriting it from scratch or packaging code in additional wrapper classes, further increasing its unnecessary complexity.

Of course, today the disorganized origin of frameworks is not as evident as before because the quality of code has risen considerably. But still, that's why most beefed-up frameworks have performance issues. That's why they are not always easy to learn. And that's why new ones emerge to cover up weaknesses of older ones. And finally that's why major frameworks provide completely rewritten 2.0 versions, which address all previously mentioned problems.

Advantages

When web application frameworks are useful:

- For more or less standard projects with dynamic content, like social networking, online stores, news portals, and so on
- For easily scalable applications that can grow from start-up to worldwide popular services without need for big changes in code

- For producing consecutive apps, in which modularity and reusability of pieces of code like controllers and views may be helpful
- For real-world development with deadlines, rotating staff, and fitful customers
- If you are, or want to be, a professional web developer, so learning how to work with frameworks is not an excessive effort

As you can see, this applies to most commercial web applications that connect to a database and allow its users to create and modify its content. Therefore, programming with web app frameworks becomes a standard and common practice in the web development world.

Disadvantages

When you should consider development without any frameworks at all:

- Purely informative web pages without user-created content, for example an artist's portfolio with fancy graphics
- Small projects with limited database connection that wouldn't benefit much from frameworks' code generation
- Really big projects that additionally need extreme performance, like the Google suite (you would be using a compiled programming language for that rather than PHP, anyway)
- With limited hardware resources that call for top performance as well (not really a likely scenario because programming costs are now always higher than hardware costs)
- Specialist or experimental applications that may evolve in completely unknown direction or work with some custom solutions, like interfaces for scientific experiments with an object-oriented database
- When you really need (and can afford) total control over the code and evolution of the application
- When you want to create a web app, but you or your co-workers don't want or, even worse, cannot learn how to use a framework

These conditions are generally fulfilled by three types of projects: *small* static websites, extremely *specialist* websites, and *failed* websites. Frameworks are created for development of common web applications with well-known standard architecture. Of course, they may be greatly extended thanks to plug-ins and modules, but complete alteration of their structure may require much painful hacking, so you should always check their capabilities with the design requirements of your project.

PHP versus Other Programming Languages

PHP for many years has been a very popular programming language; however, it was commonly judged as unprofessional. A stereotypical PHP developer was an undereducated freelancer producing cheap, low-quality code. Professionals were supposed to use Zope, ASP, or various Java technologies. Then in 2005 there was a boom of Ruby. Everyone was amazed with the elegance of this programming language; and *Ruby on Rails*, the central piece of software ever written in Ruby, was claimed to be the ultimate web applications framework. Soon clones of Ruby on Rails began popping out. That's how Python's Django and Turbogears, as well as all PHP frameworks were born.

In 2004 PHP5 was released. It was neat and object-oriented. If somebody still wrote old-styled HTML mixed with pieces of PHP script, it was only his choice, and the programming language no longer was to blame. It took some time, but people gradually considered PHP as a disciplined and professional tool. Together with the modern MVC paradigm and features styled after other frameworks, PHP begun its amazing way to the top of web development applications.

After a few years, it became evident that Ruby on Rails had various limitations. One important limitation was the low availability and high price of Ruby hostings while there was a lot of cheap hosting for PHP everywhere in the world. There was also a great community that eagerly developed early PHP frameworks. This resulted in an IT revolution that dethroned Ruby on Rails as the most popular framework and placed a council of PHP frameworks in its place.

Figure 1-1 illustrates the change in interest in various frameworks over time expressed as search volume in the Google search engine in the *Computers & Electronics* category. The figure was created with *Google Insights for Search*, which is a more advanced form of the well known *Google Trends* tool. You can check these search terms yourself to obtain results beyond mid-2010 (that's when this book was written), at the website `www.google.com/insights/search/`.

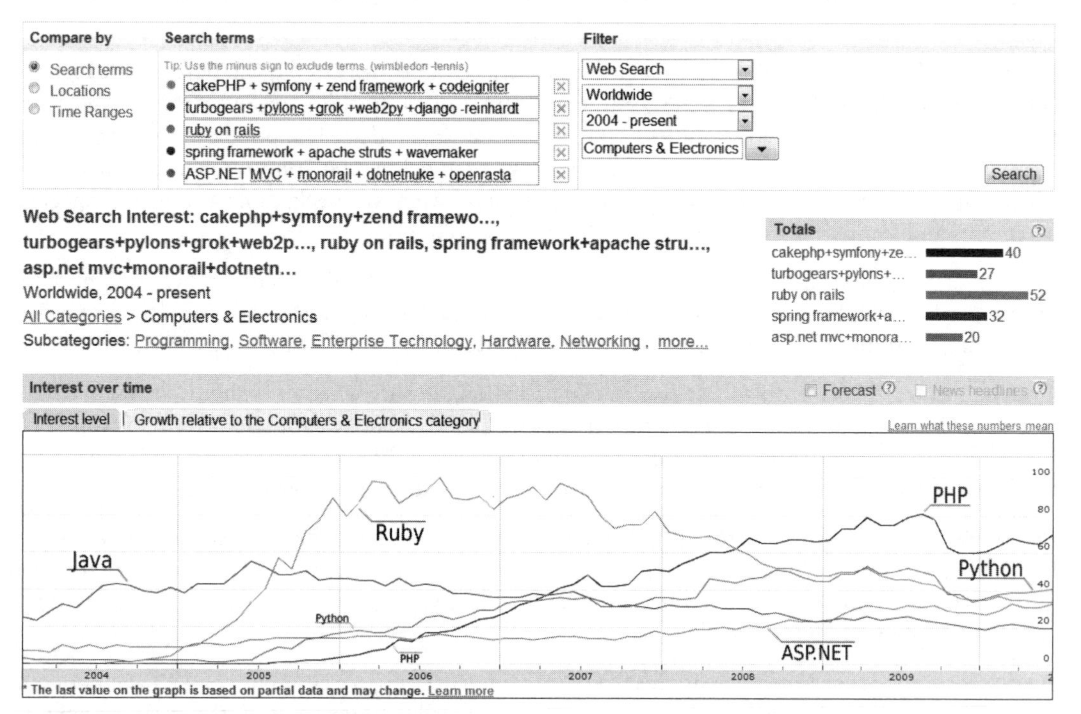

FIGURE 1-1: Search volumes of frameworks in various programming languages

OPEN SOURCE PHP WEB FRAMEWORKS

Another question we want to answer is why we have chosen these three particular frameworks. Are they really *better* in any way, or are we biased or perhaps have some financial interest in promoting them? Well, starting with that last question, we are completely independent open source enthusiasts and we wanted to compare free ("free" as free speech) software only, so there is certainly no *Evil Corporation* behind us, and nobody told us which frameworks to choose. We answer the question of whether they're better than other frameworks in the following sections.

There were once closed source PHP frameworks as well, but due to widespread success of the free frameworks, nowadays closed source frameworks are a thing of the past.

Comparison of Popular Interest

We have chosen Symfony, CakePHP, and Zend Framework due to their popularity in the web developers' community, including our own experience in PHP. We believe that open source programming tools show at least some correlation between their *popularity* and *quality* because they are used only if they are really useful. In that way they are different from things like proprietary software or pop music, in which quality can be easily replaced by aggressive *marketing* as the *popularity* gaining factor.

It turns out that the public interest in web frameworks can be measured quite objectively. Figure 1-2 shows search volumes for various PHP frameworks in *Google Insights for Search*. You can easily see that there are four leading competitors. All the others *combined* are less popular than *any one* of these four. The Lithium and Prado frameworks have been deliberately omitted because their names are nonunique, which generates *false positives* in trends. We have checked these names in specific categories and found that they are not significant as search terms, either.

When users search for information on a framework, the search results usually reflect talk about it on various blogs and forums, items about learning this technology, and finally developing applications using it. So public interest in a web framework results in real, long-term use of it.

CodeIgniter was really problematic for us. We had a long debate whether it should be included as one of the main frameworks. Perhaps now it is as frequently searched for as Symfony or CakePHP, but what matters more is the *area under the graph* because it reflects how many people have found the answers they sought and have probably used this knowledge for their projects.

Of course this graph shows nothing more than search volume, and when you see such fast growth it is hard to distinguish a long-lasting trend from temporary hype. We know that CodeIgniter is really good, so it is definitely more than a fad, and perhaps in a year or two it will have its place among the leading web tools.

We finally agreed that *three men* against *four frameworks* is not an equal fight. We have not completely forsaken CodeIgniter, though; its features are described, along with Lithium and Agavi, in Appendix B, where a simple application is developed using each one of them.

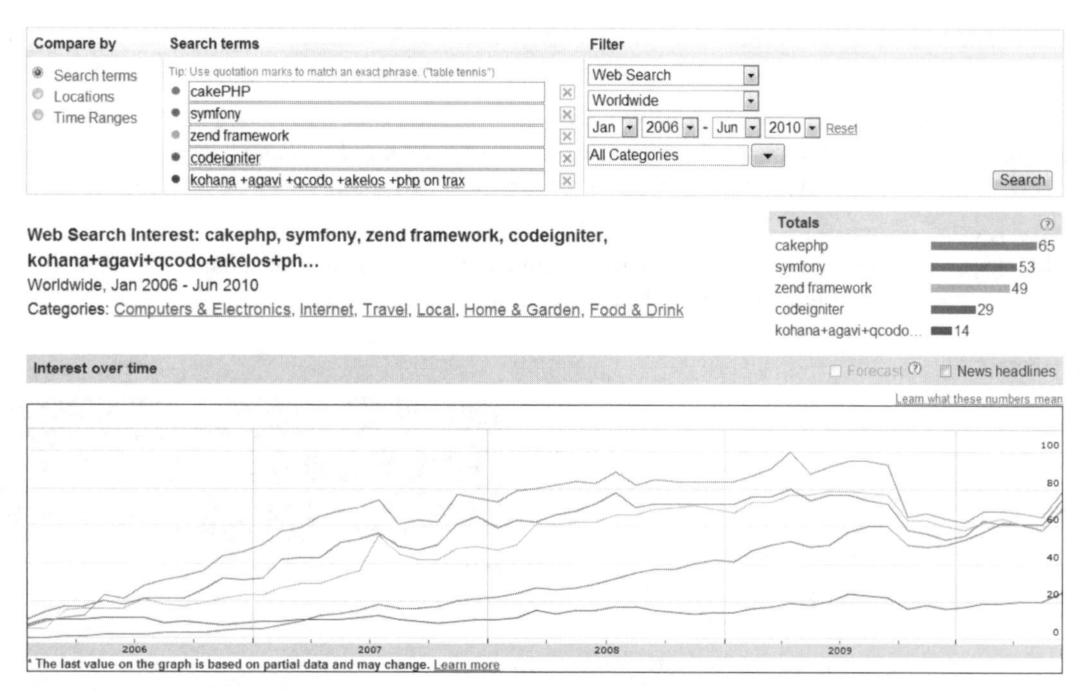

FIGURE 1-2: Comparison of search volumes of different PHP frameworks

The First Look

The first look at the frameworks really gives us little information on their individual features. Their websites just try to impress you with marketing descriptions and a list of features that vary little from one framework to another:

> *"**Symfony** is a full-stack framework, a library of cohesive classes written in PHP. It provides an architecture, components and tools for developers to build complex web applications faster. Choosing symfony allows you to release your applications earlier, host and scale them without problem, and maintain them over time with no surprise. Symfony is based on experience. It does not reinvent the wheel: it uses most of the best practices of web development and integrates some great third-party libraries."*

> *"**CakePHP** is a rapid development framework for PHP that provides an extensible architecture for developing, maintaining, and deploying applications. Using commonly known design patterns like MVC and ORM within the convention over configuration paradigm, CakePHP reduces development costs and helps developers write less code."*

> *"Extending the art & spirit of PHP, **Zend Framework** is based on simplicity, object-oriented best practices, corporate friendly licensing, and a rigorously*

tested agile codebase. Zend Framework is focused on building more secure, reliable, and modern Web 2.0 applications & web services."

Now see whether you can spot three differences. Well, the websites are not really informative about unique features of their frameworks. You can find more in various blogs and forums, but still there is little verified data, and general discussions tend to exchange purely personal opinions.

That is why we have written this book. In fact, the differences between frameworks are not really obvious, and it takes some time and practical examples to see them and then harness them in business solutions. Let's begin with some most basic facts.

Symfony

Started: 2005

License: MIT

PHP versions:

- Symfony 1.4: PHP 5.2.4+
- Symfony 2.0: PHP 5.3+

FIGURE 1-3: Symfony logo

Its logo is shown in Figure 1-3. Website: `www.symfony-project.org`

Symfony was produced in a French web development company, *Sensio Labs*, by Fabien Potencier. First it was used for the development of its own applications and then in 2005 it was released as an open source project. Its name was "symfony," but it is sometimes capitalized (as we do in this book) in order to make it more distinct.

Symfony was based on an ancient Mojavi MVC framework, with some inevitable influences from Ruby on Rails. It also integrated Propel Object-Relational Mapper and took advantage of the YAML Ain't Markup Language (YAML) serialization standard for configuration and data modeling. The default object-relational mapping (ORM) solution has been later changed to Doctrine.

Today Symfony is one of the leading web frameworks. It has a large active community and a lot of documentation — mainly free e-books. Symfony 2.0 is being released in late 2010. It offers various new features and greatly enhanced performance.

CakePHP

Started: 2005

License: MIT

PHP versions: 4.3.2+

Its logo is shown in Figure 1-4. Website: `http://cakephp.org`

FIGURE 1-4: CakePHP logo

CakePHP was started in 2005 by the effort of Polish web developer Michał Tatarynowicz. Heavily inspired by Ruby on Rails, CakePHP is an entirely community-driven open source project with lead developer Larry Masters (*aka* PhpNut). The next major release of CakePHP has also been announced, but its release date is still unknown.

The most important goals of CakePHP are its friendliness, development speed, and ease of use. And it really excels in that. Works out of the box (or oven), with no configuration. It has perfect documentation with working examples for most of its features. And it has really a lot of features to use. That allows the most rapid development with a smaller amount of code.

One of the most controversial features of CakePHP is its compatibility with PHP4. While once it allowed deployment on old cheap hosts that did not support PHP5, now it is more a drawback hindering CakePHP's development. Fortunately, version 2.0 will use PHP 5.3+. There are also reports of CakePHP's really bad performance, but they were mainly due to disabled caching by default.

Zend Framework

Started: 2005

License: new BSD

PHP versions: 5.2.4 since ZF 1.7.0

Its logo is shown in Figure 1-5. Website: `http://framework.zend.com`

FIGURE 1-5: Zend Framework logo

Zend Framework is sponsored by the U.S.-Israeli company, Zend Technologies Ltd., which was cofounded by Andi Gutmans and Zeev Suraski, the core developers of PHP. Strategic partners of Zend Technologies Ltd. include Adobe, IBM, Google, and Microsoft. The company offers various commercial products; however, Zend Framework is an open source project released under the "corporate friendly" *new BSD* license.

ZF is meant to be simple, component-based, and loosely coupled. This means that it is a *library of components*, which you can use as you wish, and usage of MVC architecture is optional. This lowers the learning curve and increases its flexibility. The documentation is great, and the source code is of very high quality, both because it's fully object oriented and thoroughly unit-tested. Zend announced an upcoming 2.0 version as well, but its release date is still unknown.

Other Frameworks

There are *hundreds* of PHP frameworks. This is not an exaggeration if you count all of them, including ancient and already abandoned projects, as well as brilliant younger startups and some useless short-lived junk. The web app market is a big one, but the amount of PHP tools is disproportionally huge and perhaps somewhat excessive. Here is an overview of a few more notable ones that we have found to be used successfully to develop web applications.

CodeIgniter

Started: 2006

License: modified BSD

PHP versions: 4.3.2+

Its logo is shown in Figure 1-6. Website: `http://codeigniter.com`

FIGURE 1-6: CodeIgniter logo

CodeIgniter is developed and maintained by a privately-owned software development company, Ellis Labs. It is focused on having a very small footprint, while allowing a big increase in performance. It follows the MVC pattern only partially, for the models are optional. It is loosely coupled and in the words of Rasmus Lerdorf, it's "the least like a framework." Its lightweight approach has earned a wide recognition in the developers' community, but it is sometimes criticized for conformance with PHP 4.

CodeIgniter is a good choice for less complex web applications that would benefit from using a framework, but the heavier ones would either hinder the applications' performance with excessive features, or their configuration would take too much time. The structural simplicity of CodeIgniter makes it also a frequent pick by beginners who choose it as learning platform before moving to a full MVC framework.

Lithium

Started: 2009

License: BSD

PHP versions: 5.3+

Its logo is shown in Figure 1-7. Website: `http://lithify.me`

FIGURE 1-7: Lithium logo

Lithium took all the best that CakePHP had to offer and moved it to PHP 5.3. First it was a branch of CakePHP called Cake3, now it is a separate project run by some former CakePHP developers. It is lightweight, fast, and extremely flexible with extensive plug-in support. It has many truly experimental and innovative functions like a filter system and an integrated test suite.

The second search result Google showed us for "Lithium framework" is a page titled "CakePHP is dead...Lithium was born." This claim is still far from true, however, with the advantages provided by Lithium's support for PHP 5.3, Lithium may really endanger CakePHP in the future unless the latter takes immediate action.

Agavi

Started: 2005

License: LGPL

PHP versions: 5.2.0+ (recommended 5.2.8+)

Its logo is shown in Figure 1-8. Website: `www.agavi.org`

FIGURE 1-8: Agavi logo

Like Symfony, Agavi is based on the Mojavi framework. It was started in 2005, but the 1.0.0 version was worked upon until early 2009. The source code is very polished and sometimes called the best-written MVC OOP framework. However, it has not gained much popularity, perhaps due to scarce documentation.

It was never meant to be popular. The authors stress that Agavi is not a website construction kit, but a serious framework built with power and extensibility in mind. Its target applications are long-term specialist projects that need full control of their developers.

Kohana

Started: 2007

License: BSD

PHP versions: 5.2.3+

FIGURE 1-9: Kohana logo

Its logo is shown in Figure 1-9. Website: `http://kohanaphp.com`

Kohana is a community-supported offshoot of CodeIgniter. In contrast with CodeIgniter, Kohana is designed for PHP5 and is fully object oriented. While boasting higher elegance of code, it still has all the qualities of CodeIgniter: It is extremely lightweight, flexible, and easy to learn. The community behind Kohana is large and active, so despite its young age it should be considered a stable and reliable framework.

Prado

Started: 2004

License: revised BSD

PHP versions: 5.1.0+

FIGURE 1-10: Prado logo

Its logo is shown in Figure 1-10. Website: `www.pradosoft.com`

Prado stands for *PHP Rapid Application Development Object-oriented*. It enjoyed moderate popularity some time ago, but now its development seems a bit sluggish. However, it is still a mature framework well-suited for most business applications. One of its interesting features is that it nicely supports event-driven programming. It has some similarities with ASP.NET.

Yii

Started: 2008

License: BSD

PHP versions: 5.1.0+

Its logo is shown in Figure 1-11.
Website: www.yiiframework.com

FIGURE 1-11: Yii logo

Yii was founded by a developer of Prado and it continues many of its conventions. Yii is very fast (leading in most benchmarks) and extensible, modular, and strictly object oriented. It has a rich set of features and decent documentation. It uses no special configuration or templating language, so you don't have to learn anything apart from object-oriented PHP to use it. Also, unlike many other frameworks, it follows pure MVC architecture with data being sent directly from Model to View.

Akelos

Started: 2006

License: LGPL

PHP versions: 4 or 5

Its logo is shown in Figure 1-12. Website: http://www.akelos.org, http://github.com/bermi/akelos

FIGURE 1-12: Akelos 2 logo

While all PHP frameworks are more or less inspired by Ruby on Rails, Akelos aims to be its direct port. It is focused on internationalization (provides multilingual *models* and *views* as well as Unicode support without extensions) and can run on low-cost shared hostings (that's why it has support for PHP4).

The author of Akelos announced the completely rewritten Akelos 2. It drops support for PHP4 and uses autoloading and lazier strategies for loading functionality. Its hallmarks will be advanced routing methods and strong REST orientation (REST is described in Chapter 12). It is to be released in late 2010 and it looks very promising.

Seagull

Started: 2001

License: BSD

PHP versions: 4.3.11+

FIGURE 1-13: Seagull logo

Its logo is shown in Figure 1-13. Website: http://seagullproject.org

Seagull is a true veteran among PHP frameworks — it was founded in 2001. Years of development made it solid, stable, and tested. It is no longer actively developed, so perhaps it is not the best choice when starting a new project, but there are still numerous successful applications that were built with it. It has contributed greatly to the development of all other PHP frameworks.

Qcodo

Started: 2005

License: MIT

PHP versions: 5.x

Its logo is shown in Figure 1-14. Website: `www.qcodo.com`

FIGURE 1-14: Qcodo logo

Qcodo is an MVC framework that excels in code generation from database design. It has a very powerful code generator that analyzes the structure of the data model, and creates PHP object code and also HTML pages for database manipulation. Perhaps this is not one of the more popular frameworks you are likely to hear about during a casual conversation, but several top institutions (including NASA) have applied it for their projects. Qcodo was created by Mike Ho of *QuasIdea Development* and is now developed by an active community. It also has a completely community-driven fork called Qcube.

Solar

Started: 2005

License: New BSD

PHP versions: 5.2+

Its logo is shown in Figure 1-15. Website: `http://solarphp.com`

FIGURE 1-15: Solar Framework logo

SOLAR stands for *Simple Object Library and Application Repository.* Its structure and naming conventions are similar to those of Zend Framework. One of the biggest differences is how you construct objects — all are created with a *unified constructor* and configured with an array in a config file. It has many helpful built-in example applications.

PHP On Trax

Started: 2007

License: GPL

PHP versions: 5.x

Its logo is shown in Figure 1-16. Website: `www.phpontrax.com`

FIGURE 1-16: PHP on Trax logo

As the name cleverly suggests, this framework was designed as an exact PHP copy of Ruby on Rails. At least it was meant to be because it still lacks many features and it is highly unlikely that it will finally realize this goal. It is just one of many good-looking frameworks that have eventually failed.

DESIGN PATTERNS IN WEB FRAMEWORKS

There are certain abstractions that can be transported between applications in order to make the development process faster. This section takes a closer look at these abstractions and the way they shape the web application frameworks.

It is not absolutely necessary to understand design patterns in order to start working with frameworks, so if you are bored, you can skip to the next chapter and come back here later. However, design patterns are fairly fundamental to these frameworks and application development as a whole, so we insist that you really come back here if you decide to skip this section now.

What Is a Design Pattern?

The definition of design pattern states that it is a *general solution to a commonly occurring problem in software design*. There is really not much more formal foundation because design patterns are a generally practical means that make up for a lack in formal mechanisms. Most often they are created when programming languages do not provide abstract mechanisms that become undeniably useful during the development of real-world applications.

A good analogy for design patterns is the game of chess. A novice player needs just to know the rules. It's like learning the basic syntax of a programming language. Still, knowing how a bishop moves doesn't make you a successful chess player, just like knowing how to open braces doesn't make you a PHP programmer. Skilled players are able to predict a few moves forward and respond with a winning scheme. That's like an experienced programmer who can, in fact, produce working software.

As you begin to master the game of chess, you begin to see patterns emerging. You can barely glance at the chessboard to classify the situation into one of these patterns and provide a proven response, both for present and future risks. You can perceive these patterns just intuitively, or you may try to name them. It's the same with software design patterns: when you are truly proficient, you use them all the time. There is a good chance that you have used some of them without even knowing it.

Naming design patterns is not necessary, but is indeed good for two things. First is an aid for thinking with patterns, because when you name something abstract, it is much easier to implement it in practice. Then you may further analyze this pattern, draw diagrams of it, and take full advantage of it. And the other thing is that you can share your experience. Chess players love to talk about various openings and gambits, and programmers can learn a lot by exchanging knowledge of design patterns as well.

And even more important, if you want another programmer to add some functionality to a fixed class and then tell him to use the Decorator pattern, you can expect that it will be done the way you want it rather than with a random makeshift solution. Thus design patterns have a great potential for preventing future problems.

Model-View-Controller as the Main Structural Design Pattern

Web frameworks take advantage of most, if not all, design patterns. However, MVC is the absolute structural backbone of all frameworks. The main idea of MVC is dividing the application into three layers:

- **Model** — Represents the business logic of the application. It is more than just the raw data; the Model has to represent the structure of data with all relationships and dependencies. It may comprise one or more classes that correspond to logic objects of the application and provide an interface for manipulating them. The Model is the only layer that uses persistent storage. It should completely encapsulate all database connections. The model should also notify the View when its internal state changes, so the View can be refreshed.
- **View** — The output displayed to the user. The most important thing is that the View never modifies the application data; it only presents it. There may be multiple Views for the same data, such as traditional HTML, PDF, Flash, or WML for mobile devices. They should be interchangeable without modifying the other layers.
- **Controller** — The part of an application responsible for handling user interaction and taking all other actions. The Controller should be created with simplicity in mind — it should be the controlling part that uses methods provided by the Model and the View; it shouldn't do everything by itself.

Figure 1-17 illustrates the relations between the three layers.

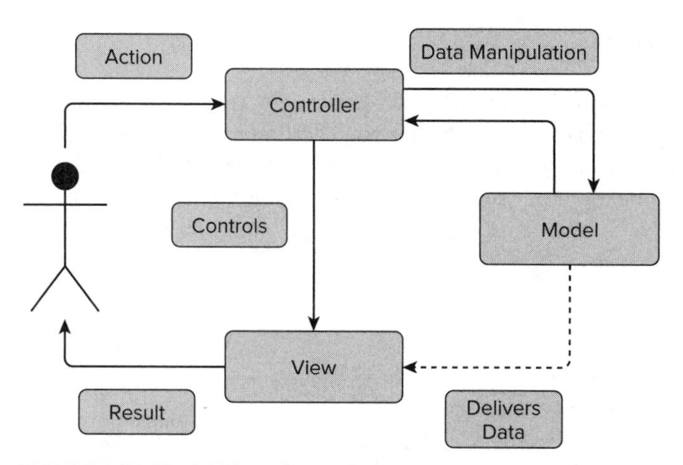

FIGURE 1-17: Model-View-Controller pattern

MVC versus MVP

MVC is an old design pattern, dating back to the 1979 work "Applications Programming in Smalltalk-80: How to use Model–View–Controller." by Trygve Reenskaug. Since that time, it was often used in non-web applications, mostly graphical user interfaces in compiled languages like C++ or Java. There it was easy and natural to implement an exact MVC pattern, but for web applications, it was somewhat modified.

Model-View-Presenter (MVP), shown in Figure 1-18, is a derivative of MVC. It is a three-tier application structure, where the Presenter acts as a middle layer between the View and the Model. The Presenter differs from the Controller in that it loads data from the Model and delivers it to the View.

Most so-called MVC frameworks follow the MVP pattern. While it is not bad itself because MVP seems even better suited to the task, this naming convention may be somewhat confusing. As long as MVP is derived directly from MVC, it is not a big problem, so in this book we will follow the names conferred by the authors of the frameworks. So we will call all frameworks *Model-View-Controller*, even if the Controller does the majority of data-transferring work.

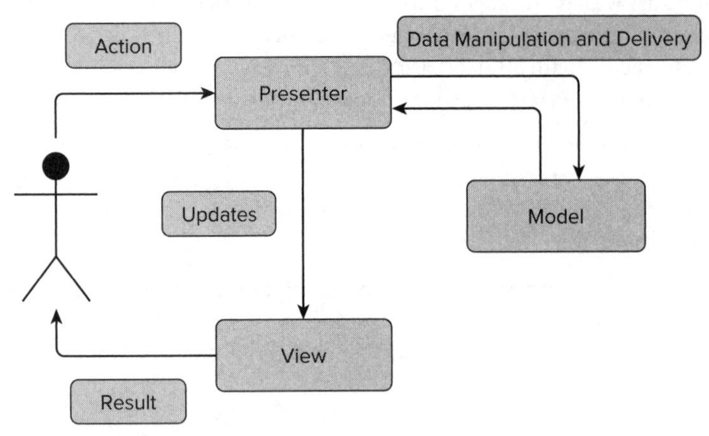

FIGURE 1-18: Model-View-Presenter pattern

Overview of Other Design Patterns

Design patterns can be divided into *creational*, *behavioral*, and *structural* patterns. Full description of all design patterns is well beyond the scope of this book, but you can find it in the most influential book on this subject: *Design Patterns: Elements of Reusable Object-Oriented Software*, by Erich Gamma, Richard Helm, Ralph Johnson, and John Vlissides (the *Gang Of Four*). However, we want to provide you with just a short overview of design patterns that are commonly used in web frameworks.

Singleton

This design pattern, which is so trivial it is often called an *antipattern*, is very useful. The purpose of the *Singleton* pattern is to ensure that a class has only one instance and to make this instance globally accessible. Whenever another object needs access to the Singleton, it calls a static, globally accessible function that returns reference to the single instance. You can see the structure of the Singleton in Figure 1-19.

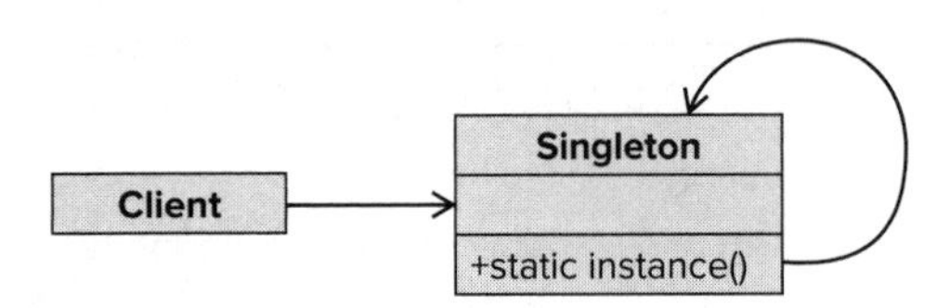

FIGURE 1-19: Singleton pattern structure

The trick behind *Singleton* is to make the instance and all its constructors *private*. So there is no way to demand creation of a `Singleton` class instance. How is the first and only instance created? The `instance()` method checks whether this object already exists; if not, it creates the single instance before returning it. Let's look at how this works with the PHP code.

```
<?php
class CarSingleton {
    private $make = 'Dodge';
    private $model = 'Magnum';
    private static $car = NULL;
```

```
        private static $isRented = FALSE;
        private function __construct() {
        }
        static function rentCar() {
            if (FALSE == self::$isRented ) {
                if (NULL == self::$car) {
                    self::$car= new CarSingleton();
                }
                self::$isRented = TRUE;
                return self::$car;
            } else {
                return NULL;
            }
        }
        function returnCar(CarSingleton $carReturned) {
            self::$isRented = FALSE;
        }
        function getMake() {return $this->make;}
        function getModel() {return $this->model;}
        function getMakeAndModel() {return $this->getMake().' '.$this->getModel();}
    }
    ?>
```

code snippet /singleton/CarSingleton.class.php

The class in the preceding code is a Singleton representing one concrete specimen of a Dodge Magnum car in a car rental business. The `__construct()` function is the constructor of this class. Note that it is set to `private` to prevent usage from outside of the class. The double underscore indicates that `__construct()` is one of the *magic functions* in PHP (special functions provided by the language), and declaring the constructor in a class will override the default one.

`CarSingleton` does provide an interface for renting and returning the car as well as pretty obvious getters. The `rentCar()` function checks first whether the car is already rented. This is not part of the Singleton pattern, but is important for the logic of our example. If the car wasn't rented, the function checks if the `$car` variable is `NULL` before returning it. If it equals `NULL`, it is constructed before the first use. Thus, `rentCar()` corresponds to the `instance()` method of the design pattern.

The `Customer` class in the following example represents a person who uses the services of the car rental business. He can rent the car (there is only one), return it, and tell the *make* and *model* of the car, provided that he drives it at the moment.

Available for download on Wrox.com

```
<?php
include_once('CarSingleton.class.php');
class Customer{
    private $rentedCar;
    private $drivesCar = FALSE;
    function __construct() {
    }
    function rentCar() {
        $this->rentedCar = CarSingleton::rentCar();
        if ($this->rentedCar == NULL) {
            $this->drivesCar = FALSE;
```

```
        } else {
            $this->drivesCar = TRUE;
        }
    }
    function returnCar() {
        $this->rentedCar->returnCar($this->rentedCar);
    }
    function getMakeAndModel() {
        if (TRUE == $this->drivesCar ) {
            return 'I drive '.$this->rentedCar->getMakeAndModel().' really fast!';
        } else {
            return "I can't rent this car.";
        }
    }
}
?>
```

code snippet /singleton/Customer.class.php

We can test these classes with the following code. It creates two customers, who both want to rent the car at the same time. But the second one will have to wait until the car is returned.

Available for download on Wrox.com

```
<?php
include_once('Customer.class.php');
$Customer_1 = new Customer();
$Customer_2 = new Customer();
echo 'Customer_1 wants to rent the car. <br />';
$Customer_1->rentCar();
echo 'Customer_1 says: ' . $Customer_1->getMakeAndModel() . '<br />';
echo '<br />';
echo 'Customer_2 wants to rent the car. <br />';
$Customer_2->rentCar();
echo 'Customer_2 says: ' . $Customer_2->getMakeAndModel() . '<br />';
echo '<br />';
$Customer_1->returnCar();
echo 'Customer_1 returned the car.<br />';
echo '<br />';
echo 'Customer_2 wants to rent the car. Again.' . '<br />';
$Customer_2->rentCar();
echo 'Customer_2 says: ' . $Customer_2->getMakeAndModel() . '<br />';
echo '<br />';
?>
```

code snippet /singleton/Test.php

The output of this code will look like this:

```
Customer_1 wants to rent the car.
Customer_1 says: I drive Dodge Magnum really fast!

Customer_2 wants to rent the car.
Customer_2 says: I can't rent this car.

Customer_1 returned the car.
```

```
Customer_2 wants to rent the car. Again.
Customer_2 says: I drive Dodge Magnum really fast!
```

The Singleton pattern is used often in other design patterns such as Prototype, State, Abstract Factory, or Facade. Apart from that, it can be used in all classes where you need a single instance with global access, but there is no way to assign it to another object, and perhaps you can also benefit from initialization on the first use. Be wary, though, because it is easy to overuse Singletons, and they may be dangerous, just like global variables. Another problem with Singletons is that they carry their state throughout the execution of the program, which seriously harms unit testing. Some experts even argue that Singleton is a bad idea and it generally should be avoided.

Frameworks use Singletons for various reasons. One of them is storing user data for security purposes. You want to have a single instance of a user that holds authentication data and make sure that no second instance can be created. This approach is represented, for example, by the `sfGuard` class of Symfony.

Prototype

The *Prototype* pattern is useful when you need the flexibility of parameterized object creation and when you want to avoid using the `new` operator. Object creation is done here by creating a parent class with an abstract `clone()` method and a few subclasses implementing `clone()`. Each of these subclasses comes with one instantiated Prototype object, which clones itself when you call for a new instance. This results in easiness and flexibility of object creation — you don't have to hard-wire the concrete subclass name in your code. Instead you can pass the name of the class as a string or reference to the appropriate Prototype.

This pattern also greatly supports deep copying of objects. Instead of cloning the Prototype, you can clone an existing object, receiving an exact copy as the result. You can even copy objects from a container with mixed objects of various subclasses. The only requirement is that they implement the `clone()` interface. Copying objects this way is much faster than creating objects with `new` and assigning values. A general diagram of this pattern is shown in Figure 1-20.

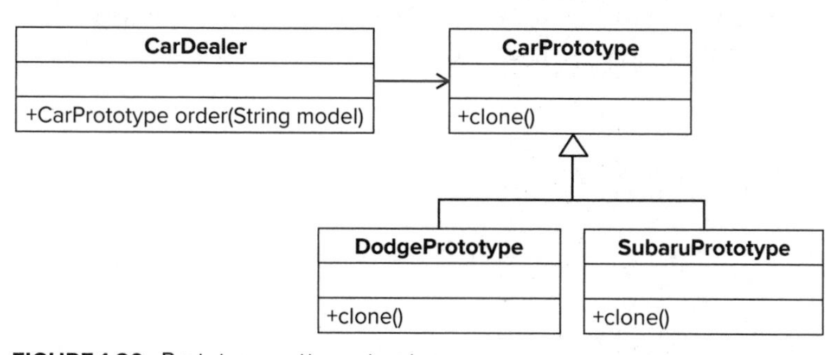

FIGURE 1-20: Prototype pattern structure

PHP has another *magic function*: `__clone()` does most of the work for you. All you have to do in the following example is to create an abstract `CarPrototype` class and subclasses for different producers. The `__clone()` function is declared `abstract`, so subclass methods are used by default when this method is called.

Available for download on Wrox.com

```
<?php
abstract class CarPrototype {
    protected $model;
    protected $color;
    abstract function __clone();
    function getModel() {
        return $this->model;
    }
    function getColor() {
        return $this->color;
    }
    function setColor($colorIn) {
        $this->color= $colorIn;
    }
}
class DodgeCarPrototype extends CarPrototype {
    function __construct() {
        $this->model = 'Dodge Magnum';
    }
    function __clone() {
    }
}
class SubaruCarPrototype extends CarPrototype {
    function __construct() {
        $this->model = 'Subaru Outback';
    }
    function __clone() {
    }
}
?>
```

code snippet /prototype/CarPrototype.class.php

Cars are quite an accurate example here, because in real life a prototype is created by a manufacturer and then different models are based on this prototype and filled with unique features. The following code tests the preceding classes. First, it creates two Prototype objects as showcase cars and then clones one of them to serve the customer. Then the color can be picked by the uniform interface.

Available for download on Wrox.com

```
<?php
include_once('CarPrototype.class.php');
$dodgeProto= new DodgeCarPrototype();
$subaruProto = new SubaruCarPrototype();
echo 'Which car do you want? <br />';
$customerDecision = 'Subaru';
if( $customerDecision == 'Subaru' ){
   $customersCar = clone $subaruProto;
} else {
   $customersCar = clone $dodgeProto;
}
echo $customersCar->getModel().'<br />';
echo 'What color do you want?<br />';
$customersCar->setColor('red');
```

```
echo 'Fine, we will paint your '.$customersCar->getModel().
     ' '.$customersCar->getColor().'.<br />';
?>
```

code snippet /prototype/Test.php

The previous code will result in the following messages:

```
Which car do you want?
Subaru Outback.
What color do you want?
Fine, we will paint your Subaru Outback red.
```

The Prototype pattern is used commonly in different modules of frameworks. An example can be nesting of forms within forms in Symfony or the `AppController` class of CakePHP.

Decorator

Subclassing is a great mechanism, but it has some serious limitations. Suppose that you want to produce a car. You put all your effort into designing a good yet affordable standard model of the car. It is a complete design that defines the *look and feel* of this model and it is a reference for any possible modifications. Then you seek to provide some optional equipment that improves the quality of the car and adds some new functionalities. For example, it may be all-wheel drive instead of front-wheel drive. It may be automatic transmission instead of manual. The car may also come in different trim levels with electric leather seats, sunroof, better audio, or GPS satellite navigation. However the basic interface remains the same — you can drive this car and feel good doing it.

When you face such alternatives, the number of possible combinations rises really fast. Figure 1-21 shows some combinations for just three improvements, described as inheritance hierarchy.

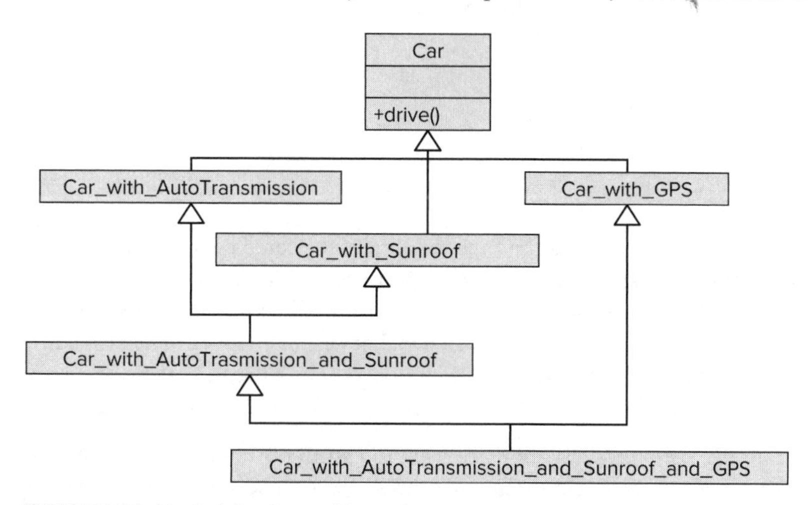

FIGURE 1-21: Nasty inheritance hierarchy

The answer to this problem is the *Decorator* pattern. The Decorator is a class that shares the interface with the decorated class (in our example, it is the basic car). It encapsulates an instance of the decorated object and extends its responsibilities dynamically. It is like putting a gift into a solid box and then wrapping it with colorful paper — it is still a gift, but durable and decorated. The inheritance structure of the Decorator pattern is presented in Figure 1-22.

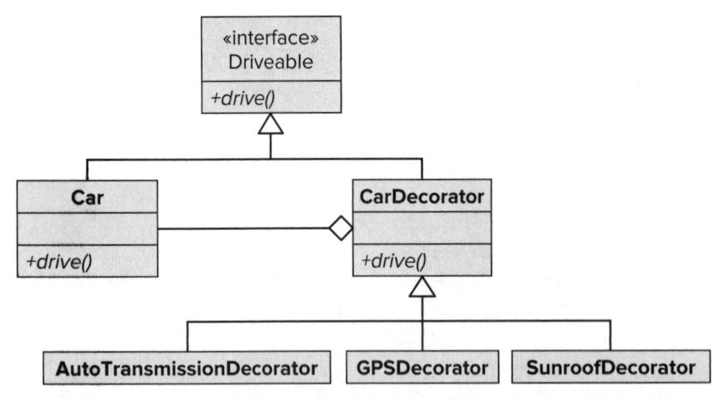

FIGURE 1-22: More reasonable inheritance hierarchy with Decorator

You can put the decorated object into other Decorators without limitations. This way you can add as many optional modules as you wish. Decorators can have their own inheritance hierarchy, and within this hierarchy they encapsulate the core object recursively.

The code below creates a standard `Car` class without optional equipment.

```
<?php
class Car{
  public $gearMessage = 'Remember to shift up.';
  public $comfortMessage = 'standard.';
  function drive() {
    return 'Accelerating ' . $this->gearMessage .
           ' Driving comfort is ' . $this->comfortMessage;
  }
}
?>
```

code snippet /decorator/Car.class.php

The following classes are responsible for extending the functionality of the car. The first one, `CarDecorator`, is the first level of wrapping. It stores the `$car` variable and a copy of `$comfortMessage`. This variable will be changed by a Decorator, so we create a copy to avoid changing the original `$car` object. On the other hand, `$gearMessage` is changed internally. The `drive()` function is also subclassed to use the proper variables `$car->model` and `$this->gearMessage` because we want to access the core object here, but `$this->comfortMessage` because we want to use the amended value.

Second-level Decorators wrapping the `CarDecorator` are used to install optional components, as shown below. `AutomaticTransmissionDecorator` installs the `$gearMessage` directly into the core `$car`, but `GPSDecorator` is installed into the `CarDecorator` instead. Note that all decorators share the common interface and additionally provide specific installers.

Available for download on Wrox.com

```
<?php
    class CarDecorator {
      protected $car;
      protected $gearMessage;
      protected $comfortMessage ;
      public function __construct(Car $car_in) {
        $this->car = $car_in;
        $this->comfortMessage = $car_in->comfortMessage;
      }
      function drive() {
        return 'Accelerating. ' . $this->car->gearMessage .
               ' Driving comfort is ' . $this->comfortMessage;
      }
    }

    class AutomaticTransmissionDecorator extends CarDecorator {
      protected $decorator;
      public function __construct(CarDecorator $decorator_in) {
        $this->decorator= $decorator_in;
      }
      public function installAutomaticTransmission(){
        $this->decorator->car->gearMessage = 'Auto transmission shifts up.';
      }
    }
    class GPSDecorator extends CarDecorator {
      protected $decorator;
      public function __construct(CarDecorator $decorator_in) {
        $this->decorator= $decorator_in;
      }
      public function installGPS(){
        $this->decorator->comfortMessage= 'very high.';
      }
    }
?>
```

code snippet /decorator/CarDecorator.class.php

We can test these classes with the following code.

Available for download on Wrox.com

```
<?php
  include_once('Car.class.php');
  include_once('CarDecorator.class.php');
  $car = new Car();
  $decorator = new CarDecorator($car);
  $transmission = new AutomaticTransmissionDecorator($decorator);
  $gps = new GPSDecorator($decorator);
  echo 'Driving standard car: <br />';
  echo $car->drive().'<br />';
  $transmission->installAutomaticTransmission();
  $gps->installGPS();
  echo 'Driving fully decorated car: <br />';
  echo $decorator->drive() . '<br />';
```

```
    echo 'Driving the car without decoration: <br />';
    echo $car->drive() . '<br />';
?>
```

code snippet /decorator/Test.php

And the result will be the following:

```
Driving standard car:
Accelerating. Remember to shift up. Driving comfort is standard.
Driving fully decorated car:
Accelerating. Auto transmission shifts up. Driving comfort is very high.
Driving the car without decoration:
Accelerating. Auto transmission shifts up. Driving comfort is standard.
```

First we call the basic `Car` model. Next we install the optional equipment and call the `drive()` function of the `CarDecorator`. Finally we choose to drive the car not using the Decorator wrapping. Note that after calling the `$car` then, its transmission is still automatic. That's because the Decorator changed it permanently.

Going back to frameworks, the Decorator pattern is used among others for layouts and templates. It is very useful for adding optional visual components or extending the user interface when new widgets are needed. An example may be adding scrollbars when user input exceeds the field area.

Chain of Responsibility

The three preceding design patterns concerned object creation and inheritance structure. *Chain of Responsibility* is a pattern of another kind, because it applies to the behavior of objects. Its main intent is to decouple the *sender* of a request from its *receiver*. Let's see how it works with an automotive example.

Imagine that there is an emergency on the road and you need to quickly stop the car. In other words, `stop` is the emitted request. In most cases, hitting the brake pedal is a sufficient solution, but there are rare cases when you find the brakes broken; that's when *Chain of Responsibility* comes in handy. If brakes cannot handle the request, they pass it to the handbrake. If for any reason the handbrake is broken, too, and you are going to hit the obstacle, at least airbags should open potentially saving your life. Airbags are the most *generic solution* to most road emergencies. They are less preferred than more specialized solutions (braking, evading), but still better than nothing if those maneuvers fail. It's the same with your applications — it is better to give the request a chain of potential handlers, as shown in Figure 1-23, instead of letting it fail without even an error message.

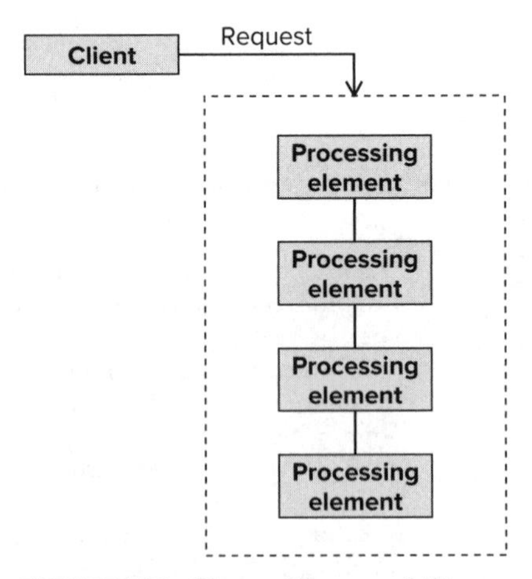

FIGURE 1-23: Chain of Responsibility as a response to a request

So, how do you create such Chain of Responsibility? The main idea of this pattern is to process a request by a list of consecutive handlers to avoid any hard-wired mappings. The initial client holds a reference only to the first element in the chain of handlers. Then each handler holds a reference to the handler afterward. The last handler must always accept the request to avoid passing it to a `NULL` value.

A good class structure supporting this behavioral pattern is shown in Figure 1-24. It consists of a parent `Handler` class that calls the `handle()` method to delegate the request to the next concrete handler `nextHandler`. This `Handler` class is subclassed by concrete handlers that try to do something with the request; if they fail, they call the `handle()` method of their superclass.

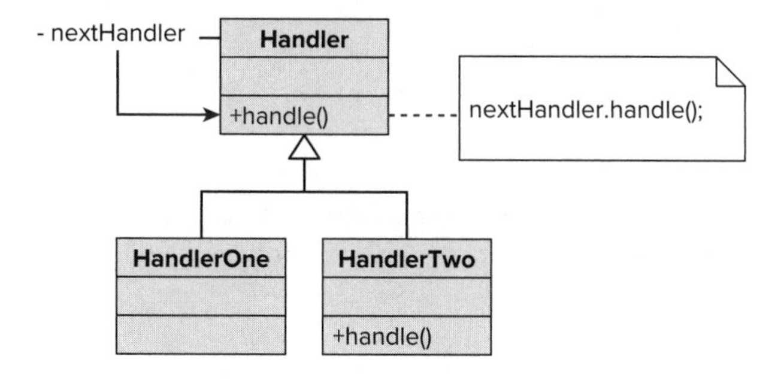

FIGURE 1-24: Chain of Responsibility pattern structure

Chain of Responsibility is commonly used for filters. One example of filtering is when a user request is being processed. First it checks whether the given controller exists or not. If it doesn't exist, a *404 error* is displayed. If it does exist, the request is passed to the controller, which handles it further. It checks whether a user tries to access an unsecured page; if it's true, it redirects the request to an SSL-secured page. Then it is checked for authentication, and so forth.

State

Sometimes you want a component to behave differently for various possible states of the application. First, define an abstract `State` class, which is a common interface for various `ConcreteStates`. All states provide a `handle()` method that provides various behaviors of your component. The `Context` class is the core class that wraps a `ConcreteState` *`state`* object. This design pattern makes sense when `Context` is a complete class that also provides state-independent functionalities. Otherwise, simple subclassing of `Context` would be more efficient.

`Context` calls the `state->handle()` method when processing its own requests. `Context` also has methods for switching between States. Depending on which `ConcreteState` the *`state`* variable holds, the `state->handle()` method provides different behaviors. This can be regarded as emulation of a partial type change at runtime. You can see a diagram of this pattern in Figure 1-25.

The State pattern, although rather simple, is very useful for application development. One example is database connection — the database abstraction layer may change its behavior depending on the current connection state. Another example can be the state of a transaction in an online store — the application may display different pages depending on which steps are needed to complete the transaction.

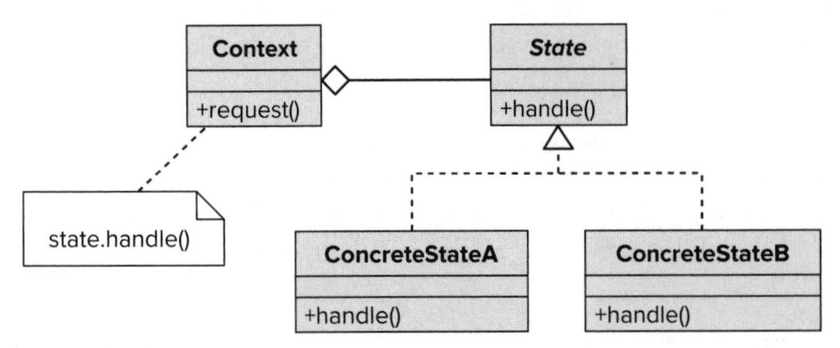

FIGURE 1-25: State pattern structure

Iterator

There are many kinds of aggregate objects and many ways to traverse them. One simple example is an array traversed by consecutive integers supplied to the *array operator*. To print out a five-element `myArray`, you could use the following:

```
for ($i=0;$i<=4;$i++) {
echo $myArray[$i];
}
```

However, this solution is not at all elegant. First of all, you have to take care of `i` variable values. PHP is not C/C++, so it is not catastrophic to call for `myArray[100]` here — it will not return random trash from memory. However, it is still easy to skip some values with hard-wired ranges. Another problem is that such an approach exposes the underlying representation of this aggregation. It makes the traversal procedure dependent on this specific representation and thus is not reusable. Object-oriented programming aims to encapsulate the internal structure of aggregate objects and provide a uniform, safe, and useful interface like this one provided by PHP:

```
interface Iterator{
function current(); // Returns the value of element under current key
function key(); // Returns the current key
function next(); // Moves the internal pointer to the next element
function rewind(); // Moves the internal pointer to the first element
function valid(); // Returns true if the element under current key is valid
}
```

Now every class implementing this interface can use the `foreach` structure. The following snippet of code produces the same output as the previous `for` loop:

```
foreach ($myArray as $value) {
echo $value;
}
```

The abstraction behind this mechanism is the *Iterator* design pattern, pictured in Figure 1-26. The `Client` application has access to two abstract classes: `Collection`, which is the aggregate object interface, and `TraversalAbstraction`, which is created by a corresponding `Collection`. The underlying concrete collections can be as different as a *List* and a *Map*, yet corresponding methods of traversal can be produced for both of them. When `Client` calls the `next()` method, different ordering algorithms are executed for *List* and for *Map*, but in both cases a subsequent element is found.

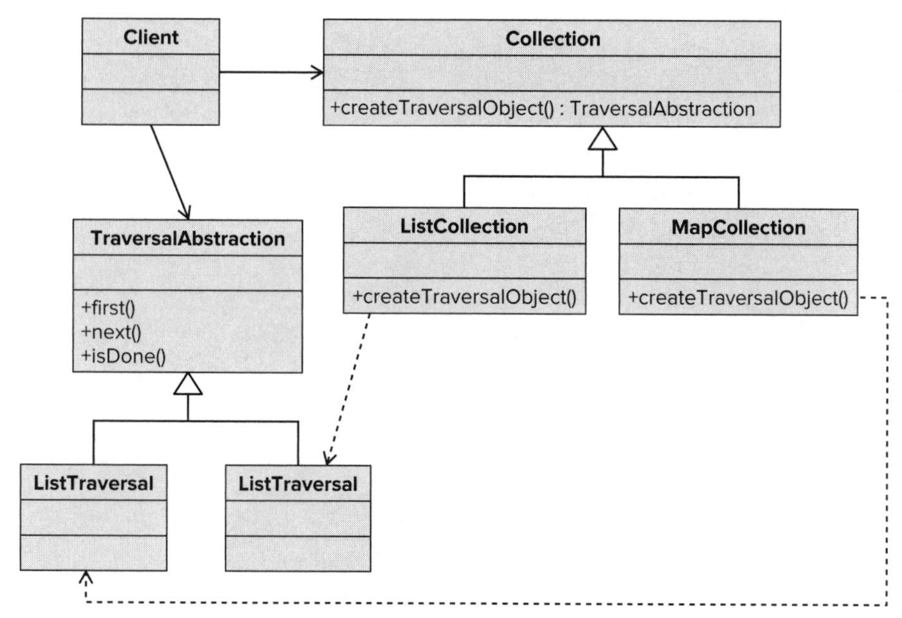

FIGURE 1-26: Iterator pattern structure

In web frameworks the Iterator pattern is used mainly for pagination. You need a uniform interface to divide web content into adequate pieces, turn them into separate web pages, and then traverse through them.

2

Getting Started

If you think your users are idiots, only idiots will use it.

— Linus Torvalds

WHAT'S IN THIS CHAPTER?

- Setting up the hosting environment.
- Installing and configuring frameworks.
- Creating a Hello World application.
- Using integrated development environments (IDEs).

Before you start developing applications with the frameworks, you need to follow a few simple steps. Web applications cannot operate alone; they need to be placed in a special hosting environment. This chapter will show you how to install and configure all software required to get your frameworks going and let you produce working web apps.

Web applications and web frameworks are system-independent, but must be configured properly for the hosting environment they're in. We will show you how to set up workspaces for Windows 7 64-bit, Ubuntu Desktop 10.04.1 64-bit and Mac OS 10.6 Snow Leopard. Of course, these instructions should work for most related operating systems such as Windows Vista or other flavors of Linux.

REQUIREMENTS

In order to successfully build web applications with web frameworks you need the following server software:

- An HTTP server that accepts incoming connections and returns displayed websites

- A relational database based on SQL for persistent storage of all kinds of data
- A PHP interpreter to turn your PHP code into system calls, database queries, and dynamic web page content

To run the application on the client side, you just need a web browser. Examples presented in this book were tested on Mozilla Firefox 3.6.10 and Google Chrome 6.0.472.63 browsers, although they should work well on any modern browser.

XAMPP

The server software requirements presented in the preceding list are common for most web applications. Therefore, the open source community has begun to create packages of the best solutions to satisfy these needs. Combining the Linux operating system, Apache web server, MySQL database, and PHP interpreter, the popular LAMP bundle emerged in the same way WAMP did for Apache, MySQL and PHP for Windows, and MAMP for Mac OS.

XAMPP stands for X = cross platform, Apache, MySQL, PHP, and Perl. It is a wonderful server package that saves hours (okay, maybe just minutes, but minutes are precious, too) of work needed to install all these components independently and make them work together. It is available for all major operating systems. In addition to its main components it also provides some other useful free software, including the following:

- **PEAR package manager** — Discussed later in this chapter.
- **phpMyAdmin** — An immensely clever PHP application that allows MySQL database administration from the level of your browser. It allows modifying whole databases, tables, and individual fields, executing raw SQL statements, and importing and exporting data into various formats, among other tasks. You can see the main page in Figure 2-1.
- **OpenSSL** — A cryptographic library implementing SSL and TLS protocols, used for secure connections.
- **SQLite** — Embedded database system (also discussed later in this chapter).

After installing XAMPP, you may notice a security warning on the phpMyAdmin main page: `http://localhost/phpmyadmin` (see Figure 2-1). That's because phpMyAdmin notices that your database's `root` user has no password, which is indeed an open door for intrusion. XAMPP is configured this way for your convenience — in a development environment it's much easier to have privileged access to the database without needing to type in any passwords.

However, before moving to any production environment you must make XAMPP secure. You can use the `http://localhost/security/` page to monitor your security settings and also fix most basic security issues. Making a web server fully secure is enough material for another thick book, so we will not even begin to discuss it here.

XAMPP for Windows

Just go to the XAMPP website (`www.apachefriends.org/en/xampp.html`), download the Windows version, and run the installer. After the files are extracted, a command window will open and ask you a few questions. The default installation is advised. After the successful installation, you should be able to run the XAMPP Control Panel Application, as shown in Figure 2-2. Try to run Apache and MySQL.

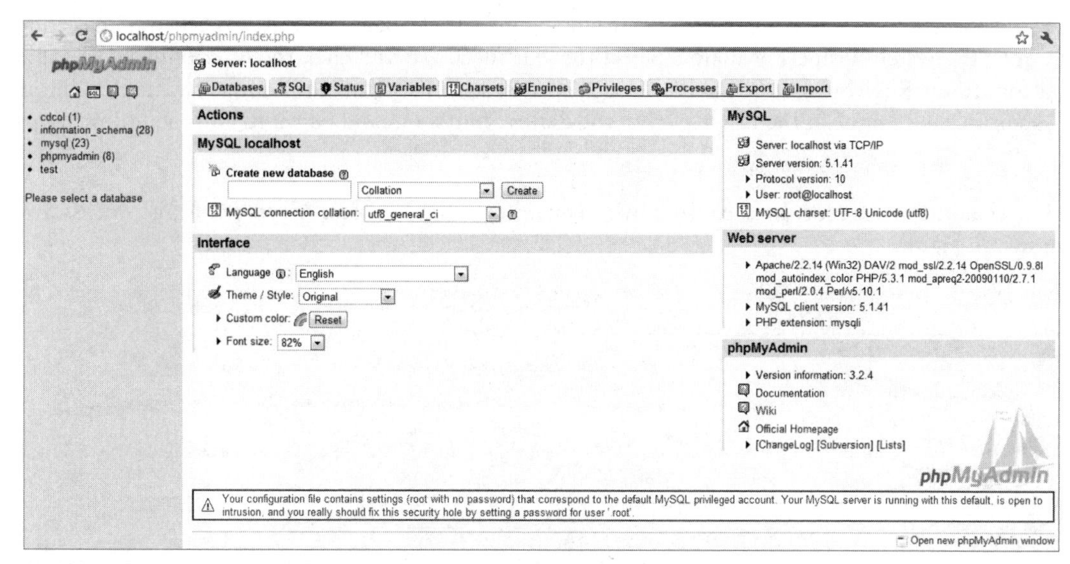

FIGURE 2-1: Main page of the phpMyAdmin database management tool

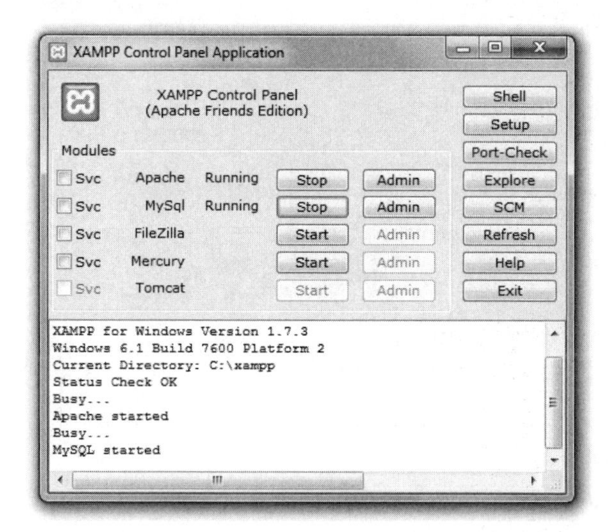

FIGURE 2-2: XAMPP Control Panel with Apache and MySQL running

If any of these modules doesn't start, first check your firewall settings. Apache uses ports: `80` (HTTP), `81` (WebDAV), and `443` (HTTPS). MySQL uses port `3306`. For Apache and MySQL to start properly, these ports must not be blocked by a firewall nor used by any other program. You can use the Port-Check button in the XAMPP Control Panel to find out if any other program uses these ports. A common conflict-maker here is Skype. You need to close such conflicting programs first or change their settings not to block these ports.

On Windows Vista, a problem was reported with the User Account Control (UAC). To deactivate it, type `msconfig` in the start menu; then go to Tools and disable User Access Control.

Another thing you need to do is set the PATH environment variable. Right-click Computer and select Properties from the context menu. In the window that opens, click Advanced system settings to open the System Properties dialog. Select the Advanced tab and click the Environment Variables button. In the Environment Variables dialog you will see a list of all environment variables. In the System variables pane in the lower part of the dialog, find `Path` and edit it to add the following path:

```
;C:\xampp\php;C:\xampp\mysql\bin
```

Note that all entries must be separated by a semicolon and no spaces. All steps of this process are shown in Figure 2-3.

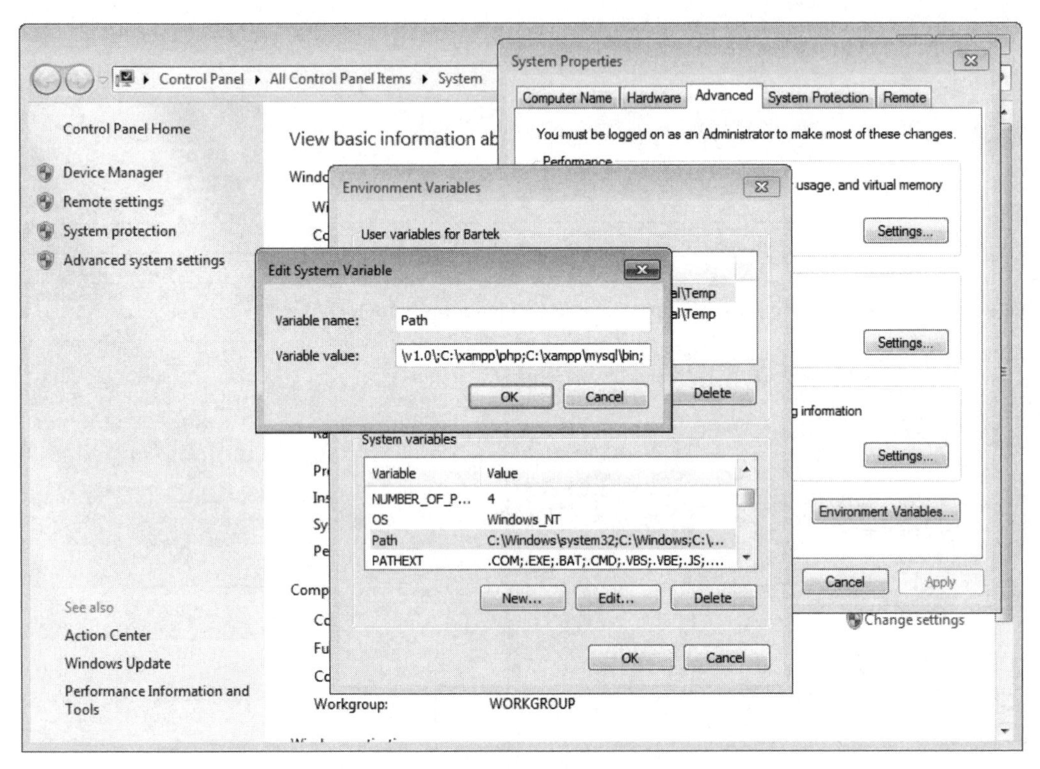

FIGURE 2-3: Setting the PATH environment variable

You will know that your XAMPP is working fine when you type `http://localhost` in your browser and you see a welcome screen.

XAMPP for Linux

Although there are also downloadable installation files of XAMPP for Linux, most Linux users prefer to install all components separately using package managers because it is even faster and simpler than downloading a compressed folder from the Internet. This will be covered in the next few pages. It is also consistent with Linux methodology that recommends using package managers for installation whenever possible because it allows easy management and automated updating of your software. As one somewhat radical friend commented, "No true Tuxhead would ever use that!"

XAMPP for Mac OS

Download the Mac OS package from the XAMPP website (`www.apachefriends.org/en/xampp.html`). A window will open (see Figure 2-4).

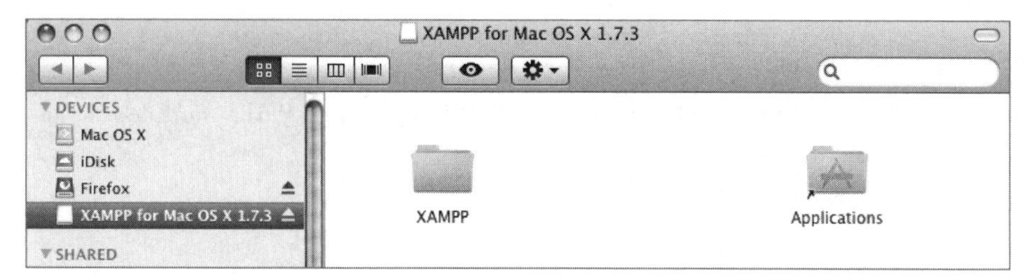

FIGURE 2-4. Mac OS XAMPP package

It is a `.dmg` installer, so just drag and drop it into the `/Applications` folder. You will see a progress bar like the one shown in Figure 2-5.

FIGURE 2-5. Mac OS XAMPP installer progress bar

Finally, go to `/Applications/XAMPP` and run the XAMPP controls. You will see a nice little Control Panel (see Figure 2-6).

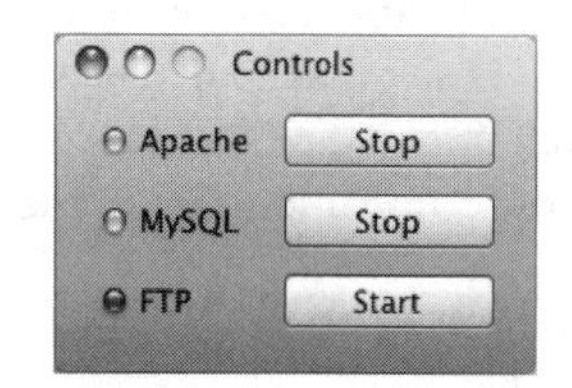

FIGURE 2-6. Mac OS XAMPP Control Panel

Now add `/Applications/XAMPP/xamppfile/bin` to your environment variables. You can do it in a few ways, including using the following command:

```
$ export PATH=${PATH}:/Applications/XAMPP/xamppfile/bin/
```

Apache

Apache, the most popular HTTP web server, is used to host the majority of websites around the world. It is an open source project, maintained and developed by the Apache Software Foundation.

Windows Installation

Apache is installed as a part of XAMPP, so you don't have to install it separately.

Linux Installation

You can get Apache for all flavors of Linux. The following command installs it for Ubuntu:

```
# sudo aptitude install apache2
```

When you go to `http://localhost/` in your browser, you should see a welcome message from the server (see Figure 2-7).

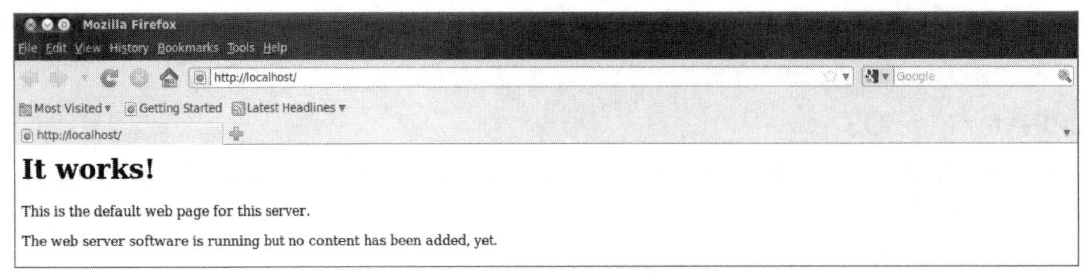

FIGURE 2-7: Apache welcome message

Your installation is not done yet. You need to install the PHP5 engine and PHP5 module for the server:

```
# sudo aptitude install php5 libapache2-mod-php5
```

Then restart Apache with following command:

```
# sudo /etc/init.d/apache2 restart
```

MacOS Installation

Just as with Windows, Apache is installed with XAMPP on Mac OS.

Database

All web applications need persistent data storage. The most widely used mechanisms are relational database management systems (RDBMSs). They are not really perfectly matched for object-oriented web applications (this is further discussed in Chapter 3), but they are standard technologies used by most companies and by the frameworks.

Now let's focus on installing a database solution.

MySQL

MySQL is one of the leading open source databases. First it was developed by a Swedish company, MySQL AB; then the company was bought by Sun Microsystems, which in turn was bought by Oracle Corporation in 2010. MySQL is equipped with innovative features such as triggers, views, replication, and stored procedures. It is written in C/C++, is multithreaded, and is among the fastest RDBMSs with client-server architecture.

XAMPP includes MySQL, so you don't have to install it anymore on Windows and Mac OS. To install MySQL and PHP5 support under Ubuntu, type the following into the console:

```
# sudo aptitude install mysql-server mysql-client php5-mysql
```

The package manager will ask you if you want to set up a root password. Although such a password is strongly recommended for production environments, it is easier to develop our applications without this password. If you need to set it (for example, if phpMyAdmin wants it), you can do it any time with following command:

```
# sudo mysqladmin -u root password NEW_PASSWORD
```

SQLite

Most databases are built on client-server architecture, in which the database is a standalone process of the operating system, and all applications need to establish connections with it. SQLite is completely different. It works as a statically or dynamically linked programming library that is embedded into applications, allowing communication with the database by function calls (which is much more efficient). This approach also removes the necessities of installation and administration. The whole database is stored in a single file with a mechanism of locking it for read and write operations. SQLite is light, but fast and capable. It is generally ACID-compliant (atomicity, consistency, isolation, durability), but the programmer must manually impose integrity constraints on data types; otherwise, it is possible to insert incorrect data types. SQLite lacks some features of heavier databases, such as views or triggers.

XAMPP also includes SQLite. To install both SQLite and PHP5 support under Ubuntu, just type the following:

```
# sudo aptitude install sqlite php5-sqlite
```

phpMyAdmin — Linux

If you envy XAMPP users the phpMyAdmin application, you can install it now with following command:

```
# sudo aptitude install phpmyadmin
```

It will automatically configure your Apache and MySQL database. You only need to include into `/etc/apache2/apache2.conf` the following line:

```
Include /etc/phpmyadmin/apache.conf
```

You can access phpMyAdmin at `http://localhost/phpMyAdmin`.

PEAR

PEAR stands for PHP Extension and Application Repository. It is a distribution system, sometimes also called a *framework*, and can be very helpful in PHP development. PEAR provides modules of PHP code, called *packages*, and a package manager for easy installation of these. The full list of packages can be found at `http://pear.php.net/packages.php`.

To install some packages, go to the command line. To call a Windows command line with PEAR support, go to the XAMPP Control Panel and click the Shell button. Find on the package list at the PEAR website the name of the package you want to install; for example, let it be a tool for Fibonacci series computation: `Math_Fibonacci-0.8`. You can install it using following command:

```
# pear install Math_Fibonacci-0.8
```

As you can see in Figure 2-8, this package is dependent on another package: `Math_Integer`. You can install it automatically with following switch:

```
# pear install --alldeps Math_Fibonacci-0.8
```

Now you have the package installed and you can include its classes into your applications.

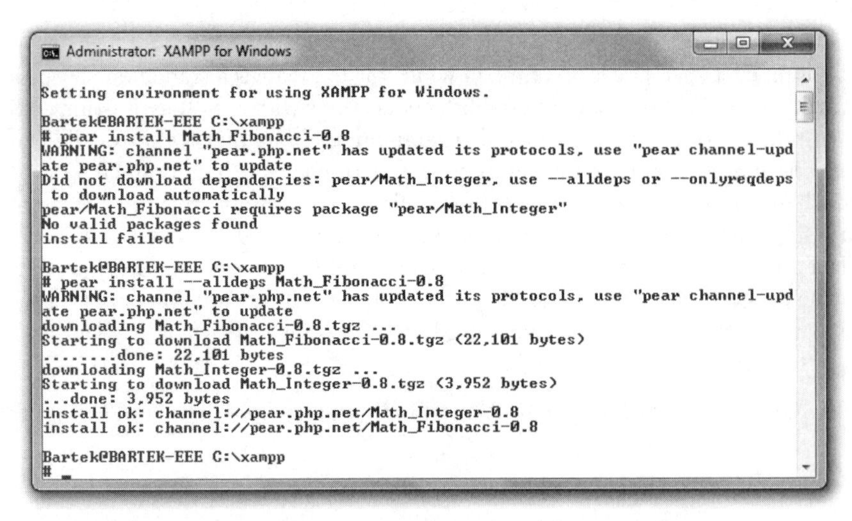

FIGURE 2-8: Installing PEAR packages with XAMPP shell for Windows

PEAR also provides an `upgrade` tool for easy updating of packages. A special example is upgrading the PEAR itself with following command, (which is a recommended action, by the way):

```
# pear upgrade pear
```

Windows

PEAR is included within the XAMPP package.

Linux

PEAR is included into some Linux distributions. If it's not, you can easily install it with package managers:

```
# apt-get install php-pear
```

Mac OS

PEAR is already installed within XAMPP.

Subversion (SVN)

Subversion is a revision control system founded in 2000 by CollabNet Inc. Its popular name, SVN, is derived from its shell command `svn`. It is not required for installation of web frameworks, nor for further development with them, so this installation is optional.

This tool is essential in most community projects, so even if you do not use it to install the frameworks, you will surely run across it one way or another. If you have never used this tool, you should become familiar with it.

The features of Subversion include the following:

- Full tracking of the past versions of the project

- Allows branching and merging of code
- Interrupted commit operations do not break the files (they are atomic)
- Efficient storage using differences between versions
- Program messages are translated into many languages.

You can learn more about SVN and get download instructions at `http://subversion.apache.org/`.

Installation Overview

At this point you have all your required software downloaded and set up. Generally there is more than one way to install the frameworks. Installation with PEAR is generally the easiest way. You can also download sandbox applications that need just extraction to a chosen folder. Package managers provide a Linux way of fast managed installation, but some distributions use very obsolete versions (see the following table for consideration of Ubuntu packages). Finally, there is the possibility of SVN checkout for advanced users to get fresh, updated code.

The following table compares availability of the installation methods.

	PEAR	SANDBOX	PACKAGE MANAGER	VERSION CONTROL SYSTEM
SYMFONY	Works	Yes	Obsolete	SVN
CAKEPHP	Not available	Yes	Obsolete	SVN\Git
ZEND FRAMEWORK	Works*	Just archive	Works	SVN

* Only unofficial channel available

INSTALLATION

This section covers the installation of Symfony, CakePHP, and Zend Framework for Windows 7 64-bit, Ubuntu 10.04.1 Desktop Edition 64-bit, and Mac OS 10.6 Snow Leopard. Of course, this should work with little or no modifications for other versions of these operating systems. We assume that you have all your required software installed and properly configured. Installation of frameworks varies little between different operating systems. Generally we will provide one installation guide, and minor differences will be put into square braces: [ ].

Symfony

Although there are many ways to install Symfony, we will show only the simplest approaches in this section. The sandbox is a fast preview — you don't have to follow this installation, but we believe it might be useful if you have never installed any frameworks before. PEAR is our default installation for Windows and for Linux as well. Advanced developers will probably want to check out from SVN (and they will need no guidance), but this involves setting up an SVN environment, which is not necessary and might be an effort for beginners. Package managers provide (for Ubuntu) the obsolete 1.0 version, so they will be disregarded here.

Installation instructions are for Symfony 1.4.8. By the time you read this book, Symfony 2.0 should be available to download with PEAR. At the time of writing, the 2.0 beta is available for preview as a sandbox application and that's how we installed it to describe Symfony 2.0 features.

Sandbox

Sandbox is the absolutely fastest way to start playing with Symfony because all you need to do is download a package from `http://www.symfony-project.org/installation` and unzip the `/sf_sandbox` folder into the web root directory:

- **Windows** — `C:\xampp\htdocs`
- **Linux** — `/var/www`
- **Mac OS** — `/Applications/XAMPP/htdocs/`

Then you can type `http://localhost/sf_sandbox/web/` into your browser to see your sample project.

Well, even if the sample project is working, it probably lacks CSS and images. If that's the case, you will see this message:

> *This project uses the symfony libraries. If you see no image in this page, you may need to configure your web server so that it gains access to the symfony_data/web/sf/ directory.*

This page with no CSS is shown later in this chapter in Figure 2-11, where it is the output of the default project generator. When you look at the web page source, you see that the image links point to nonexistent folders. This may lead to lots of confusion because you might expect that a sandbox application would really run out of the box, just like the Symfony developers promised!

You do not really need these images because you will shortly transform this example into your first application, but it's educative to do it anyway. The simplest way to enjoy these images is to add an alias to your Apache server, redirecting the nonexistent directory to the proper path. To do that, go to `C:\xampp\apache\conf` in Windows, `/etc/apache2/` in Linux, or `/Applications/XAMPP/etc/` in Mac OS and then add the following line at the end of the `httpd.conf` file:

- Windows:

  ```
  Alias /sf_sandbox/web/sf "C:\xampp\htdocs\sf_sandbox\lib\vendor\symfony\data\web\sf"
  ```

- Linux:

  ```
  Alias /sf_sandbox/web/sf var/www/sf_sandbox/lib/vendor/symfony/data/web/sf
  ```

- Mac OS:

  ```
  Alias /sf_sandbox/web/sf /Applications/XAMPP/xamppfiles/lib/php/pear/data
  /symfony/web/sf/
  ```

Restart the Apache server. The resulting webpage will look like Figure 2-9.

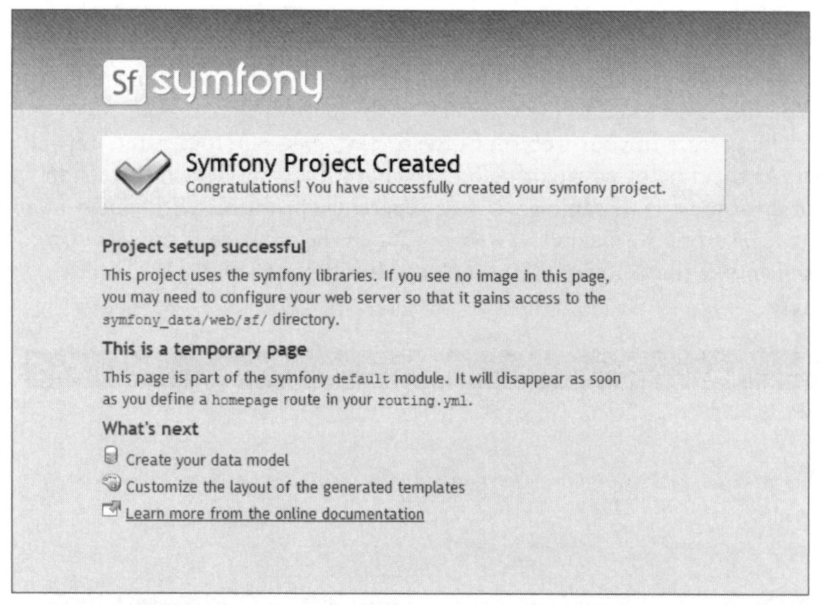

FIGURE 2-9: Sample Symfony project

It is perfectly okay to use the sandbox version of Symfony stored in the web root folder for learning and development because it is a complete installation of Symfony. However, for production environments you have to separate the configuration files from the web presentation files for security reasons. Otherwise, vulnerable files such as `/config/databases.yml` will be accessible to the public.

To uninstall the sandbox, simply delete the `/sf_sandbox` folder and undo the modification in `httpd.conf`.

PEAR

This method is also fast and simple. Just open your command line and type (`sudo` for Linux) the following:

```
# pear channel-discover pear.symfony-project.com
# pear install symfony/symfony
```

The most up-to-date version of Symfony will be installed. This book was written using Symfony 1.4.8, so if you want to install this specific version, type this instead:

```
# pear channel-discover pear.symfony-project.com
# pear install symfony/symfony-1.4.8
```

A great advantage of this approach is that the `symfony` command has been integrated with the console. You can check it with this:

```
# symfony
```

You will get a list of available tasks.

CakePHP

CakePHP installation is extremely straightforward because in contrast with Symfony, everything works out of the box. You just need to go to the CakePHP website (`http://cakephp.org`) and download the package. Then create in your web root directory a `/cakephp` folder and unpack the package contents into it. At the time of writing this book, the most recent CakePHP version was 1.3.4, and we have used it for most code samples. If you experience problems with a newer version, you can download 1.3.4 from the CakePHP website. When the package is unpacked, you should see a welcome screen like that shown in Figure 2-10 after typing `http://localhost/cakephp` in your browser.

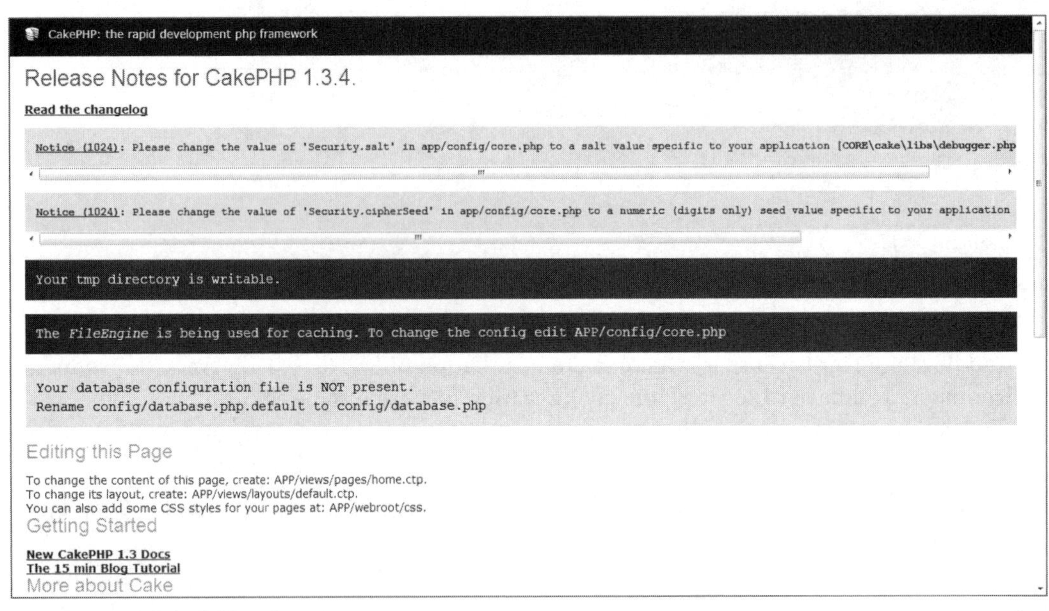

FIGURE 2-10: CakePHP welcome page

Linux users probably will not see a page like this because of default Linux settings. If images are missing and you get warnings that some files are not writeable, you need to do a few things more. First, recursively change the web root directory to be writeable:

```
$ sudo chmod -R 777 /var/www
```

The second thing is to make sure that `mod_rewrite` is activated. To do it, invoke the following command:

```
$ sudo a2enmod rewrite
```

And finally edit `/etc/apache2/sites-enabled/000-default`. Locate the following block:

```
<Directory /var/www/>
   Options Indexes FollowSymLinks MultiViews
   AllowOverride None
   Order allow,deny
   allow from all
</Directory>
```

Change `AllowOverride None` to `AllowOverride All`. Restart your Apache. It should now work as shown in Figure 2-10.

Apart from this sandbox application, you can also install development versions of CakePHP using the Git online revision control tool, but stable versions are highly recommended.

Zend Framework

Zend Framework has a wide choice of install options. Our recommended approach is to use the PEAR channel. This is an unofficial PEAR channel, yet it is regularly updated and works just fine. However, just in case it is ever broken or discontinued, we also present the installation from archive. The version that was used to write this book is 1.10.8, so you may look for it if you experience compatibility issues with the latest version.

You can also install Zend Framework bundled with Zend Server Community Edition (CE), which is a nice and easy way to start development with Zend Server. However, in this book we will not follow this approach in favor of approaches that are easier to compare between frameworks.

There are also almost up to date Ubuntu packages of Zend Framework. Perhaps there is not a regular update schedule, but if you feel adventurous, you can try installing ZF with package managers. Of course, SVN checkout is possible as well.

PEAR

The PEAR channel provides the fastest and simplest installation method. Just go to your console and type the following:

```
# pear channel-discover pear.zfcampus.org
# pear install zfcampus/zf
```

Zend Framework libraries will be installed and the command-line tool will be integrated with your shell.

Archive

First download a *Full* package of Zend Framework from its website, `http://framework.zend.com/download/latest`. There is also a *Minimal* package, but it lacks several modules you will need later. ZF doesn't provide any sandbox application, so installing from archive means just extracting its contents to a directory of your choice.

CONFIGURATION

There are some minor tasks that need to be done before you can create your sample projects. The solutions presented here are absolutely the simplest methods to make things work and sometimes are not elegant. If you are experienced in operating systems and web development, you can add several upgrades such as separating your development environment from the web root and creating a personalized `/public_html` folder, but it's not needed for a quick start. Also we will not configure frameworks to connect to the databases. The next chapter is focused on everything associated with databases and data models, and they will be explained in detail there.

Symfony

There is not much configuration for Symfony here. Some configuration will be done during the Hello World example, but there is nothing to prepare before getting to that point. However, don't be lulled into a sense of complacency by this fact, as you will configure many things in Symfony later on.

CakePHP

Remember the welcome page of CakePHP (Figure 2-10) at `http://localhost/cakephp`? It displayed some notices to attract your attention, and now we will deal with them.

First, change the `Security.salt` and `Security.cipherSeed` values in `/app/config/core.php`, as shown in the following code. They are needed for security purposes — you need to provide random values generated by yourself. Security issues are further described in Chapter 8.

```
/**
 * A random string used in security hashing methods.
 */
Configure::write('Security.salt', 'nrhG93b0qyJfIxfs3guVoUubWwvniR2G0dgaC9mi');
/**
 * A random numeric string (digits only) used to encrypt/decrypt strings.
 */
Configure::write('Security.cipherSeed', '468593096574535434967416836451');
```

The two top yellow (light grey in Figure 2-10) blocks should be gone now. While you are in the `/app/config` directory, make a copy of the `database.php.default` file and change the name of the copy to `database.php`.

When all other configuration steps are done, the last thing is to add the `cake` command to the command-line interface:

- **Windows** — Add to the PATH environment variable (the process was shown during XAMPP installation) following path:

  ```
  ;C:\xampp\htdocs\cakephp\cake\console
  ```

- **Linux** — The following command is a smart way to add the path to the environment of the current user. The `/home/username/.profile` file is modified as the result:

  ```
  echo 'export PATH=/var/www/cakephp/cake/console:$PATH' >> ~/.profile
  ```

- **Mac OS** — You can export the path with the following command:

  ```
  $ export PATH=${PATH}:/Applications/XAMPP/htdocs/cakephp/cake/console
  ```

Zend Framework

Once you have your framework installed, you need to do two things. The first one is to make sure that the ZF's command-line tool is added into the PATH environment variable. This tool is found here:

- **Windows** — `/path_to_zf/bin/zf.bat`
- **Linux** — `/path_to_zf/bin/zf.sh`
- **Mac OS** — `/Applications/XAMPP/xamppfiles/bin/zf`

The good thing about PEAR is that this will be already done during the installation.

The second thing is to add the Zend `/library` to the PHP `include_path`. To do it, you need to find a corresponding line in `php.ini` and add the path to `/path_to_zf/library`. This file can be found here:

- **Windows** — `C:\xampp\php`
- **Linux** — `/etc/php5/apache2`
- **Mac OS** — `/Applications/XAMPP/xamppfiles/etc`

Also check `register_globals` and `magic_quotes_gpc` and make sure they are both `Off`.

HELLO WORLD!

It is finally the time to create and run your first framework application. If you have used a sandbox, most of the work has been already done. That's why we recommend the PEAR installs wherever possible — they are the easiest to configure and you can still learn how to use the command-line interface to create your projects.

Symfony

Go to your web root and create a new directory there, for example `/symfony`. Then open the console, navigate to this new folder, and turn it into a Symfony project:

```
$ symfony generate:project symfony
```

Inside this project, create an application. Let it be named `frontend` because it will produce the output for the user:

```
$ symfony generate:app frontend
```

Still inside the main project folder, execute the following statement to create a `hello` module of the `frontend` application:

```
$ symfony generate:module frontend hello
```

You can now go with your browser to `http://localhost/symfony/hello` and admire the web page of your default generated project, shown in Figure 2-11. If you played with the sandbox installation, notice that it's the same image-less page.

We want to change this default view to a view of our new module. Locate the file `/symfony/apps/frontend/config/routing.yml` and change the `homepage` parameter from the `default` module to the `hello` module. After editing, these lines should look as follows:

Available for download on Wrox.com

```
homepage:
  url:   /
  param: { module: hello, action: index }
```

code snippet /symfony/apps/frontend/config/routing.yml

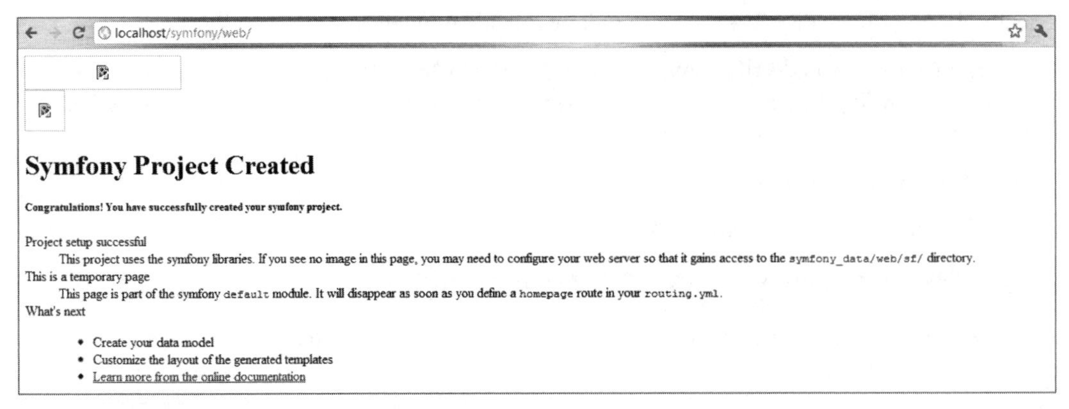

FIGURE 2-11: Web page of the default Symfony project

This code redirected the main page of this application to our module. You can check this in your browser, but you need to clear the cache from the command line:

```
# symfony cc
```

Now when you go to `http://localhost/symfony/hello`, you should see Figure 2-12.

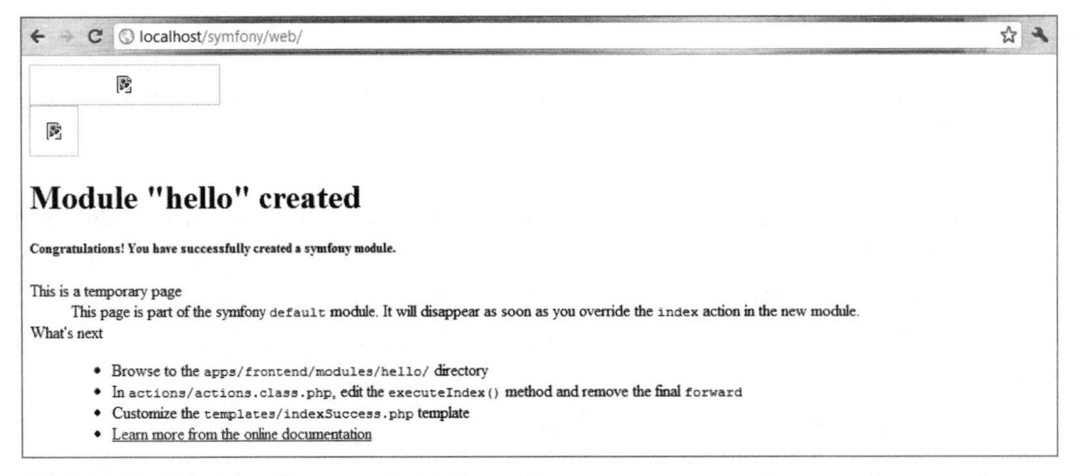

FIGURE 2-12: Web page of the generated hello module

It is just a bit better, but you are still in the `default` module. To be able to display your own module, go to `/symfony/apps/frontend/modules/hello/actions/actions.class.php` and comment out the forwarding function, just like this:

```
<?php
class helloActions extends sfActions {
  public function executeIndex(sfWebRequest $request) {
    //$this->forward('default', 'module');
  }
}
```

code snippet /symfony/apps/frontend/modules/hello/actions/actions.class.php

Now the browser will display a blank page because the index view for the `hello` module is empty. To change that, go to `/symfony/apps/frontend/modules/hello/templates/indexSuccess.php` and put the following there:

Available for download on Wrox.com

```
<h1>Hello World!</h1>
```

code snippet /symfony/apps/frontend/modules/hello/templates/indexSuccess.php

Now check `http://localhost/symfony/hello` again. You should see a big black Hello World! message, as shown in Figure 2-13. Well done!

FIGURE 2-13: Hello World example in Symfony

CakePHP

It's time to create the first application in CakePHP. You will need a controller, a model, and a view. First, let's make the controller. Create a new file in `/app/controllers` and name it `hello_controller.php`. Names are important in CakePHP because they indicate the default file for the `hello` controller. You need to add into this controller the following code:

Available for download on Wrox.com

```
<?php
class HelloController extends AppController{
    function index(){
        $this->set( 'test', "Hello World!");
    }
}
?>
```

code snippet /cakephp/app/controllers/hello_controller.php

It is possible to create a controller that uses no model, but we want to include a dummy model instead into our example. When you set the `$useTable` property to `false`, it makes a model that does not use a database. Your database is not connected yet, so that's exactly what you need now.

Available for download on Wrox.com

```
<?php
class Hello extends AppModel{
    var $useTable = false;
}
?>
```

code snippet /cakephp/app/models/hello.php

Create the view that will present the data to the user. In the controller, you have set a `test` variable that can be displayed in the associated view. You need to create an additional `/hello` folder inside `/app/views`. Note also that this view needs a peculiar CakePHP template file `.ctp` extension.

Available for download on Wrox.com

```
<html>
<body><h1><?php echo $test ?></h1>
```

```
<p>Congratulations! You have created your first CakePHP project.
</body>
</html>
```

code snippet /cakephp/app/views/hello/index.ctp

Go to the file `/app/config/routes.php` and comment out the two default routing schemes. Write a rule that redirects connections from the web root to the `hello` controller and sets `index()` as the default action.

```
// Router::connect('/', array('controller' => 'pages', 'action' =>
 'display', 'home'));
// Router::connect('/pages/*', array('controller' => 'pages', 'action' =>
 'display'));

Router::connect('/', array('controller' => 'hello', 'action' => 'index'));
```

The result is presented in Figure 2-14. Notice that the CakePHP default stylesheet was used.

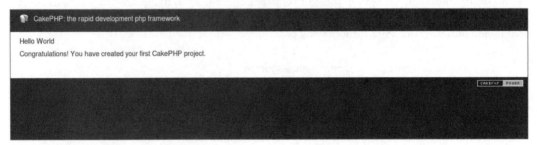

FIGURE 2-14. Hello World example in CakePHP

Zend Framework

Navigate with your command line to the place where you want to set up your Hello World application. In this case, it will be the web root folder. Then use ZF's command-line tool to create a project template:

```
$ zf create project zfhello
```

Now you can go to your browser and type in this link: `http://localhost/zfhello/public`. You will hopefully see a blue image (its grayscale version is presented in Figure 2-15).

The default controller and view were already created by the `zf create project` command, so there is not much work to be done. But take a look at them anyway. First the controller:

```
<?php
class IndexController extends Zend_Controller_Action
{
    public function init()
    {
        /* Initialize action controller here */
    }
    public function indexAction()
    {
```

```
            // action body
        }
    }
```

code snippet /zfhello/application/controllers/IndexController.php

FIGURE 2-15: The default web page of a new Zend Framework project

As you can see, it has only stubs of actions. You will fill them later and write new ones as well.

Second, take a look at the view. It is located at `/zfhello/application/views/scripts/index/index.phtml`. Notice the `.phtml` extension. It is a pre-HTML template that is preprocessed before being served as an HTML page. It may also have PHP scripts embedded. You can type a paragraph or two into it. For example, in the following code you add a Hello World message under the `<h3>` title:

```
<style>
    // various style definitions
</style>
<div id="welcome">
    <h1>Welcome to the <span id="zf-name">Zend Framework!</span></h1>
    <h3>This is your project's main page</h3>
    <div id="more-information">
        <p><img src="http://framework.zend.com/images
          /PoweredBy_ZF_4LightBG.png" /></p>
        <p>
            Helpful Links: <br />
            <a href="http://framework.zend.com/">Zend Framework Website</a> |
            <a href="http://framework.zend.com/manual/en
              /">Zend Framework Manual</a>
        </p>
    </div>
</div>
```

code snippet /zfhello/application/views/scripts/index/index.phtml

We couldn't leave without showing a Hello World example, so we have edited this file a little and you can see the effect in Figure 2-16.

FIGURE 2-16: Hello World example in Zend Framework

That's it! You've managed to install all frameworks, configure them, and create your sample Hello World applications.

STRUCTURE

This section will take a look at the structure of folders and the most important files after the default installation and creation of a project. The default installation method is PEAR for Symfony and Zend Framework, and the sandbox application for CakePHP.

Symfony

Symfony framework core installation — that is, all files installed by PEAR will be called the *global files*, while the place where your application is developed with all files generated by Symfony will be referred to as *local files*. In the sandbox installation, global and local files are placed together, so if you decided to use it, you will have to make the appropriate adjustments to follow the information in this section.

The global files are divided into two folders. The first folder, `/data/symfony`, is located in the user space of your operating system. Under Linux, it is in the standard directory, `C:\xampp\php\PEAR\data\symfony`, but under Windows. You must look for it at `C:\Users\Username\pear\data\symfony\web`. This folder contains Symfony's command-line tool and media files for web templates — check `/data/symfony/web/sf/sf_default` if you want styles for your default Symfony website. The hierarchy for this folder is the following:

```
/data/symfony
    bin
    web
```

The second global folder contains Symfony libraries, as shown in the following list. If you have installed XAMPP, it will be located at `/xampp/php/PEAR/symfony`. Under Linux it will be `/usr/share/php5/symfony/`.

```
/symfony
    action
```

```
        addon
        autoload
        cache
        command
        config
        controller
        database
        debug
        escaper
        event_dispatcher
        exception
        filter
        form
        generator
        helper
        i18n
        log
        mailer
        plugin
        plugins
        request
        response
        routing
        storage
        task
        test
        user
        util
        validator
        vendor
        view
        widget
        yaml
```

The local folder is created by you in the web root or in any other location you prefer. It consists of the following folders:

```
/symfony
    apps
    cache
    config
    data
    lib
    log
    plugins
    test
    web
```

The important thing about Symfony is that it generates three levels of applications. The root local `symfony` folder is the project folder. In `/apps` there may be multiple applications. And each of these applications has a `/modules` folder where you create individual modules folders, resulting in organized, yet needlessly long, paths to individual files.

CakePHP

After installation, CakePHP has the following folder structure:

```
/cakephp
    app
    cake
    vendors
    plugins
    .gitignore
    .htaccess
    index.php
    README
```

- `app` — The folder of your application. It contains a template folder structure and some default files.
- `cake` — Contains core components of CakePHP. You should never edit it.
- `vendors` — Placeholder for third-party libraries.
- `plugins` — Here you can install CakePHP plug-ins.
- `.htaccess` — Server access rule that redirects you to `/app/webroot`, where the welcome message and a script verifying your installation are located.
- `index.php` — PHP redirection in case `mod_rewrite` was not enabled.

The `/app` folder is especially interesting and you will use it often:

```
/app
    config
    controllers
    libs
    locale
    models
    plugins
    tests
    tmp
    vendors
    views
    webroot
    .htaccess
    index.php
```

The names are mostly self-explanatory, but please note the following folders:

- `config` — CakePHP follows a *convention over configuration* approach. There are only a few necessary configuration files and they are stored there.
- `controllers`, `models` **and** `views` — The MVC pattern in action.
- `plugins` & `vendors` — There are also folders with these names in the main `/cakephp` folder. These additional folders allow better customization of multiple applications.

- `tmp` — Stores temporary data-like logs or session information. It must be writeable.
- `webroot` — The document root of your application for production environments. Contains CSS, images, JavaScripts, and other deployable files.

Zend Framework

The full downloadable package after installation includes these directories:

```
/ZendFramework-1.10.8
    bin
    demos
    externals
    extras
    incubator
    library
    resources
    src
    tests
    INSTALL.txt
    LICENSE.txt
    README.txt
```

Of these, the most important is the `/library` folder that holds the majority of the framework itself. That's why ZF is sometimes called "more a library than a framework." You can unpack this whole structure to any directory, as long as it is a fixed place. If installed with PEAR, only libraries and binaries are installed. The command-line binaries are exported into the shell then. You will find the libraries in the following folders:

Under Windows:

```
C:\xampp\php\PEAR\Zend
```

Under Linux (usually):

```
/usr/share/php/Zend/
```

And under Mac OS:

```
/Applications/XAMPP/xamppfiles/lib/php/pear/Zend/
```

When you create a project using command-line tools, it looks like this:

```
/zfhello
    application
        Bootstrap.php
        configs
            application.ini
        controllers
            ErrorController.php
            IndexController.php
        models
        views
            helpers
```

```
            scripts
                error
                    error.phtml
                index
                    index.phtml
    library
    public
        htaccess
        index.php
    tests
        application
            bootstrap.php
        library
            bootstrap.php
        phpunit.xml
```

An important file here is `/zfhello/application/Bootstrap.php`. It allows mapping URLs to controller actions. It also defines which components and resources should be initialized.

IDE SUPPORT

In this book, we will show you how to build web applications using pure frameworks and their plug-ins with as little third-party support software as possible. That's the best way to understand the nature of each framework and grasp its unique qualities. However, once you get familiar with them, you might want to use an integrated development environment (IDE) to further speed up and organize your development process. There are a few IDE solutions that you can integrate with your frameworks; the most notable are NetBeans, Eclipse, and Zend Studio.

These IDE integrations are purely optional and not required for further chapters of this book. Moreover, you can integrate an IDE while in any part of this book, so you can skip it now. As a rule of thumb, you should use an IDE only if you exactly know *how* you will benefit from it.

NetBeans

NetBeans is written entirely in Java, so it is commonly called "a Java tool." Many developers do not know that it is also a great IDE for PHP development. It provides built-in support for Symfony and Zend Framework. It offers a few development enhancements like:

- Autocompletion for both application and framework classes
- Running framework commands by keyboard shortcuts or convenient menus with searching and documentation
- Automated creation of frontend and backend apps
- Support for YAML syntax
- Error messages printed with red font — simple yet useful

You can download NetBeans from `http://netbeans.org/downloads/index.html`. Then you need to include the framework's library in NetBeans preferences and set some framework-specific options. If you did it well, you should be able to create a new Framework project with the New PHP Project wizard, as shown in Figure 2-17.

Despite efforts of the community, NetBeans still doesn't have built-in support for CakePHP. That situation is about to change in the upcoming 7.0 version, but for now you can, with some effort, use only some of the most basic IDE functions. Fortunately, you can also integrate CakePHP with Eclipse, which seems the best IDE solution for CakePHP now.

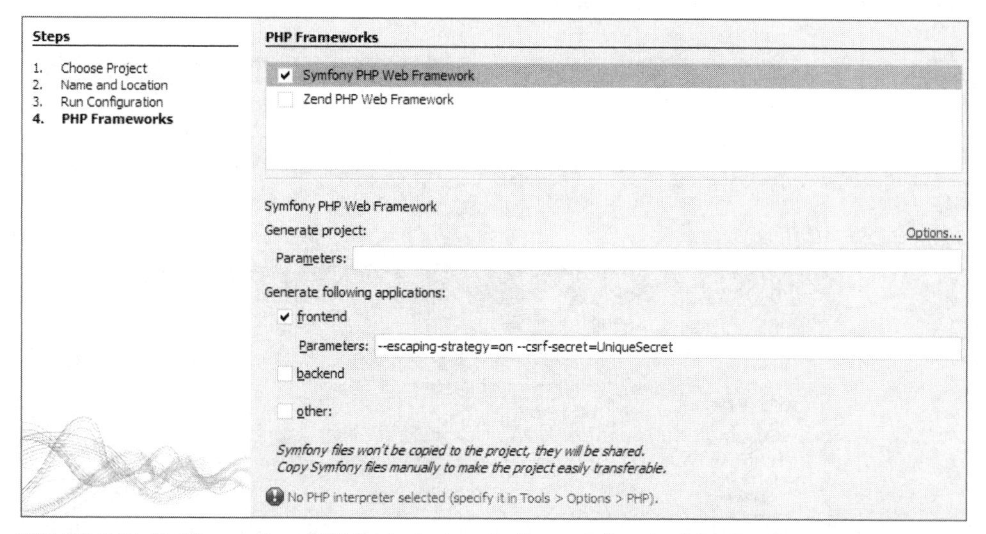

FIGURE 2-17: NetBeans New PHP Project wizard's framework selection

Eclipse

Eclipse is a generic IDE, but it provides several tools for PHP development, for instance the intuitively named PHP Development Tools (PDT) project. You can download it from `http://www.eclipse.org/pdt/`. While Eclipse has no direct support for any of the frameworks, it can be configured with little effort for each one to provide several basic enhancements such as autocompletion. The preferred solution for both Symfony and Zend Framework is NetBeans, so we will show you how to integrate Eclipse with CakePHP.

First, download both CakePHP and Eclipse with the PDT pack. There are no installers, so just unpack them to separate folders on your hard drive. Run `eclipse.exe` from the Eclipse main folder. Set a convenient workspace — a good idea is a web server's applications folder such as `C:\xampp\htdocs`. Then copy CakePHP's `/app` folder into this workspace and rename it as you wish (in this example, it is named `cake_example`). In Eclipse's File menu create a new PHP project and name it just like the folder you have previously renamed. You should see the folder name in the source list, and when you click Finish, there will be a tree of all subfolders that were once inside the original `/app` folder.

Once you have your application imported, you can make several development upgrades; the two most important are linking the project with the CakePHP core and the integration of Cake's `bake` script with Eclipse's Run External Tool command. The first thing can be done by creating a separate PHP project for CakePHP and pointing to the core files as existing sources. Then right-click the `cake_example` project in the source list and select Configure Include Path. Then include the CakePHP project as shown in Figure 2-18. Then you should have autocompletion for all core CakePHP classes.

The integration of Symfony and Zend Framework is almost the same. You can also use Eclipse to provide an IDE for other less-known frameworks.

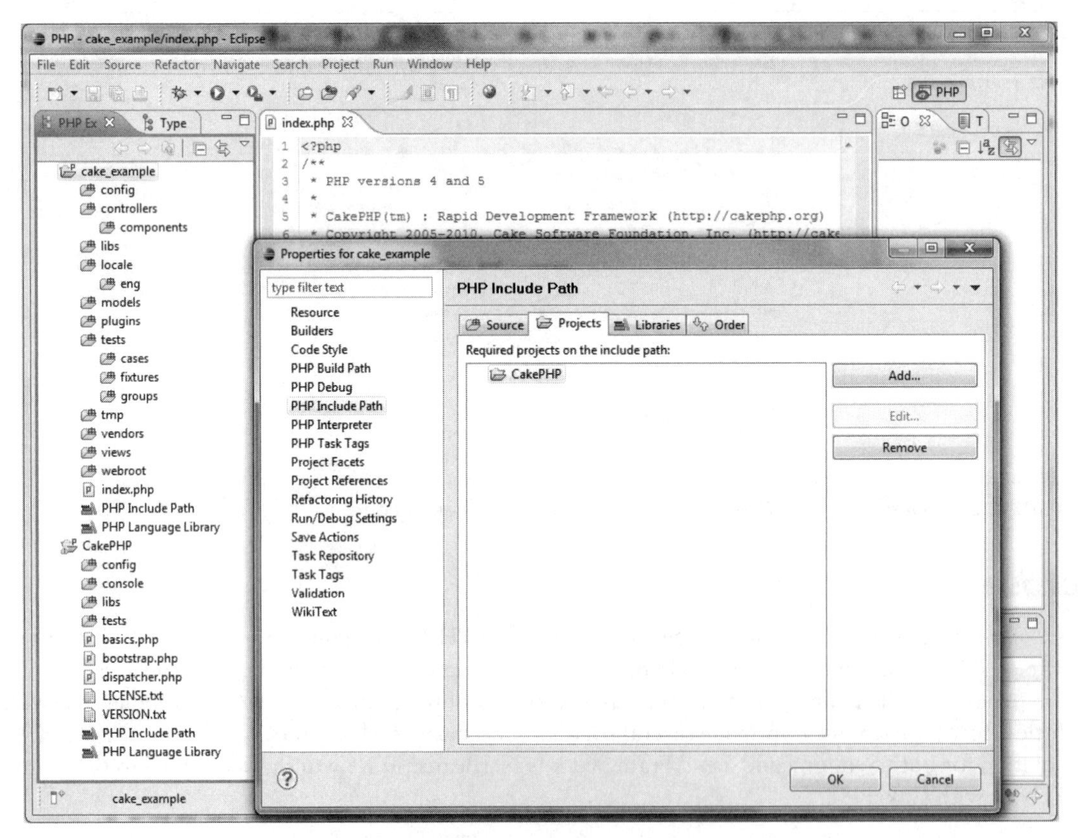

FIGURE 2-18: Including CakePHP core files into an example application

Zend Studio

Zend Studio offers great functionalities for extending the Zend Framework, including code generation, an integrated debugger, and integration with Zend Server. However it is proprietary software. In this book we focus on open source solutions for individual developers and small companies, so we will not use this IDE in further chapters. However, you are encouraged to download a 30-day trial version at `http://www.zend.com/en/products/studio/`. Figure 2-19 shows creating a new ZF project with Zend Studio.

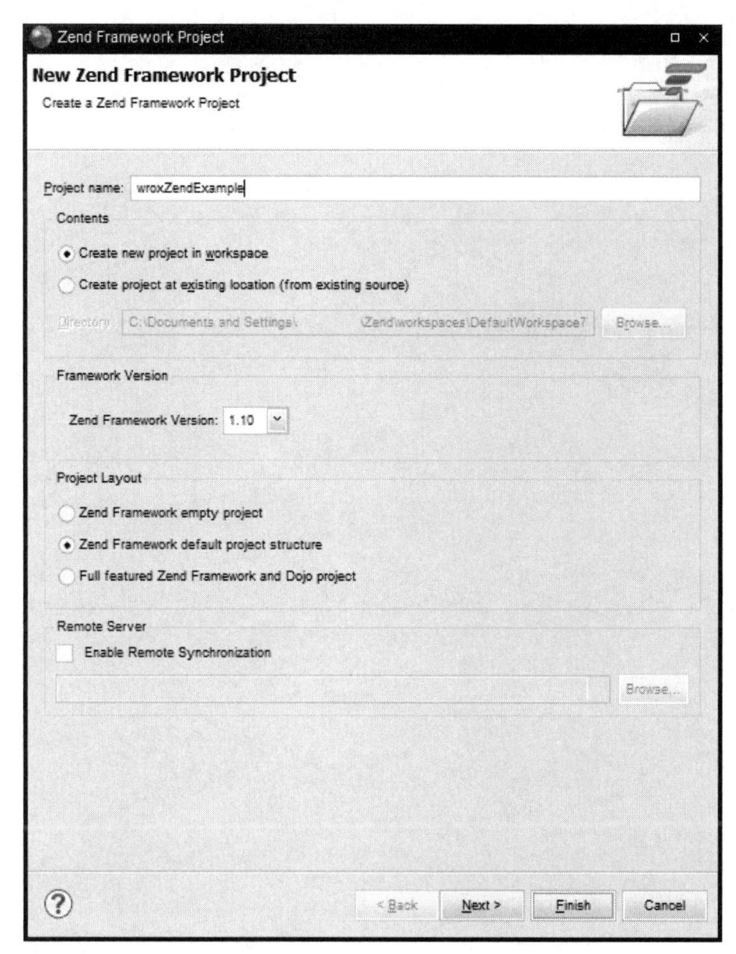

FIGURE 2-19: Zend Studio project creation wizard

3

Working with Databases

To forget one's purpose is the commonest form of stupidity.

— Friedrich Nietzsche

WHAT'S IN THIS CHAPTER?

- Understanding various approaches to object-relational mapping (ORM).
- Configuring different database engines.
- Writing schemas of object models.
- Using the command-line interface.

In order to produce your first application, you need to know how to communicate with your database. To communicate with it, the database must be configured properly for use with your framework. And before the configuration can be made, you should know how the frameworks join with database systems and perhaps choose your preferred object-relational mapping (ORM) solution.

To help you with that before you move to coding the sample app, this chapter takes a close look at the ORM concept, which is essential for almost every PHP framework available. The rest of the chapter covers configuring various databases for chosen ORM solutions and how to communicate with them efficiently. In the next chapter, you will write an address book example in each framework. The good thing is that with ORM support, communicating with databases is really straightforward. You no longer need to write lengthy SQL queries manually nor join tables each time you need to call another object by reference. So this little bit of overhead is certainly worth the effort.

OBJECT-RELATIONAL MAPPING

ORM is one of the core concepts of PHP frameworks. It creates an abstraction layer between relational database management systems (RDBMSs) and object-oriented business logic. There are specialized ORM-only frameworks that can be used alone in any PHP code or combined with Model-View-Controller (MVC) frameworks. The three frameworks provide the following ORM solutions:

- **Symfony** — Versions 1.x offer Propel and Doctrine as plug-ins. Since Symfony 1.3, Doctrine has been the default ORM plug-in. Since Symfony 2.0, support for Doctrine 2.0 only is provided. Other ORMs can also be used.
- **CakePHP** — Uses its own integrated ORM solution. Other ORMs can also be used.
- **Zend Framework (ZF)** — Provides only some database access tools, but a full ORM third-party framework can be easily installed. Future versions will integrate Doctrine by default.

Figure 3-1 shows the structure of applications built atop an ORM tool. The application has a data model, which is used by the ORM mapper to create corresponding tables. ORM tools commonly use PHP Data Objects (PDOs) to execute particular queries.

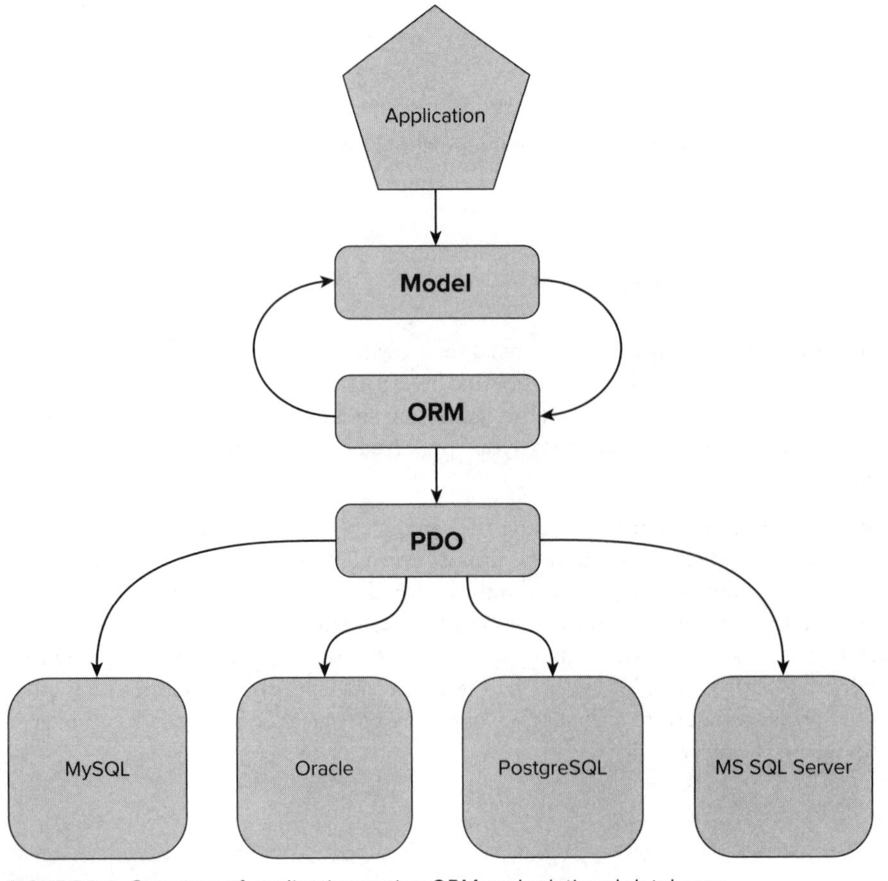

FIGURE 3-1: Structure of applications using ORM and relational databases

Object-Relational Impedance Mismatch

Object-relational impedance mismatch is a term coined to encompass several difficulties related to persistence of object-oriented data in relational databases. These problems are not only technical but also conceptual and even cultural (if database administrators and software developers are seen as two different cultures). Among the most common problems are the following:

- **Inheritance** — Relational databases do not support inheritance. There are ways to simulate inheritance in databases by using some special tricks in object-oriented programming (OOP) language classes (for example, a separate table for each subclass), but at the cost of increasing complexity of code, adding new tables, leaving large amounts of NULL cells or repeating source code, and greatly raising maintenance costs.
- **Encapsulation** — OOP emphasizes hiding objects' private data behind interfaces provided by the objects themselves. This notion is not known to RDBMSs, in which data is accessible globally, protected only by mechanisms of user roles and permissions.
- **References** — Relational databases never use attributing by reference (nor pointers), although it is one of the most basic properties of OOP.
- **Data types** — There are various differences between data types used in RDBMSs and OOP. For example, String types in RDBMSs have fixed maximum length, have specified collation, and ignore trailing spaces. On the other hand, OOP string types usually have variable, unlimited length, and do not trim white spaces unless commanded otherwise. Also, they are collation-free and must be provided separately for any sorting algorithms.
- **Data structures** — OOP uses heavily nested data structures with object lists of previously unspecified length. RDBMSs use a "flat" data model with relations characterized by primary and foreign keys. The number of fields in each row is predefined. Although some RDBMSs can dynamically add a column when needed, it is not a trivial operation.
- **Constrains** — RDBMSs extensively use declarative constrains imposed on variables and tables. OOP languages do not provide such mechanisms; the closest things are assertions and exceptions, but they affect the application's state after certain operations instead of being an internal part of the data model.
- **Transactions** — The closest counterpart of RDBMS transactions is data access in concurrent programming. It does not include all the subtleties of atomicity, consistency, isolation and durability (ACID), and even when it does, transaction-like behavior is ensured by the application, not by the language. OOP languages use small, low-level operations and do not need transactions. RDBMSs do need them, however, to ensure transactional persistence of objects, for example.
- **Conceptual differences** — Relational thinking is based on sets, OO thinking is based on graphs, databases see data as interface, OOPs favor interface via actions, databases are oriented on fixed structure, OOPs are directed toward dynamic behavior, and so on. These different approaches can lead to fundamental misunderstandings between database administrators and programmers.
- **Responsibilities** — According to the old school of computer systems design, the database schema is carefully constructed to reflect reality, and software is built on top of the database

to access and modify data. ORM tools allow you to create databases that reflect only the schema of objects. This reversal often leads to poorly designed databases.

- **Maintenance** — Introducing new classes of objects often requires changes in database schema. Database administrators who are not willing to make unnecessary changes may block development of software attempting such changes. And unreasonable requests by software developers can damage the database. Even if such extremes do not occur, the mismatch greatly increases maintenance costs.

One way to solve this impedance mismatch is to abandon OOP completely. We bet that no developer considers this solution when it comes to any serious web application, unless he has really important reasons to do so.

Object-oriented database management systems (OODBMSs) are another way to solve the problems mentioned in the preceding list. Although OODBMSs are still limited (mainly to some scientific projects), some of the world's biggest databases are object-oriented ones. However, the relational approach is still the prevailing approach in commercial web applications. Its establishment in the market is so strong that it will take years before databases fully adapt to OOP, so we will not concentrate on the OODBMS approach.

Object-relational databases are RDBMS bases that support the object-oriented data model. Although they support inheritance and by-reference behavior, they are still inferior in terms of performance. However, they may help to bridge the gap from the database side, whereas ORMs bridge it from the software side.

Propel

Introduced in 2005, Propel was the first open-source ORM solution for PHP. First it was built on top of Creole, but since version 1.2 it has used PDOs instead. Both Creole and PDO are database access application programming interfaces (APIs) that provide uniform communication with various database engines. Creole was a Propel subproject, whereas PDO is an official extension of the PHP language. That's why when PDO was introduced, it was adopted by Propel, and Creole was no longer developed.

Propel gained great popularity when it became part of Symfony — first as a core component and then as default plug-in competing with Doctrine. However, Propel's development is less active today (its abandonment is even being unofficially talked about).

Propel was inspired by and based on a Java ORM implementation: Torque. Solutions used in both Propel and Torque are simple and effective, resulting in great performance, but also have some drawbacks. One drawback is one-to-one mapping (each class is mapped to one database table). With this approach, it is necessary to create additional join tables and write some code to reflect many-to-many relations in the database.

One of the requirements for ORM in Propel is to create an XML file that describes both database schema and object model of application as well as their connections. This file can also be generated by Propel from an existing database. With the XML schema, Propel can generate PHP model classes. Propel can also generate nice visual schema diagrams.

The usage of Propel in source code is really straightforward. All you need to do is create an object and then use its `save()` method, as in the following code. The object is now written into a database. For more complex operations, Propel uses Criteria objects to formulate SQL statements.

```php
<?php
   $user = new User();
   $user->setForename('Karol');
   $user->setSurname('Przystalski');
   $user->save();
?>
```

code snippet /examples/propel.php

Doctrine

The Doctrine project was started in 2006, so it had to face the competition of already-popular Propel. Doctrine is based on one of the leading ORM solutions: Java Hibernate. Doctrine's popularity is increasing rapidly and since mid-2009 it is more frequently searched than Propel (based on the Google Insights Web Development category).

The programmer does not have to create and update the database schema in an XML file because Doctrine can generate a PHP model or a YAML Ain't Markup Language (YAML) schema, reflecting an existing database. It is also possible to create a YAML schema to specify the mapping manually.

From the perspective of PHP code, the basic syntax of Doctrine is very similar to Propel's. The configuration of a YAML schema is preferred over XML, and it can be written manually or generated by an ORM engine. The basic example of Doctrine usage in PHP code, shown in the following snippet, is the same as for Propel; however, there are differences for more advanced features, mainly searching.

```php
<?php
   $user = new User();
   $user->setForename('Leszek');
   $user->setSurname('Nowak');
   $user->save();
?>
```

code snippet /examples/doctrine.php

Doctrine is now a top ORM solution mainly because it supports many-to-many relationships. Doctrine's other exclusive features include data fixtures, migration, behaviors, full text searching, and Doctrine Query Language (DQL) (based on Hibernate's HQL) for a generation of advanced SQL operations through the `Doctrine_Query` class. Doctrine's documentation is also a big plus.

Even though Doctrine's performance is sometimes lower than Propel's, it is now a superior ORM from the programmer's perspective, because of its advanced features like DQL language. Its development also seems faster and better organized than Propel's, which is why we use Doctrine as our default ORM.

CakePHP's ORM

CakePHP comes with a bundled ORM. Unfortunately, it does not support inheritance, which is a big drawback compared with other ORMs. Another weakness of this ORM is its lack of a PDO database extension layer. This is because of Cake's compatibility with PHP 4, which forbids use of extensions specific to PHP 5.

Object persistence is organized by saving arrays of data. Arrays contain pairs of field names and values. This approach is different because it resembles preparing data for individual tables rather than simple persistency of objects. It may look less object-oriented, but it is useful for web apps that get data from organized forms. The following example demonstrates this use of arrays for data persistence:

Available for download on Wrox.com

```
<?php
    $this->data(array('forename'=>'Bartosz',
                      'surname'=>'Porebski'));
    $this->User->save($this->data);
?>
```

code snippet /examples/cakeORM.php

Zend_Db

ZF provides database access tools from the `Zend_Db` family:

- The `Zend_Db_Adapter` class is used to connect RDBMSs with the application. There are separate adapters for different databases both using PDO drivers and using PHP extensions only. Note that you must have these PHP extensions enabled in your PHP environment to use a corresponding adapter.
  - MySQL: `pdo_mysql`, `mysqli`
  - Oracle: `pdo_oci`, `oci8`
  - IBM DB2: `pdo_ibm`, `ibm_db2`
  - Microsoft SQL Server: `pdo_dblib`
  - PostgreSQL: `pdo_sql`
  - SQLite: `pdo_sql`
  - Firebird/Interbase: `php_interbase`

Adapter classes are created by appending one of the preceding names (uppercase first letter) to `Zend_Db_Adapter`. The following code is a simple example of a MySQL database adapter using PDO:

Available for download on Wrox.com

```
$db = new Zend_Db_Adapter_Pdo_Mysql( array(
  'host' => '127.0.0.1',
  'username' => 'user',
  'password' => 'pass',
  'dbname' => 'dbtest'
));
```

code snippet /examples/zendDB.php

- The Zend_Db_Profiler class provides tools for profiling SQL queries. This is useful for inspecting recent queries and their execution time. Advanced filtering by query type and elapsed time is also provided. Specialized profilers can be made through inheriting Zend_Db_Profiler by custom classes.
- The Zend_Db_Statement class, based on PDOStatement from the PDO extension, provides a convenient way to execute SQL statements and fetch results. It allows the use of parameterized statements, fetching single rows and columns from a result set, and fetching a row as an object by passing the row's values to a constructor of a specified class.
- The Zend_Db_Select class enables object-oriented methods for creation of SQL SELECT queries. Here's an example:

```
$select = $db->select()
->from('table1')
->joinUsing('table2', 'column1')
->where('column2 = ?', 'foo');
```

code snippet /examples/zendDB.php

- The Zend_Db_Table is a family of classes for creating and managing tables and relations. When you want to operate a database table, all you need to do is to simply instantiate Zend_Db_Table (available since ZF 1.9) or extend the Zend_Db_Table_Abstract class. Relations may be set between table objects based on the database schema. Other classes from this family include Zend_Db_Row, Zend_Db_Rowset, and Zend_Db_Table_Definition.

Generally, Zend_Db is more of a lightweight wrapper for unified PDO layers rather than a full ORM solution. Even if this set of tools can be useful and sufficient for a small to middle-sized project, you will probably need a more comprehensive approach for anything more serious. There are some experimental classes aiming for true ORM, but their development stage is still far from maturity. That's why many developers integrate Zend with a proven solution such as Propel or Doctrine. Doctrine is a prevailing choice, not only because of its recent popularity in the development community but also because of its chances of being officially integrated into Zend. The lead developer of a data mapper for ZF called Zend_Entity announced that it will be discontinued in favor of integrating Doctrine into future versions of ZF.

Other ORM Solutions

There are various other ORM solutions, both closed- and open-source. Among the most advanced technologies are Hibernate for Java, ActiveRecord (part of Ruby on Rails), Python framework, Django, and Microsoft's .NET. ORMs for PHP are generally younger and usually borrow the best solutions from other languages. Propel and Doctrine are the best and most successful examples to date. They are now well established and popular in the PHP community, so new ORMs must be experimental and innovative to gain some market share. Among the most interesting are the following:

- **RedBean** — A very experimental project with high aspirations. It needs absolutely no configuration; it creates a database schema by analyzing classes in PHP code instead. It can be easily integrated into ZF and CodeIgniter.

- **Qcodo** — A whole web application framework with an integrated ORM, inspired by .NET. Qcodo features object-relational model code generation as well as generation of web pages for object management, called Qforms. Its structure is completely object-oriented and therefore contributes to rapid development of elegant code.
- **php-activerecord** — Inspired by Ruby on Rails Active Record architecture, it creates an object-oriented database representation that can be used by programmers.

DATABASE CONFIGURATION

As mentioned previously, all ORMs use PDO as a database abstraction layer. Another solution is Creole, which was used by Propel some time ago. An *abstraction layer* is a very useful solution that makes it possible to change a database that an application is using. Let's use a simple example to make it clear. Let's say that you need to develop a small application that will use MySQL. In pure PHP, the code should look like this:

Available for download on Wrox.com

```
<?php
$con = mysql_connect("localhost","wroxuser","wroxpassword") or die("cannot connect");
mysql_select_db("wroxdb") or die("database doesn't exist");
$query = "SELECT * FROM users; ";
while($row=mysql_fetch_array($response)) {
    // do a lot of things
}
mysql_close($con);
?>
```

code snippet /examples/mysql.php

Suppose that you use fragments of this code in many places in your application. This code may be very important, providing some crucial features of your application. Because you are almost done with your application, the product owner says that your previously approved requirements and specifications have changed. You need to switch to PostgreSQL because of a very important reason that is known only to the product owner. So you are considering how it will be done.

A trivial solution would be to change your PHP functions such as `mysql_connect()` to equivalents for PostgreSQL. This is a very time-consuming process and is only a theory in web application development; nobody follows this approach. From an architect's perspective, if you know that there is even the smallest chance that a database would be changed, you should think about a solution that implements a database abstraction layer idea. The idea is that you need only to change the configuration of your application, not its functions, because the functions are chosen in the lower layer of your application. As an example, let's look at the database-specific configuration of your frameworks.

Open Database Connectivity (ODBC)

Open Database Connectivity (ODBC) is an API standard that provides database management and configuration, independent of the database engine, operating system, or programming language. Let's think about ODBC as another layer between an application and the database. ODBC configuration is needed to make it possible to connect to the MS SQL Server, but can optionally be used for other databases as well. PHP uses the `pdo_odbc` extension to work with ODBC. Be sure that it is present in the PHP `/ext` directory.

ODBC is a standard created by the SQL Access Group and was developed by Microsoft for Windows, but its implementations are available for other operating systems such as Linux, MacOS, and OS/2. There are many different ODBC implementations, and among the most important open-source ones are Independent ODBC (iODBC), which is platform independent; and unixODBC, which is designed for all flavors of UNIX and Linux. There is also Java Database Connectivity (JDBC), which bridges Java-based applications to native ODBC drivers.

An important notion is a data source name (DSN) — not to be confused with a domain name system (DNS). It is a data structure that contains information on a data source (in this case, a database) in order to provide the ODBC driver all the information it needs to establish a connection to this data source. It is similar in structure to a URL address and contains the following information:

- Name of driver connecting to the database
- Data source address
- Name of the data source
- Username accessing the database
- Password for user validation

An example of a valid DSN for MySQL connection is the following:

```
mysql://username:password@host/db_name
```

SQLite

SQLite is supported by all major ORMs. Thanks to SQLite's lightweight embedded structure, generally all you need to do is to specify the path to the file containing the whole database. You connect to the database without a username or login, but obviously SQLite can support all modern security mechanisms.

Propel

Configuring Propel for use with SQLite is pretty much the same as with Doctrine. The only difference is another parameter in the `param:` section, in which you need to specify the class that Propel will use to connect with the database. Because Creole is universally replaced by PDO, we assume that it is going to be used, and set the `classname:` as `PropelPDO`.

Available for download on Wrox.com

```
all:
  propel:
    class:        sfPropelDatabase
    param:
      classname:  PropelPDO
      dsn:        sqlite:///<?php echo dirname(__FILE__); ?>/sample.db
```

code snippet /sqlite/symfony/config/database.yml

Doctrine

Doctrine uses PDO as the abstraction layer to connect with databases. All you need to do is edit the `config/databases.yml` file. In the `doctrine:` section, you set `class:` as `sfDoctrineDatabase`; and in the `param:` section, you should define the DSN for the database. The `dsn:` should define the path to the file containing the SQLite database, starting with `sqlite://` as the resource descriptor. We assume that it is located in the same folder as the configuration file, the path to which is returned by the PHP expression `<?php echo dirname(__FILE__); ?>`. If the database is in another location, the path must be changed accordingly. The extension of the database file can also be `.sqlite`. A short example is shown here:

Available for download on Wrox.com

```
all:
  doctrine:
    class:      sfDoctrineDatabase
    param:
      dsn:      sqlite:///<?php echo dirname(__FILE__); ?>/sample.db
```

code snippet /sqlite/symfony/config/database.yml

CakePHP

In CakePHP, you configure the database with the `DATABASE_CONFIG` class. It has a `$default` variable, which is an array containing all necessary information about the default environment. There can be several different environments for testing, developing, or releasing, but for now you should focus on the default one.

First, set the driver as `sqlite`. Note that CakePHP does not support PDO because of its backward compatibility with PHP 4. It is a big drawback, although you can try to avoid all problems that may be generated by it. The line `'persistent' => false` determines whether the connection should be permanent or initialized in lazy mode, which affects performance. In the following example, you should replace `<path_to_cakephp>` with a full path to your CakePHP folder (or wherever SQLite is installed):

Available for download on Wrox.com

```
<?php
class DATABASE_CONFIG {
    var $default = array(
        'driver' => 'sqlite',
        'persistent' => false,
        'database' => '<path_to_cakephp>/sample.db'
    );
?>
```

code snippet /sqlite/cakephp/app/config/database.php

Zend_Db

In ZF, you have to choose the specific driver that `Zend_Db` will use. SQLite has only a PDO-dependent driver, but for other databases there may also be non-PDO variants. `APPLICATION_PATH` is the path to the application folder. This example is for the production environment, which we consider to be the default:

Available for download on Wrox.com

```
[production]
...
resources.db.adapter = "PDO_SQLITE"
resources.db.params.dbname = APPLICATION_PATH "/data/db/sample.db"
...
```

code snippet /sqlite/zf/application/configs/application.ini

PostgreSQL

PostgreSQL is also universally supported by ORM software. Like most client-server databases, PostgreSQL requires user authentication.

Propel

The configuration file `config/databases.yml` is the same as for Doctrine, but again you need to specify the `classname:` parameter as `PropelPDO`:

Available for download on Wrox.com

```
all:
  propel:
    class:          sfPropelDatabase
    param:
      classname:    PropelPDO
      dsn:          pgsql:dbname=sample;host=localhost
      username:     login
      password:     secret
```

code snippet /postgres/symfony/config/database.yml

Doctrine

The DSN for a standard server database is quite different from the database in a file. Here in the `param:` section, you must specify the type of DSN resource along with the database name and host (`localhost` in this example). In the following lines, `username` and `password` are used for authentication in PostgreSQL:

Available for download on Wrox.com

```
all:
  propel:
    class:          sfDoctrineDatabase
    param:
      dsn:          pgsql:dbname=sample;host=localhost
      username:     login
      password:     secret
```

code snippet /postgres/symfony/config/database.yml

CakePHP

CakePHP's object-oriented approach boils down to an array of values determining the database connection in the default environment: the driver type, connection mode, database name, host name, username, and password:

Available for download on Wrox.com

```
<?php
class DATABASE_CONFIG {
    var $default = array(
        'driver' => 'pgsql',
        'persistent' => false,
        'database' => 'sample',
        'host' => 'localhost',
        'login' => 'login',
        'password' => 'secret'
    );
?>
```

code snippet /postgres/cakephp/app/config/database.php

Zend_Db

The PostgreSQL adapter with PDO support is used as a database abstraction layer. Then you must set four fields of connection parameters:

Available for download on Wrox.com

```
[production]
...
resources.db.adapter = "PDO_PGSQL"
resources.db.params.host = "localhost"
resources.db.params.username = "login"
resources.db.params.password = "secret"
resources.db.params.dbname = "dbname"
```

code snippet /postgres/zf/application/configs/application.ini

MySQL

MySQL has two different drivers that allow connections. The first one is `mysql`, which is used by ORMs and provides a standard API mapped by PDO. The other driver is `mysqli` ("i" for "improved"), an extension that allows several improvements for communication with newer versions of MySQL (4.1.3+) from PHP 5 source code. These improvements include object-oriented interface, transaction support, prepared statements, or debugging with PHP 5 exceptions.

Propel

For Propel, there is only one single difference from PostgreSQL:

Available for download on Wrox.com

```
all:
  propel:
    class:        sfPropelDatabase
    param:
```

```
        classname:  PropelPDO
        dsn:        mysql:dbname=sample;host=localhost
        username:   login
        password:   secret
```

code snippet /mysql/symfony/config/database.yml

Doctrine

The following example is the same as for PostgreSQL, except the DSN driver is changed from `pgsql` to `mysql`:

```
all:
  propel:
    class:        sfDoctrineDatabase
    param:
      dsn:        mysql:dbname=sample;host=localhost
      username:   login
      password:   secret
```

code snippet /mysql/symfony/config/database.yml

CakePHP

The same is true for CakePHP as for Propel and Doctrine — the code is the same as for PostgreSQL, with the driver as the only difference:

```
<?php
class DATABASE_CONFIG {

    var $default = array(
        'driver' => 'mysql',
        'persistent' => false,
        'database' => 'sample',
        'host' => 'localhost',
        'login' => 'login',
        'password' => 'secret'
    );
?>
```

code snippet /mysql/cakephp/app/config/database.php

Zend_Db

The driver used for `Zend_Db` is `PDO_MYSQL`:

```
[production]
...
resources.db.adapter = "PDO_MYSQL"
resources.db.params.host = "localhost"
resources.db.params.username = "login"
```

```
resources.db.params.password = "secret"
resources.db.params.dbname = "dbname"
```

code snippet /mysql/zf/application/configs/application.ini

Microsoft SQL Server

Microsoft SQL Server runs only on the Windows platform. So in order to connect to this database, the best solution is to configure it using ODBC. The following steps walk you through the various windows that will collect the same data as were previously written into configuration files.

1. To access the ODBC Data Source Administrator under Windows, simply open *Data Sources (ODBC)* in Control Panel. You should see the ODBC Data Source Administrator window shown in Figure 3-2.

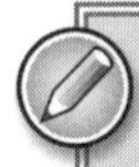

This screenshots in this section were created using Windows XP SP2. This process will work on Windows 7 and Windows Vista as well, although the windows will look slightly different.

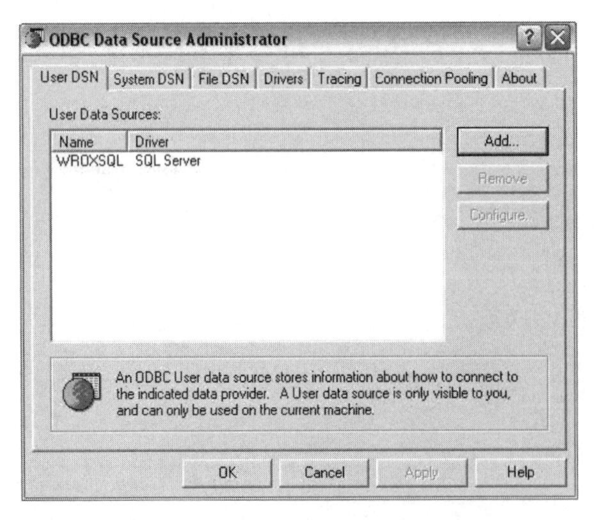

FIGURE 3-2: The ODBC Data Source Administrator window

The User DSN and Drivers tabs are the most important for you. The User DSN tab shows defined DSNs for your databases, and the Drivers tab shows available drivers. Click Add to create a new data source.

The window shown in Figure 3-3 will display with a list of drivers for different database engines. Select SQL Server and click Finish.

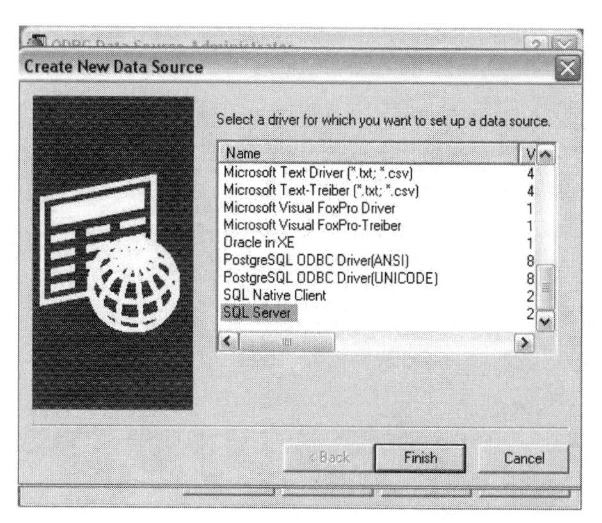

FIGURE 3-3: Choosing an ODBC driver

2. The Create a New Data Source to SQL Server window will appear (see Figure 3-4). Type a name and a brief description for the data source. From the drop-down list, select the server you want to connect to.

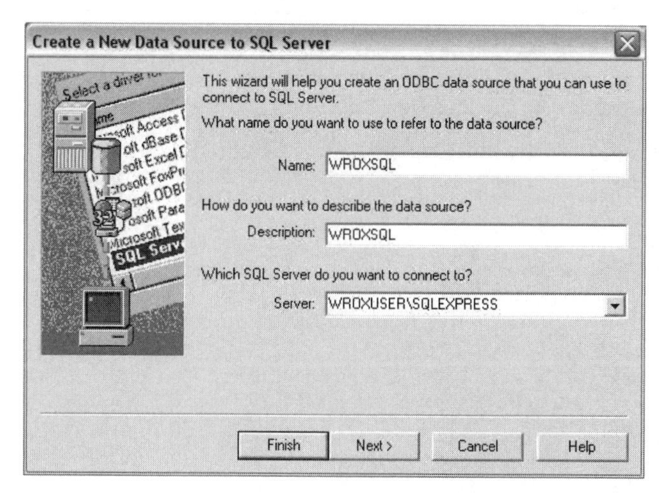

FIGURE 3-4: Defining properties of database connection

To access a SQL Server (refer to Figure 3-4), two services must be running. The first, SQL Server (SQLEXPRESS), is working by default, but the second, SQL Server Browser, may be set to be activated manually from the SQL Server Configuration Manager (see Figure 3-5).

3. Next is user authentication, shown in Figure 3-6. Type your login ID and password for the server.

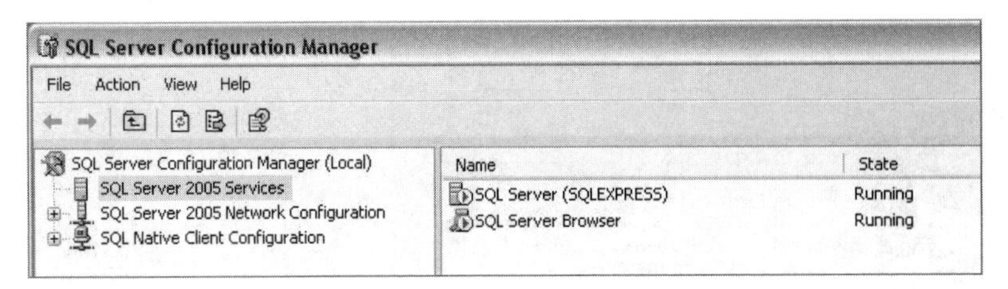

FIGURE 3-5: Configuring ODBC using Server Configuration Manager

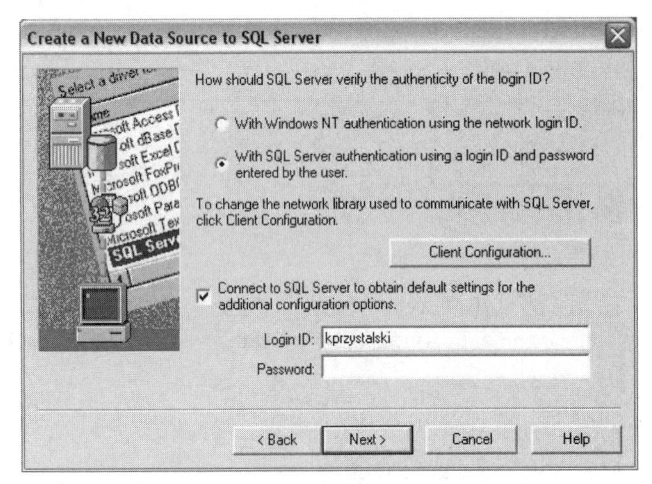

FIGURE 3-6: User authentication with Create a New Data Source to SQL Server

4. Click Next two times. Figure 3-7 lists all properties of the created data source.

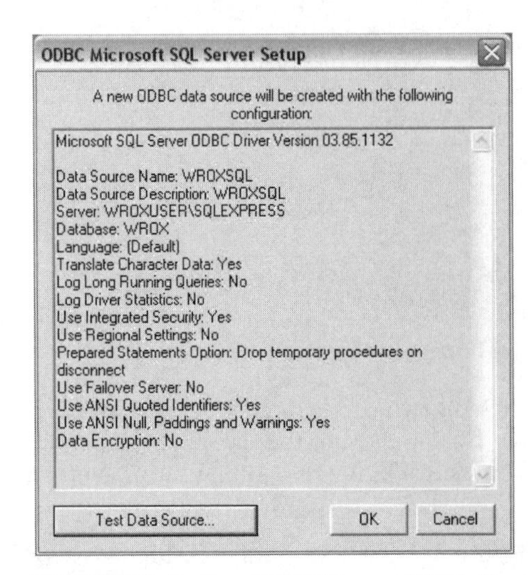

FIGURE 3-7: Testing ODBC Microsoft SQL Server Setup

If you see an entry like the one shown in Figure 3-8, the new data source has been successfully added.

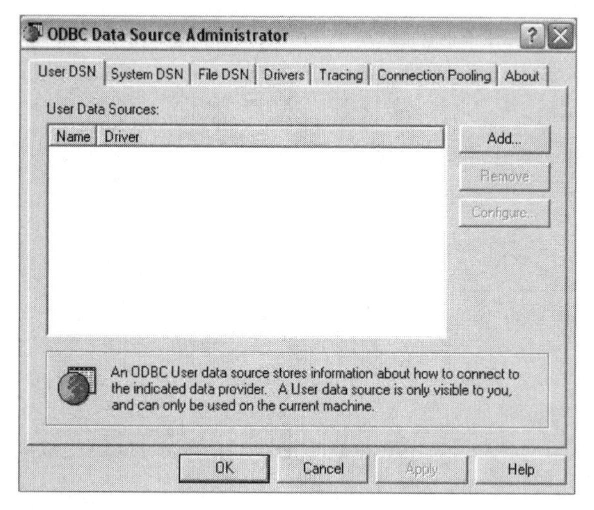

FIGURE 3-8: A successfully added entry

Propel

As usual, the only difference between Propel and Doctrine is `classname: PropelPDO`:

```
all:
  propel:
    class:        sfPropelDatabase
    param:
      classname:  PropelPDO
      dsn:        odbc:WROXSQL
      username:   login
      password:   secret
```

code snippet /mssql/symfony/config/database.yml

Doctrine

When the data source is properly installed, configuring Doctrine is even simpler than before. All properties of the connection are stored in ODBC, so all you need to do is to add your username and password. Note that the name you have given to the ODBC data source is now the only identifier for the ODBC driver.

```
all:
  propel:
    class:        sfDoctrineDatabase
    param:
      dsn:        odbc:WROXSQL
      username:   login
      password:   secret
```

code snippet /mssql/symfony/config/database.yml

CakePHP

Just point to ODBC as the driver. You don't need to specify the host because that information is already stored in ODBC.

```
<?php
class DATABASE_CONFIG {
    var $default = array(
        'driver' => 'odbc',
        'persistent' => false,
        'database' => 'WROXSQL',
        'login' => 'login',
        'password' => 'secret'
    );
?>
```

code snippet /mssql/cakephp/app/config/database.php

Zend_Db

Just point to the `PDO_ODBC` adapter and then specify the login name, password, and database name.

```
[production]
...
resources.db.adapter = "PDO_ODBC"
resources.db.params.username = "login"
resources.db.params.password = "secret"
resources.db.params.dbname = "WROXSQL"
```

code snippet /mssql/zf/application/configs/application.ini

Oracle

Oracle has its own ODBC-like solution, called Oracle Call Interface (OCI). It provides a PHP interface for database communication. You can also connect to Oracle by ODBC, but here you use this native driver instead.

Propel

Propel is the same as in Doctrine, except for the addition of the `classname` parameter.

```
all:
  propel:
    class:        sfPropelDatabase
    param:
      classname:  PropelPDO
      dsn:        oci:host=localhost
      username:   login
      password:   secret
```

code snippet /oracle/symfony/config/database.yml

Doctrine

The IP address you have used is an equivalent for `localhost hostname`.

Available for download on Wrox.com

```
all:
  propel:
    class:          sfDoctrineDatabase
    param:
      dsn:          oci:host=127.0.0.1
      username:     login
      password:     secret
```

code snippet /oracle/symfony/config/database.yml

CakePHP

For CakePHP, you don't need the database name, only the host address.

Available for download on Wrox.com

```
<?php
class DATABASE_CONFIG {

    var $default = array(
        'driver' => 'oci',
        'persistent' => false,
        'host' => '127.0.0.1',
        'login' => 'login',
        'password' => 'secret'
    );
?>
```

code snippet /oracle/cakephp/app/config/database.php

Zend_Db

The driver for OCI in `Zend_Db` is `PDO_OCI`.

Available for download on Wrox.com

```
[production]
...
resources.db.adapter = "PDO_OCI"
resources.db.params.host = "localhost"
resources.db.params.username = "login"
resources.db.params.password = "secret"
```

code snippet /oracle/zf/application/configs/application.ini

DB2

The IBM DB2 database is officially supported only by ZF and CakePHP, which is a disadvantage of using Symfony. DB2 can be accessed with ODBC, however, so you could use it with Propel and Doctrine, as in the MS SQL example, and it should work fine.

CakePHP

CakePHP provides support for DB2, so you can set a native driver and general configuration as in all the other cases:

Available for download on Wrox.com

```
<?php
class DATABASE_CONFIG {
    var $default = array(
        'driver' => 'db2',
        'persistent' => false,
        'database' => 'WROX',
        'host' => 'localhost',
        'login' => 'login',
        'password' => 'secret'
    );
?>
```

code snippet /db2/cakephp/app/config/database.php

Zend_DB

In ZF, you can configure DB2 support by native `PDO_IBM` and `IBM_DB2` adapters or through the `PDO_ODBC` adapter after configuring the data source. Here we demonstrate the second approach. In this case, `WROX` is not the name of the database; it's a DSN name created with ODBC `config`.

Available for download on Wrox.com

```
[production]
...
resources.db.adapter = "PDO_ODBC"
resources.db.params.host = "localhost"
resources.db.params.username = "login"
resources.db.params.password = "secret"
resources.db.params.dbname = "WROX"
```

code snippet /db2/zf/application/configs/application.ini

COMMUNICATION WITH A DATABASE

Every web framework should deliver enhancements that are normally included as scaffolding tools. Some of these enhancements are intended for databases and can be divided into five classes:

- **Schema** — Represents the database structure
- **Fixtures** — Sample data that is used mostly in testing
- **SQL** — Language for communicating with databases
- **CLI** — Command-line interface tools
- **Model** — Database model representing your database in the OO approach

The relationships between these enhancements are shown in Figure 3-9.

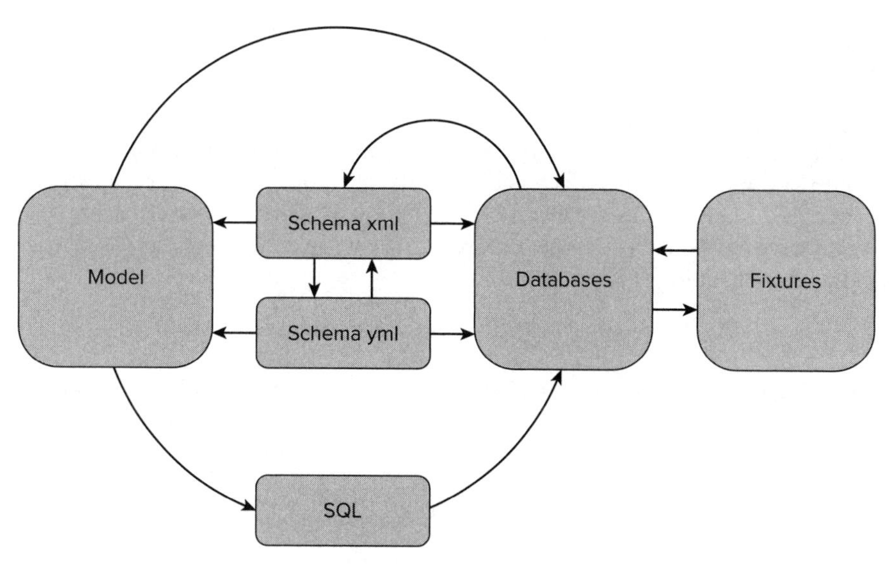

FIGURE 3-9: Relationships between framework database issues

Schema

Every ORM is, or should be, designed so that the database structure is not dedicated for only one specific database engine such as MySQL or PostgreSQL. That's why schemas were invented. A schema describes a database blueprint for ORMs that describes the database in ORM known types.

Propel

A different approach to writing a schema is proposed in Propel. Java developers probably appreciate this approach because XML is used here. It looks like this:

```
<?xml version="1.0" encoding="UTF-8"?>
  <database name="propel" defaultIdMethod="native" noXsd="true" package="lib.model">
    <table name="users" phpName="Users">
      <column name="id" type="integer" required="true" primaryKey="true"
         autoIncrement="true" />
      <column name="surname" type="varchar" size="255" />
      <column name="forename" type="varchar" size="255" />
      <column name="created_at" type="timestamp" />
    </table>
  </database>
```

code snippet /communication/symfony/config/schema.xml

This code demonstrates Propel's advantage. At the beginning, you declare an XML-specific header. The next line provides the database name (in this example, it is `propel`, but it could be named any other name). The `DefaultIdMethod` tells you about currently used ID incrementation methods that are specific for every database. For example, MySQL uses `auto_increment`, and PostgreSQL uses `sequences`. The `native` keyword says that Propel should use database native methods. Set `noXsd` to `true` if you don't want your schema to be validated before generating the model. `table` has two attributes: `name` is for the database name, and `phpName` is the name that will be used in your PHP code. This is the name that your class for that table will have. Declaring columns is mostly obvious.

Propel 1.5 provides these types: `boolean`, `numeric`, `tinyint`, `smallint`, `integer`, `bigint`, `double`, `decimal`, `float`, `real`, `double`, `char`, `varchar`, `longvarchar`, `clob`, `binary`, `varbinary`, `longvarbinary`, `blob`, `date`, `time`, and `timestamp`. Each field type also has some attributes such as `size`, `primaryKey`, and `autoIncrement`. These attributes are well known from database structure on MySQL 5. These types have equivalents for other databases. We will describe these types in later chapters as we will be using them in practical solutions.

Doctrine

A schema represents a database structure, as described in an XML or a YAML file. Let's look at an example:

Available for download on Wrox.com

```
Users:
  actAs: { Timestampable: ~ }
  columns:
   forename: string(30)
   lastname: string(30)
```

code snippet /communication/symfony/config/doctrine/schema.yml

This is a Doctrine schema. First, it describes that you want a table named Users with 2 columns that are an array of 30 chars. By default, Doctrine adds an ID field that is a primary key. The second line says what you also want to have. `Timestampable` is an attribute that adds a `created_at` column. This feature is used often in all kinds of applications because it is very practical.

A schema in Doctrine is described in the `schema.yml` file. YAML is also used in Propel. This is a good language for describing a schema, but it's very frustrating for beginners because of tab characters. Tabs are not allowed in YAML and should be replaced with spaces. This is important because in case of an error, no proper message is shown.

Doctrine provides a lot of data types: `boolean`, `integer`, `decimal`, `float`, `timestamp`, `time`, `date`, `blob`, `clob`, `string`, `array`, `object`, `enum`, and `gzip`. Additionally, `integer` is divided into `integer(1)`, `integer(2)`...`(5)`. This division corresponds to MySQL `tinyint`, `smallint`, `mediumint`, `int`, and `bigint` types. The same is true for `blob(255)`, which corresponds to MySQL `tinyblob/tinytext`, `blob(65532)` to `blob/text`, and `blob(16777215)` to `mediumblob/mediumtext`. The `gzip` type is very interesting because it compresses a string in the database. Each type and table has some behaviors that you can set in your schema file: `geographical`, `i18n`, `nestedset`, `searchable`, `sluggable`, `softdelete`, `timstampable`, and `versionable`. We will use these types in later chapters.

CakePHP

This solution is placed between ZF and Symfony in terms of schema creation and utilization. It is far less complex and useful than in Symfony, but also more advanced than in ZF. You use PHP code to declare a schema. Here's an example:

Available for download on Wrox.com

```
<?php
class AppSchema extends CakeSchema
{
    var $name = 'App';
    function before($event = array())
        {
        return true;
        }
    function after($event = array())
        {
        }
    var $user = array(
        'id' => array('type' => 'integer', 'null' => false, 'default' => NULL,
           'key' => 'primary'),
        'forename' => array('type' => 'string', 'null' => false, 'default' => NULL,
           'length' => 25),
        'surname' => array('type' => 'string', 'null' => true, 'default' => NULL,
           'length' => 25),
        'created' => array('type' => 'datetime', 'null' => false, 'default' =>
           NULL),
        'indexes' => array('PRIMARY' => array('column' => 'id', 'unique' => 1))
    );
}
?>
```

code snippet /communication/cakephp/app/config/schema/schema.php

It is possible to declare only some basic types of data, such as `string`, `text`, `integer`, `datetime`, `date`, and so on. Developers are free to use the `before()` and `after()` methods to implement code before and after callback to the schema. The variable `$user` is the name of the table that you want to operate on.

Zend Framework

Both solutions described previously represent an approach that depends on command-line tools. The next solution shows a manual way of developing models. Zend and CakePHP frameworks assume that models should be written from scratch instead of being generated, as they were in Symfony. Regardless, Doctrine and Propel can also be installed on Zend and CakePHP instead of their native solutions. The following example is a ZF model, which is equivalent to the Doctrine schema you saw earlier in this section:

Available for download on Wrox.com

```
<?php
class Application_Model_User
{
   protected $_forename;
   protected $_surname;
   protected $_created;
   protected $_email;
   protected $_id;

   public function __construct(array $options = null) {
```

```
    }
    public function __set($name, $value) {
    }
    public function __get($name) {
    }
    public function setForename($text) {
      $this->_forename = (string) $text;
      return $this;
    }
    public function getForename() {
      return $this->_forename;
    }
     /**
     * here should be also methods for each column,
     */
    public function getId() {
      return $this->_id;
    }
    public function setId($text) {
      $this->_id = (int) $id;
      return $this'
    }
}
```

code snippet /communication/zf/application/models/User.php

Table columns are protected fields. They are available only by using table model class methods. That's why you need each field to declare a setter and getter method. This pattern is commonly used. A class constructor should also be defined as well as default getter and setter methods.

You should add a relationship between your model and `DbTable` by creating a file in your models directory (in the `DbTable` directory). This file should be called as your database table. In this example, it will be `User.php`, and it should look like this:

```
<?php
class Application_Model_DbTable_User extends Zend_Db_Table_Abstract {
  protected $_name = 'User';
}
```

code snippet /communication/zf/application/models/DbTable/User.php

You have just one important line that describes your database table. This can be done quickly by using ZF's command-line tools. We will describe these tools later in this chapter.

The primary functionality of ORM is to map relationships between tables and deliver them as objects that are easier to use for developers. To make this mapping possible, you need to write this mapper class manually in Zend. This can be a boring process if you do it for a lot of tables. Unfortunately, ZF's command-line tools provide only some basic facilities. The following code is an example of `User` table mapping.

```
<?php
class Application_Model_UserMapper {

          protected $_dbTable;

          public function setDbTable($dbTable) {
              if (is_string($dbTable)) {
                  $dbTable = new $dbTable();
              }
              if (!$dbTable instanceof Zend_Db_Table_Abstract) {
                  throw new Exception('Invalid table data gateway provided');
              }
              $this->_dbTable = $dbTable;
              return $this;
          }

          public function getDbTable() {
              if (null === $this->_dbTable) {
                  $this->setDbTable('Application_Model_DbTable_User');
              }
              return $this->_dbTable;
          }

          public function save(Application_Model_User $user) {
              $data = array(
                  'forename' => $user->getForename(),
                  'surname' => $user->getSurname(),
          'email'   => $user->getEmail(),
                  'created' => date('Y-m-d H:i:s'),
              );

              if (null === ($id = $user->getId())) {
                  unset($data['id']);
                  $this->getDbTable()->insert($data);
              } else {
                  $this->getDbTable()->update($data, array('id = ?' => $id));
              }
          }

          public function find($id, Application_Model_User $user) {
              $result = $this->getDbTable()->find($id);
              if (0 == count($result)) {
                  return;
              }
              $row = $result->current();
              $user->setId($row->id)
                        ->setForename($row->forename)
                        ->setSurname($row->surname)
                        ->setEmail($row->email)
                        ->setCreated($row->created);
          }
```

```
            public function fetchAll() {
                $resultSet = $this->getDbTable()->fetchAll();
                $entries   = array();
                foreach ($resultSet as $row) {
                    $entry = new Application_Model_User();
                    $entry->setId($row->id)
                          ->setForename($row->forename)
                          ->setSurname($row->surname)
                          ->setEmail($row->email)
                          ->setCreated($row->created);
                    $entries[] = $entry;
                }
                return $entries;
            }
}
```

code snippet /communication/zf/application/models/UserMapper.php

The `setDbTable()` and `getDbTable()` methods make clear which model is currently being used. The next three methods are just simple methods for manipulating with database data. The `save()`, `find()`, and `fetchAll()` methods are using some methods that you have previously defined in your model.

The last thing we'll discuss related to ZF's schema is how the database is built. Unfortunately, ZF prefers a database schema in the form of a SQL query. This pattern is not really useful because it makes your application database-dependent. For MySQL 5 it looks like the following:

```
CREATE TABLE users (
  id INTEGER NOT NULL PRIMARY KEY AUTO_INCREMENT,
  forename VARCHAR(25) NULL,
  surname VARCHAR(25) NULL,
  email VARCHAR(32) NOT NULL,
  created DATETIME NOT NULL
);
```

code snippet /communication/zf/library/sql/User.sql

Fixtures

Fixtures in computer science are sample data pieces that can often be used for testing purposes. They can also be useful when you want to show some sample data in your application (for example, to show added products in an e-commerce website). Each framework takes a different approach to this problem, just like ORMs.

Symfony

Symfony prefers YAML in schemas. That's why Symfony fixtures are more legible and more independent from currently used databases. An exemplary fixture for a user table looks like the following:

Available for download on Wrox.com

```
User:
  kprzystalski:
    forename: Karol
    surname: Przystalski
    email: karol.przystalski@wrox.com
```

code snippet /communication/symfony/data/fixtures/fixtures.yml

CakePHP

Compared with Zend and Symfony, CakePHP prefers more coding than configuring. Looked at as an advantage, it's a very good practice when a developer can't work with the command line — for example, when using file transfer protocol (FTP) and Secure Shell (SSH) is not allowed. In other cases it results in more code than in Symfony though. Another advantage of this approach is its friendly OO approach.

Available for download on Wrox.com

```
<?php
class UserTestFixture extends CakeTestFixture {
   var $name = 'UserTest';

   var $fields = array(
      'id' => array('type' => 'integer', 'key' => 'primary'),
      'forename' => array('type' => 'string', 'length' => 25, 'null' => false),
      'surname' => array('type' => 'string', 'length' => 25, 'null' => false),
      'email' => array('type' => 'string', 'length' => 25, 'null' => false),
      'created' => 'datetime');

   var $records = array(
      array (
           'id' => 1,
           'forename' => 'Karol',
           'surname' => 'Przystalski',
           'email' => 'karol.przystalski@wrox.com',
           'created' => '2010-10-01 10:39:23'));
}
?>
```

code snippet /communication/cakephp/app/tests/fixtures/user_test_fixture.php

Zend Framework

Zend prefers pure SQL files. This is not an approach that we recommend for these fixtures because this solution depends on specific database behavior (for example, differences between the `enum` type in MySQL and PostgreSQL). This simple example works fine on MySQL and PostgreSQL:

Available for download on Wrox.com

```
INSERT INTO users (forename,surname, email, created) VALUES
('Karol', 'Przystalski','karol.przystalski@wrox.com',
DATETIME('NOW'));

INSERT INTO users (forename,surname, email, created) VALUES
('Bartosz', 'Porebski','bartosz.porebski@wrox.com',
```

```
DATETIME(,NOW'));

INSERT INTO users (forename,surname, email, created) VALUES
('Leszek', 'Nowak','leszek.nowak@wrox.com',
DATETIME(,NOW'));
```

code snippet /communication/zf/library/sql/User.sql

There are two ways to load fixtures in Zend: copy and paste the SQL code or use the console.

```
$ mysql -u user -p < data.mysql.sql
```

A completely different approach is to write a script, as shown in the following code:

Available for download on Wrox.com

```
// Initialize the application path and autoloading
defined('APPLICATION_PATH')
    || define('APPLICATION_PATH', realpath(dirname(__FILE__) . '/../application'));
set_include_path(implode(PATH_SEPARATOR, array(
    APPLICATION_PATH . '/../library',
    get_include_path(),
)));

require_once 'Zend/Loader/Autoloader.php';
Zend_Loader_Autoloader::getInstance();

$getopt = new Zend_Console_Getopt(array(
    'withdata|w' => 'Load database with sample data',
    'env|e-s'    => 'Application environment for which to create database (defaults
        to development)',
    'help|h'     => 'Help -- usage message',));

try {
    $getopt->parse();
} catch (Zend_Console_Getopt_Exception $e) {
    // Bad options passed: report usage
    echo $e->getUsageMessage();
    return false;
}

if ($getopt->getOption('h')) {
    echo $getopt->getUsageMessage();
    return true;
}

$withData = $getopt->getOption('w');
$env      = $getopt->getOption('e');
defined('APPLICATION_ENV')
    || define('APPLICATION_ENV', (null === $env) ? 'development' : $env);

$application = new Zend_Application(
    APPLICATION_ENV,
    APPLICATION_PATH . '/configs/application.ini'
```

```
);

// Initialize and retrieve DB resource
$bootstrap = $application->getBootstrap();
$bootstrap->bootstrap('db');
$dbAdapter = $bootstrap->getResource('db');


if ('testing' != APPLICATION_ENV) {
    echo 'Writing Database Guestbook in (control-c to cancel): ' . PHP_EOL;
    for ($x = 5; $x > 0; $x--) {
        echo $x . "\r"; sleep(1);
    }
}

$options = $bootstrap->getOption('resources');
$dbFile  = $options['db']['params']['dbname'];
if (file_exists($dbFile)) {
    unlink($dbFile);
}

try {
    $schemaSql = file_get_contents(dirname(__FILE__) . '/schema.sqlite.sql'); //
       important line
    $dbAdapter->getConnection()->exec($schemaSql);
    chmod($dbFile, 0666);

    if ('testing' != APPLICATION_ENV) {
        echo PHP_EOL;
        echo 'Database Created';
        echo PHP_EOL;
    }

    if ($withData) {
        $dataSql = file_get_contents(dirname(__FILE__) . '/data.sqlite.sql'); //
          important line
        // use the connection directly to load sql in batches
        $dbAdapter->getConnection()->exec($dataSql);
        if ('testing' != APPLICATION_ENV) {
            echo 'Data Loaded.';
            echo PHP_EOL;
        }
   }

} catch (Exception $e) {
    echo 'AN ERROR HAS OCCURED:' . PHP_EOL;
    echo $e->getMessage() . PHP_EOL;
    return false;
}

return true;
```

code snippet /communication/zf/library/scripts/load.sqlite.php

This code is described on the ZF web page. To be honest, we don't know why this code is not included out of the box. There are two very important lines in which you should set your database schema and data files:

```
$schemaSql = file_get_contents(dirname(__FILE__) . '/schema.sqlite.sql');
$dataSql = file_get_contents(dirname(__FILE__) . '/data.sqlite.sql');
```

To run this script to load your fixtures into a database, run it with the `--withdata` parameter.

```
$ php scripts/load.sqlite.php --withdata
```

Command-line Interface

CLI tools are very useful because they generate code automatically and save a lot of time, so an application can be developed significantly faster. It's important when *time is money.*

Symfony — Propel

Propel, just like Doctrine, provides a strong CLI. As mentioned earlier, your schema can be written in two file types: YAML and XML. That's why there are two special commands available to convert both schemas (`schema-to-xml` and `schema-to-yml`).

The following are the CLI commands provided by Propel:

```
propel
        :build
        :build-all
        :build-all-load
        :build-filters
        :build-forms
        :build-model
        :build-schema
        :build-sql
        :data-dump
        :data-load
        :graphviz
        :insert-sql
        :schema-to-xml
        :schema-to-yml
```

Another new command is `build-all`, which is equivalent to the `build --all` command in Doctrine. This task also has an extension that loads defined fixture data: `build-all-load`. `Build-schema` is a command we did not describe in the Doctrine discussion, but it's available there as well. With this task, you can build a schema from an existing database. This is very useful when you switch from a legacy application that was written in a different framework, language, and so on.

Another great feature that Propel offers is the ability to generate graphs from a model. Just create a schema, build a model, and then table relationships can be built. To do this, you should use the `graphviz` command, which will generate a `.dot` file in the `/graph` directory. To convert `.dot` to `.png`, you can use the `graphviz` tool, which is available for free from `www.graphviz.org`. Use the following command to convert it to PNG:

```
$ cd graph/
$ dot -Tpng -oGraph.png propel.schema.dot
```

For a simple schema with two tables and a simple relationship, you should see a picture similar to Figure 3-10.

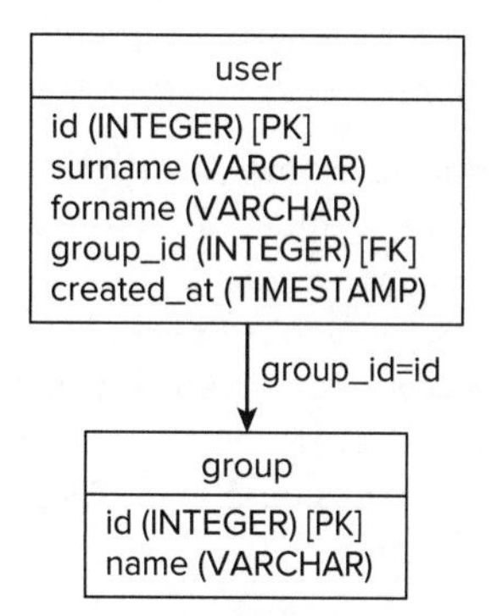

FIGURE 3-10: Schema visualized with the graphviz tool

Symfony — Doctrine

The following are the CLI commands provided by Doctrine:

```
doctrine
           :build
           :build-db
           :build-filters
           :build-forms
           :build-model
           :build-schema
           :build-sql
           :clean-model-files
           :create-model-tables
           :data-dump
           :data-load
           :delete-model-files
           :dql
           :drop-db
           :insert-sql
```

As mentioned before, Doctrine's architecture is inspired by Hibernate. Hibernate uses Hibernate Query Language (HQL) and so Doctrine uses very similar Doctrine Query Language (DQL), a specific language used only by Doctrine. It can be executed directly from the command line:

```
$ symfony  doctrine:dql "FROM User"
```

This command returns a list of users added previously. Use this query only if you have few users in the database, otherwise you will get your console flooded. Thanks to DQL, developers can work with databases without knowing details. In complicated projects, it's likely that using specific database tools and features will be necessary.

The most important Doctrine console command is `build`. This is an all-in-one command, a compilation of all other tasks that begin with `build` and will probably be the command you use most if Doctrine is the right ORM for you.

The following command builds a model from your schema; a database is based on that model:

```
$ symfony  doctrine:build --all
```

Forms, filters, and SQL files are also generated by this command. (We will discuss more about forms and filters in later chapters.) Forms, filters, and models are stored in the `/lib` directory; SQL is stored in the `/data` directory.

While developing an application, your tables can change; some may need to be deleted; others have to be added. If you remove tables from your schema, to keep your code clean you can use the `clean-model-files` command to delete no-longer-used models. To delete all model files, use `delete-model-files`; to delete a database, use `drop-db`. The last "cleaning" command is `create-model-table`, which deletes existing tables and creates a new one for your model. Doctrine also provides a command for executing a SQL query (`insert-sql`) that is used with the `build` or `build-sql` command. You can also add some specific SQL queries by editing the `.sql` file in `/data/sql/schema.sql`.

The last tasks that we want to show are designed to operate on fixtures. `data-load` loads your fixture YAML files into a database. You can also do it in another way (`data-dump`), exporting data from a database to a YAML fixture.

CakePHP

Cake gives developers two main branches of basic but necessary command-line tools: `bake` and `schema`.

```
cake bake
cake schema
        schema view
        schema generate
        schema dump <filename>
        schema run create <schema> <table>
        schema run update <schema> <table>
```

The first branch, `bake`, provides some basic options such as creating a model, controller, view, project, or other database configuration-related tasks. They are asked as questions after executing `bake`, so there are no specific options for this command.

From the command line, type **d** for database configuration, and Cake will ask a series of questions about database details, as shown in the following code:

```
Name:
[default] >
Driver: (db2/firebird/mssql/mysql/mysqli/odbc/oracle/postgres/sqlite/sybase)
[mysql] >
Persistent Connection? (y/n)
[n] >
Database Host:
[localhost] >
Port?
[n] >
User:
[root] >
Password:
>
Database Name:
[cake] >
Table Prefix?
[n] >
Table encoding?
[n] >
```

Next you are asked to confirm all database information. If confirmed, Cake will save it into `database.php`. If not confirmed, you will be asked again or default values will be assumed. You can then connect to the database. You need to make sure that all environments (*development*, *testing*, *production*) have been configured, not just the *default* one. To configure other environments, just change the proposed `[default]` to another one.

As mentioned earlier, Cake provides some tools for working with a schema. The simplest one is `view`, which just prints your `schema.php` file. You can manipulate a schema in two ways. `generate` option allows you to build a schema file from a database. It's useful if you have designed the database manually. A different approach is available with the `run` option. Both `create` and `update` parameters can create new tables, if they are not present, otherwise they will just update tables already existing in the database. With the `-s` parameter of the `run` command, you can make snapshots of schema changes. This is useful if you want to do a dry run of a new schema (the `-dry` parameter should be used). An example of using `-dry` to simulate creating `users` table from `users` schema looks as follows:

```
$ cake schema run create users users -dry
```

The last option is `dump`, which generates a `.sql` file. It contains all queries needed to build the database structure. Like all files related to a schema, `.sql` files are stored in the `/app/config/sql` directory.

Zend Framework

Each framework has its CLI tools that offer some scaffolding enhancements. Although you can work without these tools, they let you save a lot of time. There are many kinds of enhancements, but we want to show here only those that are applicable to databases. ZF offers two simple commands, shown in the following snippet:

```
$ zf configure db-adapter dsn section-name[=production]

$ zf create db-table name actual-table-name module force-overwrite
```

The first command adds `db-adapter` configuration in `application.ini`. This can be done very quickly (also manually). Here's an example of how it should be used:

```
$ zf configure db-adapter "adapter=PDO_MYSQL&dbname=WROX&username=wroxuser&password
   =secret&hostname=127.0.0.1" -s production
```

The above command will add the line below into `application.ini`.

Available for download on Wrox.com

```
[production]
...
resources.db.adapter = "PDO_MYSQL"
resources.db.params.dbname = "WROX"
resources.db.params.username = "wroxuser"
resources.db.params.password = "secret"
resources.db.params.hostname = "127.0.0.1"
```

code snippet /communication/zf/application/configs/application.ini

Database settings should be made separately for each of the three environments: *production*, *testing*, and *development*. In most cases, different databases are used for each environment.

The following command generates `db-table` files, which can be done in two different ways. The simplest method is to generate a `DbTable` file for a given model and database table:

```
$ zf create db-table users Users
```

The second method is to generate these files from database tables (the database should be configured before running this method):

```
$ zf create db-table.from-database
```

Both methods prepare only basic files without any methods for manipulating data. This is a disadvantage, but gives developers flexibility while developing applications, especially complex ones.

Your First Application in the Three Frameworks

— *Your mother ate my dog!*

— *Not all of it.*

— Braindead

WHAT'S IN THIS CHAPTER?

- Designing an address book application.
- Implementing in Symfony, CakePHP, and Zend Framework.

This chapter will take you through the process of designing and developing your first application: an online address book. This application will be built on top of a simple database, used for storing information about your contacts. Each entry consists of a few fields (first name, last name, address, phone number, e-mail address), and the basic functionality is to perform all create, read, update, and delete (CRUD) operations for each database entry.

Because this is your first step of developing applications using frameworks, we want it to be as simple as possible, introducing you to benefits offered by presented frameworks. This chapter should show how with little or no effort, you can achieve great results, all thanks to the frameworks' basic functionality.

DESIGN

At this point we assume that you have done the all steps from the previous chapters and you have your frameworks up and running. Before you can continue, you need to make sure that your server is running (Apache, for example), a database connection is configured, and a framework is installed and configured accordingly.

Project Requirements

When working on a project, it is good to have some expectations defined before any coding is done. A properly planned project greatly enhances workflow and helps you avoid unnecessary development issues.

In this project you will be using MySQL as the default database. So, we will specify requirements for the database that will be needed to build the address book application.

For storing typical address data such as first name, last name, address, e-mail address, and telephone number, one table is required. At this point, we assume that every contact in your address book has only one phone number and only one e-mail address.

Later in this book we will explain how to work with multiple tables containing related data and handle them with one controller.

In addition to the fields already mentioned, the project table will contain a few other fields that will be used for additional functionality:

- **ID** — A unique integer value that identifies every address in your address book
- **created/modified** — Fields that introduce additional functionality and will be used in the future to present autocompletion functions of the frameworks

The structure we suggest for the addresses table is shown in Figure 4-1.

You need to make sure that this table is created before you can proceed. To do this you can use various methods. For example, you can use phpMyAdmin to do it manually, use the SQL query (introduced later in this chapter), or (for Symfony and CakePHP) generate the required table using command-line tools. Before that you should define it in `schema.yml\schema.xml` (Symfony) or `schema.php` (CakePHP). How to work with schemas was explained in Chapter 3.

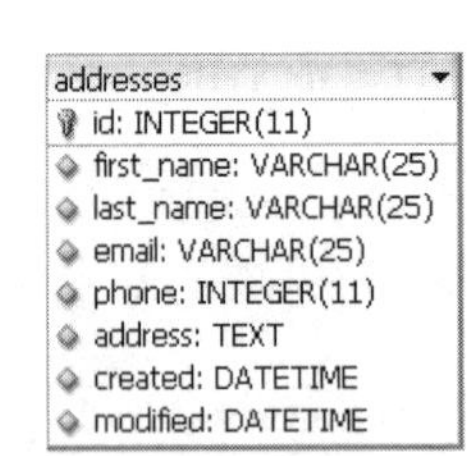

FIGURE 4-1: Database design for the address book table

The suggested encoding for the database is UTF-8 because it supports various localizations and special characters. To use that encoding in Doctrine, you should invoke the following methods to `ProjectConfiguration.class.php` in the `/config` directory:

Available for download on Wrox.com

```
<?php
  public function configureDoctrine(Doctrine_Manager $manager) {
     $manager->setCollate('utf8_unicode_ci');
     $manager->setCharset('utf8');
  }
```

code snippet /symfony/config/ProjectConfiguration.class.php

Propel has two files that you need to change. They should be modified in the same way, which is why it can sometimes be confusing. First you should set UTF-8 encoding in `database.yml`:

```
all:
  propel:
    class: sfPropelDatabase
    param:
      encoding: utf8
```

Next, edit the `propel.ini` config file and set it as "`utf8`" (it should be set as the default):

```
propel.database.encoding = utf8
```

CakePHP allows you to change that option in the database configuration:

```
var $default = array( 'encoding' => 'utf8' );
```

In Zend Framework (ZF), you use a pure SQL query because you have no schema.

```
CREATE TABLE IF NOT EXISTS 'addresses' (
  'id' int(11) unsigned NOT NULL AUTO_INCREMENT,
  'first_name' varchar(25) NOT NULL,
  'last_name' varchar(25) DEFAULT NULL,
  'email' varchar(25) DEFAULT NULL,
  'phone' int(11) DEFAULT NULL,
  'address' text,
  'created' datetime NOT NULL,
  'modified' datetime NOT NULL,
  PRIMARY KEY ('id')
) ENGINE=MyISAM  DEFAULT CHARSET=utf8 COLLATE=utf8_unicode_ci;
```

There is another important issue that should be handled for each framework. You should create not only individual tables, but also your whole database with the default encoding set as UTF-8. For example, here's how to do this in MySQL (and PostgreSQL as well):

```
CREATE DATABASE foo_bar_db CHARACTER SET utf8 COLLATE utf8_unicode_ci;
CREATE DATABASE foo_bar_db WITH ENCODING 'UTF8'
```

There are equivalent queries for other database servers.

SYMFONY

So far we have briefly discussed the first application that you are going to develop and you know what functionalities it is going to provide. Now it is time to see the frameworks in action.

Project

In previous chapters, you configured the Symfony installation; now you can use console commands to automatically generate various parts of the application. You can now create a new project using the `generate:project` command. To do so, you need to create a new folder in your `/htdocs` directory, where your project will be stored. In this case, let it be named /htdocs/symfony. In this location, a new project called addressBook will be installed.

```
$ cd htdocs/symfony
$ symfony generate:project addressBook
```

With the new project created, it is possible to add a new application to it by typing the symfony generate:app command at the command line. When you do so, the application files will be created in the directory you specify. The following command creates the /htdocs/symfony/apps/frontend directory:

```
$ symfony generate:app frontend
```

In previous chapters we showed you how to configure proper aliases and directories with Apache and LightPad. If everything is set properly, you should be able to see your project start page at http://localhost/frontend_dev.php.

Model

Now you can use Doctrine to generate the model, SQL, modules, and database tables for the project. To do this, you need to edit the schema.yml file located in /symfony/config/doctrine/, as shown in following code.

Available for download on Wrox.com

```
Addresses:
   actAs:
      Timestampable:
         created:
            name: created
            type: timestamp
            format: Y-m-d H:i:s
            notnull: false
         updated:
            name: updated
            type: timestamp
            format: Y-m-d H:i:s
            notnull: false
   columns:
      first_name: { type:string(40), notnull: false }
      last_name: { type:string(40), notnull: false }
      email: { type:string(40), notnull: false }
      phone: { type:integer(40), notnull: false }
      description: { type:object, notnull: false }
   options:
      type: MYISAM
      collate: utf8_general_ci
```

code snippet /symfony/config/doctrine/schema.yml

While editing schema.yml it is very important not to use any tabulation because that may prevent proper execution of the file. The schema in Listing 4-1 was also discussed in Chapter 3, but the last three lines are new. This is another solution for setting proper encoding; in this case you set it directly in the schema instead of in the database configuration. All three solutions — Symfony, CakePHP, and ZF — can be set at the same time.

The next step is to use the command line to call doctrine:build --all command. This will create tables in the project database according to the schema.yml file.

```
$ symfony doctrine:build --all
```

Controller

There are two main ways to create a controller. The first one uses project branch tasks, and the second one uses object-relational mapping (ORM)-based tasks. The project method generates only a template of the controller and a simple view. The ORM method generates more functional controllers with a lot of ready-to-use code. Here, we present one kind of these ORM-generated controllers. The command that you need to type is doctrine:generate-module, which will generate all the CRUD files. The parameters that need to be passed to this command are the application name, the generated module name, and the database table that CRUD operations are created for.

```
$ symfony doctrine:generate-module frontend addressBook Addresses
```

The project files generated by Doctrine are located in /symfony/apps/frontend/modules:

```
/modules
   /addressbook
      /actions
         actions.class.php
      /templates
         _form.php
         editSuccess.php
         indexSuccess.php
         newSuccess.php
```

First, look into one of the generated files: actions.class.php. Doctrine generates a controller class that contains all methods needed to provide CRUD functionality, and also provides form validation. Forms are generated at the same time when building models, during the execution of these tasks: build, build-all, or build-forms.

```
<?php
class addressbookActions extends sfActions {
    public function executeIndex(sfWebRequest $request) { }
    public function executeNew(sfWebRequest $request) { }
    public function executeCreate(sfWebRequest $request) { }
    public function executeEdit(sfWebRequest $request) { }
    public function executeUpdate(sfWebRequest $request) { }
    public function executeDelete(sfWebRequest $request) { }
    protected function processForm(sfWebRequest $request, sfForm $form) { }
}
```

Address List

The executeIndex() method lists all available items from a database table (in this case, only the User table). To get all available entries from the User table, you should use Doctrine's getTable() method. Next you need to execute a query on the selected table. Parameter a is passed to a query method. This is the name for the parameter that will be used in your table, when using some of the more complex queries; for example, to set an equal expression such as `a.firstName=='John'`.

Available for download on Wrox.com

```
public function executeIndex(sfWebRequest $request) {
  $this->users = Doctrine::getTable('User')
    ->createQuery('a')
    ->execute();
}
```

code snippet /symfony/apps/frontend/modules/addressbook/actions/actions.class.php

The results of the query execution are stored in the `$this->users` variable. In Symfony any variable that is created in controllers and is marked as `$this->variable` is automatically forwarded to the view layer after the controller method is executed properly.

Adding and Editing Entries

The `ExecuteNew()` method, which is responsible for creating new users, is very simple: It contains only one line, which creates a form for the user table and at the same time renders the view layer. `UserForm` definitions are stored in `/lib/forms/` directory.

Every method in `addressbookActions` class gets a parameter of `sfWebRequest` type. This variable contains all the data that the user can submit through the forms. In the case of the `executeNew()` or `executeIndex()` methods, `sfWebRequest` is not relevant because it is not used in those methods, as you can see in the following code. In all other methods, the `sfWebRequest` variable is important because `GET` or `POST` parameters are used in these methods.

Available for download on Wrox.com

```
public function executeNew(sfWebRequest $request) {
  $this->form = new UserForm();
}
```

code snippet /symfony/apps/frontend/modules/addressbook/actions/actions.class.php

As you can see in the following code, Symfony provides some methods that help you secure your application against simple attacks:

```
public function executeCreate(sfWebRequest $request) {
$this->forward404Unless($request->isMethod(sfRequest::POST));
  $this->form = new UserForm();
  $this->processForm($request, $this->form);
  $this->setTemplate('new');
}

public function executeEdit(sfWebRequest $request) {
  $this->forward404Unless($user = Doctrine::getTable('User')->
           find(array($request->getParameter('id'))),
           sprintf('Object users does not exist (%s).',
           $request->getParameter('id')));
  $this->form = new UserForm($user);
}
```

```
public function executeUpdate(sfWebRequest $request) {
    $this->forward404Unless($request->isMethod(sfRequest::POST)
                        || $request->isMethod(sfRequest::PUT));
    $this->forward404Unless($user = Doctrine::getTable('User')->
            find(array($request->getParameter('id'))),
            sprintf('Object users does not exist (%s).',
           $request->getParameter('id')));
    $this->form = new UserForm($user);
    $this->processForm($request, $this->form);
    $this->setTemplate('edit');
  }
```

code snippet /symfony/apps/frontend/modules/addressbook/actions/actions.class.php

For example, in `executeEdit()` the `forward404Unless()` method is used and it checks if a given user exists in the database. If not, a 404 Not Found error message is shown. In case of an error, the rest of the code is not executed. This is a good practice because you don't need to do anything else when you cannot retrieve selected user data. The same is true with request type. If you expect a `POST` request, you should not proceed any further for security purposes.

The next security feature is the `checkCSRFProtection()` method, which protects you against cross-site request forgery (CSRF) attacks. You can find more about this and other kinds of attacks in Chapter 8. The `Update` method creates a new user form — `UserForm($user)`. In this case, you should send as a parameter user data that is to be intercepted by the constructor. All given `$request` data and also `$form` data is sent to the `processForm()` method, which binds all the data together. You can observe it in the following code snippet. The `$request` variable is also needed because of any files that could be uploaded within forms. Form method `processForm()` and other forms-related topics are described in detail in Chapter 5.

```
protected function processForm(sfWebRequest $request, sfForm $form) {
  $form->bind($request->getParameter($form->getName()),
              $request->getFiles($form->getName()));
  if ($form->isValid()) {
    $user = $form->save();
    $this->redirect('addressbook/edit?id='.$user->getId());
  }
}
```

code snippet /symfony/apps/frontend/modules/addressbook/actions/actions.class.php

Deleting an Address

As shown in the following code, to delete a user you can just invoke the `delete()` method of your object. After deletion, you should redirect to another site that will inform users that the delete operation was successful.

```
public function executeDelete(sfWebRequest $request) {
  $request->checkCSRFProtection();
```

```
    $this->forward404Unless($user = Doctrine::getTable('User')->
            find(array($request->getParameter('id'))),
            sprintf('Object users does not exist (%s).',
            $request->getParameter('id')));
    $users->delete();
    $this->redirect('addressbook/index');
  }
```

code snippet /symfony/apps/frontend/modules/addressbook/actions/actions.class.php

View

By default, Symfony generates some basic views for a new module: index, new, edit, and form. As we mentioned in Chapter 1, it is important not to repeat yourself. That's why the *form* view is a separate view and it can be re-used this way both in *new* and in *edit* templates.

Editing/Updating Addresses

For each method that begins with `execute`, a template is created. The only exception in your case is the update method because this template would be the same as the edit method, so they can share one view. That's why the `setTemplate()` method is used: to let Symfony know which templates should be currently applied.

In previous Symfony releases, a form view was generated for each template. Now you need to change the form only once. Both new and edit templates import the form template by invoking the `include_partial()` helper, as shown in the following code:

Available for download on Wrox.com

```
<h1>New Addresses</h1>
<?php include_partial('form', array('form' => $form)) ?>
```

code snippet /symfony/apps/frontend/modules/addressbook/templates/newSuccess.php

The same `include_partial()` helper is present in an edit template. Everything that is added to the template before and after the `include_partial()` method is displayed as normal HTML code while being viewed in a web browser. The `include_partial()` method inserts another template into the view; in this example, it is a form template. As you can see in the preceding code, the second parameter in the `include_partial()` method is an array. In this array, you assign to the form name a `$form` object that you get from the controller. The `'form'` string describes the name of the variable that is available in the form (`_form.php`) partial template. That's why it's possible to have access to the `$form` object in `_form.php`.

Every partial template name should start with an underscore ('_'). The first two lines of the following code are responsible for adding form-specific cascading style sheets (CSSs) and JavaScript code.

The following code, which displays the form, validates it and handles errors, may look rather complicated — that's because it's a piece of HTML structure intertwined with PHP code blocks.

```
<?php use_stylesheets_for_form($form) ?>
<?php use_javascripts_for_form($form) ?>

<form action=" <?php echo url_for('addressbook/'.
          ($form->getObject()->isNew() ? 'create' : 'update').
          (!$form->getObject()->isNew() ? '?id='.$form->getObject()->getId() : ''))
?>" method="post"
<?php $form->isMultipart() and print 'enctype="multipart/form-data" ' ?> >

<?php if (!$form->getObject()->isNew()): ?>
<input type="hidden" name="sf_method" value="put" />
<?php endif; ?>
  <table>
    <tfoot>
      <tr>
        <td colspan="2">
          <?php echo $form->renderHiddenFields(false) ?>
             <a href="<?php echo url_for('addressbook/index') ?>">Back to list</a>
          <?php if (!$form->getObject()->isNew()): ?>
            <?php echo link_to('Delete',
                              'addresbook/delete?id='.$form->getObject()->
                                    getId(), array('method' => 'delete',
                                    'confirm' => 'Are you sure?'))
            ?>
          <?php endif; ?>
          <input type="submit" value="Save" />
        </td>
    </tr>
    </tfoot>
    <tbody>
      <?php echo $form->renderGlobalErrors() ?>
      <tr>
        <th><?php echo $form['forname']->renderLabel() ?></th>
        <td>
          <?php echo $form['forname']->renderError() ?>
          <?php echo $form['forname'] ?>
        </td>
      </tr>
      <tr>
        <th><?php echo $form['lastname']->renderLabel() ?></th>
        <td>
          <?php echo $form['lastname']->renderError() ?>
          <?php echo $form['lastname'] ?>
        </td>
      </tr>
      <tr>
        <th><?php echo $form['created_at']->renderLabel() ?></th>
        <td>
          <?php echo $form['created_at']->renderError() ?>
         <?php echo $form['created_at'] ?>
       </td>
   </tr>
```

```
        <tr>
          <th><?php echo $form['updated_at']->renderLabel() ?></th>
          <td>
            <?php echo $form['updated_at']->renderError() ?>
            <?php echo $form['updated_at'] ?>
          </td>
          </tr>
      </tbody>
    </table>
  </form>
```

code snippet /symfony/apps/frontend/modules/addressbook/templates/_form.php

When you split the preceding listing into parts, you will see that most of the code generates the action link. First you have a logical operator:

```
$form->getObject()->isNew() ? 'create' : 'update'
```

It tells you if the object that you want to create is a new one or just an update of an existing one. Note that you have one form for the `create` and `update` methods. If the `isNew()` method returns `true`, you put into your link a `'create'` string. In the other case, you would use `'update'`. This is obvious because if you want to add a new user, you should process the form data to the controller's `create` method.

The logical operator (?) used in the code below returns an empty string in the case of new data. Otherwise, the ID of an existing user is returned. The ID is concatenated with the `'?id='` string, which in conjunction with the previously returned string gives you a proper link for the action attribute of the form.

```
!$form->getObject()->isNew() ? '?id='.$form->getObject()->getId() : ''
```

Additionally you should add the `enctype` attribute if you plan to upload files. Without `enctype="multipart/form-data"`, your form will work, but will not upload any files.

```
 $form->isMultipart() and print 'enctype="multipart/form-data" '
```

But let's go back to the controller. As shown in the following code, the `PUT` method is also added automatically. This is described in the "RESTful News Reading" section in Chapter 12.

```
<?php if (!$form->getObject()->isNew()): ?>
<input type="hidden" name="sf_method" value="put" />
<?php endif; ?>
```

The `PUT` method simulates only the `PUT` request. In this case, the method does nothing because a false parameter is sent by default. Normally, this method should generate all the needed hidden input fields. This is further explained in Chapter 5. The following code prevents generating hidden fields in embedded forms.

```
 echo $form->renderHiddenFields(false)
```

Deleting Addresses

An edit template should provide an address deletion option. The easiest way to do that is to add a link that should allow you to invoke the controller's `delete` method. There are two new elements introduced here. First, you use another HTTP request method. This time, it is `delete`. This is described in more detail in Chapter 12. Second, Symfony allows the `link_to()` helper to add some simple JavaScript that will confirm your choice. Simple, isn't it?

```
echo link_to('Delete',
            'addresbook/delete?id='.$form->getObject()->getId(),
            array('method' => 'delete',
                  'confirm' => 'Are you sure?'))
```

Both the edit and new forms should look like those shown in Figure 4-2.

FIGURE 4-2: The New Address and Edit Address forms in Symfony

Address List

Timestamp fields don't look very user-friendly, but they provide some basic functionality that serves your purpose for now. Chapter 5 describes how to make them trendier.

The last issue is to list all available addresses. In the index method you send all user data as a `$users` variable to the index view. For each user, data is printed as shown in the following code:

Available for download on Wrox.com

```
<h1>Address List</h1>
<table>
  <thead>
    <tr>
      <th>Id</th>
      <th>FirstName</th>
      <th>Lastname</th>
      <th>Email</th>
      <th>Phone</th>
      <th>Description</th>
      <th>Created at</th>
      <th>Updated at</th>
    </tr>
  </thead>
  <tbody>
    <?php foreach ($userss as $users): ?>
    <tr>
      <td><a href="<?php echo url_for('addresbook/edit?id='.$users->getId()) ?>">
              <?php echo $users->getId() ?>
          </a>
      </td>
      <td><?php echo $users->getFirstName() ?></td>
      <td><?php echo $users->getLastName() ?></td>
```

```
        <td><?php echo $users->getEmail() ?></td>
        <td><?php echo $users->getPhone() ?></td>
        <td><?php echo $users->getDescription() ?></td>
        <td><?php echo $users->getCreatedAt() ?></td>
        <td><?php echo $users->getUpdatedAt() ?></td>
      </tr>
      <?php endforeach; ?>
    </tbody>
  </table>

    <a href="<?php echo url_for('addresbook/new') ?>">New</a>
```

code snippet /symfony/apps/frontend/modules/addressbook/templates/indexSuccess.php

Figure 4-3 shows how the index view should look in the web browser.

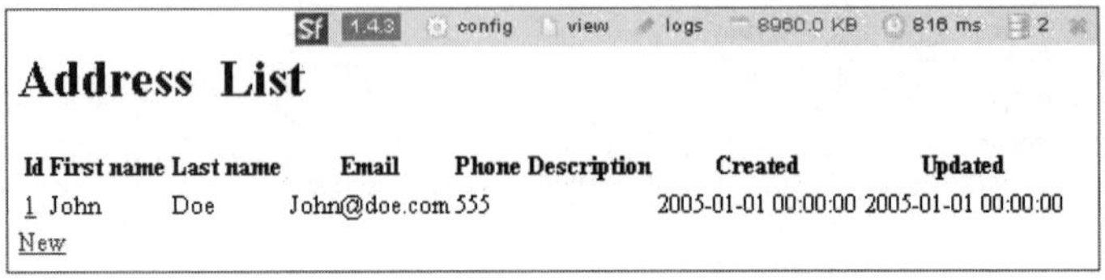

Sf 1.4.3 config view logs 8960.0 KB 816 ms 2

Address List

Id	First name	Last name	Email	Phone	Description	Created	Updated
1	John	Doe	John@doe.com	555		2005-01-01 00:00:00	2005-01-01 00:00:00

New

FIGURE 4-3: The Address List in Symfony

CAKEPHP

You will now produce an address book in CakePHP, just like you did in Symfony. With all the experience you have gained so far, it should not be a hard task.

Project

Before you start building an application, you should make sure that the database you are working with is properly created for this purpose. This project will use a database that is named Cake, and this database should contain one table called addresses, with a structure the same as that shown in the "Design" section of this chapter.

The following code shows the files used to build the address book application:

```
/cake_installation
   /app
      /config
         routes.php
         database.php
         core.php
   /controllers
      addresses_controller.php
   /models
```

```
      address.php
   /views
      /addresses
         add.ctp
         edit.ctp
         index.ctp
         view.ctp
```

Routing

Previous chapters should have left you with a fresh CakePHP framework installation in the /webroot directory. With that in place, you can start writing the functionality. At this point, you will repeat the steps used in previous chapters and begin with connecting your current application to a URL that you choose.

For example, you would like to access your address book project by typing http://localhost/cake/the-book in the browser. What you need to do now is to add an instruction to the CakePHP routing file that will make that URL point to the proper controller and its functions. To do this, it is necessary to edit the routes.php file and add another line:

```
Router::connect('/the-book',
                array('controller' => 'addresses',
                      'action' => 'index'));
```

code snippet /cakephp/app/config/routes.php

This will map /the-book to the execute action index of controller addresses. Now take a look at the model and controller.

Model

So far, you have created the routing directive. Now it's time to create the model for the project. It should be located in the /models directory (see the file structure listed right under "Project" above). It needs to look like this:

```
<?php
class Address extends AppModel {
  var $name = 'Address';
}
?>
```

code snippet /cakephp/app/models/address.php

For this application, leave it as it is now; that way the framework will try to read the model information from the structure of the addresses table.

Schema

We mentioned in Chapter 3 that you can create all needed tables in two different ways. One way is to do it manually (as in ZF), and the other is to use a schema. In this case, the schema should look like this:

```
var $_schema = array(
     'id' => array('type' => 'string', 'length' => 30),
     'first_name' => array('type' => 'string', 'length' => 30),
     'last_name' => array('type' => 'string', 'length' => 30),
     'email' => array('type' => 'string','length' => 30),
        'phone' => array('type' => 'string','length' => 30),
     'address' => array('type' => 'text'),
     'created' => array('type' => 'date'),
     'modified' => array('type' => 'date')
);
```

code snippet /cakephp/app/config/schema/schema.php

Don't forget to run the appropriate commands to complete this task (see in the previous chapter — CakePHP part of "Command-line Interface" section). However, for the purpose of this example, you will use the manual approach instead of using a schema.

Controller

You have created the routing for the URL of your choice, and you have linked it with the `'addresses'` controller, as shown in the following code:

```
<?php
class AddressesController extends AppController {
  var $name = 'addresses';
}
?>
```

code snippet /cakephp/app/controllers/addresses_controller.php

Now is a good time to say a word or two about naming conventions because they can be a little confusing.

Naming conventions in CakePHP are applied to make the use of the Model-View-Controller (MVC) as easy as possible. In your address book, the controller will be used to handle actions performed on data (addresses) that your address book will contain. Knowing this, you will need to name your controller addresses. As you know, CakePHP will automatically try to look for a model to connect with. The model's name is singular, unlike the controller's file and views' folder names. Therefore, if you want to use the automatic functions of the CakePHP framework, you need to use plural names for the controller, database tables, and views folders. Singular names will be used only for the model.

List of All Addresses

Now create some actions for the controller. As discussed with the routing file, the `index()` action should be executed while viewing `http://localhost/cake/the-book address`. Now you need to create this action, so add a `function index` inside the brackets of the addresses controller:

```
class AddressesController extends AppController {
  var $name = 'addresses';
    function index($id = null) {
        $this->set('address_list', $this->Address->find('all'));
    }
}
```

code snippet /cakephp/app/controllers/addresses_controller.php

This action finds all addresses available in your database. It is the same as this SQL query:

```
SELECT * FROM addresses;
```

That way, whenever someone types `http://localhost/cake/the-book` into a web browser window, an `index()` action will be called, and all data contained in addresses table will be read and saved into the `address_list` variable. The `set()` method used in this example creates a variable (in this case, it is `address_list`) and assigns data to it (here it is a list of all addresses) so later it can be read and used in a view template to display its content.

Note that for every controller method that is supposed to display something, a view file should be created (`index.ctp`, `add.ctp`, and so on).

Adding a New Address

Now you know how to pass variables into view templates. Suppose that you create an *add* link to add some new data. If you click it, you will get an error about missing the `add()` action, so you can create a new function that will handle adding new addresses to the database.

Putting `function add()` into the `addresses_controller.php` file should get you where you want to go. The following code will handle adding new addresses to the database:

```
function add() {
    if (!empty($this->data)) {
        if ($this->Address->save($this->data)) {
            $this->Session->setFlash('New address has been saved.');
            $this->redirect(array('action' => 'index'));
        }
    }
}
```

code snippet /cakephp/app/controllers/addresses_controller.php

Now we will explain what this function does. The first `if` statement checks to see whether there is anything in `$this->data`, which is data submitted by the form. In CakePHP, `$this->data` is a known variable where form data can also be found. If any data has been sent, it is saved using information from the address model. Then a confirmation message is generated to be displayed in the page. Finally, redirection to the index action is done, and the confirmation message is shown.

Editing an Address

Because you now have a list of all addresses and can add new addresses, you can move on to editing entries. To do so, you will add another action to the addresses controller and create a new view file. Add the `edit()` function as follows:

Available for download on Wrox.com

```
function edit($id = null) {
    $this->Address->id = $id;
    if (empty($this->data)) {
        $this->data = $this->Address->read();
    } else {
        if ($this->Address->save($this->data)) {
            $this->Session->setFlash('New address has been saved.');
            $this->redirect(array('action' => 'index'));
        }
    }
}
```

code snippet /cakephp/app/controllers/addresses_controller.php

This function is very similar to the `add()` function and is divided into two sections. The first section is responsible for loading selected address information into data (`$this->data`) that will be displayed by an edit form. The second section is responsible for saving submitted form data into the database. This is intuitive because you use the `edit()` method to display and save entry data. The first `if` statement determines whether you want to display the data or save it. As you can see, all `GET` data that you want to get is intercepted as method parameters.

Deleting a Selected Address

Now that you have created most of the application's functionality, the last thing to do is add the delete option. Add the new `delete()` action as follows:

Available for download on Wrox.com

```
function delete($id) {
    $this->Address->delete($id);
    $this->Session->setFlash('Address with id: '.$id.' has been deleted.');
    $this->redirect(array('action'=>'index'));
}
```

code snippet /cakephp/app/controllers/addresses_controller.php

As before, this file uses most of the framework's functionality, and by running `$this->Address->delete($id)`, it removes every entry with the given ID from the database without writing any database queries. The next line generates a message to be displayed after redirection is done. This method should be used very carefully because of security issues (see Chapter 8).

Viewing a Selected Address

This is the most obvious and simplest task. As before, you need to add a new action to `addresses_controler.php` according to the following code:

```
function view($id = null) {
    $this->Address->id = $id;
    $this->set('address', $this->Address->read());
}
```

code snippet /cakephp/app/controllers/addresses_controller.php

You get the address's ID and assign it to `$this->Address`, which is the same as saying this: Get an address with an ID of `$id` (where `$id` is a number). That's why in the next line you need only assign a chosen address to a view variable. The rest of the work to find the proper address is done by Cake.

View

Now is a good time to take care of the view part by adding a few lines of code to the `index.ctp` file.

Address List

To display all data from the database, use an HTML table as shown here:

```
<table>
    <tr>
        <th>Id</th>
        <th>First name</th>
        <th>Last name</th>
        <th>Email</th>
        <th>Phone</th>
        <th>Address</th>
        <th>Options</th>
    </tr>
<?php
    foreach ( $address_list as $line ) {
    $address = $line['Address'];
        echo
        '<tr>'.
            '<td>'.$address['id'].'</td>'.
            '<td>'.$address['first_name'].'</td>'.
            '<td>'.$address['last_name'].'</td>'.
            '<td>'.$address['email'].'</td>'.
            '<td>'.$address['phone'].'</td>'.
            '<td>'.$address['address'].'</td>'.
            '<td></td>'.
        '</tr>';
    };
?>
</table>
```

code snippet /cakephp/app/views/addresses/index.ctp

You can see all addresses saved to the database through the Add New Address form. As mentioned previously in the "Controller" section, you get all data in the `$address_list`.

Now you have all the prerequisites to fill the add view file. Add a link to the top of `index.ctp`:

Available for download on Wrox.com

```
<?php
    echo $html->link('Add new address', array('action'=>'add'));
?>
```

code snippet /cakephp/app/views/addresses/index.ctp

You can now see the results of your work. It is not much, but typing `http://localhost/cake/the-book` into a web browser window should display your index page. Here you can see the standard CakePHP header and footer, as well as the content created by us, which should be a single link called Add New Address. This link, if clicked, will call the same controller, but a different action, which in this case will be the add action. The address list with the Add New Address link is displayed in Figure 4-4.

New address has been saved.

Add new address

Id	First name	Last name	Email	Phone	Address	Options
1	John	Doe	john.doe@mail.com	555		

FIGURE 4-4: The Address List with the Add new address link

Forms

Adding forms in CakePHP is very simple. This framework creates all needed input fields for a given model. The necessary code is shown as follows:

Available for download on Wrox.com

```
<?php
    echo $form->create('Address');
    echo $form->inputs();
    echo $form->end('Save address');
?>
```

code snippet /cakephp/app/views/addresses/add.ctp

This code creates a form like the one shown in Figure 4-5. Note that only three form methods were used: form starting and ending tag methods, and an input generation method. The last method generates all needed input files. This is a time-saving approach because it gets the `create()` parameter, which is in fact the name of the model and automatically returns all needed input fields based on model information. You might wonder why the two additional methods are necessary. The answer is that they're needed because the HTML form tag can be customized, as can the submit button.

The form displayed in Figure 4-5 will be slightly different from the one you will see in your web browser because the stylesheet has been modified for the purpose of generating smaller images for this book.

FIGURE 4-5: The New Address form in CakePHP

Editing an Address

To edit an entry, you need to add a proper link that will redirect you to the edit form page. To do that, you need to edit `index.ctp` and change it a little bit, as shown in the following code:

Available for download on Wrox.com

```
<?php
    foreach ( $address_list as $line ) {
    $address = $line['Address'];
        echo
        '<tr>'.
            '<td>'.$address['id'].'</td>'.
            '<td>'.$address['first_name'].'</td>'.
            '<td>'.$address['last_name'].'</td>'.
            '<td>'.$address['email'].'</td>'.
            '<td>'.$address['phone'].'</td>'.
            '<td>'.$address['address'].'</td>'.
            '<td>'.$html->link('edit',
                            array('action'=>'edit',
                                  'id'=>$address['id'])).'</td>'.
    '</tr>';
    };
?>
```

code snippet /cakephp/app/views/addresses/index.ctp

We didn't explain what `$html->link()` does earlier while creating the `add.ctp` template, but we will do so now. The `link()` function added in this template has two parameters. The first is the text that will be displayed as a link, and the second is an array that allows you to set various parameters, such as the action name that will be called when the generated link is clicked and the `id` parameter that will be passed by the `$_GET` variable to identify which address will be edited.

At this point, the edit action is still missing a view file, so create one as follows:

```
<?php
    echo $form->create('Address', array('action' -> 'edit'));
    echo $form->inputs();
    echo $form->end('Save address');
?>
```

code snippet /cakephp/app/views/addresses/edit.ctp

Note that this file is nearly identical to `add.ctp`. The only difference is that you have added another parameter to the `$form->create()` function, which is an array defining what action will be called after sending the form data. It is set to `add` by default, which is why you need to change it to `edit`. Check the result shown in Figure 4-6 and compare it with the New Address form shown in Figure 4-5.

The Edit Address form is generated by the file that you have just created and looks identical to the form that handles adding new addresses, except that it contains the data of a selected address rather than being blank.

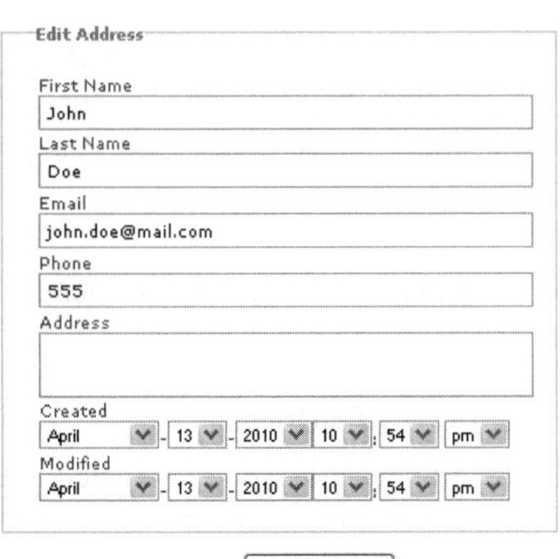

FIGURE 4-6: The Edit Address form in CakePHP

Viewing a Selected Address

Now create a view that will allow you to see detailed address information using a custom view. The most intuitive approach is to click an address entry from the address list. To do this, change the `index.ctp` file again:

```
<?php
    foreach ( $address_list as $line ) {
    $address = $line['Address'];
        echo
        '<tr>'.
            '<td>'.$address['id'].'</td>'.
            '<td>'.$html->link($address['first_name'],
                                array('action'=>'view',
                                       'id'=>$address['id'])).'</td>'.
            '<td>'.$address['last_name'].'</td>'.
            '<td>'.$address['email'].'</td>'.
            '<td>'.$address['phone'].'</td>'.
            '<td>'.$address['address'].'</td>'.
            '<td>'.$html->link('edit',
                                array('action'=>'edit',
                                'id'=>$address['id'])).'</td>'.
        '</tr>';
    };
?>
```

code snippet /cakephp/app/views/addresses/index.ctp

The added line works the same way as when you added an edit link. It makes the `first_name` value clickable and allows it to call the `view` action that will display the following file, which you need to create in the `/views` folder:

```
<?php
    $address = $address['Address'];
    echo $html->link('Back to list', array('action'=>'index'));
    echo '<h1>'.$address['first_name'].' '.$address['last_name'].'</h1>'.
        '<p>Email: '.$address['email'].'</p>'.
        '<p>Phone: '.$address['phone'].'</p>'.
        '<p>Street: '.$address['street'].'</p>'.
        '<p>Address: '.$address['address'].'</p>';
?>
```

code snippet /cakephp/app/views/addresses/index.ctp

After creating this file, you can browse through your address book and view selected entries. When an entry is selected, the page shown in Figure 4-7 should be displayed.

Back
John Doe
Email: john.doe@mail.com
Phone: 555
Address:

FIGURE 4-7: An address book entry

Deleting an Entry

Now that the code responsible for deleting entries has been created, modify the `index.ctp` file in the `/views` directory so that it allows you to select an entry for deletion. The bold font in the following code snippet shows how it is done:

```
<?php
    foreach ( $address_list as $line ) {
    $address = $line['Address'];
        echo
        '<tr>'.
            '<td>'.$address['id'].'</td>'.
            '<td>'.$html->link($address['first_name'],
                        array('action'=>'view',
                        'id'=>$address['id'])).'</td>'.
            '<td>'.$address['last_name'].'</td>'.
            '<td>'.$address['email'].'</td>'.
            '<td>'.$address['phone'].'</td>'.
            '<td>'.$address['address'].'</td>'.
            '<td>'.$html->link('edit',
                        array('action'=>'edit',
                            'id'=>$address['id'])).
          ' '.$html->link('delete',
                      array('action'=>'delete',
                      'id'=>$address['id'])).'</td>'.
        '</tr>';
    };
?>
```

code snippet /cakephp/app/views/addresses/index.ctp

This concludes the creation of a basic CRUD functionality.

ZEND FRAMEWORK

ZF suffers from not having a proper ORM tool to generate useful code without much effort. You have to write many lines of code using Zend_Db instead. (That's why this section is more than twice as long as previous ones.)

Project

As was mentioned in Chapter 3, there are a few ways to start a project with ZF. Let's say that you have done everything properly, as described in Chapter 3, and are ready to move on. In the command-line interface, type `<path>` (use the path to the directory in which you want to start developing your application):

```
$ zf create <path>
```

There is also another way to do that. Just type the project name (for example, `addressBook`):

```
$ zf create project addressBook
```

The only difference between these two methods is that the first one just creates all needed project files in the current directory, whereas the second command does the same but also creates the project directory with the name given as the parameter.

Routing

Zend has no routing configuration like Symfony has. There are two main controllers: index and error. The first one is the root controller in which all applications start. The main routing rules are defined in the `.htaccess` file of the `mod_rewrite` module, which is a good approach to allow for reusing code and tools. There is a default main rule that says that the first given parameter is the controller's name and the second is the action of this controller. All additionally given parameters are sent as `GET` parameters to the action method (for example, `http://localhost/addressBook/address/delete/id/1`). Your root path is `http://localhost/addressBook` in this case.

Model

The following SQL code creates a table that is used in your address book application. Remember to `create` and `use` the database first:

Available for download on Wrox.com

```
CREATE TABLE IF NOT EXISTS 'AddressBook' (
  'id' int(11) unsigned NOT NULL AUTO_INCREMENT,
  'first_name' varchar(25) NOT NULL,
  'last_name' varchar(25) NOT NULL,
  'email' varchar(25) NOT NULL,
  'phone' int(11) DEFAULT NULL,
  'address' text,
  'created' datetime NOT NULL,
```

```
  `modified` datetime NOT NULL,
  PRIMARY KEY (`id`)
) ENGINE=MyISAM DEFAULT CHARSET=utf8;
```

code snippet /zf/library/sql/addressbook.sql

Creating data models is probably the most difficult issue when developing with ZF. You need to create an additional model, mapper, and Db_Table model for each table. That's three files for each table! Although this approach is not the best because most of this code could be autogenerated, go with it anyway.

Model Class

Start with the model:

```
$ zf create model AddressBook
```

This command generates a template model of `AddressBook`. Model files are placed in the `/application/models/` folder. A generated template is an empty class definition, as shown in the following code, which needs to be filled out:

```
<?php
class Application_Model_AddressBook {
}
```

This template needs to be filled out with proper code. As mentioned in Chapter 3, you need to create two methods for each field. Additionally, there is a constructor and two default methods needed. The following code snippet shows how the address book template should be filled with code:

Available for download on Wrox.com

```
<?php
class Application_Model_AddressBook
{
   protected $_firstName;
   protected $_lastName;
   protected $_email;
   protected $_phone;
   protected $_address;
   protected $_created;
   protected $_modified;
   protected $_id;
   public function __construct(array $options = null) {
   }
       public function __set($name, $value) {
        $method = 'set' . $name;
        if (('mapper' == $name) || !method_exists($this, $method)) {
            throw new Exception('Invalid property');
        }
        $this->$method($value);
       }

       public function __get($name) {
      $method = 'get' . $name;
```

```
    if (('mapper' == $name) || !method_exists($this, $method)) {
          throw new Exception('Invalid property');
    }
      return $this->$method();
     }
public function setOptions(array $options) {
     $methods = get_class_methods($this);
      foreach ($options as $key => $value) {
          $method = 'set' . ucfirst($key);
          if (in_array($method, $methods)) {
              $this->$method($value);
          }
      }
      return $this;
}

public function setFirstName($text) {
  $this->_firstName = (string) $text;
  return $this;
}
public function getFirstName() {
  return $this->_firstName;
}
public function setLastName($text) {
  $this->_lastName = (string) $text;
  return $this;
}
public function getLastName() {
  return $this->_lastName;
}
public function setEmail($text) {
  $this->_email = (string) $text;
  return $this;
}
public function getEmail() {
 return $this->_email;
}
public function setPhone($text) {
 $this->_phone = (string) $text;
  return $this;
}
public function getPhone() {
  return $this->_phone;
}
public function setAddress($text) {
   $this->_address = (string) $text;
   return $this;
 }
 public function getAddress() {
   return $this->_address;
 }
 public function setCreated($text) {
   $this->_created = (string) $text;
   return $this;
```

```
    }
    public function getCreated() {
      return $this->_created;
    }
    public function setModified($text) {
      $this->_modified = (string) $text;
      return $this;
    }
    public function getModified() {
      return $this->_modified;
    }
    public function  getId() {
      return $this->_id;
    }
    public function setId($text) {
      $this->_id = (int) $id;
      return $this'
    }
}
```

code snippet /zf/application/models/AddressBook.php

This is a long but very simple piece of code. Getter and setter methods can be easily generated by any Eclipse-based integrated development environment (IDE) such as Zend Studio. If you use Zend Studio, just use the Source option in the main menu and select Generate Getters/Setters. Note that a proper class file needs to have the focus. You can see now what the individual methods shown in the preceding code are responsible for:

```
    public function __get($name) {
        $method = 'get' . $name;
        if (('mapper' == $name) || !method_exists($this, $method)) {
              throw new Exception('Invalid property');
        }
        return $this->$method();
}
```

code snippet /zf/application/models/AddressBook.php

This is a common `get()` method, which takes the name of the model's field (for example, `firstName`) as a parameter. First, the method that is responsible for getting data from this field is searched for. If the method exists, the returned value of the invoked method is given as the result. So for `$name='firstName'`, this method throws `'John'`, for example.

The `set()` method works in much the same way, but accomplishes something quite different. The `$name` and `$value` fields are needed as parameters. Like previously, the proper method is searched for. If it exists, it is invoked, and the result is returned, as shown in the following code:

```
public function __set($name, $value) {
    $method = 'set' . $name;
    if (('mapper' == $name) || !method_exists($this, $method)) {
          throw new Exception('Invalid property');
```

```
        }
        $this->$method($value);
    }
```

code snippet /zf/application/models/AddressBook.php

The last method is `setOptions()`, which just gets an array that is a kind of a hashtable/dictionary. Each key represents a field. For each key, a value is assigned, even if it is just a null value. For each key/value pair an appropriate method is searched for. If it exists, the value is set. An object with all fields filled out is returned as the result. This method is very useful when you get an array that you want to assign directly to an existing instance of a model object:

Available for download on Wrox.com

```
    public function setOptions(array $options) {
        $methods = get_class_methods($this);
        foreach ($options as $key => $value) {
            $method = 'set' . ucfirst($key);
            if (in_array($method, $methods)) {
                $this->$method($value);
            }
        }
        return $this;
    }
```

code snippet /zf/application/models/AddressBook.php

Unfortunately, this is not everything you need to do to make a working model. To develop it, you need to define some basic methods to load and save data into a database. This is why you need to define a mapper for the `AddressBook` table.

Mapper

The next step is to define a mapper class. The model class is only responsible for how the table looks. The mapper class is designed to be responsible for manipulating data. The relations between each of the three classes (Db_Table, mapper, and model) are shown in Figure 4-8.

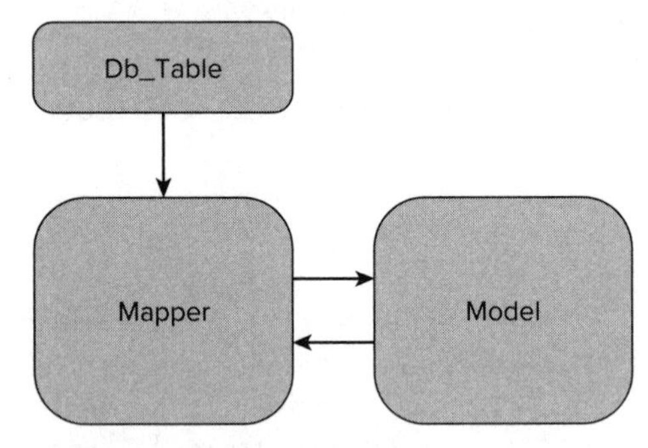

FIGURE 4-8: Relations between classes in ZF

The mapper class is shown in the following code. It should be placed as `AddressBookMapper.php` in the `/application/models/` folder.

Available for download on Wrox.com

```
<?php
class Application_Model_AddressesBookMapper {

        protected $_dbTable;

        public function setDbTable($dbTable) {
        }

        public function getDbTable() {
```

```
            }
            public function deleteOne($id) {
            }
            public function save(Application_Model_AddressBook $address) {
            }

            public function find($id, Application_Model_AddressBook $address) {
            }

            public function fetchAll() {
            }
}
```

code snippet /zf/application/models/AddressBookMapper.php

First, you need to set the right `Db_Table`. You can just create a new instance of it by putting a string as the parameter or a concrete instance to assign. This method is responsible for assigning a proper `Db_Table` class instance to the mapper. Note in the following code that the `Db_Table` class implements `Zend_Db_Table_Abstract`:

```
public function setDbTable($dbTable) {
    if (is_string($dbTable)) {
        $dbTable = new $dbTable();
    }
    if (!$dbTable instanceof Zend_Db_Table_Abstract) {
        throw new Exception('Invalid table data gateway provided');
    }
    $this->_dbTable = $dbTable;
    return $this;
}
```

code snippet /zf/application/models/AddressBookMapper.php

The same thing goes with getting a `Db_Table` instance, but in this a case, a proper `Db_Table` class instance is returned.

```
public function getDbTable() {
    if (null === $this->_dbTable) {
        $this->setDbTable('Application_Model_DbTable_AddressBook');
    }
    return $this->_dbTable;
}
```

code snippet /zf/application/models/AddressBookMapper.php

The preceding two methods are responsible for establishing the relationship with the `Db_Table` model class shown in Figure 4-8.

Now you can focus on methods that are commonly used when working with the model. Previously created model methods are used here. You need to consider what should really be done in the `save()` method because there is a difference between an existing address entry that needs to be saved after editing and a new one that is to be added. First, the `$data` array is prepared to save all needed entry information. Only the modified field is changed when the `save()` method is invoked. The rest of the form is filled out with existing information or just with empty data (from the database's perspective). In the following code, notice that the created field is filled only when a new entry is added:

```
public function save(Application_Model_AddressBook $address) {
            $data = array(
                'firstName' => $address->getFirstName(),
                'lastName'  => $address->getLastName(),
                'email'     => $address->getEmail(),
                'phone'     => $address->getPhone(),
                'address'   => $address->getAddress(),
                'created'   => $address->getCreated(),
                'modified'  => date('Y-m-d H:i:s'),
            );

            if (null === ($id = $user->getId())) {
                unset($data['id']);
                $data['created']=date('Y-m-d H:i:s');
                $this->getDbTable()->insert($data);
            } else {
                $this->getDbTable()->update($data, array('id = ?' => $id));
            }
}
```

code snippet /zf/application/models/AddressBookMapper.php

The `find()` method is used only to find just one specific entry. Because in almost all cases, `id` is the primary key and also a common identifier, it is needed as a parameter in this method so you know what to search. Additionally, an address's model instance is needed to collect all found information. In the first line, the `find()` method is invoked on an instance of the `Db_Table` object. Results are then prepared to be returned as your model object. To set all needed data models, set methods are used, as shown in the following code:

```
public function find($id, Application_Model_AddressBook $address) {
       $result = $this->getDbTable()->find($id);
       if (0 == count($result)) {
         return;
       }
       $row = $result->current();
       $address->setId($row->id)
              ->setFirstName($row->firstName)
              ->setLastName($row->lastName)
              ->setEmail($row->email)
              ->setPhone($row->phone)
              ->setAddress($row->address)
              ->setCreated($row->created)
              ->setModified($row->modified);
}
```

code snippet /zf/application/models/AddressBookMapper.php

The `find()` method shown in the preceding code is used only in cases where one entry is expected to be returned. To get all entries, the `fetachAll()` method, shown in the following code, is the proper choice:

Available for download on Wrox.com

```
public function fetchAll() {
        $results = $this->getDbTable()->fetchAll();
        $entries = array();
        foreach ($results as $row) {
          $entry = new Application_Model_Addresses();
          $entry->setId($row->id)
            ->setFirstName($row->firstName)
            ->setLastName($row->lastName)
            ->setEmail($row->email)
            ->setPhone($row->phone)
            ->setAddress($row->address)
            ->setCreated($row->created)
            ->setModified($row->modified);
         $entries[] = $entry;
      }
      return $entries;
}
```

code snippet /zf/application/models/AddressBookMapper.php

To see all the available methods for the `Zend_Db_Table` *class, go to* `http://framework.zend.com/apidoc/1.10/`*. From the Packages drop-down menu at the top of the page, choose Zend_Db and select Table from the list of choices in the left pane.*

The last method is a tiny one that deletes a row. `Db_Table` is also used here. The row is identified by the `'id='` field because the table's primary key could be also named `address_id` or something similar.

Available for download on Wrox.com

```
public function deleteOne($id) {
      $this->getDbTable()->delete('id = '. (int)$id);
  }
```

code snippet /zf/application/models/AddressBookMapper.php

In your sample application, only these four methods are needed. We could also implement more complex methods with defined criteria, but for now this is enough.

Db_Table Model

All the methods just covered are very similar to equivalents in Symfony and CakePHP. The last thing to do to get them working is to define a relation between the `Db_Table` model and the real name of the table to which it is dedicated, as shown in the following code:

Available for download on Wrox.com

```
<?php
class Application_Model_DbTable_AddressBook extends Zend_Db_Table_Abstract {
  protected $_name = 'AddressBook';
}
```

code snippet /zf/application/models/DbTable/AddressBook.php

A different approach to create `Db_Table` files is to invoke the `zf` command, which does this for each table:

```
$ zf create db-table.from-database
```

Controller

Zend also provides some commands for controllers. To easily create a controller, you can use this command:

```
$ zf create controller AddressBook
```

This command generates a basic controller with two default methods. Controllers are placed in the `/application/controllers` folder (for example, `IndexController.php`, shown in the following code). The first method is invoked when initializing, and the second method is just an index action. Let's skip `init()` because it is not needed in this example. Note, however, that the `init()` method is very often used in more complex applications.

Available for download on Wrox.com

```
<?php
class IndexController extends Zend_Controller_Action {

    public function init() {
    }

    public function indexAction() {
    }
}
```

code snippet /zf/application/controllers/IndexController.php

Note, that in this code the default index controller is shown. The only difference between `Index` and `AddressBook` is the controller's name. Use the default controller because there is less code to write.

List of All Addresses

First, show all entries in your address book. To do that, you need to create a mapper object; then the `fetchAll()` method should be invoked. The results are sent to the view layer by the `$this->view->addresses` variable. Every time you assign a value to `$this->view->`*`var`*, this variable is sent to the view layer as `$this->`*`var`*. Then just present all entries in the view layer.

Available for download on Wrox.com

```
public function indexAction() {
    $addresses = new Application_Model_AddressBookMapper();
    $this->view->addresses = $addresses->fetchAll();
}
```

code snippet /zf/application/controllers/IndexController.php

Adding a New Address

Adding entries is a bit more complex than the `fetchAll()` method. The following steps should be done:

1. Get data if the form is filled.
2. If not, show an empty form.
3. If given data is valid, proceed to save it.
4. After adding, just redirect to index page.

And this is how the `addAction()` method looks in PHP:

Available for download on Wrox.com

```
public function addAction() {
      $form = new Application_Form_AddressAdd();
      $request = $this->getRequest();
      if ($this->getRequest()->isPost()){
        if ($form->isValid($request->getPost())) {
            $entry = new Application_Model_Addresses($form->getValues());
            $mapper = new Application_Model_AddressesMapper();
            $mapper->save($entry);
            return $this->_helper->redirector('index');
        }
      }
      $this->view->form = $form;
}
```

code snippet /zf/application/controllers/IndexController.php

Forms are described later in this chapter.

Editing an Entry

The edit action is more complex because this is an all-in-one method. It shows a form with current data and also processes submitted data. It begins like the `add()` action. If `$this->getRequest()->isPost()` is true, this means that some data was submitted. Next, validation of submitted data needs to be done. (Form validation is described in more detail in Chapter 5.)

If the validation process is successful, `$form->getValues()` is called, which returns submitted data. That submitted data is subsequently sent to the `AddressBook` model. The `$entry` variable now contains all submitted data. As described previously, to work with data in databases, invoking mapper methods is required. Note that it doesn't matter whether the data given as a parameter to the `save()` method is completely new or just an update because it is checked inside the mapper's method. At the end or the process, the user is redirected to an index page. Redirection is done by using the Zend helper methods.

If no data is submitted, the ID should be intercepted. If the user clicks an edit link, the ID should be sent to the edit action (for example, `http://localhost/addressbook/edit/id/1`. To get any parameter that is sent using `GET`, the `getParam()` method should be used. As the parameter to `getParam()`, the proper parameter name should be given (for example, `ID`). Then the initialization of both the model and mapper classes needs to be done because they are needed to get data from the database. The mapper class's `find()` method selects a row from the `AddressBook` table with an ID specified as `$id`. The `$entry` variable is your model object filled with data after invoking the `find()` method.

The next step is to create an array of previously prepared data and set it inside the `value=""` HTML input/textarea attribute by using the `setDefaults()` method. Note in the following code that an

`Application_Form_AddressEdit` object is created at the beginning. If everything runs successfully without any exceptions, the form is assigned to the `$this->form` view variable:

```
public function editAction() {
      $form = new Application_Form_AddressEdit();
      $request = $this->getRequest();
      if ($this->getRequest()->isPost()){
        if ($form->isValid($request->getPost())) {
          $entry = new Application_Model_AddressBook($form->getValues());
          $mapper = new Application_Model_AddressBookMapper();
          $mapper->save($entry);
          return $this->_helper->redirector('index');
        }
      }else{
       $id=$this->getRequest()->getParam('id');
       $entry = new Application_Model_AddressBook();
       $mapper = new Application_Model_AddressBookMapper();
       $result = $mapper->find($id,$entry);
       $data = array(
                  'id' => $id,
                  'firstName' => $entry->getFirstName(),
                  'lastName'  => $entry->getLastName(),
                  'email'     => $entry->getEmail(),
                  'phone'     => $entry->getPhone(),
                  'address'   => $entry->getAddress(),
                  'created'   => $entry->getCreated(),
                  'modified'  => date('Y-m-d'),
             );
       $form->setDefaults($data);
      }
     $this->view->form = $form;
}
```

code snippet /zf/application/controllers/IndexController.php

Delete

The delete action is easy to create. In the first line of the following code, the identifier is taken from `GET` (see `$_GET` on `http://php.net`) as in the edit action. Next, a mapper is created, and the `deleteOne()` method is invoked. The `$id` parameter is given because you need to show which data to delete. After that, the user is redirected to the index page:

```
public function deleteAction() {
        $id = $this->getRequest()->getParam('id');
        $addresses = new Application_Model_AddressBookMapper();
        $addresses->deleteOne($id);
        return $this->_helper->redirector('index');
    }
```

code snippet /zf/application/controllers/IndexController.php

Forms

To make sure that the forms invoked in the code snippet above are working properly, they should be first defined. Forms are placed in the /application/forms directory (for example, AddressAdd.php). As shown in the following code, a form should inherit the Zend_Form class and have an init() method:

Available for download on Wrox.com

```
<?php
class Application_Form_Addresses extends Zend_Form {
    public function init() {
        $this->setMethod('post');
        /* form here */

        $this->addElement('submit', 'submit', array(
            'ignore'   => true,
            'label'    => 'Save',
        ));

    }
}
```

code snippet /zf/application/forms/Addresses.php

There are two methods that should be invoked when defining forms: setMethod() and addElement() — shown in the following code. The setMethod() method defines the form's method attribute. The post attribute is commonly used with the setMethod() method. The next method, addElement(), is responsible for adding form elements such as inputs or textareas. Because there are a few different types of input in Zend, they are represented by their type: text, textarea, submit, hidden. Each field can also have parameters such as label and filters, or it can be defined as a required field or not. Attributes are given as an array (a hashmap, really). The filters parameter defines which filter for data should be applied, (for example, String):

Available for download on Wrox.com

```
public function init() {
      $this->setMethod('post');
      $this->addElement('text', 'firstName', array(
             'label'   => 'Your first name:',
             'required'   => false,
             'filters'    => array('StringTrim'),
              )
      );
      $this->addElement('text', 'lastName', array(
             'label'   => 'Your last name:',
             'required'   => false,
             'filters'    => array('StringTrim'),
             )
      );
      $this->addElement('text', 'email', array(
            'label'   => 'Your e-mail address:',
            'required'   => false,
            'filters'    => array('StringTrim'),
```

```
            )
        );
        $this->addElement('text', 'phone', array(
             'label'    => 'Your phone:',
             'required'    => false,
             'filters'     => array('StringTrim'),
             )
        );
        $this->addElement('textarea', 'address', array(
            'label'    => 'Your Address:',
            'required'    => false,
            'filters'     => array('StringTrim'),
            )
        );
        $this->addElement('submit', 'submit', array(
              'ignore'    => true,
              'label'     => 'Save'
       ));
    }
```

code snippet /zf/application/forms/Addresses.php

To complete the forms for this example, two forms need to be defined: `AddressEdit` and `AddressAdd`. They should be the same except for the name. Although each of the forms can be used alone, the code is easier to understand with two separate forms.

View

First of all, a layout needs to be created. To do this, the `enable` parameter should be used. This command also creates the following layout in the `/application/layouts/scripts` directory:

```
$ zf enable layout
```

There are two main view templates: `index.phtml` and `error.phtml`, which are placed in the `/application/views/scripts/` directory. The first one is (by default) the ZF welcome page. The second one, shown in the following code, is the page that shows all errors and exceptions that happen while executing your code. As you can probably guess, it's better not to see this page too often.

Available for download on Wrox.com

```
<h1>An error occurred</h1>
 <h2><?php echo $this->message ?></h2>

 <?php if (isset($this->exception)): ?>

 <h3>Exception information:</h3>
 <p>
     <b>Message:</b> <?php echo $this->exception->getMessage() ?>
 </p>

 <h3>Stack trace:</h3>
 <pre><?php echo $this->exception->getTraceAsString() ?>
 </pre>
```

```
<h3>Request Parameters:</h3>
<pre><?php echo var_export($this->request->getParams(), true) ?>
</pre>
<?php endif ?>
```

code snippet /zf/application/views/scripts/error/error.phtml

The index template is the first page that should be changed, so change it to a list of addresses. Below the ZF welcome page, the view code is shown:

```
<style>
    a:link,
    a:visited
    {
        color: #0398CA;
    }

    span#zf-name
  {
       color: #91BE3F;
   }

    div#welcome
    {
        color: #FFFFFF;
        background-image: url(http://framework.zend.com/images/bkg_header.jpg);
        width:  600px;
        height: 400px;
        border: 2px solid #444444;
        overflow: hidden;
        text-align: center;
    }

    div#more-information
    {
        background-image:
            url(http://framework.zend.com/images/bkg_body-bottom.gif);
        height: 100%;
    }
</style>
<div id="welcome">
    <h1>Welcome to the <span id="zf-name">Zend Framework!</span></h1>

    <h3>This is your project's main page</h3>

    <div id="more-information">
        <p>
          <img src="http://framework.zend.com/images/PoweredBy_ZF_4LightBG.png" />
        </p>
        <p>
            Helpful Links: <br />
            <a href="http://framework.zend.com/">Zend Framework Website</a> |
```

```
                <a href="http://framework.zend.com/manual/en/">
                    Zend Framework Manual
                </a>
            </p>
        </div>
    </div>
```

code snippet /zf/application/views/scripts/index/index.phtml

List of All Addresses

Because the main page can be also the address book index page, the preceding code can be replaced by a simple loop, shown here:

```
<style>
    a:link, a:visited {
        color: #0398CA;
    }
    span#zf-name  {
       color: #91BE3F;
    }
    td {
      background: #cdcdcd;
    }
</style>

<div id="header-navigation" style="float: left; width: 100%;">
Address Book
</div>
<div style="float: left; ">
<table>
    <tr>
       <td>ID</td>
       <td>First Name</td>
       <td>Last Name</td>
       <td>E-mail</td>
       <td>Phone Number</td>
       <td>Address</td>
       <td>Created</td>
       <td>Modified</td>
       <td>Options</td>
    </tr>
    <?php foreach ($this->addresses as $entry): ?>
    <tr>
       <td><?php echo $entry->getId(); ?></td>
       <td><?php echo $entry->getFirstName(); ?></td>
       <td><?php echo $entry->getLastName(); ?></td>
       <td><?php echo $entry->getEmail(); ?></td>
       <td><?php echo $entry->getPhone(); ?></td>
       <td><?php echo $entry->getAddress(); ?></td>
       <td><?php echo $entry->getCreated(); ?></td>
       <td><?php echo $entry->getModified(); ?></td>
    </tr>
```

```
    <?php endforeach  ?>
</table>
</div>
```

code snippet /zf/application/views/scripts/index/index.phtml

Note that `$this->addresses` was passed from the controller. This variable is an instance of `AddressBook`. That's why in order to show proper data, the `AddressBook` model methods are used (for example, `getAddress()`). As a result, you should see something similar to what is shown in Figure 4-9 (it can be a little different because all links are added here).

AddressBook Add a new entry

ID	First Name	Last Name	E-mail	Phone Number	Address	Created	Modified	Options
21	Leszek	Nowak	dr.leszek.nowak@gmail.com	123456789	Here I am	2010-06-03	2010-06-03	Delete Edit
20	Bartosz	Porębski	bartosz.porebski@gmail.co	123456789	Foo bar	2010-06-03	2010-06-03	Delete Edit
19	Karol	Przystalski	kprzystalski@gmail.com	123456789	Homeless	2010-06-03	2010-06-03	Delete Edit

FIGURE 4-9: The Index page of ZF's CRUD application

Adding an Entry Page

To make it possible to add any kind of data, a link to the add page needs to be included, as shown in the following code:

```
<div id="header-navigation" style="float: left; width: 100%;">
Address Book
     <a href="<?php echo $this->url(
                  array('action'=>'add')); ?>">Add a new entry</a>
</div>
```

code snippet /zf/application/views/scripts/index/index.phtml

To do that, the `$this->url()` helper method can be used. An array should be given as the parameter. The array should consist of information that makes it possible to determine exactly what kind of URL should be generated. It can be an action, as shown, but also a controller. Because this URL is inside a template, which is a part of the `Index` controller, there is no need to also add the controller attribute, because it is set by default to the currently used controller.

The previously described form should be included inside the `add.phtml` template. Only one line of code is needed:

```
<?php echo $this->form;?>
```

code snippet /zf/application/views/scripts/index/add.phtml

You then see a page that includes a form (see Figure 4-10).

Editing an Address Entry

To edit address book entries, a link to the add action is needed, as is a link that redirects the user to the proper place. Additionally, the ID needs to be added with the `$this->url()` parameter, as shown in the following code, which generates a link like `http://localhost/addressbook/edit/id/1`:

Available for download on Wrox.com

```
<td><?php echo $entry->getId(); ?></td>
        <td><?php echo $entry->getFirstName(); ?></td>
        <td><?php echo $entry->getLastName(); ?></td>
        <td><?php echo $entry->getEmail(); ?></td>
        <td><?php echo $entry->getPhone(); ?></td>
        <td><?php echo $entry->getAddress(); ?></td>
        <td><?php echo $entry->getCreated(); ?></td>
        <td><?php echo $entry->getModified(); ?></td>
        <td><a href="<?php echo $this->url(
                  array('action'=>'edit','id'=> $entry->getId())); ?>">Edit</a></td>
```

code snippet /zf/application/views/scripts/index/index.phtml

FIGURE 4-10: The Add form in ZF

The following code displays the form template:

```
<?php echo $this->form;?>
```

The form with proper data is shown in Figure 4-11.

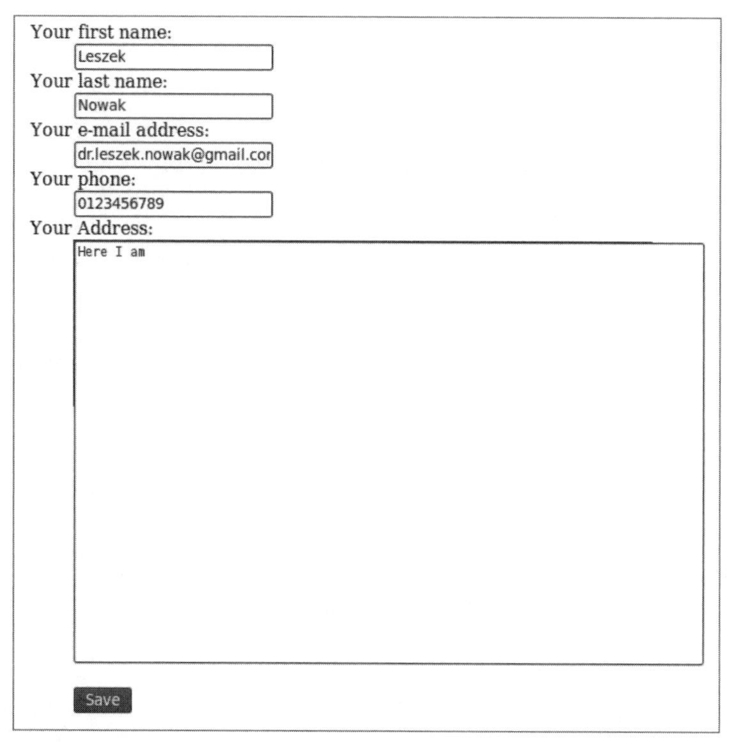

FIGURE 4-11: The Edit form in ZF

Deleting an Entry

No view template code is needed to delete an entry because redirection to an index page is done after deletion. That's why no `delete.phtml` file is needed. You only need to add a URL in `index.phtml` (almost the same process as editing):

Available for download on Wrox.com

```
<td><?php echo $entry->getId(); ?></td>
      <td><?php echo $entry->getFirstName(); ?></td>
      <td><?php echo $entry->getLastName(); ?></td>
      <td><?php echo $entry->getEmail(); ?></td>
      <td><?php echo $entry->getPhone(); ?></td>
      <td><?php echo $entry->getAddress(); ?></td>
      <td><?php echo $entry->getCreated(); ?></td>
      <td><?php echo $entry->getModified(); ?></td>
      <td><a href="<?php echo $this->url(
            array('action'=>'delete','id'=> $entry->getId())); ?>">Delete</a>
       <a href="<?php echo $this->url(
            array('action'=>'edit','id'=> $entry->getId())); ?>">Edit</a></td>
```

code snippet /zf/application/views/scripts/index/index.phtml

5

Forms

Computers are like Old Testament gods; lots of rules and no mercy.

— Joseph Campbell

WHAT'S IN THIS CHAPTER?

- Field validation.
- Customizing forms.
- Using Captcha as spam protection.

Input forms have become so common and natural that users probably do not even notice when they fill them in. There is also nothing strange about a form noticing that our e-mail address is incorrect or requesting us to write down some barely recognizable characters. This chapter explores forms: form creation and the various common tasks associated with them, such as customization and validation. Several automatic functions of frameworks regarding building forms and their validation are presented here as well.

Web forms can be found at various websites throughout the Internet. They are used in all sorts of situations, allowing users to pass data that is later processed by server-side scripts. By including forms in your web application, you allow visitors to register and enter their unique content. Furthermore, forms can also be used for ordering various products online, voting in polls, and other sorts of user input. In some situations, forms can also be used when you must implement some mechanisms to ensure the security of transmitted data. (More about form security and secured connections can be found in Chapter 8.) This chapter focuses on form validation and customization. We also discuss Captcha tests as a spam protection instrument.

FIELD VALIDATION

One of the most important parts of any web application is data validation. It is most helpful in ensuring that entered data is consistent with a web application's assumed data model. There are many common field validation methods, and they are (or should be) applied to most input forms. For example, you may want to make sure that the user creating a new account in your application enters a unique username, or that the password is no shorter than six characters and no longer than twelve. Of course, there are also more complex rules used during form validation; for example, they allow passing of only alphanumeric characters or even only strings that follow a certain predefined pattern.

There is also one very important, but often overlooked aspect of form validation. Obviously, form handling is much easier when validation rules are defined, but at the same time those rules are protecting the application from web-bots that are looking for vulnerable sites that can later be used for posting spam messages, or be targeted with other methods of attack. Later in this chapter we discuss Captcha, the second line of defense against these forms of attack. Chapter 8 of this book addresses injection and cross-site request forgery (CSRF) attacks, a special attack on a web application that utilizes poorly protected forms as an attack point.

Chapter 4 left us with a basic web application, but with no data validation, and now we will add it. We will also show alternative methods of creating forms in the project.

The address book that we created has a few fields that will require validation, so we want to add these rules:

- `first_name` — This field will be obligatory and at least 3 characters long, but no longer than 25.
- `last_name` — This field is optional; it should be no longer than 25 characters.
- `email` — Must be an e-mail format and no longer than 25 characters.
- `phone` — Integer value no longer than 11 digits.
- `created` — Date format (MDY).

Field length values here are related to database design. It is a good practice to consider database restrictions while including validation in the project. Because, for example, if a name 10 characters long is put into a `VARCHAR(5)` type field in a database, the input data will be truncated accordingly. This can be avoided by adding field validation that would prohibit sending improper data into the database.

How Does Form Validation Work?

Form validation verifies submitted data against a set of validation rules. When any information is about to be submitted via a form, validation decides whether the information is correct and can be processed or not.

There are two levels of validation that can be applied to an application. The first one can be applied before any data is sent to a server and it is done on the client side using JavaScript. This is quite useful because in case of bigger forms, the user can be informed whether a field is valid or not. This validation can be easily omitted by disabling JavaScript in a user's browser. The second stage of validation is done by sending the form input to the application server where it will be validated, and a proper reply will be sent back to the user, informing him of any errors.

Let's consider the simplest case of server-only validation, as shown in Figure 5-1. We assume that a user is about to post a comment to a blog post via a web form. Here we can decide that there have to be some values submitted for the UserName and Comment fields. The first stage of validation will check if the UserName and the Comment fields have any values assigned, and if they do, this data is further validated by a set of predefined rules. Those rules may check whether the comment contains any unwanted scripts or contains any offensive words. Later, based on validation results, an action is performed. In this case, it is saving the submitted comment into a database. On the other hand, if the user has not filled in the UserName or the Comment fields, the form validation will generate an appropriate error message, and the page will be reloaded displaying it.

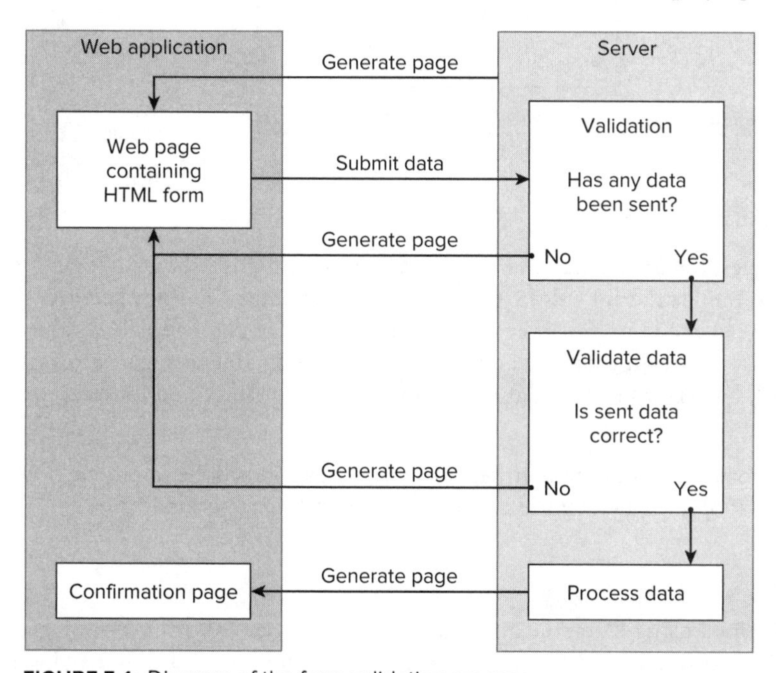

FIGURE 5-1: Diagram of the form validation process

Now let's consider an example that employs JavaScript as the most commonly used client-side validation method. This example will use the scheme shown in Figure 5-2 to illustrate how client-side form validation works.

As before, the user fills in the HTML comment form and then clicks the submit button to send data. When the submit button is clicked, the JavaScript `validator` function is called, which checks whether the UserName and the Comment fields have been both filled in. If any of those fields has no values inside, the `validator` function returns `false`, and an appropriate message is displayed to the user. If the UserName and the Comment fields have been filled in properly and the submit button was clicked by the user, the `validator` function can verify form data against a set of rules.

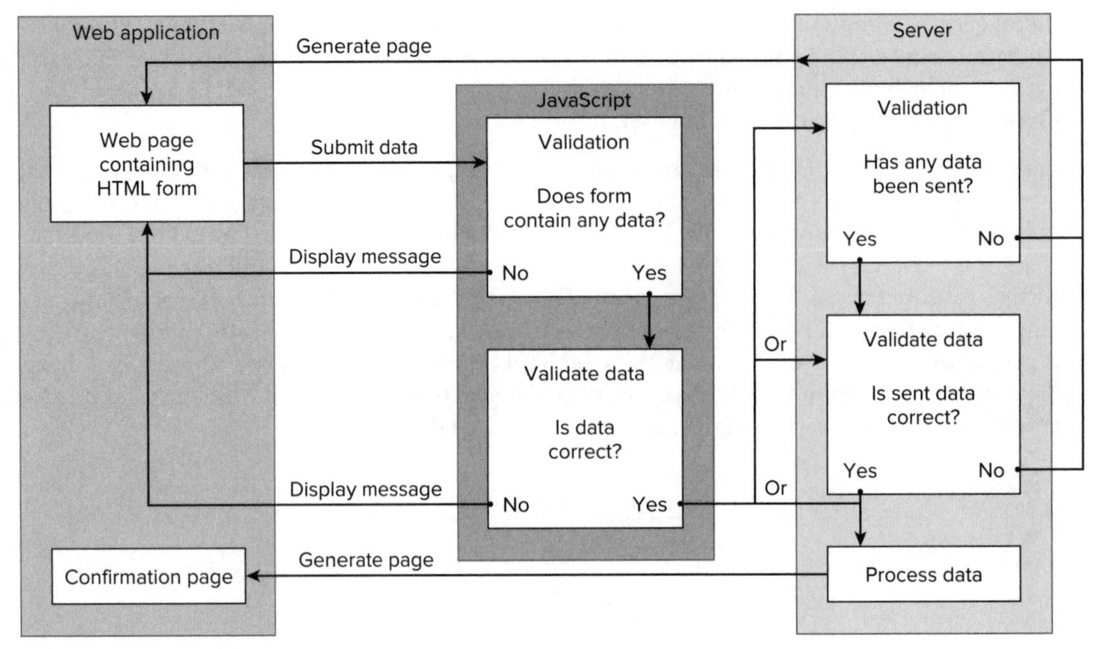

FIGURE 5-2: JavaScript form-validation process

After passing all validation rules, the form data is sent to the server, where it is validated again. Server rules can be similar to the JavaScript rules from the previous example, but any security filtering should necessarily be repeated on the server side because JavaScript can be easily disabled. It is a good practice to always validate all submitted data on the server side, due to security reasons. JavaScript validation may still be performed as an auxiliary for user convenience and to reduce server workload.

So far, we have dealt with theory; now is the time to see how the validation is done in practice. We will focus on server-side validation provided by the three frameworks' core functionality.

Symfony

In Chapter 4, the app was created using Doctrine and it automatically created forms by using a command-line interface (CLI) parameter: `doctrine:build --all`. Forms created that way have classes represented by validators and widgets. These classes provide a way to manage forms in an easy manner. Every field of a form has its own validator and widget.

While developing the first application, we used Doctrine and basic form validation rules were created. These rules can be found in the file `/lib/form/doctrine/base/BaseAddressesForm.class.php`.

In the following code, you can see the `setup()` function that calls two important methods: `setWidgets()` and `setValidators()`.

Available for download on Wrox.com

```
<?php
abstract class BaseAddressesForm extends BaseFormDoctrine {
  public function setup() {
    $this->setWidgets(array(
```

```
        'id'          => new sfWidgetFormInputHidden(),
        'first_name'  => new sfWidgetFormInputText(),
        'last_name'   => new sfWidgetFormInputText(),
        'email'       => new sfWidgetFormInputText(),
        'phone'       => new sfWidgetFormInputText(),
        'address'     => new sfWidgetFormInputText(),
        'created'     => new sfWidgetFormDateTime(),
        'updated'     => new sfWidgetFormDateTime(),
      ));
      $this->setValidators(array(
        'id'         => new sfValidatorDoctrineChoice(array(
                          'model' => $this->getModelName(),
                          'column' => 'id', 'required' => false)),
        'first_name' => new sfValidatorString(array(
                          'max_length' => 40, 'required' => false)),
        'last_name'  => new sfValidatorString(array(
                          'max_length' => 40, 'required' => false)),
        'email'      => new sfValidatorString(array(
                          'max_length' => 40, 'required' => false)),
        'phone'      => new sfValidatorInteger(array('required' => false)),
        'address'    => new sfValidatorPass(array('required' => false)),
        'created'    => new sfValidatorDateTime(),
        'updated'    => new sfValidatorDateTime(), ));
      $this->widgetSchema->setNameFormat('address[%s]');
      $this->errorSchema = new sfValidatorErrorSchema($this->validatorSchema);
      $this->setupInheritance();
      parent::setup();
    }
    public function getModelName(){ return 'Addresses'; }
  }?>
```

code snippet /validation/symfony/lib/form/doctrine/base/BaseAddressesForm.class.php

Those basic validation rules were generated according to the `schema.yml` file that was used to generate the first application project.

`sfValidatorSchema` is an array that holds the validators of the form. The `setValidators()` method is used to fill `sfValidatorSchema` with validation rules.

Symfony offers a wide range of available validators that can be defined in various ways. The `setOption()` and `setMessage()` methods can be used to customize validators.

```
$value = new sfValidatorString();
$value ->setOption('required', true);
$value ->setMessage('required', 'This value is required.');
```

It is possible to define more than one rule to a validator by using the `setOptions()` and `setMessages()` methods.

```
$name= new sfValidatorString();
$name->setOptions(array ('min_length' => 4, 'max_length' => 12));
$name->setMessages(array (
          'min_length' => 'Supplied name must be at least 4 characters long',
          'max_length' => 'Supplied name cannot be longer than 12 characters'));
```

The same validation rules can be defined like this:

```
$this->setValidators(array('name'  => new sfValidatorString(
       array( 'min_length' => 4, 'max_length' => 12 ),
       array('min_length' => 'Supplied name must be at least 4 characters long',
             'max_length' => 'Supplied name cannot be longer than 12 characters'))
));
```

Let's look at a few of the most commonly used validators:

- `sfValidatorString` — Used to validate a string. It converts the input value to a string.

```
$value = new sfValidatorString();
$value ->setOption('required', true);
$value ->setMessage('required', 'This value is required.');
```

- `sfValidatorPass` — Passes the value unmodified.

```
$value= new sfValidatorPass();
```

- `sfValidatorInteger` — Validates an integer value. It converts the input value to an integer value.

```
$age => new sfValidatorInteger(array('min' => 0,'max' => 100,'required' => false));
```

- `sfValidatorNumber` — Used to validate a number (integer or float). It converts the input value to a float value.

```
$percent = new sfValidatorNumber( array( 'min'  => 0, 'max'  => 99.99,),
               array('min' => 'Percentage must be grater than 0%',
                     'max' => 'Percentage cannot exceed 99.99%',));
```

- `sfValidatorEmail` — Used to validate e-mail format.

```
$email = new sfValidatorEmail();
```

- `sfValidatorChoice` — Used to check if the given value is one of the expected values.

```
$fruit = new sfValidatorChoice(array('required' => false,
                 'choices' => array('banana', 'apple', 'pear')));
```

- `sfValidatorTime` — Used to validate time format. It converts the input value to a valid time format.

```
$time = new sfValidatorTime();
```

- `sfValidatorDate` — Used to validate a date format. It converts the input value to a valid date format.

```
$value = new sfValidatorDate(array('with_time' => true));
```

- `sfValidatorUrl` — Used to verify whether a given value is a valid URL address. It has protocol options that allow specifying what protocols are allowed.

```
$url = new sfValidatorUrl(array(
          'protocols' => array('http', 'https', 'ftp', 'ftps')));
```

- `sfValidatorRegex` — Validates a value with a user-defined regular expression.

```
$ip = new sfValidatorRegex(array(
             'pattern' => '^[0-9]{3}\.[0-9]{3}\.[0-9]{2}\.[0-9]{3}$'));
```

For full list of validators, please refer to the Symfony documentation.

Now modify your application so that the validation rules better match the purpose of the project, as shown in the following code. Set the `required` option of the `first_name` field to `true` so that it no longer will be possible to add empty entries. Next, create some messages to inform the user if the supplied values are incorrect. Finally, you should add an e-mail validation rule.

Available for download on Wrox.com

```
<?php
abstract class BaseAddressesForm extends BaseFormDoctrine {
  public function setup() {
    $this->setWidgets(array(
      'id'         => new sfWidgetFormInputHidden(),
      'first_name' => new sfWidgetFormInputText(),
      'last_name'  => new sfWidgetFormInputText(),
      'email'      => new sfWidgetFormInputText(),
      'phone'      => new sfWidgetFormInputText(),
      'address'    => new sfWidgetFormInputText(),
      'created'    => new sfWidgetFormDateTime(),
      'updated'    => new sfWidgetFormDateTime(),
    ));
    $this->setValidators(array(
      'id'         => new sfValidatorDoctrineChoice(array(
         'model' => $this->getModelName(),'column' => 'id','required' => false)),
      'first_name' => new sfValidatorString(
         array('max_length' => 25, 'required' => true),
         array ('max_length' => 'First name must be no longer than 25 characters',
                'required' => 'First name is required' ) ),
      'last_name'  => new sfValidatorString(
         array( 'max_length' => 25, 'required' => false),
         array ('max_length' => 'Last name must be no longer than 25 characters')),
      'email'      => new sfValidatorEmail(array('required'=>false),
                      array('invalid'=>'Supplied email address email is invalid')),
      'phone'      => new sfValidatorInteger(array('required' => false)),
      'address'    => new sfValidatorPass(array('required' => false)),
      'created'    => new sfValidatorDateTime(),
      'updated'    => new sfValidatorDateTime(),
    ));
    $this->widgetSchema->setNameFormat('address[%s]');
    $this->errorSchema = new sfValidatorErrorSchema($this->validatorSchema);
    $this->setupInheritance();
    parent::setup();
  }
  public function getModelName(){ return 'Addresses'; }
}?>
```

code snippet /validation/symfony/lib/form/doctrine/base/BaseAddressesForm.class.php

In addition to the core validation helpers offered by Symfony, there are a few plug-ins available that offer additional validation options.

Plug-ins

HTML5 is making its way into the web applications world quickly, so it is natural that web frameworks incorporate new features that are offered by it.

The sfHtml5FormPlugin supplies your application with an additional set of widgets and validators to be used with the new HTML5 input types.

To install the sfHtml5FormPlugin, you simply need to type following command into console from your project folder:

```
$ symfony plugin:install sfHtml5FormPlugin
```

To activate the newly installed plug-in, it is necessary to modify the `/config/ProjectConfiguration.class.php` file and add the following line:

```
$this->enablePlugins(array('sfHtml5FormPlugin'));
```

The `ProjectConfiguration.class.php` file should now contain code that looks like this:

```
class ProjectConfiguration extends sfProjectConfiguration {
  public function setup() {
    $this->enablePlugins('sfDoctrinePlugin');
    $this->enablePlugins(array('sfHtml5FormPlugin'));
  }
}
```

As of this writing, the current version of the sfHtml5FormPlugin is version 0.49 and it provides validators such as `sfValidator5Color`, `sfValidator5Date`, `sfValidator5DateTimeLocal`, `sfValidator5DateTime`, `sfValidator5Email`, `sfValidator5Month`, and `sfValidator5Time`.

Another useful plug-in is sfJqueryFormValidationPlugin. As the name implies, it is a Symfony plug-in that introduces client-side forms validation that is performed using the jQuery library and the jQuery Validation plug-in. So how does it work? It creates JavaScript client-side validation rules and messages, according to validation rules and messages from the validation schema. This solution has a few features that are worth mentioning here. First, when an HTML page is generated, there is no need to generate additional JavaScript code because the validation is added using progressive-enhancement techniques. The second important feature is that there is no need to create new containers for client-side error messages; they are written using the same HTML elements as the server-side validation.

Installation of sfJqueryFormValidationPlugin requires modification of a few files located in the `/config` folder of Symfony installation.

First, it is necessary to include the jQuery library and the jQuery Validation plug-in into your site in `view.yml`. This can be done either by downloading them or by simply including them from their respective content delivery network (CDN), as shown here:

```
default:
    javascripts:
        [http://ajax.googleapis.com/ajax/libs/jquery/1.4/jquery.min.js,
        http://ajax.microsoft.com/ajax/jquery.validate/1.7/jquery.validate.min.js]
```

code snippet /validation/symfony/app/frontend/config/view.yml

To install the sfJqueryFormValidationPlugin, you can type the following command into the console from your project folder:

```
$ symfony plugin:install sfJqueryFormValidationPlugin
```

The `filters.yml` file should contain the following filter:

```
jquery_form_validation:
    class: sfJqueryFormValidationFilter
```

code snippet /validation/symfony/app/frontend/config/filters.yml

The next module should be enabled in your `settings.yml` by adding the following line:

```
all:
    .settings:
        enabled_modules: [default, sfJqueryFormVal]
```

code snippet /validation/symfony/app/frontend/config/settings.yml

Finally, the cache should be cleared by typing the following in the console:

```
$ symfony cc
```

There are some additional configuration options for this plug-in. For more information, please refer to the plug-in documentation.

CakePHP

Core validation rules that are offered by CakePHP make model data validation an easy task. These rules can automatically handle many often-used validation tasks that otherwise would need to be written manually. CakePHP is equipped with a powerful validation engine that allows a number of built-in rules such as e-mail address, postal number, IPv4, Social Security number, credit card numbers, and so on. You can also add your own validation rules that can be used the same way as built-in rules.

Previously, when the first application was created we created a model file. Basically, it was an empty class with no validation present at all.

In the following example, the same model file is expanded by a `$validate` array:

```
<?php
class Address extends AppModel {
  var $name = 'Address';
  var $validate = array( 'first_name' => 'notEmpty' );
} ?>
```

code snippet /validation/cakephp/app/models/address.php

The newly added `$validate` array tells CakePHP how data fields will be validated when values are sent and the `save()` method is called. The first rule introduced is very simple: It requires only that the `first_name` field should not be empty, but this rule will not generate any error message when that field is left empty. As well, no message will be generated when longer data is passed than the database can accept (`VARCHAR(25)`).

The key of the `$validate` array is the name of the form field, for which the validation rule is created, and it can take a single value or (more commonly) an array.

The following example illustrates the simplest method of defining a validation rule. The general syntax for defining rules in a model file looks like this:

```
var $validate = array('first_name' => 'alphaNumeric',
                      'last_name' => array('rule' => array('maxLength', 25)) );
```

The `'rule'` key defines the validation method and takes either a single value or an array. An array is used when the rule requires some parameters as is illustrated by the rule created for the `last_name` field. The rule may be the name of a method added in your model file, a name of the core validation rule, or even a regular expression.

In this model, any data sent by a `first_name` field will be validated against the `alphaNumeric` rule, which means that the data must contain only letters and numbers. And a second rule restricts `last_name` to be no longer than 25 characters.

Probably the most commonly used validation rule is the `email` rule. It ensures that the user is providing a properly formatted e-mail address through the `email` field.

```
var $validate = array('email' => 'email');
```

Creating validation rules in a model file allows us to define error messages that will be displayed when the data submitted does not match the defined rules. The following example uses the `isUnique` rule in conjunction with an error message to be displayed if the supplied phone number is not unique.

```
var $validate = array( 'phone' => array('rule' => 'isUnique',
               'message' => 'This phone number has already been saved.' ));
```

To verify data passed by a `Checkbox` field, a `boolean` rule can be applied that can be used as a protection against any code injection.

The data for the `AgreeCheckbox` field must be a `boolean` value. Values that are accepted are `true` or `false`, integers `0` or `1`, or strings '`0`' or '`1`'.

```
var $validate = array( 'AgreeCheckbox' => array( 'rule' => 'boolean' ));
```

Next, rules ensure that data meets the minimum length and maximum length requirements.

```
var $validate = array('password' => array('rule' => array( 'minLength', 6),
            'message' => 'Password must be at least 6 characters long' )
                      'login' => array('rule' => array('maxLength', 16),
            'message' => 'Usernames must be no larger than 15 characters long.'));
```

Date format validation is done by using a date rule to ensure that submitted data has a valid format. By setting the value of a rule array, it is possible to specify which date format is considered valid. This value can be one of the following: `dmy`, `mdy`, `ymd`, `dMy`, `Mdy`, `My`, `my`. The following code demonstrates date validation:

```
var $validate = array('birth_date' => array( 'rule' => array( 'date', 'ymd' ),
                      'message' => 'Enter a date in YY-MM-DD format.',
                      'allowEmpty' => true ));
```

In a practical application of form validation, a single field may have multiple validation rules. Let's look at how these rules are defined in the model file:

Available for download on Wrox.com

```
<?php
class User extends AppModel {
  var $name = 'User';
  var $validate = array(
  'login' => array('login_1' => array('rule' => array('minLength', 6),
                   'message' => 'Login must be at least 6 chars long'),
                   'login_2' => array( 'rule' => array('isUnique'),
                   'message' => 'This login is already taken', 'last' => true) ),
  'email' => array('email_1' => array ( 'rule' => 'email',
                   'message' => 'Please enter valid email address'),
                   'email_2' => array ( 'rule' => array('isUnique'),
                   'message' => 'This email address was already used') ) );
} ?>
```

code snippet /validation/cakephp/app/models/user.php

A new validation parameter has been introduced here. Setting the last key as `true` will cause the validator to stop on the rule if it fails instead of continuing with the next rule. This can be used if you want validation to stop if a selected rule has failed.

The examples shown so far are some of the most common validation rules that can be found in various online forms. (Of course, there are more validation options than have we presented here.) Other useful rule names include `between`, `blank`, `cc` *(credit card),* `comparison`, `date`, `decimal`, `equalTo`, `extension`, `file`, `IP`, `money`, `multiple`, `inList`, `numeric`, `phone`, `postal`, `range`, `ssn`, *and* `url`. *For more examples, please refer to the CakePHP documentation.*

In addition to already built-in validation rules, it is possible to create your own custom regular expression validation rules, simply by creating the desired regular expression and placing it into a validation rule according to following example:

```
var $validate = array( 'login' => array( 'rule' => '/^[a-z0-9]{3,}$/i',
    'message' => 'Only letters and integers, min 3 characters'
    ));
```

If none of the predefined rules meets our requirements, there is one more thing we can do about form validation in CakePHP. While using a model to apply validation rules, it is possible to add your own validation methods simply by creating them inside the model file. In a normal situation, while not using any web framework, it is necessary to write your own functions to validate form data. When writing a validation method in a model file, this situation is the same, but you keep all the validation in one file.

The following example indicates how this should be done:

```
<?php
class Item extends AppModel {
```

```
    var $name = 'Item';
    var $validate = array('field_value' => array('rule' => array('myValidation', 20),
                          'message' => 'Supplied value must be lower than 20',));
       function myValidation($check, $limit) { return $check< $limit; }
    } ?>
```

The rule array takes the method name `myValidation()` as a key. That way, this method is called when validation is done. The `myValidation()` function takes two parameters: `$check` and `$limit`. The first one is a value posted through the form, and the second variable takes a value that is specified in a rule array (e.g., `20`).

Zend Framework

When you work with Zend Framework, you can use the `Zend_Form` object in order to create a web form. It is a more than adequate tool for most cases of form building and validation. It is possible to create single form elements while encapsulating it with options that allow you to configure validation, error messages, filtering (character escaping and data normalization), and rendering. For this section, we will focus on forms data-validation options, and later you will see how to customize forms some more.

In the previous chapter, we created this file to be responsible for generating an "Add a new entry" form in the address book application:

Available for download on Wrox.com

```
<?php
class Application_Form_AddressAdd extends Zend_Form {
    public function init() {
      $this->setMethod('post');
      $this->addElement('text', 'firstName', array('label' => 'Your first name:',
                        'required' => false, 'filters' => array('StringTrim'),));
      $this->addElement('text', 'lastName', array('label' => 'Your last name:',
                        'required' => false,'filters' => array('StringTrim'),));
      $this->addElement('text', 'email', array('label' => 'Your e-mail address:',
                        'required' => false,'filters' => array('StringTrim'),));
      $this->addElement('text', 'phone', array('label' => 'Your phone:',
                        'required' => false, 'filters' => array('StringTrim'),));
      $this->addElement('textarea', 'address', array('label' => 'Your Address:',
                        'required' => false, 'filters' => array('StringTrim'),));
      $this->addElement('submit', 'submit', array('ignore' => true,
                        'label' => 'Save',));  }
} ?>
```

code snippet /validation/zf/application/forms/AddressAdd.php

The `addElement()` method of the `Zend_Form` object is responsible for creating form elements, and it can take parameters that will create field validators. Let's see the simplest method of defining a validation rule for the preceding code:

```
$this->addElement('text', 'firstName', array( 'validators' => array('alnum'),
                 'label'  => 'Your first name:', 'required' => false,
                 'filters' => array('StringTrim'), ));
```

By adding the `'validators'` key, it is possible to include various validation parameters. Here we used the `'alnum'` option. It verifies if any data sent through the `firstName` field is `alphanumeric` (letters and numbers) type. If any special characters are passed, an automatic error message will be generated and displayed. As you can see, the `addElement()` method received the`'required'` and `'filters'` keys. The first one can be used in validation to specify whether a field can be empty or not; this actually creates a `'NotEmpty'` validator that will be the first one validating a field to ensure that the verified element has a value when required. And by setting `'filters'` you can filter certain form data before it will be validated. For example, it is possible to strip all HTML and PHP tags from form input simply by using the following:

```
'filters' => array('StripTags')
```

For more information about using filters, refer to the Zend Framework documentation.

The `Zend_Validate` module provides a set of commonly used validators. It also provides a simple validator mechanism that allows chaining multiple validators to be applied on data in a user defined order.

It is possible to specify multiple validation rules by adding them as values in the `validators` array.

```
$this->addElement('text', 'firstName', array(
    'validators' => array( array('stringLength', true, array(5, 15)), 'alnum'),
));
```

Validators created in this example ensure that the data provided is alphanumeric and 5 to 15 characters long. The first validator is `stringLength` and in this case it is configured by a `true/false` parameter and the array. The second parameter of the validation array is set to true and it means that the validation chain will be broken when the rule is not met, which means no following validation rules will be applied. The third parameter is an array that allows us to define the range in which the `firstName` value must be contained.

Now let's see how to validate the format of an e-mail address. Of course, there is a validator for that as well.

```
$this->addElement('text', 'email', array(
    'validators' => array( array('EmailAddress', false, array('domain' => true)))
));
```

If more complex validation options are required, the `EmailAddress` validator can be configured through various parameters that can regard domain, hostname, and local names. But for a basic and the most common application, this example should be adequate. As before, we use three parameters to create the validator. The third one allows us to decide if we want to validate the domain or not; by setting it to `false`, we tell the validator to ignore the domain part of an e-mail address.

`Zend_Validate` is automatically equipped with a broad range of error messages, but if there is a need to customize any of these messages, it is possible to do so by adding another parameter to the validation array. In the following example, the `'messages'` key is added, and an array is created that defines two error messages:

```
$this->addElement('text', 'email', array(
    'validators' => array( array('EmailAddress', false,
                               array('domain' => true, 'messages' =>array(
     Zend_Validate_EmailAddress::INVALID => 'Please enter a valid email address',
     Zend_Validate_EmailAddress::INVALID_FORMAT => 'Invalid email format' )))
));
```

To modify a desired message, it is necessary to know its error code. These codes can be found in the Zend Framework documentation.

Basic date format validation can be as simple as this:

```
$this->addElement('text', 'productionDate', array(
    'validators' => array(array('Date', false,array('YYYY-MM-dd HH:mm')))
));
```

But there is a whole `Zend_Date` API to give developers maximum control over things that can be done with dates. As in previous examples in this chapter, the validator array contains a third parameter that is an array of options. In this case, it defines an acceptable date format.

Zend Framework gives you quite a few ways to do the same thing, and you can do things according to your liking or habit. So let's look at how validators can be created by calling the `addValidators()` method:

```
$form = new Zend_Form;
$form->addElement('text', 'firstName');
$firstName->addValidators(array( array('NotEmpty', true), array('alnum'),
    array('stringLength', false, array(5, 15)), ));
```

A more verbose version of the same code can look like this:

```
$form = new Zend_Form;
$form->addElement('text', 'firstName');
$firstName->addValidators(array(
    array('validator' => 'NotEmpty','breakChainOnFailure' => true),
    array('validator' => 'alnum'),
    array('validator' => 'stringLength', 'options' => array(5, 15)), ));
```

CUSTOMIZING FORMS

Building validated forms manually can take quite a long time. To build a functional form with form data validation, it is necessary to enter the same values in multiple places, like in the view, the field's error messages, and the field itself. Most of this is done automatically by frameworks, giving developers tools to easily build custom forms.

A common form can contain various input elements such as text fields, checkboxes, select lists, textareas, labels, and so on. In Chapter 4, we have created basic forms, by using tools offered by frameworks. Excluding Zend Framework, we didn't have much influence on how the forms were built and how will the final result looked. It is time to change that.

You will modify forms generated for your first application. We will show you how to change labels, replace input fields, and modify their functionalities. To do that, you will use built-in core helpers and some external plug-ins.

Symfony

As discussed in the validation part of this chapter, Symfony offers a wide range of validators and widgets that give you all sorts of possibilities for building your forms. There are two main classes that you will use when building forms: `sfForm` and `sfWidget`. These classes are the root classes, and every other form or widget inherits from one of them. Widgets are a type of add-on that allows you to add content to your form, such as input fields, for example. You can define your own widget that can be a customized input field not commonly used anywhere else. You can add proper widgets that are delivered within a framework by using the `setup()` method. Note that there are two main types of forms. The first are defined by developers; the second are generated by object-relational mapping (ORM). In this case, it's Doctrine. When you use the following command:

```
$ symfony doctrine:build --all
```

or

```
$ symfony doctrine:build-forms
```

forms will be generated by Doctrine for each model that you defined earlier. This can be very useful, especially when building the back end. These forms are stored in the project's `/lib/form` directory. The second directory is the application's `/lib` directory, in which you will store all defined forms. Doctrine also generated `BaseForm` classes that inherit from `sfForm`. These `BaseForm` classes are stored in the `/lib/form/doctrine/base` directory. An exemplary file can contain the following lines:

```
abstract class BaseAddressesForm extends BaseFormDoctrine {
    public function setup() {
    }
}
```

While not using Doctrine to build your application, you would usually have an exemplary `AddressesForm.class.php` in a `/lib/form` directory that should contain the following class:

```
class BaseAddressesForm extends BaseForm {
    public function setup() { }
}
```

Let's look at the `setup()` function that was built by Doctrine when first project was created in the previous chapter.

```
public function setup() {
  $this->setWidgets(array(
    'id'          => new sfWidgetFormInputHidden(),
    'first_name'  => new sfWidgetFormInputText(),
    'last_name'   => new sfWidgetFormInputText(),
    'email'       => new sfWidgetFormInputText(),
    'phone'       => new sfWidgetFormInputText(),
    'address'     => new sfWidgetFormInputText(),
    'created'     => new sfWidgetFormDateTime(),
    'updated'     => new sfWidgetFormDateTime(), ));
  $this->setValidators(array(
    'id' => new sfValidatorDoctrineChoice(array('model' => $this->getModelName(),
                    'column' => 'id','required' => false)),
    'first_name'  => new sfValidatorString(array(
                          'max_length' => 40, 'required' => false)),
    'last_name'   => new sfValidatorString(array(
                          'max_length' => 40, 'required' => false)),
    'email'       => new sfValidatorString(array(
                          'max_length' => 40, 'required' => false)),
    'phone'       => new sfValidatorInteger(array('required' => false)),
```

```
        'description' => new sfValidatorPass(array('required' => false)),
        'created'     => new sfValidatorDateTime(),
        'updated'     => new sfValidatorDateTime(), ));
      $this->widgetSchema->setNameFormat('address[%s]');}
```

There are a few widgets in there that correspond to fields in a database. Those widgets were created to match field types in the database and are as simple as possible. This solution worked earlier; we wanted to see how quickly we could create a project, so we didn't interfere with the forms because they were doing their task. The fragment of HTML code responsible for displaying form fields generated by this script looks like this:

```
<tr><th><label for="address_first_name">First name</label></th>
    <td><input type="text" name="address[first_name]" id="address_first_name" />
    </td></tr>
<tr><th><label for="address_last_name">Last name</label></th>
    <td><input type="text" name="address[last_name]" id="address_last_name" />
    </td></tr>
<tr><th><label for="address_email">Email</label></th>
    <td><input type="text" name="address[email]" id="address_email" />
    </td></tr>
<tr><th><label for="address_phone">Phone</label></th>
    <td><input type="text" name="address[phone]" id="address_phone" />
    </td></tr>
<tr><th><label for="address_description">Description</label></th>
    <td><input type="text" name="address[description]" id="address_description" />
    </td></tr>
```

Figure 5-3 illustrates how input fields for the preceding code should look in a browser.

FIGURE 5-3: Form fields created in first application

Now we want to know how customize or build these forms ourselves, so let's consider this simple example:

```
public function setup() {
    $this->setWidgets(array('id'          => new sfWidgetFormInputHidden(),
                            'first_name'  => new sfWidgetFormInputText(),
                            'description' => new sfWidgetFormTextarea(),));
    $this->widgetSchema->setNameFormat('address[%s]');}
```

The `setup()` function calls for the `setWidgets()` method that is used to define widgets that will be used to create form elements. This method accepts an associative array. Field names are accepted as the keys; as the values, the widget objects are given. The last line invokes the `setNameFormat('%s')` method that sets the naming convention for the name and ID attributes of HTML tags that will be form fields. For example, the name attribute of `first_name` input will look like this:

```
<input type="text" name="address[first_name]" />
```

Let's move on to field creation. In this example, three types of widgets are used.

The first one is `sfWidgetFormInputHidden()` and it corresponds to a hidden HTML field. The `id` field is the unique ID of the entry and this shouldn't be viewable to the user. When generated the field will look like this:

```
<input type="hidden" name="address[id]" id="address_id" />
```

Next there is a `sfWidgetFormInputText()` widget that will generate standard a HTML field as follows:

```
<tr><th><label for="address_first_name">First name</label></th>
    <td><input type="text" name="address[first_name]" id="address_first_name" />
</td></tr>
```

The last widget in this example is `sfWidgetFormTextarea()`. It is responsible for creating HTML textarea form fields that look like this:

```
<tr><th><label for="address_description">Description</label></th>
    <td><textarea rows="4" cols="30"name="address[description]"
                 id="address_description"></textarea> </td></tr>
```

Of course, every widget can take a number of parameters that will allow us to customize generated HTML code and the behavior of created form fields.

While the automatic generation of labels is very useful, the framework allows you to define personalized labels for multiple fields using the `setLabels()` method.

```
$this->widgetSchema->setLabels(array('name' => 'Your name',
'email' => 'Your email address','message' => 'Your message',));
```

You can also only modify a single label using the `setLabel()` method:

```
$this->widgetSchema->setLabel('email', 'Your email address');
```

There is another way to customize HTML code generated by widgets and it enables us to pass multiple parameters to specify functionality and attributes of form fields.

```
$this->setWidgets(array(
    'first_name'  => new sfWidgetFormInputText(
            array('label' => 'Different label'), array('class' => 'fname'))));
```

As illustrated in the previous example, the widget `sfWidgetFormInputText()` is used, and three arrays are given. These parameters affect how the HTML code will be generated:

```
<tr><th><label for="first_name">Different label</label></th>
<td><input class="fname" type="text" name="first_name" id="first_name" /></td></tr>
```

We can see that the class argument of the input tag is the same as the class parameter supplied for `sfWidgetFormInputText()`.

Now let's look at another example of form code that can be used as a simple mailing form.

```
public function setup() {
  $this->setWidgets(array(
    'name'    => new sfWidgetFormInput(array('label' => 'Name')),
```

```
        'email'   => new sfWidgetFormInput(array('label' => 'Email')),
        'subject' => new sfWidgetFormSelect(array(
                        'label' => 'Select subject',
                        'choices' => array('Item 1', 'Item 2', 'Item 3'))),
        'message' => new sfWidgetFormTextarea(array('label' => 'Message')),
      ));
      $this->widgetSchema->setNameFormat('contact[%s]');
    }
```

One new thing about this example is the `sfWidgetFormSelect()` widget. It is responsible for creating the select HTML tag.

Figure 5-4 illustrates how the mailing form should look in a web browser.

Name	
Email	
Select subject	Item 1
Message	

FIGURE 5-4: Example mailing form

The widget `sfWidgetFormSelect()` is an array of selectable items, so it requires parameter choices to be defined. As a result of using this widget, the following HTML code is created:

```
<tr><th><label for="address_created">Select subject </label></th>
    <td><select name="contact[subject]" id="contact_subject">
            <option value="A">Subject A</option>
            <option value="B">Subject B</option>
            <option value="C">Subject C</option></select></td></tr>
```

Widgets

Symfony has a large variety of widgets that can be used to build complex forms for web applications. The following list presents selected widgets with code implementation. It illustrates the range of available options. Those that can be found in most common web forms and are simplest to implement are the following:

- `sfWidgetFormInput` — Represents a simple HTML input tag.
- `sfWidgetFormInputPassword` — Represents a password HTML input tag.
- `sfWidgetFormTextarea` — Represents a textarea HTML tag.
- `sfWidgetFormInputCheckbox` — Represents an HTML checkbox input.
- `sfWidgetFormInputFile` — Represents an upload file HTML input tag.

The following code is an example of how to use these widgets in your form class:

Available for download on Wrox.com

```
$this->setWidgets(array(
    'first_name'  => new sfWidgetFormInputText(array('label' => 'Name')),
    'pass'        => new sfWidgetFormInputPassword (array('label' => 'Password')),
```

```
        'agreement'   => new sfWidgetFormInputCheckbox(array('label' => 'I agree')),
        'description' => new sfWidgetFormTextarea (array('label' => 'Description')),
        'file'        => new sfWidgetFormInputFile(array('label' => 'Upload file:')),
));
```

code snippet /customization/symfony/apps/frontend/lib/form/ExampleForm.class.php

And to make sure that all these widgets will display correctly, your template should contain code similar to the following:

```
<tr><th><?php echo $form['first_name']->renderLabel() ?></th>
    <td><?php echo $form['first_name']->renderError() ?>
        <?php echo $form['first_name'] ?></td></tr>
<tr><th><?php echo $form['pass']->renderLabel() ?></th>
    <td><?php echo $form['pass']->renderError() ?>
        <?php echo $form['pass'] ?> </td></tr>
<tr><th><?php echo $form['agreement']->renderLabel() ?></th>
    <td><?php echo $form['agreement']->renderError() ?>
        <?php echo $form['agreement'] ?></td></tr>
<tr><th><?php echo $form['description']->renderLabel() ?></th>
    <td><?php echo $form['description']->renderError() ?>
        <?php echo $form['description']?> </td></tr>
<tr><th><?php echo $form['file']->renderLabel() ?></th>
    <td><?php echo $form['file']->renderError() ?>
        <?php echo $form['file'] ?></td></tr>
```

code snippet /customization/symfony/apps/frontend/modules/exampleForm/templates/_form.php

The image shown in Figure 5-5 should be rendered in the browser.

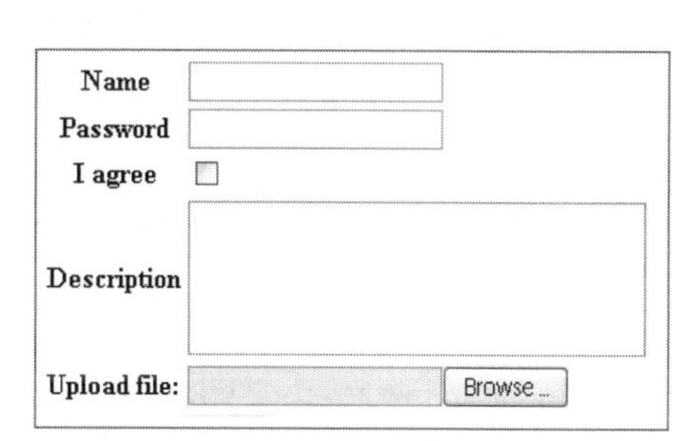

FIGURE 5-5: Form fields created in Chapter 4

Next you can see an interesting widget because it can work four different ways, depending on how you set the `'expanded'` and `'multiple'` parameters for this widget. You will see how to implement and how to configure each option separately. Implementation is straightforward, and it is done in the same way as previous examples.

`sfWidgetFormChoice` — this widget can represent HTML select tag, checkbox, radiobutton, and list input types. The first configuration works like the select tag and toggled by setting the `expanded` and `multiple` parameters to `false`. The output is shown in the Figure 5-6.

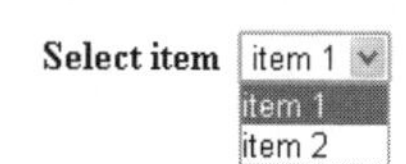

FIGURE 5-6: Drop-down select field generated by the sfWidgetFormChoice widget

```
sfWidgetFormChoice(array('label' => 'Select item',
    'expanded' => false, 'multiple' => false,
    'choices' => array('1' =>'item 1', '2'=>'item 2')))
```

The second configuration shown in Figure 5-7 represents a selection from an expanded list, and it is achieved by setting the `multiple` parameter to `true`. This form element allows multiple item selection by holding down the Ctrl or Shift key while clicking the item selected. Item 2 was selected manually in this figure.

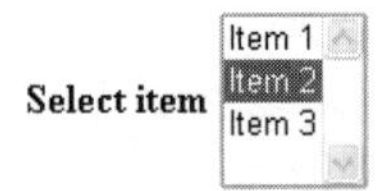

FIGURE 5-7: Multiselection field generated by the sfWidgetFormChoice widget

```
sfWidgetFormChoice(array('label' => 'Select item',
      'expanded' => false, 'multiple' => true,
      'choices'  => array('Item 1', 'Item 2', 'Item 3')))
```

The next configuration represents a radiobutton select input (see Figure 5-8), which is done by setting the `expanded` parameter to `true`.

```
sfWidgetFormChoice(array('label' => 'Select item',
      'expanded' => true, 'multiple' => false,
      'choices'  => array('Item 1', 'Item 2', 'Item 3')))
```

Select item
- Item 1
- Item 2
- Item 3

FIGURE 5-8. Multiradiobutton list generated by the sfWidgetFormChoice widget

Finally when both parameters are set to `true`, multiple checkboxes are displayed, as shown in Figure 5-9. Items 1 and 3 were selected manually.

```
sfWidgetFormChoice(array('label' => 'Select items',
    'expanded' => true, 'multiple' => true,
    'choices'  => array('Item 1', 'Item 2', 'Item 3')))
```

Select items
- Item 1
- Item 2
- Item 3

FIGURE 5-9. Multicheckbox list generated by the sfWidgetFormChoice widget

Symfony offers a number of widgets that generate date-time form inputs. Next, you will see how seven of them can be implemented in your form. First you should become familiar with the four most common date-time widgets:

- `sfWidgetFormTime` — Represents a time selection input.
- `sfWidgetFormDate` — Represents a date selection input.
- `sfWidgetFormDateRange` — Represents a date range selection input.
- `sfWidgetFormDateTime` — Represents a date-time selection input.

The next widgets presented are those designed to help with internationalization of the forms. They include a list of months and days translated to multiple languages that can be specified by setting the `culture` parameter.

- `sfWidgetFormI18nTime` — Represents a time selection input that is very similar to the `sfWidgetFormTime` widget in terms of HTML generation.

- `sfWidgetFormI18nDate` — Represents a date selection input that can be customized in terms of language.
- `sfWidgetFormI18nDateTime` — Represents a date and time selection input that can be customized in terms of language.

The following code illustrates how each of above widgets can be configured for your form. Note that by setting the `culture` parameter in the last three widgets you can specify in which language months are written.

Available for download on Wrox.com

```
$this->setWidgets(array(
    'Time'         => new sfWidgetFormTime (array(
                        'label' => 'Select Time')),
    'Date'         => new sfWidgetFormDate(array(
                        'label' => 'Select Date')),
    'DateRange'    => new sfWidgetFormDateRange(array(
                        'from_date' => new sfWidgetFormDate(),
                        'to_date'   => new sfWidgetFormDate(),
                        'label' => 'Select DateRange' )),
    'DateTime'     => new sfWidgetFormDateTime(array(
                        'label' => 'Select DateTime')),
    'I18nTime'     => new sfWidgetFormI18nTime (array(
                        'label' => 'Select I18nTime',
                        'culture' => 'en')),
    'I18nDate'     => new sfWidgetFormI18nDate(array(
                        'label' => 'Select I18nDate',
                        'culture' => 'fr')),
    'I18nDateTime' => new sfWidgetFormI18nDateTime(array(
                        'label' => 'Select I18nDateTime',
                        'culture' => 'de')),
));
```

code snippet /customization/symfony/apps/frontend/lib/form/I18NForm.class.php

To make sure that all widgets are rendered in your form, you need to have in your form template a code similar to the one shown here:

Available for download on Wrox.com

```
<tr><th><?php echo $form['Time']->renderLabel() ?></th>
    <td><?php echo $form['Time']->renderError() ?>
        <?php echo $form['Time'] ?></td></tr>
<tr><th><?php echo $form['Date']->renderLabel() ?></th>
    <td><?php echo $form['Date']->renderError() ?>
        <?php echo $form['Date'] ?></td></tr>
<tr><th><?php echo $form['DateRange']->renderLabel() ?></th>
    <td><?php echo $form['DateRange']->renderError() ?>
        <?php echo $form['DateRange'] ?></td></tr>
<tr><th><?php echo $form['DateTime']->renderLabel() ?></th>
    <td><?php echo $form['DateTime']->renderError() ?>
        <?php echo $form['DateTime'] ?></td></tr>
<tr><th><?php echo $form['I18nTime']->renderLabel() ?></th>
    <td><?php echo $form['I18nTime']->renderError() ?>
```

```
        <?php echo $form['I18nTime'] ?></td></tr>
    <tr><th><?php echo $form['I18nDate']->renderLabel() ?></th>
      <td><?php echo $form['I18nDate']->renderError() ?>
        <?php echo $form['I18nDate'] ?></td></tr>
    <tr><th><?php echo $form['I18nDateTime']->renderLabel() ?></th>
      <td><?php echo $form['I18nDateTime']->renderError() ?>
        <?php echo $form['I18nDateTime'] ?></td></tr>
```

code snippet /customization/symfony/apps/frontend/modules/i18nForm/templates/_form.php

When you run the preceding code, your browser will render the form illustrated in Figure 5-10.

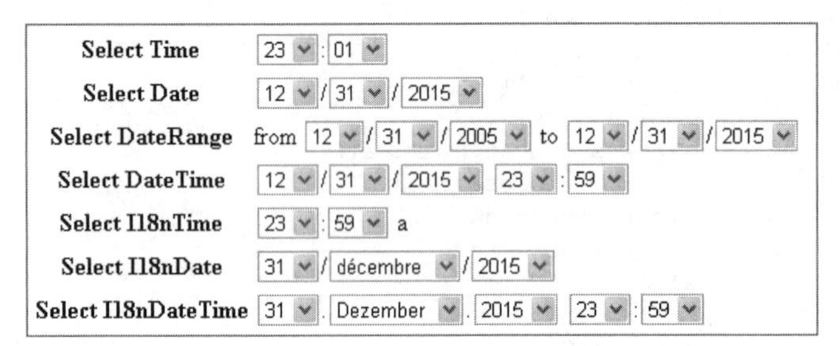

FIGURE 5-10. Various date-time form input fields generated by Symfony widgets

Finally, you can use a few more widgets that help with internationalization of your forms, three of which are listed here:

- `sfWidgetFormI18nChoiceCountry` — Represents a country HTML select tag that can be customized in terms of language (see Figure 5-11).

  ```
  sfWidgetFormI18nChoiceCountry(array('label' => 'Select country','culture' =>
  'fr'))
  ```

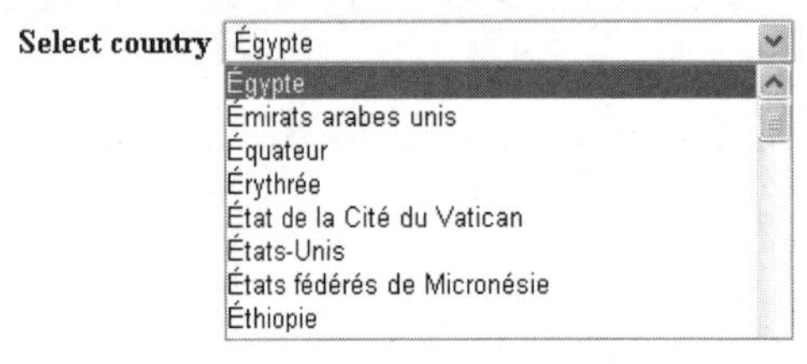

FIGURE 5-11. Country selection element generated by the sfWidgetFormI18nChoiceCountry widget

- `sfWidgetFormI18nChoiceCurrency` — Represents a currency HTML select tag that can be customized in terms of language (see Figure 5-12).

  ```
  sfWidgetFormI18nChoiceCurrency( array('label' => 'Select currency',
                                        'culture' => 'en'))
  ```

- `sfWidgetFormI18nChoiceLanguage` — Represents a language HTML select tag that can be customized in terms of language (see Figure 5-13).

  ```
  sfWidgetFormI18nChoiceLanguage (array('label' => 'Select language',
                                        'culture' => 'en'))
  ```

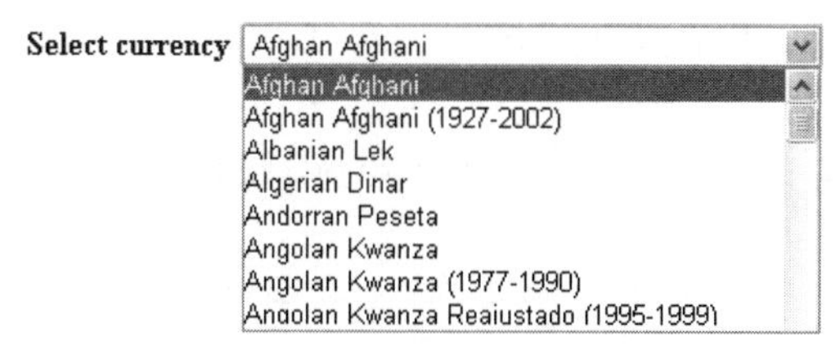

FIGURE 5-12. Currency selection element generated by the sfWidgetFormI18nChoiceCurrency widget

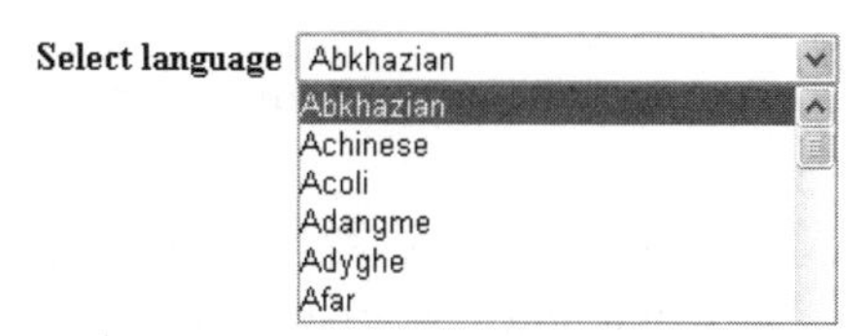

FIGURE 5-13. Language selection element generated by the sfWidgetFormI18nChoiceLanguage widget

For a full list of widgets and more specific examples, please refer to the Symfony documentation.

Plug-ins

It is possible to introduce even more customization options in Symfony forms by using plug-ins. This section looks at two plug-ins that extend the possibilities of automated form building.

sfFormExtraPlugin

This plug-in is a collection of very specific validators, widgets, and forms that extend the main Symfony package. Those components have some external dependencies.

To install the sfFormExtraPlugin, you simply need to type the following command into console from your project directory:

```
$ symfony plugin:install sfFormExtraPlugin
```

Next you may clear cache data by typing the following command into the console:

```
$ symfony cache:clear
```

This command will make available a new set of widgets to be used in our project. Those components may depend on the jQuery library to be displayed. Some of these widgets are as follows:

- `sfWidgetFormJQueryDate` — Displays a date picker using jQuery.
- `sfWidgetFormJQueryAutocompleter` — Displays an input tag with auto complete support using jQuery.
- `sfWidgetFormTextareaTinyMCE` — A rich textarea rendered with TinyMCE WYSIWYG editor.
- `sfWidgetFormSelectUSState` — Creates a select menu of U.S. states.

To use jQuery-based widgets it is necessary to include into the project a jQuery UI package that will contain the `jquery-1.4.2.min.js` and `jquery-ui-1.8.2.custom.min.js` libraries and a graphic theme that consists of the `jquery-ui-1.8.2.custom.css` style sheet and images. You can get it at `http://jqueryui.com/`.

To make it all come together, it is necessary to put jQuery libraries into the `/symfony/web/js/` directory and the theme folder into `/symfony/web/css/`.

Finally the `/symfony/apps/frontend/config/view.yml` file needs to be modified, so that it includes jQuery libraries:

```
javascripts:    [jquery-1.4.2.min.js, jquery-ui-1.8.2.custom.min.js]
```

And the style sheet needs to be included as well using the path to the theme.

```
stylesheets:    [main.css, [theme name]/jquery-ui-1.8.2.custom.css]
```

After these changes are made, clearing the cache may be required. Again it can be done by typing `symfony cache:clear` into the command console.

Let's now see how to use the `sfWidgetFormJQueryDate()` widget to give the user an option to pick a date from a jQuery calendar. To see how it is done, we can modify the earlier example simply by changing `sfWidgetFormDateTime()` to `sfWidgetFormJQueryDate()`.

```
public function setup() {
  $this->setWidgets(array(
    'id'          => new sfWidgetFormInputHidden(),
    'first_name'  => new sfWidgetFormInputText(),
    'last_name'   => new sfWidgetFormInputText(),
    'email'       => new sfWidgetFormInputText(),
    'phone'       => new sfWidgetFormInputText(),
    'address'     => new sfWidgetFormInputText(),
    'created'     => new sfWidgetFormJQueryDate( array('config' => '{}') ),
    'updated'     => new sfWidgetFormDateTime(), ));
```

As a result, you should see a new form in the web browser, as shown in Figure 5-14.

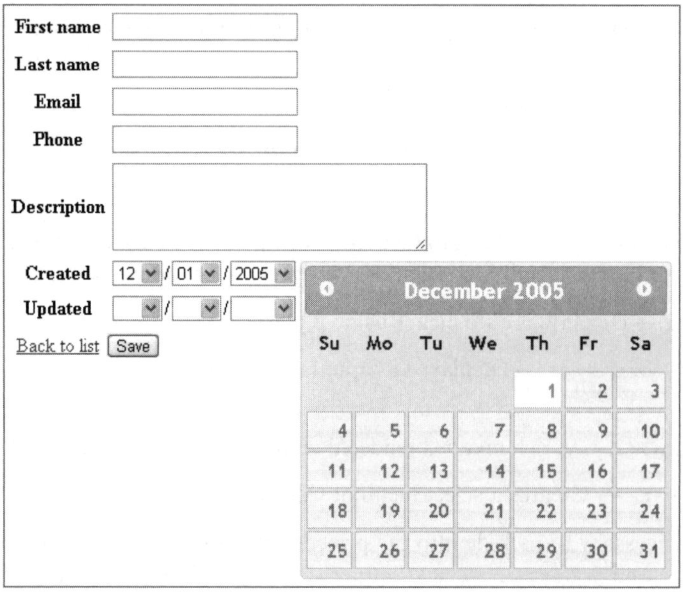

FIGURE 5-14. Form with jQuery date picker

CakePHP

For data validation, CakePHP has FormHelper, which offers many useful automatic functions; the most common will be described here.

While writing the add new address action in Chapter 4, you used the following code:

```
<?php
    echo $form->create('Address');
    echo $form->inputs();
    echo $form->end('Save address');
?>
```

code snippet /customization/cakephp/views/addresses/add.ctp

This solution is quick and good for creating backend applications that give you full access to information stored in a database. For example, information such as the date when an entry was created should not be available for modifications. As a result of those three lines, the following HTML code is generated. Note that date selection lists have been removed to improve code readability.

```
<form id="AddressAddForm" method="post" action="/cake/addresses/add">
<fieldset style="display:none;">
    <input type="hidden" name="_method" value="POST" />
</fieldset>
<fieldset>
    <legend>New Address</legend>
    <input type="hidden" name="data[Address][id]" value="" id="AddressId" />
<div class="input text required">
    <label for="AddressFirstName">First Name</label>
    <input name="data[Address][first_name]"
           type="text" maxlength="25"
           value=""
           id="AddressFirstName" />
</div>
<div class="input text">
    <label for="AddressLastName">Last Name</label>
    <input name="data[Address][last_name]"
           type="text"
           maxlength="25"
           value=""
           id="AddressLastName" />
</div>
<div class="input text">
    <label for="AddressEmail">Email</label>
    <input name="data[Address][email]"
           type="text"
           maxlength="25"
           value=""
           id="AddressEmail" />
</div>
<div class="input text">
    <label for="AddressPhone">Phone</label>
    <input name="data[Address][phone]"
           type="text"
```

```
                maxlength="11"
                value=""
                id="AddressPhone" />
</div>
<div class="input textarea">
    <label for="AddressAddress">Address</label>
    <textarea name="data[Address][address]"
            cols="30"
            rows="6"
            id="AddressAddress" >
    </textarea>
</div>
<select>
            // select form goes here
</select>
</fieldset>
<div class="submit">
    <input type="submit" value="Save address" />
</div>
</form>
```

The form rendered by the browser will have the same input composition as the one shown in Figure 5-15.

FIGURE 5-15. Form generated for the first application in Chapter 4

Now you will see how to build your own custom form input using the `input()` method of the FormHelper. The following code example invokes the `input()` method a number of times to create a web form that is identical to the one generated by the previous solution:

Available for download on Wrox.com

```
<?php echo $form->create('Address', array('type' => 'post', 'action' => 'add'));
echo '<fieldset><legend>New Address</legend>';
echo $form->input( 'first_name' ).
        $form->input( 'last_name' ).
        $form->input( 'email' ).
```

```
        $form->input( 'phone' ).
        $form->input( 'address', array('rows' => '5', 'cols' => '5')).
        $form->input( 'created' ).
        $form->input( 'modified' );
echo'</fieldset>';
echo $form->end( 'Save address' ); ?>
```

code snippet /customization/cakephp/views/addresses/add.ctp

In this example of using the `input()` method, the form fields are generated according to specifications defined in the corresponding model file. It is possible to override model information and force certain input types. To do so, you need to define some additional parameters that are passed into this `input()` method. The following example illustrates how: By adding the `'type'` parameter to the option array you can customize rendered form input. You can force normal text input to be rendered as password type form input. The implementation is shown here:

```
<?php
    echo $form->input('first_name');
    // input based on model data
    echo $form->input('first_name', array('type' => 'password'));
    // input with modified type field
?>
```

The following HTML code snippet illustrates how the `<input>` tag is modified when the `'type'` parameter is set:

```
<div class="input text required">
    <label for="AddressFirstName">First Name</label>
    <input name="data[Address][first_name]"
           type="text" maxlength="25" value="" id="AddressFirstName" /></div>
<div class="input password required">
    <label for="AddressFirstName">First Name</label>
    <input name="data[Address][first_name]"
           type="password" value="" id="AddressFirstName" /></div>
```

Customizing Generated HTML

The form generated using `$form->input()` function has some additional HTML code added to every form field. This includes putting elements into a `<div>` tag or adding labels to a created field. This can be modified to better match your preferences using an options array that is passed into the `input()` method.

For example, it is possible to modify label text assigned to a field simply by setting the `'label'` option:

```
<?php echo $form->input('last_name',
           array('label' => array('text' => 'Label text'))); ?>
```

The same way can be used to disable label generation. It is done by setting the `'label'` option to `false`, just like this:

```
<?php echo $form->input('last_name', array('label' => false)); ?>
```

Similarly, we can disable the `<div></div>` tags that surround a form field or set a class name to a field:

```
<?php echo $form->input('last_name',
         array('div' => false, 'class'=>'last_name_class')); ?>
```

It is possible to add a class name to a `<div>` containing form field by setting an option array as shown here:

```
<?php echo $form->input('last_name',
         array('div' => array('class'=>'div_class'))); ?>
```

There are a few more options that will be shown here. First there are options that can be used to define the number of `<textarea>` field rows and columns, and they work like this:

```
<?php echo $form->input('address', array('rows' => '5', 'cols' => '5')); ?>
```

The next thing that FormHelper allows you to do is to generate complex `<select>` inputs in very simple way. Suppose you want to add a group option to your address book in order to classify entries to groups such as Family, Friends, Client, or Co-worker. You need to add a new field to your database and you can use the following code to create the `<select>` field:

```
<?php echo $form->input('group', array( 'options' => array(
         'Work' => array('Value 1'=>'Client', 'Value 2'=>'Coworker' ),
         'Private' => array( 'Value 3'=>'Family', 'Value 4'=>'Friends' ))
));?>
```

Finally, let's look at how to customize the date field. It is possible to set the time and date format. For time, there are two formats: `'12'` and `'24'`; for date, it is possible to set it to `'DMY'`, `'MDY'`, `'YMD'`, and `'NONE'`. The `'minYear'` and `'maxYear'` options are self-explanatory.

```
<?php echo $form->input('created',
                    array( 'timeFormat'=>'24', 'dateFormat' => 'MDY',
                    'minYear' => date('Y') - 20, 'maxYear' => date('Y') )); ?>
```

CakePHP FormHelper allows developers to create a large variety of different form inputs that are created using the `input()` method. A list of a few selected form elements is presented here:

- `file` — Represents file selection input.
- `checkbox` — Represents standard checkbox input.
- `gender` — Represents gender selection input.
- `dateTime` — Represents a date-time selection input.

The implementation code for the previous input types can look as follows:

```
echo $form->create('Address', array( 'enctype' => 'multipart/form-data',
                                      'type' => 'post', 'action' => 'add'));
echo '<fieldset>';
echo $form->input('file', array( 'type' => 'file'));
echo $form->input('Agreement', array('type'=>'checkbox','label' => 'I agree'));
echo $form->input('gender', array('type' => 'select',
                          'options' => array('M' => 'Male','F' => 'Female')));
echo $form->input('dateTime', array('type' => 'datetime', 'label' => 'Date-time',
                  'minYear' => date('Y') - 5, 'maxYear' => date('Y'),
                  'dateFormat' => 'DMY', 'timeFormat' => '12' ));
echo'</fieldset>';
echo $form->end('Save address'); ?>
```

You can see that the input types utilize a set of options that are used for configuration. On form submission, most input fields send their value, but in the case of file input, an array is given. It contains the following:

- `name` — Name of a submitted file.
- `type` — File extension and type (e.g., `'application/pdf'`).
- `tmp_name` — Temporary patch filename for uploaded file.
- `error` — Variable that returns `0` if upload is successful.
- `size` — Uploaded file size in bytes.

Note that the array is generated by PHP.

As a result of running the preceding script, the following HTML form is generated:

```
<form enctype="multipart/form-data" id="AddressAddForm" method="post"
  action="/cake/addresses/add">
<fieldset style="display:none;">
  <input type="hidden" name="_method" value="POST" />
</fieldset>
<fieldset>
<div class="input checkbox">
  <input type="hidden" name="data[Address][Agreement]" id="AddressAgreement_"
  value="0" />
  <input type="checkbox" name="data[Address][Agreement]" value="1"
  id="AddressAgreement" />
  <label for="AddressAgreement">I agree</label>
</div>
<div class="input file">
  <label for="AddressFile">File</label>
  <input type="file" name="data[Address][file]" value="" id="AddressFile" />
</div>
<div class="input select">
  <label for="AddressGender">Gender</label>
  <select name="data[Address][gender]" id="AddressGender">
    <option value="M">Male</option>
    <option value="F">Female</option>
  </select>
</div>
<div class="input datetime">
<label for="AddressDateTimeMonth">Date-time</label>
  <select name="data[Address][dateTime][day]" id="AddressDateTimeDay">
    <option value="01">1</option>
    <option value="02">2</option>
    ...
  </select>-<select name="data[Address][dateTime][month]"
  id="AddressDateTimeMonth">
    <option value="01">January</option>
    <option value="02">February</option>
    ...
  </select>-<select name="data[Address][dateTime][year]" id="AddressDateTimeYear">
    <option value="2010" selected="selected">2010</option>
    <option value="2009">2009</option>
```

```
    ...
  </select><select name="data[Address][dateTime][hour]" id="AddressDateTimeHour">
    ...
  </select>:<select name="data[Address][dateTime][min]" id="AddressDateTimeMin">
    ...
  </select> <select name="data[Address][dateTime][meridian]"
  id="AddressDateTimeMeridian">
    <option value="am">am</option>
    <option value="pm" selected="selected">pm</option>
  </select>
</div>
</fieldset>
<div class="submit">
  <input type="submit" value="Save address" />
</div>
</form>
```

This example will render the web form illustrated in Figure 5-16.

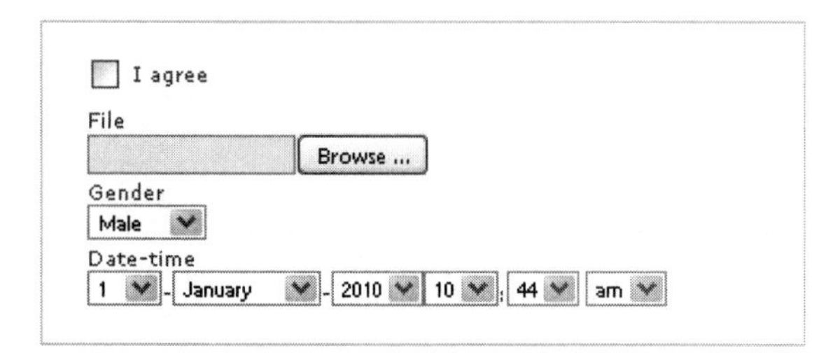

FIGURE 5-16. Web form with example input fields

Of course, this is not all in terms of forms customization that CakePHP can offer. For a full list of options, please refer to the FormHelper section in the CakePHP documentation.

Zend Framework

As you saw in the preceding section, "How Does Form Validation work?" Zend Framework allows you to easily create form validation rules, and customization is done in a similar manner. The `Zend_Form_Element` module corresponds to a single HTML form input (e.g., text field, textarea, and so on). Such elements are used to create a web form. And to make it easier, Zend Framework is equipped with element classes that encapsulate most of the HTML form input types.

It is possible to further influence HTML code generated by utilizing decorators to modify elements of a form. These decorators have access to the elements and the methods of the web content being generated.

Let's look at the `init()` function that was built while creating the first project in the previous chapter.

```
class Application_Form_AddressAdd extends Zend_Form {
    public function init() {
      $this->setMethod('post');
      $this->addElement('text', 'firstName', array(
```

```
                'label'    => 'Your first name:',
                'required' => true,
                'filters'  => array('StringTrim'),
                )
        );
        $this->addElement('text', 'lastName', array(
                'label'    => 'Your last name:',
                'required' => false,
                'filters'  => array('StringTrim'),
                )
        );
        $this->addElement('text', 'email', array(
               'label'    => 'Your e-mail address:',
               'required' => false,
               'filters'  => array('StringTrim'),
               )
        );
        $this->addElement('text', 'phone', array(
              'label'    => 'Your phone:',
              'required' => false,
              'filters'  => array('StringTrim'),
              )
        );
        $this->addElement('textarea', 'address', array(
             'label'    => 'Your address:',
             'required' => false,
             'filters'  => array('StringTrim'),
             )
        );
        $this->addElement('submit', 'submit', array(
               'ignore' => true,
               'label'  => 'Save'
       ));
    }
}
```

code snippet /customization/zf/application/forms/AddressAdd.php

You can see that there are a few `addElement()` methods in this file, and every `addElement()` method corresponds to a field in your form. Those elements take a list of parameters that allow you to create field types matching those of database fields.

The following HTML code fragment is a result of execution of the script above. It is responsible for displaying a form in a web browser.

```
<form enctype="application/x-www-form-urlencoded" method="post" action="">
<dl class="zend_form">
    <dt id="firstName-label">
        <label for="firstName" class="required">Your first name:</label>
    </dt><dd id="firstName-element">
        <input type="text" name="firstName" id="firstName" value="">
    </dd><dt id="lastName-label">
```

```
            <label for="lastName" class="optional">Your last name:</label>
        </dt><dd id="lastName-element">
            <input type="text" name="lastName" id="lastName" value="">
        </dd><dt id="email-label">
            <label for="email" class="optional">Your e-mail address:</label>
        </dt><dd id="email-element">
            <input type="text" name="email" id="email" value="">
        </dd><dt id="phone-label">
            <label for="phone" class="optional">Your phone:</label>
        </dt><dd id="phone-element">
            <input type="text" name="phone" id="phone" value="">
        </dd><dt id="address-label">
            <label for="address" class="optional">Your address:</label>
        </dt><dd id="address-element">
            <textarea name="address" id="address" rows="24" cols="80"></textarea>
        </dd>
        <dt id="submit-label"> </dt>
        <dd id="submit-element">
            <input type="submit" name="submit" id="submit" value="Save"></dd>
    </dl>
    </form>
```

You can see in Figure 5-17 how input fields for the preceding HTML code should look in a browser. Note that the textarea field can be made larger using CSS styles.

FIGURE 5-17. Web form created for the first application in Chapter 4

Now you are familiar with how forms are generated step by step, it is time to move on to customization of form elements.

`Zend_Form` provides several accessories for adding and removing form elements.

The most basic way to add an element to your form is to use the `addElement()` method. This method can take either an object of a class extending `Zend_Form_Element` or a list of arguments that specify `addElement()` behavior. These include element type, field name, and number of configuration options.

Because there is a choice of how to add a new form element, we will present two possibilities here. The first one looks as follows:

```
$element = new Zend_Form_Element_Text('fieldName');
$form->addElement($element);
```

You can see that a `Zend_Form_Element_Text` object is created with a `'fieldName'` value. This value is the name of the form field that will be generated in the web page. Next, the `addElement()` method is invoked using the `$element` parameter. This will generate a standard text input field.

Building a form this way requires the developer to use long names of classes that encapsulate fields' functionality (e.g., `Zend_Form_Element_Text` or `Zend_Form_Element_Submit`).

Exactly the same HTML output can be achieved using the next presented way for creating form elements. It is shorter and it requires passing some parameters to the `addElement()` method. An example of how it is done looks as follows:

```
$form->addElement('text', 'fieldName');
```

As a result of running the preceding code, a standard text type form input field is rendered. Parameters passed to this method are the type of a form field (e.g., text, textarea, submit, and so on) and a name for the field that will be used to handle form data. And as you can see in following example, there is a third parameter that is an array and allows customization as well as adding functionality such as filters or validators:

```
$form->addElement('text', 'fieldName', array('label' => 'Enter a value:') );
```

This example is different from the previous one simply by the label that says: `'Enter a value:'` right above the input field.

Zend Framework has a variety of element classes that cover most HTML form elements that are used in web forms.

The following is an implementation of `Zend_Form_Elements` that can be used in your applications:

- `Zend_Form_Element_Hidden` — Generates a hidden field that can hold data that is invisible to users.

  ```
  $this->addElement('hidden', 'userId', array('value' => '123') );
  ```

  This element will generate the following HTML code:

  ```
  <dt id="userId-label"> </dt>
  <dd id="userId-element">
      <input type="hidden" name="userId" value="123" id="userId"></dd>
  ```

  Note that this will not render any visible form input.

The next example you will see is built using the following form elements:

- `Zend_Form_Element_Text` — Generates a standard input field.
- `Zend_Form_Element_Password` – Generates a standard password form field.
- `Zend_Form_Element_Textarea` — Generates a standard textarea HTML tag.
- `Zend_Form_Element_Button` — Represents an HTML button input.
- `Zend_Form_Element_Submit` — Generates a standard submit button that is used for sending form data.
- `Zend_Form_Element_Reset` — Standard element that generates a form reset button.
- `Zend_Form_Element_Image` — Creates an image type button. To render this element, it is necessary to give an image path either by an image parameter or by an src parameter. In this case, the path is set to the image that is located in an `/addressBook/public/images` directory.

The purpose of the following code is to illustrate an implementation of the elements introduced previously because the resulting form may have little use in a real-world application:

```
class Application_Form_ExampleAdd extends Zend_Form {
public function init() {
 $this->setMethod('post');
 $this->addElement('text', 'name', array('label' => 'Your name:'));
 $this->addElement('password', 'pass', array( 'label' => 'Enter password:'));
 $this->addElement('textarea', 'comment', array('label' => 'Enter your comment:'));
 $this->addElement('button', 'button', array('label' => 'Click Me' ));
 $this->addElement('submit', 'submit', array('ignore' => true, 'label' => 'Save'));
 $this->addElement('reset', 'reset', array('label' => 'Reset form data'));
 $this->addElement('Image', 'imgButton', array('label' => '',
                 'image' => '../images/imageButton.png', 'alt' => 'Submit' ));
}}
```

code snippet /customization/zf/applications/forms/ExampleAdd.php

This example will render the form illustrated in Figure 5-18.

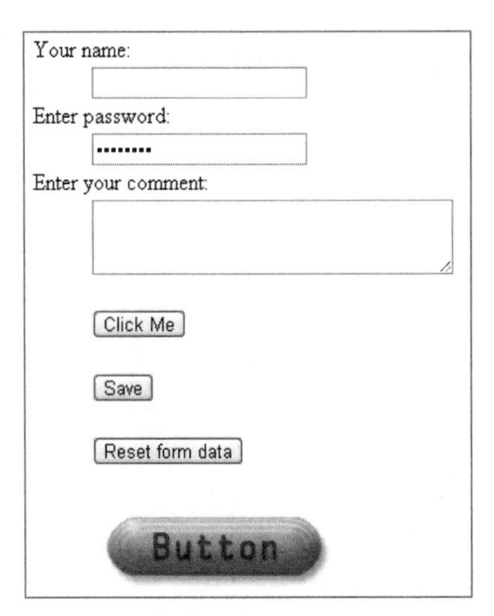

FIGURE 5-18. Form generated using the addElement() method

The form elements presented next are responsible for rendering various selection inputs such as checkboxes, radiobuttons, and select lists.

- `Zend_Form_Element_Checkbox` — Represents an HTML checkbox input and allows you to return a specific value (basically, it works as a boolean value). When the checkbox is checked, the value is submitted; otherwise, nothing is submitted.

```
$this->addElement('Checkbox', 'option',
          array('label' => 'Option', 'checkedValue' => '1',
                'uncheckedValue' => '0', 'value' => '1'));
```

The preceding example will render a single standard checkbox field. It is possible to define the behavior of this element by setting a number of options. By setting the value option to `1`, the rendered checkbox is checked by default.

- `Zend_Form_Element_MultiCheckbox` — This element is one of the nonstandard input field types. It allows you to group a set of related checkboxes. A `MultiCheckbox` ensures that on form submission, the selected options are passed as an array. The following code illustrates implementation of the `MultiCheckbox` element:

```
$this->addElement('MultiCheckbox', 'options',
                  array('label' => 'Select your options:',
                  'multiOptions' => array('opt_1' => 'Option 1',
                                          'opt_2' => 'Option 2',
                                          'opt_3' => 'Option 3',)));
```

To set some of the options as checked by default, you need to add another parameter to an options array, and it is a value array. The code for this should look like this:

```
$this->addElement('MultiCheckbox', 'options', array(
    'label' => 'Select your options:', 'multiOptions' => array(
                'opt_1' => 'Option 1', 'opt_2' => 'Option 2',
                'opt_3' => 'Option 3', 'opt_4' => 'Option 4'),
    'value' => array( 'opt_1', 'opt_3' )));
```

As a result of setting the value array, two options are checked by default. Figure 5-19 illustrates how this form element is rendered by the browser.

Select your options:
☑ Option 1
☐ Option 2
☑ Option 3
☐ Option 4

FIGURE 5-19. Form element rendered using the MultiCheckbox option

- `Zend_Form_Element_Radio` — Renders a radio button element that is quite similar in terms of code implementation to the `MultiCheckbox` element. The difference comes with a `value` parameter that indicates a single radio button to be checked by default. The rendered form element is illustrated in Figure 5-20.

```
$this->addElement('Radio', 'radioOption', array(
    'label' => 'Select option', 'multiOptions' => array(
        'opt_1' => 'Choice 1', 'opt_2' => 'Choice 2', 'opt_3' => 'Choice 3'),
    'value' => 'opt_2'));
```

Select option
○ Choice 1
◉ Choice 2
○ Choice 3

FIGURE 5-20. Form element rendered using the Radio option

- `Zend_Form_Element_Select` — An HTML select tag is rendered by this element and is nearly identical in functionality and implementation to the element introduced previously, as you can see in the following code. The difference is that the rendered form element is a drop-down selection list, like the one illustrated in Figure 5-21.

```
$this->addElement('Select', 'items', array(
    'label'   => 'Select an item:', 'multiOptions' => array(
        '1' => 'Item 1', '2' => 'Item 2', '3' => 'Item 3', ),
    'value' => '2'));
```

By setting the `value` parameter to the value of an item, it is possible to specify which item is selected by default.

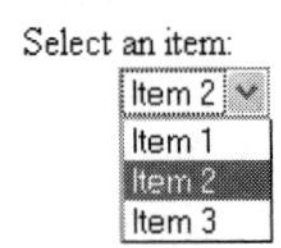

FIGURE 5-21. Form element rendered using the Select option

- `Zend_Form_Element_Multiselect` – Allows a user to select multiple items from a selection list by holding the Shift or Control key. The `value` parameter allows you to define multiple items that are selected by default. The rendered element is presented in Figure 5-22.

```
$this->addElement('Multiselect', 'items', array(
    'label'   => 'Select multiple items:',
    'multiOptions' => array(
        '1' => 'Item 1', '2' => 'Item 2', '3' => 'Item 3',
        '4' => 'Item 4', '5' => 'Item 5', '6' => 'Item 6', ),
    'value' => array('2','3','5')));
```

Select multiple items:
Item 1
Item 2
Item 3
Item 4
Item 5
Item 6

FIGURE 5-22. Form element rendered using the Multiselect option

- `Zend_Form_Element_File` — Provides a mechanism that makes file upload handling easier.
- `Zend_File_Transfer` — Used to handle internal file transfers. It is possible to influence file uploads by setting parameters such as destination that say where uploaded files should be saved, or by adding validators. Validators can automatically verify if an uploaded file has an acceptable file extension or that the file size does not exceed a defined limit. The following example illustrates how basic image uploading can be done:

```
$this->addElement('File', 'file', array( 'label'   => 'Upload an image:',
    'destination' => 'upload', 'validators' => array(
        'Extension'=> array( false, 'jpg,png,gif' ),
        'Size' => array( false, 102400 )), ));
```

The form element rendered by the preceding code is a standard file selection input that allows users to browse through local files. Figure 5-23 illustrates this element.

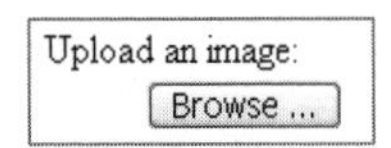

FIGURE 5-23. Form element rendered using the File option

Decorators

So far when building forms, `<dl>` and `<dt>` tags were used every time the `addElement()` method was used. As a result, a form with a single text input field could look like this:

```
<form enctype="application/x-www-form-urlencoded" method="post" action="">
<dl class="zend_form">
```

```
        <dt id="firstName-label">
            <label for="firstName" class="required">Your first name:</label>
        </dt><dd id="firstName-element">
            <input type="text" name="firstName" id="firstName" value="">
        </dd><dt id="submit-label">
        </dt><dd id="submit-element">
            <input type="submit" name="submit" id="submit" value="Save"> </dd>
    </dl></form>
```

Zend_Form comes with decorators that can be used to customize the way the forms are rendered. These decorators can be applied to form elements to influence how the HTML code is generated. It can be used for setting the appearance of error messages or defining where field labels are displayed in relation to their input fields.

As a default behavior, the decorator wraps forms in a definition list <dl> tag and form elements in an item description <dd> tag. A decorator responsible for creating tags of a form element looks as follows:

```
$form->setDecorators(array('FormElements', array('HtmlTag',
                                           array('tag' => 'dl')),'Form'));
```

This code creates HTML output like the following:

```
<form action="/form/action" method="post">
    <dl></dl>
</form>
```

The following is a list of five decorators that are used by Zend_Form_Element by default:

- ViewHelper — Simply specifies a view helper that is used to render the element.
- Errors — Used to add error messages to the element. If not specified, no message is added.
- Description — Can be used to specify the element description. As the default, the description is rendered in a <p> tag with a class of 'description'. If not specified, no description is added.
- HtmlTag — Is used to wrap the element and errors messaged in an HTML tag. By default, it is the <dd> tag.
- Label — Defines a label to the element, and by default wraps it in a <dt> tag. If no label is specified then only the <dt> tag is rendered.

These decorators can be used to modify rendered form elements. The following code is an example of a basic login form with two fields — login name and password generated — without setting any custom decorators. Code required to render such a form can look like the following:

```
$this->addElement('text', 'login', array( 'label' => 'Enter login:',));
$this->addElement('password', 'password', array( 'label' => 'Enter password:',));
```

As a result the following HTML code is created:

```
<dt id="login-label">
    <label for="login" class="optional">Enter login:</label>
</dt><dd id="login-element">
    <input type="text" name="login" id="login" value="">
</dd><dt id="password-label">
```

```
    <label for="password" class="optional">Enter password:</label>
</dt><dd id="password-element">
    <input type="password" name="password" id="password" value="">
</dd>
```

Form fields are inside <dd> tags, and labels are in <dt> tags. This makes the web browser render a form like that displayed in Figure 5-24.

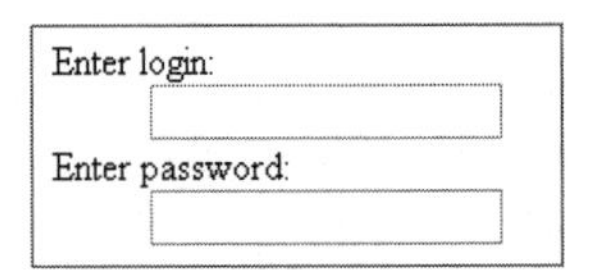

FIGURE 5-24. Basic login form rendered by a web browser

It is possible that, for some reason, you may want to have different HTML output than this solution offers. The following example illustrates how such modification can be done:

```
$this->addElement('text', 'login', array( 'label'    => 'Enter login:',
    'Decorators' => array('ViewHelper', 'Errors', 'Description',
        array('HtmlTag', array('tag' => 'div', 'class' => 'login')),
        array('Label',  array('tag' => 'b', 'placement' => 'prepend',
                    'class' => 'loginLabel')), ), ));
$this->addElement('password', 'password', array( 'label'    => 'Enter password:',
    'Decorators' => array(
        'ViewHelper', 'Errors', 'Description',
        array('HtmlTag', array('tag' => 'div', 'class' => 'password')),
        array('Label', array('tag' => 'b', 'placement' => 'prepend',
                    'class' => 'passwordLabel')), ), ));
```

You can see that code from the previous example has been extended by adding the `Decorators` parameter to the `addElement()` method. In both elements, decorators are used to make labels precede input fields and to be enclosed in a <b></b> tags to display the text of the label in bold font. Input fields are also modified to be enclosed by <div> </div> tags. For each newly set <div> and <b> tag, classes are set to allow possible styling.

As a result of introducing these decorators, the HTML code is generated as follows:

```
<b id="login-label">
    <label for="login" class="loginLabel optional">Enter login:</label>
</b>
<div class="login">
    <input type="text" name="login" id="login" value="">
</div>
<b id="password-label">
    <label for="password" class="passwordLabel optional">Enter password:</label>
</b>
<div class="password">
    <input type="password" name="password" id="password" value=""></div>
```

And if no additional CSS styles are included, the form illustrated by Figure 5-25 would be rendered.

As you can see, it is possible to customize forms rendering by setting a number of parameters while creating form fields.

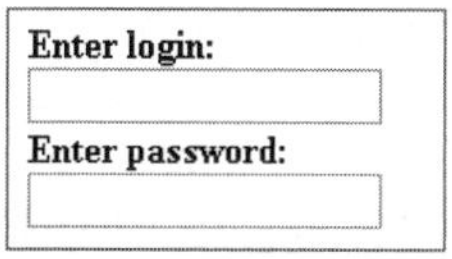

Enter login:

Enter password:

FIGURE 5-25. Modified login form rendered by a web browser

USING CAPTCHA AS SPAM PROTECTION

Spam refers not only to unwanted mail but also to any messages that can be displayed to any group of users after being posted by automated software through an unsecured form. A *Captcha*, which stands for Completely Automated Public Turing Test to Tell Computers and Humans Apart, is a program designed to protect websites against automated bots by generating tests that humans can pass but current computer programs cannot.

Problem

We all are accustomed to regular e-mail spam. If someone gets your e-mail address, you can anticipate your inbox getting filled with all kinds of junk. Web form spam is a slightly different problem.

Spam-bots are automated programs that surf the Web in search of web forms that can be used for spamming. Once a proper form is found, it is analyzed by a spambot to determine whether the form is usable for spamming purposes. Later, the targeted form is filled with data, hyperlinks, and content that is supposed to be exposed.

If a website contains at least one web form (e.g., registration, comments, message board, and so on), it is highly likely that spambots will infest this website soon enough. When that happens, forums are flooded with unwanted content and spam messages are posted on websites and displayed to the site visitors.

Why Should I Use Captcha?

Captcha is a technology that is used as a security system by websites, aiming to allow only data submitted by humans. This mechanism is commonly used when we want to allow only users to pass any data through a form, or we want to prevent passing any values generated by computers. One good example of automatically generated values may be automated software that browses websites and automatically creates accounts on popular web applications. When Captcha is present in the registration form on such websites, this software cannot figure out what to enter into the Captcha field to pass the form validation. Other popular applications of Captcha are to protect systems vulnerable to e-mail spam or to block automated posting to blogs or forums.

Captcha protection is most commonly applied as automatically generated images (usually random sets of characters or random words) that must be recognized. It is possible for people to read the image, but computers should find that reading it is very difficult.

Unfortunately, many authors that design their own Captcha mechanisms are convinced that if an image is difficult to read for them, it will be difficult for the machine as well. This is not always the case.

Optical character recognition (OCR) software can be used to attempt to defeat Captcha. This software has a wide range of tools at its disposal that are dedicated to recognizing various fonts or handwritten characters. You can find online articles that describe how Captcha systems used by Windows Live, Gmail, or Yahoo have been broken. Examples of filtered-out Captcha tests are shown in Figures 5-26 and 5-27.

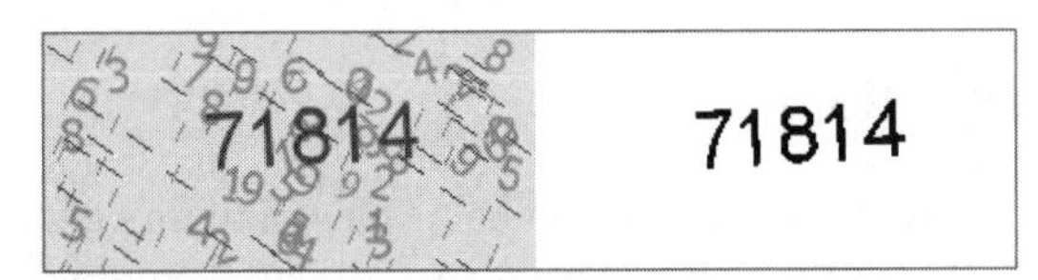

FIGURE 5-26. Example of how a Captcha image can be cleaned by software

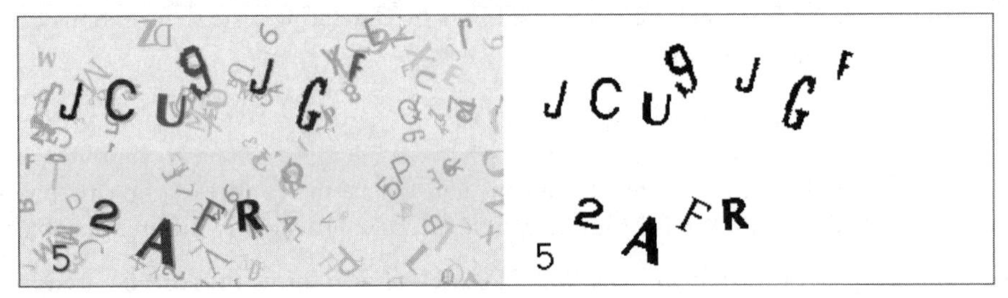

FIGURE 5-27. Another pair of examples of how a Captcha image can be cleaned

Captcha's strength lies elsewhere, namely in fact that it takes time to break a certain variation of the standard Captcha, and these variations can be easily changed.

Various Implementations of Captcha

Text-based Captcha, in which the user has to type a few letters that are displayed on the screen to complete the form submission, is not the only type of Captcha used on the Internet. There are other types of Captcha as well:

- Math Captcha — User has to solve a mathematical equation (for example: What is the result of 2+2?).
- Question Captcha — Solution requires answers to questions regarding some context (for example: What day is it today?).
- Audio Captcha — User has to type a word that is played-back through speakers. This solution is similar to text-based Captcha and is frequently combined with it.

However, in those solutions, automatic generation is the usual problem.

In addition to this form-protection arsenal, there is the following:

- ReCaptcha — a free antibot service that according to the authors of this service: "It helps digitize books, newspapers and old time radio shows." (See Figure 5-28).

We have mentioned that OCR programs are used for text recognition. During the digitization process of the scanned text (e.g., books), unintelligible fragments can often occur, for which the OCR software cannot give a clear result. Because humans are better than machines at dealing with the recognition of such fragments, the institutions involved in the digitization of library resources employ staff whose task is to verify the OCR results.

The idea of reCaptcha is that it can replace the work of the people who verify OCR results with a random group of users who can solve everyday millions of Captcha tasks. This solution can save thousands of work hours a day that otherwise would have to be done by employees working on scanned text digitization. This solution is important because it utilizes users' online activity to aid in the recognition of scanned text fragments that OCR software cannot handle. It combines websites' protection mechanisms with the beneficial work of digitization of library resources.

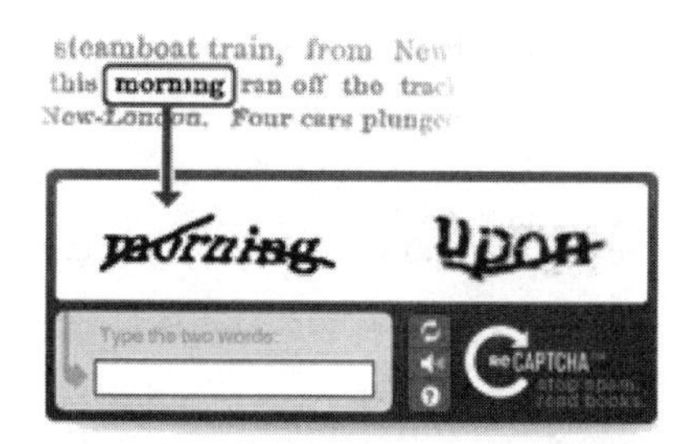

FIGURE 5-28. Dialog box of the reCaptcha plug-in

Writing Your Own Captcha

There are a few things to keep in mind while designing your own text-based Captcha system. If letters are close together, there is a high chance that two characters will be interpreted as one. Next, if nonlinear transformations are applied to a generated image, this transformation is difficult to identify on the basis of the outline of the text. Rotating or fluctuating a text string is not hard to undo automatically. More troublesome is the "fish-eye" effect applied in a few random places.

OCR usually gives several possible answers that are then checked in the dictionary, which makes it easier to choose the final text. For example when OCR recognizes a text like "thir," it assumes that it is the most probable word, "this," and not "their" or "third." That's why a completely random set of letters is much more difficult than dictionary words.

Solution

Let's proceed with implementing some Captcha protection in our forms. We will go through framework-specific solutions and those offered online. We will use a different solution for each framework because the implementation should be fairly similar regardless of framework chosen.

Symfony

In the "Customizing Forms" section of this chapter, plug-ins were used to add multiple new elements that expanded functionality of the forms. To add Captcha elements to secure your forms from unwanted web-bots, you need to install plug-ins as well. Symfony offers various Captcha plug-ins that you can install easily. Plug-ins available to install are `sfFormExtraPlugin`, `sfCaptchaGDPlugin`, `sfReCaptchaPlugin`, `gyCaptchaPlugin`, `sfPHPCaptchaPlugin`, and `sfCryptoCaptchaPlugin`. Of these plug-ins, only the first three are available for the newest Symfony version. All unavailable plug-ins are also graphical systems similar to those described in the following section.

sfWidgetFormReCaptcha

The `sfWidgetFormReCaptcha` widget is available when the sfFormExtraPlugin is installed. The sfFormExtraPlugin was used in the "Customizing Forms" section of this chapter. If you haven't read that section, you can follow these instructions.

To install sfFormExtraPlugin you simply need to type the following command into the console from your project directory:

```
symfony plugin:install sfFormExtraPlugin
```

Next it is recommended to clear cache data by typing the following command into the console:

```
symfony cache:clear
```

If you haven't done so already, you need to acquire public and private keys by registering on the reCaptcha website at `www.google.com/recaptcha`.

Now it is possible to use `sfWidgetFormReCaptcha()` and `sfValidatorReCaptcha()`in your project. You can use the `sfWidgetFormReCaptcha()` widget to render the reCaptcha form element. This will require you to add one line to an array that is used in `setWidgets()`, and the same thing needs to be done for the `setValidators()` array.

Note that `sfWidgetFormReCaptcha()` requires you to set the `public_key` value, and `sfValidatorReCaptcha()` requires the `private_key` value. The public and private keys are are those values received from the reCaptcha website.

An example of the extended form used in Chapter 4 is shown here:

```
public function setup() {
  $this->setWidgets(array(
    'id'         => new sfWidgetFormInputHidden(),
    'first_name' => new sfWidgetFormInputText(),
    'last_name'  => new sfWidgetFormInputText(),
    'email'      => new sfWidgetFormInputText(),
    'phone'      => new sfWidgetFormInputText(),
    'address'    => new sfWidgetFormInputText(),
    'created'    => new sfWidgetFormDateTime(),
    'updated'    => new sfWidgetFormDateTime(),
    'captcha'    => new sfWidgetFormReCaptcha(
            array('public_key'=>'6Ldq_QkAAAAAAKEyHHrEbMz9FkDJaxwVGi7hjh22')), ));
  $this->setValidators(array(
    'id'          => new sfValidatorDoctrineChoice(array(
                     'model' => $this->getModelName(), 'column' => 'id',
                     'required' => false)),
    'first_name'  => new sfValidatorString(array(
                     'max_length' => 40, 'required' => false)),
    'last_name'   => new sfValidatorString(array(
                     'max_length' => 40, 'required' => false)),
    'email'       => new sfValidatorString(array(
                     'max_length' => 40, 'required' => false)),
    'phone'       => new sfValidatorInteger(array('required' => false)),
    'description' => new sfValidatorPass(array('required' => false)),
    'created'     => new sfValidatorDateTime(),
    'updated'     => new sfValidatorDateTime(),
    'captcha'     => new sfValidatorReCaptcha(
         array('private_key' => '6Ldq_QkAAAAAAJ-pdmnNYWxhe7GM1apcL6YI2B1_')), ));
```

code snippet /captcha/symfony/apps/frontend/lib/form/RegistrationForm.class.php

Now you need to make sure that the newly added form element will be rendered properly. To do so, add the following code into the `_form.php` file:

```
<tr><th><?php echo $form['captcha']->renderLabel() ?></th>
    <td><?php echo $form['captcha']->renderError() ?>
        <?php echo $form['captcha'] ?></td></tr>
```

As the result of the preceding code, a web form is rendered like the one illustrated in Figure 5-29.

FIGURE 5-29. Form with the reCaptcha form element

CakePHP

There are various Captcha solutions for CakePHP that you could include in your forms, but only OpenCaptcha and reCaptcha will be shown here because they are free solutions.

OpenCaptcha

Installation of OpenCaptcha is quite easy, so let's incorporate it with one of the forms you created earlier in this chapter while upgrading your first application.

To begin, you need to dynamically create a filename (`www.opencaptcha.com/img/{random}.jpgx`) that will be displayed in the form page. The following code shows how to insert Captcha into your form. Basically it needs to be placed somewhere between the `$form->create()` and `$form->end()` functions:

```
<?php
echo $form->create('Address', array('type' => 'post', 'action' => 'add'));
echo '<fieldset><legend>New Address</legend>';
echo $form->input('first_name', array('type' => 'password')).
     $form->input('last_name', array('div' => array(
                                     'class'=>'last_name_class'))).
     $form->input('email').
     $form->input('phone').
     $form->input('address', array('rows' => '5','cols' => '5')).
     $form->input('group', array('options' => array(
                 'Work' => array('Value 1'=>'Client', 'Value 2'=>'Coworker' ),
```

```
                'Private' => array('Value 3'=>'Family', 'Value 4'=>'Friends')) )).
     $form->input('created', array('timeFormat'=>'24', 'dateFormat' => 'MDY',
                             'minYear' => date('Y') - 20, 'maxYear' => date('Y') ))
     $form->input('modified');
if( isset($opencaptcha) && $opencaptcha=='failed' ) {
   echo " <script> alert('You Did Not Fill In The Security Code Correctly');
          </script>";
}
$date = date("Ymd");
$rand = rand(0,9999999999999);
$img    = "$date$rand.jpgx";
$height = "80";
$width  = "240";
echo "<input type='hidden' name='img' value='$img'>";
echo "<img src='http://www.opencaptcha.com/img/$img'
           alt='captcha' width='240' height='80' /><br />";
echo „<input type='text' name='code' value='Enter Above Code' size='35' />";
echo'</fieldset>';
echo $form->end(‚Save address');
?>
```

code snippet /captcha/cakephp/views/addresses/add.ctp

To generate a random filename, we have used the current timestamp and a random number. And to indicate a failed verification, a JavaScript alert is generated. An example of this plug-in is shown in Figure 5-30.

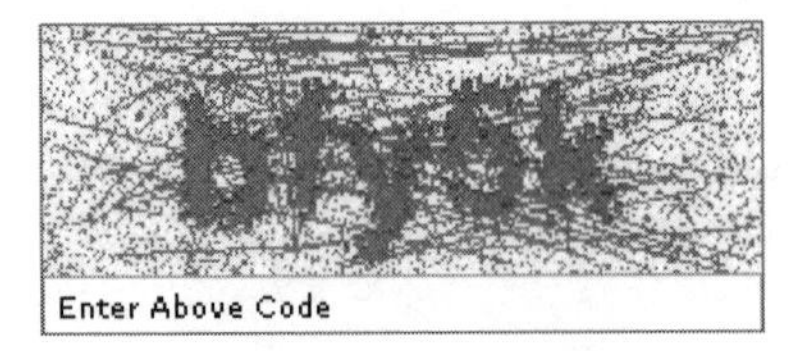

FIGURE 5-30. Dialog box of the OpenCaptcha plug-in

In the `addresses_controller.php` file, it is necessary to check whether `www.opencaptcha.com/validate.php?img={imageName}&ans={usersAnswer}` returns "`pass`" or "`fail`", as shown in the following code:

```
<?php
class AddressesController extends AppController {
  var $name = 'addresses';
  function add() {
    if (!empty($this->data) ) {
      if (file_get_contents("http://www.opencaptcha.com/validate.php?ans=".$_POST
      ['code']."&img=".$_POST['img'])=='pass' && $this->Address->save
      ($this->data) )
      {   $this->Session->setFlash('New address has been saved.');
          $this->redirect(array('action' => 'index'));
      } else { $this->set('opencaptcha', 'failed');
       $this->Session->setFlash('You Did Not Fill In The Security Code Correctly');
      }
```

```
            }
        }
    } ?>
```

code snippet /captcha/cakephp/controllers/addresses_controller.php

This should be enough to get OpenCaptcha working in our form. Alternatively, you could use the CakePHP `$this->Session->setFlash()` function to generate a message that will be displayed in case of Captcha verification failure.

reCaptcha

Earlier you learned how to include reCaptcha into your Symfony application using two different methods. In this section, you learn how to use reCaptcha in CakePHP forms.

First obtain the private and public keys as was shown in the Symfony section. Then visit the Bakery web page for CakePHP and get the reCaptcha component and helper. Those files can be found at `http://bakery.cakephp.org/articles/view/recaptcha-component-helper-for-cakephp`.

The component file should be downloaded and placed in the `/app/controllers/components/` directory and the helper file in the `/app/views/helpers/` directory.

If you have acquired both reCaptcha keys as well as the component and helper files, you can modify your controller file by adding the `$components` array and a function `beforeFilter()`, as shown in the following code:

```
class AddressesController extends AppController {
  var $name = 'addresses';
  var $components = array('Recaptcha');  //new line
  function beforeFilter() {
   $this->Recaptcha->publickey = "6Ldq_QkAAAAAAKEyHHrEbMz9FkDJaxwVGi7hjh22";
   $this->Recaptcha->privatekey = "6Ldq_QkAAAAAAJ-pdmnNYWxhe7GM1apcL6YI2B1_"; }
}
```

Next you can modify your view so that the reCaptcha element is rendered. Just call the `display_form()` method of the `$recaptcha` object in your code.

```
<?php
    echo $form->create('Address', array('type' => 'post', 'action' => 'add'));
    echo '<fieldset><legend>New Address</legend>'.
    $form->input('first_name', array('type' => 'password')).
    $form->input('last_name', array('div' => array('class'=>'last_name_class'))).
    $form->input('email').
    $form->input('phone').
    $form->input('address', array('rows' => '5', 'cols' => '5')).
    $recaptcha->display_form('echo').
    .'</fieldset>'.
    $form->end('Save address');
?>
```

The preceding example renders a form similar to the one presented in Figure 5-31. Any difference should be only in the element styles.

FIGURE 5-31. Form containing the reCaptcha element

And finally, validation should be added in a controller file, as shown in the following example:

```
function add() {
    if (!empty($this->data) ) {
        if($this->Recaptcha->valid($this->params['form'])) // recaptcha validation
        {
            $this->Address->save($this->data)
            $this->Session->setFlash('New address has been saved.');
            $this->redirect(array('action' => 'index'));
        } else {
            $this->Session->setFlash('Invalid reCaptcha code');
        }
    }
}
```

Zend Framework

In this section, you will see how to implement `Zend_Captcha` into your `Zend_Form`. Zend Framework comes with four Captcha solutions to work with: Image, Figlet, Dumb, and ReCaptcha. Three of these are available by using `Zend_Form_Element_Captcha`; the other one relies on using `Zend_Service_ReCaptcha`.

First, `Zend_Captcha_Image` will be implemented because it is probably the most common type of Captcha used throughout the Internet. It relies on a user's ability to read obscured and disfigured text from an image. To add this type of Captcha in your form, you simply need to create a new form element using the `addElement()` method the same way it was done earlier with form building. The main difference is a set of options that can be used to customize the Captcha element. This solution requires a folder that has write permission. This is where Captcha images will be generated and saved. This folder should be located in the `/public` folder. (For this example, it will be in the `./public/captcha/` folder.) The following code shows that it is possible to specify your own font used to generate the Captcha image.

```
$this->addElement('captcha', 'captchaImage', array(
    'label' => 'Enter image code:',
```

```
'captcha' => array( 'captcha' => 'Image', 'wordLen' => 6, 'timeout' => 300,
    'imgDir' => 'captcha/', 'imgUrl' => '../captcha/',
    'width' => 250, 'height' => 150,
    'font' => 'font/font.ttf', 'fontSize' => 34, ) ));
```

In addition to the standard parameters that are used to customize form elements, there is a `captcha` parameter that is associated to an option array you can modify:

- `captcha` — Specifies the type of Captcha that is used. In this case. it is `image` type Captcha.
- `wordLen` — Specifies how long the words generated in the image are.
- `timeout` — A number seconds after which image will become invalid. Here it is set to 5 minutes (300s).
- `imgDir` — A directory for storing generated images.
- `imgUrl` — Patch to generated images. It is used for display purposes.
- `width` — Width of the generated image.
- `height` — Height of the generated image.
- `font` — Patch to a font file.
- `fontSize` — Font size parameter.

The image rendered by a web browser looks like the one shown in Figure 5-32.

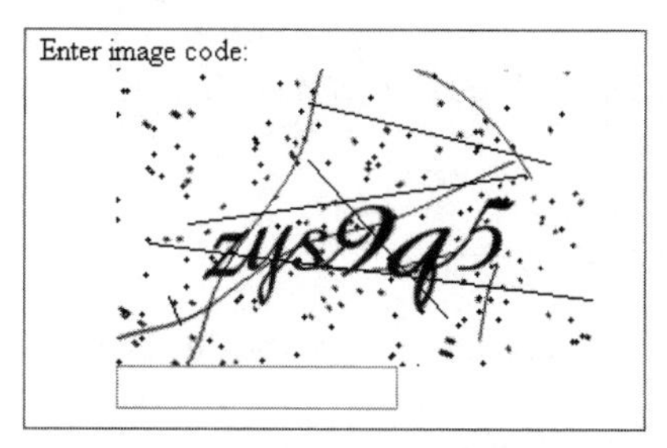

FIGURE 5-32. Form element rendered by the Zend_Captcha_Image adapter

A form element generated that way has full functionality, and no additional coding is required to verify whether a user posted a valid image code.

The second implementation is `Zend_Captcha_Figlet`, and the implementation is quite similar to the previous one. The difference is only in the number of options that are used for customization.

```
$this->addElement('captcha', 'captchaFiglet', array(
    'label' => 'Enter image code:',
    ,captcha' => array( ,captcha' => ,Figlet', ,wordLen' => 6, ,timeout' => 300,)
));
```

As you can see, the `Captcha` parameter is changed from `image` to `figlet`, and only the `wordLen` and `timeout` parameters are set. Functionality is similar to the previous example, and it requires a user to read the text from an image that is generated using only ASCII characters to form the text. Following is the HTML code that forms the text for a user to read:

```
<pre>
              ___        ______      _______     ______     ______
  _____      / _ \\      / ____//    /_     _//   / _____||   | _____||
 |     \\   | / \ ||    \\____ \\     -| ||-    / //---`'    | ||__
 | []  ||   | \_/ ||    /      //     _| ||_    \ \\____     | ||__
 |   __//    \\___//   /_____//     /______//    \\______||  |______||
 |_|`-`       `---`   `------`      `------`     `-----`     `-----`
  `-`
</pre>
```

The resulting web form rendered for this example will contain an "image" similar to the one presented in Figure 5-33.

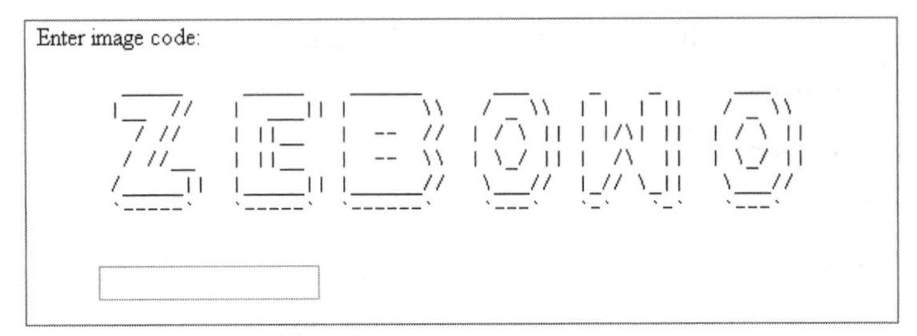

FIGURE 5-33. Form element rendered by the Zend_Captcha_Figlet adapter

Next you will see the one of the simplest Captcha elements: `Zend_Captcha_Dumb`. What it does is write random sets of letters and requires a user to write it backward into a text field. The implementation is as simple as this:

```
$this->addElement('captcha', 'captchaDumb', array(
    'captcha' => array( 'captcha' => 'Dumb', 'wordLen' => 6, 'timeout' => 300,) ));
```

No label is set in this example because the text next to the field is generated automatically. Figure 5-34 illustrates rendered `Zend_Captcha_Dumb`.

Please type this word backwards: **ukuqog**

FIGURE 5-34. Form element rendered by the Zend_Captcha_Dumb adapter

Finally `Zend_Captcha_ReCaptcha` is the reCaptcha service used to secure your forms. It requires having public and private keys that are given to registered users on the reCaptcha website.

When you have the required keys, you need to create an object for the reCaptcha Zend service, and the rest goes the same as previously:

```
$publicKey = "6Ldq_QkAAAAAAKEyHHrEbMz9FkDJaxwVGi7hjh22";
$privateKey = "6Ldq_QkAAAAAAJ-pdmnNYWxhe7GM1apcL6YI2B1_";
$recaptcha = new Zend_Service_ReCaptcha($publicKey, $privateKey);

$this->addElement('captcha', 'captchaRecaptcha', array(
    'captcha' => array( 'captcha' => 'ReCaptcha', 'service' => $recaptcha ) ));
```

Again, the value of the `captcha` parameter has been changed to `ReCaptcha`, and a new parameter defining the service is set. As a result, you will get a reCaptcha form element that looks like the one in Figure 5-35.

FIGURE 5-35. Form element rendered by the Zend_Captcha_ReCaptcha adapter

Mailing

The more technologically advanced the medium, the more primitive, trivial and useless messages are transmitted through it.

— Stanisław Lem

WHAT'S IN THIS CHAPTER?

- Sending plain text and HTML-formatted e-mail.
- Including attachments and adding carbon copies.
- Configuring SMTP servers and setting secure connections.
- Overview of the most popular mailing engines.

E-mail predates the first web pages and even the Internet itself, and compared to other web technologies, mailing has not changed much over the years. However e-mail is still the backbone of all advanced web services and the Internet could not work without it. Apart from user-to-user communication, mailing is indispensable for creating accounts, reminding users about passwords they've forgotten, sending newsletters, keeping up with newsgroups, and so on.

You can't develop web apps without mailing, and this chapter explains how to do it efficiently and effortlessly. Using the mailing engines presented here is easy and straightforward, so this chapter will be a piece of cake for you — a piece of very nutritious cake, in fact, taking into account how many beneficial uses of mailing there are.

CREATING MAILING APPLICATIONS

Developers need to make sure that e-mail is automated and works as designed. Most of the commonly encountered problems are associated with the following:

- Establishing connections
- Sending HTML-formatted e-mail
- Sending e-mail to multiple receivers
- Carbon copies

All these problems can be easily solved with mailers. Mailers are ready-to-use solutions that are included within web application frameworks or separate modules that can be added to a web framework.

Mailing Approaches and Web Servers

One of the biggest nuisances of web development is when you deploy your application on a hosting server and your mailing module stops working. This often happens because of configuration issues. One hosting server may work fine with mailing enabled in the PHP configuration and a properly configured mail server such as Sendmail or Postfix, but others may have the mailing server disabled. In most cases, you cannot force the administrators to configure the server and enable mailing. They don't want to do that, mostly for security reasons — which is a good point by the way. Unfortunately it's not a good point for you because you need to do more work on your side in this case.

The more complete details of the e-mail-sending process are beyond the scope of this chapter, but in general it looks like Figure 6-1.

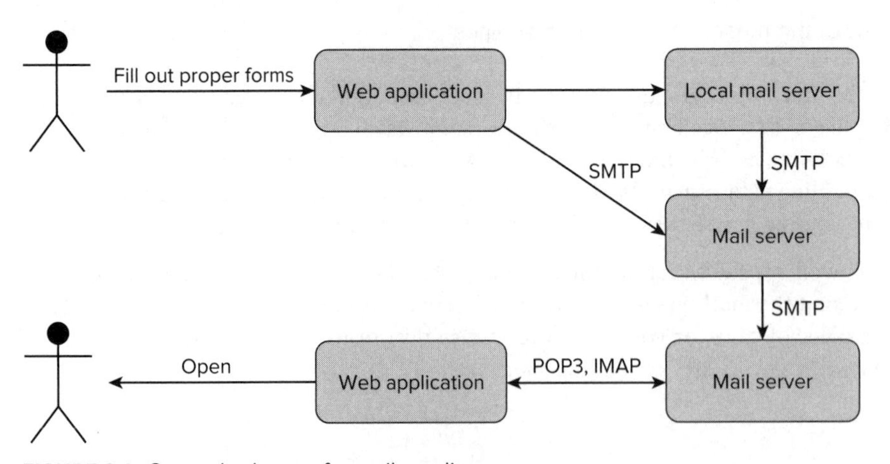

FIGURE 6-1: General schema of e-mail sending

After you create the e-mail's content and click the Send button, all data is collected from the text fields and sent either to a remote mail server or a local mail server if you have an e-mail server where the application is deployed.

In most cases, a remote SMTP server is used, even when it's on the same machine (it's not really remote, but it's treated as such).

Connecting to a remote mail server has some advantages. In almost all cases, this kind of connection requires a username and password because of the authentication process. While you are authenticated, your e-mail can be sent to any other mail server without being treated as spam. After the e-mail is sent from the remote mail server, it moves through the SMTP protocol to the destination mail server and can be read by the recipient through a web application or it can be requested by the recipient through the POP3/IMAP protocol.

PHP Configuration

The `php.ini` file is used to configure PHP settings. It is placed in the `/etc/php5/apache2/` directory under UNIX systems and in the `C:\xampp\php\` under Windows if you use XAMPP. Important parts of this file are shown in Figures 6-2 and 6-3.

safe_mode_include_dir	no value	no value
sendmail_from	no value	no value
sendmail_path	no value	no value
serialize_precision	100	100
short_open_tag	Off	Off
SMTP	localhost	localhost
smtp_port	25	25

FIGURE 6-2: PHP's php.ini configuration file represented through the phpinfo() function

You can set the default SMTP hostname, SMTP port, and Sendmail's *path* and *from* values. You can also configure some mail-specific issues such as creating headers or a log file.

mail.add_x_header	Off	Off
mail.force_extra_parameters	no value	no value
mail.log	no value	no value
max_execution_time	60	60

FIGURE 6-3: PHP's php.ini configuration file represented through the phpinfo() function

After editing `php.ini`, you should have something similar to these values:

```
[mail function]
SMTP = localhost
smtp_port = 25
;sendmail_from = me@example.com
;sendmail_path =
;mail.force_extra_parameters =
mail.add_x_header = On
;mail.log =
```

To apply an entry, you need to remove the semicolon that comments it out.

SMTP Server Configuration

Sendmail, like almost all leading mail servers, is available both for UNIX and Windows systems.

UNIX

To install Sendmail, you can use a package manager like Sendmail:

```
# apt-get install sendmail
```

Now, you should configure Sendmail by executing the following command with root privileges:

```
# sendmailconfig
```

You can now easily send an e-mail from the command line. Create a file called `mail.txt` and fill it with some text.

```
$ touch mail.txt
$ echo "Test mail" > mail.txt
$ mail -s "Hello world" john@wroxexample.com < mail.txt
```

At the end, you need to execute the `mail` command, as shown previously. Replace the example e-mail with your own text, send it, and check your mailbox. Probably it will be delivered but filtered as spam, so search your spam inbox as well.

Windows

This may come as a surprise, but despite the fact that Sendmail is a UNIX application, it is delivered within XAMPP for Windows, so if you followed XAMPP installation in Chapter 2, you don't have to install anything else. The file structure of Sendmail for Windows is presented below.

```
c:\xampp\sendmail\
    libeay32.dll
    sendmail.exe
    sendmail.ini
    ssleay32.dll
```

Sendmail is also used by PHP under Windows to send e-mail.

SWIFTMAILER

SwiftMailer is available not only as part of Symfony, but also as a separate application (see Figure 6-4). It is available for every framework considered in this book.

FIGURE 6-4: SwiftMailer logo

Symfony

SwiftMailer is Symfony's default mailer and is included within framework libraries, so you don't need to install any additional libraries. The code snippets in this section can be put wherever you like into the controllers' actions.

Sending Simple E-mail

You can employ SwiftMailer in Symfony by invoking the `getMailer()` method as shown here:

```
$mailer = $this->getMailer();
```

Creating and sending simple e-mail can be easily done using one method only: `composeAndSend()`, as shown in the following code. This is very useful when you are developing a big application in which the mailing code is not really the important part, but you need to close some functionalities that depend on sending e-mail.

FIGURE 6-5: Symfony debug toolbar

```
$mailer->composeAndSend(
        'example@wroxexample.com',
        'example@wroxexample.com',
        'Hello World!!!!',
        'John Smith'
);
```

After executing this code through a browser, you should be able to see in the right corner of the debug toolbar an envelope with the count of sent e-mail (see Figure 6-5).

When you click the envelope, you should see details of each e-mail on the left (see Figure 6-6).

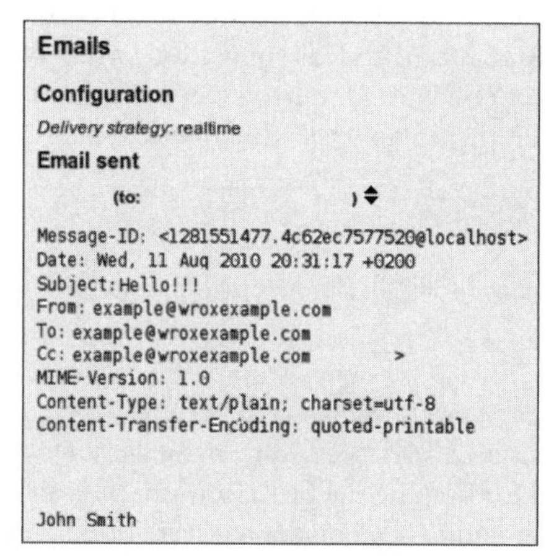

FIGURE 6-6: E-mail details toolbar

Sending HTML E-mail

You can send not only plain text e-mail but also HTML-formatted messages. You may specify what kind of e-mail you want to send with the `setBody()` method. It gets two parameters: message body (content) and message type. In the following example, an HTML message is sent:

```
$message = Swift_Message::newInstance('Hello World Subject!', 'foobar message');
$message->setBody('foobar <p style="font-weight: bold;">message</p>', 'text/html');
$this->getMailer()->send($message);
```

Additionally you can use Symfony's partial files for the message body. To get partial content, you should use the `getPartial()` method. As the second parameter, you send an array with key variables and their assigned values.

```
$message = Swift_Message::newInstance('Hello World Subject!', 'foobar message');
$htmlBody = $this->getPartial('activation',array('name'=>'John Smith'));
$message->setBody($htmlBody,'text/html');
$this->getMailer()->send($message);
```

To run this example, you need to create a partial file that should be saved as `_activation.php` in `/modules/<example>/templates/` directory. Note that you replace *`<example>`* with your module name. The partial file's content can look like this:

```
Hello World!
<?php echo $name; ?>
```

Adding Attachments

The *`Swift_Attachment`* class is responsible for creating attachments in SwiftMailer. Attachments can be added in two major ways:

- Using the path to an existing file
- Dynamically

Depending on your business strategy and application architecture, you can store attachment files directly under a file system path or in a database. When you store attachments just as files, you can attach them using the `fromPath()` method and the file's path. An example e-mail code is shown following. Note that you can also set a proper content-type value. This is not obligatory, and you can omit this parameter, but it can be helpful for some e-mail clients to let them know the attachment type.

```
$message = Swift_Message::newInstance('Hello World Subject!', 'foobar message');
$message->setFrom('producer@wroxexample.com');
$message->setTo('example@wroxexample.com');
$attachment = Swift_Attachment::fromPath('C:\funny.jpg', 'image/jpeg');
$message->attach($attachment);
$this->getMailer()->send($message);
```

To hide files from public, sometimes they are kept with strange names such as `frt4754fehrt954643g-fwe0.jpg`. Such names are very hard to guess, so they cannot be easily accessed from outside. This approach can't be called real security, but proves to be good for keeping the files out of the view of general public. In this case, you can set another filename that will be seen by the receiver. To do that, you should use the `setFilename()` method as follows:

```
$message = Swift_Message::newInstance('Hello World Subject!', 'foobar message');
$message->setFrom('producer@wroxexample.com');
$message->setTo('example@wroxexample.com');
$attachment = Swift_Attachment::fromPath(
  'C:\xampp\public_html\cake\app\webroot\attach\frt4754fehrt954643gfwe0.jpg')
  ->setFilename('funny.jpg');
$message->attach($attachment);
$this->getMailer()->send($message);
```

However, most developers keep files in databases, especially when attachments are dynamic and change very often, or if they differ for each e-mail. You can easily attach a file that was saved before in a database. Assume that your `Attachments` table structure looks as follows:

```
field name      type
id              int(3) primary key auto_increment
fileName        varchar(32)
content         BLOB
```

You can get attachment's content using Doctrine, as shown in the following code:

```
$attachData = Doctrine_Core::getTable('Attachments')->find(1);
$data=$attachData->getContent();
$fileName=$attachData->getFileName();
$message = Swift_Message::newInstance('Hello World Subject!', 'foobar message');
$message->setFrom('producer@wroxexample.com');
$message->setTo('example@wroxexample.com');
$attachment = Swift_Attachment::newInstance($data, $fileName);
$message->attach($attachment);
$this->getMailer()->send($message);
```

That's really easy to implement.

Carbon Copy

Adding more than one recipient can be done in few ways. The simplest way is to add more recipients in the TO field as follows:

```
$message = Swift_Message::newInstance('Hello World Subject!', 'foobar message');
$message->setFrom('producer@wroxexample.com');
$message->setTo(array('example@wroxexample.com','john@wroxexample.com'));
$this->getMailer()->send($message);
```

In some cases this solution is not the proper one. That's why carbon copies (CC) and blind carbon copies (BCC) were invented. You can add carbon copies using the `addCc()` method of the `Swift_Message` object.

```
$message = Swift_Message::newInstance('Hello World Subject!', 'foobar message');
$message->setFrom('producer@wroxexample.com');
$message->setTo('example@wroxexample.com');
$message->addCc('boss@wroxexample.com', 'John Kowalski');
$this->getMailer()->send($message);
```

Adding blind carbon copies is similar to adding carbon copies.

```
$message = Swift_Message::newInstance('Hello World Subject!', 'foobar message');
$message->setFrom('producer@wroxexample.com');
$message->setTo('example@wroxexample.com');
$message->setBcc(array(
    'pm@wroxexample.com',
    'boss@wroxexample.com' => 'John Kowalski',
));
$this->getMailer()->send($message);
```

Both in CC and BCC, you can apply more than one recipient, as shown previously.

Remote SMTP Servers

SwiftMailer is integrated with Symfony. Therefore, you can configure an SMTP connection in application configuration files. By editing the `factories.yml` file in an application's `/config` directory, you can add some configuration entries dedicated to Symfony's default mailer. You can enable or disable logging for SwiftMailer, and set default charset and delivery options. But most interesting are the SMTP configuration entries. You can set `user`, `password`, `host name` and `port` for all sent e-mail. So you don't need to set it anywhere else when sending e-mail. Exemplary SwiftMailer entries for all environments can be set as follows:

```
all:
  routing:
    class: sfPatternRouting
    param:
      generate_shortest_url:            true
      extra_parameters_as_query_string: true
  view_cache_manager:
    class: sfViewCacheManager
    param:
      cache_key_use_vary_headers: true
      cache_key_use_host_name:    true
  mailer:
    class: sfMailer
    param:
      logging:           %SF_LOGGING_ENABLED%
      charset:           %SF_CHARSET%
      delivery_strategy: realtime
      transport:
        class: Swift_SmtpTransport
        param:
          host:       localhost
          port:       25
          encryption: ~
          username:  ~
          password:  ~
```

Secure Connections

Because nonsecure connections (shown in the preceding code snippet) are very rarely used, you will most likely be using secure connections. You can easily change the configuration according to your needs. For example, for a secure connection, the configuration entries could be as follows:

```
all:
  routing:
    class: sfPatternRouting
    param:
      generate_shortest_url:            true
      extra_parameters_as_query_string: true
  view_cache_manager:
    class: sfViewCacheManager
    param:
      cache_key_use_vary_headers: true
      cache_key_use_host_name:    true
  mailer:
    class: sfMailer
    param:
      logging:           %SF_LOGGING_ENABLED%
      charset:           %SF_CHARSET%
```

```
delivery_strategy: realtime
transport:
  class: Swift_SmtpTransport
  param:
    host:       smtp.gmail.com
    port:       465
    encryption: ssl
    username:  wroxexample@gmail.com
    password:  wroxexample123
```

See Chapter 8 to read more about the differences between secured and nonsecured connections.

In some situations, one global configuration for all sent e-mail is not a good solution. Let's assume that you use a few accounts on different SMTP servers. In this case, it's better to use `Swift_SmtpTransport` to define connection parameters for each e-mail module, as follows:

```
$transport = Swift_SmtpTransport::newInstance('smtp.example.org', 25)
->setUsername('your username')
->setPassword('your password');
```

Next you need to send the authentication data to `Swift_Mailer` as a parameter:

```
$mailer = Swift_Mailer::newInstance($transport);
```

You can also define a secure connection with the same effect as described previously:

```
$transport = Swift_SmtpTransport::newInstance('smtp.example.org', 465, 'ssl');
```

All in One

To summarize, the following code shows a registration module example in which all previously described features are presented.

```
<?php
class RegistrationActions extends sfActions {
    public function executeRegister() {
           $transport = Swift_SmtpTransport::newInstance('smtp.gmail.com', 465, 'ssl')
           ->setUsername('wroxexampleregistration@gmail.com')
           ->setPassword('wroxexample123');
      $mailer = Swift_Mailer::newInstance($transport);
      $message = Swift_Message::newInstance('Hello World Subject!', 'foobar
message');
      $message->setFrom('wroxexampleregistration@gmail.com');
      $message->setTo('example@wroxexample.com');
      $message->setCc(array(
                          'admin@wroxexample.com' => 'John Kowalski',
      ));
     $attachment = Swift_Attachment::fromPath(
       '/home/wrox/public_html/symfony/web/attachments/subscription_pack.zip',
       'application/zip');
```

```
            $message->attach($attachment);
            $mailer->send($message);
        }
    }
```

code snippet /swiftmailer/symfony/app/frontend/modules/registration/actions/actions.class.php

CakePHP

SwiftMailer is not integrated with CakePHP the way it is in Symfony. That's why you need to use SwiftMailer through CakePHP's `/vendor` library path. You can download SwifMailer files from `http://swiftmailer.org/download`. After extraction, your directory structure should be as follows:

```
app/vendors/swift_mailer/
        CHANGES
        lib/
            classes/
            dependency_maps/
            mime_types.php
            preferences.php
            swift_init.php
            swift_required_pear.php
            swift_required.php
       tests/
       test-suite/
       LICENSE
       README
       VERSION
```

Now you can use the SwiftMailer library by importing it within the controller. The missing mailing code will be shown later in this section.

```
<?php
App::import('Vendor', 'Swift', array('file' =>
'swift_mailer'.DS.'lib'.DS.'swift_required.php'));
class RegistrationController extends AppController {
    var $name = 'registration';
    function send() {
        /* mailing code */
    }
}
?>
```

Sending Simple E-mail

After you import SwiftMailer, you can send e-mail as you can in Symfony. The only difference is that you need to set transport parameters through `Swift_SmtpTransport` every time you use SwiftMailer. The following code shows sending an e-mail with SwitfMailer via Gmail.

```
$transport = Swift_SmtpTransport::newInstance('smtp.gmail.com', 465, 'ssl')
                ->setUsername('wroxexample@gmail.com')
                ->setPassword('wroxexample123');
$mailer = Swift_Mailer::newInstance($transport);
```

```
$message = Swift_Message::newInstance('Cake SwiftMailer','Hello World!');
$message->setFrom('wroxexample@gmail.com');
$message->setTo('example@wroxexample.com');
$mailer->send($message);
```

Sending HTML E-mail

You can easily add message content using the `setBody()` method. But what about message templates? Can they be made as shown in Symfony using partials? Template loading is possible with CakePHP's `View` class.

```
$viewPath='email';
$type='html';
$viewName='registration';
$view = new View($this);
$view->layout=$this->layout;
$content=$view->element($viewPath.DS.$type.DS.$viewName, array('name' => "John
Smith"), true);
$htmlBody= $view->renderLayout($content);
```

Note that in the preceding example you get a page with the layout used by the current controller as the `$htmlBody` variable. To see any results, you need to create a `registration.phtml` template element, which should be placed in the `/app/views/elements/email/html/` directory. If you print the `$htmlBody` content with the `echo` command, you will see something similar to Figure 6-7.

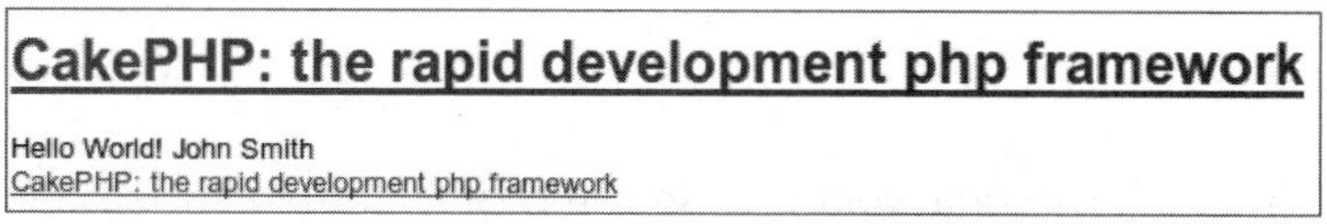

FIGURE 6-7: CakePHP SwiftMailer–delivered mail content

Your `registration.ctp` should be as follows:

```
Hello World!
<?php echo $name; ?>
```

The output shown in Figure 6-7 is probably not exactly the one you expected. This is because the default layout was used. To replace the default layout, you need to assign the layout's name to the `$this->layout` variable instead of assigning the current layout, which is by default the default layout. For example if you set the layout as follows:

```
$this->layout='mailing';
```

then you should also create `mailing.ctp` in the `/app/views/layouts/` directory with the following content:

```
<?php echo $content_for_layout; ?>
```

The preceding layout has only one line, which includes the template's content. It works in the same way as it does in a usual application. After merging, your code should look like the following:

```
$viewPath='email';
$type='html';
$viewName='registration';
$view = new View($this);
```

```
$view->layout=$this->layout;
$content=$view->element($viewPath.DS.$type.DS.$viewName,
  array('name' => "John Smith"), true);
$htmlBody= $view->renderLayout($content);
$transport = Swift_SmtpTransport::newInstance('smtp.gmail.com', 465, 'ssl')
                ->setUsername('wroxexample@gmail.com')
                ->setPassword('wroxexample123');
$mailer = Swift_Mailer::newInstance($transport);
$message = Swift_Message::newInstance();
$message->setSubject('swiftExample');
$message->setFrom('wroxexample@gmail.com');
$message->setTo('example@wroxexample.com');
$message->setCc(array('admin@wroxexample.com' => 'John Kowalski',));
$message->setBody($htmlBody,'text/html');
$mailer->send($message);
```

Note that it is a good practice to keep HTML and plain e-mail in separate folders in the `elements/email/` directory.

```
views/elements/email/html/
views/elements/email/text/
```

Adding Attachments, Carbon Copy, and SMTP Connection

These are done exactly as described in the "Symfony" section earlier in this chapter, so it will not be covered again here.

All in One

When you merge all code described in this section, your code should be similar to following code.

```
<?php
App::import('Vendor', 'Swift', array('file' =>
'swift_mailer'.DS.'lib'.DS.'swift_required.php'));
class RegistrationController extends AppController {
    var $name = 'registration';
    function send() {
        $transport = Swift_SmtpTransport::newInstance('smtp.gmail.com', 465, 'ssl')
                ->setUsername('wroxexample@gmail.com')
                ->setPassword('wroxexample123');
        $mailer = Swift_Mailer::newInstance($transport);
        $message = Swift_Message::newInstance();
        $message->setSubject('swiftExample');
        $message->setFrom('wroxexample@gmail.com');
        $message->setTo('example@wroxexample.com');
        $message->setCc(array('admin@wroxexample.com' => 'John Kowalski',));
        $viewPath='email';
        $type='html';
        $viewName='registration';
        $view = new View($this);
        $view->layout=$this->layout;
        $content=$view->element($viewPath.DS.$type.DS.$viewName,
          array('name' => "John Smith"), true);
        $htmlBody= $view->renderLayout($content);
        $message->setBody($htmlBody,'text/html');
```

```
            $attachment = Swift_Attachment::fromPath(
              '/home/wrox/public_html/symfony/web/attachments/subscription_pack.zip',
              'application/zip');
            $message->attach($attachment);
            $mailer->send($message);
        }
    }
    ?>
```

code snippet /swiftmailer/cakephp/app/controllers/registration_controller.php

Note that you also need to create proper template files and attachments to make this example runnable.

Zend Framework

Using SwiftMailer in Zend Framework is done the same way as in CakePHP. You need to unpack SwiftMailer into your project's `/library` path. Your directory structure should look as follows:

```
library/swiftmailer/
    CHANGES
    lib/
        classes/
        dependency_maps/
        mime_types.php
        preferences.php
        swift_init.php
        swift_required_pear.php
        swift_required.php
    tests/
    test-suite/
    LICENSE
    README
    VERSION
```

You can now add the SwiftMailer library:

```
<?php
require_once('swiftmailer/lib/swift_required.php');
class RegistrationController extends Zend_Controller_Action {
}
```

Sending Simple E-mail

The rest of the code within the controller is almost the same as in Symfony and CakePHP.

```
        $mailer = Swift_Mailer::newInstance($transport);
        $message = Swift_Message::newInstance();
        $message->setSubject('swiftExample');
        $message->setFrom('wroxexample@gmail.com');
        $message->setTo('example@wroxexample.com');
        $message->setBody("Hello World",'text/plain');
        $mailer->send($message);
```

The only difference, explained in the following section, is in getting the view template because it depends on the framework's architecture and libraries.

Sending HTML E-mail

To get a template and send it as an HTML e-mail, you need to use `Zend_View` class.

```
$view = new Zend_View();
$view->addScriptPath(APPLICATION_PATH . '/application/views/scripts/email/');
$view->assign('name','John Smith');
$htmlBody = $view ->render(registration.phtml');
$mail->setBody($htmlBody,'text/html');
```

Your template should be saved as `/application/views/scripts/email/registration.phtml` and can look as follows:

```
Hello World! <br />
<?php echo $this->name; ?>
```

Note that the *`APPLICATION_PATH`* variable is defined in `/application/public/index.php`.

```
<?php
defined('APPLICATION_PATH')
    || define('APPLICATION_PATH', realpath(dirname(__FILE__) . '/../application'));
```

All in One

Your merged efforts will result in following code.

Available for download on Wrox.com

```
<?php
require_once('swiftmailer/lib/swift_required.php');
class RegistrationController extends Zend_Controller_Action {
    function send() {
        $transport = Swift_SmtpTransport::newInstance('smtp.gmail.com', 465, 'ssl')
                ->setUsername('wroxexample@gmail.com')
                ->setPassword('wroxexample123');
        $mailer = Swift_Mailer::newInstance($transport);
        $message = Swift_Message::newInstance();
        $message->setSubject('swiftExample');
        $message->setFrom('wroxexample@gmail.com');
        $message->setTo('example@wroxexample.com');
        $message->setCc(array(
                                'admin@wroxexample.com' => 'John Kowalski',
        ));
        $view = new Zend_View();
        $view->addScriptPath(APPLICATION_PATH .
 '/application/views/scripts/email/');
        $view->assign('name','John Smith');
        $htmlBody = $view ->render(registration.phtml');
        $message->setBody($htmlBody,'text/html');
        $attachment = Swift_Attachment::fromPath(
          '/home/wrox/public_html/symfony/web/attachments/subscription_pack.zip',
          'application/zip');
        $message->attach($attachment);
```

```
            $mailer->send($message);
        }
    }
    ?>
```

code snippet /swiftmailer/zf/application/controllers/RegistrationController.php

CAKEPHP'S MAILING COMPONENT

CakePHP delivers within itself a ready-for-use mailing component. You can find it in the `/cake/libs/controller/components` directory. The component filename is very meaningful because it's called `email.php`. You can check it for default variables like the following:

```
var $replyTo = null;
```

You can change this variable if there is an address that is usually used.

To add this component to a controller to work with, you need to add the component name to the `$components` variable. Let's create an exemplary controller (`MailController`) with one method: `sendEmail()`. Your code should look like the following:

```
<?php
class MailController extends AppController {
    var $components = array('Email');
    var $uses = '';
    function sendEmail() {
    }
}
```

The bold line demonstrates how you can add components in CakePHP. Assume that the `sendEmail()` action is invoked every time when you want to send an e-mail with a fixed content. You can modify it to make the content dynamic, but to simplify the problem we will use fixed values such as subject, message, and so on.

Sending Simple E-mail

To begin this example, we want to send a simple e-mail with "Hello World!" as the message. You can do it by accessing the `Email` component's methods and variables through `$this->Email`. The code that sends a plain text e-mail should look like the following:

```
$this->Email->to = 'john.smith@localhost';
$this->Email->subject = 'Just want to say Hi';
$this->Email->replyTo = 'noreply@wrox.com';
$this->Email->from = 'Example <noreply@wrox.com>';
$this->Email->send('Hello World!');
```

This piece of code sends an e-mail. The parameter given to the `send()` method is the body of the message. It's useful only when we want to send short messages, but what if we want to do more? We can define a variable where we can hold a bigger message. In CakePHP, there is also a different approach available. We can use layouts to send messages, which is an advantage of CakePHP. This feature facilitates working with e-mail because you can work only with code and then someone else prepares the e-mail layouts. To make it possible, we need to create an `/email` directory in the view's `/layouts` directory. We should also separate plain text and HTML layout directories, so the default text layout path will be `/views/layouts/email/text/default.ctp`. To make it possible to assign a layout as the message of an e-mail, you need to assign it as a template. You can do it with the following line:

```
$this->Email->template = 'default';
```

The content of `default.ctp` could be as follows:

```
Hello World!
```

Note that you don't add the `.ctp` extension to the template name. The line adding the template needs to be placed before the `send()` method is invoked. As mentioned before, we can send an e-mail in multiple formats. To mark a concrete format, we need to assign it to the `sendAs` variable like this:

```
$this->Email->sendAs = 'text';
```

As the default value, text is used here. So the prepared e-mail will be sent as a text with message defined within the `detault.ctp` file. Note that if you set a template to be the message within the `Email` object, you don't need to set it as a parameter of the `send()` method.

Sending HTML E-mail

Usually you want to produce HTML-formatted e-mail because they look much better and almost all e-mail clients (web or standalone applications) can interpret them. The CakePHP mailer component supports HTML e-mail. As with plain text e-mail, we need to create a template layout. This time, you need to place `default.ctp` in the `/views/layouts/email/html/` directory. Also in this case you need to point to the template that should be used.

```
$this->Email->template = 'default';
```

Note that you can create more than one template and assign only the one that is now needed.

To have this e-mail sent as HTML, we need to assign the proper mail format:

```
$this->Email->sendAs = 'html';
```

Because sometimes only one format can be interpreted by an e-mail client, we can send e-mail in both formats, so in worst case the client can read plain text. When you send both formats, the client can skip one of them and read the preferred one. To send both formats you need to set both values as below:

```
$this->Email->sendAs = 'both';
```

You will use mailing probably more often with dynamic data than with static data. To use information generated with templates, you need to use the `set()` method to assign some data to a variable, which is next sent to the template. An example of this may be the following:

```
$this->set('name', 'John Smith');
```

And now your template can look like this:

```
<p>Hello World!</p>
Regards,
<?php echo $name; ?>
```

Using e-mail templates allows you to separate the presentation layer from the core mailing and thus maintain an organized structure of business logic. You can create generic messages and store all mailing code in one place, conforming to the DRY principle.

Adding Attachments

Adding attachments in the CakePHP e-mail component can be a little annoying. You first need to set the path or paths where attachments are placed. Next, the filename of the attachment or multiple attachments needs to be given. Example code could look like this:

```
$this->Email->filePaths=array(getcwd().'/');
$this->Email->attachments = array('foo.doc');
```

Note that this approach makes it impossible to include an attachment directly from a database, so it must have been saved previously and accessible by a file system path. In the preceding code, we added the `getcwd()` method, which returns the current path for the attachments. You may need to change it to your path for the attachments.

Carbon Copy

There are two ways to add a copy of a message for someone else: through carbon copy (CC) or blind carbon copy (BCC). The difference between them is the visibility. When you use CC, the copy receiver is visible to the original recipient. Addresses from the BCC list are not visible to the recipient nor to anyone else who is copied on the message. In CakePHP's mailer, you can use these copies this way:

```
$this->Email->cc=array('foo@bar.com');
$this->Email->bcc=array(''foo@bar.com');
```

You can add more than one e-mail in CC and/or BCC arrays.

Remote SMTP Servers

As described earlier in this chapter, in many cases we need to use a remote SMTP server to send e-mail. You need to provide a username and password with which you sign in. A hostname and SMTP port number are also required. An unsecure SMTP server port number is set by default to `25`. In CakePHP, you need to set all these parameters as `smtpOptions` in the following way:

```
$this->Email->smtpOptions = array(
    'port'=>'25',
    'timeout'=>'30',
    'host' => 'smtp.wroxexample.com',
    'username'=>'john.smith@wroxexample.com',
    'password'=>'secretPassword123'
);
$this->Email->delivery = 'smtp';
$this->Email->send();
```

Additionally you need to change the delivery mode to `smtp` because by default it's set to `mail`. Note that everything, including SMTP options, need to be set before `Email`'s `send()` method is used. If you have some problems with this option, you can check `smtpError` where all errors are stored. You can access this variable as follows:

```
$this->Email->smtpError;
```

Remember that unlike previous variables, you should use it after the `send()` method is invoked.

Secure Connections

In most cases, you should use secure connections. For a secure SMTP connection through SSL/TLS, port `465` is reserved. A secure connection in CakePHP's e-mail component looks like this:

```
$this->Email->smtpOptions = array(
    'port'=>'465',
    'timeout'=>'30',
    'host' => 'ssl://smtp.gmail.com',
    'username'=>'wroxexample@gmail.com',
    'password'=>'secretPassword123',
);
```

In this example, Gmail's SMTP server was used.

All in One

To summarize, a full example is presented below. Assume that your attachment is placed in `/home/wrox/public_html/cake/app/webroot/attachments/schedule.doc`. Additionally, you need to create two e-mail templates that should be placed in `/home/wrox/public_html/cake/app/views/layouts/email/html/schedule.ctp` and `/home/wrox/public_html/cake/app/views/layouts/email/text/schedule.ctp`. In Windows, equivalent paths to attachment and e-mail templates would be `C:\xampp\htdocs\cake\app\webroot\attachments\schedule.doc`, `C:\xampp\htdocs\cake\app\views\layouts\email\html\schedule.ctp` and `C:\xampp\htdocs\cake\app\views\layouts\email\text\schedule.ctp`.

Available for download on Wrox.com

```
<?php
class MailController extends AppController {
    var $components = array('Email');
    var $uses = '';
    function sendEmail() {
        $this->Email->to = 'john.smith@localhost';
        $this->Email->subject = 'Schedule';
        $this->Email->replyTo = 'hr@wroxexample.com';
        $this->Email->from = 'Example <noreply@wroxexample.com>';
        $this->Email->filePaths =
          array('/home/wrox/public_html/cake/app/webroot/attachments/');
        $this->Email->attachments = array('schedule.doc');
        $this->Email->cc=array('pm@wroxexample.com');
        $this->Email->template = 'schedule';
        $this->Email->sendAs = 'both';
```

```
            $this->Email->smtpOptions = array(
                'port'=>'465',
                'timeout'=>'30',
                'host' => 'ssl://smtp.wroxexample.com',
                'username'=>'mailing-list@wroxexample.com',
                'password'=>'secretPassword123',
            );
            $this->Email->send();
        }
    }
```

code snippet /cakeMailer/cakephp/app/controllers/mail_controller.php

Such a prepared mailer will work if you change SMTP options to those that are relevant to you. If you want to send e-mail one by one, you should use the `reset()` method.

```
$this->Email->send();
```

This method resets all variables to default values, which can prevent mistakes.

ZEND MAILER

Zend mailer is located in `C:\xampp\php\Zend\Mail.php` or `/usr/share/php/Zend/Mail.php` under UNIX. You can view all methods and variables at `http://framework.zend.com/apidoc/1.10/Zend_Mail/Zend_Mail.html`. An example controller could be like this:

```
<?php
class MailingController extends Zend_Controller_Action {
    public function sendMail() {
    }
}
?>
```

The `sendMail()` method in our example is invoked when you want to send an e-mail.

Sending Simple E-mail

To send a simple e-mail, you need to fill in the `sendMail()` method with the following code:

```
$mail = new Zend_Mail();
$mail->setBodyText('Hello World!');
$mail->setFrom('noreply@wrox.com', 'Example');
$mail->addTo(john.smith@localhost', 'John Smith');
$mail->setSubject('Just want to say Hi');
$mail->send();
```

This code gives almost the same result as in CakePHP's mailer component. The only difference between these two solutions is that in Cake you assigned data through variables, whereas in Zend you use methods to complete all mail information.

Sending HTML E-mail

Zend's approach is not as comfortable as CakePHP's. You cannot use e-mail templates as easily as in CakePHP. Usually you will also need another method for sending an HTML-formatted e-mail:

```
$mail = new Zend_Mail();
$mail->setBodyText('Hello World!');
$mail->setBodyHtml('<div class="text-weight: bold;">Hello World!</div>');
$mail->setFrom('noreply@wrox.com', 'Example');
$mail->addTo(john.smith@localhost', 'John Smith');
$mail->setSubject('Just want to say Hi');
$mail->send();
```

But not-so-easy doesn't equal impossible. Assigning a proper view template content to a variable can be done by using `Zend_View`.

```
$htmlTemplate = new Zend_View();
$htmlTemplate->addScriptPath(APPLICATION_PATH.'/views/scripts/email/');
$htmlTemplate->assign('name','Administrator');
$html_body = $htmlTemplate ->render('test.phtml');
```

After adding the rest of the mailing code, your code should be as follows:

```
$view = new Zend_View();
$view->addScriptPath(APPLICATION_PATH . '/application/views/scripts/email/');
$view->assign('name','John Smith');
$htmlBody = $view ->render(email.phtml');
$mail = new Zend_Mail();
$mail->setBodyHtml($htmlBody);
$mail->setFrom('wroxexample@gmail.co', 'Example');
$mail->addTo('kprzystalski@gmail.com', 'Karol');
$mail->setSubject('Just want to say Hi');
$mail->send();
```

You should also create a view template that should be saved as `email.phtml` in the `/application/views/scripts/email/` directory.

```
<p>Hello World!</p>
Regards,
<?php echo $name; ?>
```

Adding Attachments

The easiest way to attach a file within a mail with `Zend_Mail` is to get the file content and send it as the parameter to the `Zend_Mail createAttachment()` method. To get the content from any file, you can use the PHP `file_get_contents()` function.

```
$fileContents = file_get_contents('schedule.doc');
```

Because you get only the content of the file, you should also set the filename that will be shown. You can also provide a file type.

```
$mail = new Zend_Mail();
$mail->setBodyText('Hello World!');
$mail->setFrom('noreply@wrox.com', 'Example');
```

```
$mail->addTo(john.smith@localhost', 'John Smith');
$mail->setSubject('Just want to say Hi');
$fileContents = file_get_contents('schedule.doc');
$attachment = $mail->createAttachment($fileContents);
$attachment->filename='schedule.doc';
$attachment->type='application/msword';
$mail->send();
```

Carbon Copy

Adding more recipients is as easy as in CakePHP's mailing component: Just use the `addCc()` or `addBcc()` methods.

```
$mail = new Zend_Mail();
$mail->setBodyText('Hello World!');
$mail->setFrom('noreply@wrox.com', 'Example');
$mail->addTo(john.smith@localhost', 'John Smith');
$mail->setSubject('Just want to say Hi');
$mail->addCc('john@wroxexample.com', 'John Smith');
$mail->addBcc('topsecret@wroxexample.com', 'Top Secret Recipient');
$mail->send();
```

You can add more than one recipient in CC/BCC by invoking the `addCc()` or `addBcc()` method again. This is a good approach when getting e-mail from a database in an iterative way.

Remote SMTP Servers

You will probably send e-mail through remote servers. In `Zend_Mail` you need to define an array for configuration with expected keys: `auth`, `username`, and `password`. This array should be sent as the second parameter when initializing a `Zend_Mail_Transport_Smtp` object instance. The `auth` key can be set to `plain`, `login`, or `crammd5`. If you want to send an e-mail through a remote server, you should use `login`.

```
$config = array('auth' => 'login',
                'username' => 'username',
                'password' => 'password');
$transport = new Zend_Mail_Transport_Smtp('mail.wroxexample.com', $config);
$mail = new Zend_Mail();
$mail->setBodyText("Hello World!");
$mail->setFrom('wroxexample@gmail.co', 'Example');
$mail->addTo('kprzystalski@gmail.com', 'Karol');
$mail->setSubject('Just want to say Hi');
$mail->send($transport);
```

The `Zend_Mail_Transport_Smtp` configuration should be set as the parameter for the `send()` method if you want to use these configuration entries for sending an e-mail.

Secure Connection

To secure the connection between your application and an SMTP server, you need to set two additional configuration entries: `ssl` and `port`. The `port` option is not really a security configuration entry, but remote servers usually use a different port number for secured SMTP connections.

```
<?php
$config = array('auth' => 'login',
                'username' => 'wroxexample@gmail.com',
                'password' => 'wroxexample123',
                'ssl' => 'ssl',
                'port' => 465);
$transport = new Zend_Mail_Transport_Smtp('smtp.gmail.com', $config);
$mail = new Zend_Mail();
$mail->setBodyHtml("Hello World!");
$mail->setFrom('wroxexample@gmail.co', 'Example');
$mail->addTo('kprzystalski@gmail.com', 'Karol');
$mail->setSubject('Just want to say Hi');
$mail->send($transport);
```

All in One

Merging all the examples shown previously, you will get the following piece of code. It should be saved as `MailingController.php` in the `/application/controllers/` directory.

Available for download on Wrox.com

```
<?php
class MailingController extends Zend_Controller_Action {
    public function sendAction() {
        $config = array('auth' => 'login',
                        'username' => 'wroxexample@gmail.com',
                        'password' => 'wroxexample123',
                        'ssl' => 'ssl',
                        'port' => 465);
       $transport = new Zend_Mail_Transport_Smtp('smtp.gmail.com', $config);
       $htmlTemplate = new Zend_View();
       $htmlTemplate->addScriptPath(ROOT_DIR .
           '/application/views/scripts/templates/');
       $htmlTemplate->assign('name','Administrator');
       $html_body = $htmlTemplate ->render(htmlEmailExample.phtml');
       $mail = new Zend_Mail();
       $mail->setBodyHtml($html_body);
       $mail->setFrom('sender@test.com', 'Some Sender');
       $mail->addTo('recipient@test.com', 'Some Recipient');
       $mail->addCc('someone@example.com', 'Someone Else');
       $mail->addBcc('topsecret@example.com', 'Top Secret Recipient');
       $fileContents = file_get_contents('schedule.doc');
       $attachment = $mail->createAttachment($fileContents);
       $attachment->filename='schedule.doc';
       $attachment->type='application/msword';
       $mail->addAttachment($attachment);
       $mail->setSubject('TestSubject');
       $mail->send($transport);
    }
}
```

code snippet /zendMailer/zf/application/controllers/MailingController.php

PHPMAILER

FIGURE 6-8: PHPMailer logo

PHPMailer (see Figure 6-8) is not included in any of the frameworks presented in this chapter. However it is fairly popular and you may wish to add it as a separate mailer application, as in CakePHP and Zend Framework, or as a Symfony plug-in. You can find more about PHPMailer at `http://phpmailer.worxware.com`. As you can see, there are also a few add-ons available for PHPMailer on this page (`PHPMailer-FE`, `PHPMailer-ML`, `PHPMailer-BMH`). Additionally, you can also get support for PHPMailer from its founder: Worx International (not to be confused with Wrox Press, of course).

Symfony

Symfony doesn't support PHPMailer since version 1.2. There was a plan to include PHPMailer as a part of Symfony 2.0, but SwiftMailer won this battle and it's still a part of Symfony. If you want to check how PHPMailer works with Symfony, you can try earlier versions of Symfony (1.2 and earlier) and install PHPMailer as a plug-in using the following command:

```
$ symfony plugin:install sfPHPMailerPlugin
```

If you really need to use PHPMailer, it's also possible to use PHPMailer in Symfony in a different way, similar to the way it's used in CakePHP, but you will break the strategy of adding add-ons in Symfony then. Anyway, we don't recommend this option. You should rather consider a different mailer to use with Symfony.

CakePHP

Unfortunately, CakePHP bases this installation on its individual components. But as in case of SwiftMailer, you can still use PHPMailer. To download PHPMailer, go to `http://sourceforge.net/projects/phpmailer/files/phpmailer%20for%20php5_6/`. Probably you have noticed that there are more versions available, including a Lite version, but we will describe in this chapter only the most popular PHPMailer for PHP5/6. To integrate PHPMailer with CakePHP, you need to unpack the proper PHPMailer package to the CakePHP application's `/vendors` directory. After unpacking, your directory structure should look like this:

```
app/vendors/phpmailer/
    docs/
    examples/
    language/
    test/
    LICENSE
    README
    aboutus.html
    changelog.txt
    class.phpmailer.php
    class.pop3.php
    class.smtp.php
```

All in One

The individual code snippets demonstrating PHPMailer are discussed in the Zend Framework section. For CakePHP developers, there is a merged example presented below and the discussion in the Zend Framework section applies to this example as well. Almost all PHPMailer code used in CakePHP example is the same as in Zend Framework.

```
<?php
App::import('Vendor', 'PHPMailer', array('file' =>
'phpmailer'.DS.'class.phpmailer.php'));
class MailController extends AppController {
    var $uses = '';
    function sendEmail() {
        $mail = new PHPMailer();
        $mail->IsSMTP();
        $mail->SMTPAuth = true;
        $mail->SMTPSecure = 'ssl';
        $mail->Host = 'smtp.gmail.com';
        $mail->Port = 465;
        $mail->Username = "wroxexample@gmail.com";
        $mail->Password = "wroxexample123";
        $mail->SetFrom("wroxexample@gmail.com", "PHPMailer Wrox Example");
        $mail->Subject = "PHPMailer example";
        $mail->AddAddress("kprzystalski@gmail.com");
        $viewPath='email';
        $type='html';
        $viewName='registration';
        $view = new View($this);
        $view->layout=$this->layout;
        $content=$view->element($viewPath.DS.$type.DS.$viewName,
          array('name' => "John Smith"), true);
        $htmlBody= $view->renderLayout($content);
        $mail->MsgHTML($htmlBody);
        $mail->Send();
    }
}
```

code snippet /phpMailer/cakephp/app/controllers/registration_controller.php

As you did with SwiftMailer, you need to include the PHPMailer libraries using the `import()` method. Note that you also need to use the `View` class to create e-mail contents using templates.

Zend Framework

In Zend Framework, after unpacking PHPMailer, your directory structure should be as follows:

```
library/phpmailer/
    docs/
    examples/
    language/
    test/
    LICENSE
    README
```

```
aboutus.html
changelog.txt
class.phpmailer.php
class.pop3.php
class.smtp.php
```

The file highlighted with bold in the preceding code is one you need to include (as shown in the following code), as is the case with every other add-on.

```
<?php
require_once('phpmailer/class.phpmailer.php');
class RegistrationController extends Zend_Controller_Action {
    function send() {
    }
}
```

Sending Simple E-mail

To send an e-mail with PHPMailer, you need to create an instance of `PHPMailer` and set some commonly known attributes.

```
$mail = new PHPMailer();
$mail->SetFrom("boss@wroxexample", "Boss");
$mail->Subject = "PHPMailer example";
$mail->Body = "Hello World!";
$mail->AddAddress("john@wroxexample.com");
$mail->Send();
```

Sending HTML E-mail

HTML e-mail can be sent using the `MsgHTML()` method. PHPMailer has a nice attribute, `AltBody`, which allows you to set a message that is shown when recipient can't receive HTML e-mail. Getting templates is done in the same way as in SwiftMailer.

```
$mail = new PHPMailer();
$mail->SetFrom("boss@wroxexample", "Boss");
$mail->Subject = "Wrox example";
$htmlTemplate = new Zend_View();
$htmlTemplate->addScriptPath(APPLICATION_PATH.'/views/scripts/email/');
$htmlTemplate->assign('name','Foo Bar');
$htmlBody = $htmlTemplate ->render('registration.phtml');
$mail->AltBody="To view the message, use an HTML compatible e-mail viewer!";
$mail->MsgHTML($htmlBody);
$mail->AddAddress("john@wroxexample.com");
$mail->Send();
```

Adding Attachments

PHPMailer has options very similar to the CakePHP mailing component. You can attach a file using its file system path.

```
$mail = new PHPMailer();
$mail->SetFrom("boss@wroxexample", "Boss");
$mail->Subject = "PHPMailer example";
$mail->MsgHTML("Hello World!");
```

```
$mail->AddAddress("john@wroxexample.com");
$mail->AddAttachment("attachments/schedule.doc");
$mail->AddAttachment("attachments/fnf84y534thb38h53.doc","plan.doc");
$mail->Send();
```

Additionally, you can set the name of the attachment that will be shown to the recipient.

Carbon Copy

This solution delivers three methods with which we can set the reply address, add additional recipients, and add hidden recipients: `AddReplyTo()`, `AddCC()`, and `AddBCC()`.

```
$mail = new PHPMailer();
$mail->SetFrom("boss@wroxexample", "Boss");
$mail->Subject = "PHPMailer example";
$mail->MsgHTML("Hello World!");
$mail->AddAddress("john@wroxexample.com");
$mail->AddReplyTo("pm@wroxexample.com","PM");
$mail->AddCC("john.smith@wroxexample.com,"John Smith");
$mail->AddBCC("foo.bar@wroxexample.com", "foo bar");
$mail->Send();
```

Remote SMTP Servers

To connect to a remote SMTP server, you need to express it directly by invoking the `isSMTP()` method. Additionally you need to set all commonly needed attributes such as `host name`, `port number`, `username`, and `password`. PHPMailer also has additional functionalities dedicated to specific mail servers such as Qmail, Sendmail, or Gmail.

```
$mail = new PHPMailer();
$mail->IsSMTP();
$mail->SMTPAuth = true;
$mail->Host = 'smtp.wroxexample.com';
$mail->Port = 25;
$mail->Username = "admin@wroxexample.com";
$mail->Password = "wroxexample123";
$mail->SetFrom("admin@wroxexample.com", "Admin");
$mail->Subject ="PHPMailer example";
$mail->Body ="Hello World!";
$mail->AddAddress("john@wroxexample.com");
$mail->Send();
```

Secure Connection

For a secure connection you need only to set the `SMTPSecure` attribute to `ssl` and change the port to a secured one.

```
$mail = new PHPMailer();
$mail->IsSMTP();
$mail->SMTPAuth = true;
$mail->SMTPSecure = 'ssl';
$mail->Host = 'smtp.gmail.com';
$mail->Port = 465;
$mail->Username = "wroxexample@gmail.com";
$mail->Password = "wroxexample123";
```

```
$mail->SetFrom("wroxexample@gmail.com", "Admin");
$mail->Subject = "PHPMailer example";
$mail->Body = "Hello World!";
$mail->AddAddress("john@wroxexample.com");
$mail->Send();
```

All in One

Your merged code should be as shown here.

```
<?php
require_once('phpmailer/class.phpmailer.php');
class RegistrationController extends Zend_Controller_Action {
    function send() {
        $mail = new PHPMailer();
        $mail->IsSMTP();
        $mail->SMTPAuth = true;
        $mail->SMTPSecure = 'ssl';
        $mail->Host = 'smtp.gmail.com';
        $mail->Port = 465;
        $mail->Username = "wroxexample@gmail.com";
        $mail->Password = "wroxexample123";
        $mail->SetFrom("wroxexample@gmail.com", "PHPMailer Wrox Example");
        $mail->Subject = "PHPMailer example";
        $mail->AddAddress("kprzystalski@gmail.com"));
        $htmlTemplate = new Zend_View();
        $htmlTemplate->addScriptPath(APPLICATION_PATH.'/views/scripts/email/');
        $htmlTemplate->assign('name','Foo Bar');
        $htmlBody = $htmlTemplate ->render('registration.phtml');
        $mail->MsgHTML($htmlBody);
        $mail->Send();
    }
}
```

code snippet /phpMailer/zf/application/controllers/RegistrationController.php

7

Searching

If you type "Google" into Google, you can break the Internet. So please, no one try it, even for a joke. It's not a laughing matter. You can break the Internet!

— Jen, The IT Crowd

WHAT'S IN THIS CHAPTER?

- Introducing full-text searching and indexing.
- Sphinx searching engine with Symfony.
- Apache Lucene with Zend Framework.
- Google Custom Search with CakePHP.

With the advent of Web 2.0, web content was no longer generated solely by webmasters and dedicated editors, but by communities of end users themselves. One side effect of this transformation was a huge increase in web content that needs to be stored and occasionally searched.

In this chapter, we are going to show you how to integrate search engines with the frameworks. There are many search engines on the market, but we chose only three because of their usefulness, efficiency, and popularity; we also discuss important differences between them. The engines we describe are Lucene, Sphinx, and the Google API. Apache Lucene is a popular, Java-based, open-source engine that has spawned several successful subprojects. Sphinx was written in C++ by a sole dedicated software engineer with top performance and scalability in mind. The Google AJAX Search API allows you to easily embed web search capability into your website. It is unfortunately not open-source, but it is so cool we couldn't ignore it.

PROBLEM

When you have a small database of a few thousand records and you need to run a query as rarely as once a minute, the search method doesn't really matter. You may use the SQL WHERE clause and built-in database mechanisms then. But when the query count increases, you simply cannot afford to run each search separately. You need to look for a more advanced mechanism.

Matters further complicate when you want to broaden your results to synonyms of your search phrase. You may expect that if somebody looks for `guns` he would be interested in `firearms`, too. However, the situation gets really messed up if you decide that searching should be intelligent and filter out irrelevant hits like `Guns N' Roses`. Of course that's messed up unless you integrate your application with a search engine. If you do, everything gets much simpler.

Full Text Searching

There is a good chance that you have used Google, Yahoo, or another web search engine. You were using full-text searching then. The web search engines are the most prominent examples of search engines, but there are also other solutions, especially those called enterprise search engines used for applications' internal resources. The only difference is that they do not crawl the Internet to get the content, but instead they search and index databases or files filled with content written by web app users. The type of data source is not that important as long as you have full access to it.

The problem with full-text searching is that you want to quickly get a large number of relevant results. It is hard to achieve that goal, and relevance seems to decrease as the number of results increases. To quantify these results, two important notions were defined:

- **Recall** — The ratio of the quantity of returned relevant results to the quantity of all relevant items. In other words, it is the ratio of those items that you intended to hit and actually did to all items that you wanted to hit.
- **Precision** — The ratio of the quantity of returned relevant results to the quantity of all returned results, including irrelevant ones. In other words, it is the ratio of those items you wanted to hit and did to all items you hit whether you wanted them or not.

These notions are illustrated in Figure 7-1. Recall is increased when relevant items are returned, and precision is increased mainly if irrelevant items are not returned (but also by increasing recall). The density of dots roughly represents the fact that most items are not relevant and stay within the database.

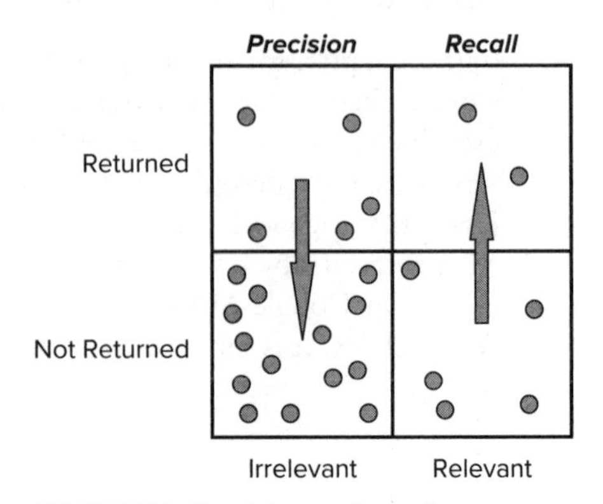

FIGURE 7-1: Precision and recall

Indexing

As you probably expect, naive scanning of all data looking for exact matches is the worst option possible. If you look for `"how to feed cats"`, this process compares this exact phrase with the beginning of every string in the database, moves one letter forward, compares it again, and so on. If 100 users look for `"how to feed cats"`, the process is repeated from scratch. Moreover, such an exact phrase search cannot hit a sentence like `"The favorite food of my cat is raw fish"`, which seems quite a relevant answer.

There are many indexing algorithms, but the thing they all have in common is that they initially analyze the database to decrease the work that needs to be done later, possibly increasing the recall of search. The index itself needs to be stored, but it is usually not much bigger than a few thousand commonly used words, so it is a little tradeoff for its effectiveness. Some common steps done during indexing include the following:

- **Tokenization** — Continuous strings need to be segmented into individual words, called *tokens*. In most Western languages, words are clearly separated by spaces, but even then some problems may occur. For example, in English, `"killer whale"` is the same as `"orca"`, but when indexed as separate words may lead to `"whale killers"`, meaning `"whalers"`. Proper tokenization of the German language may be even more difficult, as it tends to dynamically create compound words such as `"Tempolimit"`, which is `"speed limit"`. Eastern languages are even less clearly whitespace-delineated, which makes tokenization challenging.
- **Stop words** — Some words are themselves meaningless, extremely common, or otherwise unwanted, and you want them filtered out from the index. Some common stop words are `"the"`, `"it"`, `"how"`, `"to"`, or `"however"`.
- **Stemming** — Many words may be derived from a common stem. For example, `"painting"`, `"painted"`, `"paints"`, and `"painter"` have a common stem `"paint"` and can be stored as one concept word under one index. This can dramatically improve recall, but at the cost of precision. A more sophisticated form of stemming is *lemmatization*. The word is first identified as a part of speech (e.g., a noun), and then an appropriate rule is used to find the stem. This allows better precision as the word `"painting"` may be either a noun, like `"Caravaggio's painting"`, or a verb, like `"Mary likes painting"`.
- **Entity extraction** — Some phrases in text can be identified as named entities and stored under their own indexes. This may include places like `"Great Barrier Reef"`, organizations like `"Free Software Foundation"`, currencies, dates recognized from multiple formats, or others.
- **Experimental methods** — There is still much that can be done to improve general indexing algorithms and even more regarding language-specific indexing algorithms. There are some interesting methods introducing human-like fuzziness, like those indexing the phonetic sound of words. Some other systems try to match synonyms of various words to index pure concepts that can be expressed using several different words. Sometimes even semantic webs are constructed that allow the calculation of conceptual distance between particular words.

As you can see, this is quite a complex issue, perhaps more related to linguistics than information technology or computer science in general. Fortunately you do not have to go deep and you can focus on application development instead as each of the search engines discussed in this chapter provides its own indexing methods.

Search Query

When users enter a search query, some magic can be done by the search engine. There are some well-known techniques for increasing the quality of returned hits:

- **Boolean operators** — Queries can be more precise when you are able to specify that you want only results with all queried words or exclude results with some unwanted words.
- **Wildcards** — Special characters that may substitute any other character or an indefinite amount of other characters.
- **Regular expressions** — The preceding methods can be further refined to create a full syntax that allows for matching a word/character pattern with indexed items.
- **Fuzzy search** — If fuzziness was not introduced in the index itself, you can do it during the search to improve the recall.
- **Field match** — If the data source is a database of known structure, you can employ field-specific searching. For example, you can search only `Title` fields or filter old results using the `Date_Created` field.

SOLUTIONS

In web application development, three search engine solutions are most commonly used: Sphinx, Lucene, and the Google Custom Search API. Because this book is not a never-ending story, we decided to integrate each search engine with only one web framework. It's an exception from the rule we've followed generally in this book that we show how to do exactly the same thing for each of the frameworks. The reason was to give every framework full-text search capabilities, rather than integrate it with a concrete search engine. Moreover, each search engine can be integrated with each web framework, often with few modifications. So after reading this, you should be able to get all combinations working (for example, Sphinx with CakePHP), even one that wasn't explained explicitly. We believe it's better than showing three nearly identical integrations.

Sphinx

Sphinx is a free search engine licensed under General Public License version 2. It was developed by a Russian software engineer, Andrew Aksyonoff. To get more detailed information about Sphinx, go to `http://sphinxsearch.com`. This section describes how to use Sphinx within Symfony. Sphinx is also available as a CakePHP plug-in or you can just use Sphinx's libraries to integrate it with Zend Framework. The Sphinx logo is shown in Figure 7-2.

FIGURE 7-2: Sphinx search engine logo

Installing Sphinx

Before you can use Sphinx inside your application, you need to install it first. Sphinx is a stand-alone application that is accessed rather than included by your web applications. Therefore, before using any framework's extension or enhancement, you need to install the engine separately. For some systems (for example, Windows and Ubuntu Linux), a binary version of Sphinx is available.

For Windows, the binaries are the default solution. You can grab them from Sphinx's homepage. Under Linux distributions, it is best to create binaries from the newest sources to avoid version compatibility issues. To do that, you first need to install some additional packages that are needed for the building process:

```
# apt-get install build-essential
```

When installation is complete, you can run the configuration script to set up your Sphinx to work with a chosen database engine, as it's done here:

```
# ./configure --with-mysql
# make
# make install
```

You need to edit the configuration file. On Linux, you can find it at /`etc/sphinxsearch/sphinx.conf` or `/usr/local/etc/sphinx.conf`, depending on the Sphinx version. On Windows, choose the file called `sphinx-min.conf.in` located in the main Sphinx installation directory and make a copy for editing called `sphinx.conf`. The reference manual recommends that you install Sphinx at `C:\Sphinx`, so we will follow this convention.

The following code snippet shows how this configuration file should look on Ubuntu Linux. You need to include a named data source with an SQL query that gets data from a database table. You also need to specify details for connecting to this database. The second thing you need to include is a named index. Set the data source as the source of this index and provide a path to store it.

```
source wroxSrc {
    type                    = mysql
    sql_host                = localhost
    sql_user                = foo
    sql_pass                = bar
    sql_db                  = sphinx
    sql_port                = 3306
    sql_query               = \
        SELECT id, title, description \
        FROM news
    sql_query_info          = SELECT * FROM news WHERE id=$id
}
index wroxIndex {
    source                  = wroxSrc
    path                    = /home/wrox/sphinx/source/wroxSrc
    docinfo                 = extern
    charset_type            = sbcs
}
indexer {
    mem_limit               = 32M
}
searchd {
    port                    = 3312
    log                     = /var/log/sphinxsearch/searchd.log
    query_log               = /var/log/sphinxsearch/query.log
    read_timeout            = 5
    max_children            = 30
    pid_file                = /var/run/searchd.pid
    max_matches             = 1000
```

```
        seamless_rotate         = 1
        preopen_indexes         = 0
        unlink_old              = 1
}
```

code snippet /sphinx/sphinx.conf

The next thing that needs to be done is adding the directory, where executable files are stored, to the PATH variable of your environment. This allows you to use available Sphinx tools: `indexer`, `indextool`, `search`, `searchd`, `spelldump`. On UNIX-like operating systems, after you execute `make install`, the symlinks are automatically added into `/usr/bin/` or another directory that was already included into the system's PATH environment variable. On Windows you need to include the `C:\Sphinx\bin` directory using dialog windows (refer to Chapter 2).

Create the target folder for your index folder (Linux — `/home/wrox/sphinx/source`; Windows — `C:\Sphinx\data`) and an empty `wroxSrc.spl` file inside it. As always, make sure the paths are valid for your operating system. In the Windows configuration file, you will see in some places, the `@CONFDIR@` variable. It is a placeholder and you must change these paths to correct ones like `C:\Sphinx\data\wroxSrc`.

Using the following tool, you can create the index (the parameter is the name of the index created in the configuration file):

```
$ indexer wroxIndex
```

It will consume the `wroxSrc.spl` file and create these files in the `/data` directory:

```
wroxSrc.spa
wroxSrc.spd
wroxSrc.sph
wroxSrc.spi
wroxSrc.spl
wroxSrc.spm
wroxSrc.spp
```

Now, run the Sphinx daemon so your application can access it to conduct search queries. It is a compiled C++ application, so it runs really fast. On Linux, you can run it just like this:

```
/etc/init.d/sphinxsearch start
```

On Windows, you need to add it to Windows Services first. It will be more convenient than starting it from the console every time manually. Create another folder: `/log`, in `C:\Sphinx`. You need to run the console as administrator. Find the `cmd.exe` executable (type `cmd` in the Windows 7 start menu), right-click it, and choose the shielded option. When you've got the admin console, run the following command:

```
$ searchd --install --config C:\Sphinx\sphinx.conf --servicename SphinxSearch
```

The console output should look like Figure 7-3 if everything went well.

```
c:\sphinx>searchd --install --config C:\Sphinx\sphinx.conf --servicename SphinxS
earch
Sphinx 1.10-beta (r2420)
Copyright (c) 2001-2010, Andrew Aksyonoff
Copyright (c) 2008-2010, Sphinx Technologies Inc (http://sphinxsearch.com)

Installing service...
Service 'SphinxSearch' installed succesfully.

c:\sphinx>_
```

FIGURE 7-3: Installing Sphinx as a Windows Service

Now, when you go to Windows Services, you can start this SphinxSearch daemon, as shown in Figure 7-4. Automatic startup means that this service will be started on demand, so you don't have to do it manually.

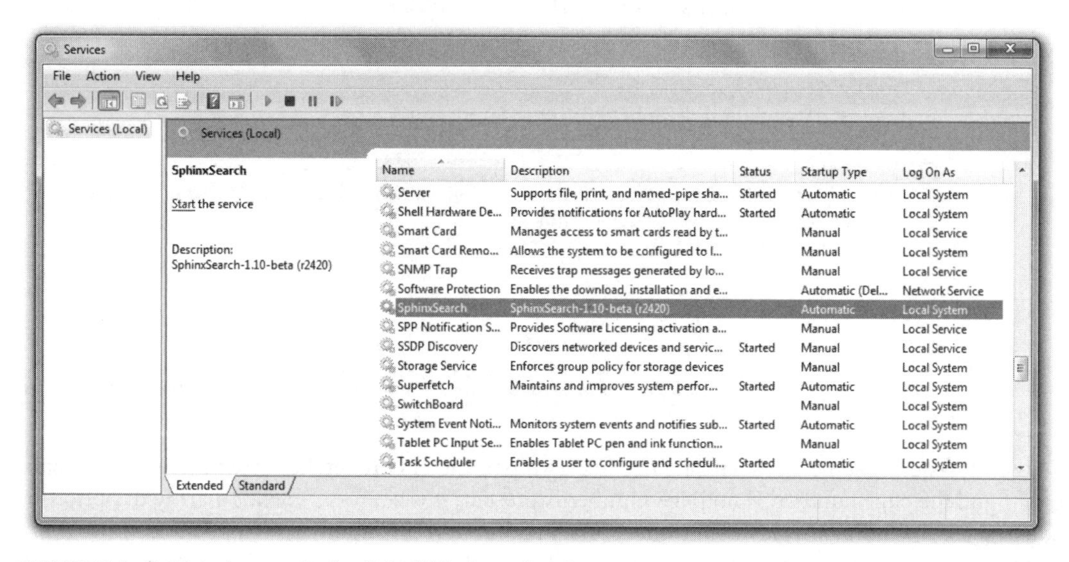

FIGURE 7-4: Sphinx daemon in the list of Windows Services

Symfony

In Symfony, there is a plug-in for almost everything, including Sphinx. You can read more about it at `http://www.symfony-project.org/plugins/sfSphinxPlugin`. To install it through the command line, you need to type the following command:

```
$ symfony plugin-install sfSphinxPlugin
```

Installing the Symfony plug-in gives you the possibility to access the Sphinx daemon.

As shown in the following code, generate the `mysearch` project that contains the `frontend` application and a nice `search` module:

```
$ symfony generate:project mysearch
$ symfony generate:app frontend
$ symfony generate:module frontend search
```

Controller

Fill the controller file with the index action as in the following code:

```
<?php
class searchActions extends sfActions {

  public function executeIndex(sfWebRequest $request) {
    $this->query = $this->getRequestParameter('search');
    $this->page = $this->getRequestParameter('p', 1);
    $options = array(
      'limit'   => 5,
      'offset'  => ($this->page - 1) * 5,
      'weights' => array(100, 1),
      'sort'    => sfSphinxClient::SPH_SORT_EXTENDED,
      'sortby'  => '@weight DESC',
      );
    if (!empty($this->query)) {
      $this->sphinx = new sfSphinxClient($options);
      $res = $this->sphinx->Query($this->query, 'wroxIndex');
      $this->pager =
         new sfSphinxDoctrinePager('News', $options['limit'], $this->sphinx);
      $this->pager->setPage($this->page);
      $this->pager->init();
    }
  }
}
```

code snippet /sphinx/symfony/apps/frontend/modules/search/actions/actions.class.php

This code requires some explanation. The first two parameters are fetched from the web request: the query and the page number. If no page number is present, it is set to `1`. Then, an array of options is constructed, including display count limit, offset in search result number, weights, and sorting method. If the query is not empty, an instance of `sfSphinxClient` is created and then used to execute the query. Note that the second argument of the `Query()` function is the name of the index created before. The next line creates a Doctrine pager. There is also a pager for Propel called `sfSphinxPager`. Set the page and run the `init()` method that initializes the pager and results in pagination.

Displaying Results

The next step is to create the search form. The following snippets are segments of one template file, `sindexSuccess.php`.

As shown in the following code, you should include the Search helper because it will be helpful for displaying data. Create a simple GET form with an input field and a submit button:

Available for download on Wrox.com

```
<?php use_helper('Search') ?>
What are you looking for?
<form action="<?php echo url_for('/index.php/search') ?>" method="get">
<input type="text" name="search" value="<?php echo $query; ?>" />
<input type="submit"  name="submit" value="search" />
</form>
```

code snippet /sphinx/symfony/apps/frontend/modules/search/template/indexSuccess.php

If the query is empty then, well, `return` and that's all:

Available for download on Wrox.com

```
<?php if (empty($query)): ?>
<?php return ?>
<?php endif ?>
```

code snippet /sphinx/symfony/apps/frontend/modules/search/template/indexSuccess.php

If the query is not empty, handle it appropriately. The bold section in the following code is important because it displays in a loop all the titles and descriptions of the results of this query. Moreover, the search result in these texts gets highlighted.

Available for download on Wrox.com

```
<?php $res = $pager->getResults() ?>
<?php if (empty($res)): ?>
No result matches your query
<?php else: ?>
<?php if ($sphinx->getLastWarning()): ?>
Warning: <?php echo $sphinx->getLastWarning() ?>
<?php endif ?>
<ol start="<?php echo $pager->getFirstIndice() ?>">
<?php foreach ($res as $news): ?>
  <li>
    <?php echo link_to(highlight_search_result($news->getTitle(), $query),
       'news?id=' . $news->getId()) ?>
    <?php echo highlight_search_result($news->getDescription(), $query) ?>
  </li>
<?php endforeach ?>
</ol>
<?php endif ?>
```

code snippet /sphinx/symfony/apps/frontend/modules/search/template/indexSuccess.php

Pagination

Now, prepare the pagination module. If there is enough content to be paginated, the following code will split it into pages and provide the well-known navigation links:

Available for download on Wrox.com

```
<?php if ($pager->haveToPaginate()): ?>
  <?php echo link_to('&laquo;', 'index.php/search?q=' . $query . '&p=' .
    $pager->getFirstPage()) ?>
```

```
  <?php echo link_to('&lt;', 'index.php/search?q=' . $query . '&p=' .
    $pager->getPreviousPage()) ?>
  <?php $pages = $pager->getLinks() ?>
  <?php foreach ($pages as $page): ?>
    <?php echo ($page == $pager->getPage()) ? $page : link_to($page,
      'index.php/search?q=' . $query . '&p=' . $page) ?>
  <?php endforeach ?>
  <?php echo link_to('&gt;', 'index.php/search?q=' . $query . '&p=' .
    $pager->getNextPage()) ?>
  <?php echo link_to('&raquo;', 'index.php/search?q=' . $query . '&p=' .
    $pager->getLastPage()) ?>
<?php endif ?>
```

code snippet /sphinx/symfony/apps/frontend/modules/search/template/indexSuccess.php

The last thing you need to include in your template is the number of matches found as the query result. It can be achieved with the following line:

```
Sphinx search "<?php echo $query; ?>" found
<?php echo $pager->getNbResults(); ?> matches.
```

code snippet /sphinx/symfony/apps/frontend/modules/search/template/indexSuccess.php

Testing

It would be nice to test the search engine on a data set, wouldn't it? Well, that's what fixtures are for. Create a `fixturex.yml` fixture file. It may be as simple as the one following, but you are free to generate a really big file. You can read more about fixtures and testing in Chapter 15.

```
news:
  first:
    title: first news
    description: important news
  second:
    title: second news
    description: important news
  third:
    title: third news
    description: important news
  fourth:
    title: fourth news
    description: important news
  fifth:
    title: fifth news
    description: important news
  sixth:
    title: sixth news
    description: important news
  seventh:
    title: seventh news
    description: important news
```

code snippet /sphinx/symfony/data/fixtures/fixtures.yml

Load the data with following command. The database must be configured before and contain a `news` table with `id` (autoincremented `INT`), `title` (`VARCHAR`), and `description` (`VARCHAR` too, but bigger) fields.

```
$ symfony doctrine:data-load
```

To see the output you've been waiting for (see Figure 7-5), go to your browser, enter `http://localhost/index.php/search` in the address bar (remember to configure the routing), and then search for a phrase that can be found in the fixtures' titles.

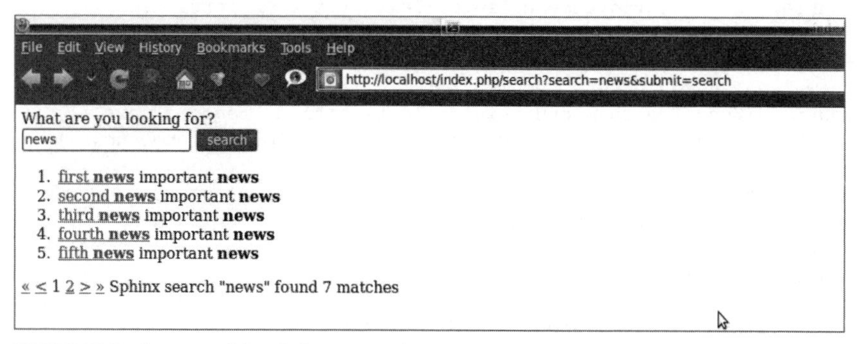

FIGURE 7-5: Output of the Sphinx search application in Symfony (mouse pointer irrelevant)

If you need continuous indexing, you have to set Linux `cron` or Windows Scheduler to systematically run the `indexer` tool.

CakePHP and Zend Framework

Integrating Sphinx is nearly as easy and straightforward in any other framework as it is in Symfony. When working with CakePHP, it's best to use the `SphinxClient` class in the model. In ZF, use it as an adapter. However, the Symfony plug-in makes it even easier, which is why we chose this combination in this chapter.

Lucene

Lucene was written originally by Dave Cutting, but now, it is developed and supported by the Apache Software Foundation. At first, it was Jakarta family Java software, but it has been ported to many other programming languages, including PHP. You can read more about Lucene at its website: `http://lucene.apache.org/java/docs/index.html`. The Lucerne logo is shown in Figure 7-6.

FIGURE 7-6: Apache Lucene search engine logo

Zend Framework

Using Lucene and Zend Framework together is not a big deal because Lucene is already integrated with Zend Framework by default. `Zend_Search_Lucene` included in Zend Framework is one of the most successful ports of the Apache Lucene project. You can read more about this Zend component in the official documentation: `http://framework.zend.com/manual/en/zend.search.lucene.html`.

Creating an Index

Go to /application/controllers/IndexController.php and create an indexing action that will be responsible for generating the index. All indexed items in Zend Lucene are instances of the Zend_Search_Lucene_Document class. The following code creates the documents, fills them with sample data, and adds them to the index:

```
public function indexingAction() {
    $index = Zend_Search_Lucene::create('/home/wrox/public_html/lucene/');
    $doc = new Zend_Search_Lucene_Document();
    $doc->addField(Zend_Search_Lucene_Field::Text('title', 'first news'));
    $doc->addField(Zend_Search_Lucene_Field::Text('description','hot news'));
    $index->addDocument($doc);
    $doc = new Zend_Search_Lucene_Document();
    $doc->addField(Zend_Search_Lucene_Field::Text('title', 'second news'));
    $doc->addField(Zend_Search_Lucene_Field::Text('description','hot news'));
    $index->addDocument($doc);
    $doc = new Zend_Search_Lucene_Document();
    $doc->addField(Zend_Search_Lucene_Field::Text('title', 'third news'));
    $doc->addField(Zend_Search_Lucene_Field::Text('description','hot news'));
    $index->addDocument($doc);
    $doc = new Zend_Search_Lucene_Document();
    $doc->addField(Zend_Search_Lucene_Field::Text('title', 'fourth news'));
    $doc->addField(Zend_Search_Lucene_Field::Text('description','hot news'));
    $index->addDocument($doc);
    $doc = new Zend_Search_Lucene_Document();
    $doc->addField(Zend_Search_Lucene_Field::Text('title', 'fifth news'));
    $doc->addField(Zend_Search_Lucene_Field::Text('description','hot news'));
    $index->addDocument($doc);
    $doc = new Zend_Search_Lucene_Document();
    $doc->addField(Zend_Search_Lucene_Field::Text('title', 'sixth news'));
    $doc->addField(Zend_Search_Lucene_Field::Text('description','hot news'));
    $index->addDocument($doc);
  }
```

code snippet /lucene/zf/application/controllers/IndexController.php

Create the associated view. It can be as simple as this one.

```
indexing..
```

code snippet /lucene/zf/application/views/scripts/index/indexing.phtml

When you execute this action through your browser with the following link: http://localhost/index.php/index/indexing, you will see the simple view, as shown in Figure 7-7, and the index will be created in the background.

This is a makeshift solution designed as an example illustrating how to implement searching in Lucene. In a production environment, you can't create a single controller with hard-coded values to create an index. Instead, the index should be updated when new data is entered into or deleted from the database. We hope that it's clear for you.

FIGURE 7-7: Creating the search index using a controller

Searching

In the same `IndexController.php`, edit the `indexAction()` as shown in the following code. The searched query is retrieved using the `$this->_getParam()` method with `'search'` as the argument.

```
if ($this->_getParam('search') == "") {
    $searchQuery = "";
}else {
    $searchQuery =$this->_getParam('search');
}
$this->view->search = $searchQuery;
$index = Zend_Search_Lucene::open('/home/username/lucene/');
$this->view->results = $index->find($searchQuery);
```

code snippet /lucene/zf/application/controllers/IndexController.php

The phrase is searched using the index created before, and the results are returned to the view as the `$this->results` variable.

Displaying Results

Create a view that allows you to enter the queries with a form and displays the results at the same time. The following code realizes these goals:

```
<form method="get" action="/index.php/index">
  Something missing?
  <input type="text" name="search" value="<?php echo $this->search; ?>" />
  <input type="submit" name="submit" value="search" />
</form>
<ol>
    <?php foreach ($this->results as $res): ?>
        <li><?php   echo $res->title.' - '.$res->description; ?></li>
    <?php endforeach; ?>
</ol>
```

code snippet /lucene/zf/application/views/scripts/index/index.phtml

Pagination

Pagination is only a little bit more complicated; you need to use the `Zend_Paginator` library. All you have to do is to supply the `Zend_Paginator::factory()` method with the results. This factory method produces the `$pager` paginator that is really easy to use. Just set the current page number and items per page. The full index action grows to look something like this:

Available for download on Wrox.com

```
public function indexAction() {
    if ($this->_getParam('search') == "") {
        $searchQuery = "";
    }else {
        $searchQuery =$this->_getParam('search');
    }
    $this->view->search = $searchQuery;
    $index = Zend_Search_Lucene::open('/home/username/lucene/');
    $results = $index->find($searchQuery);
    if ($this->_getParam('page') == "") {
        $page = 1;
    } else {
        $page = $this->_getParam('page');
    }
    $pager = Zend_Paginator::factory($results);
    $pager->setCurrentPageNumber($page);
    $pager->setItemCountPerPage(3);
    $this->view->results=$pager;
    $this->view->page = $page;
}
```

code snippet /lucene/zf/application/controllers/IndexController.php

You need also to update the view to use the pagination as shown in the following code. Notice the `$res->score` fragment; Zend allows you to access the relevance score determined by Lucene for each queried word.

Available for download on Wrox.com

```
<form method="get" action="/index.php/index">
  Something missing?
  <input type="text" name="search" value="<?php echo $this->search; ?>" />
  <input type="submit" name="submit" value="search" />
</form>
<?php // print_r($this->results); ?>
<?php if(!empty($this->results)): ?>
<ol>
  <?php foreach ($this->results as $res): ?>
    <li><?php echo $res->title.' - '.$res->description.', score: '.$res->score; ?>
    </li>
  <?php endforeach; ?>
</ol>
<?php echo $this->paginationControl(
    $this->results, 'Jumping','index/pager.phtml',
    array('search'=>$this->search));?>
<?php else: ?>
  No result matches your query
<?php endif; ?>
```

code snippet /lucene/zf/application/views/scripts/index/index.phtml

Zend's `paginationControl()` method highlighted in bold calls another view, here named `pager.phtml`, to do the pagination. There are also various scrolling styles available. According to Zend documentation, they are as follows:

- **Elastic** — A Google-like scrolling style that expands and contracts as a user scrolls through the pages.
- **Jumping** — As users scroll through, the page number advances to the end of a given range and then starts again at the beginning of the new range.
- **Sliding** — A Yahoo!-like scrolling style that positions the current page number in the center of the page range or as close as possible. This is the default style.

The pagination view `pager.phtml` mentioned before is presented in the following code. The first section is responsible for checking whether the `Previous` link is applicable; if so, link it with the previous page. The middle section shows pages from the neighborhood determined by the `$this->`*`pagesInRange`* variable. And the last section is responsible for the `Next` button.

```
<?php if ($this->pageCount): ?>
  <?php if (isset($this->previous)): ?>
      <a href="
         <?php echo $this->url(array('search'=>$this->search,
             'page' => $this->previous)); ?>
         ">Previous </a>
  <?php else: ?>
    Previous
  <?php endif; ?>
  <?php foreach ($this->pagesInRange as $page): ?>
      <?php if ($page != $this->current): ?> <a
          href="<?php echo $this->url(array('search'=>$this->search,
             'page' => $page)); ?>"> <?php echo $page; ?></a>
      <?php else: ?>
      <?php echo $page; ?>
      <?php endif; ?>
  <?php endforeach; ?>
  <?php if (isset($this->next)): ?>
      <a href="
         <?php echo $this->url(array('search'=>$this->search,
             'page' => $this->next)); ?>
         "> Next</a>
  <?php else: ?>
      Next
  <?php endif; ?>
<?php endif; ?>
```

code snippet /lucene/zf/application/views/scripts/index/pager.phtml

The final output of this application is displayed in Figure 7-8.

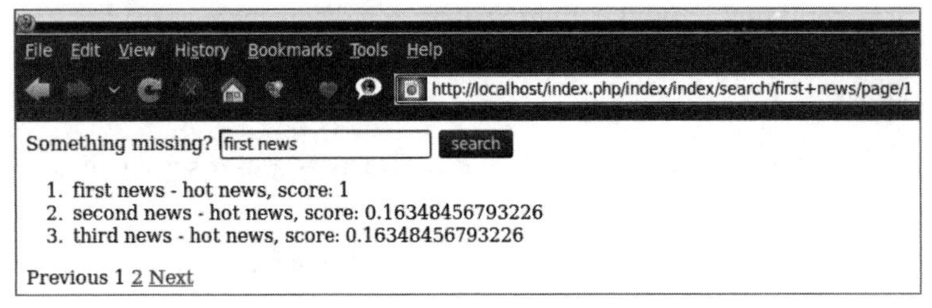

FIGURE 7-8: The Zend_Search_Lucene application with match scores

Please notice that this is a full-featured fuzzy search. The search term was `first news`, but there were many other results displayed with lower match scores. A big advantage of Zend Framework is that it includes a search engine of such capabilities out of the box.

Symfony and CakePHP

The Symfony integration is also rather simple because a Lucene plug-in is available at `www.symfony-project.org/plugins/sfLucenePlugin`. CakePHP developers are not so lucky, and again, they would have to write a special component to handle Lucene searching. This is not very hard, but it is rather time-consuming.

Google Custom Search

The previous two search engines were oriented for searching a named data source, preferably a local database. The solution presented here is powered by the Google Search Engine and allows you to use its vast database of indexed websites. The Google logo is shown in Figure 7-9.

FIGURE 7-9: Google logo (the caption is obvious).

The first web-search API from Google was called the Google SOAP search API, and it is no longer supported. A newer solution was the Google AJAX Search API. We were going to present it here, but it became deprecated as we were writing this chapter. Therefore, the newest solution from the Google search family will be used here: the Google Custom Search.

Setting up Google Custom Search

Go to the following web page and follow the white rabbit: `http://www.google.com/cse`.

Click the Create a Custom Search Engine button. You'll need a Google account for this, so create it if you don't have one. The first step is shown in Figure 7-10.

Provide the name and description of the search engine. Chose the websites your search engine will focus on. In most cases, this will be your own website, but you can include some friends' sites as well or create a search engine for any other combination of places. Well, that's why it's called custom. Accept the terms of service and free or ads-free edition. Proceed to the second step shown in Figure 7-11.

Google custom search | My Account | Sign out

1. Set up your search engine 2. Try it out 3. Get the code

Describe your search engine

Name: phpframeworks

for example, Real Climate Search Engine

Description: phpframeworks description

for example, Climate Science from Climate Scientists

Language: English

Define your search engine

Sites to search: http://phpframeworks.org/

List one URL per line.

Learn more about URL formatting.

Select an edition

Editions: **Standard edition**: Free, ads are required on results pages.

Site Search: Starts at $100 per year, no ads on results pages.

Learn more about each edition.

I have read and agree to the Terms of Service.

Next

FIGURE 7-10: Step 1 — Setting up the search engine

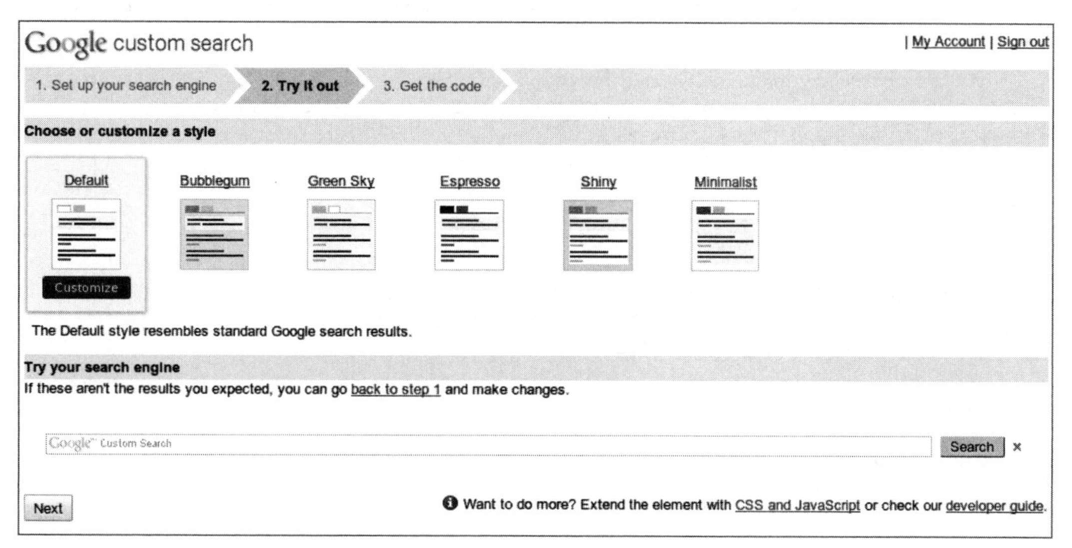

FIGURE 7-11: Step 2 — Picking a stylesheet

Pick one of the ready-to-use stylesheets or customize them to your liking. You can test the outputs with the following form. Proceed to the last step shown in Figure 7-12.

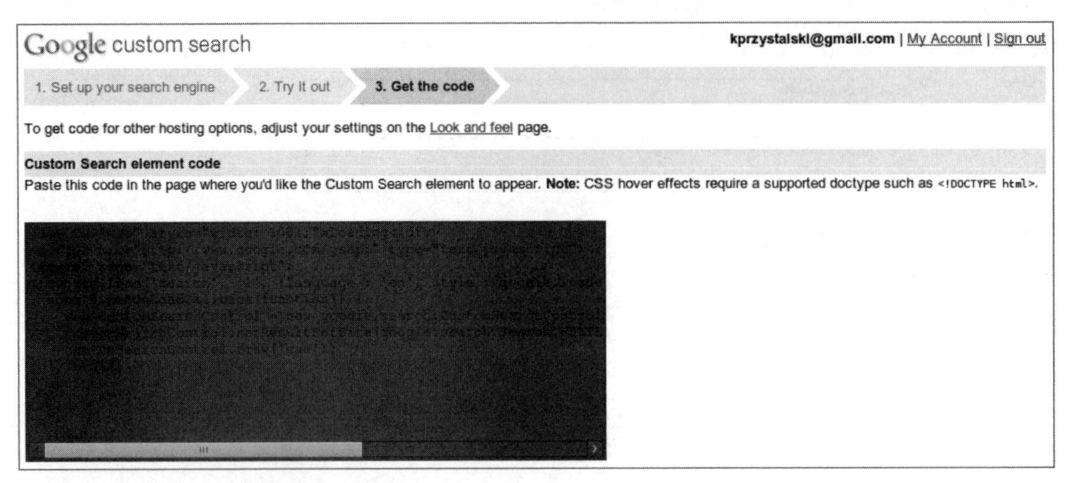

FIGURE 7-12: Step 3 — Getting the code

All you have to do is to copy the code and paste it into your web page. That's all.

CakePHP

Symfony had Sphinx and Zend had Lucene, so we will show how to integrate Google Custom Search with CakePHP only. Well, "integration" is surely too strong a word here as it boils down to inserting a bunch of Google code into a view. It just couldn't be easier.

Take a view and insert the obtained code into it. It will look similar to the following snippet, although not exactly the same because the keys will vary.

```
<div id="cse" style="width: 100%;">Loading</div>
<script src="http://www.google.com/jsapi" type="text/javascript"></script>
<script type="text/javascript">
  google.load('search', '1', {language : 'en'});
  google.setOnLoadCallback(function() {
    var customSearchControl =
        new google.search.CustomSearchControl(
        '008847152987572801710:baanh-mj9ly');
    customSearchControl.setResultSetSize(
        google.search.Search.FILTERED_CSE_RESULTSET);
    customSearchControl.draw('cse');
  }, true);
</script>
```

The result is shown in Figure 7-13.

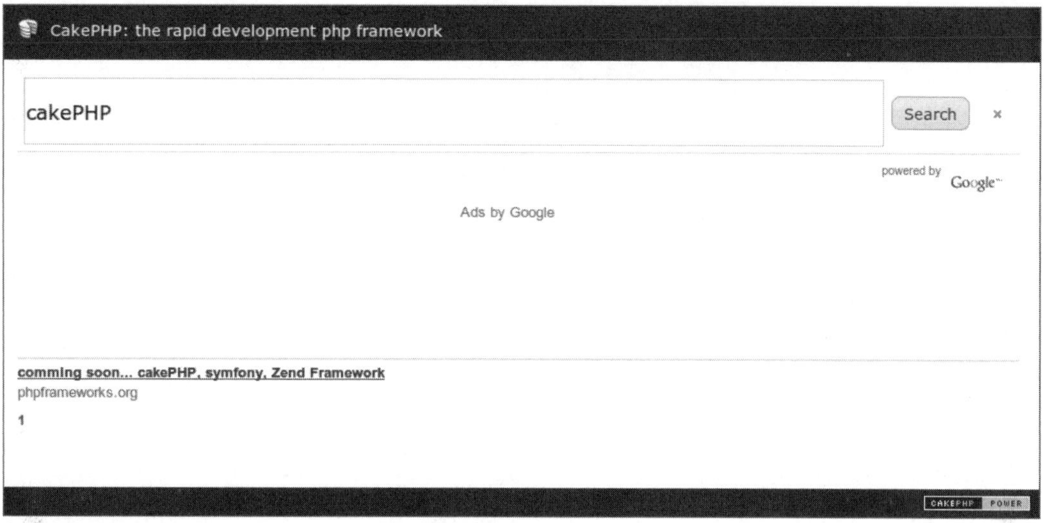

FIGURE 7-13: Google Custom Search in a CakePHP view

Symfony and Zend Framework

In Symfony and Zend Framework, Google Custom Search works exactly the same way. You just copy the Google code as presented previously, put it into any framework's view or static web page, and it will work. That's why separate sections for every framework would be redundant.

Security

Knowledge is power. Guard it well.

— WARHAMMER 40,000: DAWN OF WAR

WHAT'S IN THIS CHAPTER?

- Setting secure SSL connections
- Defending against XSS injection attacks
- Securing forms against CSRF session hijacking

Security enforcement is one of the best things that frameworks have to offer. While basic functionalities of a web application are mostly straightforward and obvious, proper dealing with security takes a lot of work and knowledge. This is also very responsible work. When you mess up something trivial like mailing, this error shows right away, and you can fix it before the application is launched. On the contrary, when there is a hole in security, it remains completely unseen until somebody exploits it; then the damage may be catastrophic.

When you are an inexperienced programmer, frameworks do a great job of taking care of the best security practices for you. If you are a professional, they are still valuable because they save you from writing a lot of not really exciting fragments of code. This chapter takes a closer look at various security problems like setting safe HTTPS connections that allow sending vulnerable data. Next we'll show how to defend against a cross-site scripting (XSS) attack that injects malicious code into a website, and a cross-site request forgery (CSRF) that hijacks the security context of an inconspicuous user.

SETTING SECURE CONNECTIONS

In most cases, sending unsecured data is a normal behavior, but when an application has more to do with business (for example, e-commerce), then security matters. There are ways to secure connections between customers and the server where the web application is deployed. However, you must remember that a Secure Socket Layer (SSL) connection is just a tool and it does not guarantee full security of data transfer. There is currently no secure way to have mixed HTTP/HTTPS access to a site.

Problem

There are many reasons to hide sent information, so you want to make the connection as secure as possible. For web application frameworks, the main problem is closely coupled with secure connection protocols such as HTTPS. Other protocols are very rarely used, so in this section we describe how to prevent information sniffing using HTTPS. But why should you use a secure connection at all? Because you usually don't want to share data transferred to and from clients with third parties. These strangers can use the data to do really nasty things to the application or users, such as stealing passwords or credit card numbers.

Here's an example of data sniffing when someone tries to log on to a web application with HTTP and with HTTPS. We used Wireshark (`www.wireshark.org/`) to sniff packet transmissions.

Under Linux, you need to run Wireshark with root privileges.

For Linux distributions, it's easier to install Wireshark using the specific distribution's package manager.

On Wireshark's homepage, you can download a version for Windows and Mac OS X as well.

So, let's try to sniff some packets. To sniff the proper data, you need to define the capture options. There is an icon below the main menu that shows the capture options window, as shown in Figure 8-1.

FIGURE 8-1: Wireshark main menu

Next, a capture filter needs to be defined. On the capture filter list (shown in Figure 8-2), there is an entry called TCP or UDP port 80 (HTTP) that perfectly satisfies your needs now.

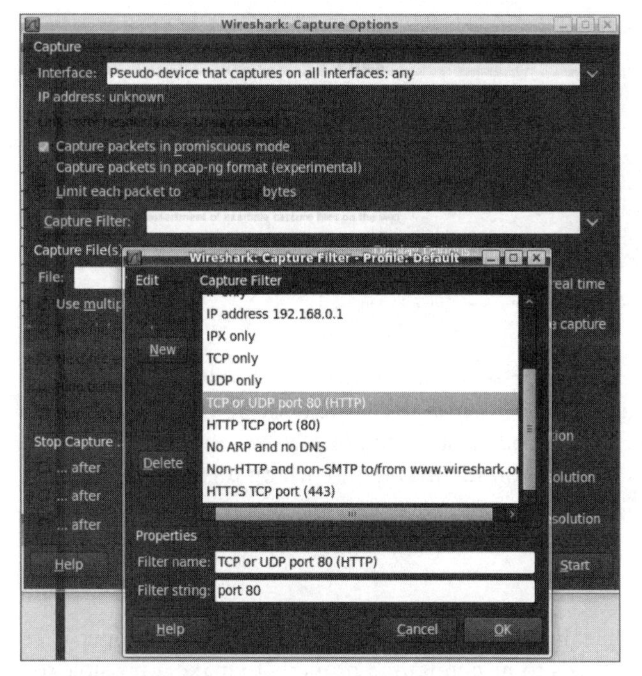

FIGURE 8-2: Wireshark capture filter selection

In this example, you can use a simple login form. To capture packets, you need to click the Start button, which is shown on the bottom right of Figure 8-2. Enter random data in the login and password form input fields; then submit this form. In Wireshark, you should be able to see something like Figure 8-3. If the next page appears, capturing can be switched off because you don't need any more data.

```
63 7.411834   127.0.0.1   HTTP   GET /ch85symfony/sf/sf_web_debug/images/error.png HTTP/1.1
64 7.411922   127.0.0.1   HTTP   HTTP/1.1 304 Not Modified
65 7.444448   127.0.0.1   TCP    56825 > http [ACK] Seq=7075 Ack=9192 Win=49408 Len=0 TSV=2232057 TSER=2232053
67 10.910523  127.0.0.1   HTTP   POST /ch85symfony/index.php/security/login HTTP/1.1  (application/x-www-form-urlencoded)
68 10.943807  127.0.0.1   TCP    http > 56825 [ACK] Seq=9192 Ack=7738 Win=48512 Len=0 TSV=2232407 TSER=2232403
```

FIGURE 8-3: Sniffed HTTP POST request

Captured requests and responses are shown in Figure 8-4. (Note that we assume that the web application is on the same PC where Wireshark is working.) That's why 127.0.0.1 is shown as the address (refer to Figure 8-3) and the pseudo-interface *any* (refer to Figure 8-2) is set in the capture options. Your captured data can differ a bit from the data shown in Figures 8-3 and 8-4. The highlighted HTTP request in Figure 8-3 shows the submit action, which is in fact a `POST` request to a specific URL. After clicking the highlighted entry in Figure 8-3, you will see something similar to Figure 8-4 at the bottom of the Wireshark's window. This is the captured information that is sent to the server. This data is sent as plain text, so it can be sniffed and is easily readable by humans.

```
0210  0d 0a 43 6f 6f 6b 69 65  3a 20 73 79 6d 66 6f 6e   ..Cookie : symfon
0220  79 3d 6c 72 33 73 6e 6a  72 6b 70 70 76 6a 6f 37   y=lr3snj rkppvjo7
0230  76 6b 31 36 73 6d 64 63  65 76 73 31 0d 0a 43 6f   vk16smdc evs1..Co
0240  6e 74 65 6e 74 2d 54 79  70 65 3a 20 61 70 70 6c   ntent-Ty pe: appl
0250  69 63 61 74 69 6f 6e 2f  78 2d 77 77 77 2d 66 6f   ication/ x-www-fo
0260  72 6d 2d 75 72 6c 65 6e  63 6f 64 65 64 0d 0a 43   rm-urlen coded..C
0270  6f 6e 74 65 6e 74 2d 4c  65 6e 67 74 68 3a 20 38   ontent-L ength: 8
0280  36 0d 0a 0d 0a 6c 6f 67  69 6e 3d 4b 61 72 6f 6c   6....log in=Karol
0290  2b 50 72 7a 79 73 74 61  6c 73 6b 69 26 70 61 73   +Przysta lski&pas
02a0  73 77 6f 72 64 3d 70 61  73 73 77 6f 72 64 26 5f   sword=pa ssword&_
02b0  63 73 72 66 5f 74 6f 6b  65 6e 3d 62 37 64 65 66   csrf_tok en=b7def
02c0  64 37 64 63 64 65 37 37  30 36 30 30 63 62 35 38   d7dcde77 0600cb58
02d0  31 62 38 32 61 30 66 63  39 62 64                  1b82a0fc 9bd
```

FIGURE 8-4: Sniffed HTTP POST packets

In the example, the intercepted information is rather useless because you sniffed data that was sent by you to your own web application. But the same can be done at any node between the client and the server. In most cases, such a node is a switch or a server that is relaying the packets, which is why it's so dangerous to send confidential data with an unsecured channel such as HTTP.

Configuring the Web Server

The solution for this problem is really simple. First you need to start with generating proper X.509 keys with OpenSSL. Next, the web server needs to be configured properly to make it possible to connect using HTTPS.

Before running Apache with HTTPS enabled, you need to generate a server certificate, which is used every time when connecting to Apache using the HTTPS protocol. The certificate needs to be signed by someone. In this example, you will sign the certificate yourself. The following approach should be used for testing only. In real business applications, each certificate should be signed by a trusted company. Many companies offer certificates signed by a certificate authority (CA), which promises that the signed certificate is valid.

In the example, you need only a private and public key. The first step is to install OpenSSL, which is really straightforward.

You can get OpenSSL for Linux here: `www.openssl.org/`*, and for Windows here:* `www.openssl.org/related/binaries.html`.

For Linux, you can also install OpenSSL using the distribution's package manager.

As the first step after installation, a private key needs to be created, which can be done with this command:

```
openssl genrsa -out /etc/apache2/ssl/apache.key 1024
```

This gives you a private key file with `.key` extension that is generated using an RSA algorithm with key strength of 1024 bytes. This strength size is now commonly used because 512 may be too weak, and bigger ones are not properly interpreted by some applications. This key should not be published anywhere because it's the private key needed to decrypt encrypted information. The second step is to generate a public key for the private key. This key is published to everyone who wants to connect to the server and is used to encrypt any information sent from clients to the server:

```
openssl req -new -x509 -days 365 -key /etc/apache2/ssl/apache.key
    -out /etc/apache2/ssl/apache.crt
```

Notice that if the previous folder doesn't exist, you need to create it; otherwise, both commands will print an error message. The previous command needs to include the key standard and expiration time, as well as the private key path and the path for the newly created public key as the parameters. X509 and updated standards derived from the same idea are commonly used standards in private and public key cryptography. The time expiration should be given as the number of days from the present that this key is valid. In this example, the public key is valid for one year. Note that if you are using Windows, you should replace the `/etc/...` path with the Windows equivalent; for example, `C:\xampp\apache\ssl\...`. OpenSSL will ask you some questions about key details such as city, region, country, and e-mail address. If you don't like filling in your details, just put in some random data. This doesn't matter in the example, but does in a real production environment. In that case, you should buy a certificate like those offered by VeriSign.

Now Apache or the other web server installed by you needs to know about the generated keys, so you need to make some changes in one configuration file. In XAMPP for Windows, you should edit the `httpd-ssl.conf` file, which is placed in the `C:\xampp\apache\conf\extra\` directory. Ubuntu stores Apache configuration files in `/etc/apache2/sites-enabled/000default-ssl`. Note that Ubuntu sometimes asks to enable sites with SSL. To enable them, create a link in `/sites-enabled` to the file `default-ssl` placed in the `\sites-available` directory. In other distributions, it can be stored under other configuration file names, but you should easily find it because it contains the name `ssl` or `https`.

```
# cd /etc/apache2/sites-enabled
# ln -s /etc/apache2/sites-available/default-ssl 000default-ssl
```

Lines to be changed are those that point to the key files. `SSLCertificateFile` handles the public key file, and `SSLCertificateKeyFile` handles the private key file.

Available for download on Wrox.com

```
SSLEngine on

SSLOptions +FakeBasicAuth +ExportCertData +CompatEnvVars +StrictRequire

SSLCertificateFile /etc/apache2/ssl/apache.crt
SSLCertificateKeyFile /etc/apache2/ssl/apache.key
```

code snippet ssl/configuration/default-ssl

Don't forget to turn `SSLEngine` on if it's turned off. After the configuration, it's time to start or restart Apache web server:

```
/etc/init.d/apache2 restart
```

This should not take long. For this example, you can use (as with the case of the unsecured page) the login form used previously in this chapter. Because the certificate is not signed by a real CA, a security message is displayed in Firefox, shown in Figure 8-5. This is good security from the browser. To proceed, you need to get this certificate and confirm it as an exception.

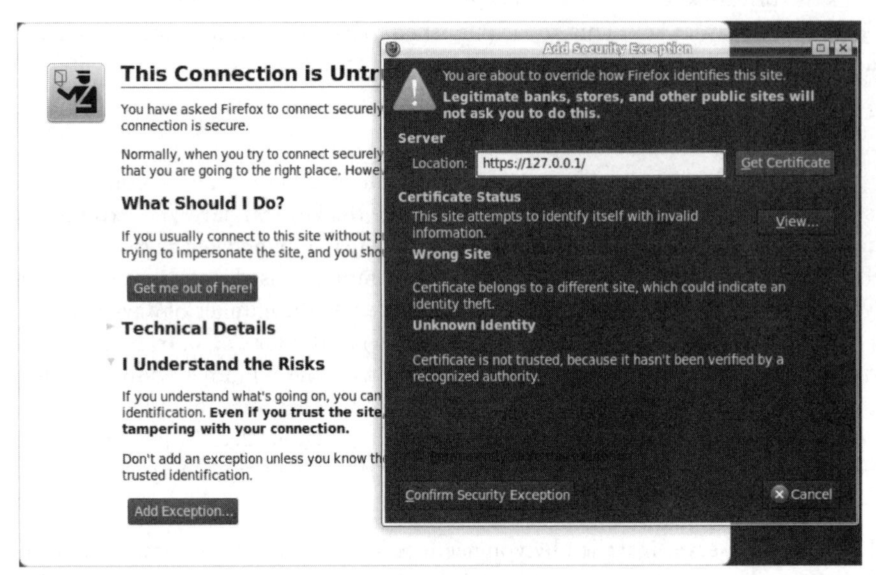

FIGURE 8-5: Firefox unknown certificate security page

When you go to `https://127.0.0.1/index.php/`, you should see that `127.0.0.1` has a blue background in the navigation bar. For the purpose of this example, we used Firefox as the browser, so if you use a different browser, the window might look a little bit different from Figure 8-6. When you click on it, a new window appears. This window shows more details about the certificate.

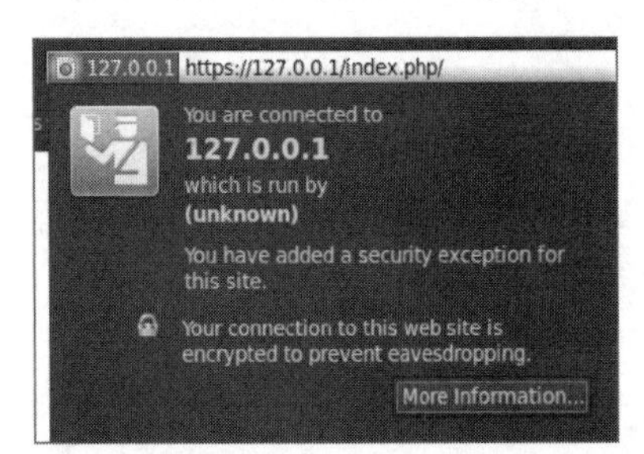

FIGURE 8-6: Secured connection information

There is also a second window with full certificate information. In Firefox, it looks like Figure 8-7. This window also shows your certificate details given as answers for OpenSSL questions.

Let's see what the sniffed information looks like. Instead of HTTP in the capture filter options, you should set HTTPS. It's the last entry in the list in Figure 8-2. After repeating the steps as in HTTP, you should see something similar to Figure 8-8.

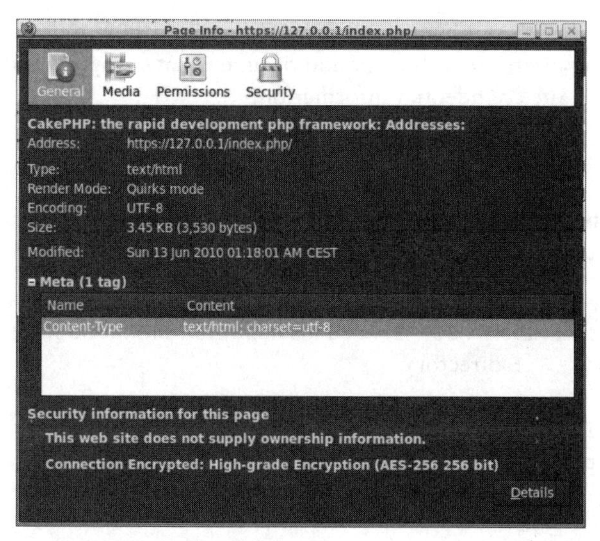

FIGURE 8-7: Certificate information

```
 4 0.000309    127.0.0.1    SSL     Client Hello
 5 0.000335    127.0.0.1    TCP     https > 43820 [ACK] Seq=1 Ack=369 Win=33920 Len=0 TSV=2249834 TSER=2249834
 6 0.006020    127.0.0.1    TLSv1   Server Hello, Certificate, Server Key Exchange, Server Hello Done
 7 0.006033    127.0.0.1    TCP     43820 > https [ACK] Seq=369 Ack=1413 Win=35712 Len=0 TSV=2249835 TSER=2249835
 8 0.008744    127.0.0.1    TLSv1   Client Key Exchange, Change Cipher Spec, Encrypted Handshake Message
 9 0.012025    127.0.0.1    TLSv1   Change Cipher Spec, Encrypted Handshake Message
10 0.012390    127.0.0.1    TLSv1   Application Data
11 0.046495    127.0.0.1    TLSv1   Application Data, Application Data, Application Data, Application Data
12 0.053301    127.0.0.1    TLSv1   Application Data
13 0.053510    127.0.0.1    TLSv1   Application Data
14 0.069316    127.0.0.1    TLSv1   Application Data
15 0.069495    127.0.0.1    TLSv1   Application Data
```

FIGURE 8-8: Sniffed HTTPS POST request and key exchange

As you can see in the figure, there is a key exchange at the beginning, after which the data is sent. Highlight the Application Data entry and you should see something similar to Figure 8-9 at the bottom of the screen.

```
0120  d1 d9 90 ab 5c 33 58 b7  2d a4 c8 4d d8 50 20 64   ....\3X. -..M.P d
0130  a2 3e 74 df 1c ec 43 73  90 a0 d7 6b 98 7e d1 fb   .>t...Cs ...k.~..
0140  12 41 b7 0d da 57 6e b9  ed d4 f0 a6 70 10 d2 b8   .A...Wn. ....p...
0150  da 9b 43 bb 4e 47 af cb  d6 4b 15 43 d1 a7 22 cf   ..C.NG.. .K.C..".
0160  06 bc 4b 6f d3 87 cf a7  4f dc da ac 4e 54 4f d1   ..Ko.... O...NTO.
0170  df 1e 4e 2d a7 c3 16 70  43 7a 2a 38 4d bb c4 ad   ..N-...p Cz*8M...
0180  cb 26 e1 90 7b 65 2c 62  03 54 09 f8 69 a5 79 f8   .&..{e,b .T..i.y.
0190  45 f3 23 f7 49 10 a9 90  0b 87 ab b4 cd ee 31 f8   E.#.I... ......1.
01a0  71 05 84 61 90 d9 9b d8  d1 0e 07 de 96 4f 6b 18   q..a.... .....Ok.
01b0  51 de e4 86 f0 61 79 e5  7b ce 22 c0 73 91 c1 5e   Q....ay. {.".s..^
01c0  2f 69 a8 82 76 1b d1 7d  c7 6a 03 f7 e7 a8 8c f9   /i..v..} .j......
01d0  ae d3 6c a1 ff 46 80 b5  64 7f 6b f8 e0 20 21 fd   ..l..F.. d.k.. !.
01e0  42 17 e7 df c6 de d6 2e  80 30 cb d9 bf b3 94 aa   B....... .0......
01f0  f0 48 00 70 0a 54 52 f3  fe 83 2c f3 bb ee 89 11   .H.p.TR. ..,.....
0200  9c 52 8c 1b de 2f fa 36  b7 9d 5f 29 db 0b 9d 8c   .R.../.6 .._)....
0210  d4 91 ce 74 14 46 41 d4  16 95 ea 65 89 28 7f 57   ...t.FA. ...e.(.W
0220  4c 56 aa 1a f9 67 6d e8  5b 51 cc fa ad 5e f5 13   LV...gm. [Q...^..
0230  fa 91 f4 6d dc a1 97 2c  ed df e7 f3 d2 a0 09 8b   ...m..., ........
0240  20 7c d4 e0 a0 26 93 eb  48 db 96 f9 37 6d 25 e8    |...&.. H...7m%.
0250  37 25 96 dd c5 b6 75 f5  11 b4 e2 8c 13 00 61 e3   7%....u. ......a.
0260  f4 b6 91 ae a2 c9 e7 cf  44 62 f4 ea e2 36 15 7c   ........ Db...6.|
0270  53 da 84 84 27 56 62 f1  79 b6 06 1c 15 cd 94 0e   S...'Vb. y.......
0280  bb 92 01 9c 3b 33 76 6a  3a c5 49 dc 6d d8 cf 91   ....;3vj :.I.m...
0290  b5 f1 f6 7a 88 22 9e 53  e3                        ...z.".S .
```

FIGURE 8-9: Encrypted HTTPS POST request packets

Try to read it now. This is an encrypted text, so it's not human-friendly. We can't promise that decrypting it is impossible, but it's almost impossible in a short period of time. That's why using the HTTPS protocol is very useful when sending any confidential information.

Symfony

Symfony provides filters, which are methods executed before sending any data to the client. Filters are implemented as a design pattern called *chain of responsibility*. (This pattern is described in Chapter 1 of this book).

To create a filter, you need to make a class that inherits `sfFilter`. This definition should be stored as `sslFilter.class.php` in the application's `/lib` directory.

```
<?php
class sslFilter extends sfFilter {
     public function execute($filterChain) {
         $context = $this->getContext();
         $request = $context->getRequest();
         if (!$request->isSecure()) {
             $secure_url = str_replace('http', 'https', $request->getUri());
             return $context->getController()->redirect($secure_url);
         } else {
             $filterChain->execute();
         }
     }
}
```

code snippet /ssl/symfony/apps/frontend/lib/sslFiler.class.php

The main method that is invoked when the filter is running is `execute()`. The preceding code checks whether the current page is secured (that this action has an `is_secure` entry in the `/config/security.yml` file of modules). To access this action, you must have privileges, so you need to be authenticated first. In other words, if the current action is available for the public, it should replace `http` with `https` in the URL and redirect to a page prepared this way. If the current action is not available for the public, return the handle to the next filter. To enable a filter, add an entry in `filters.yml` in the configuration directory of the application. Call this entry SSL, as in the following code. It is important to set the class name so it reflects the name of the filter it refers to.

```
ssl:
    class: sslFilter

rendering: ~
security:  ~

cache:     ~
execution: ~
```

code snippet /ssl/symfony/apps/frontend/config/filters.yml

Another important thing to note is where this filter is placed in `filters.yml`. Symfony goes through `filters.yml` from the beginning to the end, and invokes each filter. The last invoked filter is `execution`. It doesn't matter whether there is any filter after this one because it will not be invoked. That's why SSL is the first filter in the preceding code, but it could also be placed after `rendering` or `security`. The list of executed filters is available in Symfony's web debug logs (see Figure 8-10).

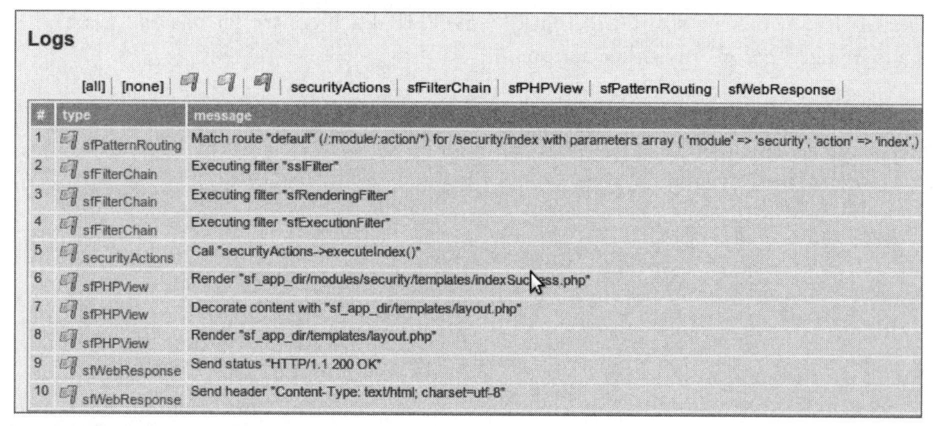

FIGURE 8-10: Web debug logs

If you want to use HTTPS in one module, you can easily get the current module name by invoking this method: `$context->getModuleName()`. Now you need only to create a simple `if-else` statement.

CakePHP

In CakePHP, the process is a little bit different and much easier to implement. Because HTTPS is used only when confidential data is sent, it is more useful to place every confidential action into one controller. CakePHP controllers are built so that the `beforeFilter()` method is executed, as in Symfony, before any other action is invoked.

```
function beforeFilter() {
   if(!$this->RequestHandler->isSSL()) {
      $this->redirect('https://' . env('SERVER_NAME') . $this->here);
      exit();
   }
}
```

code snippet /ssl/cakephp/app/controller/ssl_controller.php

This code redirects to a secured web page if the `isSSL()` method doesn't return a `true` value. The *`$this->here`* variable stores the module name and action, which you can give as a fixed string. The `isSSL()` method is a part of the `RequestHandler` component that needs to be added prior to `beforeFilter()`.

```
var $components  = array('RequestHandler');
```

code snippet /ssl/cakephp/app/controller/ssl_controller.php

At the end, the exit() method should be invoked for security purposes because nothing else should be executed after redirecting.

Zend Framework

Zend Framework offers a solution similar to that of CakePHP. Each controller has an init() method, which is invoked before any other actions.

Available for download on Wrox.com

```
<?php
require_once 'Zend/Controller/Action.php';
class IndexAction extends Zend_Controller_Action {
     function init() {
        $path = "/";
         if( empty($_SERVER["HTTPS"])) {
             $hostname = $_SERVER["HTTP_HOST"];
             $url = 'https://'.$hostname .$path;
             $this->_redirect($url);
         }
     }
}
```

code snippet /ssl/zf/applications/controllers/IndexController.php

Because you are in the default index controller, the $path variable is set to /. In the lines that follow, the HTTPS protocol is checked. If it is being used, nothing happens; if it isn't being used, the $url of the application is set, and the redirection method is invoked for it. This is a good solution when you are in the default controller. A more generic solution is presented in the following code:

Available for download on Wrox.com

```
function init() {
        $request = $this->getRequest();
        $module = $request->getModuleName();
        $controller = $request->getControllerName();
        $action = $request->getActionName();
        $path = $module .'/'.$controller.'/'.$action;
        /* as previously */
```

code snippet /ssl/zf/applications/controllers/IndexController.php

In this piece of the code module, the controller and action names are retrieved. Next, a proper $path for current module and action is built. In the case of an index action in the index controller, the $path variable would look like index/index, so you would be redirected to https://127.0.0.1/index/index, for example.

SECURING A PROFILE FORM AGAINST XSS AND INJECTION ATTACKS

Cross-site scripting (XSS) and all kinds of injection attacks are a real threat that must always be taken into account when developing web applications. These attacks are commonly used by hackers because of their simplicity. The only knowledge one needs is just some basics of SQL, HTML, JS, CSS, and general web application structure.

Problem

XSS and injection attacks are different security problems, but they use almost the same web application vulnerabilities. This section explains how each attack works and how is it used.

What Is XSS?

Unlike CSRF, XSS is not dedicated against a particular user, but against the website. XSS utilizes the injection mechanism. Figure 8-11 shows an example of how it works.

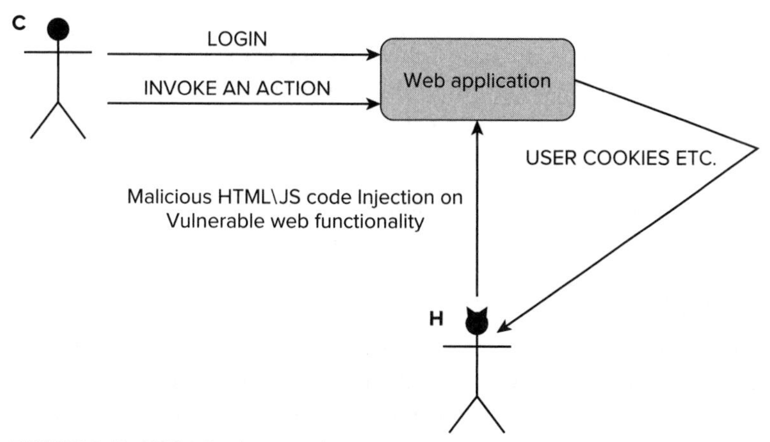

FIGURE 8-11: XSS attack example

This example starts with a vulnerable functionality of a web application. This security bug can be used to add some malicious code to the website that will be executed every time a user invokes this functionality (for example, it displays a profile on a social network). Because it's invoked for every user who executes it, this code can send user confidential information (for example, session cookies) to the attacker. The problem is that the web application doesn't check the data that is sent to it.

Why SQL Injections Are So Dangerous

SQL injection attacks exploit the vulnerability that occurs when the data entered into a form on the website (or otherwise sent to the server) is not properly validated. If someone enters a string that contains an apostrophe or quote into a web form, various things can happen — from simple SQL query execution errors to erasing all data from a database. Suppose that a web page contains the following form:

```
<form method="post" action="login.php">
    Login: <input type="text" name="login">
    Password: <input type="password" name="pass">
    <input type="submit" value="Login">
</form>
```

Now suppose that after form data is submitted, a PHP script is executed with the following query:

```
SELECT user FROM users WHERE login = '$login' AND password = $pass
```

The `$login` and `$pass` variables contain the username and password entered within the form. Of course, this is a simplified example and in real applications, passwords are never stored in databases as plain text, but as MD5 or SHA1 hashes. However, no matter what the storage technique is, when you enter the following string as a password:

```
' OR '1'='1
```

the resulting query to be executed is as follows:

```
SELECT user FROM users WHERE login = 'admin' AND password='' OR '1'='1'
```

The form input has changed the query that checks the password, and now it uses two logical conditions. Although the first might be false, the other one is always true. So it is possible to log in having only a valid login name.

The next example is more aggressive. After inserting the following code as the password, the users table and all its contents are removed from the database. This could be truly catastrophic because you have a table called `users`.

```
'; DROP TABLE users;
```

Attacks exploiting SQL injection vulnerability can steal, modify, or remove information from databases, as well as grant unauthorized access, so they are very dangerous.

How Do Other Injection Attacks Work?

Besides SQL injections, there are also JavaScript, HTML, and CSS injection attacks. JavaScript injection is commonly used in XSS attacks. If there is a security vulnerability in web applications that enables an attacker to inject client-side code, which is then displayed in a web page viewed by other users, it can mislead them to perform undesirable actions. Scripts located in the affected site can bypass some of the mechanisms that control access to user data held by the browser. A potential attacker can find ways of injecting malicious scripts into web pages in order to gain greater privileges to access sensitive page content, session cookies, and other information stored for the user by the web browser.

One of the most common forms of JavaScript injection is when web page content is generated directly from data submitted to a server by parameters in an HTTP query, or simply by an HTML form. It is possible only when no proper sanitizing of the submitted data is present. At first glance, submitting a JavaScript injection input to the website does not seem to be a serious problem because the user would could influence only his own security (his own browser cookies, cache data, and so on). A potential attacker can prepare malicious code sections to modify web-page content by adding hidden frames or misleading links that can cause a viewer's browser to navigate to other URLs. This process can happen completely in the background; in such a case, an attacker can interact with a user without his knowledge, which can threaten his security. For example, the following code can be put into a browser's URL bar:

```
javascript:void(document.cookie="login=true");
```

JavaScript will modify the content of a cookie. This example illustrates how simple it is to interfere with information held by the browser. The next example shows how easy it is to view session cookie content stored by the browser:

```
javascript:alert(document.cookie);
```

There is a more persistent variation of JavaScript injection that can be used to attack vulnerable web applications. It relies on the fact that the data submitted by the attacker is later saved on the server;

then this data (whenever it is malicious script or simple text) is displayed on a web page displayed to other users while they are browsing affected content. Without proper HTML escaping, this can be a serious security flaw.

Most malicious JavaScript programs act upon the document object model (DOM) and modify the structure and content of a web page by injecting them with dynamically generated data.

For example, a persistent attack can look like this. A social network allows posting of HTML-formatted messages on an online message board. An attacker prepares a message containing malicious code and posts it on that board. While a user views that message board, his cookies and session data are stolen and sent to the attacker. At this point, the attacker can use the stolen cookie to use the user's session and impersonate him.

Solution

HTML *sanitization* (validation, escaping, filtering) is a method to eliminate some XSS vulnerabilities. This solution also works against injection attacks. To sanitize is to validate incoming data and reject undesired characters or replace them with acceptable ones. Of course, simple character replacement isn't the only solution to this problem. The appropriate method may depend on the context in which the problem occurs. These methods rely on escaping all unwanted data and leaving only the content that is correct for the context. In this way, it is possible to apply a proper escaping scheme, depending on where the sanitized input needs to be placed. For example, sanitization can be done by JavaScript escaping, HTML escaping, CSS escaping, and so on. By using these methods, protection against injection attacks can be a fairly simple task as long as the web application does not require rich data storage.

Look at some examples of how to protect scripts against injection attacks. The primary way to protect against SQL injection is to prevent unauthorized changes of queries executed by the database engine. In PHP, this can be done by executing the PHP built-in function `addslashes()` on the text in each parameter used for the construction of queries. This function adds the backslash before characters, such as `'`, `"`, or `\`, so that the characters are not treated as special characters. There are also functions specific to each database, such as that offered by the MySQL server: `mysql_real_escape_string()`. This function works like `addslashes()`, with the difference that it takes into account the character set used in the MySQL connection. The following example shows how to utilize the server `mysql_real_escape_string()` function while building an SQL query.

```
$user = mysql_real_escape_string($_POST['user_name']);
$sql = "SELECT * FROM users WHERE username = '$user'";
```

PHP delivers functions that can be used to sanitize strings. There are two commonly used PHP functions: `htmlentities()` and `htmlspecialchars()`.

```
htmlentities($str);
htmlspecialchars("<a href='test'>Test</a>");
```

These commands are very similar. They change HTML tags such as <a>link</a> to <a>link</a>. A user will see strange text, but thanks to the above commands, it will not be executed as an HTML or JavaScript code.

Symfony

In Symfony, it's very easy to protect against XSS and injection attacks. Symfony does it globally; you need only to edit the application's `settings.yml` configuration file and turn on the escaping.

```
all:
 .settings:
   escaping_strategy: on
   escaping_method: ESC_SPECIALCHARS
```

code snippet /xss/symfony/app/frontend/config/settings.yml

There are a few escaping methods in Symfony. As described before, PHP delivers two main functions, which are used in Symfony as follows:

```
ESC_SPECIALCHARS - htmlspecialchars(),
ESC_ENTITIES - htmlentities().
```

Symfony also has two methods dedicated to JavaScript escaping:

```
ESC_JS,
ESC_JS_NO_ENTITIES.
```

These methods are used when you want to use dynamically changed HTML code or just a string inside JavaScript. If you don't want to escape any values, just set *`ESC_RAW`* as the method or turn escaping off.

CakePHP

The *`Sanitize`* class is responsible for escaping in CakePHP. To use its methods, you need to add it at the beginning of the controller.

```
App::import('Sanitize');
class xssController extends AppController {
}
```

code snippet /xss/cakephp/app/controller/xss_controller.php

Sanitizing allows the use of four methods: `clean()`, `escape()`, `html()`, and `paranoid()`.

```
Sanitize::clean($data, $options);
```

The `clean()` method changes the `$data` input and outputs as given in `$options`. Available options are `odd_spaces`, `encode`, `dollar`, `carriage`, `unicode`, `escape`, and `backslash`. Each option cleans the input string or array. To enable them, set them as `true`, as shown in the following code:

```
Sanitize::clean($data, array('backslash'=>true));
```

code snippet /xss/cakephp/app/controller/xss_controller.php

The escape() method escapes a SQL statement where $database is the variable that describes the used database (see database.php in the configuration directory); for example, 'default'.

```
Sanitize::escape(string $SQL, string $database)
```

code snippet /xss/cakephp/app/controller/xss_controller.php

The html() method cleans a string of HTML tags:

```
$HTMLString = '<a href='test'>Test</a>';
echo Sanitize::html($HTMLString);
```

code snippet /xss/cakephp/app/controller/xss_controller.php

The method in the preceding code will print <a href="test">Test</a>:

```
echo Sanitize::html($HTMLString, array('remove' => true));
```

If you set the remove option to true, you get a string that doesn't contain any HTML tag.

The last method is paranoid(), which removes all special characters such as ;, :, <, >, @, #.

```
$HTMLString = "<a href='test'>Test</a>";
echo Sanitize::paranoid($HTMLString);
```

code snippet /xss/cakephp/app/controller/xss_controller.php

The preceding code prints a href=testTesta.

Zend Framework

Zend Framework delivers the Zend_Filter class, which is responsible for sanitizing. Additionally, ZF offers a method that is available as a helper in the view layer.

```
$this->escape($this->testData);
```

Some developers prefer a strategy to escape only the output that is shown to the user. This is usually a good practice because XSS and injection attacks are based on showing malicious code. If it's escaped before it's sent to the user, the attack fails.

A second approach in ZF is to filter the bad code within the controller. To do this, you need to create an instance of Zend_Filter_HtmlEntities and invoke filter() with a parameter that is the filtered data. The filter() method returns an escaped value, so it's clean and ready to safely use.

```
$entityFilter = new Zend_Filter_HtmlEntities();
$goodData = $entityFilter->filter($HTMLString);
```

code snippet /xss/zf/application/controllers/IndexController.php

It is possible to specify filters still while building a web form, as shown here:

```
$this->addElement('text', 'firstName', array(
    'label'  => 'Your first name:',
    'required'   => false,
   'filters'    => array('StripTags'),
));
```

code snippet /xss/zf/application/forms/Addresses.php

A filter created this way will return the input string, with all HTML and PHP tags removed from it. Yet it is possible to specify which tags are allowed and which are not.

CSRF

Cross-site request forgery (CSRF) attacks are commonly mistaken for XSS attacks because of similarities in their outcomes. They work completely differently, however. While for XSS the attacker must put malicious code on a targeted website, for CSRF all he needs is to make you click a prepared link. That's all; there is no JavaScript required, and you can even have scripting disabled in your browser.

Problem

Developers have some problems defending against this kind of attack because it takes much knowledge to know how to do it properly. And there is no limit on the severity of these attacks. Fortunately, all this knowledge is already included in the frameworks, so this section describes how to secure against CSRF fast and simply.

What Is CSRF?

This attack is linked with form security and exploits some form vulnerabilities. Unlike XSS attacks, CSRF attacks are more user-oriented, and they do more harm to users than to web applications. Figure 8-12 illustrates a short CSRF example. *C* is the unaware *Customer*, and *H* stands for the *Hacker*.

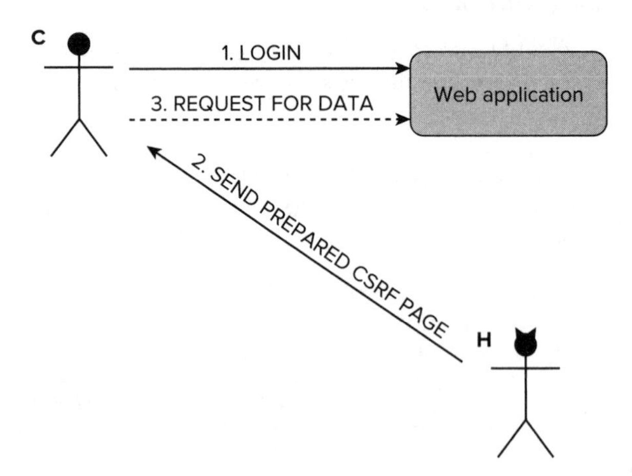

FIGURE 8-12: CSRF attack example

Because CSRF attacks can be carried out only in some situations, to make this attack possible, some additional favorable circumstances need to be fulfilled. Let the web application in Figure 8-12 be an e-commerce application. *H* wants to get profile data. To get it, *H* needs to execute a piece of code such as the following on the attacked side. *C* needs to be logged in to the web application, and then *H* makes him execute this script by a prepared link.

```
<script>
var url = 'http://example.com/profile;
setTimeout(30000, "window.open(url)");
</script>
</html>
```

So here's how it works: Customer *C* logs in to the web application. Next, *H* sends a link to the prepared web page. As shown in the preceding code, a fixed URL is opened in a new window after a period of time. This window displays the profile data. This script could be even more malicious and save this data somewhere or buy something expensive. *C* doesn't know about this attack because the malicious web page can be opened in another tab in his browser or even completely in the background. Therefore, this kind of attack is very popular, but it also needs some information about the attacked person to make it possible.

Solution

To defend against CSRF attacks, a small change needs to be done in all forms that could be potentially used for this attack. *Hacker* needs to collect some information about *Customer* and also about the web application that he uses. Suppose that *H* is also a customer that has his own account in the example e-commerce web application. *H* can collect information about form structure and fields, so he can prepare a malicious web page on this basis.

Each form has some input fields (`name`, `forename`, `email`, and so on). Values that are entered into these fields are different for each user, but fields usually still have the same names (`<input name="">`). In some applications, the fields may differ for each user, which makes this attack more difficult, but it's still possible. If the attacker can figure out the form names that are expected to be sent from *C*, this attack may succeed.

Symfony

Symfony delivers CSRF protection utilities out of the box, just as all the frameworks described in this book do. By default, these protection utilities are enabled in `settings.yml`, which is placed in the application's `/config` directory.

```
all:
  .settings:
    csrf_secret:                vxfdb8wrh34ni3th93y
```

code snippet /csrf/symfony/apps/frontend/config/settings.yml

For security purposes, you need to change the `csrf_secret` value. When this value is correctly set, an additional input field will be placed in each form, called *`_csrf_token`*.

```
<input type="hidden" name="_csrf_token" value="58702cd53a37190250899563f3dd9928"
    id="csrf_token" />
```

code snippet /csrf/symfony/apps/frontend/modules/csrfExample/templates/indexSuccess.php

The value of this field is different from that given in the configuration file because `csrf_secret` in the `settings.yml` config file is a *salt*, or random seed, used to generate the token. The salt is only one of the items that produce the resulting token value. All other items can be known to the attacker in some cases, but the salt is and should be always kept in secret.

CakePHP

CakePHP allows for securing a web application against CSRF attacks as well. Instead of setting a common variable in configuration files, as in Symfony, CakePHP gives the possibility to secure each controller separately.

To secure all forms that are generated with a controller, add this line at the top of it:

```
public $components = array('Security');
```

After adding it, an exemplary controller looks like the following:

Available for download on Wrox.com

```
<?php
class AddressesController extends AppController {
  var $name = 'addresses';
  var $components = array('Security');
  function index($id = null) {
    $this->set('address_list', $this->Address->find('all'));
  }
```

code snippet /csrf/cakephp/app/controller/xss_controller.php

As with Symfony, a salt needs to be set. This can be done in `core.php`, which is placed in the `/config` directory.

Available for download on Wrox.com

```
Configure::write('Security.salt', 'vxfdb8wrh34ni3th93y');
```

code snippet /csrf/cakephp/app/config/core.php

Unlike Symfony, CakePHP generates not one, but two CSRF tokens.

Available for download on Wrox.com

```
<form id="AddressEditForm"
    method="post"
    action="/index.php/addresses/edit/addresses/edit"
    accept-charset="utf-8">
    <div style="display:none;">
        <input type="hidden" name="_method" value="POST" />
        <input type="hidden" name="data[_Token][key]"
            value="7f72422a68cfce07a88966cade00118025b034a8"
            id="Token1034995606" />
    </div>
```

code snippet /csrf/cakephp/app/view/csrf/index.ctp

The first one is placed after `<form>` start tag, and the second one is placed in the bottom part of the following code:

Available for download on Wrox.com

```
    <div class="submit">
        <input type="submit" value="Save address" />
    </div>
```

```
    <div style="display:none;">
        <input type="hidden" name="data[_Token][fields]"
            value="5d49a9573ceb05291667243fcc672d85f1
            bdbd25%3An%3A1%3A%7Bv%3A0%3Bf%3A10%3A%22Nqqerff.vq%22%3B%7D"
            id="TokenFields1736401509" />
    </div>
</form>
```

code snippet /csrf/cakephp/app/view/csrf/index.ctp

These keys are both checked after each submit. If they are not the same, an error message is shown. The preceding code prevents CSRF attacks because token values are different for each user, and the attacker can't know the values for each user.

Zend Framework

In contrast with the previous two frameworks, each form is secured separately in Zend Framework. To enable CSRF protection, you need to add an additional element of type `hash` into the form definition.

```
<?php
class Application_Form_Guestbook extends Zend_Form {
    public function init() {
        $this->addElement(
            'hash', 'csrf_token', array('salt' => 'vxfdb8wrh34ni3th93y'));
    }
}
```

code snippet /csrf/zf/application/forms/Guestbook.php

In ZF, a salt is also employed, which generates a form field as follows:

```
<dt id="csrf_token-label"> </dt>
<dd id="csrf_token-element">
    <input type="hidden"
        name="csrf_token"
        value="5e7b35565c404102c04697fa4637f4c7"
        id="csrf_token">
</dd>
```

code snippet /csrf/zf/application/views/scripts/index/index.phtml

This field is checked during form validation. The same result can be achieved as well with the following code:

```
$token = new Zend_Form_Element_Hash('token');
$token->setSalt(md5(uniqid(rand(), TRUE)));
$token->setTimeout(Globals::getConfig()->authentication->timeout);
$this->addElement($token);
```

code snippet /csrf/zf/application/forms/Guestbook.php

A timeout can also be set for the token to make it lose validity after a certain amount of time.

Templates

Beware the Jabberwock, my son!
The jaws that bite, the claws that catch!
Beware the Jubjub bird, and shun
The frumious Bandersnatch!

— Lewis Carroll

WHAT'S IN THIS CHAPTER?

- Creating an image gallery using Lightbox
- Integrating chosen template engines with frameworks
- Pros and cons of using template engines
- Overview of popular template engines

Previous chapters discussed frameworks' innards; this chapter focuses on the presentation layer instead. So what are these template engines, and why are they so important? In web development, PHP code processes all data, so it's responsible for the business logic. The view layer represented by template engines is the presentation part of your site. A template engine allows you to develop websites with various different layouts or themes for the same core functionality.

Template engines are very popular tools among PHP projects that do not use any frameworks. Despite their popularity however, they are not often used along with web frameworks. In this chapter, we will explain why it is so and show a few tricks to make them get along with each other.

CREATING A SIMPLE IMAGE GALLERY BY USING HELPERS AND LIGHTBOX

The following script renders an index page. It uses some PHP functions to generate the page content intertwined with HTML blocks. (This is a programming style from the year 2000, when PHP was a new thing altogether.)

```
<?php
$head_title = 'Title';
$block_name ='News block';
display_content();
function_1();
function_2();
?>

<html>
    <head>
        <title>
            <?php echo $head_title; ?>
        </title>
</head>
<body>
    <tag>
        <tag>
            <?php echo $block_name; ?>
        </tag>
    </tag>
    <tag>
        <?php echo display_content(); ?>
    </tag>
</body>
</html>
```

Today, more advanced template engines are used to separate the view layer from PHP code, which is used for the business logic. This allows developers to work on the code of the system without interfering with the designers who create different layouts for it. This is a good programming practice just like the Model-View-Controller (MVC) architecture offered by the frameworks.

A second commonly known good practice that can be used here is Don't Repeat Yourself (DRY). You can use just one template file for a few functionalities if the template code is the same in all of them. This is possible because of separating business logic from the view. The following pseudocode example demonstrates how PHP scripts should be separated from an HTML template:

```
<?php
$variable1;
$variable2;
$variable3;

function_1();
function_2();
function_3();
function_4();
render_template (template.tpl);
?>
```

This code presents a quasi-controller that renders the following template file:

```
<html>
<head>
    <title></title>
</head>
<body>
    <tag>
        <tag></tag>
    </tag>
    <tag></tag>
    <tag></tag>
</body>
</html>
```

The template fragment can still contain PHP scripts, but usually it requires a template language to indicate segments that are to be filled with content by a script. These languages vary from one template engine to another, but usually cover the same functions.

Presentation Layer Helpers

Before you move to the template engines, we will discuss a nice and easy topic concerning the presentation layer as well. We'll show you how to create an image gallery in your frameworks by using the frameworks' helper classes and the Lightbox JavaScript application.

Helpers are classes that encapsulate certain frequently used functionalities and allow developers to use these complex functions easily without the need for much coding. Usually helpers are designed for the view part of the MVC pattern because most repeated code lines are located in the view files. You can use helpers to format and prepare output data easily using a single function/method.

The three frameworks that you work with in this book have a number of useful helpers. In previous chapters, helpers were used many times in a very natural manner, without the necessity to learn their usage or even to explain it too much. Well, look at the following example:

```
<?php echo $html->text('UserName') ?>
```

This line from a view file can create the standard HTML text input tag with the `name` attribute set to `UserName`, but it also may encapsulate this input field in `<p></p>` tags or `<div></div>` tags just like this:

```
<div class="form-Input">
    <input type="text" name="UserName" />
</div>
```

It all depends on how this HTML helper is designed. Now, knowing only this example and the common HTML form tags, you can assume that when you write the following line:

```
<?php echo $html->password('UserPass') ?>
```

it should render a password input field with `name` attribute set to `UserPass`, just like this:

```
<div class="form-Input">
    <input type="password" name="UserPass" />
</div>
```

The preceding code snippets illustrate how intuitive helpers can be. Similar helpers are available for formatting data, field validation, time-date operations, and so on. Custom helpers can also be added to facilitate other aspects of web development.

Now we will focus on the main topic of this section: for every web developer there comes a time when he needs to have an image gallery in the project that he is working on, be it his own portfolio or a different random project. The most basic image gallery can be created using only an HTML page with multiple thumbnails or plain links connected to large images that can be opened in a new page or different frame. This solution is rather outdated because the user can spend more time navigating the gallery than viewing it.

Lightbox

Today, in most cases, image galleries are built using JavaScript. JavaScript requires more work for the developer and makes it more difficult to modify an existing gallery, but most JavaScript libraries provide a few additional features — for example, opening images with some basic navigation, such as next and previous buttons.

Now if you wonder whether you can learn how to create your own image gallery from this book, the answer is *no*. We would love to show it, but the book would grow another 50 pages or so and it would not really be framework-related code. Instead you will learn how to implement one of the most common, lightweight, and dynamic ready-to-use image galleries: the Lightbox.

Lightbox is a JavaScript application, written by Lokesh Dhakar, used to display image galleries utilizing a popup window. This script has gained wide popularity, mostly due to easy implementation and great presentation style that fits any website. You can read more about Lightbox at its author's website: `www.huddletogether.com/projects/lightbox2`. Now you will learn how to include Lightbox 2 in your application, developed for all three frameworks.

Symfony

There are several solutions that allow you to create web image galleries simply by adding one of the available Symfony plug-ins. First you will learn how to implement one of these solutions that enables you to display image galleries in your application using the popular Lightbox script. Later you will find a short description of two selected alternative solutions.

sfJQueryLightBoxPlugin

If you've read this book chapter by chapter, you probably already know the routine and will not be surprised by anything written in this section. sfJQueryLightBoxPlugin allows you to use the sfJQuery-Lightbox helper that transforms image links into a Lightbox image gallery. You can find details about this plug-in at `www.symfony-project.org/plugins/sfJQueryLightboxPlugin`. First of all, the sfJ-QueryLightBoxPlugin requires you to have sfJqueryReloadedPlugin already installed. To install it, simply execute the following command in your project command line:

```
$ symfony plugin:install sfJqueryReloadedPlugin
```

For details on this plug-in, please refer to its website: `www.symfony-project.org/plugins/sfJqueryReloadedPlugin`. If you already have sfJqueryReloadedPlugin, you can proceed to sfJQueryLightboxPlugin installation.

To install sfJQueryLightboxPlugin, you need to simply type the following command into the console at your project directory:

```
$ symfony plugin:install sfJQueryLightBoxPlugin
```

Next, you can clear the cache data by typing the following command into your console:

```
$ symfony cache:clear
```

Assuming that you created a project and a sample `frontend` application, at this point you should be ready to start editing the files of your project. Let's create a sample module:

```
$ symfony generate:module frontend lightexample
```

You need only one method for this example. What is more, this method should be empty because all the gallery presentation is done in the view layer:

```
public function executeIndex() {
}code snippet
```

In order to use features that were installed by sfJQueryLightBoxPlugin, you need to modify the module's view file located in `/apps/frontend/modules/lightexample/templates`. It is necessary to indicate there that you want to use the jQuery helper required by the sfJQueryLightbox helper to make it work. To do so, just add the following line in your `indexSuccess.php` file:

```
<?php use_helper("jQuery") ?>
```

code snippet /gallery/symfony/apps/frontend/modules/lightexample/templates/indexSuccess.php

Once it is done, you can now do the same for the JQueryLightbox helper. Just add another line:

```
<?php use_helper("sfJQueryLightbox") ?>
```

code snippet /gallery/symfony/apps/frontend/modules/lightexample/templates/indexSuccess.php

Now in the same template file, you can use the `light_image()` function for the image that you want to have the Lightbox effect. It is done like this:

```
<?php echo light_image(
                       $thumbnail_url,
                       $full_image_url,
                       array('title' => $image_title ),
                       $thumb_options
                       );
?>
```

code snippet /gallery/symfony/apps/frontend/modules/lightexample/templates/indexSuccess.php

The example of a simple gallery can look as follows:

Available for download on Wrox.com

```
<?php use_helper( 'jQuery', 'sfJQueryLightbox') ?>
<h1>Lightbox Logos Gallery</h1>
<?php echo light_image(
    'http://www.symfony-project.org/images/symfony_logo.gif',
    'http://www.symfony-project.org/images/symfony_logo.gif',
    array('title' => 'Symfony Logo'),
    array('border' => 0)); ?>
<br />
<?php echo light_image(
    'http://cakephp.org/img/cake-logo.png',
    'http://cakephp.org/img/cake-logo.png',
    array('title' => 'CakePHP Logo' ),
    array('border' => 0)); ?>
<br />
<?php echo light_image(
    'http://framework.zend.com/images/logo.gif',
    'http://framework.zend.com/images/logo.gif',
    array('title' => 'Zend Framework Logo' ),
    array('border' => 0)); ?>
```

code snippet /gallery/symfony/apps/frontend/modules/lightexample/templates/indexSuccess.php

Note that in this example, the same image is used for the thumbnail as well as for the normal-size image. The preceding example should be rendered by the browser the same way as it is illustrated by Figure 9-1.

FIGURE 9-1: Example of an image gallery using sfJQueryLightBoxPlugin

If your image gallery misses some graphics, such as the next or close buttons, it may be due to having a different web root than the one assumed by the plug-in. The default directory for Lightbox graphics is `/sfJQueryLightboxPlugin/images/`.

It is possible to change paths for every image used by Lightbox. To do this, you need to add a few code lines into the `app.yml` file. For this example, the first slash character had to be removed from the image paths, in order to make Lightbox display all elements correctly. This is shown in the following code:

```
all:
  sf_jquery_lightbox:
    css_dir: '/sfJQueryLightboxPlugin/css/'
    js_dir:  '/sfJQueryLightboxPlugin/js/'
    imageLoading: 'sfJQueryLightboxPlugin/images/lightbox-ico-loading.gif'
    imageBtnClose: 'sfJQueryLightboxPlugin/images/lightbox-btn-close.gif'
    imageBtnPrev: 'sfJQueryLightboxPlugin/images/lightbox-btn-prev.gif'
    imageBtnNext: 'sfJQueryLightboxPlugin/images/lightbox-btn-next.gif'
    imageBlank: 'sfJQueryLightboxPlugin/images/lightbox-blank.gif'
    txtImage: 'Image'
    txtOf: 'of'
```

code snippet /gallery/symfony/apps/frontend/config/app.yml

sfLightboxPlugin

sfLightboxPlugin is an alternative to sfJQueryLightBoxPlugin introduced earlier. After installation, sfLightboxPlugin provides you with LightboxHelper that allows you to create image galleries and slideshows very easily.

It may be a little less popular among users of the Symfony framework, but on the other hand it is compatible with older versions of Symfony. Installation files and examples for this plug-in can be found at `www.symfony-project.org/plugins/sfLightboxPlugin`.

sfMediaBrowserPlugin

sfMediaBrowser is a plug-in that works directly on the file structure to allow users to manage file uploads. It comes with a complete user interface for managing files as well as folders that are contained in a specific directory. What is unusual about sfMediaBrowser is that it does not use any database.

This plug-in comes with a widget and a validator that can be used in any form to replace the standard HTML file upload input field. You can get installation files from the following website: `www.symfony-project.org/plugins/sfMediaBrowserPlugin`.

CakePHP

Using Lightbox in Cake is nearly as straightforward as in any static website. To demonstrate this example of Lightbox 2, you need to download the package from the author's website: `www.huddletogether.com/projects/lightbox2`. The example gallery will consist of three links to framework logos, as illustrated in Figure 9-2.

Lightbox Logos Gallery

Symfony Logo
CakePHP Logo
Zend Framework Logo

FIGURE 9-2: Links to framework logos

When you have the Lightbox2 package, it is time to put all the files into your CakePHP application directory. Lightbox uses the Prototype and Scriptaculous libraries to render some effects while displaying images. Assuming that you follow the standard CakePHP installation, you need to put the following JavaScript libraries inside the CakePHP `/app/webroot/js/` directory:

- builder.js
- effects.js
- lightbox.js
- prototype.js
- scriptaculous.js

The same thing goes for the Lightbox CSS file (`lightbox.css`) that you need to place into the `/app/webroot/css/` directory.

The Lightbox styles use the `../images/` path to display images, so you also need to make sure that any paths to images in the CSS are correct. If you placed the `lightbox.css` file as instructed, all images used by Lightbox should be located in the `/app/webroot/images/` directory. That is all you need to do in terms of Lightbox installation.

Next there are a few things that need to be done to use the installed Lightbox in your application. Add the following lines of code to your site's layout that is located in the `/app/views/layouts/` directory and you're good to go. In this example, the `default.ctp` layout file is used. CakePHP allows you to easily link CSS and JavaScript files into your site's head section of layout. The layout used for this example looks as follows:

```
<html>
  <head>
    <?php
      echo $html->css ( "lightbox", "stylesheet");
        if ( isset ( $javascript ) ):
          echo $javascript->link ("/app/webroot/js/prototype.js" );
          echo $javascript->link(
                      "/app/webroot/js/scriptaculous.js?load=effects,builder");
          echo $javascript->link ("/app/webroot/js/lightbox.js" );
        endif;
    ?>
    </head>
  <body>
    <?php echo $content_for_layout ?>
  </body>
</html>
```

code snippet /gallery/cakephp/app/views/layouts/default.ctp

The routing file should contain the following line:

```
Router::connect('/lightbox', array(
    'controller' => 'lightbox','action' => 'index'));
```

code snippet /gallery/cakephp/app/config/routes.php

Now you can use the `http://localhost/lightbox` URL to test your project.

You need to prepare the controller for this example. To use Lightbox in your view files, the controller needs to have the `$helpers` value specified and set to use Javascript. This will define which helper is used in this example. If you have already specified `$helpers` within your controller, you can just append another value at the end of your helper array, and set it to `"Javascript"`. The controller file used in this example looks like this:

```
<?php
  class LightboxController extends AppController {
    var $name = 'lightbox';
    var $helpers = array ( "Javascript" );
    function index() {
    }
  }
?>
```

code snippet /gallery/cakephp/app/controllers/lightbox_controller.php

In the model file, you need to indicate that this small project does not use any database table by setting the `$useTable` variable to `false`. If you don't, a missing table error message will be displayed.

```
<?php
class Lightbox extends AppModel {
  var $useTable = false;
}
```

code snippet /gallery/cakephp/app/models/lightbox.php

The last thing to do is to create your view file that will contain the image gallery and will use Lightbox to display images. At this point, you only need to add the `rel="lightbox"` parameter to a link in order to use Lightbox. The `rel` parameter used for this example looks different because it is possible to group image sets using brackets, just like in the following view file:

```
<h1>Lightbox Logos Gallery</h1>
<a href="http://www.symfony-project.org/images/symfony_logo.gif"
    rel="lightbox[logos]"
    title="Symfony Logo">Symfony Logo</a>
<br />
<a href="http://cakephp.org/img/cake-logo.png"
    rel="lightbox[logos]"
    title="CakePHP Logo">CakePHP Logo</a>
<br />
<a href="http://framework.zend.com/images/logo.gif"
    rel="lightbox[logos]"
    title="Zend Framework Logo">Zend Framework Logo</a>
```

code snippet /gallery/cakephp/app/views/lightbox/index.ctp

Finally, you should be able to run Lightbox through the `http://localhost/lightbox` page, and by clicking any of the image links, an image like the one illustrated in Figure 9-3 will be displayed as the result. Note that text links can be replaced with image thumbnails simply by adding an `<img>` tag between the `<a>` and `</a>` tags.

Now you have Lightbox up and running, and if you wish to use any other external JavaScript file, this example should give you a general idea how to do it.

FIGURE 9-3: Images displayed using Lightbox

Zend Framework

Using Lightbox2 in Zend Framework is not a complicated task; the installation is very similar to the one done in CakePHP. To begin, you need to download the Lightbox2 package from `www.huddletogether.com/projects/lightbox2`. After downloading and unpacking the libraries, you need to copy the JavaScript files into your application's `/public/lightbox/js/` directory. Then the stylesheet `lightbox.css` goes to: `/public/css/`, and finally images used by Lightbox go to: `/public/images/`. If any of these directories does not exist, create it.

At this point, the `/appDirectory/public/` directory should contain the following:

```
js/
    lightbox/
        builder.js
        effects.js
        lightbox.js
        prototype.js
        scriptaculous.js
css/
    lightbox.css
images/
    closelabel.gif
    ...
```

If you have this directory structure, you can create the controller file. To use Lightbox inside an existing project, you probably need to add another action to your controller, as in the following code:

Available for download on Wrox.com

```
<?php
class IndexController extends Zend_Controller_Action {
    public function init() {
    }
    public function lightboxAction() {
    }
}
```

code snippet /gallery/zf/application/controllers/IndexController.php

The controller file does not require any additional code lines added in order to use Lightbox because it is all done in the layout file.

The following is the listing of the `layout.phtml` file that uses helpers to append Lightbox libraries into the application:

Available for download on Wrox.com

```
<html>
  <head>
    <title>Lightbox Logos Gallery</title>
    <?php
        echo $this->headLink()->appendStylesheet(
            $this->baseUrl('/css/lightbox.css') );
        echo $this->headScript()->appendFile(
            $this->baseUrl('/js/lightbox/prototype.js') );
        echo $this->headScript()->appendFile(
            $this->baseUrl('/js/lightbox/scriptaculous.js?load=effects,builder'));
        echo $this->headScript()->appendFile(
            $this->baseUrl('/js/lightbox/lightbox.js') );
    ?>
  </head>
  <body>
    <?php echo $this->layout()->content; ?>
  </body>
</html>
```

code snippet /gallery/zf/application/layouts/layout.phtml

As you can see, `$this->headLink()->appendStylesheet()` is used to append the CSS file, and the `$this->headScript()->appendFile()` lines append the JavaScript files.

Now you have all files in their places and you can use the standard HTML syntax to turn any image link into a Lightbox effect gallery using `rel="lightbox"`. You can also group a number of images using the `rel="lightbox[groupname]"` syntax.

The following code is an example view file that renders an image like the one shown in Figure 9-4 when you type `http://localhost/appName/public/index/lightbox` into your browser:

Available for download on Wrox.com

```
<h1>Lightbox Logos Gallery</h1>
<a href="http://www.symfony-project.org/images/symfony_logo.gif"
    rel="lightbox[logos]"
    title="Symfony Logo">Symfony Logo</a>
<br />
<a href="http://cakephp.org/img/cake-logo.png"
    rel="lightbox[logos]"
    title="CakePHP Logo">CakePHP Logo</a>
<br />
<a href="http://framework.zend.com/images/logo.gif"
    rel="lightbox[logos]"
    title="Zend Framework Logo">Zend Framework Logo</a>
```

code snippet /gallery/zf/application/views/scripts/index/index.phtml

FIGURE 9-4: Image gallery using Lightbox

If your Lightbox window happens to be missing the loading image or close button image, you can fix it by modifying the corresponding paths in the `lightbox.js` file at lines 49 and 50. In this example, the paths look as follows:

```
LightboxOptions = Object.extend({
    fileLoadingImage:        '../images/loading.gif',
    fileBottomNavCloseImage: '../images/closelabel.gif',
```

code snippet /gallery/zf/public/js/lightbox/lightbox.js

USING TEMPLATE ENGINES WITHIN WEB FRAMEWORKS

So far we have described only the advantages of the framework template engines. However, to be honest with you, opinions on their usefulness are varied. They are often praised by teams where PHP programmers deal with business logic only and leave the presentation layer for the designers. However, individual developers tend to judge template engines as nearly useless.

PHP is an interpreted programming language that can act as a template engine. This means that the template engines are not necessary, and when you use them, they must be interpreted separately by PHP. Template engines provide an interpreted language inside the PHP-interpreted language, and that requires the templates to be parsed two times. This looks like an additional overhead that degrades performance of web apps, but in fact most of today's templating engines have caching features that make parsing necessary only once per template. The performance is no longer a big issue while using templates.

The following code illustrates how plain PHP can be a natural substitute for the Smarty template engine, which is described more fully in the following section. Smarty code first:

```
{if $user eq 'Martin'}
    Martin has logged in.
{elseif $ user eq 'Susie'}
    Susie has logged in.
{else}
    Anonymous has logged in.
{/if}
```

And the regular PHP equivalent:

```
<?php
if ($user == 'Martin') {
```

```
    echo ' Martin has logged in.';
} elseif ($user == 'Susie') {
    echo 'Susie has logged in.';
} else {
    echo 'Anonymous has logged in.';
}
?>
```

Another reason for negative opinions about template engines is that there is a learning curve tied to any template system because most PHP templates have their own set of tags or even their own language. However, don't be prejudiced against template engines before you try them out. Many developers value them as an elegant way of view representation, and even if you won't like them, perhaps your fellow web designers will, so it's valuable to get to know this technology anyway.

Smarty

Over the years, Smarty has gained lots of popularity and became probably the best known web template system written in PHP. Its logo is presented in Figure 9-5. Many newly created template engines were created based on Smarty because it has been for a long time a popular tool for separating system logic from HTML templates. Version 3 of Smarty is coming in big steps and will address shortcomings of its predecessor as well as add new features. This new version of Smarty is object-oriented, written from scratch, and written entirely in PHP 5.0. Moreover, tests indicate that it will offer much better performance than the current version.

FIGURE 9-5: Smarty template engine logo

You can install Smarty in various ways. The most basic is downloading the most recent release from the Smarty website: `www.smarty.net`. Then unpack it to your PHP library folder.

There is also a PEAR channel provided by a GoogleCode project. You can use it with the following console commands:

```
# pear channel-discover pear-smarty.googlecode.com/svn
# pear install smarty/smarty
```

UNIX/Linux has packages for various package managers, so you can install Smarty with the following command:

```
# apt-get install smarty3
```

Web content generated by Smarty relies on Smarty tags placed within documents (templates), later to be processed and substituted with PHP code. This is done by the template engine, allowing people working on application development to keep their work more organized and less reliant on the progress of others.

Smarty tags can be functions, loops, variables, or logical statements. These directives are enclosed in template delimiters and are used by Smarty's parser while the template is processed later. It is possible for PHP programmers to define custom functions that can be invoked using Smarty tags.

The following code is an example implementation of Smarty. First is the PHP file that acts as the controller:

Available for download on Wrox.com

```
<?php
require 'libs/Smarty.class.php';
$smarty = new Smarty;
$smarty->template_dir = 'templates/';
$smarty->compile_dir = 'templates/compile/';
$smarty->cache_dir = 'templates/cache/';
$smarty->assign('title', 'Smarty example');
$smarty->assign("frameworks", array( 'Symfony', 'CakePHP', 'Zend Framework'));
$smarty->display('index.tpl');
?>
```

code snippet /templates/smarty/index.php

On top of the standard inclusion of a template engine class and the creation of its object, you usually need to set three paths for Smarty. The template directory is where Smarty looks for template files. Next the compile and cache files, which need to be writable, are placed where the processed templates will be compiled and cached. The variable assignment is done through the `$smarty->assign()` function that takes two parameters. The first parameter is the name of the variable, through which it will be visible in the template file, and the second parameter is the value to be passed to the template.

The template file used by this PHP script may look like this:

Available for download on Wrox.com

```
<!DOCTYPE html PUBLIC "-//W3C//DTD XHTML 1.1//EN"
      "http://www.w3.org/TR/xhtml11/DTD/xhtml11.dtd">
<html>
  <head>
    <title> {$title} </title>
    <meta http-equiv="content-type" content="text/html; charset=utf-8" />
  </head>
  <body>
    <h1>List of covered frameworks</h1>
    {* Smarty comment *}
    <div>
      {section name=row loop=$frameworks}
        {strip}
          {$smarty.section.row.index}) {$frameworks[row]} <br />
        {/strip}
      {/section}
    </div>
  {include file="footer.tpl"}
  </body>
</html>
```

code snippet /templates/smarty/templates/index.tpl

To print the passed variables into the template file the `{$variable}` syntax is used. The syntax for commenting looks like this: `{* comment *}`. `{section}`. It is used to encapsulate fragments of Smarty code; in this case, it is Smarty's equivalent of the `foreach` loop. And at the end, `{include}` is used to include other templates. In the preceding code, the template file is `footer.tpl`. It is not introduced here, so just create another empty template. The resulting image for this example is shown in Figure 9-6.

List of covered frameworks

1) Symfony
2) CakePHP
3) Zend Framework

FIGURE 9-6: Printing the passed variables in the template file

As you can see in the preceding example, the mechanics offered by Smarty allow web page functionality to be modified separately from the presentation part. This allows developers to simplify and enhance workflow as well as the software maintenance process.

You read at the beginning of this section that template engines receive some criticism. This is no different with Smarty because it replicates features offered natively by PHP, causing additional processing overhead. Actually, this general opinion could have originated from Smarty; at the early development stage of Smarty, server resources were not as cheap as they are today, to say the least. Today Smarty3 offers caching that greatly mitigates this problem; however, it was one of the first template engines and its early versions have influenced the general opinion. Additionally, any developers who wish to use Smarty need to learn the Smarty new pseudo-language.

PHP frameworks' view components usually provide most of the benefits offered by Smarty without sacrificing performance and adding the unnecessary complexity of learning a new language. This makes integration of such template engines with frameworks rather questionable. To make things worse, without well-maintained plug-ins or at least strong documentation, the template engines can be really hard to integrate with any framework.

Smarty for Zend Framework

The integration of Smarty with Zend Framework is a good example of how loosely coupled framework architecture results in its extensibility. Combined with good documentation on both sides, the process is fairly simple.

First you need to build a Smarty handling library. And of course, you must have Smarty installed prior to this. This library just replaces Zend View calls by Smarty methods. It extends the `Zend_View` class by an interface that has all the `Zend_View` methods; that's why this integration is so easy.

Create the `SmartyView.class.php` file in the `/library` folder of ZF. At the beginning of this file, import Smarty. (The path shown in the following code in bold is relevant for standard Linux installations; you need to provide the valid path for your environment.)

Create the constructor for your `Zend_View_Smarty` adapter class. It will take at least two arguments: the path to your template files folder, the path to the compilation results folder, and an optional array of extra parameters. Most of this class consists of getters and setters that translate

Zend View arguments into Smarty fields. The last method passes a rendering of the view to the Smarty template. Now fill the `SmartyView.class.php` file with following code:

Available for download on Wrox.com

```
<?php
require_once("/usr/share/php/smarty/Smarty.class.php");
class Zend_View_Smarty implements Zend_View_Interface {
  public $_smarty;
  public function __construct($tmplPath = null, $cmplPath = null,
                              $extraParams = array()) {
            $this->_smarty = new Smarty;
            if (null !== $tmplPath) {
                $this->setScriptPath($tmplPath);
                $this->setCompilePath($cmplPath);
            }
            foreach ($extraParams as $key => $value) {
                $this->_smarty->$key = $value;
            }
  }
  public function getEngine() {
            return $this->_smarty;
  }
  public function setScriptPath($path) {
            if (is_readable($path)) {
                $this->_smarty->template_dir = $path;
                return;
            }
            throw new Exception('Invalid path provided');
  }
  public function getScriptPaths() {
            return array($this->_smarty->template_dir);
  }
  public function setCompilePath($path) {
            if (is_readable($path)) {
        $this->_smarty->compile_dir = $path;
                return;
            }
            throw new Exception('Invalid path provided');
  }
  public function getCompilePaths() {
            return array($this->_smarty->compile_dir);
  }
  public function setBasePath($path, $prefix = 'Zend_View') {
            return $this->setScriptPath($path);
  }
  public function addBasePath($path, $prefix = 'Zend_View') {
            return $this->setScriptPath($path);
  }
  public function __set($key, $val) {
            $this->_smarty->assign($key, $val);
  }
  public function __isset($key) {
      return (null !== $this->_smarty->get_template_vars($key));
  }
  public function __unset($key) {
```

```
                $this->_smarty->clear_assign($key);
   }
   public function assign($spec, $value = null) {
                if (is_array($spec)) {
                    $this->_smarty->assign($spec);
                    return;
                }
                $this->_smarty->assign($spec, $value);
   }
   public function clearVars() {
                $this->_smarty->clear_all_assign();
   }
   public function render($name) {
                return $this->_smarty->fetch($name);
   }
}
```

code snippet /templates/zf/library/SmartyView.class.php

Create the controller and load your adapter library, shown in bold in the next snippet. Now ZF's `init()` method comes in handy because you can easily replace the view of this controller before any other methods are called. This single line (segmented to fit the page) is shown in bold as well. Again you need to supply the proper paths for your environment.

The next few lines demonstrate the power of Zend Framework libraries. They allow you to get the `ViewRenderer` helper and then configure paths and the file suffix to work neatly with the adapter view. Create the `IndexController.php` file and fill it with following code:

```
<?php
require_once("../library/SmartyView.class.php");
class IndexController extends Zend_Controller_Action {
  public function init() {
    $this->view =
        new Zend_View_Smarty(
                 "/home/wrox/public_html/application/views/templates/",
                 "/home/wrox/public_html/application/views/compile/"
                            );
    $viewRenderer =
        Zend_Controller_Action_HelperBroker::getStaticHelper('ViewRenderer');
    $viewRenderer->setView($this->view)
           ->setViewBasePathSpec($this->view->_smarty->template_dir)
           ->setViewScriptPathSpec(':controller/:action.:suffix')
           ->setViewScriptPathNoControllerSpec(':action.:suffix')
           ->setViewSuffix('tpl');
  }
  public function indexAction() {
    $this->view->name = "Wrox";
  }
}
```

code snippet /templates/zf/application/controller/IndexController.php

This controller handles all its methods, but you can go even further and include the `init()` part into the bootstrap. You will then have all the controllers use the adapter view by default.

Finally, create a simple index view file like the following:

```
Smarty works! {$name}
```

code snippet /templates/zf/application/views/templates/index/index.tpl

Note that the path of this view is created with a pattern very similar to the Zend View views: /`templates/`*`controller`*`/`*`action`*. The `{$name}` Smarty tag produces the `$this->view->name` variable set in the `indexAction()` method of the controller. The output is presented in Figure 9-7.

FIGURE 9-7. Smarty template in Zend Framework

Smarty for Symfony and CakePHP

Integrating Smarty with Symfony and CakePHP, even when using ready-to-use plug-ins, can be a real pain in the neck and the profits still are marginal. The Symfony plug-in installation doesn't work. You can install Smarty manually instead, but you have to put in a lot of work to get this solution working with Symfony's command-line interface (CLI) code-generating tools.

Smarty can be integrated with CakePHP using SmartyView; it was recently updated to work with CakePHP 1.3 only, and it appears to have problems working without conflict with various versions of the Smarty engine. So you can waste a lot of time to figure out a working set among CakePHP, SmartyView, and Smarty. In the best-case scenario, you end up with a non-upgradable application using old versions of both the framework and the template engine.

You should not try these solutions unless you are a really experienced developer who has some spare time.

Dwoo

The Dwoo template engine (the logo is shown in Figure 9-8) is quite similar to Smarty, but is written entirely in PHP 5.0. In many aspects, Dwoo is compatible with Smarty's templates and plug-ins because Dwoo's authors based it on the general ideas that Smarty has introduced to the world of web development. Dwoo takes advantage of the new features offered by PHP 5.0, so it is a well-written, object-oriented template engine that allows easier and faster development compared with Smarty, and still it is compatible enough to allow developers using Smarty to make a smooth

FIGURE 9-8: Dwoo template engine logo

transition to Dwoo — and vice versa. What's more, Dwoo offers adapters that help developers integrate it into web frameworks such as CakePHP, Zend Framework, Code Igniter, Agavi, or Yii. Utilizing this feature, you will learn how to integrate Dwoo into CakePHP.

The Dwoo template engine is released under a modified BSD license. (The Dwoo website is `http://dwoo.org/`.)

CakePHP

To make your application use Dwoo, first you need to get the package from `http://dwoo.org/` and extract the library to the `/vendor` directory of your application (for example, `/app/vendors/dwoo`). You can use a different directory if you wish, but it requires an additional adjustment of line 3 in the `dwoo.php` file. By default, it looks like this:

```
App::import('vendor', 'dwoo', array("file" => 'dwooAutoload.php'));
```

The second step is to place the `/Dwoo/Adapters/CakePHP/dwoo.php` file from the package into the `/app/views` directory of your application. In the last step, you need to create the `/app/tmp/dwoo/cache` and the `/app/tmp/dwoo/compile` directories. Those directories should have write privileges.

It is possible to use a different template file extension than the default `.tpl`. To do so, you need to modify the `dwoo.php` file. Line 44 has the following line, which gives you the option to change the template file extension that Dwoo will use:

```
$this->ext = '.tpl';
```

code snippet /templates/cakephp/app/views/dwoo.php

Let's move on with the example. As usual, you must set the routing for this project by adding the following line in the `routes.php` file:

```
Router::connect('/dwoo', array('controller' => 'dwooexample', 'action' => 'index'));
```

code snippet /templates/cakephp/app/config/routes.php

Next you need to create a model file and configure it not to use the database:

```
<?php
class Dwooexample extends AppModel {
  var $useTable = false;
}
```

code snippet /templates/cakephp/app/models/dwooexample.php

Then there is the controller file, in which you need to import `dwooAutoload.php` and set the `beforeFilter()` function with `autoRender` set to `false`. It is marked with bold in the following code. Doing so disables the standard CakePHP template files. The rest of Dwoo-related code is located in the `index()` function. Three objects are created: one is the main Dwoo object, the second object loads the template file, and the last one creates the object for storing data:

```
<?php
  App::import('Vendor', 'dwoo', array('file' => 'dwooAutoload.php'));
  class DwooexampleController extends AppController {
    function beforeFilter() {
      $this->autoRender = false;
    }
    function index() {
      $dwoo = new Dwoo();
      $tpl = new Dwoo_Template_File('../views/dwooexample/index.tpl');
      $data = new Dwoo_Data();
      $frameworks = array( 'sf' => 'Symfony',
                           'ck' => 'CakePHP',
                           'zf' => 'Zend Framework');
      $data->assign('frameworks', $frameworks);
      $dwoo->output($tpl, $data);
    }
  }
?>
```

code snippet /templates/cakephp/app/controller/dwooexample_controller.php

At the end, the data is assigned to be displayed by the template file, and finally the template file is rendered.

Now you can use Dwoo template files to display data, as shown in the following code:

```
<h1>List of covered frameworks</h1>
<p>{$frameworks[sf]}</p>
<p>{$frameworks[ck]}</p>
<p>{$frameworks[zf]}</p>
```

code snippet /templates/cakephp/app/views/dwooexample/index.tpl

The resulting image is shown in Figure 9-9.

Unfortunately, this solution is not really what you want to get. It allows you to use only Dwoo templates, while CakePHP templates are not rendered, including the main layout file. This is similar to using Dwoo as a stand-alone application with a library that provides you with CakePHP controller functions.

List of covered frameworks

Symfony

CakePHP

Zend Framework

FIGURE 9-9: Dwoo template engine example in CakePHP

This section has demonstrated just a crude example of how to get things done. To make Dwoo global for the whole project you would have to write a component that would map Dwoo to the CakePHP view, but this is beyond the scope of this book. Frankly speaking, this is a job that should be done by Dwoo developers if they really want it integrated with CakePHP.

Dwoo for Symfony and Zend Framework

You could try to integrate Dwoo with Symfony, but it would be hard because Symfony's file–generation CLI tools do not work with it, and there is no Dwoo plug-in for Symfony. You can also try to develop a new plug-in that would support Dwoo. For today, however, Symfony doesn't support Dwoo.

You can use Dwoo in Zend Framework by integrating its libraries with a ZF project. This is not an easy task, mainly because of Dwoo's disastrous documentation, some sections of which are now written in three different languages at random, so we don't recommend using ZF with Dwoo. In fact, it is hard to recommend using Dwoo with any framework, even if it is a worthy template engine for stand-alone projects.

Twig

Twig is one of the most full-featured modern PHP template engines and also one of the fastest. Twig compiles the templates down to plain optimized PHP code, so the overhead is minimal. It features native template inheritance in which templates are compiled as classes, automatic auto-escaping is done during compilation, and it has a secure sandbox mode. All these features give Twig great extensibility. A flexible lexer and parser allow the developer to define his own custom tags, filters, and much more.

Website: `http://www.twig-project.org`

License: MIT

Twig (the logo is shown in Figure 9-10) was developed by Sensio Labs and is an integral part of Symfony 2.0. We can't show you how to integrate Twig with Symfony because it is compatible only with old Symfony versions, so we will show you how to use Twig with Symfony 2.0 beta. Note that many things may change between now and the stable release of this framework.

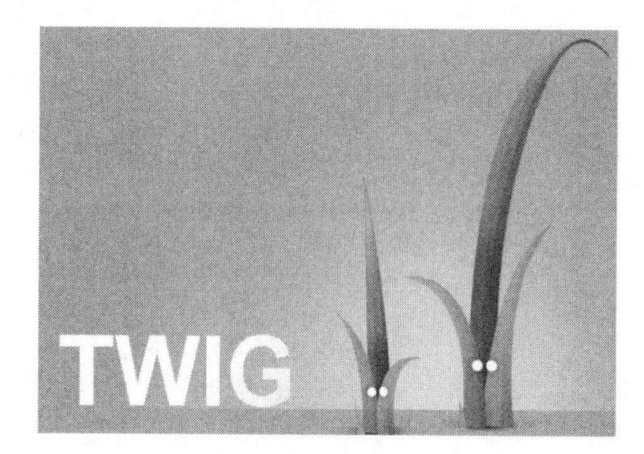

FIGURE 9-10: Twig logo

Twig is packaged together with Symfony 2.0 by default. If you downloaded the Symfony 2.0 sandbox app (the default approach used in this example), you can find the Twig libraries in following directory: `/src/vendor/twig/lib/`. You can also install Symfony 2.0 by PEAR. In both cases, you don't have to install Twig separately. However, if you want to install just the Twig alone, you can do it by PEAR using following console command:

```
$ pear channel-discover pear.twig-project.org
$ pear install twig/Twig
```

Some configuration needs to be done. Find the `config.yml` file and add the bold lines shown in the following listing:

```
kernel.config:
    charset:        UTF-8
    error_handler: null
web.config:
    csrf_secret: fsnbfw7e5y593hrt4057541y01h410t80
    router:      { resource: "%kernel.root_dir%/config/routing.yml" }
```

```
    validation:  { enabled: true, annotations: true }
web.templating:
    escaping:       htmlspecialchars
twig.config:
    auto_reload: true
```

code snippet /templates/symfony2/app/config/config.yml

You can set the environment-related options in the `config_prod.yml` and `config_test.yml` files, although it is optional. YAML is the default format, but you can switch to XML or simply PHP if you like.

Create a controller like the one shown in the following code. The only difference from a standard Symfony 2.0 controller is highlighted with bold font. It sets the Twig template to be used by this action:

Available for download on Wrox.com

```
<?php
namespace Application\WroxBundle\Controller;
use Symfony\Bundle\FrameworkBundle\Controller\Controller;
class WroxController extends Controller
{
    public function indexAction($name)
    {
        return $this->render('WroxBundle:Hello:index:twig', array('name' => $name));
    }
}
```

code snippet /templates/symfony2/src/Application/Bundle/WroxBundle/Controller/WroxController.php

The final page will be rendered using two files. First change the main layout into something like this:

Available for download on Wrox.com

```
{% extends "::layout" %}
{% block body %}
    <h1>Wrox Example</h1>
    {% block content %}{% endblock %}
{% endblock %}
```

code snippet /templates/symfony2/src/Application/Bundle/WroxBundle/Resources/views/layout.twig

It will print the "Wrox Example" title for every view.

And finally, make a view to fill the `{% block content %}{% endblock %}` tags. The view uses the `$name` variable from the controller. The `|upper` switch makes it uppercase:

Available for download on Wrox.com

```
{% extends "WroxBundle::layout" %}
{% block content %}
    Hello {{ name|upper }}!
{% endblock %}
```

code snippet /templates/symfony2/src/Application/Bundle/WroxBundle/Resources/views/Wrox/index.twig

The output is shown in Figure 9-11.

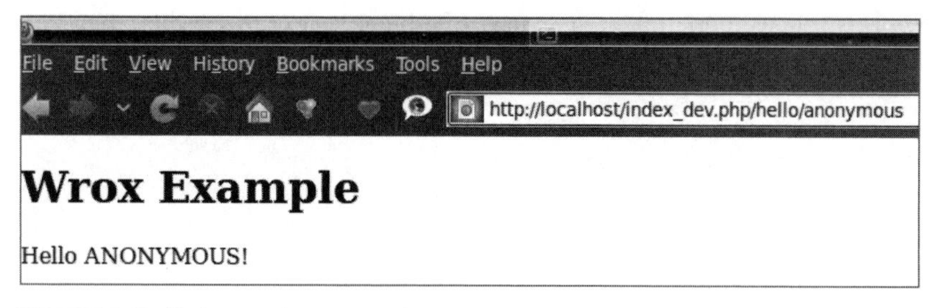

FIGURE 9-11. Twig template example

Twig is dedicated for Symfony 2.0, but you can try to include it as a library for any other framework with the following code:

```
<?php
require_once 'lib/Twig/Autoloader.php';
Twig_Autoloader::register();
$loader = new Twig_Loader_String();
$twig = new Twig_Environment($loader);
$template = $twig->loadTemplate('Wrox {{ test }}!');
$template->display(array('test' => 'example'));
```

The first two lines can go to a bootstrap file or initializing method and the next four lines allow you to use Twig within a controller.

OVERVIEW OF OTHER ADD-ON TEMPLATE ENGINES

There is a large variety of PHP template engines available for use. From more than 50 known PHP template engines, implementation of only 3 was shown in the previous section. This section presents a handful of other valuable template engines. The code snippets presented here are just plain PHP files and templates to make you familiar with the templating languages. Integration with web frameworks, if possible, should be similar to those shown in the previous section.

Template Blocks

Template Blocks is a visual template engine, which means that it uses an AJAX interface to let the developer handle everything through online forms in the browser. There is no need to write everything by yourself because a significant part of site building is done simply by dragging blocks, as you can see in Figure 9-12.

Website: `http://www.templateblocks.com`

License: GPL

Open Power Template (OPT)

One of the few template engines written natively in PHP 5.0, the Open Power Template (OPT) is a powerful and rapidly developing tool. Its logo is shown in Figure 9-13. It uses a domain-specific XML template language for creating templates. Its API is object-oriented by design, which helps in integration with frameworks. It is well documented as part of a bigger set of tools: the Open Power Library. We recommend that you check this one out!

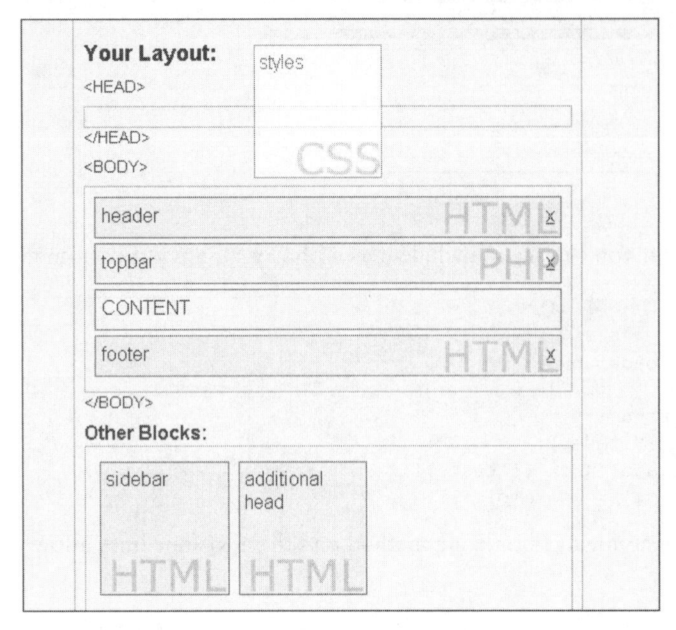

FIGURE 9-12: Page building using the Template Blocks drag-and-drop interface

Website: `http://www.invenzzia.org/en/projects/open-power-libraries open-power-template`

License:

- Open Power Template 2.0: BSD-new
- Open Power Template 1.1: GNU LGPL

FIGURE 9-13: Open Power Template logo

The following code shows an example implementation. First the controlling PHP file needs some additional configuration. The path to OPT is set, template directories are defined, the OPT object is created, and finally the `setup()` method is called:

Available for download on Wrox.com

```
<?php
require('../lib/Opl/Base.php');
Opl_Loader::setDirectory('../lib/');
Opl_Loader::register();
$tpl = new Opt_Class;
$tpl->sourceDir = 'templates/';
$tpl->compileDir = 'templates_c/';
$tpl->setup();
$view = new Opt_View('index.tpl');  // Load template
$view->pageTitle = 'List of covered frameworks';
$view->list = array( 'Sf' => 'Symfony',
                     'Cake' => 'CakePHP',
```

```
                          'ZF' => 'Zend Framework' );
$view->setFormat('list', 'Array');
$output = new Opt_Output_Http;
$output->render($view);
```

code snippet /templates/opt/index.php

Compared with other template engines, setting up OPT gives more configuration options. In OPT, templates are loaded before the variables are assigned. And as you can see in the following code, OPT gives developers some additional tags that generate common fragments of web pages or cover common tasks such as the `foreach` loop made using the `<opt:foreach>` tag. Displaying variables is exactly the same as in Smarty: by using `{$variable}`:

```
<?xml version="1.0" ?>
<opt:root>
<!-- generate an XML prolog for the browser -->
<opt:prolog version="1.0" />
<!-- generate the DTD for the browser from a template -->
<opt:dtd template="xhtml10transitional" />
<html>
  <head>
    <title>{$pageTitle}</title>
  </head>
  <body>
    <h1>List of covered frameworks</h1>
    <opt:foreach array="$list" index="short" value="value">
       <p>{@short} - {@value}</p>
    </opt:foreach>
  </body>
</html>
</opt:root>
```

code snippet /templates/opt/index.tpl

You can see the output of these two files in Figure 9-14.

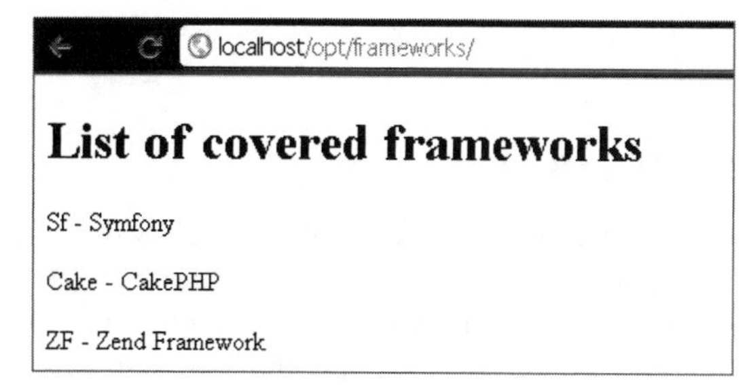

FIGURE 9-14: Page content rendered using OPT

TinyButStrong

What can be said about this template engine is that it is indeed tiny, which means one file and one PHP class! It has a few distinguishing features. It can natively work with MySQL, SQLite, and PostgreSQL. And it is not restricted to working with HTML files: it can work with XML, RTF, and WML files; and also with document files of OpenOffice and Microsoft Office.

Website: `http://www.tinybutstrong.com`

License: GNU LGPL

The following code shows an example implementation. It begins with the controlling PHP file, which is quite elegant. Then there is the standard class inclusion and template engine object creation at the beginning. Loading the template is done using the aptly named `LoadTemplate()` function. Variables are assigned as in a standard PHP file. An array variable is assigned by using the `MergeBlock()` function. Finally, the template is rendered using the `Show()` method:

Available for download on Wrox.com

```
<?php
include_once('tbs_class_php5.php');
$TBS = new clsTinyButStrong;
$TBS->LoadTemplate('index.htm');
$title = 'List of covered list';
$list = array( 'Symfony', 'CakePHP','Zend Framework' );
$TBS->MergeBlock('list', $list);
$TBS->Show();
```

code snippet /templates/tiny/index.php

Next, the following code shows the template file that uses minimalistic syntax to display variables. If the `$list` variable was set, the `[list.val;block=p]` block can be used to render blocks of `<p></p>` tags filled with the items from the `$list` variable:

Available for download on Wrox.com

```
<html>
  <head>
    <title>[onshow.title]</title>
  </head>
  <body>
    <h1>List of covered frameworks</h1>
    <p>[list.val;block=p]</p>

  </body>
</html>
```

code snippet /templates/tiny/index.htm

You can see the output of these two files in Figure 9-15.

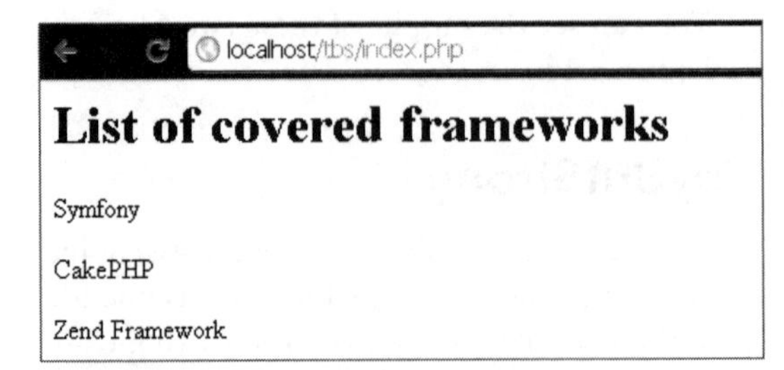

FIGURE 9-15: Page content rendered using the TinyButStrong template engine

Rain TPL

This template engine is a part of the Rain framework, but it can be used stand-alone as well. It is quite small (only two files) and comes in a package with a simple example that can help you get familiar with it.

Website: `http://www.raintpl.com`

License: GNU GPL

An example implementation is illustrated by the two following files. Again the controller goes first:

```
<?php
  //include the RainTPL class
  include "inc/rain.tpl.class.php";
  //initialize a Rain TPL object
  $tpl = new RainTPL( 'tpl' );
  //assign title variable
  $tpl->assign( "title", 'List of covered frameworks' );
  // assign array variable
  $frameworks = array( 1 => 'Symfony',
                             2 => 'CakePHP',
                             3 => 'Zend Framework' );
  $tpl->assign( "frameworks", $frameworks );
  //draw the template
  echo $tpl->draw( 'index' );
?>
```

code snippet /templates/rain/index.php

The PHP file, in this case called `index.php`, begins with the RainTPL class, and then a new Rain TPL object is created. Data preparation is done as in standard PHP code, but variables that are to be passed to the template file are assigned using the `assign()` method of the Rain TPL object. Finally, `index.html`, shown following, is rendered using prepared data:

```
<!DOCTYPE HTML PUBLIC "-//W3C//DTD HTML 4.01 Transitional//EN" >
<html>
  <head>
    <meta http-equiv="Content-Type" content="text/html; charset=utf-8" >
    <title>{$title}</title>
  </head>
  <body>
    <h1>List of covered frameworks</h1>
    {loop name="frameworks"}
    <p>
       {$key }) {$value}
    </p>
    {/loop}
  </body>
</html>
```

code snippet /templates/rain/index.html

The page title is printed using `{$title}` syntax. In the page body, three paragraphs are generated using the `{loop}{/loop}` statement. The variables `$key` and `$value` are generated automatically using `{loop}` on the `frameworks` array. The resulting page looks like the one illustrated in Figure 9-16.

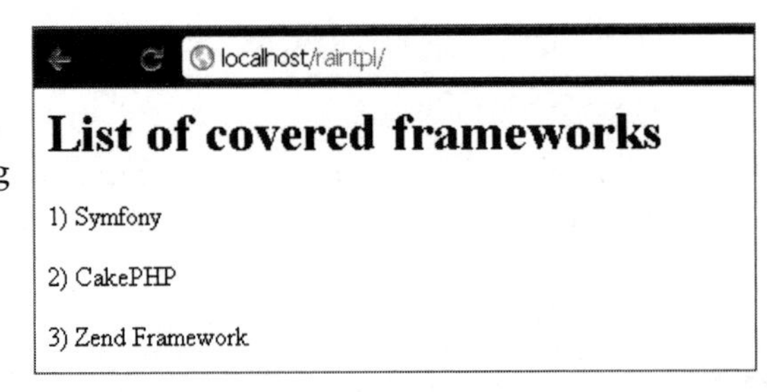

FIGURE 9-16: Page content rendered using Rain template engine

Savant

Savant (the logo is shown in Figure 9-17) is a somewhat unique template engine because of the language it uses. In most cases, developers need to learn a new markup language when they start using a new template engine. In Savant this is not the case because its templates use PHP.

Website: `http://phpsavant.com`

License: GNU LGPL

SAVANT3

THE SIMPLE, ELEGANT TEMPLATE SYSTEM FOR PHP

FIGURE 9-17: Savant3 logo

Most of Savant's syntax is identical to PHP, so in the following code the first `Savant3.php` file is included into the `index.php` file and then the `Savant3` object is created. Variables are assigned as if they were variables of the `Savant3` object called `$tpl` in this example. The template to be displayed is selected by the `$tpl->display()` method:

Available for download on Wrox.com

```
<?php
// Load the Savant3 class file and create an instance.
require_once 'Savant3.php';
$tpl = new Savant3();
// Set title
$title = "List of covered frameworks";
// Prepare data
$frameworks = array(
    array(
        'nr' => '1',
        'short' => 'Sf',
        'name' => 'Symfony'
    ),
    array(
        'nr' => '2',
        'short' => 'Cake',
        'name' => 'CakePHP'
    ),
    array(
        'nr' => '3',
        'short' => 'ZF',
        'name' => 'Zend Framework'
    )
);
```

```
// Assign values to the Savant instance.
$tpl->title = $title;
$tpl->frameworks = $frameworks;
// Display a template
$tpl->display('index.tpl.php');
?>
```

code snippet /templates/savant/index.php

The template file uses the `.tpl.php` extension; in this case, the file is the `index.tpl.php` file. Variables are displayed using the `$this` object and the `eprint()` method:

```
<!DOCTYPE HTML PUBLIC "-//W3C//DTD HTML 4.01 Transitional//EN" >
<html>
  <head>
    <meta http-equiv="Content-Type" content="text/html; charset=utf-8" >
    <title><?php echo $this->eprint($this->title); ?></title>
  </head>
  <body>
    <h1>List of covered frameworks</h1>
    <table>
      <tr>
        <th>Nr.</th>
        <th>Short</th>
        <th>Framework name</th>
      </tr>
      <?php foreach ($this->frameworks as $key => $val): ?>
      <tr>
        <td><?php echo $this->eprint($val['nr']); ?></td>
        <td><?php echo $this->eprint($val['short']); ?></td>
        <td><?php echo $this->eprint($val['name']); ?></td>
      </tr>
      <?php endforeach; ?>
    </table>
  </body>
</html>
```

code snippet /templates/savant/index.tpl.php

Standard `echo()` and `print()` functions can be used to display variables, but the `$this->eprint()` method automatically escapes the output. This helps to protect your page against XSS scripting attacks. The result of this example is illustrated in Figure 9-18.

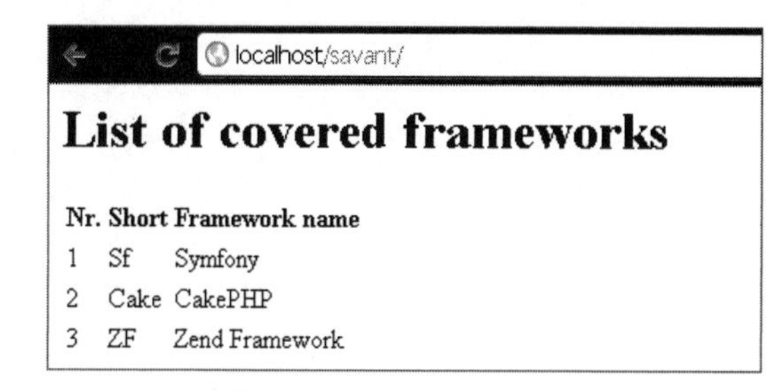

FIGURE 9-18: Page content rendered using Savant3

Because the templates in Savant are regular PHP files, it can be said that Savant is not an interpreted template system (that means they are interpreted a second time inside PHP). This feature makes Savant one of the fastest template engines available. It is also very well commented and easy to extend. Developers can use their own interpreters inside Savant to use any template markup system.

10

AJAX

It was a joke, okay? If we thought it would actually be used, we wouldn't have written it!

— Mark Andreessen, speaking of the HTML tag BLINK

WHAT'S IN THIS CHAPTER?

- Introducing AJAX
- Including autocomplete feature into your text fields
- Using pop-up windows
- Making an AJAX chat

In Greek mythology, Ajax was a Titan who supported the heavens on his back. This applies to AJAX as well, but instead of the heavens, this technology supports the whole world of modern interactive websites. (Well, OK, the Titan's name was Atlas, but it doesn't really matter as long as the trope is valid, right? Just look at what AJAX is capable of!)

In many ways, AJAX has become a hallmark of modern web applications. Users expect autocomplete, updating content without reloading, and other AJAX goodies. And sometimes they get angry with a web page that doesn't provide it.

AJAX, which stands for Asynchronous JavaScript and XML, is a web development technique that provides web developers with the capability to create dynamic and interactive web applications. Applications developed using AJAX perform all the operations on the client side and can communicate with a server to retrieve data that results from running various scripts and database queries. Data retrieved from a server using the `XMLHttpRequest` object can be used to update website content without the necessity of reloading the entire page or influencing the application's behavior.

There is also another similar technique: Asynchronous HTML and HTTP (AHAH), which uses XHTML instead of XML for data retrieval. It allows for easier development with less code, but is not as popular as AJAX.

INTRODUCING AJAX

Let's start with two clarifications concerning the AJAX name. The first letter of AJAX stands for *asynchronous* because the client communicates with the server asynchronously, mainly because of the interactive interface of AJAX web pages and the dynamic content sent back from the server. This isn't always true because the server queries do not need to be asynchronous. Also, the X in AJAX stands for XML, but the developer does not need to use XML anywhere to perform complex AJAX actions, although it is good practice in this technology.

So, what exactly is AJAX and how does it work? AJAX is not a software package; it is not a software library, a programming language, a markup language, or a communication protocol. It is actually a little of every technology used in web development tied up together to achieve some miraculous results. The easiest way to grasp the concept behind AJAX is to understand how it processes a portion of data. The following example is meant to illustrate the basic mechanics of AJAX:

Available for download on Wrox.com

```
<html>
<head>
  <script type="text/javascript">
  function loadNewContent() {
    if (window.XMLHttpRequest) { //support for IE7+, Firefox, Chrome, Opera, Safari
        xmlhttp = new XMLHttpRequest();
    }
    else { //support for IE6, IE5
        xmlhttp = new ActiveXObject("Microsoft.XMLHTTP");
    }
    xmlhttp.onreadystatechange=function() {
        if (xmlhttp.readyState==4 && xmlhttp.status==200) {
           document.getElementById("ajax_content").innerHTML=xmlhttp.responseText;
        }
    }
    xmlhttp.open("GET","ajax_script.php",true);
    xmlhttp.send();
  }
  </script>
</head>
<body>
    <div id="ajax_content">
        <h2>Page content</h2>
        <p>This content will reload after you press the button</p>
        <button type="button" onclick="loadNewContent()">Use AJAX</button>
    </div>
</body>
</html>
```

code snippet /introduction/index.html

As you can see, the `index.html` file contains a basic HTML structure with little content and one JavaScript function that is called when the button is pressed. This function is called thanks to the DHTML `onclick` action. The `loadNewContent()` function first creates a new `XMLHttpRequest` object, and then there is a function declared that is responsible for updating the content of the HTML element with `ajax_content` ID. This second function is called automatically each time the `readyState` property of the document changes. The content used for updating is a result of running `ajax_script.php` script. The code presented so far will render content like that shown at the left in Figure 10-1.

Page content

This content will reload after you press the button

Use AJAX

AJAX loaded page content

Bold title

Red color text paragraph

FIGURE 10-1: On the left — sample page content. On the right — content reloaded using AJAX

Then, when the Use AJAX button is clicked, the following code will be loaded through the AJAX `XMLHttpRequest` object:

```
<?php
echo '<h2>AJAX loaded page content</h2>
      <b>Bold title</b>
         <p style="color: red;">
         Red color text paragraph <br />
      </p>';
?>
```

code snippet /introduction/ajax_script.php

Loaded content will replace the current content without reloading the whole page, and the image illustrated to the right in Figure 10-1 will be rendered.

The `XMLHttpRequest` object has two status parameters: the `readyState` and `status`. These properties allow developers to perform certain actions corresponding to various status changes.

The `xmlhttp.readyState` variable holds the current state of the `XMLHttpRequest`. It is denoted as an integer and may have the following values:

- `0` – Request not initialized
- `1` – Server connection established
- `2` – Request received
- `3` – Processing request
- `4` – Request finished and response is ready

When the `readyState` property changes, an event is triggered. It results in execution of the function stored in `onreadystatechange`. You can store just the name of a function there instead.

The `xmlhttp.status` variable can take two values: `200` and `404`. The first one means that everything went well, and the second one means that page (or script in this case) was not found, and results in the famous "404 error."

This basic example should explain the concept of AJAX technology. In short, the Document Object Model (DOM) provides tools that allow manipulation of page content, while JavaScript and `XMLHttpRequest` objects are used to update web document structure. PHP or any scripting language used by the server can prepare web content that later is inserted into the current document structure. These scripts could be run as standalone scripts, without any participation of AJAX. Finally, AJAX utilizes HTML and CSS to present style-generated page content.

AUTOCOMPLETE

Autocomplete is a great feature that was introduced for the first time in desktop software such as command-line interpreters and code editors. In web applications, autocompletion arrived with the increasing popularity of JavaScript and found its place in online search engines such as Google, Yahoo, and Altavista. Now users expect this improvement in every web app.

There is a large variety of ready-to-use AJAX scripts that can easily be integrated with your applications, although web frameworks usually have some kind of solutions for that as well. For instance, CakePHP has an AJAX helper that gives you the option to use autocomplete very easily. Zend Framework has the ZendX library that includes jQuery autocomplete, and Symfony can use sfJqueryReloadedPlugin or sfFormExtraPlugin to achieve the same results.

Symfony

In this example, the autocomplete feature is realized for Symfony, thanks to sfJqueryReloadedPlugin. This plug-in gives you access to the `jq_input_auto_complete_tag()` function that can be used in forms to create autocomplete elements. Alternatively, sfFormExtraPlugin, used in Chapter 5, gives you access to a number of widgets that enhance the form-building process. This plug-in includes the sfWidgetFormJQueryAutocompleter widget as well, and it can be used to create autocomplete form fields.

Moving to the sfJqueryReloadedPlugin installation, it is a standard procedure, as with any Symfony plug-in. In your command console you need to call the following command from the project directory:

```
$ symfony plugin:install sfJqueryReloadedPlugin
```

Cache clearing is suggested, too:

```
$ symfony cache:clear
```

The database table used to provide suggested values in the autocomplete field is defined by the following `schema.yml` file:

Available for download on Wrox.com

```
Mails:
  connection: doctrine
  tableName: mails
  columns:
```

```
id: {type: integer(4) fixed: false unsigned: false
  primary: true autoincrement: true}
email: {type: string(32) fixed: false unsigned: false
  primary: false notnull: true autoincrement: false}
```

code snippet /autocomplete/symfony/config/doctrine/schema.yml

Then you need to build it using the following command in your console:

```
$ symfony doctrine:build --all
```

If you wish to use styles for autocomplete, it is a good idea to modify the `view.yml` file and add the `JqueryAutocomplete` stylesheet. It should look as follows:

```
default:
  metas:
    stylesheets:    [main.css, JqueryAutocomplete]
```

code snippet /autocomplete/symfony/apps/frontend/config/view.yml

The most important fragment of this implementation is the actions file, in which the `executeList()` action is defined. It is responsible for generating a list of suggested values for the autocomplete input form element. The data is taken from a database and displayed by the list view:

```
<?php
class addressbookActions extends sfActions {
    public function executeIndex(sfWebRequest $request){
    }
    public function executeList(sfWebRequest $request) {
        $query = $request->getParameter('query');
        $q = Doctrine_Query::create()
            ->from('mails')
            ->andWhere('email like ?', '%' . $query . '%')
            ->addOrderBy('email')
            ->limit(10)
            ->execute();
        $this->results = $q;
    }
}
```

code snippet /autocomplete/symfony/apps/frontend/modules/addressbook/actions/actions.class.php

The view file responsible for displaying the form element with the autocomplete option looks as follows:

```
<?php use_helper('jQuery'); ?>
<?php echo jq_input_auto_complete_tag('query','','addressbook/list',array(),array());?>
```

code snippet /autocomplete/symfony/apps/frontend/modules/addressbook/templates/indexSuccess.php

The second view file is responsible for displaying the suggestion list, prepared by the list action from the `actions.class.php` file:

Available for download on Wrox.com

```
<?php foreach($results as $res): ?>
  <?php echo $res->getEmail()."\n"; ?>
<?php  endforeach; ?>
```

code snippet /autocomplete/symfony/apps/frontend/modules/addressbook/templates/listSuccess.php

You can see the result of using the solution introduced here in Figure 10-2.

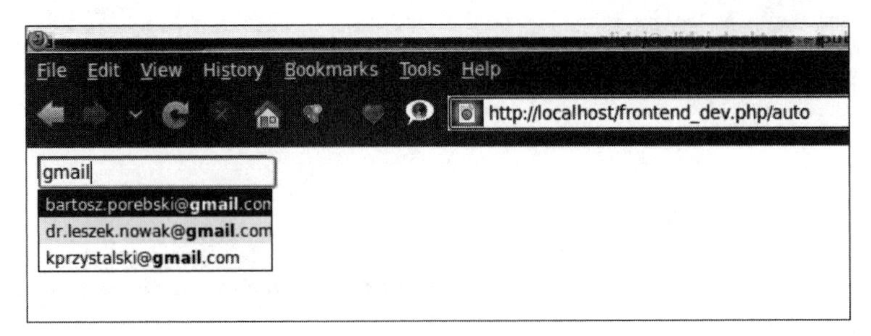

FIGURE 10-2: Autocomplete created using the `jq_input_auto_complete_tag()` function

CakePHP

There are a number of solutions that enable you to implement autocomplete in most web applications. You could use one of the many available JavaScript libraries or simply use the CakePHP AJAX core helper. Because this book is all about frameworks and their features, you will see how to use the solution native to CakePHP.

The first thing necessary to implement autocomplete is to create a database of words that will be autocompleted. In this example, you can use the following SQL script to fill the `months` table with names of months.

```
INSERT INTO 'months' ('id', 'name') VALUES
(1,'January'), (2,'February'), (3,'March'), (4,'April'),
(5,'May'), (6,'June'), (7,'July'),(8,'August'),
(9,'September'), (10,'October'), (11,'November'), (12,'December');
```

The `months` table is now a part of the CakePHP database and consists of two columns: `id` (autoincremented int) and `name` (varchar(15)) that serves as the month name. The following SQL query can help you generate this table:

```
CREATE TABLE IF NOT EXISTS `months` (
  `id` int(11) NOT NULL AUTO_INCREMENT,
  `name` varchar(15) NOT NULL,
  PRIMARY KEY (`id`)
) ENGINE=MyISAM  DEFAULT CHARSET=utf8;
```

You can use any words or phrases in the database, but we advise that you use those suggested for this example, especially if you are new to CakePHP. Otherwise, the table name and variable names might be easy to confuse. The goal for this example is to achieve a simple one-field form that allows users to input a month name, as shown in Figure 10-3.

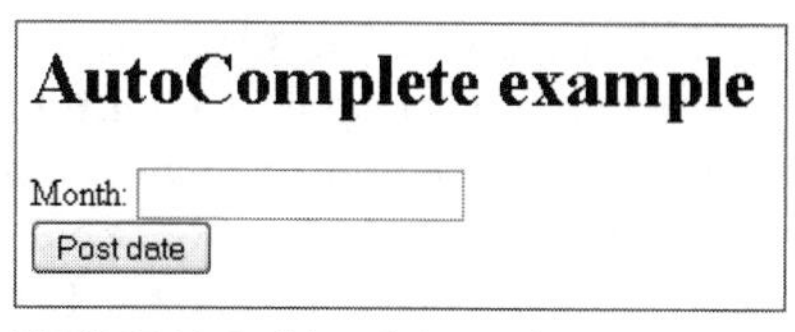

FIGURE 10-3: Month input form

Moving on to the example, the layout file should contain the JavaScript libraries used by the CakePHP AJAX helper: `prototype.js`, `scriptaculous.js`, `effects.js` and `controls.js`. Make sure that your `/app/webroot/js/` directory contains all the mentioned libraries. You can get up-to-date versions of these scripts from `www.prototypejs.org` and `http://script.aculo.us/downloads`. The layout used in this example looks as follows:

```
<html>
  <head>
  <?php
    echo $html->css ( "autocomplete", "stylesheet");
    if ( isset ( $javascript ) ):
      echo $javascript->link('prototype');
      echo $javascript->link('scriptaculous.js?load=effects');
      echo $javascript->link('controls');
    endif;
  ?>
  </head>
  <body>
    <?php echo $content_for_layout ?>
  </body>
</html>
```

code snippet /autocomplete/cakephp/app/views/layouts/default.ctp

Note the order in which the JavaScript libraries are linked, and that `autocomplete.css` is included in the `<head>` section. The `autocomplete.css` file is used to modify the style of the autocomplete box.

Set the routing to connect the web address `http://localhost/cake/autocomplete` with the controller and one of its actions by using the following line:

```
Router::connect('/autocomplete',
  array('controller' => 'autocomplete', 'action' => 'index'));
```

code snippet /autocomplete/cakephp/app/config/routes.php

Next, create the `Month` model file like this:

```
<?php
class Month extends AppModel {
  var $name = 'Month';
  var $useTable = 'months';
}
```

code snippet /autocomplete/cakephp/app/models/month.php

The most important file is the autocomplete_controller.php file located in the /app/controllers/ directory. It is responsible for processing actions, and needs to contain the autoComplete() function that will be responsible for creating the list of phrases matching text entered into a form field using autocomplete. The controller file for this example looks as follows:

```
<?php
  class AutocompleteController extends AppController {
    var $uses = 'Month';
    var $helpers = array ( 'Html', 'Javascript', 'Ajax' );
    function index() {
    }
    function autoComplete() {
          $months = $this->Month->find('all',
             array('conditions' =>
               array('Month.name LIKE' =>
                 $this->data['Date']['month'].'%'),
               'fields' => array('name')
          ));
          $this->set('months',$months);
          $this->layout = 'ajax';
    }
  }
?>
```

code snippet /autocomplete/cakephp/app/controllers/autocomplete_controller.php

So far, you should have the most important pieces needed for autocompletion already in your form, but at this point comes a twist. To use autocomplete in the form, you actually need two view files. One is the standard view matching the index action, and the second one is the view that is used to display the list of words matching the input text. Start with the view file that generates the suggestion list. It will be called and filled with data by AJAX. This file looks as follows:

```
<ul>
  <?php foreach($months as $month): ?>
    <li><?php echo $month['Month']['name']; ?></li>
  <?php endforeach; ?>
</ul>
```

code snippet /autocomplete/cakephp/app/views/autocomplete/auto_complete.ctp

Now the view file is located in the same directory, contains a small web form, and looks as follows:

```
<h1>AutoComplete example</h1>
<?php echo $form->create('Date', array('url' => '/autocomplete')); ?>
<label for="Date.month">Month:</label>
<?php echo $ajax->autoComplete('Date.month', '/autocomplete/autoComplete')?>
<?php echo $form->end('Post date')?>
```

code snippet /autocomplete/cakephp/app/views/autocomplete/index.ctp

As you can see in this code fragment, while calling the $ajax->autoComplete() function, the form field is created with the name parameter set to Date.month, and /autocomplete/autoComplete.ctp is requested to generate the suggestion list. The form shown in Figure 10-4 is rendered by the web browser.

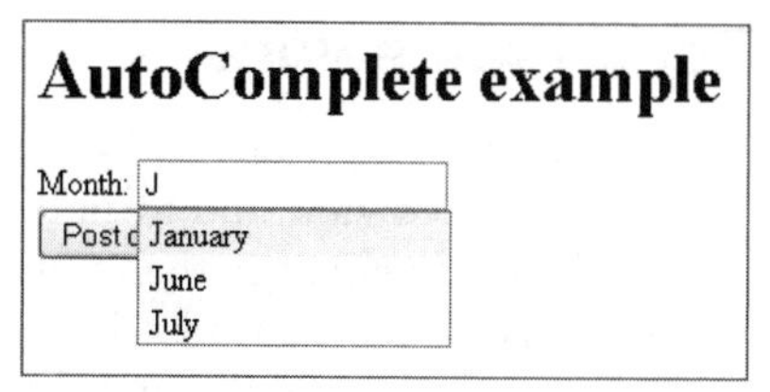

FIGURE 10-4: Month input form with the suggestion box visible

If you do not like how your suggestion box looks, you can use styles such as those shown in this example. The `autocomplete.css` stylesheet needs to be located in the `/app/webroot/css` directory:

```
div.auto_complete    {
  position :absolute;
  width :150px;
  background-color :white;
  border :1px solid #888;
  margin :0px;
  padding :0px;
}
li.selected    {
  background-color: #ffb;
}
div.auto_complete ul {
  margin:0px;
  padding:0px;
}
div.auto_complete li {
  margin:0px;
  padding:0 5px;
  list-style-type: none;
}
```

code snippet /autocomplete/cakephp/app/webroot/css/autocomplete.css

One more thing. If by any chance you have artifacts in your suggestion box like those illustrated in Figure 10-5, it is probably because of the configuration settings in the `/app/config/core.php` file that contains the following line:

```
Configure::write('debug',2);
```

It is used to set the debugging level. These artifacts are actually a summary of database queries that are run whenever the suggestion box is updated. To solve this problem, you simply need to change the debugging level by modifying the configuration line as follows:

```
Configure::write('debug',1);
```

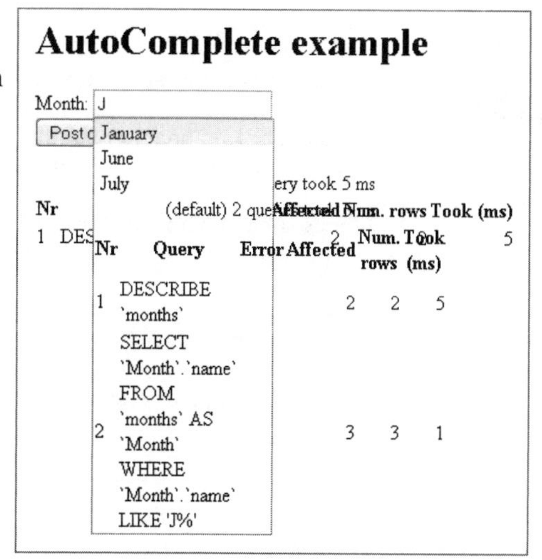

FIGURE 10-5: Artifacts displayed in the suggestion box

Zend Framework

ZendX is an additional library that includes jQuery–based view and form helpers that allow developers to enhance their applications. It contains elements such as date-picker, color-picker, slider, dialog container, and the autocomplete feature, which you will learn how to use in your application. Its stub is presented in Figure 10-6.

ZendX autocomplete example

Color name:

FIGURE 10-6: Basic form with color input field

In Zend Framework 1.10.8, the ZendX library is not a part of the standard libraries yet. To be able to use ZendX, you need to do a few things first. In the downloaded Zend Framework package, you can find the `/extras` folder containing the ZendX library. You need to copy this folder into your `/appName/library` directory.

In the next step, add `autoloaderNamespaces[]` into your `application.ini` file and set its value to `'ZendX'`. Add this line under the `[production]` tag after the database part, as shown in the following code fragment:

Available for download on Wrox.com

```
[production]
...
autoloaderNamespaces[] = "ZendX"
[staging : production]
```

code snippet /autocomplete/zf/application/configs/application.ini

By enabling `autoloader`, it is now possible to use jQuery JavaScript by loading it from the Google Ajax Library content distribution network (CDN). It gives you the possibility to load both jQuery and jQuery UI libraries. What does this mean in practice? To load JavaScript files in your layout file, the following method was generally used:

Available for download on Wrox.com

```
<html>
  <head>
    <title>Autocomplete example</title>
    <?php
      echo $this->headScript()->appendFile(
                          $this->baseUrl('/js/jquery-1.4.3.min.js')
                                      );
      echo $this->headScript()->appendFile(
                          $this->baseUrl('/js/jquery-ui-1.8.5.custom.min.js')
                                      );
    ?>
  </head>
  <body>
    <?php echo $this->layout()->content; ?>
  </body>
</html>
```

code snippet /autocomplete/zf/application/layouts/scripts/layout.phtml

This required you to have all the included scripts stored inside your application file structure (for example, in the /appName/public/js/ folder). But now you can use the following code (used also throughout this example):

```
<html>
  <head>
    <title>Autocomplete example</title>
    <?php
      echo $this->headLink();
      echo $this->jQuery()->setVersion('1.4.3')->setUiVersion('1.8.5');
    ?>
  </head>
  <body>
    <?php echo $this->layout()->content; ?>
  </body>
</html>
```

code snippet /autocomplete/zf/application/layouts/scripts/layout.phtml

By using the `$this->jQuery()` method, you make sure that whenever jQuery is needed, it is loaded. `setVersion()` specifies what version of jQuery you want to use, and `setUiVersion()` specifies what version of jQuery UI is loaded.

Now you can proceed to create the controller file. Here in the `init()` function it is necessary to define the path to the ZendX helper using the `addHelperPath()` method. The `autocompleteAction()` function creates a new element to be rendered in the view file. The form element will work because autocomplete is created using the `autocompleteElement` object. The configuration for this object consists of a field label and a list of values from which suggestions will be generated.

```
<?php
class IndexController extends Zend_Controller_Action
{
    public function init() {$this->view->addHelperPath(
      "ZendX/JQuery/View/Helper", "ZendX_JQuery_View_Helper");
    }
    public function autocompleteAction() {
        $this->view->autocompleteElement = new
            ZendX_JQuery_Form_Element_Autocomplete('ac');
        $this->view->autocompleteElement->setLabel('Color name:');
        $this->view->autocompleteElement->setJQueryParam(
              'data', array('Red', 'Green', 'Blue','Redish', 'Rose Red')
                                                          );
    }
}
```

code snippet /autocomplete/zf/application/controllers/IndexController.php

Finally, the view file needs to be created. In the following listing you can see that only the `$this->autocompleteElement` object needs to be called to make autocomplete work:

Available for download on Wrox.com

```
<h1>ZendX autocomplete example</h1>
<form>
    <?php  echo $this->autocompleteElement; ?>
</form>
```

code snippet /autocomplete/zf/application/views/scripts/index/autocomplete.phtml

The left side of Figure 10-7 illustrates the result of running the application in the browser by typing `http://localhost/appName/public/index/autocomplete`.

FIGURE 10-7: On the left — autocomplete with suggested values. On the right — autocomplete with styled suggested values

Looking at the effect of this example so far, you may not be entirely happy with the results. For one thing, you put all the autocompleting values inside the controller file, and this is a rough solution to say the least. And, of course, the appearance is somewhat crude. You can take care of the latter now because the jQuery user interface (UI) is a JavaScript library that gives you the possibility to build interactive web applications, and it comes with a number of different visual style variants. For this example, the `ui-lightness` theme was selected. You can download any of the available styles from `http://jqueryui.com/download`. After downloading the package, you need to copy the theme folder (`/ui-lightness`) into your project to the `/addressBook/public/css/` directory. When that's done, you need to link the downloaded stylesheet to your layout file using the `appendStylesheet()` method. The following code listing illustrates how this is done:

Available for download on Wrox.com

```
<html>
  <head>
    <title>Autocomplete example</title>
    <?php
      echo $this->headLink();
      echo $this->headLink()->appendStylesheet(
             $this->baseUrl('/css/ui-lightness/jquery-ui-1.8.5.custom.css')
                                                  );
      echo $this->jQuery()->setVersion('1.4.3')->setUiVersion('1.8.5');
      /*  alternative jQuery loading
      echo $this->headScript()->appendFile(
        $this->baseUrl('/js/jquery-1.4.3.min.js'));
      echo $this->headScript()->appendFile(
        $this->baseUrl('/js/jquery-ui-1.8.5.custom.min.js'));  */
    ?>
```

```
 </head>
 <body>
    <?php echo $this->layout()->content; ?>
 </body>
</html>
```

code snippet /autocomplete/zf/application/layouts/scripts/layout.phtml

If all went well, and you updated your layout file, you should get a result similar to the right side of Figure 10-7. This should be more acceptable in terms of appearance.

Now you will see how to use a database to hold your autocomplete data. Note that this topic is not about AJAX itself, and it refers to the standard application to database communication that was covered in Chapter 3 and Chapter 4. First, the database table can be created using the following SQL query:

```
CREATE TABLE IF NOT EXISTS `colors` (
  `id` int(11) NOT NULL AUTO_INCREMENT,
  `name` varchar(25) NOT NULL,
  PRIMARY KEY (`id`)
) ENGINE=MyISAM  DEFAULT CHARSET=utf8;

INSERT INTO `colors` (`id`, `name`) VALUES
(1, 'AliceBlue'), (2, 'AntiqueWhite'), ...
```

The content was filled using a list of color names that are supported by web browsers, although any other content can be entered. Next, the model file needs to be created, and for this example it can be the following:

Available for download on Wrox.com

```
<?php
class Application_Model_Color {
}
```

code snippet /autocomplete/zf/application/models/Color.php

Then create the `DbTable` model file that looks like this:

Available for download on Wrox.com

```
<?php
class Application_Model_DbTable_Colors extends Zend_Db_Table_Abstract {
    protected $_name = 'colors';
}
```

code snippet /autocomplete/zf/application/models/DbTable/Colors.php

And the `Color` mapper used for this example is like the following:

Available for download on Wrox.com

```
<?php
class Application_Model_ColorMapper {
  protected $_dbTable;
  public function setDbTable($dbTable) {
    if (is_string($dbTable)) {
      $dbTable = new $dbTable();
```

```
    }
    if (!$dbTable instanceof Zend_Db_Table_Abstract) {
      throw new Exception('Invalid table data gateway provided');
    }
    $this->_dbTable = $dbTable;
    return $this;
  }
  public function getDbTable() {
    if (null === $this->_dbTable) {
      $this->setDbTable('Application_Model_DbTable_Colors');
    }
    return $this->_dbTable;
  }
  public function fetchAll() {
    $resultSet = $this->getDbTable()->fetchAll();
    $entries = array();
    foreach ($resultSet as $row) {
      $entry = new Application_Model_Color();
      $entries[] = $row->name;
    }
    return $entries;
  }
}
```

code snippet /autocomplete/zf/application/models/ColorMapper.php

When all model files are ready, the controller needs to be modified slightly. Two new lines are introduced to the controller. The first one creates the object that gives access to database data. The second one fetches the `name` column of the `colors` table. Finally the data is passed to the `autocompleteElement`:

Available for download on Wrox.com

```
<?php
class IndexController extends Zend_Controller_Action{
    public function init() {
        $this->view->addHelperPath(
                                    "ZendX/JQuery/View/Helper",
                                    "ZendX_JQuery_View_Helper"
                                     );
    }
    public function autocompleteAction() {
      $this->view->autocompleteElement = new
             ZendX_JQuery_Form_Element_Autocomplete('ac');
      $this->view->autocompleteElement->setLabel('Color name:');
      $colors = new Application_Model_ColorMapper();
      $colorList = $colors->fetchAll();
      $this->view->autocompleteElement->setJQueryParam('data', $colorList);
    }
}
```

code snippet /autocomplete/zf/application/controllers/IndexController.php

As a result, you should have the suggestion list generated from the database. Figure 10-8 illustrates the final result of this example.

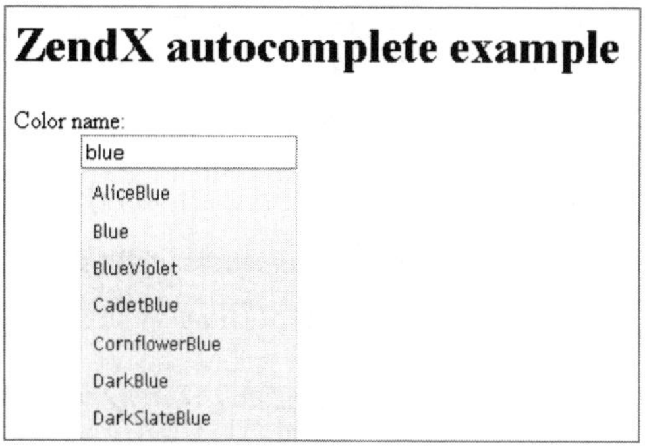

FIGURE 10-8: Autocomplete-styled suggested values read from database

DYNAMIC POPUP WINDOWS

Not long ago, popup windows were considered more of a nuisance than something useful. A popup would usually appear out of nowhere and cover the entire screen with some kind of advertisement. Of course, those popup windows had nothing to do with current AJAX technology because they used an early browser mechanism that didn't feature tabs. All web browsers currently protect users from this kind of popup.

With the appearance of AJAX, new kinds of advertising came to life, but at the same time AJAX opened a completely new set of possibilities that could be used to enhance web applications. Using AJAX it is easy to create a child window that users can interact with. Such windows are called *modal windows*. In Chapter 9 you read about Lightbox, which is an excellent example of how AJAX can generate modal windows with interactive content.

Another application of modal windows can be to display additional information on a website (for example, warning messages) without reloading it or modifying currently visible content. Another great use of modal windows is to block access to certain sections of a web application, by forcing users to interact with the window (to log in, for example).

In this section we discuss a few modal window mechanisms that all allow the same outcome and differ little in their usage. We decided to show each of them used with one framework only, but they obviously can be used with every other framework.

Symfony

For Symfony, this chapter shows two examples. One is sfFlashMessagePlugin, which allows you to change the default method of displaying messages to AJAX–based message windows. The other one illustrates how to use Lytebox script to create popup windows containing HTML content.

sfFlashMessagePlugin

This plug-in relies on JqueryReloadedPlugin, which offers easy integration of jQuery with your application. You can read about JqueryReloadedPlugin at `www.symfony-project.org/plugins/sfJqueryReloadedPlugin`, and about sfFlashMessagePlugin at `www.symfony-project.org/plugins/sfFlashMessagePlugin`.

To install JqueryReloadedPlugin, from your project directory enter the following command in your command window (if you have JqueryReloadedPlugin already installed, skip this step):

```
$ symfony plugin:install sfJqueryReloadedPlugin
```

sfJqueryReloadedPlugin gives you the possibility to use the jQuery helper in your project files.

Do the same for sfFlashMessagePlugin using the following command:

```
$ symfony plugin:install sfFlashMessagePlugin
```

Cache clearing is advised:

```
$ symfony cache:clear
```

As far as installation goes, this is all you need to do. Now you can move to the project files. First, the layout file needs to have the `include_javascripts()` function present inside the `<head></head>` tags. The code used in this example is as follows:

```
<!DOCTYPE html PUBLIC "-//W3C//DTD XHTML 1.0 Transitional//EN"
      "http://www.w3.org/TR/xhtml1/DTD/xhtml1-transitional.dtd">
<html xmlns="http://www.w3.org/1999/xhtml" xml:lang="en" lang="en">
  <head>
    <?php include_http_metas() ?>
    <?php include_metas() ?>
    <?php include_title() ?>
    <link rel="shortcut icon" href="/favicon.ico" />
    <?php include_stylesheets() ?>
    <?php include_javascripts() ?>
  </head>
  <body>
    <?php echo $sf_content ?>
  </body>
</html>
```

code snippet /popup/flash/symfony/apps/frontend/templates/layout.php

Next, the action file needs to set some example flash messages. Four message types are available here: success, notice, warning, and error. Every one of these messages has a different color when rendered. The following are the example messages used for this example:

```
<?php
class flashmessageActions extends sfActions{
  public function executeIndex(sfWebRequest $request){
    $this->getUser()->setFlash('success', 'This is success message!'); //green
    $this->getUser()->setFlash('notice', 'This is notice message!');   //yellow
    $this->getUser()->setFlash('warning', 'This is warning message!'); //orange
    $this->getUser()->setFlash('error', 'This is error message!');     //red
  }
}
```

code snippet /popup/flash/symfony/apps/frontend/modules/flashmessage/actions/actions.class.php

The view file is responsible for rendering those messages, and it usually is done as shown in the following code:

Available for download on Wrox.com

```
<h1>Flash Messages</h1>
<p>
<?php echo $sf_user->getFlash('success') ?><br />
<?php echo $sf_user->getFlash('warning') ?><br />
<?php echo $sf_user->getFlash('notice') ?><br />
<?php echo $sf_user->getFlash('error') ?></p>
```

code snippet /popup/flash/symfony/apps/frontend/modules/flashmessage/templates/indexSuccess.php

The resulting page content is rendered as shown in Figure 10-9.

Flash Messages

This is success message!
This is warning message!
This is notice message!
This is error message!

FIGURE 10-9: Standard flash messages, displayed using the getFlash() method

Now, you should use sfFlashMessagePlugin and render these messages using AJAX. To do so, you only need to prepend this file with the `use_helper()` function and set it to use the `jQuery` and `sfFlashMessage` helpers. The code of the `indexSuccess.php` view file can be shortened to the following code:

Available for download on Wrox.com

```
<?php use_helper( 'jQuery', 'sfFlashMessage') ?>
<h1>Flash Messages</h1>
```

code snippet /popup/flash/symfony/apps/frontend/modules/flashmessage/templates/indexSuccess.php

This will make your messages look like Figure 10-10.

Flash Messages

This is success message!
This is notice message!
This is warning message!
This is error message!

FIGURE 10-10: Flash messages rendered using sfFlashMessagePlugin

Messages rendered using sfFlashMessagePlugin disappear after a set amount of time, except the error message; that is visible until it is closed manually. It is possible to modify the style and display delay time by modifying the plug-in's configuration in the `app.yml` file. Here you can select a display method from the `pop` and `growl` options, and set a delay time in milliseconds, as shown here:

```
sf_flash_message:
  delay: 2500
  method: growl
```

Lytebox

The script demonstrated in this example is another variation of Lightbox, which was introduced in Chapter 9. It differs from other similar scripts mainly by its independence from other AJAX libraries such as jQuery. Lytebox, created by Markus F. Hay, offers you options to create slideshow image galleries or windows with the possibility to browse HTML content in catalog-like style. The implementation for this script is probably the easiest of all scripts presented in this chapter.

To get moving with the integration, first visit the authors' website `www.dolem.com/lytebox` and get the Lytebox package. In this example, you need to place the unpacked content (`lytebox.js` file, `lytebox.css` file, and `/images` folder) inside the `/appName/web/lytebox` folder. If you wish to separate package files to the corresponding folders inside `/appName/web` folder, you could do so, but this will require you to modify all file paths accordingly, including the `lytebox.css` file.

When you have Lytebox in place, you need to include `lytebox.js` and `lytebox.css` into your layout file. The code for `layout.php` used in this example looks like the following:

Available for download on Wrox.com

```
<!DOCTYPE html PUBLIC "-//W3C//DTD XHTML 1.0 Transitional//EN"
       "http://www.w3.org/TR/xhtml1/DTD/xhtml1-transitional.dtd">
<html xmlns="http://www.w3.org/1999/xhtml" xml:lang="en" lang="en">
  <head>
    <?php include_http_metas() ?>
    <?php include_metas() ?>
    <?php include_title() ?>
    <link rel="shortcut icon" href="/favicon.ico" />
    <?php use_stylesheet('../lytebox/lytebox.css') ?>
    <?php include_stylesheets() ?>
    <?php use_javascript('../lytebox/lytebox.js') ?>
    <?php include_javascripts() ?>
  </head>
  <body>
    <?php echo $sf_content ?>
  </body>
</html>
```

code snippet /popup/lytebox/symfony/apps/frontend/templates/layout.php

As for the actions file, only the index action is needed, as shown in the following code:

Available for download on Wrox.com

```
<?php
class lyteboxActions extends sfActions{
  public function executeIndex(sfWebRequest $request){
  }
}
```

code snippet /popup/lytebox/symfony/apps/frontend/modules/lytebox/actions/actions.class.php

For the HTML side of this example, the base content is shown in Figure 10-11.

The first two links will open a window with HTML content, in which you can browse back and forth through the items in this list. This window is shown in Figure 10-12. The third link will open a window of the size specified in the following code without the possibility of scrolling its HTML content. Note that the `rev` attribute can be used for any link in this example to change the size of the displayed window. The code of the view file in this example looks as follows:

LyteBox example

Show list item 1
Show list item 2
Show new window in full screen

LyteBox gallery example:

Symfony Logo
CakePHP Logo
Zend Framework Logo

FIGURE 10-11: Lytebox application example

```
<h1>LyteBox example</h1>
<a href="http://www.wrox.com/" title="Wrox"
   rel="lyteframe[catalog]">Show list item 1 </a><br />
<a href="http://www.wiley.com/" title="Wiley"
   rel="lyteframe[catalog]">Show list item 2 </a><br />
<a href="http://www.wrox.com/" title="Wrox"
   rel="lyteframe" rev="width: 400px; height: 300px; scrolling: no;">
   Show new window in full screen</a>
```

code snippet /popup/lytebox/symfony/apps/frontend/modules/lytebox/templates/indexSuccess.php

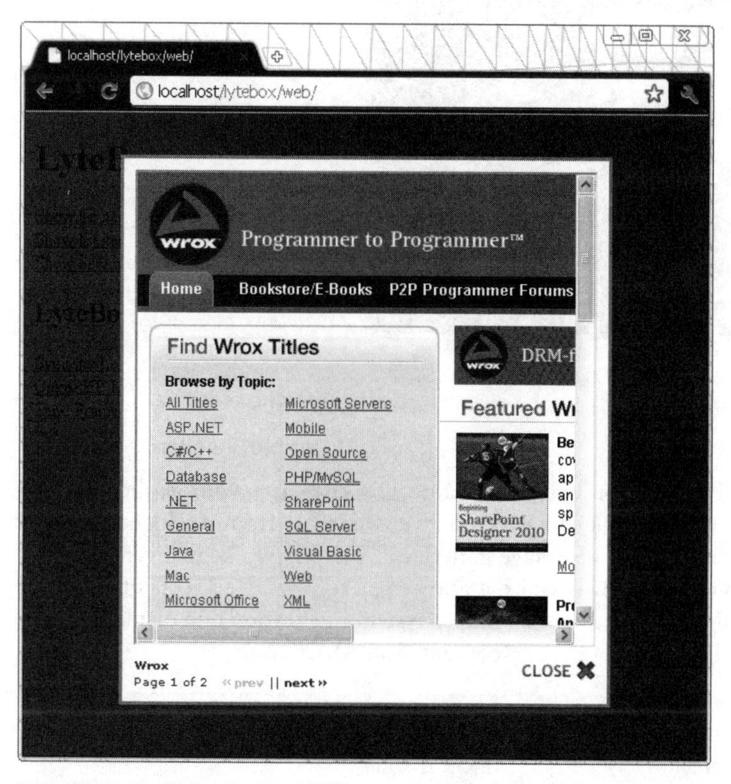

FIGURE 10-12: Gallery style, HTML content viewer using Lytebox

The gallery capabilities of the Lytebox script can be used by adding the following code into your `indexSuccess.php` view file:

Available for download on Wrox.com

```
<h2>LyteBox gallery example: </h2>
<a href="http://www.symfony-project.org/images/symfony_logo.gif"
    rel="lyteshow[logos]"
    title="Symfony Logo">Symfony Logo</a><br />
<a href="http://cakephp.org/img/cake-logo.png"
    rel="lyteshow[logos]"
    title="CakePHP Logo">CakePHP Logo</a><br />
<a href="http://framework.zend.com/images/logo.gif"
```

```
rel="lyteshow[logos]"
title="Zend Framework Logo">Zend Framework Logo</a>
```

code snippet /popup/lytebox/symfony/apps/frontend/modules/lytebox/templates/indexSuccess.php

Figure 10-13 illustrates the image gallery that is displayed when any gallery link is clicked.

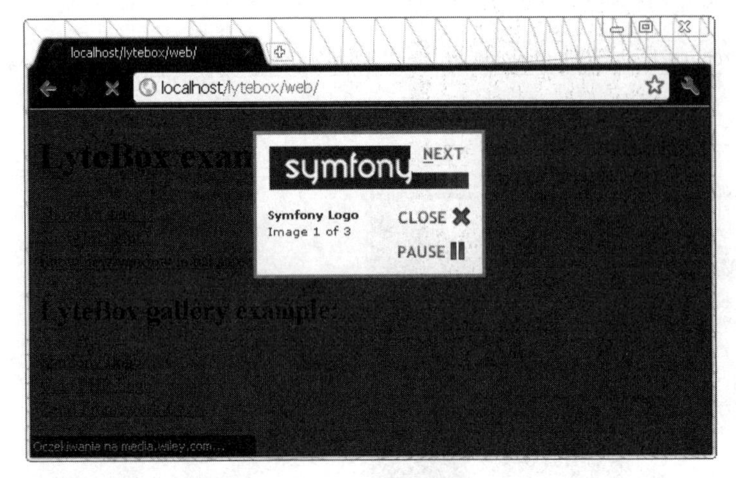

FIGURE 10-13: Lytebox image slideshow gallery

CakePHP

To create popup windows in CakePHP, you will incorporate ThickBox into your application. ThickBox is a script written by Cody Lindley in JavaScript. It originates from the Lightbox script designed to enhance websites with interactive image galleries. ThickBox works in a very similar manner, but is not restricted to images only because it allows you to display all sorts of content. There are many features behind ThickBox, such as simple system integration and displaying various kinds of content (images, `iframed` content, `inline` content, and AJAX content).

Figure 10-14 shows an example page that consists of a paragraph of text and two links using ThickBox to display content.

Modal Window

Show modal content.
Show hidden modal content.
Modal window can be used to display additional information on a website, without reloading it or modifying currently visible content.

FIGURE 10-14: Sample content with two links prepared for ThickBox

Now integrate ThickBox into your CakePHP application. The first thing to do is to download ThickBox files from the website: `http://jquery.com/demo/thickbox/`. You need to download `thickbox.js` or `thickbox-compressed.js` and place it inside the `/app/webroot/js/` directory. The `thickbox.js` and `thickbox-compressed.js` files require jQuery in order to work properly. You can download jQuery from the same page as ThickBox or you can download it from the jQuery website at `http://docs.jquery.com/Downloading_jQuery`. The jQuery library should be placed in the same folder as the ThickBox script. Next you need to download `thickbox.css` and copy it to the `/app/webroot/css/`

directory. The last file that needs to be downloaded into `/app/webroot/img/` is `loadingAnimation.gif`. When you're done, you should have the following file structure:

```
/app/webroot/
    js/
        thickbox-compressed.js
        jquery-1.4.3.min.js
    css/
        thickbox.css
    img/
        loadingAnimation.gif
```

To begin integration of ThickBox into a CakePHP application, start by creating a route in the `routes.php` file. This can look as follows:

Available for download on Wrox.com

```
Router::connect('/modalbox', array(
    'controller' => 'thickbox', 'action' => 'index'));
```

code snippet /popup/cakephp/app/config/routes.php

The layout file should contain corresponding helpers inside the `<head>` section. The three bold lines in the following code make sure that the supplied libraries are loaded properly. The layout used for this example is as follows:

Available for download on Wrox.com

```
<html>
  <head>
    <?php
      echo $html->css ( "thickbox", "stylesheet");
      if ( isset ( $javascript ) ):
         echo $javascript->link ("/app/webroot/js/jquery-1.4.3.min.js" );
         echo $javascript->link ("/app/webroot/js/thickbox-compressed.js" );
      endif;
    ?>
  </head>
  <body>
    <?php echo $content_for_layout ?>
  </body>
</html>
```

code snippet /popup/cakephp/app/views/layouts/default.ctp

This is nearly enough to use ThickBox, but you still need to define the set of helpers that your application is using. Set the `$helpers` variable in the `thickbox_controller.php` controller file. The code for this file is as follows:

Available for download on Wrox.com

```
<?php
  class ThickboxController extends AppController {
    var $name = 'thickbox';
    var $helpers = array ( "Javascript" );
    function index() {
    }
```

```
  }
?>
```

code snippet /popup/cakephp/app/controllers/thickbox_controller.php

The `thickbox.php` model file should be created and it might look like this one:

Available for download on Wrox.com

```
<?php
class Thickbox extends AppModel {
  var $useTable = false;
}
```

code snippet /popup/cakephp/app/models/thickbox.php

Finally, the `index.ctp` view file allows you to use ThickBox with your content. Assuming that you are using a standard `link` element to call popups, you will need to set the `class` attribute to the `thickbox` value, like this:

```
<a href="" class="thickbox"></a>
```

The `href` attribute needs to begin with the `#TB_inline` anchor. Next there are several options:

```
<a href="#TB_inline?height=100&width=200&inlineId=modalContent&modal=true"
    class="thickbox"></a>
```

The `height` and `width` options define the size of the popup window. The `inlineId` option is the id value of the element that will contain the ThickBox content. If the `modal` option is set as `true`, the content displayed in the window will have to contain an element with the `onclick="tb_remove()"` attribute. The following code illustrates how to use a simple message window and a yes/no message box:

Available for download on Wrox.com

```
<h1>Modal Window</h1>
<p>
<a href="#TB_inline?height=100&width=200&inlineId=modalContent"
      class="thickbox">Show modal content.</a>
<br />
<a href="#TB_inline?height=150&width=200&inlineId=hiddenModalContent&modal=true"
      class="thickbox">Show hidden modal content.</a>
</p>
<div id="modalContent" >
    <p>Modal window can be used to display additional information on a website,
      without reloading it or modifying currently visible content.</p>
</div>
<div id="hiddenModalContent" style="display:none">
    <p>Modal windows are great way to block access to certain section of web
      application, by forcing user to interact with it.</p>
    <p>Do you agree?</p>
    <input type="button" id="Login" value=" Yes " onclick="tb_remove()" />
    <input type="button" id="Login" value=" No " />
</div>
```

code snippet /popup/cakephp/app/views/thickbox/index.ctp

To the left in Figure 10-15 is the message window displayed as the result of clicking the Show modal content link.

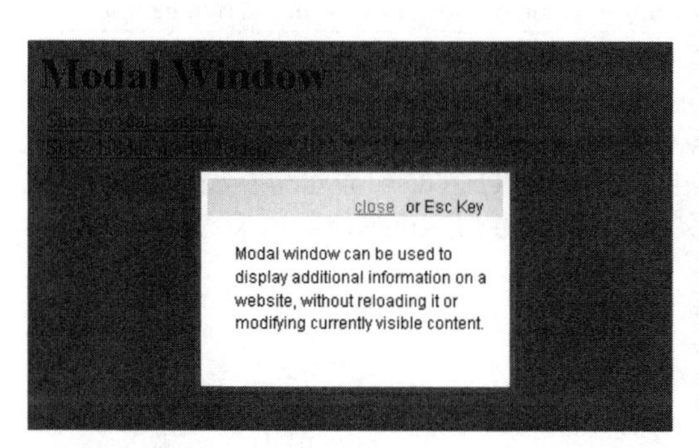

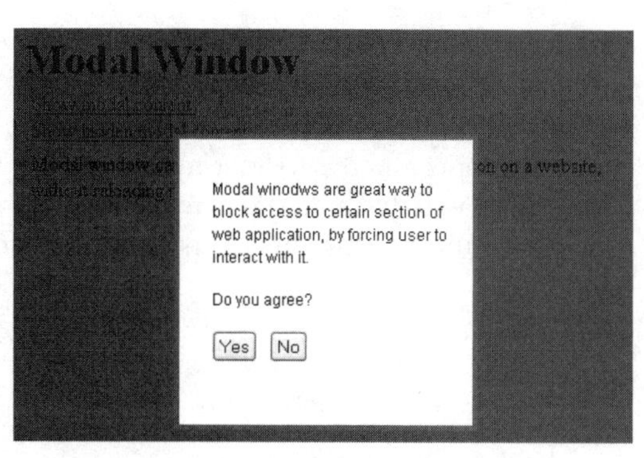

FIGURE 10-15: On the left — the ThickBox window, displayed by clicking the Show modal content link. On the right — the ThickBox window, displayed by clicking the Show hidden modal content link

To the right in Figure 10-15 you can see another message window that requires the user to click the Yes button in order to close it.

Zend Framework

To create a popup window able to display content of various types, the GreyBox JavaScript library was selected. It is an independent library, and it means that no additional AJAX libraries are required. So no jQuery this time.

Installation of GreyBox in Zend Framework is a simple and swift task. Proceeding with the installation, first you need to download the GreyBox package from its author website: `http://orangoo.com/labs/GreyBox/`. The downloaded package contains GreyBox, and various examples of usage as well. You need to copy the `/greybox` folder to the `/appName/public/js` directory of your application. The `/greybox` folder contains various files: images, scripts, and stylesheets. You could group them into separate folders, but this is unnecessary.

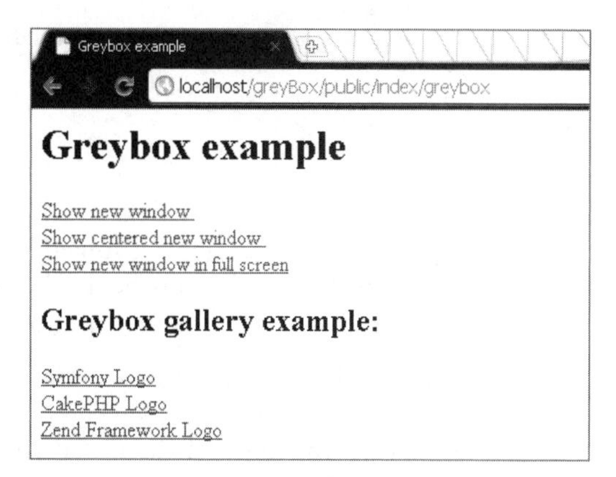

FIGURE 10-16: GreyBox example application

When the application using GreyBox is finished, it will look as shown in Figure 10-16. The links demonstrate various usage examples.

Moving to the controller file, it does not contain any additional functionality. Only the blank `greyboxAction()` is added. The following code is the listing of the controller used in this example:

```
<?php
class IndexController extends Zend_Controller_Action {
    public function init() {
    }
    public function greyboxAction() {
```

```
        }
    }
```

code snippet /popup/zf/application/controllers/IndexController.php

The layout file makes GreyBox available for use in your application. Additionally, to include the GreyBox scripts and the stylesheet, you need to set the *GB_ROOT_DIR* variable to be used in GreyBox scripts. This variable holds the path to the image files used by GreyBox. You can see in the following code what value is set to make this example work with the Zend Framework file structure:

Available for download on Wrox.com

```
<html>
  <head>
    <title>Greybox example</title>
      <script type="text/javascript">
        var GB_ROOT_DIR = "../js/greybox/";
      </script>
      <?php
        echo $this->headLink()->appendStylesheet(
                    $this->baseUrl('/js/greybox/gb_styles.css')
                                                            );
        echo $this->headScript()->appendFile($this->baseUrl('/js/greybox/AJS.js'));
        echo $this->headScript()->appendFile(
                    $this->baseUrl('/js/greybox/AJS_fx.js')
                                                        );
        echo $this->headScript()->appendFile(
                    $this->baseUrl('/js/greybox/gb_scripts.js')
                                                        );
      ?>
  </head>
  <body>
    <?php echo $this->layout()->content; ?>
  </body>
</html>
```

code snippet /popup/zf/application/layouts/scripts/layout.phtml

A CSS stylesheet in this example is linked by the `appendStylesheet()` method and it points to the folder where JavaScript is usually held. All scripts used by GreyBox here are located in the same folder, however. The JavaScript files are linked by the `appendFile()` method.

You should now have everything necessary to use the features of GreyBox with the standard HTML syntax. Using the `rel` attribute, you can now turn a hyperlink tag into a link to a new window or an image gallery. As the value for the `rel` attribute you can use a number or variables such as `gb_page`, `gb_page_fs`, `gb_imageset`, and so on. Each of these values has its own uses. For the full list of features, please refer to the GreyBox documentation. The following code illustrates various usages of the GreyBox library:

Available for download on Wrox.com

```
<h1>Greybox example</h1>
  <a href="http://www.wrox.com/"
     title="Wrox"
     rel="gb_page[790, 200]">Show new window </a> <br />
  <a href="http://www.wrox.com/"
```

```
        title="Wrox"
        rel="gb_page_center[200, 200]">Show centered new window </a> <br />
    <a href="http://www.wrox.com/"
        title="Wrox"
        rel="gb_page_fs[]">Show new window in full screen</a>
  <h2>Greybox gallery example: </h2>
    <a href="http://www.symfony-project.org/images/symfony_logo.gif"
         rel="gb_imageset[logos]"
         title="Symfony Logo">Symfony Logo</a> <br />
    <a href="http://cakephp.org/img/cake-logo.png"
         rel="gb_imageset[logos]"
         title="CakePHP Logo">CakePHP Logo</a> <br />
    <a href="http://framework.zend.com/images/logo.gif"
         rel="gb_imageset[logos]"
         title="Zend Framework Logo">Zend Framework Logo</a>
```

code snippet /popup/zf/application/views/scripts/index/greybox.phtml

Finally, you can see results by typing `http://localhost/appName/public/index/lightbox` in your web browser. Figure 10-17 illustrates a centered window displaying a web page.

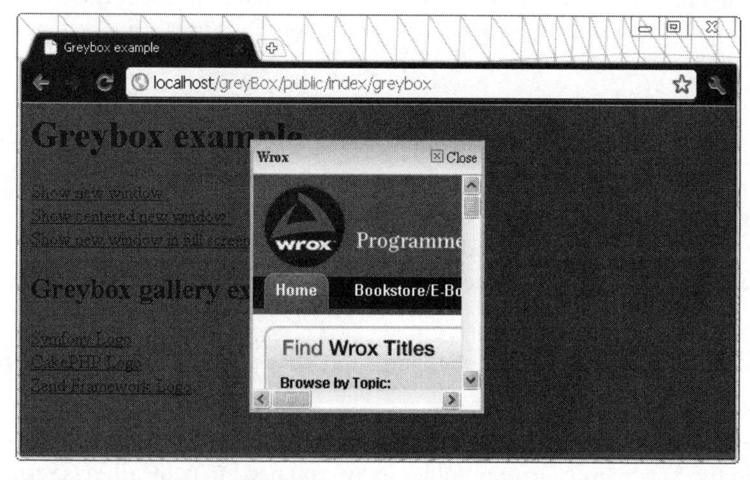

FIGURE 10-17: A new window opened using GreyBox

Figure 10-18 demonstrates how an image gallery can be realized using GreyBox. There is an issue with displaying images in a gallery reported in version 5.54 of GreyBox, where the images are not rendered the first time. If you encounter this problem, switching to version 5.53 should fix it.

AJAX USER CHAT

Web chat is a form of conference-like communication between multiple users, using a web application. Chats are usually part of larger applications, such as social networks, information services, forums, or online games. They allow users to divide into chat rooms, where various subjects can be discussed. Chat can take different forms. It can be a shoutbox, user-to-user private conversation, or Internet Relay Chat (IRC). Some of these may require special software to use. Features of chat applications can cover things such as image sending, sound messages, IP blocking, forbidden word filtering, user bans, moderation, and so on.

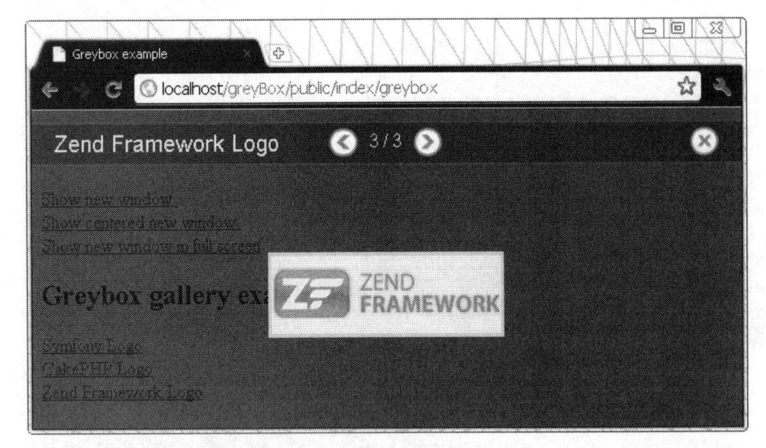

FIGURE 10-18: Image gallery using GreyBox

In this section you will learn how to implement ready-to-use chat scripts and implement them as a part of your web application, created in web frameworks. One of the solutions uses a file system for storing chat messages; the two other use a database to do this.

Symfony

To learn how a basic chat can be integrated into a Symfony application, the chat script created by Ryan Smith was chosen. This chat solution is easy to use in standalone applications, but in Symfony it needs to be slightly modified to take full advantage of the features offered by this framework. So go on and grab the AJAX chat package from `www.dynamicajax.com/tutorials/ajax_chat_1.zip`.

This package contains the following files: `chat.html`, `chat.sql`, `database.php`, `getChat.php`, and `readme.html`.

The first step is to create two files for your application: the `chat.js` file inside the `/appName/web/js` folder and the `chat.css` file in the `/symfony/web/css` folder. Now you need to copy all JavaScript code from between the `<script> </script>` tags of the `chat.html` file and paste it into the `chat.js` file of your project. You can do the same thing for styles in `chat.html`. Simply copy the style content from between the `<style> </style>` tags and place it inside `chat.css`. Later you can add your own styles inside this file to modify the visual style of the chat window and messages.

You must now modify the `chat.js` file and make sure that the AJAX `sendReq.open()` and `receiveReq.open()` requests point to the `getchat` action. This should be done in three lines, and these line numbers are 26, 38, and 84. An example of how this should be done is as follows:

Available for download on Wrox.com

```
// line 26
receiveReq.open(
                "GET",
                'index.php/moduleName/getchat?chat=1&last=' + lastMessage,
                true
```

```
                    );
// line 38
sendReq.open(
             "POST",
             'index.php/moduleName/getchat?chat=1&last=' + lastMessage,
             true
             );
// line 84
sendReq.open(
             "POST",
             'index.php/moduleName/getchat?chat=1&last=' + lastMessage,
             true
             );
```

code snippet /chat/symfony/web/js/chat.js

When you have the `chat.js` file ready, a modification to the `view.yml` file is necessary (highlighted in bold) as shown here:

```
default:
  http_metas:
    content-type: text/html
  metas:
  stylesheets:      [main.css, chat.css]
  javascripts:      [chat.js]
  has_layout:       true
  layout:           layout
```

code snippet /chat/symfony/apps/frontend/config/view.yml

When `chat.js` and `chat.css` are included in `view.yml`, you need to make sure that those files are loaded when the page is displayed. To do so, the `<head>` section of the layout file needs to contain the following code:

```
    <?php include_stylesheets() ?>
    <?php include_javascripts() ?>
```

code snippet /chat/symfony/apps/frontend/templates/layout.php

The chat application uses a database to hold all messages posted by users. The design for the database tables can be found in `chat.sql` of the original package. Alternatively you can use the following schema:

```
Message:
  connection: doctrine
  tableName: message
  columns:
    message_id: { type: integer(4) fixed: false unsigned: false
      primary: true autoincrement: true }
    user_id: { type: integer(4) fixed: false unsigned: false
      primary: false default: '0' notnull: true autoincrement: false }
    user_name:{ type: string(64) fixed: false unsigned: false
```

```
      primary: false notnull: false autoincrement: false }
    message: { type: string() fixed: false unsigned: false
      primary: false notnull: false autoincrement: false }
    post_time: { type: timestamp(25) fixed: false unsigned: false
      primary: false notnull: false autoincrement: false }
```

code snippet /chat/symfony/apps/config/doctrine/schema.yml

To generate the table described in `schema.yml`, use the following command in the command console from your project directory:

```
$ symfony doctrine:build --all
```

Now you can view the `getChat.php` file of the original package. This file is responsible for performing all database operations regarding user messages. Notice that it includes `database.php` to create a database connection. While using the Symfony framework, all this can be replaced by creating the `executeGetchat()` function in your `actions.class.php` file. The code in this function is equivalent to the code of the original package, and it looks as follows:

Available for download on Wrox.com

```
<?php
class chatActions extends sfActions {
  public function executeIndex(sfWebRequest $request) {
  }
  public function executeGetchat(sfWebRequest $request) {
    if(isset($_POST['message']) && $_POST['message'] != '') {
        $msg = new Message();
        $msg->setUserId(1);
        $msg->setUserName('unknown');
        $msg->setMessage($_POST['message']);
        $msg->setPostTime(date("Y-m-d H:i:s"));
        $msg->save();
    }
    $xml = '<?xml version="1.0" encoding="UTF-8" ?><root>';
    if(!isset($_GET['chat'])) {
        $xml .= '<message id="0">';
        $xml .= '<user>Admin</user>';
        $xml .= '<text>Your are not currently in a chat session.</text>';
        $xml .= '<time>'.date("Y-m-d H:i:s").'</time>';
        $xml .= '</message>';
    } else {
        $last = (isset($_GET['last']) && $_GET['last'] != '') ? $_GET['last'] : 0;
        $messages = Doctrine_Core::getTable('Message')
            ->createQuery('c')
            ->where('c.message_id > ?', $last)
            ->orderBy('c.message_id')
            ->execute();
        foreach($messages as $msg) {
            $xml .= '<message id="' . $msg->getMessageId() . '">';
            $xml .= '<user>' . $msg->getUserName() . '</user>';
            $xml .= '<text>'.htmlspecialchars($msg->getMessage()).'</text>';
            $xml .= '<time>' . $msg->getPostTime(). '</time>';
            $xml .= '</message>';
```

```
            }
        }
        $this->text = $xml .= '</root>';
        $response = $this->getResponse();
        $response->setContentType('text/xml');
        return $this->renderText($this->text);
    }
}
```

code snippet /chat/symfony/apps/frontend/modules/chat/actions/actions.class.php

Because `actions.class.php` contains two actions, two view files are needed; the first one is `indexSuccess.php` and must be filled with HTML code from `chat.html` from the original package. At the end of this file the `startChat()` JavaScript function needs to be called. The code used in this example is as follows:

Available for download on Wrox.com

```
<h2><a href="http://www.dynamicAJAX.com"
      style="color: #000000; text-decoration: none;">
      AJAX Driven Web Chat
      </a>
</h2>
<div id="div_chat"
      style="height: 300px; width: 500px; overflow: auto; background-color:
        #CCCCCC; border: 1px solid #555555;">
</div>
<form id="frmmain" name="frmmain" onsubmit="return blockSubmit();">
    <input type="button" name="btn_get_chat" id="btn_get_chat" value="Refresh Chat"
           onclick="javascript:getChatText();" />
    <input type="button" name="btn_reset_chat" id="btn_reset_chat"
           value="Reset Chat" onclick="javascript:resetChat();" />
    <br />
    <input type="text" id="txt_message" name="txt_message" style="width: 447px;" />
    <input type="button" name="btn_send_chat" id="btn_send_chat" value="Send"
           onclick="javascript:sendChatText();" />
</form>
<script language="JavaScript" type="text/javascript">
  startChat();
</script>
```

code snippet /chat/symfony/apps/frontend/modules/chat/templates/indexSuccess.php

Finally, in the same directory as `indexSuccess.php`, you should create a blank `getchatSuccess.php` file, and you are done. The results of this example should look as illustrated in Figure 10-19.

CakePHP

The solution used in CakePHP is an AJAX chat plug-in written by Matt Curry. It allows user communication by a web form, illustrated in Figure 10-20. This solution was selected because of its easy implementation and popularity.

FIGURE 10-19: Chat window in Symfony application

FIGURE 10-20: Chat window without any messages

You can get the plug-in package from `http://github.com/mcurry/chat`. Unpacked content needs to be placed in the `/app/plugins/chat` directory. There you will find the `chats.sql` file that contains an SQL query that is responsible for creating the `chats` database table for holding all user posts. This query is as follows:

```
CREATE TABLE `chats` (
`id` int(10) unsigned NOT NULL auto_increment,
`key` varchar(45) NOT NULL default '',
`name` varchar(20) NOT NULL default '',
`message` text NOT NULL,
`ip_address` varchar(15) NOT NULL default '',
`created` datetime default NULL,
PRIMARY KEY (`id`),
KEY `KEY_IDX` (`key`)
);
```

It is good to have the `chats` table created before proceeding. When that is done, you can begin creating the routing connection in the routing file. For this example, the following code is used:

Available for download on Wrox.com

```
Router::connect('/chat', array('controller' => 'chatbox', 'action' => 'index'));
```

code snippet /chat/cakephp/app/config/routes.php

The chat plug-in uses the jQuery library, so it needed to be included in the `default.ctp` layout file. You can get jQuery library from `http://jquery.com/`. Also, the plug-in's `chat.css` stylesheet and `chat.js` need to be linked inside the layout. In this case, the following layout is used:

Available for download on Wrox.com

```
<html>
  <head>
    <?php
      echo $html->css('/chat/css/chat.css', "stylesheet");
    if ( isset ( $javascript ) ):
       echo $javascript->link('jquery');
       echo $javascript->link('/chat/js/chat.js');
    endif;
    ?>
  </head>
  <body>
    <?php echo $content_for_layout ?>
  </body>
</html>
```

code snippet /chat/cakephp/app/views/layouts/default.ctp

We suggest not using the same name for the controller as the name of the plug-in. In this case, `ChatboxController` is used instead of `ChatController`. So moving to the controller file, you need to add the `chat.ajaxChat` value into the `$helpers` array, as well as the `Ajax` value.

Available for download on Wrox.com

```
<?php
  class ChatboxController extends AppController {
    var $uses = 'Chatpost';
    var $helpers = array('Ajax', 'chat.ajaxChat');
    function index() {
    }
  }
?>
```

code snippet /chat/cakephp/app/controllers/chatbox_controller.php

The model file is quite standard and goes like this:

Available for download on Wrox.com

```
<?php
class Chatpost extends AppModel {
  var $name = 'Chatpost';
  var $useTable = 'chats';
}
```

code snippet /chat/cakephp/app/models/chatpost.php

And finally the view file `index.ctp` needs only one line to have your chat up and running:

Available for download on Wrox.com

```
<?php echo $ajaxChat->generate('chatWindowName');   ?>
```

code snippet /chat/cakephp/app/views/index.ctp

By setting different values in the `generate()` method, it is possible to have multiple chat windows at the same time. The `index.ctp` view file used in this example goes as follows:

```
<h1>Ajax Chat  Example</h1>
<?php echo $ajaxChat->generate('chat');   ?>
```

code snippet /chat/cakephp/app/views/index.ctp

There may be some problems with displaying messages. If this happens, you need to modify one of the plug-in's files: `chat.js`. This file is located in the `/app/plugins/chat/vendors/js` directory. At the end of this file there are lines similar to those presented here. Here you can set the path to update the script of the plug-in, and you can modify the interval in which the chat box is reloaded:

```
...
$.fn.chat.defaults = {
    update: '/cake/chat/update',
    interval: 5000
};
```

code snippet /chat/cakephp/app/plugins/chat/vendors/js/chat.js

At this point you should have a working AJAX chat that looks like the one illustrated by Figure 10-21.

FIGURE 10-21: Chat window with users' messages

Zend Framework

The AJAX chat script selected to be implemented into the Zend Framework application is the Most Simple Ajax Chat Script, available from `www.linuxuser.at`. It will introduce you to the problem of implementing external scripts into your application. So why this script and not another? Well, it is a great piece of code for such a small package. It contains only three files. One is a PHP file responsible for saving and loading chat history. The other file is an HTML page with chat window and some JavaScript embedded inside it. The last is a text file that holds chat messages. This example will show you how to use AJAX chat and will set you up if you ever wish to develop the application further.

There is a huge selection of free AJAX scripts on the Internet, but most of them are quite large applications — too big to be introduced in this book. But if you have some spare time, we suggest the AJAX chat tutorial available at this page: `http://devzone.zend.com/article/1581-Ajax-Chat-Tutorial`.

Moving to the example, first get the Most Simple Ajax Chat Script package from `www.linuxuser.at/chat/index.html`. You can run it just after unpacking it to your server and see how it works. A modified example rendered in the browser is shown in Figure 10-22.

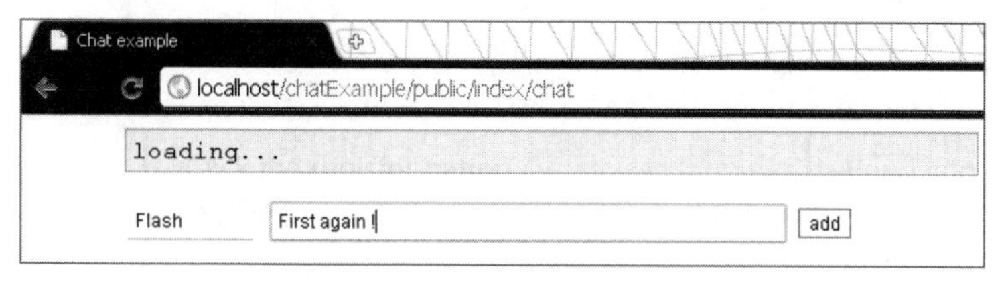

FIGURE 10-22: Chat window without messages

The package contains three files:

- `index.html` — hat form, styles sheet, JavaScript code
- `w.php` — Responsible for reading and writing content of the `chat.txt` file
- `chat.txt` — Contains chat history

First you should open the `index.html` file and prepare to split it into three files: `chat.css`, `chat.js`, and the `chat.phtml` view file. Start with cutting everything between the `<style></style>` tags from `index.html` and placing it inside `chat.css` in the `/appName/public/css` folder. For this example, the content of this file was slightly modified to achieve a white-gray theme style. When you have the CSS file ready, you can modify your layout file to include this style, as shown in the following code:

```
<html>
 <head>
    <title>Chat example</title>
    <?php
        echo $this->headLink();
        echo $this->headLink()->appendStylesheet($this->baseUrl('/css/chat.css'));
    ?>
 </head>
 <body>
<?php echo $this->layout()->content; ?>
 </body>
</html>
```

code snippet /chat/zf/application/layouts/scripts/layout.phtml

Next you should cut JavaScript from between the `<script> </script>` tags of the `index.html` file and copy the extracted content into the `chat.js` file, placed inside the `/appName/public/js/` folder. The rest of the `index.html` file needs to be copied into the `chat.phtml` file inside the /appName/application/views/scripts/index/ folder and modified so that it matches to the view file introduced next:

```
<div id="content">
<p id="chatwindow"> </p>
<!--
    <textarea id="chatwindow" rows="19" cols="95" readonly></textarea><br>
-->
<input id="chatnick" type="text" size="9" maxlength="9" > 
<input id="chatmsg" type="text" size="60" maxlength="80"
       onkeyup="keyup(event.keyCode);">
<input type="button" value="add" onclick="submit_msg();"
       style="cursor:pointer;border:1px solid gray;"><br><br>
<br>
</div>
<?php echo $this->headScript()->appendFile($this->baseUrl('/js/chat.js'));
?>
```

code snippet /chat/zf/application/views/scripts/index/chat.phtml

Notice that at the end of this file, appendFile() is used to include the chat.js file created before.

Finally the controller file contains two functions: chatAction(), which is responsible for displaying the initial view file; and chatwriteAction(), which contains the whole functionality of the w.php file.

As highlighted in the following code, you need to include $this->_helper->viewRenderer->setNoRender(); inside the chatwriteAction() action, because it is not supposed to render any view files:

```
<?php
class IndexController extends Zend_Controller_Action{
    public function init() {
    }
    public function chatAction() {
    }
    public function chatwriteAction() {
        $this->_helper->viewRenderer->setNoRender();
        // the content of w.php file goes here.
    }
}
```

code snippet /chat/zf/application/controllers/IndexController.php

The last file is the one containing the chat history. For this example the chat.txt file is located inside the newly created /appName/public/chat/ directory and it has write rights enabled.

You're nearly ready to have your chat application running, but first you need to adjust all paths pointing to the chat.txt file. The first code line of w.php and now the second line of the chatwriteAction() function is a variable containing the full path to chat.txt. For this example this path goes as follows:

```
$fn = "../public/chat/chat.txt";
```

Next the `chat.js` file needs to be modified. If you followed this example exactly without removing any comments, you have to modify lines 51, 100, and 109 of the `chat.js` file. Otherwise, you can look at the code and find the corresponding lines yourself. Modifications done for this example go as follows:

```
// line 51
intUpdate = setTimeout("ajax_read('../chat/chat.txt?x=" + ms + "')", waittime)
// line 100
ajax_write("./chatwrite?m=" + msg + "&n=" + nick);
// line 109
var intUpdate = setTimeout("ajax_read('../chat/chat.txt')", waittime);
```

Now you can run your application and enjoy the results. You should have a chat window similar to the one shown in Figure 10-23.

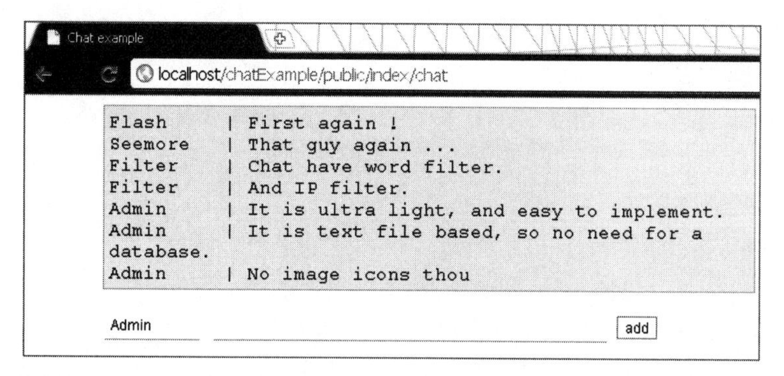

FIGURE 10-23: Chat window with various messages

Your `chatwriteAction()` allows you to set some additional options, such as IP address blocking or word filtering. The following snippet illustrates the code responsible for these options:

```
/* Set this to a minimum wait time between posts (in sec) */
$waittime_sec = 0;
/* spam keywords */
$spam[] = "ass";
$spam[] = "hell";
$spam[] = "poo";
/* IP's to block */
$blockip[] = "72.60.167.89";
/* spam, if message IS exactly that string */
$espam[] = "ajax";
```

Additionally, with a little understanding of PHP and experience in development, you can easily modify this example to use a database instead of the text file.

11

Making Plug-ins

Death seed blind man's greed
Poets' starving children bleed
Nothing he's got he really needs
Twenty first century schizoid man.

— King Crimson, In the Court of the Crimson King [1969]

WHAT'S IN THIS CHAPTER?

- Making PDF plug-ins for Symfony and CakePHP
- Introducing Zend Framework plug-in philosophy

Frameworks offer great enhancements in web development by themselves, but with plug-ins you can achieve even more! There are various ready-to-use plug-ins that greatly extend the core functionalities of the frameworks. In this chapter, we show you how to build a plug-in in all three frameworks. In Symfony and CakePHP, you will see how to create a plug-in that prepares PDF files. Plug-ins in Zend Framework are of a somewhat different nature and are dedicated to purposes different from plug-ins of other frameworks.

Plug-ins are great for two reasons. First, they help with separating code that provides certain additional functionalities from the framework's core. This way, the framework can remain lighter and achieve better performance, while the optional add-ons are installed on demand. And that's the second advantage of this approach: it is beneficial for core developers who are freed to focus on development of the framework, for the open-source community that can easily prepare and maintain plug-ins dedicated for certain solutions, for companies that may develop sophisticated commercial plug-ins, and finally for all users who can choose from the wide range of ready-to-use solutions.

SYMFONY

This section describes how to write a plug-in for generating PDF files. Actually, making PDF files can be done easily in Symfony by installing sfTCPDFPlugin using the following command:

```
$ symfony plugin:install sfTCPDFPlugin
```

However, if you have read this book up to this part, you should know how to install existing plug-ins, and using this one is not the objective of this section. We've shown this just to let you know that this ready-made plug-in exists, but in this section you will learn how to create your own plug-in for Symfony.

Plug-in Structure

Let's start with Symfony's plug-in structure. In general, it consists of folders and files as follows:

```
sfPlugin/
  config/
    sfPluginConfiguration.class.php
    routing.yml
    doctrine/
     schema.yml
  lib/
    sfPlugin.class.php
    helper/
    filter/
    form/
    model/
    task/
  modules/
    pluginModule/
      actions/
      config/
      templates/
  web/
```

You can see that there is a strong similarity between this file structure and Symfony's application file structure. You don't need to create every directory, only those that you will need when making this plug-in. The `/config` directory contains all configuration files, such as `routing.yml`, that can be used for adding a module for routing. Schema and plug-in dependencies go to this folder, too. The `/lib` folder holds tasks, helpers, forms, models, and the main plug-in class. Inside `/modules`, all ready-to-use modules are kept; inside `/web` are all images, stylesheets, and JavaScripts.

Developing the Plug-in

As you want to develop your own plug-in, you will avoid the TCPDF plug-in mentioned in the introduction to this section and use an alternative: the Free PDF PHP (FPDF) general-purpose library.

For simple PDF creation, you don't have to code much; all you need is one simple helper with one exemplary function that will generate a PDF with text. You must have the FPDF library installed before creating this helper. You can download it from `www.fpdf.org` and copy it into the PHP libraries. Under Linux, you can also install it as a package. This helper file could look like this:

```
<?php
require('fpdf/fpdf.php');
function generatePDF() {
  $pdf=new FPDF();
  $pdf->AddPage();
  $pdf->SetFont('Times','B',12);
  $pdf->Cell(40,10,'Symfony FPDF Plugin');
  $pdf->Output();
}
?>
```

code snippet /symfony/plugins/sfFPDFPlugin-1.0.0/lib/helper/sfFPDFHelper.php

Plug-in development requires a few basic facts about the plug-in. This information is stored in the `package.xml` file in the root folder of the plug-in. An example is presented here:

```
<?xml version="1.0" encoding="UTF-8"?>
  <package xmlns="http://pear.php.net/dtd/package-2.0"
    xmlns:tasks="http://pear.php.net/dtd/tasks-1.0"
    xmlns:xsi="http://www.w3.org/2001/XMLSchema-instance" packagerversion="1.8.0"
    version="2.0" xsi:schemaLocation="http://pear.php.net/dtd/tasks-1.0
    http://pear.php.net/dtd/tasks-1.0.xsd http://pear.php.net/dtd/package-2.0
    http://pear.php.net/dtd/package-2.0.xsd">
  <name>sfFPDFPlugin</name>
  <channel>pear.symfony-project.com</channel>
  <summary>Exemplary FPDF Plugin</summary>
  <description>Very short example</description>
  <lead>
    <name>Wrox</name>
    <user>Wrox</user>
    <email>foo_bar@wrox.com</email>
    <active>yes</active>
  </lead>
  <date>2011-02-27</date>
  <time>00:00:00</time>
  <version>
    <release>1.0.0</release>
    <api>1.0.0</api>
  </version>
  <stability>
    <release>stable</release>
    <api>stable</api>
  </stability>
  <license uri="http://www.symfony-project.com/license">MIT license</license>
  <notes>
    Exemplary notes
  </notes>
  <contents>
    <dir name="/">
      <file md5sum="2779dd4abdee0683069bc5ecb9721cde"
```

```
            name="lib/helper/sfFPDFHelper.php" role="data"/>
        </dir>
      </contents>
      <dependencies>
        <required>
          <php>
            <min>5.3.0</min>
          </php>
          <pearinstaller>
            <min>1.4.1</min>
          </pearinstaller>
        </required>
      </dependencies>
      <phprelease/>
    </package>
```

code snippet /symfony/plugins/sfFPDFPlugin-1.0.0/package.xml

Note that you can set the minimal version of PEAR and PHP as well as the plug-in's version and its stability. You need to supply the MD5 sum as well. This is a minimal security measure to counteract unauthorized file replacement and also helps with discovering corrupt file download.

The file structure of your plug-in should be as follows now:

```
sfFPDFPlugin-1.0.0\
    lib\
        helper\
            sfFPDFHelper.php
package.xml
```

Testing Your Plug-in

To test your plug-in, all you have to do is to pack it into an archive and install it:

```
$ symfony plugin:install /home/wrox/public_html/sfFPDFPlugin-1.0.0.tar.gz
```

Although the directory path may differ on your machine, the output will be the same:

```
>> plugin    installing plugin "/home/wrox/public_html/sfFPDFPlugin-1.0.0.tar.gz"
>> sfSymfonyPluginManager Installation successful for plugin
   "/home/wrox/public_html/sfFPDFPlugin-1.0.0.tar.gz"
```

Your helper can be now added into the configuration file of your applications. An example is presented here:

Available for download on Wrox.com

```
all:
  .settings:
    standard_helpers:       [Partial, Cache, sfFPDF]
```

code snippet /symfony/apps/frontend/config/settings.yml

And here is an example action that utilizes this helper:

Available for download on Wrox.com

```
    public function executeIndex(sfWebRequest $request)
    {
      $response = $this->getResponse();
      $response->setContentType('application/pdf');
   }
```

code snippet /symfony/apps/frontend/modules/pdfexample/actions/actions.class.php

The preceding code sets the output type as PDF. You need to execute the helper in a view as follows:

Available for download on Wrox.com

```
<?php echo generatePDF(); ?>
```

code snippet /symfony/apps/frontend/modules/pdfexample/templates/indexSuccess.php

When the routing is set to call this action, you should see a PDF file like the one in Figure 11-1.

FIGURE 11-1: Symfony PDF plug-in output

CAKEPHP

Plug-ins in CakePHP are basically mini-applications that can be deployed in different CakePHP projects and used therein. In this section, you will have the opportunity to learn how to prepare a plug-in that will be responsible for generating PDF reports. The content of this report will be a list of persons held in an addresses database table — the same one that was introduced in Chapter 4. To generate this report, the Free PDF PHP (FPDF) class is used.

To use FPDF in your application, you should download FPDF from the `http://fpdf.org/` website and place all its content into the `/app/vendors/fpdf/` directory. Later it will be called from the controller file of your plug-in.

Plug-in Structure

When a copy of `fpdf.php` is in your `/app/vendors/fpdf/` directory, you can proceed with the process of creating a CakePHP plug-in. Plug-ins in CakePHP are usually self-contained applications on their own, so the file structure for such a plug-in is nearly identical to those of a normal CakePHP application.

First you need to name your plug-in. For this example, `pdfreport` should be a good name. The basic plug-in file structure used for the `pdfreport` example plug-in looks as follows:

```
/pdfreport
    /app
    /plugins
    /pdfreport
    /controllers
    /models
    /views
    /pdfreport_app_controller.php
    /pdfreport_app_model.php
```

In the main plug-in folder, there are two important files: the `pdfreport_app_controller.php` file that is the plug-in's `AppController` and the `pdfreport_app_model.php` file that is the plug-in's `AppModel`. These files are named after plug-in's name.

Developing the Plug-in

To start building your plug-in, you need to create the file structure shown in the preceding section. The content of the `AppController` file of the plug-in in this example is a simple class extending the `AppControler` of your main application. The listing of this file is as follows:

Available for download on Wrox.com

```
<?php
  class PdfreportAppController extends AppController {
  }
?>
```

code snippet /cakephp/app/plugins/pdfreport/pdfreport_app_controller.php

The situation is similar with the `AppModel` of the plug-in. The code for this example is as follows:

Available for download on Wrox.com

```
<?php
  class PdfreportAppModel extends AppModel {
  }
?>
```

code snippet /cakephp/app/plugins/pdfreport/models/pdfreport_app_model.php

Now you have the basis of your plug-in, and it is time to create a controller that will handle all the capabilities of your plug-in. Since you want to generate PDF reports from your application, you need to create `GeneratePdfController` inside the `/controllers` folder of your plug-in. In this example, the controller file will prepare a user list that is stored in the `addresses` database table. To do this, you need to use the `$uses` variable to point out that this controller uses the `Address` model to read all the data. The controller file used in this example goes as follows:

Available for download on Wrox.com

```
<?php
class GeneratePdfController extends PdfreportAppController {
```

```
        var $name = 'GeneratePdf';
        var $uses = array('Address');
        function index() {
            $this->layout = 'pdf';
            $this->set('address_list', $this->Address->find('all'));
        }
    }
    ?>
```

code snippet /cakephp/app/plugins/pdfreport/controllers/pdfreport_app_controller.php

This controller file has an `index()` action that does two things: specify the layout file that was used to render the view file and read all data from the `Address` model and pass it to the view file as the `address_list` variable.

The layout file `pdf.ctp`, specified in the index action, needs to be created inside the `/views/layouts` folder. It will be used to render the `index.ctp` view file as PDF content instead of HTML content. The content of the layout file should be as follows:

Available for download on Wrox.com

```
<?php
  header("Content-type: application/pdf");
  echo $content_for_layout;
?>
```

code snippet /cakephp/app/plugins/pdfreport/views/layouts/pdf.ctp

You should create the model file and set the `$useTable` variable to `false` because this model does not use any database tables. Code for this file can go like this:

Available for download on Wrox.com

```
<?php
class GeneratePdf extends PdfreportAppModel {
    var $name = 'GeneratePdf';
    var $useTable = false;
}
?>
```

code snippet /cakephp/app/plugins/pdfreport/models/generate_pdf.php

Finally, the view file, `index.ctp`, needs to be created in the `/app/plugins/pdfreport/views/generate_pdf` folder. Here you will place all the PDF building commands, but first you need to import the FPDF library by using the `App::import()` command. The code used to illustrate how the PDF file is generated is listed next:

Available for download on Wrox.com

```
<?php
  App::import('Vendor', 'fpdf/fpdf');
  $pdf = new FPDF();
  $pdf->AddPage();
  $pdf->SetFont('Times', '', 16);
  $pdf->Write(5, 'Persons list');
  $pdf->Ln();
  $pdf->SetFontSize(10);
```

```
    $pdf->Write(5, 'Report of users held in database.');
    $pdf->Ln();
    $pdf->Ln(5);
    $pdf->SetFont('Arial', 'i', 10);
    $pdf->Cell(10 ,7, 'Nr.', 1);
    $pdf->Cell(20 ,7, 'Name', 1);
    $pdf->Cell(50 ,7, 'Email', 1);
    $pdf->Cell(20 ,7, 'Phone', 1);
    $pdf->Ln();
    $pdf->SetFont('Helvetica', '', 10);
    foreach ( $address_list as $line ) {
    $address = $line['Address'];
        $pdf->Cell(10 ,7, $address['id'], 1);
        $pdf->Cell(20, 7, $address['first_name'].' '.$address['last_name'], 1);
        $pdf->Cell(50, 7, $address['email'], 1);
        $pdf->Cell(20, 7, $address['phone'], 1);
        $pdf->Ln();
    }
    $pdf->Output();
?>
```

code snippet /cakephp/app/views/addresses/index.ctp

If you wish to learn more on how PDF files are created, please visit `http://fpdf.org/` because this example introduces only basic functions.

Testing Your Plug-in

This concludes writing your CakePHP plug-in, and now you probably wonder how you can use it. Well, this is quite simple. Because this plug-in was designed to generate PDFs containing a user list, it would be nice to add this option to an application that has a user list already. For this example, the application from Chapter 4 will be used, but you need to add one code line at the end of the `index.ctp` file that is responsible for displaying the address list. It will create the Get pdf report link illustrated in Figure 11-2. The report is presented in Figure 11-3. The code line that needs to be added is as follows:

```
<?php echo $html->link('Get pdf report', array('plugin' => 'pdfreport',
    'controller' => 'GeneratePdf', 'action' => 'index')); ?>
```

code snippet /app/views/addresses/index.ctp

localhost/cake/addresses

Add new address

Id	First name	Last name	Email	Phone	Address	Options
1	Johan	Doe	john.doe@mail.com	555		edit delete
2	Jake	Brown	jake.brown@hotmail.com	555		edit delete

Get pdf report

FIGURE 11-2: Address list in your application

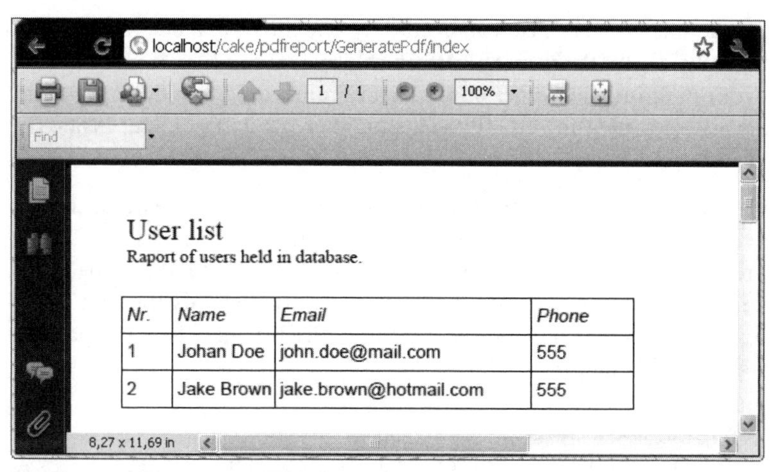

FIGURE 11-3: The user list PDF report

ZEND FRAMEWORK

In the Symfony and CakePHP sections of this chapter, you learned how to create plug-ins that allow you to generate PDF files on the fly. In this section, no such plug-in will be created. This is because of the specificity of plug-ins in Zend Framework, which is discussed in this section.

As for generating PDF files, Zend Framework is supplied with the `Zend_Pdf` component that allows you to do that. The `Zend_Pdf` component offers a number of features that allow you to load, create, modify, and save PDF documents. If you wish to learn more about generating PDF files in Zend Framework, please refer to the `Zend_Pdf` component documentation at: `http://framework.zend.com/manual/en/zend.pdf.html` or consider using the Free PDF PHP library introduced in the Symfony and CakePHP sections of this chapter.

If you think of plug-ins in general, you imagine something that you connect to an application, and that you can use as a part of a bigger whole. As a hardware example, consider a USB web camera or a game controller that you can connect to any computer, and is ready to use after the installation process. The concept is similar with plug-ins for Symfony or CakePHP, in which a plug-in can have nearly unlimited functionality and can be used in any application.

In Zend Framework, plug-ins are completely different and are designed to be used in a different manner than in Symfony or CakePHP. In Zend Framework, a plug-in is a class that contains a number of preset methods that are called every time an application page is loaded. Because of this, when you wish to create a Zend Framework plug-in, you need to keep in mind that its code will be executed every time the page is loaded. This limits your plug-ins to a small set of specific tasks that can be performed this way. It differentiates Zend Framework plug-ins from typical plug-ins, where you create a controller class that can give you access to additional helpers.

So what are Zend Framework plug-ins used for? A Zend Framework plug-in is a set of listeners that is called when certain events occur in the front controller. These events correspond to the routing and dispatch actions. So typically, Zend Framework plug-ins can be applied to application initialization, caching, routing modification, user authentication, and so on.

Creating your own plug-in is a simple task because you need only one file to make it work. You may have noticed that in Symfony and CakePHP, there is a certain folder named `plug-ins` that gives you a general idea of where your plug-ins should be. But in Zend Framework, you don't have such a folder. So where should you place your plug-in? Usually you should create a `/My` folder inside the `/Library` folder of your application.

Now let's create an example plug-in called `Pluginexample.php`, which you'll create in the `/appName/library/My/Controller` directory. Note that the path name influences how the class is named inside `Pluginexample.php`, and for `appName/library/My/Controller` the plug-in class name will be `My_Controller_Pluginexample`. The following code is a listing of a basic plug-in with a set of functions. These functions will be executed one by one when any page is loaded in the application that uses this plug-in:

```
<?php
class My_Controller_Pluginexample extends Zend_Controller_Plugin_Abstract {
  public function routeStartup(Zend_Controller_Request_Abstract $request){
    echo '<p>1. Router startup executed.</p>';
  }
  public function routeShutdown(Zend_Controller_Request_Abstract $request){
    echo '<p>2. Router shutdown executed.</p>';
  }
  public function dispatchLoopStartup(Zend_Controller_Request_Abstract $request){
    echo '<p>3. Dispatch loop startup.</p>';
  }
  public function preDispatch(Zend_Controller_Request_Abstract $request){
    echo '<p>4. Pre dispatch executed.</p>';
  }
  public function postDispatch(Zend_Controller_Request_Abstract $request){
    echo '<p>5. Post dispatch executed.</p>';
  }
  public function dispatchLoopShutdown(){
    echo '<p>6. Dispatch loop shutdown.</p>';
  }
}
?>
```

code snippet /zf/library/My/Controller/Pluginexample.php

In this file, you can place the desired functions for your application instead of the example functions we used; for example, for processing session variables or influencing routing.

To use this plug-in, you need to make sure that your application's `Bootstrap.php` contains the following line. This will register name space for your plug-in folder; in this case, its name is `/My`.

```
$autoloader->registerNamespace('My_');
```

code snippet /zf/application/Bootstrap.php

Finally, to enable a specific plug-in, you need to add the following line inside the `application.ini` file:

Available for download on Wrox.com

```
resources.frontController.plugins.param = "My_Controller_Pluginexample"
```

code snippet /zf/application/configs/application.ini

Now when you run your application, all messages contained in `My_Controller_Pluginexample` will be displayed before any content of your application is rendered. These messages will look as follows:

```
1. Router startup executed.
2. Router shutdown executed.
3. Dispatch loop startup.
4. Pre dispatch executed.
5. Post dispatch executed.
6. Dispatch loop shutdown.
```

12

Web Services

Always be wary of any helpful item that weighs less than its operating manual.

— Terry Pratchett

WHAT'S IN THIS CHAPTER?

- Creating basic CRUD-like web services with REST
- Using SOAP for enterprise web services
- Testing SOAP web services with soapUI

Web services are commonly considered by beginner programmers as something terribly hard to learn. This is only half true, as web services are advanced technologies indeed and they are mostly on the bleeding edge of development. There are also many different standards that are compliant with different web services. So they are quite hard to learn, but still it is not rocket science and if you made it through all previous chapters of this book, you can cope with web services as well.

There are good reasons for using web services. First of all, they are incredibly trendy now, especially REST with its small learning curve, allowing for rapid web development. The popularity of SOAP is declining somewhat, but it is still a successful heavyweight enterprise solution used by many companies. With the exchange of data constantly increasing between applications over networks, you can expect that the importance of web services will continue to increase.

The second reason is much more practical. Assume that you have another application. Not a web app itself, but you need to integrate it with a web app you are developing now. Using web services is the best way to deliver such a rich, elegant interface that would allow these applications to communicate with each other.

RESTFUL NEWS READING

REST stands for Representational State Transfer and any application conforming to this standard is called *RESTful*. It is a kind of stateless web software architecture that is based on HTTP requests such as the commonly known `GET`.

REST is probably the best choice to start for developers who don't have experience with web services. In this section, we will show how to develop a simple RESTful application using HTTP methods. Frameworks add-ons and features allow you to develop it easily and fast.

How Does REST Work?

REST is very simple and based on HTTP request methods: `GET`, `POST`, `DELETE`, and `PUT`. You probably remember the first two methods from developing previous example applications. The last two methods are not so popular in common application development, but `PUT` and `DELETE` can be used in the same way as `POST` and `GET`. `GET` is used every time you use an Internet browser in the usual way to gather web content. `POST` is commonly used when some data needs to be sent to an application. It's used in almost all web forms. REST is based on all four methods to implement a create, read, update, and delete (CRUD) application without filling any forms, but just by simple method-invoking. Comparing REST to CRUD operations, `GET` would be *read*, `POST` would be *create*, `DELETE` would be *delete*, and `PUT` would be *update*.

What is cURL?

cURL is tool that allows for data between miscellaneous protocols, for example http, https, ftp, telnet, or ldap. You can grab it at `http://curl.haxx.se/`. LibcURL is a library used also by PHP. It's installed with XAMPP under Windows and should also be available out of the box when installing PHP under UNIX systems. What you need to do is to make sure that cURL is enabled in `php.ini`. In Windows, there should be an entry like the following:

```
extension=php_curl.dll
```

Under Linux, you should look for something like this:

```
extension=curl.so
```

If there is no semicolon at the beginning of this line, this library should be enabled. Now you can use cURL libraries in your PHP scripts.

In this chapter, some examples will be shown using the command line `curl`. You can download Windows binaries from `http://curl.haxx.se/` or if you use a UNIX system such as Ubuntu Linux, you can install it using a native package manager. In Ubuntu, the command that installs cURL is as follows:

```
# apt-get install curl
```

This chapter discusses enterprise solutions, and Red Hat Enterprise Linux (RHEL) and its derivatives are common production environments. To install cURL on RHEL, Fedora, and other RPM-based distributions, use the following command:

```
# rpm -I curl-7.15.5-*.rpm
```

Note that if you use Windows, you need to copy all files you have downloaded with the binaries and unpack them to `C:\xampp\php\`. You will invoke `curl.exe` directly from `C:\xampp\php\`. This is important because as described in Chapter 2, you need to add the `C:\xampp\php\` directory to the `PATH` environment variable. This makes accessing it through the command line possible and not dependent on the directory where you currently invoke `curl`.

Let's try to use it and access `google.com` with the HTTP `GET` method:

```
$ curl -I http://google.com/
```

The `I` parameter returns only the header of the response. The command executed previously should give you a response that's similar to the following one:

```
HTTP/1.1 301 Moved Permanently
Location: http://www.google.com/
Content-Type: text/html; charset=UTF-8
Date: Sun, 12 Sep 2010 16:26:21 GMT
Expires: Tue, 12 Oct 2010 16:26:21 GMT
Cache-Control: public, max-age=2592000
Server: gws
Content-Length: 219
X-XSS-Protection: 1; mode=block
```

As can be seen, the response gives you the information that `http://google.com/` is in fact a redirection to `www.google.com`. So, let's try this one:

```
$ curl -I http://www.google.com/
```

And now you can observe the expected response result, which should be similar to the following:

```
HTTP/1.1 200 OK
Date: Sun, 12 Sep 2010 16:26:17 GMT
Expires: -1
Cache-Control: private, max-age=0
Content-Type: text/html; charset=ISO-8859-1
Set-Cookie:
PREF=ID=36b253584c333970:TM=1284308777:LM=1284308777:
S=SD1VOPq6YCXFl8vN;expires=Tue, 11-Sep-2012 16:26:17 GMT;
path=/; domain=.google.com
Set-Cookie: NID=38=QeuwPnG5FULmdUstQvm-RCG52Q1x2TBAmynr0G5
GREXEKCmpqMCUuxVU5xxCFhqhkSXoqsVeHLMOWMr367Rn1w4bRyupJ
_Yo5tzICyhUQQ0kXrjtp2SPjZVHTN1bDHO;
expires=Mon, 14-Mar-2011 16:26:17 GMT; path=/;
domain=.google.com; HttpOnly
Server: gws
X-XSS-Protection: 1; mode=block
Transfer-Encoding: chunked
```

If you use the `--help` parameter, you will see a lot of available options. cURL is a powerful tool with many possibilities. In this section, it will be used to get information about web application responses. We use it later in this chapter to simulate the client-side application.

Symfony

Symfony provides multiple plug-ins for most imaginable tasks. Symfony also delivers a few plug-ins that implement the REST architecture. The two most commonly used plug-ins are the following:

- **sfRestWebServicePlugin** — Offers an easy interface for REST API based on your domain model: `http://www.symfony-project.org/plugins/sfRestWebServicePlugin`
- **sfDoctrineRestGeneratorPlugin** — An additional Doctrine's task for generating RESTful modules based on defined models: `http://www.symfony-project.org/plugins/sfDoctrineRestGeneratorPlugin`

sfRestWebServicePlugin is used in this section of the chapter. The following example is about reading news through REST, so you should use a simple example model to see how it works. Let's create a simple model in `schema.yml`:

```
news:
  columns:
    title: string(50)
    description: string(50)
    content: string(255)
```

code snippet /rest/symfony/config/doctrine/schema.yml

Then you need to build the model, forms, and all the things related to the model:

```
$ symfony doctrine:build --all
```

The following code installs the sfRestWebServicePlugin plug-in:

```
$ symfony plugin:install sfRestWebServicePlugin
```

sfRestWebService has a few nice features. One of them implements a security enhancement that makes your REST services available only from fixed hosts. You can configure this enhancement directly in the plug-in configuration file `config.yml`, which is placed in the `/plugins/sfRestWebServicePlugin/config` directory. You can also add REST services you want to enable and define a model, which should be assigned to particular services. For the news model, `config.yml` could be like the following:

```
all:
  protected: true
  allowed: [127.0.0.1]
  protectedRoute: secure
  services:
    news:
      model:  news
      methodForQuery: ~
      states:
```

code snippet /rest/symfony/plugins/sfRestWebServicePlugin/config/config.yml

Additionally, you can define which states should be enabled for the current service. By default, all four states are enabled. There is also a second configuration file: `routing.yml`, shown below, in which all available routing possibilities are presented. You can also set the default response format, which is by default set to XML.

```
ws_entry:
  url: /api/:service.:sf_format
  class: sfRequestRoute
  param: { module: sfRestWebService, action: entry, sf_format: xml }
  requirements:
    id: \d+
    sf_method: [GET, POST]
ws_resource:
  url:  /api/:service/:id.:sf_format
  class: sfRequestRoute
  param: { module: sfRestWebService, action: resource, sf_format: xml }
  requirements:
    id: \d+
    sf_method: [GET, PUT, DELETE]
ws_search:
  url: /api/:service/search/:column/:value.:sf_format
  class: sfRequestRoute
  param: { module: sfRestWebService, action: search, sf_format: xml }
  requirements:
    id: \d+
    sf_method: [GET]
ws_500:
  url:  /api/error
  param: { module: sfRestWebService, action: 500 }
```

code snippet /rest/symfony/plugins/sfRestWebServicePlugin/config/routing.yml

As shown here, the search action is possible for each concrete column, which in this example would be *title* or *description*. If you type `/search/title/HotNews`, the REST module will return all news items where the title contains *HotNews*.

Getting a List of News

You don't need to configure anything else. Typing the following in the command line:

```
$ curl -X GET http://localhost/api/news/
```

you should see XML output like this:

```
<?xml version="1.0" encoding="utf-8"?>
<objects>
  <object id="1">
    <id>1</id>
    <title>Hot news</title>
    <description>Symfony REST services works!</description>
  </object>
</objects>
```

This is what is expected from a REST module. Note that you had to previously add some data to the database to get these responses.

Adding a News Item

To add a news item, you need to execute a command that will send an HTTP POST request with additional POST data:

```
$ curl -X POST -d "title=Second&description=News" http://localhost/api/news
```

Adding news doesn't require providing any additional GET parameters. You should get a proper message in XML format as the response.

Updating News

Updating an entry requires that you give the ID of the entry to be changed. PHP does not handle HTTP PUT requests well. In Symfony, this problem is solved by sending an HTTP POST request with the sf_method parameter set to PUT. The cURL command should look like this (the line has been broken to fit the page margins, but you should write this as a single line):

```
$ curl -X POST -F sf_method=PUT -F title=First -F
       description=News http://localhost/api/news/1
```

Note that you need to give the ID parameter of the news in the URL. As a result, you should get an XML response showing the changed row:

```
<?xml version="1.0" encoding="utf-8"?>
<object id="1">
      <id>1</id>
      <title>First</title>
      <description>News</description>
  </object>
```

Deleting News

Deleting entries couldn't be easier. Just invoke an HTTP DELETE request with the news ID as the parameter:

```
$ curl -X DELETE http://localhost/rest/index.php/api/news/1
```

The response should be shown as an info message like this one:

```
<?xml version="1.0" encoding="utf-8"?>
<object>
  Object has been deleted
</object>
```

CakePHP

CakePHP also supports REST. This example uses the same model as was used for Symfony in the previous section on the logical level only because the code will differ. CakePHP not only supports HTML as the output, but it can also easily give you an XML file. For example, if you request http://localhost/index.xml, this request is automatically properly interpreted by CakePHP as a request for an XML file instead of the default HTML. This can be done by invoking the parseExtensions() method, which is a part of the Router class.

To make it possible to access CakePHP modules through REST requests, you may also invoke a resource mapper method that maps REST methods (GET, POST, PUT, DELETE) to CakePHP's controller CRUD equivalents `index()`, `add()`, `edit()`, and `delete()`. Both sets of methods should be added in the `app/config/routes.php` configuration file:

```
Router::mapResources('news');
Router::parseExtensions();
```

Now you can proceed with the implementation of a controller that will handle all news requests.

Getting a List of News

Let's assume that a news controller is placed in `/controllers/news_controller.php` as shown in the following code for `index()` and `view()` actions:

```
<?php
class NewsController extends AppController {
    var $components = array('RequestHandler');
    function index() {
        $recipes = $this->News->find("all");
        $this->set(compact("news"));
    }
    function view($id) {
        $recipe = $this->News->findById($id);
        $this->set(compact("news"));
    }
}
```

code snippet /rest/cakephp/app/controllers/news_controller.php

It's very similar to the default controller, but note that PHP's `compact()` function is used to prepare an array that will be used further to display the requested XML file. This array is next serialized to be shown as an XML. Both templates, `view.ctp` and `index.ctp`, look the same:

```
<newss>
<?php echo $xml->serialize($news); ?>
</newss>
```

code snippet /rest/cakephp/app/views/news/index.ctp

Both files are placed in the `/app/views/news/xml` directory because we want to request an XML file, such as `http://localhost/news/index.xml`. CakePHP recognizes automatically that an XML file is requested and renders proper template files. When you want to get the information about just one concrete news item, you should go to `http://localhost/news/1.xml`. This could not be simpler. To get news entries you can use also cURL:

```
$ curl -I -X GET http://localhost/news/index.xml
```

The resulting response depends on what entries were added before invoking the preceding command, but it should be similar to the following:

```
<?xml version="1.0" encoding="UTF-8" ?>
<newss>
    <news id="1" title="Foo" description="Bar" />
    <news id="2" title="Hot" description="News" />
</newss>
```

Note that even when you request an XML file, templates are wrapped by a layout template. In this case, an XML layout template is placed in the project's `/cake/libs/view/layouts/xml/default.ctp` directory. That's why an array that is serialized to XML is wrapped with an XML header.

Creating New Entries

Creating new entries is done in the same way as it was in the Symfony example earlier in this chapter, through sending `POST` data. Unlike index or view actions, adding new entries cannot be done by a request to an XML file. That's why `POST` requests are sent to `http://localhost/news/add`. The problem is that CakePHP will not recognize this as an XML file request. This is not a proper behavior, but we could live with that. If we wanted to be more professional, then it would be nice to send the response as JSON or XML, because this is what the requester expects. The solution is to create a template just like the previous ones, but to keep it in the `/app/views/news` directory. To add an XML header, you need to set a proper layout path. The rest of the `add()` action is built like an action that handles the form submissions:

```
function add() {
    $this->layoutPath='xml';
    if ($this->News->save($this->data)) {
            $message = "Saved successfully";
        } else {
        $message = "Error while saving item";
        }
    $this->set('message',$message);
    $this->render('message');
}
```

code snippet /rest/cakephp/app/controllers/news_controller.php

Additional actions should also provide XML message answers. That's why you should create only one template and render it within an action. For example, a message template could look like this:

```
<message><?php echo $message; ?><message>
```

This template should be saved as `/app/views/news/message.ctp`.

To invoke an add action, you need to send data as it's done by the CakePHPs forms. Therefore, the cURL command should be as follows (again, you should write this as a single line):

```
$ curl -X POST -F data[News][title]=REST -F data[News][description]=Works!
    http://localhost/news/add
```

Updating News

Editing entries should be done almost in the same way as creating new items:

```
function edit($id) {
    $this->layoutPath='xml';
    $this->News->id = $id;
    if ($this->News->save($this->data)) {
        $message = "News updated successfully";
```

```
        } else {
            $message = "Error while updating item";
        }
        $this->set('message',$message);
        $this->render('message');
    }
```

code snippet /rest/cakephp/app/controllers/news_controller.php

One line needs to be added to let CakePHP know which news need to be updated. Unlike adding entries, in updating you need to set the news ID number in the URL:

```
$ curl -X POST -F data[News][title]=Brand -F data[News][description]=New
       http://localhost/cake/index.php/news/edit/1
```

Deleting News

Deleting news can be done very easily by using the news ID as a parameter to the model's `delete()` method:

```
function delete($id) {
    if($this->News->delete($id)) {
        $message = "News deleted successfully";
    } else {
        $message = "Error while deleting item";
    }
    $this->set('message',$message);
    $this->render('message');
}
```

code snippet /rest/cakephp/app/controllers/news_controller.php

To check out how it works, use HTTP `DELETE`:

```
$ curl -X DELETE http://localhost/cake/index.php/news/1
```

Zend Framework

Zend Framework offers quite a few possibilities to implement REST, but the easiest way is to inherit a controller from `Zend_Rest_Controller`. But before you start adding REST functionalities, you need to add some routing rules that intercept REST-specific requests and invoke proper actions. You should add the `_initRestRoute()` method within the application's bootstrap `/application/Bootstrap.php` file:

```
<?php
class Bootstrap extends Zend_Application_Bootstrap_Bootstrap {
    protected function _initRestRoute() {
        $this->bootstrap('frontController');
        $frontController = Zend_Controller_Front::getInstance();
        $restRoute = new Zend_Rest_Route($frontController);
```

```
            $frontController->getRouter()->addRoute('default', $restRoute);
        }
    }
```

code snippet /rest/zf/application/Bootstrap.php

This allows you to invoke HTTP requests without sending the action's name. So instead of `http://localhost/news/put`, you can invoke `http://localhost/news/`. Because the HTTP method is known, Zend will recognize it and invoke the proper action that is dedicated for each HTTP request; for example, the `putAction()` method will be invoked when `PUT` HTTP is requested. Now, you are ready to create the controller. As mentioned before, you should inherit from `Zend_Rest_Controller`:

Available for download on Wrox.com

```
<?php
class NewsController extends Zend_Rest_Controller {
}
```

code snippet /rest/zf/application/controllers/NewsController.php

Save the controller as `NewsController.php` in the application's controller directory. When you try now to execute any action on this controller, you get an error message because you haven't added inherited methods `indexAction()`, `getAction()`, `postAction()`, `deleteAction()`, and `putAction()`. You need to add them before proceeding to the next steps:

Available for download on Wrox.com

```
public function init() {
     $this->_helper->viewRenderer->setNoRender(true);
}
```

code snippet /rest/zf/application/controllers/NewsController.php

If you want to respond with an XML file, you should also set the `NoRender` variable to `true`. If you do that, Zend will not include layouts while executing an action. For this example, we need to create a News model, `News.php`, which should be placed in the application's `/model` directory, as shown here.

Available for download on Wrox.com

```
<?php
class Application_Model_News {
       protected $_title;
       protected $_description;
       protected $_id;
       public function __construct(array $options = null) {
       }
       public function __set($name, $value) {
            $method = 'set' . $name;
            if (('mapper' == $name) || !method_exists($this, $method)) {
                throw new Exception('Invalid property');
            }
            $this->$method($value);
       }
       public function __get($name) {
           $method = 'get' . $name;
```

```
            if (('mapper' == $name) || !method_exists($this, $method)) {
                throw new Exception('Invalid property');
            }
            return $this->$method();
        }
        public function setOptions(array $options) {
            $methods = get_class_methods($this);
            foreach ($options as $key => $value) {
                $method = 'set' . ucfirst($key);
                if (in_array($method, $methods)) {
                    $this->$method($value);
                }
            }
            return $this;
        }
        public function setTitle($text) {
           $this->_title = (string) $text;
           return $this;
        }
        public function getTitle() {
           return $this->_title;
        }
        public function setDescription($text) {
           $this->_description = (string) $text;
           return $this;
        }
        public function getDescription() {
           return $this->_description;
        }
        public function  getId() {
           return $this->_id;
        }
        public function setId($text) {
           $this->_id = (int) $text;
           return $this;
        }
}
```

code snippet /rest/zf/application/models/News.php

Additionally, as shown in the following code, you need to create a News model mapper and save it as `NewsMapper.php` at the same path.

Available for download on Wrox.com

```
<?php
class Application_Model_NewsMapper {
    protected $_dbTable;
    public function setDbTable($dbTable) {
        if (is_string($dbTable)) {
            $dbTable = new $dbTable();
        }
        if (!$dbTable instanceof Zend_Db_Table_Abstract) {
            throw new Exception('Invalid table data gateway provided');
        }
        $this->_dbTable = $dbTable;
```

```
            return $this;
        }
        public function getDbTable() {
            if (null === $this->_dbTable) {
                $this->setDbTable('Application_Model_DbTable_News');
            }
            return $this->_dbTable;
        }
        public function deleteOne($id) {
             $this->getDbTable()->delete('id = '. (int)$id);
        }
        public function save(Application_Model_News $news) {
                $data = array(
                    'title' => $news->getTitle(),
                    'description' => $news->getDescription()
                );
                if (null === ($id = $news->getId())) {
                    unset($data['id']);
                    $id = $this->getDbTable()->insert($data);
                } else {
                    $this->getDbTable()->update($data, array('id = ?' => $id));
                }
                return $id;
        }
        public function find($id, Application_Model_News $news) {
                $result = $this->getDbTable()->find($id);
                if (0 == count($result)) {
                  return;
                }
                $row = $result->current();
                $news->setId($row->id)
                       ->setTitle($row->title)
                       ->setDescription($row->description);
        }
        public function fetchAll() {
                $results = $this->getDbTable()->fetchAll();
                $entries = array();
                foreach ($results as $row) {
                  $entry = new Application_Model_News();
                  $entry->setId($row->id)
                    ->setTitle($row->title)
                    ->setDescription($row->description);
                 $entries[] = $entry;
              }
              return $entries;
        }
    }
```

code snippet /rest/zf/application/models/NewsMapper.php

To finish, the DbTable model needs to be created in the `/models/DbTable` directory:

Available for download on Wrox.com

```
<?php
class Application_Model_DbTable_News extends Zend_Db_Table_Abstract {
  protected $_name = 'News';
}
```

code snippet /rest/zf/application/models/DbTableNews.php

Getting a List of News

To get a list of news, you need to fetch it, as was done with the address list in Chapter 4, and generate an XML response.

Available for download on Wrox.com

```
public function indexAction(){
    $news = new Application_Model_NewsMapper();
    $result = $news->fetchAll();
    $xml = "<newss>";
    foreach($result as $news){
           $xml = $xml. "<news>";
           $xml = $xml. "  <id>".$news->getId()."</id>";
           $xml = $xml. "  <title>".$news->getTitle()."</title>";
           $xml = $xml. "  <description>".$news->getDescription()."</description>";
           $xml = $xml. "</news>";
    }
    $xml = $xml."</newss>";
    $this->getResponse()
           ->setHttpResponseCode(200)
           ->setHeader('Content-Type', 'text/xml')
           ->appendBody('<?xml version="1.0" encoding="utf-8"?>')
           ->appendBody($xml);
}
public function getAction(){
    $this->getResponse()
          ->setHttpResponseCode(404)
          ->setHeader('Content-Type', 'text/xml')
          ->appendBody("<message>Try index action</message>");
}
```

code snippet /rest/zf/application/controllers/NewsController.php

Note that `getAction()` is needed, but in our case, we can just redirect from it to `indexAction()` because both do the same thing. You don't need to create any template file because all response data is sent directly using the `getResponse()` method within the action. To check how the previous code works, execute the following command:

```
$ curl http://localhost/news
```

Create News

Adding news is as simple as getting a list. What you need to do is just get `POST` parameters and create an instance of `Application_Model_News` and save it. Finally, you also need to return an XML file, which should contain information on the currently added item. It should especially contain the ID number:

```
public function postAction(){
        $description = $this->_request->getPost('description');
        $title = $this->getRequest()->getPost('title');
        $entry = new Application_Model_News();
        $entry->setTitle($title);
        $entry->setDescription($description);
        $mapper  = new Application_Model_NewsMapper();
        $id  = $mapper->save($entry);
        $xml = "<newss>";
        $xml = $xml. "<news>";
        $xml = $xml. "  <id>".$id."</id>";
        $xml = $xml. "  <title>".$entry->getTitle()."</title>";
        $xml = $xml. "  <description>".$entry->getDescription()."</description>";
        $xml = $xml. "</news>";
        $xml = $xml."</newss>";        $this->getResponse()
               ->setHttpResponseCode(201)
               ->setHeader('Content-Type', 'text/xml')
               ->appendBody($xml);
}
```

code snippet /rest/zf/application/controllers/NewsController.php

You can test the success of this with the following command:

```
$ curl -X POST -d "description=Brand&title=New" http://localhost/index.php/news
```

Updating News

While developing REST methods in Zend, the method for updating news is the most annoying task because of some workarounds that you need to do. Normally when adding a new item, you need to send data through `POST`, but in this case a better way would be sending it by `GET` and marking the HTTP method as `PUT`:

```
public function putAction(){
        $params = $this->_getAllParams();
        $entry = new Application_Model_News();
        $entry->setTitle($params['title'];);
        $entry->setDescription($params['description'];);
        $entry->setId($params['id'];);
        $mapper  = new Application_Model_NewsMapper();
        $id  = $mapper->save($entry);
        $xml = "<newss>";
        $xml = $xml. "<news>";
        $xml = $xml. "  <id>".$entry->getId()."</id>";
        $xml = $xml. "  <title>".$entry->getTitle()."</title>";
        $xml = $xml. "  <description>".$entry->getDescription()."</description>";
        $xml = $xml. "</news>";
        $xml = $xml. "</newss>";
        $this->getResponse()
```

```
                  ->setHttpResponseCode(503)
                  ->appendBody($xml);
}
```

code snippet /rest/zf/application/controllers/NewsController.php

To get all sent parameters to your application, you can use the `_getAllParams()` method. The rest of the code is as in the previous add method. To test it, you should execute the cURL command like this:

```
$ curl -X PUT -G -d "description=Hot&title=News" http://localhost/index.php/news/1
```

Deleting News

To delete items, you need to get `GET` parameters with the `getParam()` method. The rest is done as in the usual CRUD `Delete` action:

Available for download on Wrox.com

```
public function deleteAction(){
     $id = $this->getRequest()->getParam('id');
     $news = new Application_Model_NewsMapper();
     $news->deleteOne($id);

    $this->getResponse()
            ->setHttpResponseCode(204)
            ->appendBody("<message>News deleted</message>");
}
```

code snippet /rest/zf/application/controllers/NewsController.php

Maybe you have noticed that in all the previous Zend examples, different response codes are used. This is the power and versatility that ZF gives to you. The following is a list of the response code meanings:

- `200 OK`
- `201 Created`
- `204 No Content`
- `404 Not Found`
- `503 Service Unavailable`

PROVIDING SOAP WEB SERVICES IN E-COMMERCE APPLICATIONS

Simple Object Access Protocol (SOAP) is a web service protocol. To work, it needs a Web Services Description Language (WSDL) method definition file. WSDL contains methods, parameters, and all other information needed to send web service requests. In fact, SOAP can be compared to invoking a server application's methods remotely.

Despite of the recent boom of REST, SOAP is still very popular and it is used in many advanced and complicated applications. It is a powerful solution and it is used mainly in enterprise solutions. In this section, you add functionality to your application that is very similar to what you added in the previous sections in this chapter, but you use SOAP.

Installing the SOAP Extension for PHP

In some cases, you will need to add the PHP SOAP extension. XAMPP delivers this extension out of the box, so you can skip this section if you are using XAMPP. In some UNIX systems, like most Linux distributions, this extension is not installed by default, but you can easily install it yourself. For example, in Ubuntu Linux you need to use a package manager to install the `php-soap` package:

```
# apt-get install php-soap
```

In both UNIX and Windows systems, you need to enable the SOAP extension if it's disabled in `php.ini` by uncommenting the proper entry:

```
extension=php_soap.dll
```

Testing with soapUI

To test SOAP functionalities, soapUI is a good choice. You can download this tool from `www.soapui.org` (you can see its logo in Figure 12-1). It's free and available for every operating system (OS) that supports the described frameworks. Download your soapUI installer and go through the Installation Wizard steps. You should be able to run it by clicking the created icons (for example, in the Start menu in Windows) or by executing the soapUI application through the command line, as in Linux systems:

```
$ soapUI-3.6
```

FIGURE 12-1: soapUI logo

What is the Difference Between SOAP and REST?

SOAP is bigger and more advanced than REST. You can do the same things, or find a workaround to implement the same tasks with REST, but in some situations SOAP is just a better solution, especially when you have to deal with communicating with enterprise applications. On the other hand, there is a common opinion that SOAP is just too big, and REST would be a better solution when you are not communicating with enterprise applications.

As shown in Figure 12-2, REST is just a request/response scheme. A client application submits an HTTP request and expects an XML response back.

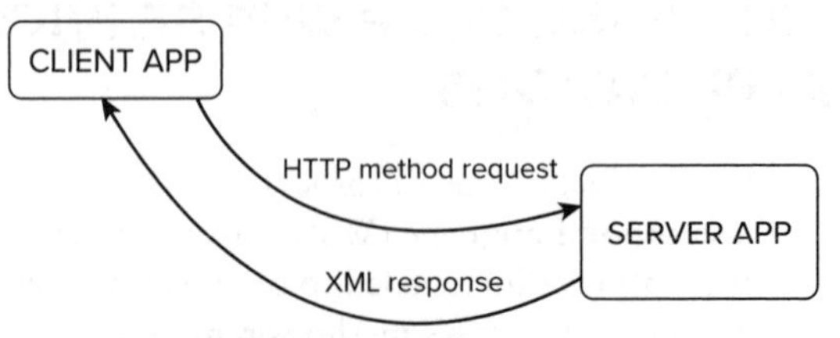

FIGURE 12-2: REST approach

As you can see in Figure 12-3, SOAP is more complicated. In REST, there are only four methods that need to be handled. In SOAP, there can be more, and there is no limit for that. That's why a client application must get a WSDL file in which all available methods are defined with parameters that are allowed. A server application location should be also within this file because the client application needs to know where to send its requests, and it's not obvious that it's the same location where WSDL is placed.

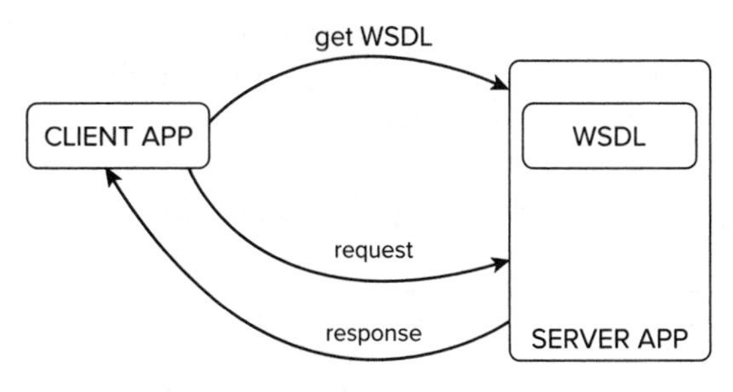

FIGURE 12-3: SOAP approach

Symfony

Symfony delivers a lot of ready-to-use plug-ins. You can easily connect to different applications such as Google Picasa, LinkedIn, or Last.fm. Here are some examples of plug-ins that you can install:

- sfPicasaPlugin — Gives you access to the Google Picasa API: `http://www.symfony-project.org/plugins/sfPicasaPlugin`
- sfGoogleLoginPlugin — Allows logging in to the Google account: `http://www.symfony-project.org/plugins/sfGoogleLoginPlugin`
- sfHarmonyPlugin — Library that provides SOAP communication for applications: `http://www.symfony-project.org/plugins/sfHarmonyPlugin`
- dbAmazonS3Plugin — Allows you to work with Amazon S3 through its API: `http://www.symfony-project.org/plugins/dbAmazonS3Plugin`
- sfMapFishPlugin — Allows you to integrate your Symfony application with MapFish application: `http://www.symfony-project.org/plugins/sfMapFishPlugin`
- WebPurifyPlugin — Enables securing web applications with WebPurify: `http://www.symfony-project.org/plugins/WebPurifyPlugin`
- wpLastFmPlugin — Provides tools to integrate with the Last.fm music network: `http://www.symfony-project.org/plugins/wpLastFmPlugin`
- sfNuSoapPlugin — Another library that enables SOAP communication: `http://www.symfony-project.org/plugins/sfNuSoapPlugin`
- sfLinkedinProfilePlugin — Allows you to show a LinkedIn profile on your page: `http://www.symfony-project.org/plugins/sfLinkedinProfilePlugin`
- sfFlexymfonyPlugin — Makes communication with Flex applications from Symfony side possible: `http://www.symfony-project.org/plugins/sfFlexymfonyPlugin`

This section uses the ckWebService plug-in to create an application with SOAP. To install the plug-in, use the following command:

```
$ symfony plugin:install ckWebServicePlugin
```

Until the installation of this plug-in, you could use only three types of application environments: dev, prod, and test. This plug-in will add the fourth: soap. So you need to configure the soap environment in your application's app.yml file, as shown in the following code:

Available for download on Wrox.com

```
all:
  enable_soap_parameter: off
soap:
  enable_soap_parameter: on
  ck_web_service_plugin:
    wsdl: %SF_WEB_DIR%/NewsApi.wsdl
    handler: NewsApiHandler
    persist: <?php echoln(SOAP_PERSISTENCE_SESSION) ?>
    soap_options:
      encoding: utf-8
      soap_version: <?php echoln(SOAP_1_2) ?>
    soap_headers:
      MySoapHeader:
        class: MySoapHeaderDataClass
```

code snippet /soap/symfony/apps/frontend/config/app.yml

By default, soap parameters are set to on, but you should turn them off for all application environments and enable them only for soap. Additionally, some plug-in–specific configuration needs to be set, such as the default WSDL file, encoding, SOAP version, and so on. In this example, adding news will be presented, so the NewsApi handler and definition will be further generated. It's already added in the preceding configuration. After you have completed the basic configuration of the SOAP application, you also should let Symfony know what will be the default SOAP environment's controller. You can define it in the application's factories.yml configuration file, as shown in the following code:

Available for download on Wrox.com

```
soap:
  controller:
    class: ckWebServiceController
```

code snippet /soap/symfony/apps/frontend/config/factories.yml

Finally, you need to enable SOAP applications to get parameters. Because that is done using filters you can set it in filters.yml:

Available for download on Wrox.com

```
rendering: ~
security:  ~
soap_parameter:
  class: ckSoapParameterFilter
  param:
    condition: %APP_ENABLE_SOAP_PARAMETER%
cache:     ~
execution: ~
```

code snippet /soap/symfony/apps/frontend/config/filters.yml

Note that in this example, the sequence of entries is important. That completes the configuration, but you still cannot add any news through SOAP now. Doctrine classes that you have used to manipulate the dates kept in the database are not available in the SOAP controller out of the box, so you need to add some hints to let everybody know that particular classes will be used in SOAP actions. You can do that easily just by adding comments before the class definitions. In case of the `news` class that you generated in the REST example, you need to add one line in the `/lib/model/doctrine/news.class.php` file:

```
<?php
/**
 * @PropertyStrategy('ckDoctrinePropertyStrategy')
 */
class news extends Basenews {
}
```

code snippet /soap/symfony/lib/model/doctrine/news.class.php

Now you can create a module that will hold your SOAP action:

```
$ symfony generate:module frontend news
```

You are halfway finished with your Hello World SOAP application. To add a new news entry, you need to get two parameters: *`title`* and *`description`*. If you read previous chapters carefully, you should know that the add action would be like the following one:

```
<?php
class newsActions extends sfActions {
  public function executeAdd($request) {
    $news = new news();
    $news->title=$request->getParameter('title');
    $news->description =$request->getParameter('description');
    $news->save();
    $this->result = $news->getId();
  }
}
```

code snippet /soap/symfony/apps/frontend/modules/news/actions/actions.class.php

It would be nice to comment what exactly this action will do. It is important also because this way, you specify which web service should handle this action while generating a new WSDL file (`@WSMethod`):

```
<?php
class newsActions extends sfActions {
 /**
   * An action for adding news
   * @WSMethod(webservice='NewsApi')
   * @param string $title Title
   * @param string $description Description
   * @return double The result
```

```
     */
    public function executeAdd($request) {
      // ...
    }
  }
```

code snippet /soap/symfony/apps/frontend/modules/news/actions/actions.class.php

Finally, you need to create a /config directory in the current module path and create a module.yml configuration file. It's needed for defining parameters and responses for SOAP. You need to add the following lines (from add: to the end, it should be written as a single line) in /modules/news/config/module.yml:

```
soap:
  add: { parameter: [title, description],
    result: { class: ckPropertyResultAdapter, param: { property: result } } }
```

code snippet /soap/symfony/apps/frontend/modules/news/config/module.yml

Before testing your first SOAP module, you need to create the WSDL definition file, as it was discussed at the beginning of this chapter. This plug-in provides a nice way to generate this WSDL file based on information given in the preceding configuration file. What you need to do is just to invoke this task using Symfony's command-line interface (CLI):

```
$ symfony webservice:generate-wsdl frontend NewsApi http://localhost/
```

Note that you need to put your URL as the last parameter. The preceding task will generate the following output:

```
>> file+     /home/wrox/public_html/soapsymfony/web/NewsApi.php
>> tokens    /home/wrox/public_html/soapsymfony/web/NewsApi.php
>> file-     /home/wrox/public_html/soapsymfony/apps/frontend/lib/
             BaseNewsApiHandler.class.php
>> file+     /home/wrox/public_html/soapsymfony/apps/frontend/lib/
             BaseNewsApiHandler.class.php
>> tokens    /home/wrox/public_html/soapsymfony/apps/frontend/lib/
             BaseNewsApiHandler.class.php
>> file+     /home/wrox/public_html/soapsymfony/web/NewsApi.wsdl
```

As shown previously, all needed files were generated. When you take a look inside NewsApi.wsdl, you will see something similar to the following code (some lines had to be broken for print; write each entry between brackets <> as a single line):

```
<?xml version="1.0" encoding="utf-8"?>
  <wsdl:definitions xmlns:wsdl="http://schemas.xmlsoap.org/wsdl/"
    xmlns="http://schemas.xmlsoap.org/wsdl/"
    xmlns:xsd="http://www.w3.org/2001/XMLSchema"
    xmlns:soap="http://schemas.xmlsoap.org/wsdl/soap/" name="NewsApi"
    targetNamespace="http://localhost/" xmlns:tns="http://localhost/"
    xmlns:soapenc="http://schemas.xmlsoap.org/soap/encoding/">
```

```
  <wsdl:types xmlns:xsd="http://www.w3.org/2001/XMLSchema">
    <xsd:schema xmlns:xsd="http://www.w3.org/2001/XMLSchema"
    xmlns="http://www.w3.org/2001/XMLSchema"
    targetNamespace="http://localhost/"/>
  </wsdl:types>
  <wsdl:portType name="NewsApiPortType">
    <wsdl:operation name="news_add" parameterOrder="title description">
      <wsdl:input message="tns:news_addRequest"/>
      <wsdl:output message="tns:news_addResponse"/>
    </wsdl:operation>
  </wsdl:portType>
  <wsdl:binding xmlns:soap="http://schemas.xmlsoap.org/wsdl/soap/"
    name="NewsApiBinding"
    type="tns:NewsApiPortType">
    <soap:binding xmlns:soap="http://schemas.xmlsoap.org/wsdl/soap/" style="rpc"
                  transport="http://schemas.xmlsoap.org/soap/http"/>
    <wsdl:operation xmlns:soap="http://schemas.xmlsoap.org/wsdl/soap/"
      name="news_add">
      <soap:operation xmlns:soap="http://schemas.xmlsoap.org/wsdl/soap/"
        soapAction="http://localhost/news_add" style="rpc"/>
      <wsdl:input xmlns:soap="http://schemas.xmlsoap.org/wsdl/soap/">
        <soap:body xmlns:soap="http://schemas.xmlsoap.org/wsdl/soap/" parts="title
          description" use="literal" namespace="http://localhost/"
          encodingStyle="http://schemas.xmlsoap.org/soap/encoding/"/>
      </wsdl:input>
      <wsdl:output xmlns:soap="http://schemas.xmlsoap.org/wsdl/soap/">
        <soap:body xmlns:soap="http://schemas.xmlsoap.org/wsdl/soap/"
          parts="result" use="literal" namespace="http://localhost/"
          encodingStyle="http://schemas.xmlsoap.org/soap/encoding/"/>
      </wsdl:output>
    </wsdl:operation>
  </wsdl:binding>
  <wsdl:message name="news_addRequest">
    <wsdl:part name="title" type="xsd:string"/>
    <wsdl:part name="description" type="xsd:string"/>
  </wsdl:message>
  <wsdl:message name="news_addResponse">
    <wsdl:part name="result" type="xsd:double"/>
  </wsdl:message>
  <wsdl:service xmlns:soap="http://schemas.xmlsoap.org/wsdl/soap/"
    name="NewsApiService">
    <wsdl:port xmlns:soap="http://schemas.xmlsoap.org/wsdl/soap/"
      name="NewsApiPort" binding="tns:NewsApiBinding">
      <soap:address xmlns:soap="http://schemas.xmlsoap.org/wsdl/soap/"
        location="http://localhost/NewsApi.php"/>
    </wsdl:port>
  </wsdl:service>
</wsdl:definitions>
```

The bold text in this file listing defines the input and output of actions, the parameters, and the result. For testing your new SOAP application, you can use soapUI, as mentioned before.

Run it and choose File from the main menu; then choose New soapUI Project. You should see a new window, as shown in Figure 12-4. Browse for the WSDL file if it's on your workstation, or you can download it from a remote machine and then use it.

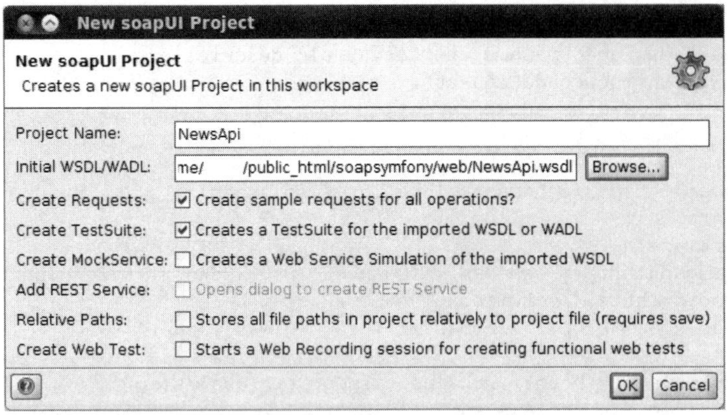

FIGURE 12-4: Wizard for adding new project in soapUI

After you click OK, you are taken to the next step, shown in Figure 12-5. Notice that the action you supplied in the previous step is automatically recognized because WSDL contains information of this kind.

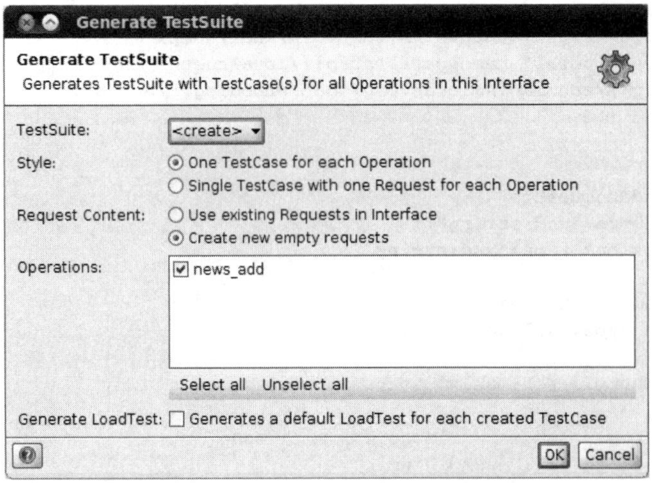

FIGURE 12-5: Adding test cases and requests in soapUI

Click OK and, as the last step, you are asked to specify a proper name for the test suite (see Figure 12-6).

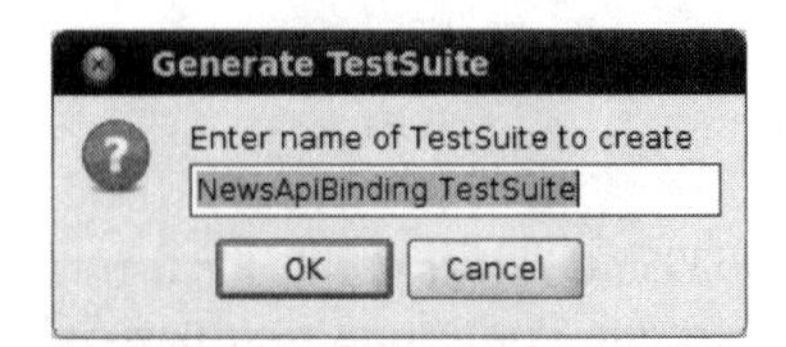

FIGURE 12-6: Specifying a name for the soapUI test suite generator

Click OK and a list of all created projects appears to the left in the next window displayed. It should look like Figure 12-7.

If you have followed the instructions in this chapter, clicking Request 1 opens a window with a new prepared request, as shown in Figure 12-8.

Change the question marks that you'll see to some data, as it's done in Figure 12-8. (Question marks were displayed there instead of `Hot` and `News`.)

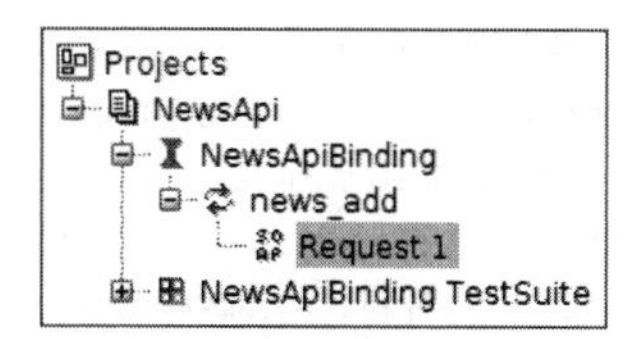

FIGURE 12-7: soapUI projects list

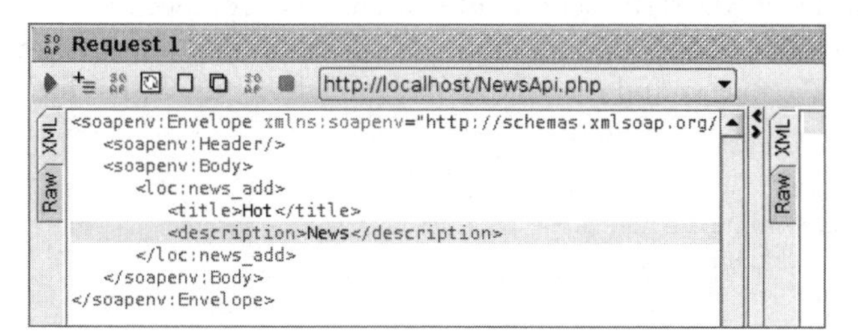

FIGURE 12-8: soapUI request definition

After clicking the green arrow visible in the top-left part of this window, you should see the application's response on the right, as shown in Figure 12-9.

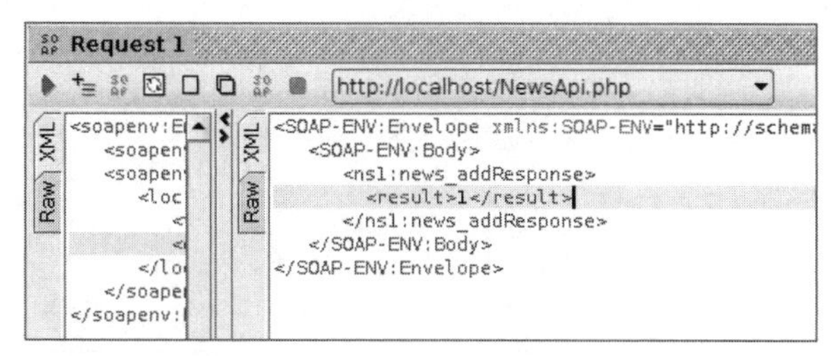

FIGURE 12-9: soapUI application's response

The result should contain the ID of the news you've added before. In this example, it is `1`.

CakePHP

CakePHP SOAP implementation is more time-consuming than the other two frameworks because you need to manually set some properties, such as the WSDL response header. WSDL files in Symfony and Zend are generated automatically and based on a given class. A model needs to be created because you will operate on a News table. You should also define a new method that you will use for SOAP, such as the method shown in the following code snippet:

```
<?php
class News extends AppModel {
    function addNewItem($title,$description) {
            $data['News']['title']=$title;
            $data['News']['description']=$description;
            $this->save($data);
            return "News id:".$this->id;
    }
}
?>
```

code snippet /soap/cakephp/app/models/news.php

The returned value is a string with the information about the currently added News ID. The model shown in the preceding code should be saved as /app/models/news.php. The controller that will handle the SOAP request should be very similar to the controller presented in the "Creating New Entries" section of the "CakePHP" section of this chapter. You need a RequestHandler component, but you will need only two methods, as shown in the following code snippet. The first is used to handle SOAP requests and the second one will show the WSDL file that makes the request possible.

```
<?php
class NewsController extends AppController {
    var $components = array('RequestHandler');
    function service() {
        $this->layout = false;
        $this->autoRender = false;
        Configure::write('debug', 0);
        ini_set("soap.wsdl_cache_enabled", "0");
        $server = new SoapServer('http://localhost/news/wsdl');
        $server->setClass("News");
        $server->handle();
    }
    function wsdl() {
        $this->layout = false;
        header('Content-Type: text/xml');
    }
}
?>
```

code snippet /soap/cakephp/app/controllers/news_controller.php

The bold line assigns the News class, which is your News model class and invokes the requested method on an object of the News type. The second method generates just an XML file; that's why a proper header needs to be set. Additionally, you need to manually write a WSDL file. This can be a very annoying issue, especially for developers who haven't met SOAP before. You can use the example shown here:

```
<wsdl:definitions name='News'
  targetNamespace='http://localhost/'
  xmlns:tns='http://localhost/'
  xmlns:soap='http://schemas.xmlsoap.org/wsdl/soap/'
  xmlns:xsd='http://www.w3.org/2001/XMLSchema'
  xmlns:soapenc='http://schemas.xmlsoap.org/soap/encoding/'
  xmlns:wsdl='http://schemas.xmlsoap.org/wsdl/'
  xmlns='http://schemas.xmlsoap.org/wsdl/'>
<wsdl:types>
    <schema xmlns="http://www.w3.org/2001/XMLSchema"
                targetNamespace="http://www.ecerami.com/schema"
                xmlns:wsdl="http://schemas.xmlsoap.org/wsdl/"
                xmlns:soapenc="http://schemas.xmlsoap.org/soap/encoding/">
        <complexType name="ArrayOfString">
            <complexContent>
                <restriction base="soapenc:Array">
                    <attribute ref="soapenc:arrayType"
                                   arrayType="string[]"/>
```

```
                </restriction>
            </complexContent>
        </complexType>
    </schema>
</wsdl:types>
<message name='addNewItemRequest'>
    <part name='title' type='xsd:string'/>
    <part name='description' type='xsd:string'/>
</message>
<message name='addNewItemResponse'>
  <part name='Result' type='xsd:string'/>
</message>
<portType name='NewsPortType'>
  <operation name='addNewItem'>
    <input message='tns:addNewItemRequest'/>
    <output message='tns:addNewItemResponse'/>
  </operation>
</portType>
<binding name='NewsBinding' type='tns:NewsPortType'>
  <soap:binding style='rpc' transport='http://schemas.xmlsoap.org/soap/http'/>
  <operation name='addNewItem'>
    <soap:operation soapAction='urn:your-urn'/>
    <input>
      <soap:body use='encoded' namespace='urn:your-urn'
        encodingStyle='http://schemas.xmlsoap.org/soap/encoding/'/>
    </input>
    <output>
      <soap:body use='encoded' namespace='urn:your-urn'
        encodingStyle='http://schemas.xmlsoap.org/soap/encoding/'/>
    </output>
  </operation>
</binding>
<service name='NewsService'>
  <port name='NewsPort' binding='NewsBinding'>
    <soap:address xmlns:soap="http://schemas.xmlsoap.org/wsdl/soap/"
      location='http://localhost/news/service'/>
  </port>
</service>
</wsdl:definitions>
```

code snippet /soap/cakephp/app/views/news/wsdl.ctp

Save the preceding code as `wsdl.ctp` in the `/views/news` directory. Now you can test your SOAP application developed with CakePHP. In soapUI, you are also able to set a URL instead of a path to your local WSDL file in the WSDL file field. For this example, it would be `http://localhost/news/wsdl` if your application is on `localhost`.

Zend Framework

Zend Framework delivers a lot of ready-to-use classes such as `Zend_Soap_Client`, `Zend_Soap_Server`, `Zend_Soap_Wsdl`, and a class for generating WSDL files, `Zend_Soap_AutoDiscover`. You can use the same News model files you used with the REST example. Creating a simple SOAP application is very similar to the one that was presented in the "CakePHP" section. First of all, you need to create a class to handle SOAP requests. Adding a news class can be done as follows:

Available for download on Wrox.com

```
<?php
require '../application/models/News.php';
require '../application/models/NewsMapper.php';
require '../application/models/DbTable/News.php';
class NewsAPI {
    /**
     * Add method
     * @param String $title
     * @param String $description
     * @return Int
     */
    public function news_add($title, $description) {
        $entry = new Application_Model_News();
        $entry->setTitle($title);
        $entry->setDescription($description);
        $mapper  = new Application_Model_NewsMapper();
        $id = $mapper->save($entry);
        return $id;
    }
}
```

code snippet /soap/zf/library/NewsAPI.php

You need to include the necessary model files on your own, as it was already described a few times in previous chapters, particularly in Chapter 4. Next you need to define a simple method that saves the News title and description within the request. You can save it in `/library` as `NewsAPI.php`. You need to include it in the controller that you will use to handle the SOAP request. To simplify, let's use the main controller. Just as in CakePHP, two methods need to be defined: one for generating WSDL and one for handling SOAP requests:

Available for download on Wrox.com

```
<?php
require_once realpath(APPLICATION_PATH .'/../library/').'/NewsAPI.php';
class IndexController extends Zend_Controller_Action {
    public function wsdlAction() {
    }
    public function serviceAction() {
    }
}
```

code snippet /soap/zf/application/controllers/IndexController.php

To generate a WSDL file, you can use `Zend_Soap_AutoDiscover`:

Available for download on Wrox.com

```
public function wsdlAction() {
     $this->_helper->viewRenderer->setNoRender();
     $autodiscover = new Zend_Soap_AutoDiscover();
     $autodiscover->setClass('NewsAPI');
     $autodiscover->handle();
}
```

code snippet /soap/zf/application/controllers/IndexController.php

The preceding code generates the WSDL file based on the `NewsAPI` class definition. This approach needs less effort than in the case of CakePHP. Next, you need to handle the SOAP request:

```
public function serviceAction() {
    $this->_helper->viewRenderer->setNoRender();
    $soapServer = new Zend_Soap_Server("http://localhost/index/wsdl");
    $soapServer->setClass('NewsAPI');
    $soapServer->handle();
}
```

code snippet /soap/zf/application/controllers/IndexController.php

In soapUI, the WSDL file's URL would be as shown as in the preceding code. It's the parameter for the `Zend_Soap_Server` constructor method. As the last task, you should set `http://localhost/index/service`.

13

Back End

Why so serious?

— Joker, the Dark Knight (Batman)

WHAT'S IN THIS CHAPTER?

- Comparison of various content management systems (CMSs).
- Introducing back-end applications for CRUD operations.

Content management systems (CMSs) are now so popular that they are a well-known standard. It is not really a problem to build a CMS from scratch, but why should you reinvent the wheel? Developing just another CMS when you need one is a waste of time because there are so many really good solutions, and you will certainly find one to suit your needs. The CMSs described in this chapter use proven design patterns and promote best programming practices, which makes using them both straightforward and educative.

But what is really good about these solutions is that they are based on the three frameworks covered in this book and they inherit the Model-View-Controller (MVC) architecture. Another benefit is that they follow their parent framework's structure and conventions, so you don't need to learn how to use a new piece of software, but instead you will feel yourself at home. It's also definitely much easier to add or change some functionalities of a CMS based on your favorite framework.

SYMFONY

Symfony has an extensive plug-in repository, including CMS plug-ins that can be installed directly from the command line. Another way of installing a CMS is to download a prepared package, complete with Symfony and CMS inside. In addition, you can use one more solution that is delivered with Symfony itself: the *admin* feature of the Doctrine object-relational mapper (ORM). For more on Doctrine and ORMs, refer to Chapter 3.

The two ready-to-use CMS plug-ins described in this section are Apostrophe and Diem (their logos are shown in Figure 13-1). Both solutions should attract your attention because they are arguably the richest of the CMSs covered in this chapter. There are also some other solutions, such as Lfcms or Sympal, but they are not as refined.

FIGURE 13-1: Apostrophe and Diem logos

Doctrine admin Modules

Symfony delivers a lot of command-line tools as described in earlier chapters. There are two commonly used tasks to generate create, read, update, and delete (CRUD) modules:

```
doctrine
  :generate-admin
  :generate-module
```

In Chapter 4, the `generate-module` task was described in detail. The `generate-admin` task generates administration controllers and views, which implement the CRUD operations. This simplifies the work when you want to build a back-end application. Let's build a simple CRUD back-end application, which will allow you to manipulate e-mail data. Assume that you have an e-mail model containing such fields as email, forename, and surname. You can create the application with the following command:

```
$ symfony generate:app backend
```

To generate an admin module, you need to use this command:

```
$ symfony doctrine:generate-admin frontend Mails
```

Now, when you go to `http://localhost/backend_dev.php/mails`, you should see something similar to the left side of Figure 13-2. The right side of Figure 13-2 shows filters for searching for records based on concrete fields. It's useful when you want to constrain your results to a few fixed fields.

FIGURE 13-2: Doctrine admin module

Note that the URL includes `localhost` because we assume that you are working on your local computer. If you go to `/apps/backend/modules/mails`, you notice that almost all the directories are empty, and no class definitions contain any defined methods; they are only inherited from other classes that reside in cache. These cache classes are generated from the libraries. So such exemplary `action.class.php` files found in this folder can be as simple as follows:

```
<?php
require_once dirname(__FILE__).'/../lib/mailsGeneratorConfiguration.class.php';
require_once dirname(__FILE__).'/../lib/mailsGeneratorHelper.class.php';
class mailsActions extends autoMailsActions {
}
```

All files are generated and placed in the `/cache` directory. The directory structure should be as follows:

```
cache/backend/dev/
                  config/
                  i18n/
                  modules/
                  template/
```

Inside the cache in a proper directory, you can find the `autoMailsActions` class definition.

You can change how files are generated by changing the `generator.yml` configuration file, as shown in the following code. The `generator.yml` configuration file is located in the `/modules/config` directory.

Available for download on Wrox.com

```
generator:
  class: sfDoctrineGenerator
  param:
    model_class:           Mails
    theme:                 admin
    non_verbose_templates: true
    with_show:             false
    singular:              ~
    plural:                ~
    route_prefix:          mails
    with_doctrine_route:   true
    actions_base_class:    sfActions

    config:
      actions: ~
      fields:  ~
      list:    ~
      filter:  ~
      form:    ~
      edit:    ~
      new:     ~
```

code snippet /symfony/app/frontend/modules/adminexample/config/generator.yml

To summarize, you need to execute just one command to get a CRUD module. You don't need to add any more lines of code. Propel also has this kind of functionality that you can use through Symfony's command-line tools. Note that generating CRUD modules is a functionality of Doctrine, so you can use this feature in any other web framework where Doctrine integration is possible. You can download Doctrine from `www.doctrine-project.org`.

Apostrophe

Apostrophe is a CMS in which the word *management* means something different than in most other CMSs. Instead of creating two different levels (*management* and *presentation*), it blurs the boundary between the *back end* and the *front end*. You can get Apostrophe from `www.apostrophenow.com`.

If you have already created a project, you can install Apostrophe as a plug-in with the following command:

```
$ symfony plugin:install apostrophePlugin
```

Note that installing only the previous plug-in will not give you all functionalities that come with Apostrophe. You should also install the following plug-ins:

```
apostropheBlogPlugin
apostrophePlugin
sfDoctrineActAsTaggablePlugin
sfDoctrineGuardPlugin
sfFeed2Plugin
sfJqueryReloadedPlugin
sfSyncContentPlugin
sfTaskExtraPlugin
sfWebBrowserPlugin
```

These plug-ins are available out of the box in the sandbox version. After unpacking, you should change the configuration filenames by deleting `.sample` at the end. You need to edit `database.yml` and fill it with proper database information. If your database doesn't exist, you need to create it before going on to the next steps (this was described in Chapters 2 and 3). Next, you need to execute the following combination of commands:

```
$ symfony cc
$ symfony plugin:publish-assets
$ symfony doctrine:build --all
$ symfony doctrine:data-load
```

The first command is executed only to make sure that there are no previously generated files within `/cache`. The second command publishes Apostrophe's web assets. After that, you need to build models, forms, and database tables, as designed in Apostrophe's `schema.yml` files. Finally you load some data to see it on the Web.

When you go to `http://localhost/`, you should be able to see something similar to what is presented in Figure 13-3.

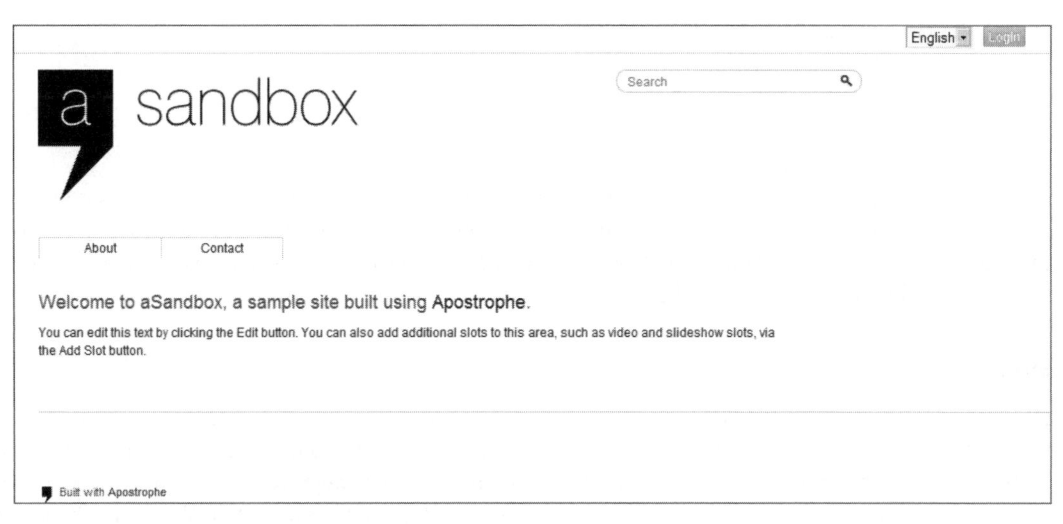

FIGURE 13-3: Apostrophe sandbox main page

If you cannot see the Apostrophe main page (refer to Figure 13-3) and you are sure that you configured the web server properly, you should check permissions by executing the following command:

```
$ symfony project:permissions
```

That command will fix directories permissions if they are set wrong.

In the right corner of the main page, you can see a Login button. This allows you to enter the administration mode. To get there, you need to fill out the login form with `admin` for the login and `demo` for the password. Now you can add, edit, or delete the contents of each page. A dialog for creating a page is shown in Figure 13-4.

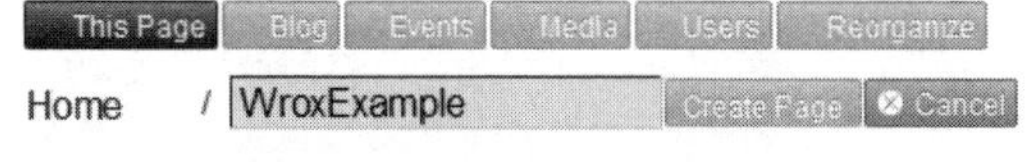

FIGURE 13-4: Adding pages with the Apostrophe CMS

As shown in the following code, Apostrophe also provides a lot of new tasks available within Symfony's command-line interface (CLI):

```
apostrophe-blog
  :fix-untitled-posts
  :migrate-page-slugs

apostrophe
  :after-deploy
  :demo-fixtures
  :deploy
  :fix-remote-permissions
  :generate-slot-type
  :import-files
  :migrate
  :migrate-data-from-pkcontextcms
  :migrate-from-pkcontextcms
  :optimize-search-index
```

```
    :rebuild-search-index
    :refresh
    :repair-tree
    :ssh
    :update-search-index
```

Apostrophe's approach gives you the capability to use CMS in a way other than how it is commonly used, where a project is divided into two parts: the front end and the back end. With Apostrophe the pages are nearly What You See Is What You Get (WYSIWYG), so the page you make changes to looks nearly the same as the page the user will see.

Diem

Diem is more than a simple CMS. It's a content management framework (CMF). It has huge capabilities because you can build your pages with blocks. It has a lot of widgets that can be placed within your website. To start using Diem, you need to download the package from `http://diem-project.org/`. Next, unpack it to a convenient directory like `C:\diem\`. The next step, shown in the following code, is to create a directory where your Diem project will be finally placed:

```
$ cd C:\xampp\htdocs\
$ mkdir diemproject
```

Now you can proceed with the installation by going to the directory you created and executing the Diem PHP install script:

```
$ cd C:\xampp\htdocs\diemproject\
$ php C:\diem\install
```

This script will create a lot of files. When it ends, you need to configure Diem by executing the following command in your Diem project directory:

```
$ symfony dm:setup
```

That command will ask you some simple questions and will do the rest of the configuration by itself. After your Diem project is configured, you will be able to execute some Diem tasks using Symfony's command-line interface, as shown in the following code:

```
dm
  :clear-cache
  :data
  :loremize
  :permissions
  :publish-assets
  :search-update
  :server-check
  :setup
  :sitemap-update
  :sync-pages
  :upgrade
```

```
dmAdmin
  :generate
  :generate-module
dmFront
  :generate
  :page-indexable-content
dmUser
  :change-password
  :promote
```

You can access the Diem admin page by typing `http://localhost/admin_dev.php/` in your browser, and you can access the front end with `http://localhost/`. The front end won't look good when you first open it because you have not built a page yet, so it's almost blank. If you go to the admin site and sign in with `admin` as both the login and the password, you will be able to change the website's details. You might notice a link at the bottom of the page to switch to the back end. After clicking it, you will have access to the Diem tool for building websites, as shown in Figure 13-5. You should see two panels: the one to the left is called Pages, and the one to the right is called Media. You need to choose a page on the left and add widgets with drag and drop. After you are done making changes to the front end, you can log out and try it out.

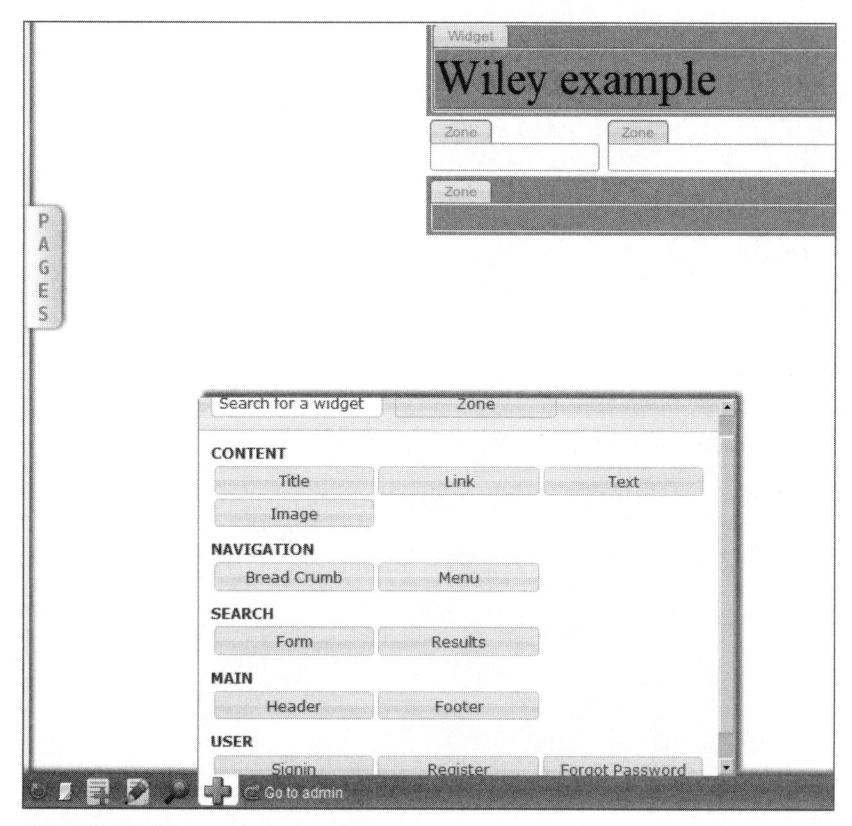

FIGURE 13-5: Diem website building

CAKEPHP

CakePHP framework has only two CMSs worth describing: Croogo and Wildflower (their logos are shown in Figure 13-6). There are also some other CMS or e-commerce solutions (such as BakeSale) that are based on CakePHP, but only these two are now in active development. CakePHP doesn't support generating default CRUD modules as Symfony does. That can be done by integrating Doctrine with CakePHP, but it needs additional effort.

Croogo

FIGURE 13-6: Croogo and Wildflower logos

Croogo

Croogo is a simple CMS that you just need to unpack to the /app directory. Croogo needs to be installed within an existing CakePHP instance as its application. You need to download it first from www.croogo.org. Unpack the content of Croogo's main directory to the /app directory. Your directory structure should look as follows:

```
app/
      config/
      controllers/
      libs/
      locale/
      models/
      plugins/
               acl/
               empty/
               example/
               extensions/
                   install/
               tinymce/
               translate/
      tests/
      tmp/
      vendors/
      views/
      webroot/
      app_controller.php
      app_error.php
      app_helper.php
      app_model.php
      .htaccess
      index.php
      LICENSE.txt
      README.mdown
      VERSION.txt
cake/
plugins/
vendors/
.htaccess
index.php
README
```

This listing doesn't show everything; only files and directories that we selected are shown here, and the most important directories are bold. The main `/app` folder contains the Croogo application downloaded in the earlier step. After this preparation, Croogo is ready to be installed. The Croogo web installer will guide you through the next configuration steps. Just type `http://localhost/` into your browser, provided you have installed the CMS on your local workstation. After the installation process ends, you need to delete the `/install` directory, shown in bold in the preceding code. Now you can run the Croogo CMS. Under `http://localhost/` you can find your front-end application, and the back end is under `http://localhost/admin`. The default login is `admin`, and the password is `password`. A front-end example page is shown in Figure 13-7.

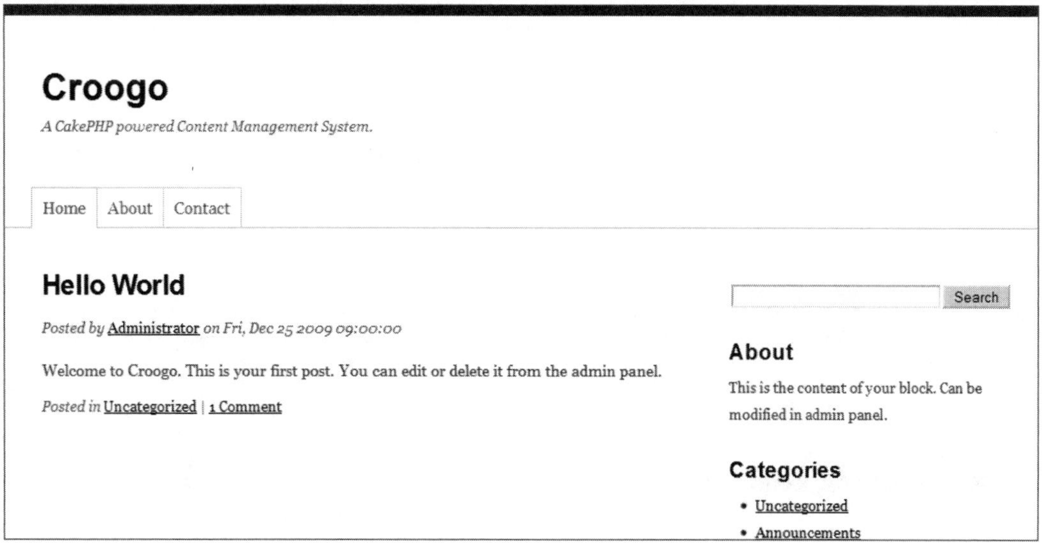

FIGURE 13-7: Croogo main web page

Croogo is a decent CMS without unusual features, so don't expect any rocket science, but at least this CMS has all the basic features everyone expects.

Wildflower

Wildflower is also a CMS based on CakePHP. It's even simpler than Croogo. Installation of Wildflower is not as easy as it is with Croogo because it hasn't got an installer. Before starting manual installation, you need to download Wildflower from `http://wf.klevo.sk/`. The downloaded package is a whole CakePHP application with CakePHP's libraries. You only need to unpack it to a proper directory.

When you're done with that, you can start working with Wildflower by changing database connection properties in `app/config/database.php`. Database connection entries should be changed as is usually done in a CakePHP application. Then you can create proper database tables and insert some example data in them. Wildflower delivers a SQL file for import with your favorite database tool. If you don't have a favorite database tool, you can import these entries from the command line as follows:

```
$ mysql -u root -D wildflower < app/config/sql/wildflower.sql
```

Note that this works if you are currently in the project directory. Otherwise, you should give the whole path to `wildflower.sql`. Now you have Wildflower installed and you can access the front end (`http://localhost/`) and back end (`http://localhost/admin`) of the application. Wildflower's back end is shown in Figure 13-8. The default password for the `admin` account is `admin321`. Wildflower is a very simple CMS, but you can develop a bigger application based on it.

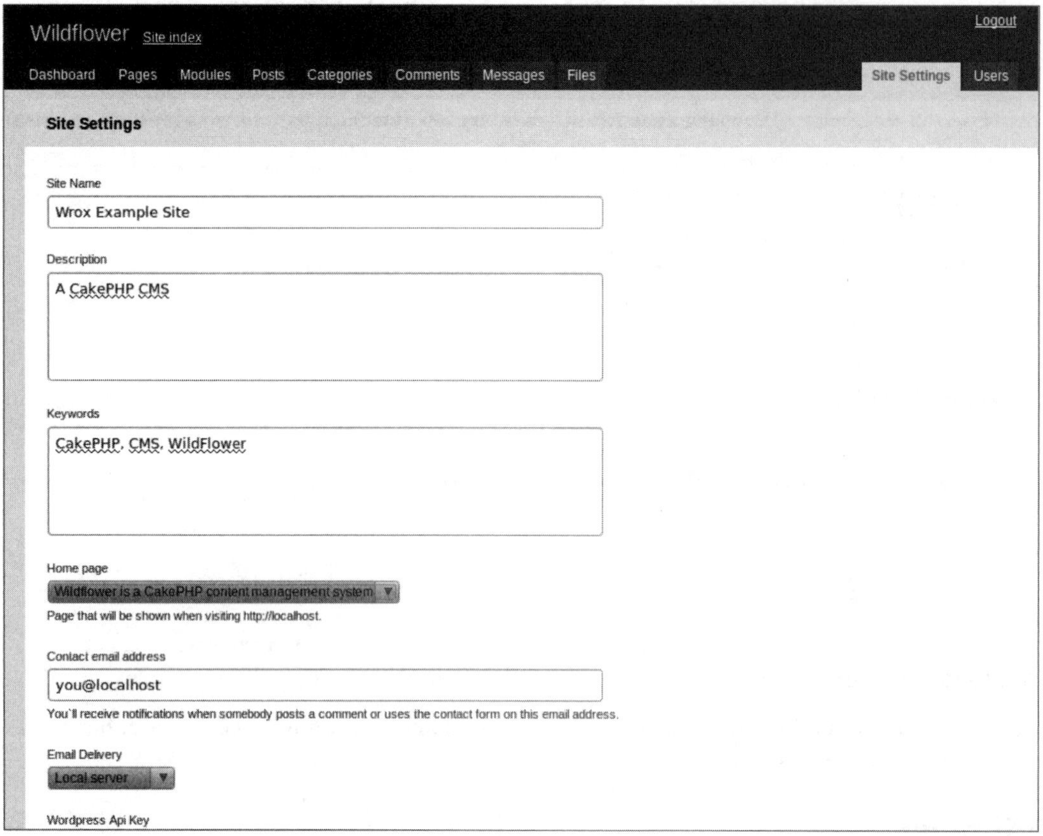

FIGURE 13-8: Wildflower's back end

ZEND FRAMEWORK

Zend Framework doesn't support generating CRUD controllers by default (except when using Doctrine as the default ORM). This is a big drawback, but you can live without that because in most cases developers spend a lot of time customizing those automatically generated controllers and views, and thus the time savings are not as great as one would expect.

A guide to building a CRUD module for Zend Framework is the same as in Chapter 4: You need to create all CRUD actions yourself manually. You can also use one of the open source CMSs and customize it to your needs. This section presents three of the best known open source CMSs based on

Zend Framework: TomatoCMS, Pimcore, and Digitalus CMS. Their respective logos are shown in Figure 13-9.

FIGURE 13-9: TomatoCMS, Pimcore, and Digitalus CMS logos

TomatoCMS

TomatoCMS comes with a handy web installer. After downloading it from `www.tomatocms.com` and unpacking to your web root directory, you can access the installer just by typing `http://localhost/` into your web browser. You should see something similar to what is presented in Figure 13-10.

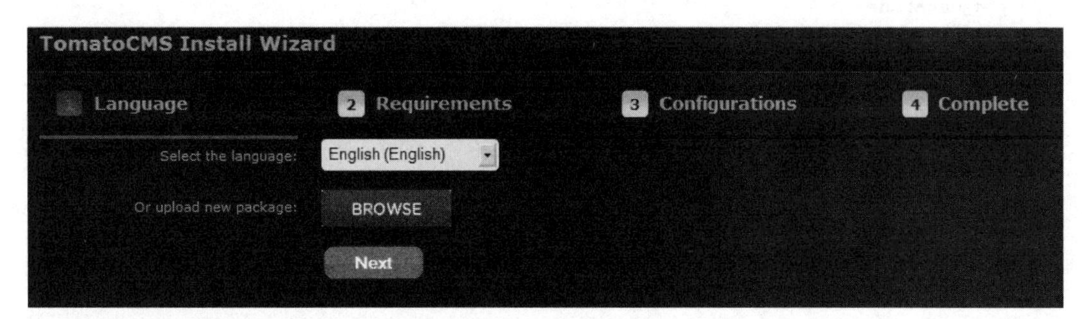

FIGURE 13-10: TomatoCMS installation wizard

The installer will guide you step by step. In Step 3, you should check Import sample data if you are using TomatoCMS for the first time. The back-end application is available at `http://localhost/admin`. The password for the admin account is generated randomly, and you should be able to see it in the last step of the installation wizard. TomatoCMS is nicely integrated with Google applications and also with Flickr and Twitter. The rest of the features are as usual in all common CMS solutions.

Pimcore

Pimcore is one of the biggest CMSs presented in this chapter. You can download it from its homepage: `www.pimcore.org`. You can install Pimcore in two ways: through a web installer or manually. We will show you the manual approach because it gives deeper insight into the CMS. When you unpack Pimcore, you will notice that the directory structure is a little bit different from that of Zend Framework. Pimcore developers made their libraries based on ZF, and although they're not the same as in ZF, they're quite close. If you know ZF, you should have no problems with Pimcore.

After unpacking, you need to set information on the database connection in the `pimcore/website/var/config/system.xml` configuration file. Lines to be edited are shown in bold:

Available for download on Wrox.com

```
<?xml version="1.0"?>
<zend-config xmlns:zf="http://framework.zend.com/xml/zend-config-xml/1.0/">
  <general>
    <timezone>Europe/Berlin</timezone>
    <domain></domain>
```

```
    <language>en</language>
    <validLanguages>en</validLanguages>
    <debug>1</debug>
    <theme>/pimcore/static/js/lib/ext/resources/css/xtheme-blue.css</theme>
    <welcomescreen>1</welcomescreen>
  </general>
  <database>
    <adapter>Pdo_Mysql</adapter>
    <params>
      <host>localhost</host>
      <username>root</username>
      <password></password>
      <dbname>pimcore_example</dbname>
    </params>
  </database>
  <documents>
    <versions>
      <days></days>
      <steps>20</steps>
    </versions>
    <default_module>website</default_module>
    <default_controller>default</default_controller>
    <default_action>default</default_action>
    <error_page>/</error_page>
  </documents>
  <objects>
    <versions>
      <days></days>
      <steps>20</steps>
    </versions>
  </objects>
  <assets>
    <webdav>
      <hostname></hostname>
    </webdav>
    <versions>
      <days></days>
      <steps>20</steps>
    </versions>
  </assets>
  <services>
    <scribd>
      <apikey></apikey>
      <secret></secret>
    </scribd>
```

code snippet /pimcore/website/var/config/system.xml

As in almost all previous cases, you need to additionally create a proper database. After that, you should load some example data if you are using it for the first time:

```
$ mysql -u wroxuser -D pimcore_example <
   /home/wrox/public_html/pimcore/pimcore_example.sql
```

Now you can access the back-end application through `http://localhost/admin` with `admin` as both login and password. It has a lot of features and nice tools that make your life easier. Pimcore's theme looks a little bit like Microsoft Outlook (see Figure 13-11).

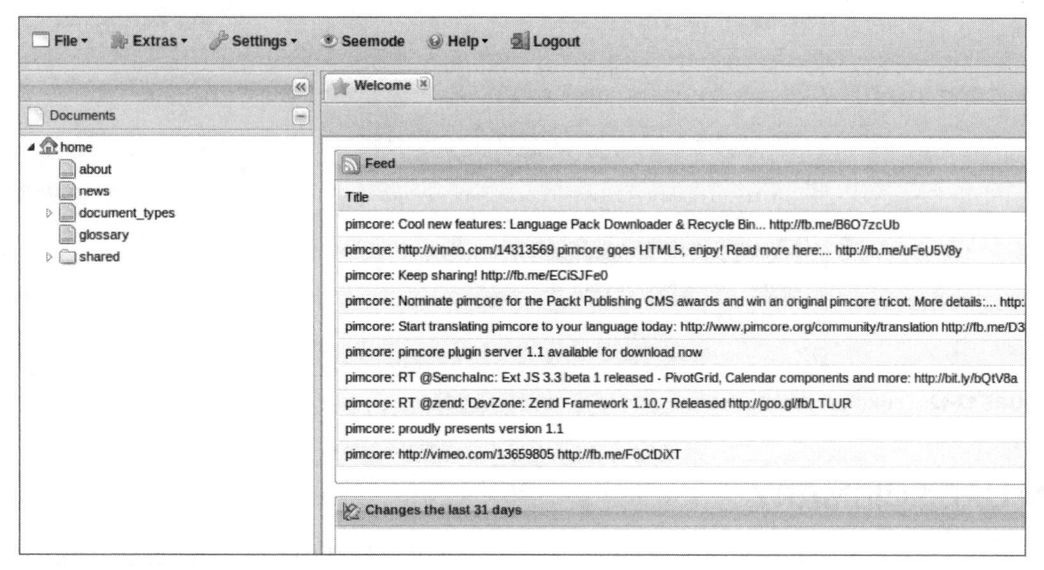

FIGURE 13-11: Pimcore admin site

You can now edit pages from the back end with a WYSIWYG editor that shows you the result of the whole web page, not only the content of it, as it is presented in most of the other CMSs.

Digitalus CMS

You can grab this CMS from `http://digitaluscms.com/`. Digitalus CMS comes with a nice installer, which checks all prerequirements and creates all needed tables. You will be asked for a user ID and password for your super-user account.

After the installation is finished, you should be able to see something similar to Figure 13-12. Digitalus comes with a rich internationalization feature. The rest of it is very similar to the other commonly used CMS solutions.

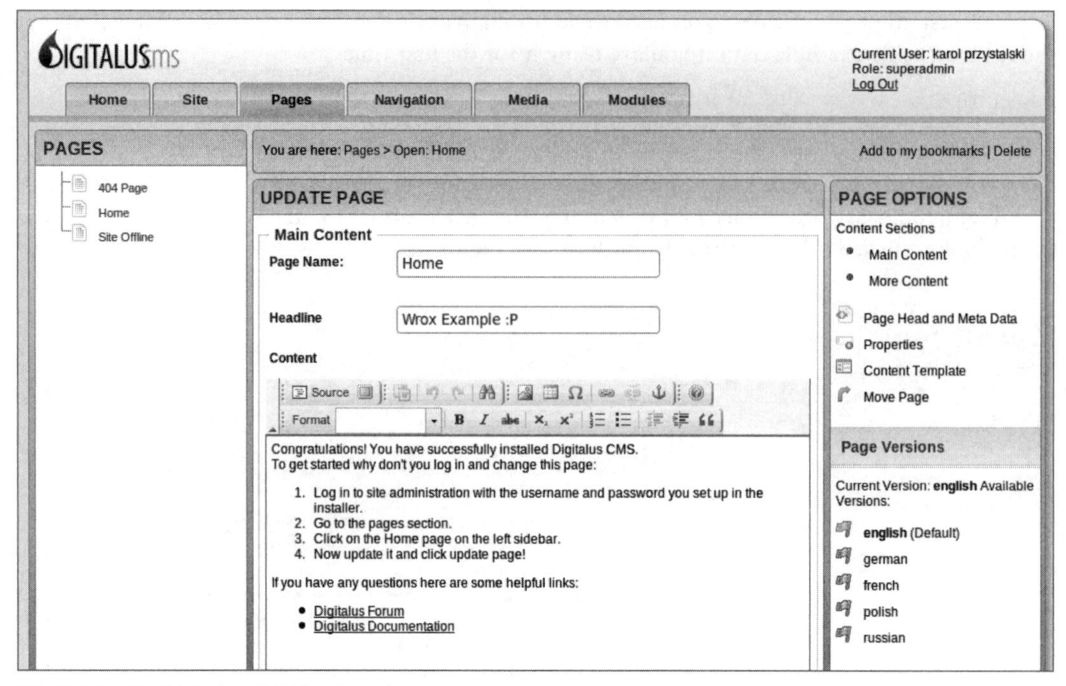

FIGURE 13-12: Digitalus CMS back end

FEATURE SUMMARY

We have prepared a short summary of the unique features of individual CMSs (see page 369). This table should be helpful for comparing them and choosing the right one for your needs.

CMS	INSTALLATION SIMPLICITY	GOOGLE ANALYTICS/ ACCOUNT INTEGRATION	PLUG-INS	LICENSE	MANAGEMENT APPROACH
Doctrine	Out of the box in Symfony	No	Yes	GPLv2	Typical back-end approach
Apostrophe	As plug-in or sandbox	No	Yes	MIT	Front-end approach
Diem	As plug-in or sandbox	Yes	Yes	MIT	Back-end and front-end approach, widget-driven
Croogo	Web installer	No	Yes	MIT	Back-end approach
Wildflower	No installer, need to change files manually	Yes	No	MIT	Back-end approach
TomatoCMS	Web installer	Yes	Yes	GPLv2	Back-end approach
Pimcore	Simple change in database connection configuration file, also a web installer	Yes	Available	BSD	From back end, but as WYSIWYG
Digitalus	Web installer	Yes	As modules	BSD	Back-end approach

(continues)

(continued)

CMS	ADDITIONAL FEATURES	MAINTENANCE	SEARCH ENGINE	DOCUMENTATION\ COMMUNITY
Doctrine	Filters, admin generator configurable via generator.yml	Manual	As all plug-ins for Symfony; this can be added separately	Very good
Apostrophe	Building website from content blocks	Can be automated; CLI command available	Lucene	Good
Diem	Widgets	Can be automated; scripts available	Lucene	Good
Croogo	Integrated reCaptcha	Manual; scripts not provided	Not available	Good
Wildflower	Integrated Wordpress	Manual; scripts not provided	Not available	Poor
TomatoCMS	Pools, integrated with Flickr and Twitter	Manual; scripts not provided	Not available	Good
Pimcore	History of changes, simple image editor, PDF/doc documents preview	Can be automated	Available as a plug-in	Good
Digitalus	Internationalization	Manual; scripts not provided	Lucene	Good

14

Internationalization

Let us be fully aware of all the importance of this day, because today within the generous walls of Boulogne-sur-Mer have met not French with English, nor Russians with Polish, but people with people.

— LUDOVIKO ZAMENHOF, THE FOUNDER OF ESPERANTO

WHAT'S IN THIS CHAPTER?

- Introducing i18n.
- Using the CLI to translate view templates.
- Displaying time and date in different locales.
- Translating form elements.
- Using a database to store translations.

Multilingual websites are becoming increasingly popular, not only among users, but also developers and important strategic partners who want to see web apps translated into their native languages. While translating into languages transcribed using Latin-derived charsets is relatively easy, there are also multiple scripts that use completely different charsets, ideographic symbols, and right-to-left text orientation. Internationalization is not only a matter of courtesy but is also an excellent tool for tapping into the great revenue potential that an international market presents.

Web frameworks widely support internationalization. They provide useful libraries or even ready-to-use solutions. In this chapter, we show you how easy it is to extend your web applications to use multiple languages and cultural settings.

INTERNATIONALIZATION DEFINED

Internationalization, often abbreviated to *i18n* because it is a long word, goes far beyond providing a full Unicode charset. It concerns many other issues such as the following:

- Text writing direction
- Character collation (character order for sorting purposes)
- Varying plural forms and suffixes affected by other words
- Formatting of numbers, especially the decimal separator and optional thousands separator
- Date and time formatting and local time display, taking into account time zones and daylight saving time
- Weights, measures, and currency
- Various other cultural traits, such as postal codes, addresses, titles, and academic degrees
- Mapping of social institutions and government documents covering the same responsibilities, such as insurance, taxation, health care, and so on
- Conformance of content with legal restrictions (for example, copyrights or alcoholic beverage advertising)

Apart from internationalization, you can also come across other terms like localization (110n) and globalization (g13n). l10n usually refers to translating the interface in to a specific language while i18n refers to offering the content in different languages. There is no strict definition for these terms, however, and they are sometimes used interchangeably.

RIGHT-TO-LEFT TEXT ORIENTATION

Right-to-left text orientation (RTL) is one of the most important i18n issues. It is very easily implemented using CSS direction property, so it can be used for every framework. The following code sets the text orientation inside a div to rtl.

```
div {
direction: rtl;
}
```

This is a universal solution supported by all modern browsers.

SYMFONY

Symfony provides, out of the box, two i18n command-line tasks: `i18n:extract` and `i18n:find`. They are both very useful. The `i18n:find` task allows you to locate untranslated template elements. You should be careful, though, because this task may return many false positives when parsing PHP files with text strings that are not intended to be displayed to the user. The `i18n:extract` task extracts all i18n strings from the given application and target culture. By default, this tool only counts the number of strings to extract; if you want to make it save them in the i18n message catalogue, use the `--auto-save` option:

```
symfony i18n:extract --auto-save application_name culture
```

Configuration

To configure internationalization in Symfony, first create a project, an application, and a module, as shown in the following code. For this example, the module is called `i18nexample`:

```
$ symfony generate:project wroxI18N
$ symfony generate:app frontend
$ symfony generate:module frontend i18nexample
```

Symfony uses a parameter of the user session called `culture`. This parameter naturally combines the language of the user and all the cultural settings of his country. You may specify the default culture of your website in the `settings.yml` file:

Available for download on Wrox.com

```
all:
  .settings:
     default_culture: en_US
```

code snippet /symfony/apps/frontend/config/settings.yml

The culture called `en_US` uses the U.S. flavor of the English language and United States locale settings.

In the same file, you have to add the following line to make the i18n module work:

Available for download on Wrox.com

```
all:
  .settings:
    i18n: true
```

code snippet /symfony/apps/frontend/config/settings.yml

You can specify which languages will be supported by particular web pages. To do that, edit `routing.yml`. The following example illustrates how to provide the news module for three language versions: English (any variant), German, and Polish:

Available for download on Wrox.com

```
news:
  url: /:sf_culture/:page
  param:
  requirements: { sf_culture: (?:en|de|pl) }
```

code snippet /symfony/apps/frontend/config/routing.yml

Note that you get clean, organized URLs this way. When you have a page about cars with an English link (`http://localhost/en/cars`), the link of the German version will be `http://localhost/de/cars`. There is also the zxI18nRoutingPlugin plug-in to make it look like `http://localhost/de/fahrzeuge`. It may have a great effect on search engine optimization (SEO) of localized websites.

You can set the culture of a user anytime using the following method:

```
$this->getUser()->setCulture('en_US');
```

The getter method is equally simple:

```
$culture = $this->getUser()->getCulture();
```

Templates

Creating a multilingual application requires a modification of your view templates. Go to the `actions.class.php` file and comment out the line responsible for redirection to the default module:

Available for download on Wrox.com

```
<?php
class i18wroxActions extends sfActions {
  public function executeIndex(sfWebRequest $request) {
  //  $this->forward('default', 'module');
  }
}
```

code snippet /symfony/apps/frontend/modules/i18nwrox/actions/actions.class.php

This way, the `indexSuccess.php` template of your module will be displayed. Go to the `/templates` folder and edit this template:

Available for download on Wrox.com

```
<?php use_helper('I18N') ?>
<?php echo __('The latest news') ?>
```

code snippet /symfony/apps/frontend/modules/i18nwrox/templates/indexSuccess.php

Using the `I18N` helper gets the work done with minimal effort. All you have to do is to surround the text to localize with a double underscore and round parentheses:

Available for download on Wrox.com

```
<?php use_helper('I18N') ?>
<?php echo __('The latest news') ?>
<?php echo "Not translated string"; ?>
```

code snippet /symfony/apps/frontend/modules/i18nwrox/templates/indexSuccess.php

The bold line is important for comparison because strings in double apostrophes will not be extracted as translatable text. Try out the `find` command-line tool, as shown in the following code. It returns all strings that are not translated, including those you don't want to translate. The output is as follows:

```
$ symfony i18n:find frontend
>> i18n    find non "i18n ready" strings in the "frontend" application
>> i18n    strings in "/apps/frontend/modules/i18nwrox/templates/indexSuccess.php"
  I18N
  The latest news
  Not translated string
```

Now the `extract` tool can be used to prepare all relevant strings to be worked by translators. Remember to set the `--auto-save` option with the name of your application and culture:

```
$ symfony i18n:extract --auto-save frontend en_US
```

The output will include only `'The latest news'` string that you marked for localization:

```
>> i18n      extracting i18n strings for the "frontend" application
>> i18n      found "1" new i18n strings
>> i18n      found "0" old i18n strings
```

Now you can check your localization dictionary, `messages.xml`. It will contain the extracted string:

```
<?xml version="1.0" encoding="UTF-8"?>
<!DOCTYPE xliff PUBLIC "-//XLIFF//DTD XLIFF//EN"
  "http://www.oasis-open.org/committees/xliff/documents/xliff.dtd">
<xliff version="1.0">
  <file source-language="EN" target-language="en_US" datatype="plaintext"
    original="messages" date="2010-10-09T06:22:52Z" product-name="messages">
    <header/>
    <body>
      <trans-unit id="1">
        <source>The latest news</source>
        <target/>
      </trans-unit>
    </body>
  </file>
</xliff>
```

code snippet /symfony/apps/frontend/i18n/en_US/messages.xml

XML Localization Interchange File Format (XLIFF) is a recognized XML standard used in localization. It was standardized in 2002 by OASIS, a group of localization service and localization tools providers, and it is used widely in the localization industry. You can grab its full specifications at its website: `http://docs.oasis-open.org/xliff/xliff-core/xliff-core.html`.

The following command deletes old (no longer used) localization strings and saves the new ones:

```
$ symfony i18n:extract --auto-save --auto-delete frontend en_US
```

To add another language, just run the `extract` command with another target culture:

```
$ symfony i18n:extract --auto-save --auto-delete frontend pl_PL
```

You will get another source-target pair in your XLIFF dictionary. Now you can add a `<target>` segment with localized text just after the `<source>` segment. Try to do that with a language of your choice, as shown in bold in the following code:

```
<?xml version="1.0" encoding="UTF-8"?>
<!DOCTYPE xliff PUBLIC "-//XLIFF//DTD XLIFF//EN" "http://www.oasis-open.org/
   committees/xliff/documents/xliff.dtd">
<xliff version="1.0">
  <file source-language="EN" target-language="pl_PL" datatype="plaintext"
```

```
    original="messages" date="2010-10-09T06:22:52Z" product-name="messages">
     <header/>
     <body>
       <trans-unit id="1">
         <source>The latest news</source>
         <target>Najnowsze wiadomości</target>
       </trans-unit>
     </body>
   </file>
</xliff>
```

code snippet /symfony/apps/frontend/i18n/pl_PL/messages.xml

Now all you have to do is to set the corresponding culture in your `i18wrox` action:

```
$this->getUser()->setCulture('pl_PL');
```

Remember to clear your cache because Symfony may hold in its cache old translated strings, which forces it to generate new files:

```
$ symfony cc
```

The result looks like Figure 14-1: the translatable string is displayed in Polish, and the other is not translated, just as you wanted.

Najnowsze wiadomości
Not translated string

FIGURE 14-1: The translated message

There is another group of useful helpers that can do wonders with dates. It is best to display dates through an internationalization filter because they can be adjusted to user culture by default. The `Date` helper is shown in the following code:

```
<?php use_helper('Date') ?>
```

It provides the following methods:

- `format_date()` — Displays a formatted date. You can use predefined formats or custom ones.
- `format_datetime()` — Formatted date and time of day
- `time_ago_in_words()` — Describes in words how much time has passed since a date; for example, *2 `months`*
- `format_daterange()` — Displays a formatted range of dates; for example, *`from 1939-09-01 to 1945-05-08`*
- `distance_of_time_in_words()` — Describes in words a time distance between two dates

The methods providing textual output will translate the output according to the user culture or the default culture.

There is also a specialized helper for numbers and currency:

```
<?php use_helper('Number') ?>
```

It provides the following methods:

- `format_number()` — Returns the number formatted according to user's culture. This includes the decimal separator and the thousands separator.
- `format_currency()` — Provides a string with the numeric value formatted as a chosen currency, with the currency symbol displayed to the correct side of the number.

An example of the `indexSuccess.php` template created for the U.S. culture is presented in the following code snippet. Figure 14-2 shows the visual output of this template. All dates, numbers, and currency are displayed using standard U.S. locale.

Available for download on Wrox.com

```
<?php
use_helper('Date');
use_helper('Number');
echo 'Date: '.format_date(time()).'<br />';
echo 'Date and time: '.format_datetime(time()).'<br />';
echo 'Number: '.format_number(123456.78).'<br />';
echo 'Currency: '.format_currency(12345, 'USD');
```

code snippet /symfony/apps/frontend/modules/i18nexample/templates/indexSuccess.php

Date: 10/19/10
Date and time: October 19, 2010 5:50:42 AM CEST
Number: 123,456.78
Currency: $12,345.00

FIGURE 14-2: Output formatted for U.S. English culture

And the same file using Polish culture looks as follows:

Available for download on Wrox.com

```
<?php
use_helper('Date');
use_helper('Number');
echo 'Data: '.format_date(time()).'<br />';
echo 'Data i godzina: '.format_datetime(time()).'<br />';
echo 'Liczba: '.format_number(123456.78).'<br />';
echo 'Waluta: '.format_currency(12345, 'PLN');
```

code snippet /symfony/apps/frontend/modules/i18nexample/templates/indexSuccess.php

Figure 14-3 shows the output. See how everything has changed: The short date is displayed using the *DD-MM-YY* pattern, the long date uses the Polish month name and 24h clock, the decimal separator is changed to the comma, and the currency symbol (`zł`) is automatically displayed to the right of the numeric value.

Data: 19-10-10
Data i godzina: 19 października 2010 05:56:34 CEST
Liczba: 123 456,78
Waluta: 12 345,00 zł

FIGURE 14-3: Output formatted for Polish culture

Forms

Symfony's Form Helper allows you to create several useful forms. First you need to include this helper:

```
<?php use_helper('Form') ?>
```

The following i18n forms are available. They allow users to choose their date and time formats as well as country, language, and other locale. There are also corresponding validators. The form names are pretty self-explanatory:

- sfWidgetFormI18nDate
- sfWidgetFormI18nDateTime
- sfWidgetFormI18nTime
- sfWidgetFormI18nChoiceCountry
- sfWidgetFormI18nChoiceCurrency
- sfWidgetFormI18nChoiceLanguage
- sfWidgetFormI18nChoiceTimezone
- sfValidatorI18nChoiceCountry
- sfValidatorI18nChoiceLanguage
- sfValidatorI18nChoiceTimezone

Most of these widgets, as well as forms in general, are described in detail in Chapter 5.

It is possible to display the same fields in multiple languages, using a schema. The following code illustrates this:

Available for download on Wrox.com

```
<?php
class NewsForm extends BaseNewsForm {
  public function configure() {
    $this->embedI18n(array('en', 'pl'));
    $this->widgetSchema->setLabel('en', 'English');
    $this->widgetSchema->setLabel('pl', 'Polski');
  }
}
```

code snippet /symfony/lib/form/doctrine/NewsForm.class.php

Generate an administration module:

```
$ symfony doctrine:generate-admin frontend news
```

Now when you access `http://localhost/index.php/news` in your browser, you can manage the module. It looks like Figure 14-4.

FIGURE 14-4: Form for multilingual news editing

Using a Database for i18n

Another advanced approach is to use a database as a repository for translated strings. This can be very efficient for larger websites. Create the following schema:

```
News:
  actAs:
    I18n:
      fields: [title,description]
  columns:
    title: { type: string(150) }
    description: { type: string(150) }
```

code snippet /symfony/config/doctrine/schema.yml

Now use the `doctrine:build` command-line tool to create tables based on this schema:

```
$ symfony doctrine:build --all
```

This code generates the following tables. There is the source `news` table that holds the `EN` strings and the `news_translation` table related to `news`. It holds the ID of the source, the translated string, and the language of translation. Note that the primary key is composed from `ID` and `lang` because a source sentence can be translated to multiple targets:

```
news table:
+-------------+-------------+------+-----+---------+----------------+
| Field       | Type        | Null | Key | Default | Extra          |
+-------------+-------------+------+-----+---------+----------------+
| id          | bigint(20)  | NO   | PRI | NULL    | auto_increment |
+-------------+-------------+------+-----+---------+----------------+
news_translation table:
+-------------+-------------+------+-----+---------+-------+
| Field       | Type        | Null | Key | Default | Extra |
+-------------+-------------+------+-----+---------+-------+
```

```
| id          | bigint(20)   | NO   | PRI | 0       |       |
| title       | varchar(150) | YES  |     | NULL    |       |
| description | varchar(150) | YES  |     | NULL    |       |
| lang        | char(2)      | NO   | PRI |         |       |
+-------------+--------------+------+-----+---------+-------+
```

Now you can easily get the translated data using the following code in a controller:

```
$this->news = Doctrine::getTable('News')->findAll();
```

Now you can get all records and choose a specific translation. Or (even better) you can create a query that returns data for the specified language only. This is how a view that utilizes the data from the above controller could look:

```
<?php foreach ($news as $n): ?>
<?php echo $n['Translation']['pl']['description']; ?>
<?php echo $n['Translation']['pl']['title']; ?>
<?php echo $n['Translation']['en']['description']; ?>
<?php echo $n['Translation']['en']['title']; ?>
<?php endforeach; ?>
```

code snippet /symfony/apps/frontend/modules/i18nexample/templates/indexSuccess.php

It displays the title and full description in both languages.

Add-ons

There are several Symfony plug-ins that can speed up and ease the i18n process:

- **mgI18nPlugin** — Adds a translation panel into the debug web panel. It displays all source-target pairs for the current page, and a form that allows you to edit the target strings: `http://www.symfony-project.org/plugins/mgI18nPlugin`
- **zxI18nRoutingPlugin** — A smart plug-in that allows you to translate routing paths: `http://www.symfony-project.org/plugins/zxI18nRoutingPlugin`
- **sfDoctrineCultureFlagsPlugin** — Automatically adds links to localized versions of your web pages and decorates them with little country flags: `http://www.symfony-project.org/plugins/sfDoctrineCultureFlagsPlugin`
- **sfI18NGettextPluralPlugin** — Allows support of complex plural forms of some languages. Also fixes a bug where Symfony doesn't tokenize plural forms: `http://www.symfony-project.org/plugins/sfI18NGettextPluralPlugin`
- **sfFormI18nNumberPlugin** — Validates numbers: `http://www.symfony-project.org/plugins/sfFormI18nNumberPlugin`

There are also some language-specific plug-ins, like these two:

- **brFormExtraPlugin** — Brazilian widgets and validators: `http://www.symfony-project.org/plugins/brFormExtraPlugin`
- **sfSlovenianPlugin** — Slovenian translations of core Symfony messages: `http://www.symfony-project.org/plugins/sfSlovenianPlugin`

CAKEPHP

CakePHP has a few nice features, such as a command-line interface (CLI) tool similar to the one offered by Symfony and a database loaded from schema, although it offers no additional i18n plug-ins and it lacks in the area of forms translation.

Configuration

CakePHP requires no special configuration; you can use its console tool right away:

```
$ cake i18n
```

Cake's i18n shell has the form of a wizard that guides you through the process. This friendly, straightforward approach makes it significantly easier for beginners to include internationalization in their web applications.

```
Welcome to CakePHP v1.2.4.x Console
---------------------------------------------------------------
App : wrox
Path: /home/wrox
---------------------------------------------------------------
I18n Shell
---------------------------------------------------------------
[E]xtract POT file from sources
[I]nitialize i18n database table
[H]elp
[Q]uit
```

The database initialization command will be used later in this section; for now, the focus is on extracting strings from the sources.

Templates

Run the `cake i18n` tool and choose `[E]` to start extracting translatable strings from the source files. Make sure that the path for extraction points to your application's root folder. When CakePHP asks you whether you want to merge all translations into one file, answer yes `[y]`, and when it asks you to name the translation output file, you can leave the default or name it after your default language. For this example, the name is `en`.

The bold parts of the following example designate the input. If no user input is present, that means the proposed value was accepted:

```
What is the full path you would like to extract?
Example: /home/wrox/public_html/i18n/myapp
[Q]uit
[/home/wrox/public_html/i18n/app] >

What is the full path you would like to output?
Example: /home/wrox/public_html/i18n/app/locale
[Q]uit
[/home/wrox/public_html/i18n/app/locale] >

Extracting...
```

```
---------------------------------------------------------------
Path: /home/wrox/public_html/i18n/app
Output Directory: /home/wrox/public_html/i18n/app/locale/
---------------------------------------------------------------
Would you like to merge all translations into one file? (y/n)
[y] >
What should we name this file?
[default] > en
Processing /home/wrox/public_html/i18n/app/index.php...
Processing /home/wrox/public_html/i18n/app/config/acl.ini.php...
Processing /home/wrox/public_html/i18n/app/config/bootstrap.php...
Processing /home/wrox/public_html/i18n/app/config/core.php...
Processing /home/wrox/public_html/i18n/app/config/database.php...
Processing /home/wrox/public_html/i18n/app/config/routes.php...
Processing /home/wrox/public_html/i18n/app/config/schema/db_acl.php...
Processing /home/wrox/public_html/i18n/app/config/schema/i18n.php...
Processing /home/wrox/public_html/i18n/app/config/schema/sessions.php...
Processing /home/wrox/public_html/i18n/app/webroot/css.php...
Processing /home/wrox/public_html/i18n/app/webroot/index.php...
Processing /home/wrox/public_html/i18n/app/webroot/test.php...
Done.
```

You can watch the files being processed one after another. The previous code will generate the `en.pot` localization file, shown in the following code:

Available for download on Wrox.com

```
#: /webroot/test.php:88
msgid "Debug setting does not allow access to this url."
msgstr ""
```

code snippet /cakephp/app/locale/default.pot

The file now contains only one translatable error message from the `/webroot/test.php` file. Add a new controller, a model, and a view to check how CakePHP's i18n works with your classes. First, create a new dummy controller called `news_controller.php`:

Available for download on Wrox.com

```
<?php
class NewsController extends AppController {
    function index() {
    }
}
```

code snippet /cakephp/app/controllers/news_controller.php

Then create a dummy `news.php` model as well:

Available for download on Wrox.com

```
<?php
class News extends AppModel {
}
?>
```

code snippet /cakephp/app/models/news.php

Also make an index view that will contain only a string to translate. The string is surrounded by `__()`, just as in Symfony. Remember that there are two underscores in the front:

```
<?php echo __("Internationalization in CakePHP"); ?>
```

code snippet /cakephp/app/views/news/index.ctp

Now execute the extract command again:

```
$ cake i18n extract
```

You will be able to observe in the output the new files created by you:

```
Processing /home/wrox/public_html/i18n/app/controllers/news_controller.php...
Processing /home/wrox/public_html/i18n/app/models/news.php...
Processing /home/wrox/public_html/i18n/app/views/news/index.ctp...
```

The resulting file, `default.po`, will contain two entries now:

```
#: /views/news/index.ctp:1
msgid "I18n in CakePHP!"
msgstr ""

#: /webroot/test.php:88
msgid "Debug setting does not allow access to this url."
msgstr ""
```

code snippet /cakephp/app/locale/default.pot

To provide translations for other languages, copy this file into the appropriate folders inside `/app/locale/`. Just as `/app/locale/eng/` is the folder for the English language, you need folders for the target languages. In this example, these folders are `/app/locale/ind/` for Hindi and `/app/locale/pol/` for Polish. Edit the `msgstr ""` line, inserting the Hindi phrase (`"CakePHP में अंतर्राष्ट्रीयकरण"`) into `/app/locale/ind/default.po` and the Polish phrase (`"Wielojęzyczność w CakePHP"`) into `/app/locale/pol/default.po`. If you have trouble writing non-ASCII characters, just write anything else instead.

Now you can edit the `Config.language` property in the controller to change the language, as shown in the following code. The outputs for these three languages are juxtaposed in Figure 14-5.

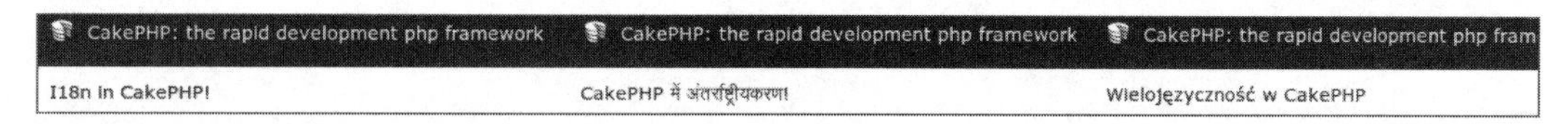

FIGURE 14-5: Internationalization in CakePHP in multiple languages

```
<?php
class NewsController extends AppController {
    function index() {
        $this->Session->write('Config.language', 'pol');
    }
}
```

code snippet /cakephp/app/controllers/news_controller.php

You can set the default language in the `core.php` configuration file by adding this line at the end of this file:

Available for download on Wrox.com

```
Configure::write('Config.language', "pol");
```

code snippet /cakephp/app/config/core.php

Forms

CakePHP has some problems with forms localization. It is not really convenient, and many other frameworks have similar problems. Unfortunately, the translatable form parts must be saved as HTML and not using the `$form` helper. The following code is a workaround that makes it possible to have form labels translated at all. The output for this example looks like the form in Figure 14-6.

Available for download on Wrox.com

```
<h1><?php echo __("Add a news"); ?></h1>
<?php echo $form->create('News'); ?>
  <label for="NewsTitle"><?php echo __("Title"); ?></label>
    <?php echo $form->input('title',array('label'=>'')); ?>
  <label for="NewsDescription"><?php echo __("Description"); ?></label>
    <?php echo $form->input('description',array('label'=>'')); ?>
  <input type="submit" name="submit" value="<?php __("Add"); ?>" />
<?php echo $form->end(); ?>
```

code snippet /cakephp/app/views/news/index.ctp

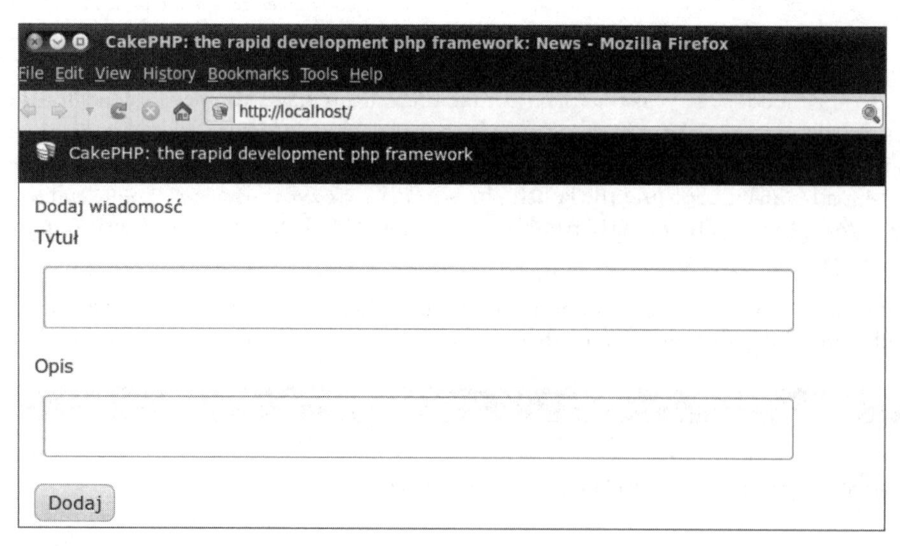

FIGURE 14-6: Form labels translated into Polish

Using a Database for i18n

Storing translations in a database is a convenient and effective way of localizing web applications in CakePHP. First you must set up your database connection in `/app/config/database.php`. Then manually create the database tables. These steps were described in detail in Chapters 3 and 4. Now you are ready to generate the schema:

```
$ cake schema generate
```

The output of schema generation is the following:

```
Welcome to CakePHP v1.x Console
---------------------------------------------------------------
App: app
Path: /home/wrox/public_html/i18n/app
---------------------------------------------------------------
Cake Schema Shell
---------------------------------------------------------------
Generating Schema...
Schema file: schema.php generated
```

Well, the `news.php` schema was generated, but where was it saved? You can find it in `/app/config/schema` and it looks like this:

Available for download on Wrox.com

```
<?php
class newsSchema extends CakeSchema {
    var $name = 'news';
    function before($event = array()) {
        return true;
    }
    function after($event = array()) {
    }
    var $news = array(
        'id' => array('type' => 'integer', 'null' => false,
            'default' => NULL, 'length' => 5, 'key' => 'primary'),
        'title' => array('type' => 'string', 'null' => true,
            'default' => NULL, 'length' => 150),
        'description' => array('type' => 'string', 'null' => true,
            'default' => NULL, 'length' => 150),
        'indexes' => array('PRIMARY' => array('column' => 'id', 'unique' => 1))
    );
}
?>
```

code snippet /cakephp/app/config/schema/news.php

You can create this file manually instead. If you want to generate this file, you need to run the following command:

```
$ cake schema create news news
```

And if everything went well, you will see the following output:

```
Welcome to CakePHP v1.x Console
---------------------------------------------------------------
App: app
Path: /home/wrox/public_html/app
---------------------------------------------------------------
```

```
Cake Schema Shell
---------------------------------------------------------------

The following table(s) will be dropped.
news
Are you sure you want to drop the table(s)? (y/n)
[n] > y
Dropping table(s).
news updated.

The following table(s) will be created.
news
Are you sure you want to create the table(s)? (y/n)
[y] > y
Creating table(s).
news updated.
End create.
```

Additionally, you have to initialize the i18n table whether the schema was created automatically or manually. Run the following command:

```
$ cake i18n
```

The CakePHP console will ask you which i18n tasks you would like to perform. Answer `[I]`:

```
Welcome to CakePHP v1.x Console
---------------------------------------------------------------
App: app
Path: /home/wrox/public_html/app
---------------------------------------------------------------
I18n Shell
---------------------------------------------------------------
[E]xtract POT file from sources
[I]nitialize i18n database table
[H]elp
[Q]uit
What would you like to do? (E/I/H/Q)
> I
```

You must answer two questions, as shown in the following listing. First you are asked if you want to drop (delete) your current i18n database. Agree unless you already have some important data there. Next you are asked if you want to re-create this table. Answer yes to finish the process.

```
Welcome to CakePHP v1.x Console
---------------------------------------------------------------
App: app
Path: /home/wrox/public_html/app
---------------------------------------------------------------
Cake Schema Shell
---------------------------------------------------------------

The following table(s) will be dropped.
i18n
Are you sure you want to drop the table(s)? (y/n)
[n] > y
```

```
Dropping table(s).
i18n updated.

The following table(s) will be created.
i18n
Are you sure you want to create the table(s)? (y/n)
[y] > y
Creating table(s).
i18n updated.
End create.
```

The following table will be created:

```
+-------------+--------------+------+-----+---------+----------------+
| Field       | Type         | Null | Key | Default | Extra          |
+-------------+--------------+------+-----+---------+----------------+
| id          | int(10)      | NO   | PRI | NULL    | auto_increment |
| locale      | varchar(6)   | NO   | MUL | NULL    |                |
| model       | varchar(255) | NO   | MUL | NULL    |                |
| foreign_key | int(10)      | NO   | MUL | NULL    |                |
| field       | varchar(255) | NO   | MUL | NULL    |                |
| content     | text         | YES  |     | NULL    |                |
+-------------+--------------+------+-----+---------+----------------+
```

Before you start translating your strings, first indicate in the model which fields should be translated, as shown here:

Available for download on Wrox.com

```
<?php
class News extends AppModel {
  var $name = 'News';
  var $actsAs = array(
    'Translate' => array(
        'title', 'description'
    )
  );
}
?>
```

code snippet /cakephp/app/models/news.php

The form used for adding content was shown in Figure 14-6. The controller method that handles this form is presented here. The bold line sets the Polish locale. You can modify it to add translations for other languages.

Available for download on Wrox.com

```
function add() {
    if ($this->data) {
        $this->News->locale = 'pol';
        $this->News->create();
        if ($this->News->save($this->data)) {
            $this->redirect(array('action' => 'index'));
        }
    }
}
```

code snippet /cakephp/app/controllers/news_controller.php

Add some content using the form and the method shown in the preceding code. In this example, "nowa wiadomość" was written into the title field, and "bardzo ważna" into description. Now when you look in the database, you can find the following data in the i18n table:

```
select * from i18n;
+----+--------+-------+-------------+-------------+----------------+
| id | locale | model | foreign_key | field       | content        |
+----+--------+-------+-------------+-------------+----------------+
|  1 | pol    | News  |           1 | title       | nowa wiadomość |
|  2 | pol    | News  |           1 | description | bardzo ważna   |
+----+--------+-------+-------------+-------------+----------------+
2 rows in set (0.00 sec)
```

As you can see, CakePHP stores the values for each translated field separately, with the field name as an identifier. If you want to get all records, you can call in a controller the find() method on a model to fill the *$data* variable with translated values, as shown here:

```
$this->set('data',$this->News->find());
```

Then display this data in a view:

```
<?php print_r($data); ?>
```

For this example, you will see the following output, each record listed with its translations:

```
Array ( [News] => Array ( [id] => 1 [title] => nowa wiadomość
  [description] => bardzo ważna [locale] => pol ) )
```

Add-ons

Unfortunately, CakePHP doesn't offer any add-ons. However, its core features seem quite sufficient, so it is not a big drawback.

ZEND FRAMEWORK

Zend Framework has two libraries designed to help you with application localization: Zend_Translate and Zend_Locale. The Zend_Translate library is focused on translating texts, while Zend_Locale deals with other aspects of localization, such as date formats or decimal separators.

Configuration

You need to set the default language. Add the following line into application.ini:

```
resources.locale.default = "en"
```

Zend_Locale provides a few libraries for various cultural settings, such as:

- Zend_Date
- Zend_Calendar
- Zend_Currency

Zend_Translate

`Zend_Translate` is a well-developed library that provides some useful translation tools. A family of adapters is one really great solution. Both Symfony and CakePHP force you to use one or two file formats, while ZF introduces an additional layer of adapters. This allows you to choose the file format of your translations from a long list of supported formats:

- `Array` — Just PHP arrays, good for special purposes.
- `csv` — Simple text, comma-separated values.
- `Gettext` — Binary files with the `.mo` extension for the Gettext GNU localization tool.
- `INI` — Text-based `.ini` files.
- `TBX` — TermBase eXchange `.tbx` files. An ISO standard for storage and exchange of terminology, used by professional-grade computer aided translation (CAT) tools.
- `TMX` — Translation Memory eXchange `.tmx` files. Open XML standard used by CAT tools for the exchange of translation memories. Translation memories store whole segments of text instead of single terms.
- `Qt` — QT Linguist `.ts` files, for use with the QT programming framework.
- `XLIFF` — XLIFF `.xliff/xml` files.
- `XMLTM` — Similar to the TMX, XML-based format.
- `SQL` — Database queries stored as `.sql` files.

XLIFF format is used by Symfony, and sometimes stored also as `.xml` files. CakePHP uses a custom POT format, similar to INI. But Zend Framework, by allowing so many formats, is the true winner here.

An example for an INI adapter is shown here:

```
$translate = new Zend_Translate(
    array(
        'adapter' => 'ini',
        'content' => /home/wrox/public_html/application/translations/en.ini,
        'locale'  => 'pl_PL'
    )
);
```

Zend_Locale

Zend introduces the `Zend_Locale` library that allows setting locale time and date according to a user's culture. The following code sets two dates: one using a U.S. locale and the second one using a Polish locale:

```
<?php
class IndexController extends Zend_Controller_Action {
    public function init() {
    }
    public function indexAction() {
```

```
        $usLoc = new Zend_Locale('en_US');
        $this->view->dateUS=new Zend_Date(date("Y-m-d"), null, $usLoc);
        $plLoc = new Zend_Locale('pl_PL');
        $this->view->datePL=new Zend_Date(date("Y-m-d"), null, $plLoc);
    }
}
```

code snippet /zf/application/controllers/IndexController.php

Create the following simple view that displays these two dates. The output is presented in Figure 14-7.

```
<?php echo $this->dateUS; ?><br />
<?php echo $this->datePL; ?>
```

code snippet /zf/application/views/scripts/index/index.phtml

```
Oct 13, 2010 12:00:00 AM
13-10-2010 00:00:00
```

FIGURE 14-7: The same date and time in two different formats

You can use the locale module directly in the view, too:

```
<?php
$date =  new Zend_Date();
echo $date; ?><br />
```

Translation

ZF provides a translation library: `Zend_Translate`. A sample view file using a simple `array` adapter is presented here (while developing a real app, you should move the translation part into a controller, leaving only the presentation in the view):

```
<html>
  <head>
    <meta content="text/html; charset=UTF-8" http-equiv="content-type">
  </head>
  <body>
    <?php
      $english = array('hello' => 'Hello World!');
      $polish = array('hello' => 'Witaj Świecie!');
      $hindi = array('hello' => 'नमस्ते विश्व!');
      $translate = new Zend_Translate(
          array('adapter' => 'array','content' => $english,'locale'  => 'en')
      );
      $translate->addTranslation(array('content' => $polish, 'locale' => 'pl'));
      $translate->addTranslation(array('content' => $hindi,  'locale' => 'hi'));
      $translate->setLocale('en');
      print $translate->_("hello").' <br />';
      $translate->setLocale('pl');
      print $translate->_("hello").' <br />';
      $translate->setLocale('hi');
```

```
        print $translate->_("hello").' <br />';
      ?>
    </body>
  </html>
```

code snippet /zf/application/views/scripts/index/index.phtml

Forms

The translation of forms works great in Zend Framework. It allows for translating form elements, which was not possible in CakePHP. The following code builds a single form and then displays it for three languages: Polish, English, and Hindi. First you need to build arrays of translations for each language. Then create an object of the `Zend_Translate` class. Use its `addTranslation()` method to feed it with the arrays for various locales. Finally you just echo the form when the chosen locale is set. You can see the results in Figure 14-8.

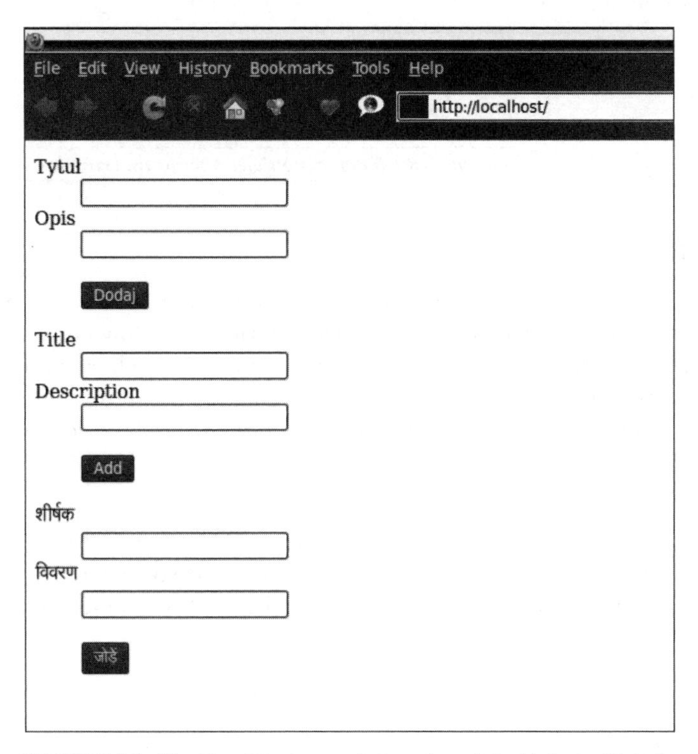

FIGURE 14-8: The Zend Framework form translated into multiple languages

```
<html>
  <head>
    <meta content="text/html; charset=UTF-8" http-equiv="content-type">
  </head>
  <body>
    <?php
      $english = array('Title' => 'Title','Description' => 'Description',Add'
```

```
            => 'Add');
        $polish = array('Title' => 'Tytuł','Description' => 'Opis',Add' => 'Dodaj');
        $hindi = array('Title' => 'शीर्षक', 'Description'=>'विवरण','Add' => 'जोड़ें');
        $translate = new Zend_Translate(
            array('adapter' => 'array', 'content' => $english,'locale'  => 'en')
        );
        $translate->addTranslation(array('content' => $polish, 'locale' => 'pl'));
        $translate->addTranslation(array('content' => $hindi,  'locale' => 'hi'));
        $form = new Zend_Form;
        $form->setAction('/news/add')->setMethod('post');
        $form->addElement('text','title',array('Label'=>'Title'));
        $form->addElement('text','description',array('Label'=>'Description'));
        $form->addElement('submit','add',array('Label'=>'Add'));
        $form->setDefaultTranslator($translate);
        $translate->setLocale('pl');
        echo $form;
        $translate->setLocale('en');
        echo $form;
        $translate->setLocale('hi');
        echo $form;
    ?>
  </body>
</html>
```

code snippet /zf/application/views/scripts/index/index.phtml

Using a Database for i18n

Getting translations from a database is supported by Zend Framework through an SQL adapter, but to achieve the same result as in Symfony or CakePHP you would have to write everything on your own. The approach using an SQL adapter allows you to translate static text, but it would be hard to support dynamic translations as it is presented in Symfony or CakePHP. One solution is to write a plug-in that will get the texts from a database. However, this solution requires a very large amount of code, and this book is meant to show what the frameworks can do rather than develop custom workarounds when they can't.

There is one more way to do this. Another functionality ZF lacks is a true ORM mapper. It turns out that if you integrate ZF with Doctrine, you can use Doctrine's features just as you can in Symfony. With one integration, you gain two important modules: an excellent ORM and full support for i18n databases.

Add-ons

Zend Framework provides so many libraries that in almost all cases there is no real need to use any external add-ons. Most of these add-ons available for use with ZF were not created solely for this framework and are not especially interesting.

15

Testing

Computers are good at following instructions, but not at reading your mind.

— Donald Knuth

WHAT'S IN THIS CHAPTER?

- Basic facts on enterprise software testing.
- Functional and unit testing.
- Using testing frameworks.
- Automated tests with Selenium.

Many people associate "testing" with measuring the performance of applications. These kinds of tests will be conducted in Chapter 17, but this chapter deals with testing on a much deeper level, namely testing whether an application works as expected or not. It is easy to underestimate this kind of testing because it may seem a trivial issue. Indeed, it is trivial for very small applications, but when they grow and gain new functionalities, testing becomes an indispensable part of the software development process. It is an area of computer science that focuses on the quality of software.

INTRODUCING TESTING

Imagine that you have just written a really cool app with abundant functionalities and you have instantly sold it at a premium price. However, after a week your customer wants his money back or even sues you because your software crashes once a day. So, you delivered a piece of software that could be really great, but in fact is useless for your customer. Generally speaking, software stability may be something not easily noticeable from a developer's point of view, but it is critical for end users who will work with this software every day in their environments.

How to Begin Testing

When starting a new project, some requirements for the final product must be established. A *requirement* is something a software quality engineer refers to while testing the software. It is good to start with making sure that all described requirements are comprehensible for everyone. That's why requirements are often presented as a list of stories and they are named as simply as possible; for example: *As a customer, I want to be able to use my credit card so that I can pay for products in my basket*. This story should then be described with as much detail as possible, but without overstatement.

There are various software development and maintenance methodologies. A good example of methodology that supports defining requirements is the Scrum methodology belonging to Agile software development techniques. Scrum provides the following template, which can be used to develop meaningful stories: As a <type of user>, I want <some goal> so that <some reason>. *It clearly defines the actor, the action, and the consequences of this story.*

Test Cases, Test Suites, and Test Coverage

Test cases, *test suites*, and *test coverage* are concepts commonly used in software quality assurance. We will start by describing these concepts in detail.

Test Case

A *test case* is nothing more than a list of steps and expected results. For example, assume that you need to test authentication functionality. To make sure that authentication works properly, you need to check that after filling out the login form we will be redirected to the main page if the authentication succeeds. So this test case could be defined as shown in the following table.

STEP	ACTION	EXPECTED RESULT
1	Go to the page `http://localhost/login`.	A page with a login form is displayed.
2	Fill out the username and password fields with `admin` and `secret` values.	Username is filled out with plain text, and password is filled out with hidden text.
3	Click the login button.	Form information is submitted.
4	Check the current page location.	The page location is `http://localhost/main`.

With the test case defined this way, you can to execute it easily because everything is clear — you know what action you need to execute and what the expectations are. All test cases must fulfill the requirements, which are defined before each functionality is implemented. Each requirement has its own acceptance criteria. Test cases also define steps to determine whether an application meets the acceptance criteria.

Note that the test case described in the preceding table doesn't really cover the requirement that authentication function properly because if the application accepted just any *username* and *password*, the test case would end successfully, but the application obviously wouldn't work properly and thus wouldn't meet the acceptance criteria. Each requirement in most cases needs more than one test case. Therefore, in the example you should also create additional test cases that check the negative scenario as well. An exemplary negative scenario test case is shown in the following table.

STEP	ACTION	EXPECTED RESULT
1	Go to the page `http://localhost/login`.	A page with a login form is displayed.
2	Fill out the username and password fields with the values `admin` and `wrongSecret`.	Username is filled out with plain text, and password is filled out with hidden text.
3	Click the login button.	Form information is submitted.
4	Check the current page location.	The page location is `http://localhost/login`.
5	Check the error message displayed.	Error message is *Wrong username/password. Please try again*.

Other test cases can be made to check the main page when it's shown after successful login. You are free to invent more test cases to cover the requirements. Each test case can end as successful or failed. If it fails, we can show exactly where it's failing, so searching for errors is easier. That's why test cases are so important when we want to deliver quality software.

Test Suite

Test suites are just collections of test cases. Test suites collect test cases testing the same general issue. Most often, test cases from one test suite are executed together to cover a whole functionality.

For the issue of login authentication, you can call the corresponding example test suite *AppLogin*, containing test cases such as *L001_PositiveLoginAdmin* and *L002_NegativeLoginAdmin*, and also *L003_PositiveLoginUser* or *L004_NegativeLoginUser*, because this test suite should cover not only administrators' authentication but also users who are not administrators. This test suite should cover all roles that are supported by this authentication module.

And what if you deliver authentication through web services as well? Should this also be covered by this test suite? In most cases, there are separate test suites because web services authentication is an additional functionality that is not implemented at the same time as web authentication. But this also depends on requirements. The same concerns all other functionalities — test suites are created to group test cases by functionality, implementation time, and application structure.

Test Coverage

Test coverage is a term that corresponds to the percentage of source code covered by test cases. It may be applied to the coverage of automated or manual tests of source code: code can be covered 50 percent through automated tests and 30 percent through manual tests. We may also speak of test coverage while testing concrete functionalities. We can say whether this functionality is covered by tests or not. A higher test coverage index usually results in higher software quality, but only if the tests are executed in a timely manner, of course.

Categories of Tests

There are two main layers of test categorization. The first layer divides tests into groups of automatic and manual tests. The second divides them into multiple purpose groups. These two layers are quite independent, so there can be a manual test used for build verification and an automatic test used for the same purpose. Let's take a closer look at the first layer of tests. The difference between them is the way they are executed. Manual tests are executed every time manually by software testers. Manual test cases need to be done step by step manually, so they are more time-consuming. On the other hand, they not only verify whether all operations provide correct output but also provide you with a look at its internal structure.

Black-box Tests

Black-box tests are so named because they follow the black-box scheme. In software testing this means that a tester doesn't know the code he is executing. Therefore we need to define the input of the application and then check the application's output (see Figure 15-1).

FIGURE 15-1: Black-box testing idea

The actual output is compared with the expected output value; if they are equal, the test case or step is checked as successful. The two authentication test cases described previously would be black-box tests if we didn't know the application's code. We don't know exactly what is done within the application's authentication module, but we know that we should be redirected to the main page if the authentication ends successfully.

To show the idea of black-box testing, we have used the Lime test framework that is used in Symfony. As you can see, the following code presents a step-by-step scenario that covers the previously defined test case. Note that we don't check each step because we assume that the `sfBrowser()` methods are doing this correctly. If login page loading fails, we should get an error within the `setField()` method because we will not be able to set a value to the username field. At the end, we check the result page. If both values are equal, the test case succeeds. Note that we are using only Lime classes and methods, so we do not interfere with the application's code.

```
<?php
include(dirname(__FILE__).'/../../bootstrap/functional.php');
$browser = new sfTestFunctional(new sfBrowser());
```

```
$browser->get('/security/index');
$browser->with('response')->begin()->isStatusCode(200);
$browser->setField('login', 'admin');
$browser->setField('password', 'secret');
$browser->click('submit');
$browser->end();
$response= $browser->getResponse();
$browser->with('response')->
isStatusCode(200);
$browser->test()->like($response->getContent(), '/Main page/');
```

White-box Tests

White-box tests, unlike black-box tests, are based on knowledge of the code that is being tested. The tester needs to have programming skills because he is testing the application at a lower level than in the case of black-box tests. The most popular tests that use white-box testing are unit tests. Unit tests cover the application at the source code level. The tester invokes methods to complete a scenario that realizes a requirement. We have used PHPUnit here to show the main assumptions of white-box testing. It is one of the most popular test frameworks for PHP. An exemplary scenario that tests the authorization module can look as follows:

```
<?php
require_once("Auth.class.php");
class AuthTest extends PHPUnit_Framework_TestCase {
     protected $_auth = null;
     protected $_adminLogin = "admin";
     protected $_adminPassword = "secret";
     protected $_wrongLogin = "badAdmin";
     protected $_wrongPassword = "wrongSecret";
     public function setUp() {
         $this->_auth = new Auth();
     }
     public function tearDown() {
         unset($this->_auth);
     }
     public function testAdminLogin() {
            $result = $this->_auth->authenticate($this->_adminLogin,
            $this->_adminPassword);
            $this->assertTrue($result);
     }
     public function testAdminLoginNegative() {
            $result = $this->_auth->authenticate($this->_wrongLogin,
            $this->_wrongPassword);
            $this->assertTrue($result);
     }
}
```

The preceding code has two test cases: *AdminLogin* and *AdminLoginNegative*. Unlike black-box testing, in this case we invoke authorization class methods, so we use the code that was written by developers. After getting the result of authentication, we need to check whether it is a `true` value. If yes, the test case ends successfully.

Grey-box Tests

Grey-box tests are in fact a combination of black- and white-box tests. Application testing is done at the black-box level, but with knowledge of the application's data structures and algorithms. Note that in black-box testing, the data that is input can be given blindly.

Smoke Tests

Smoke tests are a group of tests that check the most important functionalities. *Most important* means that these are vital functionalities that are needed for an application to make sense.

Suppose you are developing a banking application. If the funds-transfer functionality of this application has *blocking bugs* (bugs that don't allow the application to proceed to the next step), the product doesn't make sense for any bank and it must be repaired as soon as possible. Imagine what would happen if you delivered a product without the main functionalities. To prevent that situation, smoke tests should be executed before delivery of every version of the product. These tests are also used in situations when developers deliver a new module and want to know if the whole program still works as designed. Smoke tests are very short tests that should take only a small part of the execution time of all tests.

Performance, Load, and Stress Tests

Load tests and stress tests are sometimes recognized as subgroups of performance tests, but they really aren't. They are properly separate test groups because their goals are different, even if the tools used to execute them are the same.

With *performance tests,* you search for bottlenecks in your application. Performance can be measured in throughput, response times, scalability, or resource usage. The goal is to find places in our application where we can improve it to handle more web clients. For example, you can reduce HTML or CSS files when it's possible, so you need less bandwidth for the same effect.

Load tests check applications' behaviors in situations when the load is high. For example, we can start 1,000 threads that log in and log out from our application 24 hours per day. Normally, memory usage should finally fix on one value at some moment when testing begins and stays constant for 24 hours. If it is increasing all the time, you probably forgot to free the application's unused memory and should look for such bugs.

Stress tests are responsible for testing the durability of our application against peak load. As an example, let's take a banking application. Stress tests will test how many transfers your application can serve in a fixed period of time. It may be able to handle 1,000 transfers at one moment. If the application is working properly with 1,000, you should increase the amount to 10,000, and so on. If the application starts to crash or behave in an unstable way, this is probably the application's transfer limit. It depends, of course, on the hardware on which it is executed, but we still can say that on this particular machine the limit is 10,000 transfers. Then this can be scaled to a more powerful hardware configuration to achieve better results.

A popular tool for performance, load, and stress tests is *Apache JMeter*, which is discussed and applied in Chapter 17.

Regression Tests

Regression tests are tests that are executed each time a new functionality is delivered. Scrum methodology states that these tests should be executed after each iteration ends. It depends on the situation, time, and human resources, but in most cases, whole tests are executed. *Whole tests* means all test cases, including both automated and manual test cases. The main reason for executing these tests is to check that nothing changed in the application since it was tested last time. In other words, we need to check that a new functionality didn't break any functionalities that were previously working correctly (the functionality passes all tests).

When to Finish Testing

How should you determine when you've done enough testing? This is a good question. In software development, there are three main determinants of software development: *cheap*, *fast*, or *good* (see Figure 15-2).

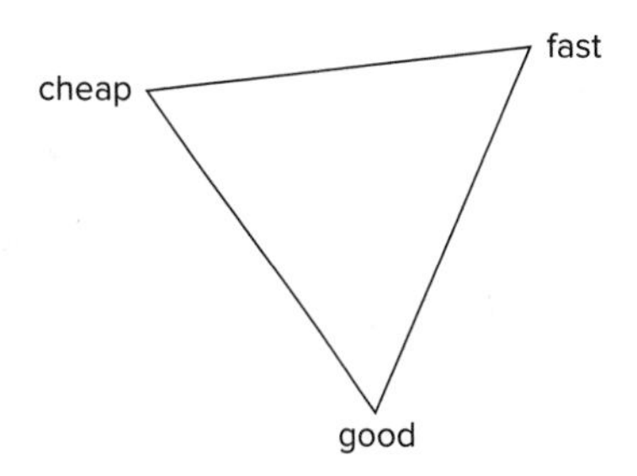

FIGURE 15-2: The testing triangle

It's important not to pay excessive attention to any single one of these requirements. A good practice is to choose the two that are most important to you and try to accomplish them. That approach will get you near the middle of the triangle shown in Figure 15-2, which is where you get the best results. You can try to reach the very middle, but it's really hard to do so. So if your application needs to be of good quality, you need to decide whether it needs to be done fast (then it cannot be done cheap) or cheap (then it cannot be done fast).

The problem is described here because it's related to testing. How many application functionalities we can cover with tests depends on how much time and money we have to do that. Each quality assurance (QA) engineer needs to be paid. Fewer QA workers need more time to cover the same functionalities. So before you start a project, you need to create a good testing plan that includes costs and time. Thanks to that plan, you can estimate when the testing would finish.

Bugs Are Your Friends

Undiscovered bugs are very dangerous because they are like ticking time bombs. You never know how much time you have left until they explode or how much damage they can inflict. You cannot be sure how many undiscovered bugs there are in your software, but the fewer of them, the better the application quality. Finding undiscovered bugs is the main job of testers. To get the best results, you need to cover as much of your code as possible with tests. Of course, this quality assurance has its price, so this goal should be balanced with your available costs and time.

The bugs you know are in fact a measure of the quality of your software. Developers make mistakes like everybody else, especially because their work is creative and innovational, so some bugs are inevitable. Up to a point, the more bugs you can locate, the better. However, there is a limit above which more bugs imply that the developers made too many mistakes and the initial quality of code was really low.

Each bug, when it is discovered, should be placed within a bug-tracking tool such as Bugzilla. The bug life cycle is shown in Figure 15-3. At the beginning, each bug has *new* status. In most cases it is then *assigned* to someone who will be responsible for it. If this is not assigned naturally to the person who wrote it, someone should be assigned to this responsibility anyway. When a bug is *assigned*, it may change the status back to *new*, but this does not happen often. More likely it may change the status from *new* to *resolved* without being *assigned*, if the problem described in a bug is fixed at once, without the need to assign anybody to it. The status is also changed from *assigned* to *resolved* when the bug is handled normally (that is, someone managed to solve it).

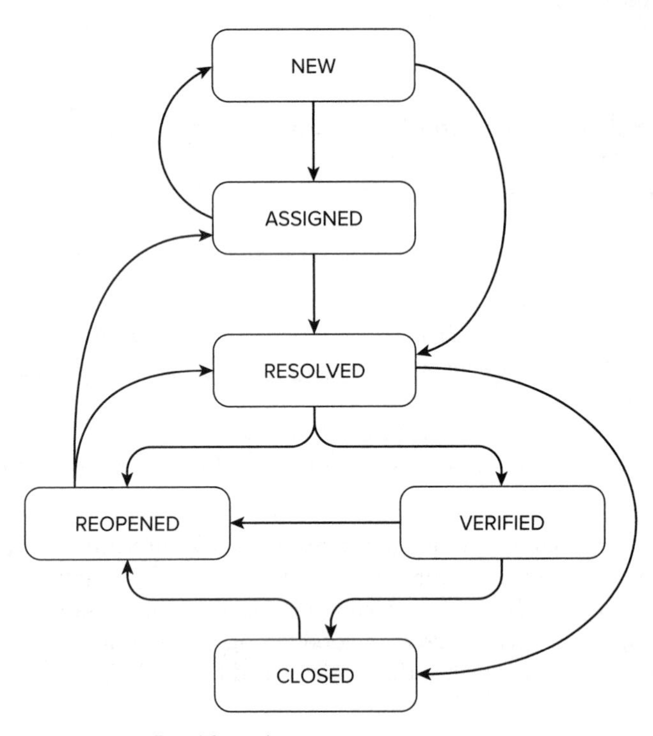

FIGURE 15-3 Bug life cycle

A bug can be handled in various ways. These conclusions are divided into the following groups, called resolutions: *duplicated*, *fixed*, *invalid*, *moved*, *won't fix*, and *works for me*. When one of these conditions is met, this bug has changed its status to *resolved*. If it's *duplicated*, this means that someone has already added a bug entry that covers this problem. There is no reason to fix the same issue more than once; that's why this bug entry needs to be ignored in future considerations. In bug-tracking tools, it's done gently by changing its status to *resolved* with its resolution set to *duplicated*. After that a *duplicated* bug can be *closed*. Most bugs, however, need to be repaired and get a *fixed* resolution afterward. Repairing or fixing bugs means repairing the problem within the application that constituted the issue within the bug description.

Invalid resolution means that this bug is not a real bug. Mostly, this resolution is added due to a mistake. Some bugs are not reproducible, so they were noticed only once. Another reason for this situation may be when you do testing on machines that are not configured properly. Each test case should be tested on a *clean machine*, which is prepared and meets all requirements. In other words, this is a machine that is identical to a typical machine the application's users will have. Let us illustrate this with an example. Assuming you are using Firefox, normally you don't install add-ons of unknown origin. One of these add-ons might interfere with your application and could generate bugs, which wouldn't exist without this add-on. Unless this add-on is commonly used or specifically required, such a conflict should not be considered a bug, but an exception. Additionally, this information should be included within the application's documentation.

The next resolution is *moved*, which means that this bug is related to a different product, so it should be moved to its bug tracker. It is not used when you develop only one application.

The next very interesting resolution is *won't fix*. This means that a developer agrees that it's a bug, but it cannot be fixed now or fixing it requires too much effort (this last case is sometimes denoted as another resolution, *postponed*). This resolution can be set only if the priority of this bug is low, it occurs in very rare situations, or it occurs in a functionality that is almost never used by users.

The last resolution is *works for me*. It is used in similar situations as in the case of the *invalid* resolution. Here a bug is also considered not to be a bug, but unlike *invalid*, a developer doesn't see any problem here at all. Another reason could be that it was confused with an actual feature. For example, some input fields may become inactive due to some other options.

Testers should check all *resolved* bugs to be certain they're really resolved. This is done mostly in situations when the resolution was set to *fixed*. In other cases, a tester should change the status to *closed*. Bugs are also *closed* after a tester ends bug verification and changes the status to *verified*. Note that closing bugs should not be done immediately after verification, but after a period of time, for example when Scrum iteration ends, the product is released, and so on. When it is *closed*, the bug normally ends its life.

When a resolved bug is verified negative, its status is changed to *reopen*. *Reopen* in most cases means the same as *assigned*, but the status was previously set as *resolved*. A reopened bug can be changed to *resolved* when a developer makes corrections based on testers' comments and suggestions. When the bug is *closed*, it shouldn't later be changed to any other status. But there are some exceptions when it can be reopened. These situations include development of a new version of the application with the old bug occurring again. The other reason can be when someone accidentally closed a bug that should not have been *closed*.

Fixtures

Fixtures are data sets created for testing purposes. Assume that you want to test some functionalities, but to make it possible, you need to have sample data imported into the database. These data sets are called fixtures. Fixtures can be stored as XML, YAML, or SQL files, but they also can be defined as a PHP class.

Imagine that you need to test a user's address list. You cannot start testing on production databases with real users because of the terrible consequences if something goes wrong. Therefore, you should use a different database for testing.

Another problem is loading and deleting a fixture's data. Note that for each test suite, you usually need different data within the database. That's why fixtures are loaded before each test suite is executed. You don't want to collect any previous testing results in the databases. Tests usually manipulate data stored in the database, but we want to have exactly the same data loaded every time. That's why you should flush the database after the test suite is done. Fixtures usage is shown in Figure 15-4.

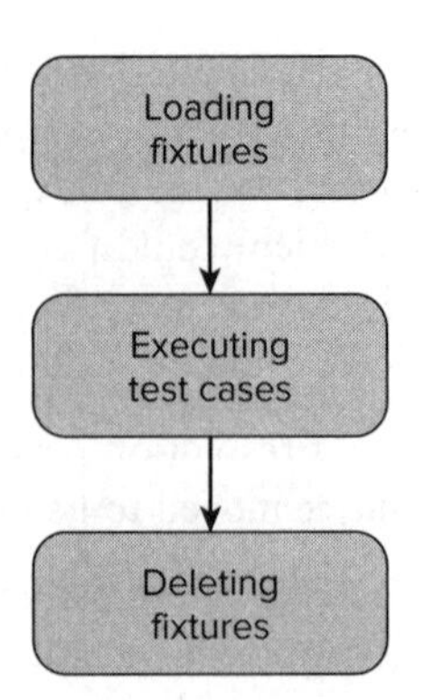

FIGURE 15-4: Fixtures usage

Mocks

You should not always test a whole application as one big system. Some functionalities need to be tested separately. But how do you test intertwined systems separately (for example, authentication without a user model)? The answer to this question: by using a *mock*. We use mocks to simulate objects to test other objects' behavior. If you create a mock that properly simulates a user model, you can test authentication for all unusual behaviors. Figure 15-5 shows how it works when you don't use mocks.

The authentication module consists of methods, classes, and libraries that are responsible for authentication. Authentication uses some libraries or models. When we put a mock between the authentication module and the user model, it will look like Figure 15-6.

As you can see, there is no connection between the user model and authentication. The connection could exist between the user model mock and the real user model if needed, but this is not the reason why we create mocks. In most cases there are no connections between mocks and the models simulated by these mocks.

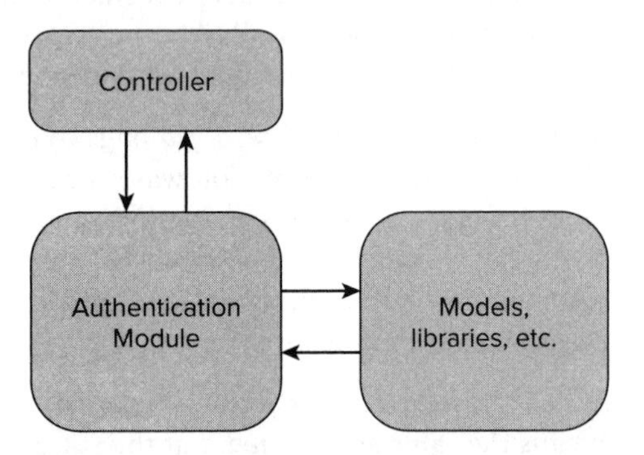

FIGURE 15-5: Exemplary authentication workflow

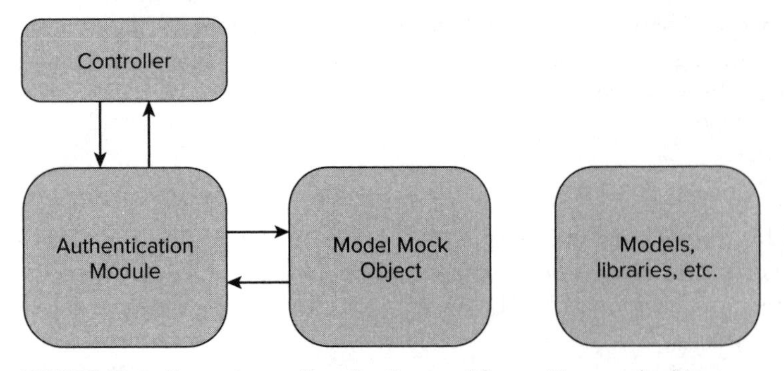

FIGURE 15-6: Exemplary authentication workflow with a mock object

Assume that you have an authentication class such as that shown in the following code. This class gets a `User` model object as the parameter while creating its instance. The `authenticate()` method returns a `true` value if the user has `$login` and `$password` fields; otherwise, it returns `false`.

```
<?php
class Authentication {
```

```
        protected $_User = null;
        public function __construct($User) {
            $this->_User = $User;
        }
        public function authenticate($login,$password) {
                $results=$User->get($login,md5($password));
                if($results) {
                    return true;
                }
                return false;
        }
    }
```

Mocks are used mostly within testing code. They could be used within development code as well, but this is not considered a good practice. A test case testing the authentication using mocks is presented here:

```
    <?php
    require_once 'Auth.php';
    class AuthTest extends PHPUnit_Framework_TestCase {
        public function testAdminAuth() {
            $UserMock = $this->getMock('User', array('get'));
            $UserMock->expects($this->any())
                     ->method('get')
                     ->will($this->returnValue(true'));
            $auth = new Authentication($UserMock);
            $this->assertTrue($auth->authenticate("admin","secret"));
        }
    }
```

The `$UserMock` variable keeps the mock that was generated by the `getMock()` method. The parameters of this method are class name and the array of methods that this mock will have. In this case, it is the `get()` method. Next you have to define the behavior of this mock. When you set `expects($this->any())`, it means that the method can be invoked many times. The `Authentication` class needs a user model, so the prepared mock is used instead of the real model. Finally, an assertion is executed. It checks whether the `authenticate()` method returns a `true` value; if not, an exception is thrown and the test case fails.

Test-Driven Development

The common approach to development is to write functionalities first and test them later. But there is another interesting approach called *test-driven development* (*TDD*). Using TDD, you don't wait for development of functionalities; you prepare test cases first. An advantage of this approach is that all requirements are well known before the first line of code is written. The main idea of TDD is shown in Figure 15-7.

After requirements are defined, we write test cases that cover these requirements. Only then do we develop modules that allow us to run these tests. If the tests fail, we need to change our source code until they succeed. Then we prepare new tests for new functionalities and iterate until all requirements are met. Of course, sometimes we need to change the tests as well if they do not cover the requirements properly.

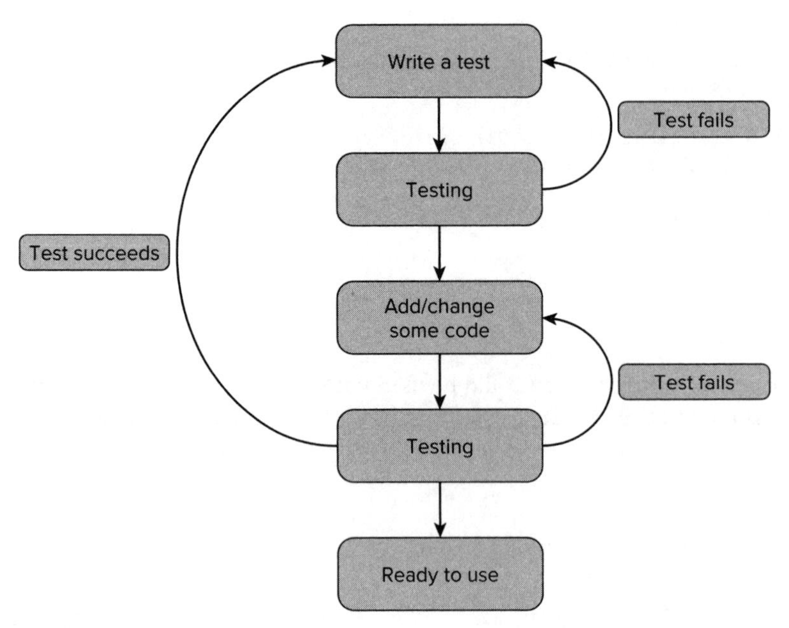

FIGURE 15-7: Graph of TDD

Test Frameworks

Each framework provides some tools and enhancements for Quality Assurance, such as specialized test frameworks and CLI commands. There are three commonly used test frameworks: *PHPUnit*, *SimpleTest*, and *Lime*.

PHPUnit

PHPUnit (the logo is shown in Figure 15-8) is probably the most popular test framework among the PHP frameworks. It's the default test framework in Symfony 2.0 and Zend Framework.

FIGURE 15-8: PHPUnit logo.

To install PHPUnit separately, you can use your Linux distribution package manager or PEAR. The latter is like installing Symfony or Zend Framework. You need to run this command first:

```
# pear channel-discover pear.symfony-project.com
```

You can also use PHPUnit's channel:

```
# pear channel-discover pear.phpunit.de
```

After adding the channel, you can commence installation using this command:

```
# pear install phpunit/PHPUnit
```

Note that you can now run the `PHPUnit` command:

```
$ phpunit
```

Symfony

If you want to install PHPUnit in Symfony 1.x, you should use the following command:

```
$ symfony plugin:install sfPhpunit2Plugin
```

Note that this command installs PHPUnit in version 2. We use the older version of PHPUnit in our Symfony examples because it's easier for beginners.

To install the newer version, you need to use the following command:

```
$ symfony plugin:install sfPhpUnitPlugin
```

After you install PHPUnit3, you can use Symfony's CLI tasks such as the following:

```
phpunit
  :generate-compat
  :generate-functional
  :generate-selenium
  :generate-unit
  :test-all
  :test-functional
  :test-selenium
  :test-unit
```

The first command makes it possible to use PHPUnit with older Symfony versions, such as 1.2. The next three commands generate sample test suites. The last four run the appropriate tests. They're very simple and easy to use. Note that all Symfony tasks are a kind of wrapper to the `phpunit` command. So you need to have PHPUnit already installed.

SimpleTest

SimpleTest (the logo is shown in Figure 15-9) is an alternative solution to PHPUnit. It is also a full-featured test framework, very popular as a stand-alone solution. Modified SimpleTest is the default framework for CakePHP.

FIGURE 15-9: SimpleTest logo.

CakePHP contributors don't include test framework libraries into CakePHP, which can be a little annoying. Do they assume that nobody tests their applications?! If the libraries are not installed, you will see the following error:

```
$ cake testsuite
Error: Sorry, Simpletest could not be found. Download it from http://simpletest.org
and install it to your vendors directory.
```

You need to download SimpleTest from `http://simpletest.org` and extract the package into the CakePHP projects `/app/vendors/` directory. Now you can start testing, and the error message will not be shown.

Apart from the `/vendors` directory where your SimpleTest libraries are placed, CakePHP also provides also a separate directory for test cases. The directory structure looks like this:

```
app/tests/
    cases/
```

```
        behaviors/
        components/
        controllers/
        helpers/
        models/
    fixtures/
    groups/
```

These directories are dedicated for test cases, fixtures, and groups of tests, respectively. Test cases are divided into those covering behaviors (such as ACL), components (such as Email), controllers, helpers, and models.

Zend Framework

ZF does not provide any CLI facilities in this case, but thanks to integrated PHPUnit, ZF gives us a lot of classes that are ready to use. If you installed Zend Framework with PEAR following the installation in Chapter 2, the test library is placed in `/usr/share/php/Zend/Test` (UNIX) or `C:\xampp\php\PEAR\Zend\Test` (Windows with XAMPP). These classes are (for example) `Zend_Test_PHPUnit_Db_Exception` or `Zend_Test_PHPUnit_ControllerTestCase`. ZF also provides a testing directory structure that looks like this:

```
application/
    bootstrap.php
library/
    bootstrap.php
phpunit.xml
```

You can configure your tests by editing `phpunit.xml`. This configuration file is used for running test cases with PHPUnit as follows:

```
$ phpunit --configuration phpunit.xml
```

Lime

This framework is used in Symfony 1.x. It is obsolete and is not used in Symfony 2.x as a part of the whole framework. We recommend that you use PHPUnit instead of Lime. We don't want to recommend bad practices, which is why we don't use Lime further in this chapter.

BLACK-BOX REGISTRATION FORM TESTING USING FUNCTIONAL TESTS

Black-box testing of web applications is done from the browser level as described earlier in this chapter. From the code-level perspective, there are two main testing approaches: unit and functional testing. Functional tests realize the black-box testing approach and we will describe them here.

Problem

First of all, you need to define an exemplary test case that will cover a simple user registration scenario, as shown in the following table. Assume a success scenario where everything goes as expected.

STEP	ACTION	EXPECTED RESULT
1	Go to the page `http://localhost/registration`.	A page with a registration form displays with login, password, repeat password, e-mail, forename, and surname fields.
2	Fill in the login, passwords, e-mail, forename, and surname fields with: login: `sampleUser`, password: `secret`, e-mail: `leszek.nowak@wrox.com`, forename: `Leszek`, and surname: `Nowak`.	The login, e-mail, forename, and surname fields are filled out with plain text, and the password fields are filled out with hidden text.
3	Click the register button.	Form information is submitted.
4	Check the current page location.	The page location is `http://localhost/thankyou`.

When someone fills out the registration form as above, a *Thank You* page will be shown. There are many other scenarios that should be considered, but to simplify let's consider only the above test case.

Solution

The solution is to implement a test case that covers the registration requirements. You need to use the frameworks' test frameworks to provide good-quality registration functionality. Assume that in each of our frameworks the registration form looks like this:

```
<form action="/registration/submit" method="POST">
<table>
     <tr>
         <th><label for="username">Username</label></th>
         <td><input type="text" name="username" id="username" /></td>
    </tr>
    <tr>
         <th><label for="password">Password</label></th>
         <td><input type="password" name="password" id="password" /></td>
    </tr>
    <tr>
         <th><label for="repeat_password">Repeat password</label></th>
         <td><input type="password" name="repeat_password" id="repeat_password"
         /></td>
    </tr>
    <tr>
         <th><label for="forename">Forename</label></th>
         <td><input type="text" name="forename" id="forename" /></td>
    </tr>
    <tr>
         <th><label for="surname">Surname</label></th>
         <td><input type="text" name="surname" id="surname" /></td>
    </tr>
    <tr>
```

```
            <th><label for="email">Email</label></th>
            <td><input type="text" name="email" id="email" /></td>
        </tr>
         <tr>
            <td colspan="2">
                <input type="submit" id="submit" name="submit" value="register" />
            </td>
         </tr>
    </table>
    </form>
```

code snippet /black-box/registration.html

It doesn't matter exactly how the form is formatted if it's within `<table></table>` or `<div></div>` HTML tags. It can be different from the HTML code perspective as long as it has `<input />` fields. After submitting it, you should use a redirecting function to move to the *Thank You* page. For Symfony and CakePHP, the redirecting function is `$this->redirect()`; for Zend Framework it's `$this->_redirect()`.

Symfony

Functional tests in Symfony are better done using Selenium. In Symfony 1.4 and later 1.x versions, the PHPUnit plug-in is delivered as a fake wrapper that in fact uses Lime in the background. PHPUnit is a solution we can recommend, while Lime leaves much to be desired. That's why we advise against using Symfony 1.x functional tests. If possible, please use Symfony 2.0 or the Selenium extension delivered within the PHPUnit2 plug-in for Symfony 1.x.

CakePHP

CakePHP is based on a modified version of the SimpleTest framework. Let's test the registration functionality. (Chapter 5 discusses what you need to do to implement a registration form.) The CakePHP testing approach requires that every test file name should end with `.test.php`. For this example, the filename will be `registration.test.php`. We are testing the controller, so you need to save this file into the `/app/tests/cases/controllers/` directory. Let's call the first test `RegistrationControllerTest` and add the `testRegistrationPositive()` method, which should load our registration page and check whether expected form fields exist. An exemplary test can look like the following:

Available for download on Wrox.com

```
<?php
class RegistrationFormTests extends WebTestCase {
    function testRegistrationPositive() {
        $this->get('http://localhost/registration');
        $this->assertField('username', '');
        $this->assertField('password', '');
        $this->assertField('repeat_password', '');
        $this->assertField('forename', '');
        $this->assertField('surname', '');
        $this->assertField('email', '');
    }
}
```

code snippet /black-box/cakephp/app/tests/cases/controllers/registration_controller.test.php

That's all you need for the first step. Why do we check to see whether form fields are blank? Because developers sometimes don't clean the code. By mistake, a *username* field can be set to something like `foo` or worse. This is a question for a QA engineer. Next, you need to fill out the registration form with proper data. The `setField()` method is used to set insert data into form input fields. The following code snippet illustrates how to do this:

```
$this->setField('username', 'admin');
$this->setField('password', 'secret');
$this->setField('repeat_password', 'secret');
$this->setField('forename', 'John');
$this->setField('surname', 'Smith');
$this->setField('email', 'john@example.com');
```

code snippet /black-box/cakephp/app/tests/cases/controllers/registration_controller.test.php

The preceding code needs to be placed after the `assertField()` methods within the `testRegistrationPositive()` method. We can, of course, believe our testing tools that they are setting form fields in the right way, but a good quality assurance engineer never trusts programs completely. That's why a good practice is to check registration form fields again. This time, we need to check whether values within the input fields are equal to those that we set earlier. We need to use the same `assertField()` method as previously, when we checked whether form fields are blank.

```
$this->assertField('username', 'admin');
$this->assertField('password', 'secret');
$this->assertField('repeat_password', 'secret');
$this->assertField('forename', 'John');
$this->assertField('surname', 'Smith');
$this->assertField('email', 'john@example.com');
```

code snippet /black-box/cakephp/app/tests/cases/controllers/registration_controller.test.php

These lines of code need to be placed after the `setField()` methods and within the `testRegistrationPositive()` method.

At this point, you are done with Step 2. In the next step, you will check whether the submit button can be pushed and whether any response is given. To click any field, you need to use the `click()` method. The `assertResponse()` method is dedicated to checking the response from the server. Step 3 should look like the following:

```
$this->click('submit');
$this->assertResponse(200);
```

This code needs to be added at the end of `testRegistrationPositive()`. In the last step, you expect to be redirected to a *Thank You* page. As shown in the following code, you need to get the current URL and compare it with the expected one. After that, you should also search page content for the expected text:

```
$current=$this->getUrl();
$this->assertEqual('http://localhost/index.php/thankyou',$current);
$this->assertText('Thank You');
```

The preceding code completes Step 4. Normally, you would be finished at this point, but when you go deeper into this test case you will see a lot of problems. What if the registration form is shown on the *Thank You* page? What if validation rules throw a validation error? These and more issues need to be coped with in further test cases. Use your imagination and write more test cases that cover the whole registration functionality.

Command-line Test Execution

CakePHP allows you to run tests from the command line. To test all written tests, you need to use the following command:

```
$ cake testsuite app all
```

This command starts with executing tests one by one. We have only one test case, so it should go fast. As a result, you see something similar to this:

```
Welcome to CakePHP v1.3 Console
---------------------------------------------------------------
App : app
Path: /home/wrox/public_html/cake/app
---------------------------------------------------------------
CakePHP Test Shell
---------------------------------------------------------------
Running app all
All App Tests
1/1 test cases complete: 15 passes.
```

As shown above, one test case is completed, and 15 assertions are passed. Note that assertions are those methods that make a test case fail if their conditions are not fulfilled. To run only the registration module, you need to run the following command:

```
$ cake testsuite app case controllers/registration
```

To learn more about allowed parameters, you need to run this command:

```
$ cake testsuite help
```

Web-based Test Execution

CakePHP, unlike Symfony or Zend Framework, delivers a great feature for web-level testing. To see all available test cases — those that you wrote and those delivered with CakePHP — you need to access `test.php` in the CakePHP `/webroot` directory. The right URL is `http://localhost/test.php` if your CakePHP application path is set in Apache to `http://localhost/`. When you access `test.php`, you should see something similar to Figure 15-10.

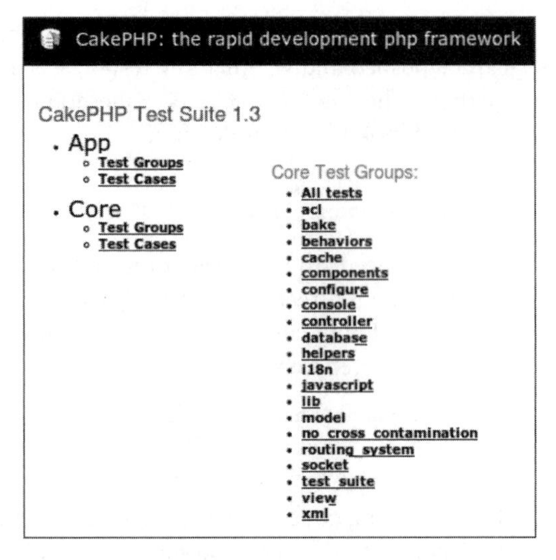

FIGURE 15-10: CakePHP — all tests from web level

If you choose Test Cases from the App group (refer to Figure 15-10), you should see only one test case, the one that you wrote if you completed the example earlier in this section. After clicking the name of the test case, you should see something similar to Figure 15-11.

You can see all assertions that have passed by clicking the Show Passes option.

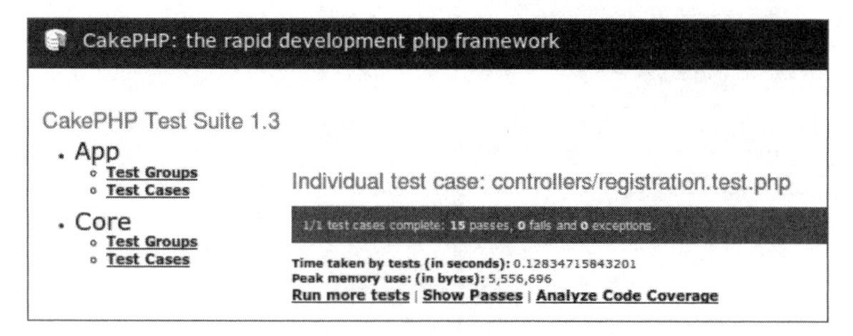

FIGURE 15-11: CakePHP — test execution results in the Web

Zend Framework

Zend Framework's functional tests are based on Selenium. We don't say that it's impossible to develop functional tests that work like CakePHP's tests, but just as with Symfony, we recommend using Selenium to accomplish this goal. The next section describes how to do this. Note that CakePHP uses SimpleTest, which doesn't support Selenium out of the box because SimpleTest has its own functional test solution. PHPUnit developers decided to use a known, existing solution and integrate it.

CMS TESTS AUTOMATION USING SELENIUM

Each tester or quality assurance engineer will confront test automation sooner or later. This section describes how to use Selenium to automate web GUI testing.

Selenium IDE Installation

Selenium consists of several components. You can see all of them at `http://seleniumhq.org/download/`. The Selenium integrated development environment (IDE) is only available for Firefox. To run your tests on other Internet browsers, you need to install Selenium Remote Control. We will work with the Selenium IDE. You don't have to install it to run the tests presented in this book, but if you have no experience with automated tests or Selenium you should try it to see how it works and get some experience with clickable test automation tools. When you click the Download link on the Selenium homepage, you will be asked whether you really want to install this add-on (see Figure 15-12).

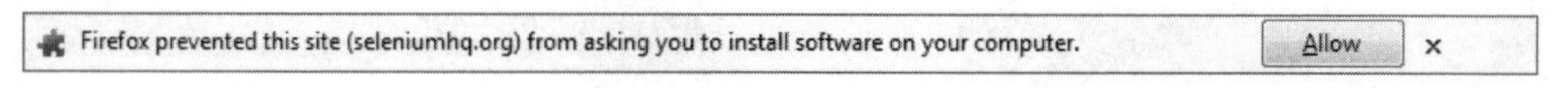

FIGURE 15-12: Selenium Firefox security notice

When you click Allow, the window shown in Figure 15-13 will be displayed. This is a second security notice. If you believe us that we are not trying to install malicious software on your machine, click Install Now.

Next, you need to reboot Firefox. After rebooting, you will be able to access Selenium through Tools ➪ Selenium IDE in the main menu on the top of the browser window. Invoke the Selenium IDE and you should see the Selenium IDE main window as in Figure 15-14.

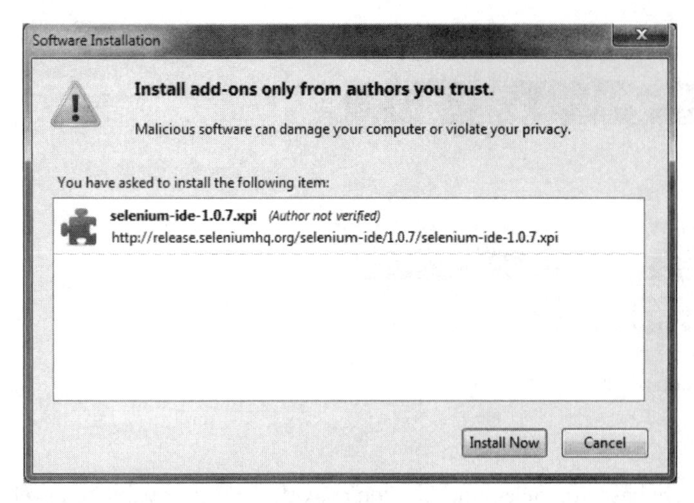

FIGURE 15-13: Selenium Firefox installation window

In the top right of the Selenium IDE main window, there is a red round button that is very similar to the well-known audio record button. In fact, it is a record button, but it records your browser actions. Push the button and do something, such as sign in to your favorite social network. After signing in, you should be able to see something similar to Figure 15-15. Your password is not hidden and is shown as plain text in Selenium IDE. But you have also recorded your steps. Click the record button again to turn it off. You can click the green arrow to run your recorded test case.

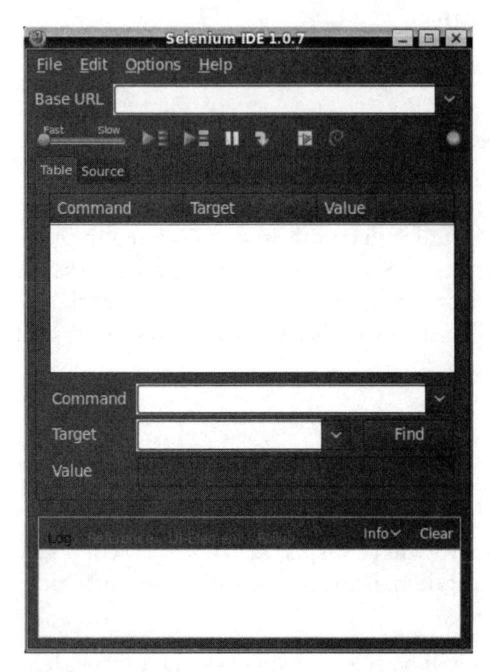

FIGURE 15-14: Selenium IDE main window

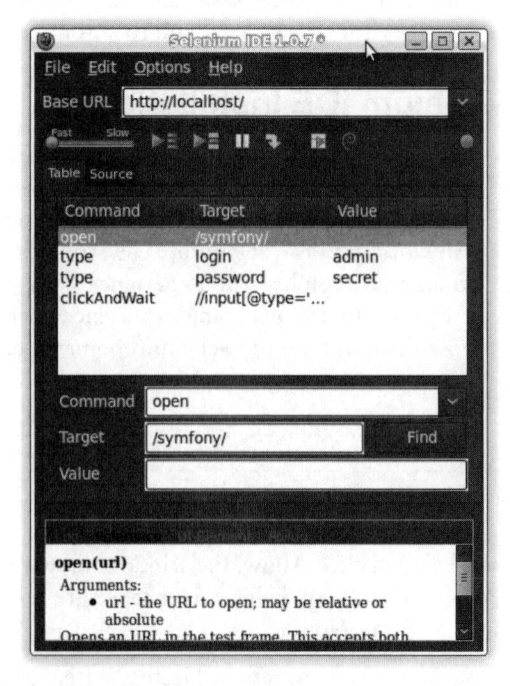

FIGURE 15-15: Selenium IDE recorded actions

What can you use this for? Selenium IDE allows you to create tests by recording actions, like mouse clicks, instead of writing code. Of course, after you record these actions, you can see the source code for them. By default, an XHTML version of the source code is shown in the Source tab. We are not interested in XHTML; a piece of PHP code would be more useful, and the good news is that Selenium IDE provides this kind of functionality. Go to the Options menu and select the format type from the Format option. Select PHP - Selenium RC. In the Source tab, you will see something similar to this code:

Available for download on Wrox.com

```
<?php
require_once 'PHPUnit/Extensions/SeleniumTestCase.php';
class Example extends PHPUnit_Extensions_SeleniumTestCase {
  protected function setUp() {
    $this->setBrowser("*chrome");
    $this->setBrowserUrl("http://change-this-to-the-site-you-are-testing/");
  }
  public function testMyTestCase() {
  }
}
?>
```

code snippet /selenium/exampleTest.php

Remember this code; you will see more Selenium PHPUnit code later in this chapter.

Selenium Remote Control Installation

With the Selenium IDE, you can click out your test cases, but only on Firefox. But what if you want to use a browser different from Firefox? This should be considered not only because someone might prefer a different browser, but also because you should test your application in all major browsers, especially when you use a lot of JavaScript in your web application. The solution is Selenium Remote Control.

You probably noticed that Selenium IDE has not generated the `setBrowser()` parameter as you might have expected. Why is it `chrome` while you were using Firefox? Because it's the default browser in Selenium, but you can replace this parameter with any browser you want to run this test case on. Note that the browser setup is set within the `setUp()` method, not in the test case method. For simplicity, we are running the Selenium test only on localhost.

To see how Selenium Remote Control works, you need to download it from `http://seleniumhq.org/download/` and unpack it. Note that you also need a Java Runtime Environment (JRE) to work with Selenium RC. If you don't have one, you can get it from the Sun website (`http://java.sun.com/`). After installing it, you can run this command from the command line:

```
java -jar selenium-server.jar
```

To run the previous command, you need to be in the Selenium RC directory. After running it, you should see something similar to this:

```
15:04:05.979 INFO - Java: Sun Microsystems Inc. 14.0-b16
15:04:05.980 INFO - OS: Linux 2.6.32-23-generic amd64
15:04:05.985 INFO - v2.0 [a2], with Core v2.0 [a2]
15:04:06.049 INFO - RemoteWebDriver instances should connect to:
 http://192.168.1.3:4444/wd/hub
```

```
15:04:06.050 INFO - Version Jetty/5.1.x
15:04:06.050 INFO - Started HttpContext[/selenium-server/driver,
 /selenium-server/driver]
15:04:06.051 INFO - Started HttpContext[/selenium-server,/selenium-server]
15:04:06.051 INFO - Started HttpContext[/,/]
15:04:06.059 INFO - Started org.openqa.jetty.jetty.servlet.ServletHandler@16a4e743
15:04:06.059 INFO - Started HttpContext[/wd,/wd]
15:04:06.062 INFO - Started SocketListener on 0.0.0.0:4444
15:04:06.062 INFO - Started org.openqa.jetty.jetty.Server@7d2a1e44
```

This is the output generated when starting Selenium RC. You will see your individual configuration such as IP address or operating system instead of what is shown here.

Problem

Selenium is one of many solutions that you can use to realize black-box testing. The great thing about Selenium is that it's free and available for all operating systems in which Java is supported. Additionally, Selenium delivers the recording feature, which is rare in most automation frameworks/ tools dedicated for web applications. Other tools, such as HP QuickTest Professional, are not free and are not dedicated only for the Web. The test case that we want to cover in this section is shown in the following table.

STEP	ACTION	EXPECTED RESULT
1	Go to the page `http://localhost/login`.	A page with a login form is displayed.
2	Fill out the username and password fields with `admin` and `secret` values.	Username is filled out with plain text, and password is filled out with hidden text.
3	Click the login button.	Form information is submitted.
4	Check the current page location.	The page location is `http://localhost/main`.

Solution

Earlier in this chapter, we described a similar test case for a functional test. We want to do the same now, but this time we want to have it working as a part of Selenium. Assume that the tested login form looks as follows:

Available for download on Wrox.com

```
<form action="/login/submit" method="POST">
<table>
     <tr>
         <th><label for="username">Username</label></th>
         <td><input type="text" name="username" id="username" /></td>
    </tr>
    <tr>
         <th><label for="password">Password</label></th>
         <td><input type="password" name="password" id="password" /></td>
    </tr>
     <tr>
```

```
            <td colspan="2">
                <input type="submit" id="submit" name="submit" value="submit" />
            </td>
        </tr>
    </table>
</form>
```

code snippet /selenium/exampleLoginForm.html

This time we present all three web frameworks because it's also possible to integrate CakePHP's SimpleTest with Selenium using PEAR packages.

Symfony

As described earlier, Symfony delivers some command-line tasks, and two are dedicated for Selenium tests. One of them generates a default test case. To do it, you need to type the following command:

```
$ symfony phpunit:generate-selenium frontend login
```

You should see output similar to this:

```
>> dir+      /home/wrox/public_html/symfony/test/phpunit/selenium/frontend
>> file+     /home/wrox/public_html/symfony/test/phpunit/selenium/frontend
             /loginActionsTest.php
>> help      run this test with: ./symfony phpunit:test-selenium frontend login
```

Generated code should be as follows:

```
<?php
require_once dirname(__FILE__).'/../../bootstrap/selenium.php';
class selenium_frontend_loginActionsTest extends sfPHPUnitBaseSeleniumTestCase {
  protected function setUp() {
    $this->setBrowser('*firefox');
    $this->setBrowserUrl('http://localhost/');
  }
  public function testPositiveAdminLogin() {
  }
}
```

code snippet /selenium/symfony/test/phpunit/selenium/frontend/loginActionsTest.php

We changed the default test case method name to make it more meaningful. Now we need to fill it out with proper code. The following code accomplishes our earlier defined test case:

```
public function testPositiveAdminLogin() {
    $this->open('http://localhost/login');
    $this->assertTitle('Login Page');
    $this->type("username", "admin");
    $this->type("password", "secret");
    $this->click("submit");
    $this->waitForPageToLoad("30000");
    $this->verifyTextPresent("Successfully logged in");
}
```

code snippet /selenium/symfony/test/phpunit/selenium/frontend/loginActionsTest.php

You can run Selenium tests with the following command:

```
$ symfony phpunit:test-selenium
```

This should give an output similar to this:

```
PHPUnit 3.4.15 by Sebastian Bergmann.
.
Time: 6 seconds, Memory: 10.00Mb
OK (1 test, 2 assertions)
```

We get plain text output, but Selenium also provides the Selenium Remote Control Web console, as shown in Figure 15-16.

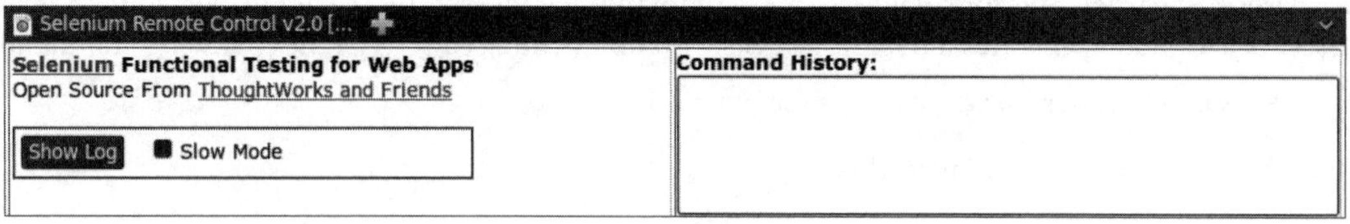

Selenium Remote Control v2.0 [...

Selenium Functional Testing for Web Apps
Open Source From ThoughtWorks and Friends

Show Log   Slow Mode

Command History:

FIGURE 15-16: Selenium Remote Control

Also, a second browser window is opened, in which all steps are executed one by one.

CakePHP

CakePHP doesn't support Selenium by default because its SimpleTest doesn't provide Selenium support, unlike PHPUnit. But this problem can be easily solved using the `Testing_Selenium` package that is available in the PEAR package database. You can download it from `http://pear.php.net/package/Testing_Selenium`. You can also install it by using the PEAR command-line installation parameter, but in this case, a better solution is to extract this package to CakePHP's `/vendors` directory. Because of dependencies within the main `Selenium.php` file, it's better to extract files from the package to the `/Testing` subdirectory. After proper extraction, your directory structure should look like the following:

```
app\vendors\Testing\
                       examples\
                       Selenium\
                       tests\
                       ChangeLog
                       readme
                       Selenium.php
                       selenium-server.jar
                       todo
```

Make sure that it's exactly the same in your case. Next, you need to make one easy change in `Selenium.php`. Find this line:

```
require_once 'Testing/Selenium/Exception.php';
```

Change it to this:

```
require_once 'Selenium/Exception.php';
```

This is only one word, but without this change you would not be able to run tests using Selenium. This PEAR package is something like a wrapper for PHPUnit Selenium classes. After making these changes, you can start implementing a sample test case. The test case can be saved as `selenium.test.php` and placed in the `/app/tests/cases/behaviors` directory.

To begin, include the Selenium wrapper. In CakePHP, you can do so by using the `App::import()` method. An exemplary test class draft can look like the following:

Available for download on Wrox.com

```
<?php
App::import('Vendor','Selenium', array('file' => 'Testing'.DS.'Selenium.php'));
class LoginSeleniumTest extends UnitTestCase {
     function setUp() {
     }
     function tearDown() {
     }
}
```

code snippet /selenium/cakephp/app/tests/cases/behaviors/selenium.test.php

The first parameter in the `import()` method, `Vendor`, states from which part of CakePHP we want to import a class. The next parameter is only an identifier; you can call it whatever you want. The last parameter is an array. For the file key, assign the path and filename of `Selenium.php`. The *`DS`* variable is the separator between paths. In Windows, it's `"\"`; in UNIX it's `"/"`. Now you can define what the `setUp()` and `tearDown()` functions will do. These methods are very common in many testing frameworks: `setUp()` is invoked when a test begins, and `tearDown()` is invoked when all invoked methods are done (except `tearDown()`). Before executing any test case, we need to define in which Internet browser the test cases should be executed and the starting URL. This method looks like the following:

Available for download on Wrox.com

```
function setUp() {
    $this->selenium =
        new Testing_Selenium("*firefox /usr/lib/firefox/firefox-bin",
            "http://localhost/login");
    $this->selenium->start();
}
```

code snippet /selenium/cakephp/app/tests/cases/behaviors/selenium.test.php

Because we don't need to work with Selenium after test cases are done, the `tearDown()` method should be as follows:

Available for download on Wrox.com

```
function tearDown() {
    $this->selenium->stop();
}
```

code snippet /selenium/cakephp/app/tests/cases/behaviors/selenium.test.php

Let's name our test case as we did in Symfony and Zend Framework: `testPositiveAdminLogin()`:

Available for download on Wrox.com

```
function testPositiveAdminLogin() {
}
```

code snippet /selenium/cakephp/app/tests/cases/behaviors/selenium.test.php

In CakePHP, follow the same steps as in Symfony. The only difference is that you do not invoke Selenium dedicated methods through `$this`, but through the `$this->selenium` wrapper. Therefore, the `testPositiveAdminLogin()` method content should be as follows:

Available for download on Wrox.com

```
$this->selenium->open('http://localhost/login');
$this->assertTrue($this->selenium->getTitle('Login page'));
$this->selenium->type("username", "admin");
$this->selenium->type("password", "secret");
$this->selenium->click("login");
$this->selenium->waitForPageToLoad("30000");
$this->selenium->verifyTextPresent("Successfully logged in");
```

code snippet /selenium/cakephp/app/tests/cases/behaviors/selenium.test.php

Now, when you go to `http://localhost/test.php`, you should be able to see two test cases, as shown in Figure 15-17.

Remember to start Selenium RC before you run any Selenium test cases. Otherwise, you will see something similar to Figure 15-18.

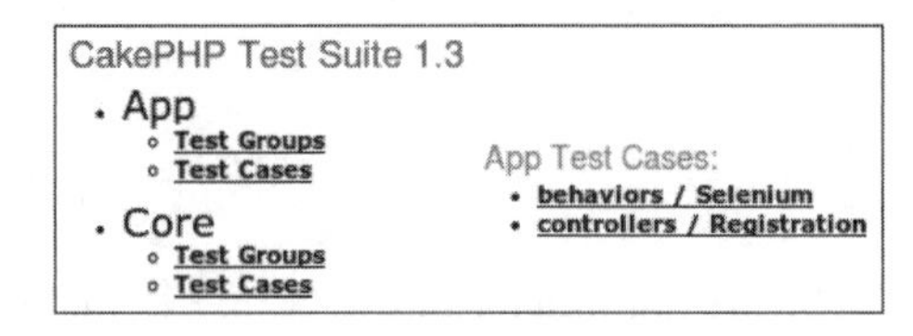

FIGURE 15-17: CakePHP test case web browser

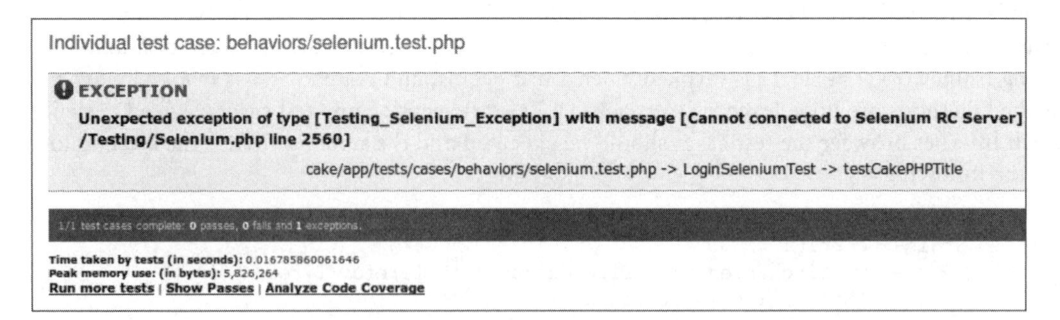

Individual test case: behaviors/selenium.test.php
EXCEPTION
Unexpected exception of type [Testing_Selenium_Exception] with message [Cannot connected to Selenium RC Server]
/Testing/Selenium.php line 2560]
cake/app/tests/cases/behaviors/selenium.test.php -> LoginSeleniumTest -> testCakePHPTitle
Time taken by tests (in seconds): 0.016785860061646
Peak memory use: (in bytes): 5,826,264
Run more tests | Show Passes | Analyze Code Coverage

FIGURE 15-18: CakePHP error when Selenium RC is not found

Zend Framework

Zend Framework doesn't support any features that help executing test cases. This is not really a problem, though, because ZF delivers PHPUnit classes, so with the `phpunit` command, you don't need anything else. To start, you need to create a directory in which you want to keep your Selenium test cases. Let it be `/tests/application/selenium`. You can save your test drafts as `LoginTestCases.php`. It should look like the following:

Available for download on Wrox.com

```
<?php
require_once 'PHPUnit/Extensions/SeleniumTestCase.php';
class LoginSeleniumTest extends PHPUnit_Extensions_SeleniumTestCase {
  protected function setUp() {
    $this->setBrowser("*chrome");
    $this->setBrowserUrl("http://localhost/");
  }
  public function testPositiveAdminLogin() {
```

```
    }
}
?>
```

code snippet /selenium/zf/tests/application/selenium/LoginTestCases.php

In fact, all the test drafts do not differ from each other a lot. The only difference is what libraries they import. In the case of ZF, Selenium libraries are stored in `C:\xampp\php\PEAR\PHPUnit` under Windows and in `/usr/share/php/PHPUnit` under UNIX systems. Note that you don't need to use Chrome or Firefox as testing browsers; you can use any of the following with `$this->setBrowser()`:

```
*firefox
*chrome
*iexplore
*googlechrome
*safari
*opera
*custom
```

`firefox`, `googlechrome`, `opera`, `safari`, and `iexplore` are obvious. Note that if you choose `chrome`, Firefox will be used. When you choose `custom`, you will be able to use other browsers not listed previously. In this case, you need to give a proper path to the browser. (This is also a good solution if you want to test more versions of a browser.)

The test case should look like this:

Available for download on Wrox.com

```
$this->open('http://localhost/login');
$this->assertTitle('Login Page');
$this->type("username", "admin");
$this->type("password", "secret");
$this->click("login");
$this->waitForPageToLoad("30000");
$this->verifyTextPresent("Successfully logged in");
```

code snippet /selenium/zf/tests/application/selenium/LoginTestCases.php

It's the same as with Symfony. The difference is in execution. In Symfony, we did it with tasks delivered out of the box. In ZF, we need to use PHPUnit's executables. In ZF, each test can be executed as follows:

```
$ phpunit application/selenium/LoginTestCases.php
```

This needs more effort because you need to automate it further when more tests are available. When you switch to the Selenium RC console, you should be able to see something similar to this:

```
11:12:43.261 INFO - creating new remote session
11:12:43.262 INFO - Allocated session 1b843f2a2f714a049305340656f72dc7 for
   http://localhost/, launching...
11:12:43.285 INFO - Preparing Firefox profile...
11:12:45.658 INFO - Launching Firefox...
```

```
11:12:48.702 INFO - Got result: OK,1b843f2a2f714a049305340656f72dc7 on session
   1b843f2a2f714a049305340656f72dc7
11:12:48.748 INFO - Command request: setTimeout[30000, ] on session
   1b843f2a2f714a049305340656f72dc7
11:12:48.755 INFO - Got result: OK on session 1b843f2a2f714a049305340656f72dc7
11:12:48.802 INFO - Command request: open[http://localhost/login, ] on session
   1b843f2a2f714a049305340656f72dc7
11:12:48.912 INFO - Got result: OK on session 1b843f2a2f714a049305340656f72dc7
11:12:48.959 INFO - Command request: getTitle[Login Page, ] on session
   1b843f2a2f714a049305340656f72dc7
11:12:48.975 INFO - Got result: OK,Login Page on session
   1b843f2a2f714a049305340656f72dc7
11:12:49.023 INFO - Command request: type[username, admin] on session
   1b843f2a2f714a049305340656f72dc7
11:12:49.053 INFO - Got result: OK on session 1b843f2a2f714a049305340656f72dc7
11:12:49.101 INFO - Command request: type[password, secret] on session
   1b843f2a2f714a049305340656f72dc7
11:12:49.128 INFO - Got result: OK on session 1b843f2a2f714a049305340656f72dc7
11:12:49.176 INFO - Command request: click[submit, ] on session
   1b843f2a2f714a049305340656f72dc7
11:12:49.288 INFO - Got result: OK on session 1b843f2a2f714a049305340656f72dc7
11:12:49.335 INFO - Command request: waitForPageToLoad[30000, ] on session
   1b843f2a2f714a049305340656f72dc7
11:12:49.358 INFO - Got result: OK on session 1b843f2a2f714a049305340656f72dc7
11:12:49.406 INFO - Command request: isTextPresent[Successfully logged in, ] on
   session 1b843f2a2f714a049305340656f72dc7
11:12:49.426 INFO - Got result: OK,true on session 1b843f2a2f714a049305340656f72dc7
11:12:49.474 INFO - Command request: testComplete[, ] on session
   1b843f2a2f714a049305340656f72dc7
11:12:49.474 INFO - Killing Firefox...
11:12:49.955 INFO - Got result: OK on session 1b843f2a2f714a049305340656f72dc7
```

This output shows what exactly was executed by Selenium RC step by step. ZF doesn't deliver any scripts to run test cases, but we still can use PHPUnit's configuration XML file to run more test cases at one time. To make it possible, edit the `phpunit.xml` file placed in the `/tests` directory. It should look like the following code:

```
<phpunit bootstrap="./application/bootstrap.php">
        <testsuite name="Wrox Example">
                <directory>./</directory>
        </testsuite>
</phpunit>
```

code snippet /selenium/zf/tests/phpunit.xml

You need to define the bootstrap file that will set up all needed variables before the test suites are executed. A test suite name should be defined as well as the test suite's directory in which PHPUnit will start to search for test cases. In the case of Zend Framework, `bootstrap.php` should be as following:

```
<?php
define('BASE_PATH', realpath(dirname(__FILE__) . '/../../'));
define('APPLICATION_PATH', BASE_PATH . '/application');
define('APPLICATION_ENV', 'testing');
```

code snippet /selenium/zf/tests/application/bootstrap.php

Note that you define the application's environment as testing, so all testing parameters, such as database connection settings, will be used. To execute tests, you can use PHPUnit's command-line application:

```
$ phpunit -configuration phpunit.xml
```

MAILING UNIT TESTING

Unit testing uses mostly white-box testing schemas. However, depending on how we use unit testing frameworks, we can also use other testing approaches. Normally, unit tests focus on the quality of the code at the code level. Formal test cases are not always defined because unit tests are implemented mostly by developers, not testers.

Problem

E-mails are often sent for subscriptions, registrations, password recovery mechanisms, and so on. Developers need to use mailing functionality many times in different controllers. According to the Don't Repeat Yourself (DRY) rule, mailing code is commonly extracted into libraries. This gives you another advantage: the possibility to encapsulate parts of code and test their quality separately.

Let's assume that you have a `Mailing` class with two methods: `sendMailSubscription()` and `sendMail()`. `sendMailSubscription()` takes only two arguments: subscription type and mail address. The `sendMail()` method takes no arguments. The first method sends a proper e-mail for a given subscription type. The next method sends one e-mail to 10 random accounts from a mailing database. For these two methods, you can define four simple test cases, two negative and two positive, as shown in the following table.

STEP	ACTION	EXPECTED RESULT
1	Invoke with the `full` and `example@wroxexample.com` arguments.	The method returns a `true` value.

Let's assume that the `sendMailSubscription()` method sends an e-mail with previously prepared content. The content is fixed, but it depends on the subscription type. Assume that there are two types of subscriptions: *full* and *trial*, and for each type there is a different content. But what happens if you invoke the method with a completely different argument? The expected action is that if the argument is not full or trial, the `sendMailSubscription()` method returns a `false` value, as shown in the following table.

STEP	ACTION	EXPECTED RESULT
1	Invoke with the `foobar` and `example@wroxexample.com` arguments.	The method returns a `false` value.

Next, test cases use the Mails model. A random e-mail address needs to be retrieved from the database, and we need to use the Mails model to do that. One test case can check a scenario in which the Mails table has valid e-mail. To do that, we need to load some sample data (fixtures), as shown in the following table.

STEP	ACTION	EXPECTED RESULT
1	Load fixtures.	Fixtures are loaded.
2	Invoke `sendMail()`.	The method returns a `true` value.
3	Delete fixtures.	Fixtures are deleted.

To keep test cases clean, you should delete fixtures when they are no longer needed, which prevents mistakes in subsequent test cases. The last test case, shown in the following table, should check the action when `sendMail()` is invoked and the table is empty.

STEP	ACTION	EXPECTED RESULT
1	Check for mail in the database.	The Mails table is empty.
2	Invoke `sendMail()`.	The method returns a `false` value.

The `Mailing` class, described in Chapter 6, looks like this:

```
<?php
/* including libraries here */
class Mailing {
    public function sendMailSubscription($type, $mail) {
        /* method content */
    }
    public function sendMail() {
        /* method content */
    }
}
```

You should feed the method's content with proper code, as described in Chapter 6.

Symfony

The `Mailing` class should be saved as `Mailing.class.php` in the project's `/lib` directory to make it available for every application.

CakePHP

In CakePHP, the `Mailing` class should be named as in Symfony and placed in the application's library path: `/app/libs`. But there is one difference. Because of CakePHP's specific behavior, it's easier to make a model object an argument of the `sendMail()` method. After this change, the `sendMail()` method should be as follows:

```
public function sendMail($mail) {
    /* method content */
}
```

Zend Framework

ZF's `Mailing.class.php` should be placed in the project's `/library` path. It should not include the CakePHP change.

Solution

As mentioned in the "Test Frameworks" section of this chapter, each framework prefers a different unit testing framework. We'll show only the most popular ones, although some frameworks can use more than one testing framework.

Symfony

Symfony 2.0 uses PHPUnit, whereas Symfony 1.0 uses Lime (except when the PHPUnit2 plug-in is installed, in which case Symfony1 uses PHPUnit). The following example is written in Symfony 1.0 with the PHPUnit2 plug-in installed. To start working with Symfony tests, you need to generate a default unit test:

```
$ symfony phpunit:generate-unit mailing
This will generate proper files:
>> dir+      /home/wrox/public_html/symfony//test/phpunit/unit
>> file+     /home/wrox/public_html/symfony//test/phpunit/unit/mailingTest.php
>> help      run this test with: ./symfony phpunit:test-unit mailingTest
```

You need to use the `Mailing` class, so it should be set up for every test case. To do that, you can use the `setUp()` and `tearDown()` methods as follows:

Available for download on Wrox.com

```
<?php
require_once dirname(__FILE__).'/../bootstrap/unit.php';
class unit_mailingTest extends sfPHPUnitBaseTestCase
{
    public function setUp() {
      $this->_mailing = new Mailing();
    }
    public function tearDown() {
      unset($this->_mailing);
    }
    /* test cases methods */
}
```

code snippet /unit/symfony/test/phpunit/unit/mailingTest.php

The first two test cases are very simple because the implementation needs only to change the attributes that are sent. Finally, the test cases should be as follows:

Available for download on Wrox.com

```
    public function testSubscriptionPositive() {
      $this->assertTrue($this->_mailing
       ->sendMailSubscription("full","example@wroxexample.com"));
    }
    public function testSubscriptionNegative() {
      $this->assertTrue(!$this->_mailing
       ->sendMailSubscription("foobar","example@wroxexample@com"));
    }
```

code snippet /unit/symfony/test/phpunit/unit/mailingTest.php

Note that `$this->_mailing` is the `Mailing` instance. The last test case doesn't need any data in the Mails table, so it can be easily implemented as follows:

```
public function testRandomMailNegative() {
  $this->assertTrue(!$this->_mailing->sendMail());
}
```

code snippet /unit/symfony/test/phpunit/unit/mailingTest.php

In both negative test cases, we place an exclamation mark to the left of `$this->_mailing` to check whether the inversed values from the returned values are `true`.

The last test case is the most complicated of all. You need to define fixtures that would be loaded before `sendMail()` is invoked. Fixture files should be placed in the project's `/data/fixtures` directory. For example, you can save the fixture file as `mailing.yml` in the `/data/fixtures/mailing` directory. This separates fixture files from the functionalities for which they are needed. `mailing.yml` should be defined as follows:

```
mails:
  john_smith:
    email:        example@wroxexample.com
    forename:     John
    surname:      Smith
    subscription: full
```

code snippet /unit/symfony/data/fixtures/mailing/mailing.yml

To load data, you need information about the project configuration, which provides information about database connections that can be used to load fixture data into proper tables. You should use sfDatabaseManager to establish a connection and Doctrine_Core to load data. After testing, the `sendMail()` method fixtures need to be deleted, as shown in the following code:

```
public function testRandomMailPositive() {
      $configuration =
        ProjectConfiguration::getApplicationConfiguration('frontend','test',true);
      $conn = new sfDatabaseManager($configuration);
      Doctrine_Core::loadData(sfConfig::get('sf_data_dir').'/fixtures/mailing/');
      $this->assertTrue($this->_mailing->sendMail());
      Doctrine_Core::getTable('mails')->findAll()->delete();
}
```

code snippet /unit/symfony/test/phpunit/unit/mailingTest.php

The test string defines which environment configuration is to be loaded. `sfConfig::get('sf_data_dir')` returns the project's `/data` path (for example, `/home/wrox/public_html/symfony/data`). To run the test, you need to execute the following command:

```
$ symfony phpunit:test-unit
```

Output is similar to that from the Selenium tests you saw earlier in this chapter.

CakePHP

In CakePHP, you should start with defining fixtures. Fixtures, which are classes that inherit from `CakeTestFixture`, are placed in the `/app/test/fixtures` directory. CakePHP presents a slightly different approach to fixtures. Fixtures are not loaded to a database as is done in Symfony or ZF. This is a kind of mock that simulates all behaviors of a model with data that can be accessed with commonly used methods such as `find()`. But first you should define a fixture as follows:

Available for download on Wrox.com

```
<?php
class MailTestFixture extends CakeTestFixture {
    var $name = 'Mail';

    var $fields = array(
        'id' => array('type' => 'integer', 'key' => 'primary'),
        'email' => 'text',
        'surname' => 'text',
        'forename' => 'text',
        'subscription' => 'text',
    );
    var $records = array(
        array ('id' => 1, 'email' => 'example@wroxexample.com',
            'surname' => 'Smith', 'forename' => 'John', 'subscription' => 'full')
    );
}
?>
```

code snippet /unit/cakephp/app/test/fixtures/app/test/fixtures

Because fixtures simulate a model, you don't need to define any connections or get configuration information. The fixture presented in the preceding code should be saved as `mail_test_fixture.php`. Now you can load this fixture file by assigning its name to the `$fixtures` variable as follows:

Available for download on Wrox.com

```
<?php
require_once('libs/Mailing.class.php');
class MailingTest extends CakeTestCase {
    var $fixtures = array( 'mail_test');
    public function setUp() {
      $this->_mailing = new Mailing();
    }
    public function tearDown() {
      unset($this->_mailing);
    }
    /* test cases methods */
}
```

code snippet /unit/cakephp/app/test/cases/components/mailing.test.php

The test case file should be placed in `/app/test/cases/components` as `mailing.test.php`. The `Mailing` class will be used. Therefore, we need to include it and get an instance of `Mailing` as shown in the preceding code. The first two test cases are obvious and look like the following:

Available for download on Wrox.com

```
    public function testSubscriptionPositive() {
      $this->assertTrue($this->_mailing->sendMailSubscription(
        "full","example@wroxexample.com"));
    }
    public function testSubscriptionNegative() {
      $this->assertTrue(!$this->_mailing->sendMailSubscription(
        "foobar","example@wroxexample@com"));
    }
```

code snippet /unit/cakephp/app/test/cases/components/mailing.test.php

To get the `Mail` object fixtures, you need to get its instance by using `ClassRegistry`:

```
public function testRandomMailPositive() {
  $this->Mail =& ClassRegistry::init('Mail');
  $this->assertTrue($this->_mailing->sendMail($this->Mail));
}
```

code snippet /unit/cakephp/app/test/cases/components/mailing.test.php

When `find()` is invoked within `sendMail()` with the given object as the argument, a list of rows defined in the fixture will be returned as the result. This is an advantage of CakePHP because this approach is very easy to use and you don't need to use the database at all. Of course, you can use the database as well and sometimes that will be necessary.

In the last test case, you need only to delete all data defined in the fixture to get an empty database. Use the `delete()` method, as shown in the following code, to clear the Mails table:

```
public function testRandomMailNegative() {
      $this->Mail =& ClassRegistry::init('Mail');
      $this->Mail->delete();
      $this->assertTrue(!$this->_mailing->sendMail($this->Mail));
    }
```

code snippet /unit/cakephp/app/test/cases/components/mailing.test.php

You can now execute the preceding test using the `http://localhost/test.php` URL.

Zend Framework

The most difficult approach for the QAs is delivered by Zend Framework. However, it is still easy to implement, just as it is in the two frameworks already discussed. To begin, you should include ZF's `Application` class, and PHPUnit's `framework` and `Mailing` classes. The first class is used to get the project's configuration, especially the database connection configuration. The second class is used to make testing with the PHPUnit framework possible. The purpose of the third class is obvious. In `setUp()`, you need to get an instance of `Mailing` and additionally get a database connection adapter. The adapter looks like the following:

```
<?php
require_once 'Zend/Application.php';
require_once 'PHPUnit/Framework.php';
require_once '../library/Mailing.class.php';
class MailingTest extends PHPUnit_Framework_TestCase {
    public function setUp() {
      $application = new Zend_Application(
         APPLICATION_ENV,
         APPLICATION_PATH . '/configs/application.ini'
      );
      $bootstrap = $application->getBootstrap();
      $bootstrap->bootstrap('db');
      $dbAdapter = $bootstrap->getResource('db');
      $this->_mailing = new Mailing();
    }
```

```
        public function tearDown() {
          unset($this->_mailing);
        }
        /* test cases methods */
    }
```

code snippet /unit/zf/tests/application/unit/MailingTest.php

Unit tests should be placed in the `/tests/application/unit` directory (for example, `/tests/application/unit/MailingTest.php`). As the following code shows, the first two test cases don't differ from Symfony and CakePHP test case implementations:

```
public function testSubscriptionPositive() {
      $this->assertTrue($this->_mailing->sendMailSubscription(
        "full","example@wroxexample.com"));
}
public function testSubscriptionNegative() {
      $this->assertTrue(!$this->_mailing->sendMailSubscription(
        "foobar","example@wroxexample@com"));
}
```

code snippet /unit/zf/tests/application/unit/MailingTest.php

You can also try to load fixtures manually, as described in Chapter 3, or try to execute this script from the code level, but in cases where the test needs to be automated, a simpler approach is available, as shown in the following code. You need to define an array of data that should be loaded into the database. Next, a model and mapper are used in the same way as they are used in controllers:

```
public function testRandomMailPositive() {
     $fixtures=array('firstName'=>'John',
                     'lastName'=>'John',
                     'email'=>'John',
     );
     $entry = new Application_Model_Mails($fixtures);
     $mapper  = new Application_Model_MailsMapper();
     $id=$mapper->save($entry);
     $this->assertTrue($this->_mailing->sendMail());
     $mapper->deleteOne($id);
}
```

code snippet /unit/zf/tests/application/unit/MailingTest.php

At the end, you need to delete the entry saved previously with `$id` that was returned through the `save()` method. All methods such as `save()` or `deleteOne()` are defined for each model, as described in Chapter 4.

The last test case is the same as in Symfony and CakePHP:

```
public function testRandomMailNegative(){
      $this->assertTrue(!$this->_mailing->sendMail());
}
```

code snippet /unit/zf/tests/application/unit/MailingTest.php

To run the unit test, you can use the `phpunit.xml` configuration file, as shown in the "CMS Tests Automation Using Selenium" section of this chapter, or you can use the following command:

```
$ phpunit tests/application/unit/MailingTest.php
```

All tests should pass if your `Mailing` class methods are done correctly. The output is similar to that obtained with Selenium.

16

User Management

The world will look up and shout 'save us' and I will look down and whisper 'no.'

— Rorschach, The Watchmen

WHAT'S IN THIS CHAPTER?

- RBAC and ACL as basic user management methods.
- Setting up LDAP.
- Advanced user management with LDAP.

How should a web application be secured against unprivileged access? We want to explore this topic as deeply as possible in this chapter because of its significance and the severe consequences of neglecting security. The first major section of this chapter, "Basic User Management," covers not only the basic security issues, but also dynamic access control and features of specific frameworks.

The second major section of this chapter, "Identifying Users Using LDAP Implementation," is focused on implementing user authorization with LDAP within the frameworks. This is an alternative industry-scale solution, so you can skip this section if you don't need it. However, this knowledge will be invaluable for more advanced users, because it is not easily accessible on the Internet, and it is highly valued among big companies and corporations.

BASIC USER MANAGEMENT

There are many ways to manage user authorization. In the frameworks featured in this book, there are two main user management approaches, RBAC and ACL. They are quite similar, but have some important differences that are described and explained in the following section.

RBAC versus ACL

RBAC, which stands for *Role-based Access Control*, is more role oriented (roles, not specific users, are authorized). This approach is generally more sophisticated, but also more practical than ACL. Figure 16-1 shows an example of what this looks like.

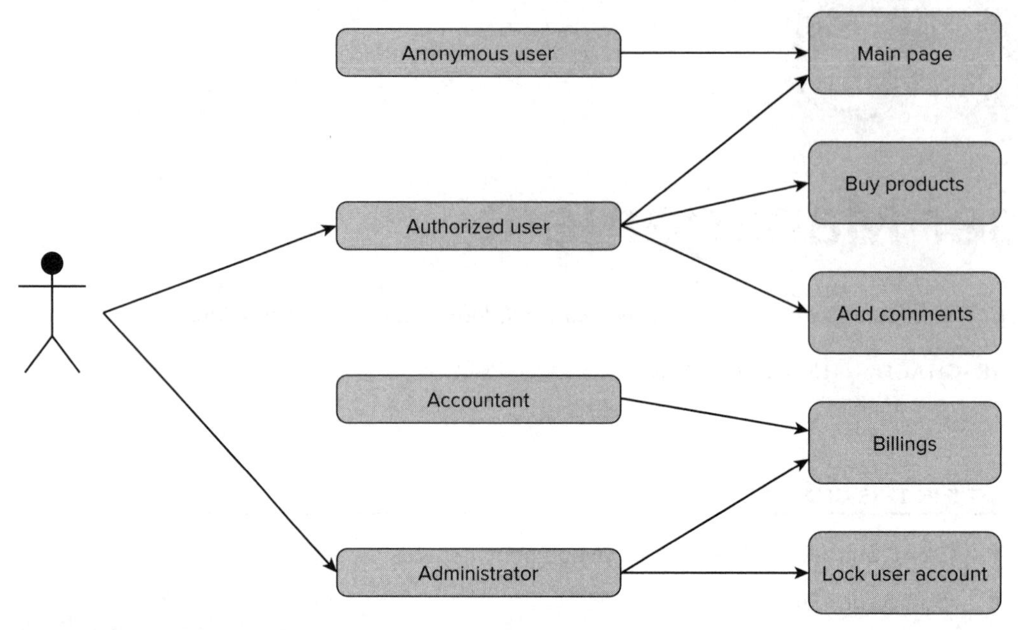

FIGURE 16-1: RBAC example.

So let's assume that we have defined four roles: anonymous, authorized user, accountant, and administrator. Each of these roles has some privileges such as adding product comments, viewing billings, and so on. All that needs to be done is to assign users to roles. As shown in Figure 16-1, the example user has two roles: authorized user and administrator. These roles combined entitle him to add comments, buy products, see billings, and so on. Roles are named after the rights they provide: administrator, accountant, customer, and so on. This is a human-friendly approach because when someone talks about the administrator or authorized user role, automatically everyone connects this with some obvious behaviors such as buying products or locking users. RBAC is used in Symfony. Solaris 10 (and probably every subsequent version) will also use RBAC, so it's not only in web frameworks that there are RBAC capabilities.

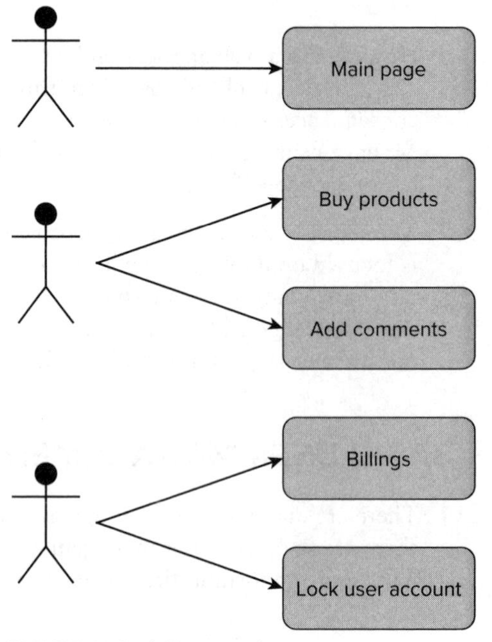

FIGURE 16-2: ACL example.

An *access control list*, or ACL (see Figure 16-2), is used in Zend and CakePHP. This solution is older than RBAC and is commonly used in almost all operating systems as the default access control methodology. This approach is also commonly used in network administration and is even implemented in network hardware. It is simpler than RBAC because it is user-oriented. Every user has a specific privilege for every object; for example, adding comments can be allowed or disallowed separately for every account.

That's why when you are setting access to buying a product, for example, you need to add the rule for each user. You must do this for each user who is to be granted access, at least, because a non-access rule can be assumed as a default rule. If an access rule to this object cannot be found for a user, it is assumed that this user has no privileges to access it. This saves lots of time needed to define all rules because you define only the part needed for allowing access. At first look, ACL seems easier to implement than RBAC, but it isn't. It is more flexible because each user can have custom rules assigned, but this means more time spent on assigning them. For example, `userA` may have the same privileges as `userB`, and there may be as many as 100 objects; for each object the rule has to be defined for both users. It's easier to create some main groups of rules and assign users to these groups. When you do so, you get something similar to RBAC, but this is not exactly the same because you are also able to assign users to objects. ACL with groups is very often mistaken for RBAC, and vice versa.

Methodologies described previously show different approaches to the problem of user access control. Let's see how the problem is solved in each framework.

Symfony

Symfony implements the RBAC idea. Before you can take advantage of RBAC, however, we must describe some Symfony configuration features. In the main configuration file `settings.yml` you can set default security modules. Symfony delivers two default modules that display login or credentials requirement information. These pages look like the welcome pages shown in Figures 16-3 and 16-4. If you want to have modules other than the default provided by Symfony, you should create an additional security module that would show these pages. Let's create a module called `security` and add two actions into it: `login` and `auth`. The first action would display an information screen stating that login is required in order to access these resources. The second would show an error message saying that the user has no proper credentials. So there is no proper role assigned to this user. These two actions are created only for informational purposes. Symfony delivers these two messages out of the box in its default layout (see Figures 16-3 and 16-4).

To change these default pages you need to make some changes in `settings.yml`. If these entries don't exist, update or create them and then change the default login and action modules to those that were just created. In the `all` and `actions` sections, change the default module and action from **default/login** to **security/login**.

```
all:
  .actions:
      login_module: default
      login_action: login
```

code snippet /basic/symfony/frontend/config/settings.yml

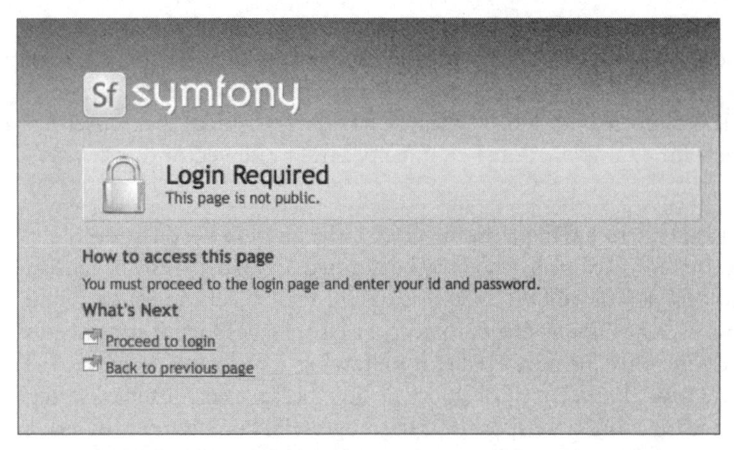

FIGURE 16-3: Symfony default login requirement information page.

This is how it should look after the changes:

Available for download on Wrox.com

```
all:
 .actions:
     login_module: security
     login_action: login
```

code snippet /basic/symfony/frontend/config/settings.yml

To change the default page that shows the credentials requirement information, you need to change a few other entries in the `settings.yml` file.

Available for download on Wrox.com

```
all:
 .actions:
     secure_module: default
     secure_action: secure
```

code snippet /basic/symfony/frontend/config/settings.yml

After modification these entries should look like this:

Available for download on Wrox.com

```
all:
 .actions:
     secure_module: security
     secure_action: auth
```

code snippet /basic/symfony/frontend/config/settings.yml

You can provide any module and action that was previously created. A usual practice is to set them both, or at least the login requirement page entry, to a login action that is not only an informational page but also has a login form within.

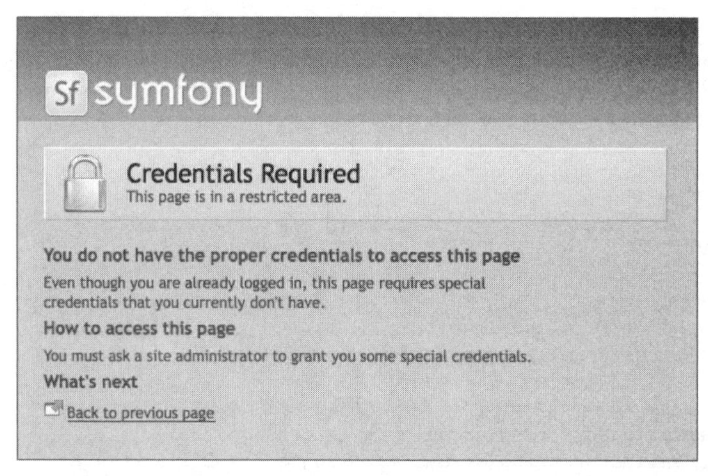

FIGURE 16-4: Symfony default credentials requirement information page.

Basic Security

In the simplest approach, no database for roles and users is needed. Let's say that for the purpose of this section you have three users and the same number of roles. The users are named with capital `A`, `B`, and `C` at the end. Available roles are *admin*, *user*, and *anonymous*. `userA` is anonymous, `userB` is just an authenticated user, and `userC` is an administrator. First, you can create a simple user module with `login` and `logout` actions. These modules should be responsible for checking user authentication, such as giving privileges and also removing them. Then create a `products` module that should be available only for authenticated users and one `secretFeature` for administrators only.

```
$ symfony generate:project securityExample
$ symfony generate:app frontend
$ symfony generate:module frontend user
$ symfony generate:module frontend products
$ symfony generate:module frontend secretFeature
```

Actions need to be added manually to the user module, as described in previous chapters. It will look like this:

Available for download on Wrox.com

```
<?php
class userActions extends sfActions {
    public function executeLogin(){
    }
    public function executeLogout() {
    }
    public function executeIndex() {
    }
}
```

code snippet /basic/symfony/frontend/modules/user/actions/actions.class.php

An index action should be created in the view layer as well as a login form with the following fields: login and password. That's why you need to create a login form definition in the /forms directory. The login form should also have some basic validation rules. Let's define it as shown here:

Available for download on Wrox.com

```
<?php
class LoginForm extends sfForm
{
  public function configure()
  {
    $this->setWidgets(array(
      'login'    => new sfWidgetFormInputText(),
      'password' => new sfWidgetFormInputPassword(),
    ));
    $this->setValidators(array(
      'login'    => new sfValidatorString(array('max_length' => 255)),
      'password' => new sfValidatorString(array('max_length' => 255)),
    ));
  }
}
```

code snippet /basic/symfony/frontend/lib/form/LoginForm.class.php

When you create the preceding form in the index action with `$this->form = new LoginForm(),`, it should be also implemented in the view.

Available for download on Wrox.com

```
<form action="<?php echo url_for('security/login'); ?>" method="POST">
  <table>
    <?php echo $form; ?>
    <tr>
      <td colspan="2">
        <input type="submit" />
      </td>
    </tr>
  </table>
</form>
```

code snippet /basic/symfony/frontend/modules/user/templates/indexSuccess.php

The generated web page should consist of all needed form fields. Notice that there is a CSRF token generated additionally by default. (CSRF is described in more detail in Chapter 8.)

```
<form action="security/login" method="POST">
<table>
  <tr>
    <th><label for="login">Login</label></th>
    <td><input type="text" name="login" id="login" /></td>
  </tr>
  <tr>
    <th><label for="password">Password</label></th>
    <td><input type="password" name="password" id="password" />
      <input type="hidden" name="_csrf_token"
             value="58702cd53a37190250899563f3dd9928"
```

```
                id="csrf_token" />
      </td>
    </tr>
    <tr>
      <td colspan="2">
      <input type="submit" />
    </td>
    </tr>
  </table>
  </form>
```

To simplify this example, user authentication is carried out with `if/else` statements. So, if `userB` or `userC` is sent as login value, the corresponding user will be authenticated.

```
<?php
class userActions extends sfActions {
    public function executeLogin(){
      if ( ($request->getParameter('login') == 'userB') ||
           ($request->getParameter('login') == 'userC')) {
         $this->getUser()->setAuthenticated(true);
         $this->redirect('products/index');
      }
    }
    public function executeLogout(){
      $this->getUser()->setAuthenticated(false);
    }
    public function executeIndex() {
        $this->form = new LoginForm();
    }
}
```

code snippet /basic/symfony/frontend/modules/user/actions/actions.class.php

The user is authenticated now. So far, this gives you nothing because all modules and actions are not yet secured; they are public. To secure an action, you need to create a `/config` directory in the `/module` directory if it doesn't exist. Next you need to create a file called `security.yml` in this `/config` directory. In this example, it should be `secretFeature/config/security.yml`. There you create two actions: `index` and `admin`. The first one should be available for both authenticated users and administrators, and the second one should be for administrators only.

```
index:
   is_secure: true
admin:
   is_secure: true
```

code snippet /basic/symfony/frontend/modules/secretFeature/config/security.yml

Now both actions are secured and cannot be viewed by unauthorized users. The next step is to organize the privileges of actions and give credentials to roles that should have access to concrete actions. For example, for the action `admin` in the `secretFeature` module in `security.yml`, the entry will look as follows:

```
admin:
   is_secure: true
   credentials: [admin]
```

code snippet /basic/symfony/frontend/modules/secretFeature/config/security.yml

In the case of the `index` action, you need to add two roles that are allowed to perform this action: `user` and `admin`. These roles should be given: `user` for authenticated users and `admin` for administrators. You can choose role names as you wish, though they should reflect the real usage. So, for the `index` action, `security.yml` should look something like this:

```
index:
   credentials: [admin,user]
```

code snippet /basic/symfony/frontend/modules/secretFeature/config/security.yml

When you want to provide access for more than one role, just add another role, separated by a comma. When you add the previous entries into `security.yml`, you cannot access these pages because you have still not assigned any of these roles to any user. Therefore the next step in Symfony is to add credentials.

```
<?php
class userActions extends sfActions {
    public function executeLogin(){
      $user = $this->getUser();
      if ($request->getParameter('login') == 'userB') {
         $user->setAuthenticated(true);
         $user->addCredential('user');
      }
      if ($request->getParameter('login') == 'userC') {
         $user->setAuthenticated(true);
         $user->addCredentials('user','admin');
      }
    }
    public function executeLogout(){
      $this->getUser()->setAuthenticated(false);
      $user->clearCredentials();
    }
```

code snippet /basic/symfony/frontend/modules/user/actions/actions.class.php

There are two methods that manipulate the credentials: `clearCredentials()` and `addCredentials()`. The `clearCredentials()` method simply erases all credentials that were given to the user. It is commonly used in `logout` actions. The second one assigns roles to users. These role names can be set as you wish, but the names must be related to role names defined in `security.yml`.

In the view layer you can check if the current user has a credential using the `hasCredential()` method. The following code shows how to do this:

Available for download on Wrox.com

```
<ul>
<?php if ($sf_user->hasCredential('admin')): ?>
<li><?php echo link_to('logout', 'user/logout') ?></li>
<li><?php echo link_to('products','products/index') ?></li>
<li><?php echo link_to('products','products/admin') ?></li>
<?php elseif ($sf_user->hasCredential('user')): ?>
<li><?php echo link_to('logout', 'user/logout') ?></li>
<li><?php echo link_to('products', products/index') ?></li>
<?php else: ?>
<li><?php echo link_to('login', 'user/login') ?></li>
<?php endif; ?>
</ul>
```

code snippet /basic/symfony/frontend/modules/user/templates/indexSuccess.php

Everything described previously is just an example of basic security authentication features. Now it is time to move on to more advanced techniques.

Dynamic Access

Authentication is not usually based on fixed values like those described previously. It's obvious because when there are more than a few users, all your code responsible for security would grow exponentially. That's why when you plan to have a lot of users you should think about a dynamic access algorithm. The easiest way to apply dynamic user access in Symfony is by installing the sfGuard plug-in, which is also available for Doctrine and Propel. You install it just like any other Symfony plug-in.

```
$ symfony plugin:install sfDoctrineGuardPlugin
```

Note that for Propel this plug-in is called sfGuardPlugin instead of sfDoctrineGuardPlugin. There are some plug-in–naming intricacies because of history legacies. In earlier Symfony versions, Propel was the default object-relational mapping (ORM), which is why sfGuardPlugin was dedicated only for Propel and there wasn't a need to name it any differently.

sfDoctrineGuardPlugin provides basic dynamic access functionality. After installation, you need to enable this plug-in within the project configuration file `ProjectConfiguration.class.php`, as shown in the following code, unless the plug-in installation script does that automatically. It's placed in the project `/config` directory.

Available for download on Wrox.com

```
<?php
class ProjectConfiguration extends sfProjectConfiguration {
    public function setup() {
        $this->enablePlugins(array(
            'sfDoctrinePlugin',
            'sfDoctrineGuardPlugin'
        ));
    }
}
```

code snippet /basic/symfony/config/ProjectConfiguration.class.php

Now you can use the features of this plug-in. The sfGuard plug-in's security logic relies on a database, as mentioned before. As is usual in situations of this kind, you need to generate models, forms, and so on because sfGuard delivers only a schema. To do that, run the following command:

```
$ symfony doctrine:build --all
```

Note that after installing sfGuardPlugin you are able to run new tasks in the `guard` group. To see the full task list, just run the `symfony` command:

```
guard
  :add-group
  :add-permission
  :change-password
  :create-user
  :promote
```

So now you can manage users, groups, and so on from the command line. For example, to create a user you can use the following command:

```
$ symfony guard:create-user nowak@wrox.com nowakuser nowakpass  Leszek Nowak
```

To change the password you can use this command:

```
$ symfony guard:change-password nwoakuser nowakpass
```

You can promote a user to be a super-user with the `promote` task:

```
$ symfony guard:promote nowak
```

These commands are nice, but it's not enough. To manage it from the application level, you need to add sfGuard modules.

Available for download on Wrox.com

```
all:
  .settings:
     enabled_modules: [default, sfGuardGroup, sfGuardUser, sfGuardPermission]
```

code snippet /basic/symfony/backend/config/settings.yml

The module gives you the ability to manage groups, users, and permissions directly from the web page, for example: `http://localhost/backend_dev.php/sfGuardUser`. It is probably a good idea to enable these modules within a back-end application. At first glance, these modules are not the pretty ones. To apply Symfony admin stylesheets to them, you need to copy them from `/usr/share/php/symfony/plugins/sfDoctrinePlugin/web/` to your project `/web` directory. For Windows XAMPP, you need to copy them from `C:\xampp\php\PEAR\symfony\plugins\sfDoctrinePlugin\web\`. After this, you should be able to see admin pages similar to those shown in Figures 16-5 and 16-6. You can also access admin pages for `sfGuardPermission` and `sfGuardGroup`.

In Figure 16-5, admin permissions are defined. Add a user and assign it to an admin permission, as shown in Figure 16-6.

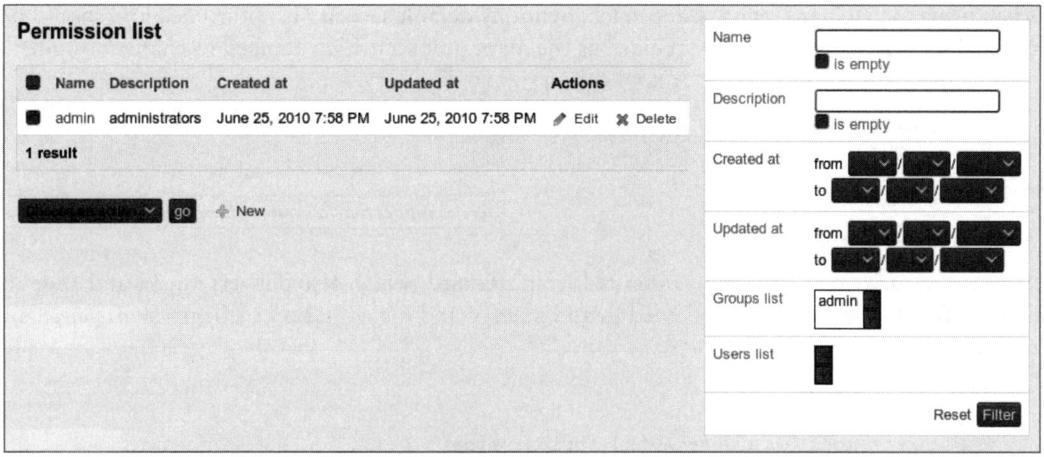

FIGURE 16-5: Symfony permissions admin page.

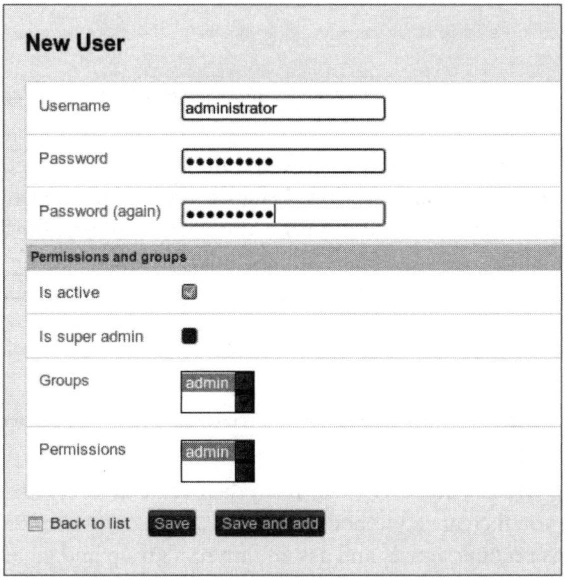

FIGURE 16-6: Symfony sfGuardUser admin page.

All the previous steps are for the back-end side. By enabling the `sfGuardAuth` module, you can gain sfGuard functionalities on the front-end side. As before, you need to enable this module within the front-end `settings.yml` configuration file, as follows:

```
all:
  .settings:
    enabled_modules: [default, sfGuardAuth]
```

code snippet /basic/symfony/frontend/config/settings.yml

When using the sfGuard security approach, Symfony default security is not needed and should be replaced with sfGuard. To apply sfGuard as the main user security, you need to change `myUser.class.php`, which is placed in the application's `/lib` directory.

Available for download on Wrox.com

```
class myUser extends sfGuardSecurityUser {
}
```

code snippet /basic/symfony/frontend/lib/myUser.class.php

Now user security management is inherited from sfGuard, which also delivers `login` and `logout` actions. To add these actions, you need to add `signin` and `signout` actions from the `sfGuardAuth` module to routing rules:

Available for download on Wrox.com

```
sf_guard_signin:
  url:   /login
  param: { module: sfGuardAuth, action: signin }

sf_guard_signout:
  url:   /logout
  param: { module: sfGuardAuth, action: signout }
```

code snippet /basic/symfony/frontend/config/routing.yml

Note that the permissions you defined in the `sfGuardPermission` back-end module are also used as credentials that were described in the basic security approach section. Because you added a permission called `admin`, which is in fact a role definition, you can add it within the `security.yml` file of a module that needs to be secured.

Available for download on Wrox.com

```
index:
  is_secure: true
  credentials: [admin]
```

code snippet /basic/symfony/frontend/modules/secretFeature/config/security.yml

As you can see, it works well. In most cases, you will not add every user from the back-end side, but within a front-end controller. For this example, you'll create a method called `executeCreateAccount()`, which will add a user, set his password, make his account active, and assign him to a group and give him permissions.

Available for download on Wrox.com

```
<?php
    class securityActions extends sfActions {
        public function executeCreateAccount() {
    $user = new sfGuardUser();
    $user->setUsername($this->getRequestParameter('username'));
    $user->setPassword($this->getRequestParameter('password'));
    $user->setIsActive(false);
    $user->save();
    $user->addGroupByName("admin");
    $user->addPermissionByName("admin");
}
```

code snippet /basic/symfony/frontend/modules/security/actions/actions.class.php

You need to create also a registration form that should have `username` and `password` fields. These fields are taken from the form. Note that the password and the salt are created appropriately as a SHA1 hash and as a random generated hash. (Salt is described in detail in the "CSRF" section of Chapter 8.) Take a look at the database to see the results. In fact, this is a nice feature because you don't need to spend time on generating secure passwords. The next step is user activation. For a `true` value, the user is activated; for `false`, it is deactivated. At the end you need to assign the user to a group and/or permission. This is important when you define roles within the application.

One commonly used extension of sfGuard is a plug-in that registers the login history. To install it, do the following:

```
$ symfony plugin:install sfDoctrineGuardLoginHistoryPlugin
```

CakePHP

CakePHP presents a different approach. Security is entirely based on an ACL. In fact, you could say that the ACL mechanism is based on relations between the requested resource and the requester.

Defining ACL Entries

CakePHP defines two main tables: *ARO* and *ACO*, which stand for *access request objects* and *access control objects*. ARO maintains users and, if needed, groups. ACO is responsible for storing controllers and actions. There is also a third table that defines the relation between these tables. This table realizes the ideology of ACLs. Each user has access to a fixed amount of actions. In CakePHP, this boils down to controlling main actions for each model. These actions are create, read, update, and delete (CRUD) actions. To create all tables needed to make user authentication and authorization operations possible, just run the following command in your `/app` project directory:

```
$ cake acl initdb
```

You can now define some basic users and actions that can be requested later. One way to do this is to use CakePHP's command line interface (CLI) commands. You need two groups: `User` and `Admin`. To create these groups, run the following commands:

```
$ cake acl create aro / Admin
$ cake acl create aro / User
$ cake acl create aro / Guest
```

These commands create two main groups. The root sign (`/`) denotes that there is nothing higher in the hierarchy, so these entries don't belong to anything. Adding users is simple as well. Instead of the root, you need to enter the right group:

```
$ cake acl create aro User UserB
```

To see which entries you already have, you can execute the following command:

```
$ cake acl view aro
```

You should see something similar to this:

```
[1]Admin
[2]User
  [4]UserB
[3]Guest
```

So you have three groups and one user that belong to the group `User`. Note that the ARO/ACO rules have a tree structure that gives you more flexibility when developing a web application. For now, you have defined only requesters. Now it's time for definitions of actions and controllers. Create a controller called `Confidential` and grant access to this controller for the `sample` user. To create this controller, you need to create a `confidential_controller.php` file in the `/controller` path with the following content:

```
<?php
class ConfidentialController extends AppController {
    var $name = 'Confidential';
    function index() {
    }
 }
```

code snippet /basic/cakephp/app/controllers/confidential_controller.php

Before granting any privileges to this controller, you need to create an appropriate ACO entry:

```
$ cake acl create aco / Confidential
```

Note that the second parameter is also the route to a controller/action in the application address (for example, `http://localhost/Confidential`). You also need to create an `index.ctp` view file for this controller in order to prevent error messages. To give `sample` user privileges to access this resource, you need to run this command:

```
$ cake acl grant sample Confidential *
```

The last sign in this command means that `sample` user has all privileges provided by `Confidential`.

Accessing Resources

First of all, you need to create a `User` controller that holds `login()` and `logout()` actions:

```
<?php
class UsersController extends Controller {
    var $name = 'Users';
    var $uses = array('User');
    var $components = array('Auth');
    function login(){
    }
    function logout(){
    }
}
```

code snippet /basic/cakephp/app/controllers/users_controller.php

Next, you need to create a view template for each method. An exemplary `login.ctp` view may look as follows:

```
<?php echo $form->create('User',
    array('action' => 'login','id'=>'main_login_form'));?>
<div class="oneline">
  <?php echo $form->input('login', array('label'=>array('text'=>'USERNAME',
```

```
        'class'=>'text_label')'class'=>'text','div'=> NULL)); ?>
    <?php echo $form->input('password',array('label'=>array('text'=>'PASSWORD',
        'class'=>'text_label'),'class'=>'text','div'=>NULL)); ?>
    <input type="submit" value="SIGN-IN" class="submit" />
</div>
<?php echo $form->end(); ?>
```

code snippet /basic/cakephp/app/views/users/login.ctp

CakePHP delivers form helpers, some of which you used previously. The first parameter of `create()` is the name of the model that is to be created. Further parameters are given as an array of `<form>` tag attributes. There are also two `input()` methods that print `<input>` tags with appropriate name attributes set to `login` and `password`. These fields are not the default ones provided by the `Auth` component responsible for user authentication. To change these settings, edit `Auth.php`, which is placed in the `cake/libs/controller/components/` folder of the project. You need to find the lines shown here and change the `username` and `password` values:

```
var $fields = array('username' => 'login', 'password' => 'password');
```

The same is true for the model that is used for authentication. By default, it is `User`. To change the default value, you also need this line in `Auth.php`:

```
var $userModel = 'User';
```

To do anything with users, you need to create a `User` model in `/app/models` as `user.php`, which should at least contain the following code:

```
<?php
class User extends AppModel {
  var $name = 'User';
}
```

code snippet /basic/cakephp/app/models/user.php

As described earlier, the user authentication controller should contain `login()` and `logout()` actions. For the given login form (as described previously), the `login()` action should look like the following:

```
function login() {
    if(!empty($this->data)) {
        $this->Auth->login($this->data);
        if($this->Auth->user()){
             $this->redirect('/', null, true);
        }
    }
}
```

code snippet /basic/cakephp/app/controllers/users_controller.php

If the form data is not empty, it should proceed to the `Auth login()` method, which checks whether the `/login/password` entry exists in the model with defined fields. If it does, then the user is redirected to the main page; otherwise, the login form is shown.

The Auth component also delivers a logout() method that does everything automatically. For security reasons, the Session should also be destroyed. Then the user is redirected to the main page:

```
function logout() {
     $this->Auth->logout();
     $this->Session->destroy();
     $this->redirect('/', null, true);
}
```

code snippet /basic/cakephp/app/controllers/users_controller.php

The authentication mechanism is not working yet because there is one more thing still missing. To enable access control security for each controller, you need to edit the AppController.php, which is placed in the /app directory. Code that is stored within beforeFilter() is executed before everything else. Also because all controllers that a developer normally defines inherit from the AppController, this code is executed for every other controller as well:

```
<?php
class AppController extends Controller {
  var $components = array('Auth', 'Acl');
  function beforeFilter() {
    $this->Auth->loginAction = array('controller'=>'users','action'=>'login');
    $this->Auth->logoutRedirect = array('controller'=>'pages','action'=>'index');
    $this->Auth->loginRedirect = array('controller'=>'pages','action'=>'index');
    }
```

code snippet /basic/cakephp/app/app_controller.php

First of all, authorization and authentication components need to be loaded. Next login and logout actions are defined. These are the default ones if CakePHP points out that the current user has no credentials to access a controller/action. Note that the default ARO-ACO relation defines the access to four CRUD actions. Not every controller defines only these actions, which is why those mostly used are mapped by default in Auth.php to proper CRUD actions. The mapping is as follows:

```
var $actionMap = array(
    'index'       => 'read',
    'add'         => 'create',
    'edit'        => 'update',
    'view'        => 'read',
    'remove'      => 'delete'
);
```

code snippet /basic/cakephp/cake/lib/controller/components/auth.php

You can search for this in Auth.php.

Dynamic ACL Creation

To define access control rules, you have used CLI commands. This is a hard way to execute them from PHP code. CakePHP also delivers aro and aco classes. To define a User group, as done previously with CLI, you need to invoke the following code:

Available for download on Wrox.com

```
$aro = new aro();
$aro->create();
$aro->save(array(
      'model'=>'User',
      'foreign_key'=>null,
      'parent_id'=>null,
      'alias'=>'User'));
```

code snippet /basic/cakephp/app/controllers/acl_controller.php

A foreign key is used to point to a concrete ID of a given model; for example, user, with an ID equal to 1. Because aro/aco lists can be tree hierarchies, there can be groups and users within other groups. That's why parent_id is used — to point to the parent entry from the list. Defining an ACL list usually requires more effort than in the RBAC case because concrete users are assigned to every resource (controller/action). To decrease this effort, users are grouped. This is the code you need to invoke when you want to assign a user to a previously created User group:

Available for download on Wrox.com

```
$parent = $aro->findByAlias('User');
$parentId = $parent['Aro']['id'];
$aro->create();
$aro->save(array(
      'model'=>'User',
      'foreign_key'=>1,
      'parent_id'=>$parentId,
      'alias'=>'User::1'));
```

code snippet /basic/cakephp/app/controllers/acl_controller.php

At the beginning, you need to search for a group called User. If this group exists, its ID is retrieved. Because the exemplary user has an id equal to 1, the foreign key is set to 1. Additionally, the alias should be unique; that's why it's commonly a concatenate of the model name and the foreign key, separated with a double colon.

The next step is to define an ACO entry. Let it be the User controller. The following code should solve this:

Available for download on Wrox.com

```
$aco = new Aco();
$aco->create();
$aco->save(array(
     'model'=>'User',
     'foreign_key'=>null,
     'parent_id'=>null,
     'alias'=>'User'));
```

code snippet /basic/cakephp/app/controllers/acl_controller.php

Analogically, in the case of ARO you can define groups. To allow users in the User group to access all actions in the User controller, you need to execute this code:

Available for download on Wrox.com

```
$this->Acl->allow('User', 'User', '*');
```

code snippet /basic/cakephp/app/controllers/acl_controller.php

The first parameter is the ARO, and second one is ACO.

Available for download on Wrox.com

```
var $component = array('Acl');
```

code snippet /basic/cakephp/app/controllers/acl_controller.php

Don't forget to enable the Auth component in the controller where you want to use the previous code.

Zend Framework

Zend Framework (ZF) doesn't support any CLI commands for ACLs or authentication. Nevertheless you can accomplish user access control just as you do in CakePHP or Symfony. ZF delivers two classes (Zend_Acl and Zend_Auth) that you use to realize the authentication and authorization mechanisms.

Authentication

To authenticate users, you need to make it possible to get their username and password from them. Therefore, you need to define a login form with username and password fields. As you know from Chapter 5, you need to create a form definition in the application's /forms directory. The login form should look like this:

Available for download on Wrox.com

```
<?php
class Application_Form_Login extends Zend_Form {
    public function init() {
      $this->setMethod('post');
      $this->addElement('text', 'username', array(
             'label'    => 'Username:',
             'required'   => false,
             'filters'    => array('StringTrim'),
              )
      );
      $this->addElement('password', 'Password:', array(
             'label'    => 'Password:',
             'required'   => false,
             'filters'    => array('StringTrim'),
             )
      );
      $this->addElement('submit', 'submit', array(
            'ignore'   => true,
            'label'    => 'Login'
     ));
```

```
        }
    }
    ?>
```

code snippet /basic/zf/application/forms/Login.php

That's quite obvious. Now, you need to add this form to the `login` method in `IndexController.php`. This controller is used in the example to simplify it. Add this form as follows:

```
public function login() {
    $form = new Application_Form_Login();
     if ($this->getRequest()->isPost()){
        if ($form->isValid($request->getPost())) {
            /* authentication code here */
        }
    }
    $this->view->form = $form;
}
```

code snippet /basic/zf/application/controllers/IndexController.php

As soon as the form data is sent and validated, the authentication can proceed. First, database credentials need to be set. To do that, you need to create an array with database information that will be used for user authentication. In the example, this configuration is as follows:

```
$config= array('dbname'=>'addressBook',
                  'username'=> 'dbUser',
                  'password' =>'secret',
                  'hostname' => 'localhost',
                  );
```

code snippet /basic/zf/application/controllers/IndexController.php

The preceding configuration needs to be loaded into a proper database adapter. Let's say that you use MySQL as the database, so the configuration should be loaded like this:

```
$db = new Zend_Db_Adapter_Pdo_Mysql($config);
```

Next, you need to create a proper table within your database. This table will store information about users and will be used to verify them.

```
CREATE TABLE IF NOT EXISTS users (
  uid int(11) NOT NULL AUTO_INCREMENT,
  username varchar(32) NOT NULL,
  password varchar(32) NOT NULL,
  PRIMARY KEY (uid)
);
```

You also need to add an example user:

```
INSERT INTO users (username, password) VALUES ('admin', 'secret');
```

After that, you can add the MySQL database adapter and create an instance of `DbTable`. You also need to define which table and which fields should be taken into consideration.

Available for download on Wrox.com

```
$adapter = new Zend_Auth_Adapter_DbTable($db);
$adapter
    ->setTableName('users')
    ->setIdentityColumn('username')
    ->setCredentialColumn('password');
```

code snippet /basic/zf/application/controllers/IndexController.php

The rest of the code is dedicated to authenticate concrete users. The following shows an example setting using `username` and `password` as the authentication values:

Available for download on Wrox.com

```
$adapter
    ->setIdentity($form->getValue('username'))
    ->setCredential($form->getValue('password'));
```

code snippet /basic/zf/application/controllers/IndexController.php

An instance of `Zend_Auth` needs to be created because it does all the authentication work. The `authenticate()` method with the adapter attribute checks the table and fields for a given username and password. The result is stored in the *`$result`* variable.

Available for download on Wrox.com

```
$auth = Zend_Auth::getInstance();
$result = $auth->authenticate($adapter);
```

code snippet /basic/zf/application/controllers/IndexController.php

If the result of the `isValid()` method returns `true`, the user is authenticated successfully, and is redirected to the `index` action.

Available for download on Wrox.com

```
if($result->isValid()) {
    return $this->_helper->redirector('index');
}
```

code snippet /basic/zf/application/controllers/IndexController.php

Authentication data is stored, and to delete that data you need to use the `clearIdentity()` method of `Zend_Auth`.

Available for download on Wrox.com

```
public function logout() {
    $auth = Zend_Auth::getInstance();
    $auth->clearIdentity();
}
```

code snippet /basic/zf/application/controllers/IndexController.php

A good approach is to create a link that redirects the user to the `logout` action that clears all credentials, as shown previously.

Authorization

The shortest way to put an ACL approach into practice is to define ACLs within, for example, `.AddressBookAcl.php`. It should be placed in the `/library` directory.

Available for download on Wrox.com

```
<?php
class AddressBookAcl extends Zend_Acl {
     public function __construct() {
        /* ACL roles, resources and privileges */
     }
}
```

code snippet /basic/zf/library/AddressBookAcl.php

You store `AddressBookAcl.php` in the `/library` path because these rules need to be available for all controllers. You need to define the resources that should be secured:

Available for download on Wrox.com

```
$this->add(new Zend_Acl_Resource('index'));
$this->add(new Zend_Acl_Resource('confidential'));
$this->add(new Zend_Acl_Resource('backend'));
```

code snippet /basic/zf/library/AddressBookAcl.php

These are the controller names. Next, roles should be defined:

Available for download on Wrox.com

```
$this->addRole(new Zend_Acl_Role('guest'));
$this->addRole(new Zend_Acl_Role('user'), 'guest');
$this->addRole(new Zend_Acl_Role('admin'), 'user');
```

code snippet /basic/zf/library/AddressBookAcl.php

Note that the user role inherits from the guest role because the user role includes guest privileges.

Available for download on Wrox.com

```
$this->allow('guest', 'index');
$this->allow('user', 'confidential');
$this->allow('admin');
```

code snippet /basic/zf/library/AddressBookAcl.php

The last thing is to define the relations between resources and roles so the constructed access list meets your needs. You can also build ACLs more dynamically by loading them from the database. This is a good approach only if the access list is short because loading a long access list would take time and reduce performance. To enable `AddressBookAcl` you need to include its class definition within the application's `Bootstrap.php`.

Available for download on Wrox.com

```
<?php
require_once("AddressBookAcl.php");
class Bootstrap extends Zend_Application_Bootstrap_Bootstrap
{
```

code snippet /basic/zf/application/Bootstrap.php

Finally, you need to add ACLs within each controller. A good place is the `init()` method because it's invoked each time any action of this controller is executed.

```
<?php
class IndexController extends Zend_Controller_Action {
     function init(){
        $controller = $request->getControllerName();
        $acl = new AddressBookAcl();
        $acl->isAllowed($auth->getIndentity(),$controller);
   }
```

code snippet /basic/zf/application/controllers/IndexController.php

IDENTIFYING USERS USING LDAP IMPLEMENTATION

In almost all cases, authentication mechanisms are built using databases. This is a good approach in general because it is easy to set up and configure, so it is attainable for everyone. But there is a faster and more maintainable solution, based on directory services and commonly used by corporations: the *Lightweight Directory Access Protocol* (*LDAP*), based on the X.500 standard, has various implementations. Authentication mechanisms based on LDAP are much faster than those based on relational databases, because they are just simpler. This is one of the reasons why LDAP is used for authentication purposes instead of relational databases.

In the following examples, you will be using OpenLDAP, which is an open source project; and *Active Directory Application Mode* (ADAM), which is an LDAP implementation offered by Microsoft. ADAM is free for use and is still very close to the LDAP standard, so it will be used here instead of Active Directory — another Microsoft LDAP implementation. Please, do not mistake ADAM (and its newer version called AD LDS) with Active Directory, which is a different and much more complex product.

Microsoft also delivers an LDAP implementation that is called *Active Directory Lightweight Directory Services* (*AD LDS*), which is a newer version of ADAM. In fact, it is just the same as ADAM, but it is a renamed version released for Windows 7 and later operating systems. The most important changes are the name and Windows 7 integration. In the examples you'll be using both ADAM and AD LDS. You will probably not see any differences, but when there are considerable ones, we will discuss them. There are also other LDAP implementations, such as IBM Tivoli Directory Server or Red Hat 389 Directory Server. They should work as well, but they are not within the scope of this book.

Requirements

There are no special requirements needed to start. ADAM and AD LDS installation will be presented for Windows operating systems, while on Linux you need to install the LDAP PHP extension.

For ADAM you need to download the installation files. The file used here was `ADAMSP1_x86_English.exe`, which is available at the Microsoft downloads web page.

```
www.microsoft.com/downloads/en/details.aspx?familyid=96
88f8b9-1034-4ef6-a3e5-2a2a57b5c8e4&displaylang=en
```

The name may change in the future, but probably not much. You can type **Microsoft ADAM** into Google, and you should see a link to this page in the results. There is additionally a multilingual add-on available with `MUI` (Multilingual User Interface) in the name of the installer. Notice that these installers are available for two processor architectures: x86 and x64.

If you are using Windows 7, you should download AD LDS, which you can find here:

```
http://www.microsoft.com/downloads/en/details.aspx?familyid=A45
059AF-47A8-4C96-AFE3-93DAB7B5B658&displaylang=en
```

You can access this web page easily by typing **Microsoft AD LDS download** into Google. The proper installation file is called `Windows6.1-KB975541-x86.msu`. The `.msu` extension is a Windows Update extension, so this is not just a separate application but also an extension of the Windows operating system.

Before installing any LDAP implementations, please make sure that you are not running any other implementation of LDAP because ports can be blocked, which could be troublesome. So before doing anything with LDAP in PHP, you need to see whether PHP's LDAP extension is installed. XAMPP delivers it out of the box. Under UNIX systems, you usually need to install this extension separately. Under Ubuntu, you need to run this command with root privileges:

```
# apt-get install php-ldap
```

Under RHEL, after downloading the proper RPM package from one of the RPM repository sites, you need to use the following command to install LDAP support in PHP:

```
# rpm -i php-ldap-*.rpm
```

You must, of course, install PHP first, because it's a prerequisite.

Under FreeBSD you need to go to `/usr/ports/net/php5-ldap/` and invoke the following command:

```
# make
```

To make sure that the PHP LDAP extension is installed, you need to find the `php.ini` file in the PHP extension directory. If you use Windows and XAMPP, that directory will be `c:\<XAMPP PATH>\php\ext\`, where `<XAMPP PATH>` is the directory in which you have installed XAMPP. In UNIX systems, the directory is almost always `/usr/lib/php/`.

```
;extension=php_ldap.dll
```

You generally also need to enable the LDAP extension in the `php.ini` config file, most often found in `/etc/php5/apache/`. (To *enable* means to delete the comma or hash before an extension library name.) Sometimes these config entries are separate files for each module (in Ubuntu, for example) placed in `/etc/php5/apache/conf.d`.

```
extension=ldap.so
```

In Windows, the extensions are stored in `.dll` files; under UNIX, they are stored in `.so` files.

How Does LDAP Work?

LDAP stores data records just like ordinary relational databases. The difference between these two is that databases are flat and LDAP has a tree structure in which each object can be subordinate to another one. Additionally, in LDAP each object can have a different structure. So LDAP is heterogeneous, unlike databases. In databases, each record in a table has the same structure. Each record is identified by its primary key. In LDAP, each record is identified by its *distinguished name* (*DN*) like `cn=przystalski, ou=authors, o=wrox, c=us`. So a company like Wrox will have its global information stored in `o=wrox, c=us`, but information on authors will be available in `ou=authors, o=wrox, c=us`. Similarly, when you want to see some information about an editor you should ask about `cn=dinse, ou=editors, o=wrox ,c=us`; or to see all editors, just `ou=editors, o=wrox, c=us`. In databases, you would do a SQL query like this one: `SELECT * from editors;` or `SELECT * FROM editors WHERE surname='Dinse';`

Preparing LDAP

In the following sections, you install each LDAP engine and you can decide which best suits your needs. First, we describe the installation of ADAM. Next you move to OpenLDAP installation and configuration.

ADAM Installation

After downloading the proper installer, run it and a welcome dialog should be displayed (see Figure 16-7).

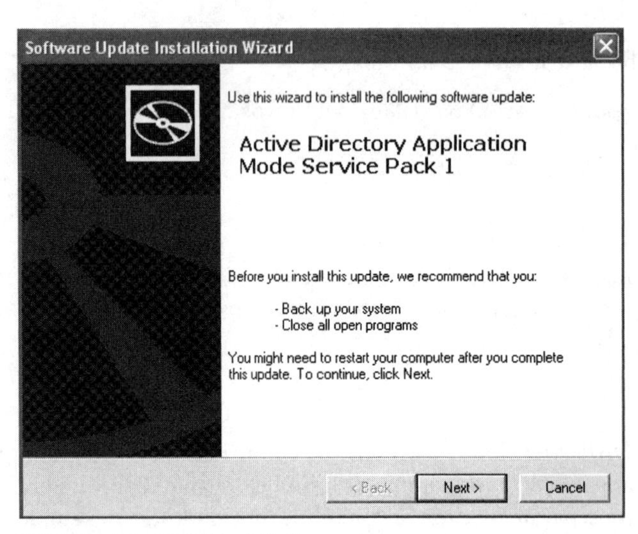

FIGURE 16-7: ADAM installation welcome page.

The next steps are very common to any other installations. Just read the license, click Next a few times and Finish at the end. That's all you do to install ADAM. In Windows 7, it looks a little bit different (see Figure 16-8). Just answer Yes and the installation moves on.

This update installs AD LDS shortcuts in the Windows Control Panel.

OpenLDAP Installation

With OpenLDAP, it's probably easier. You only need to choose which distribution to use. Although each of them can call OpenLDAP in a different way, in most cases it's with `openldap`.

FIGURE 16-8: AD LDS installation welcome page.

Ubuntu

Installation is very simple, but in Ubuntu the OpenLDAP package is called `slapd`. This can be confusing.

```
# apt-get install slapd
```

FreeBSD

Installation is nothing special; just `make` the `openldap` package that belongs to the `net-nds` group.

```
# cd /usr/ports/net-nds/openldap
# make
```

Gentoo

Installation is accomplished as with FreeBSD, but by using `emerge`.

```
# emerge -av openldap
```

Other

With Linux distributions such as Red Hat, you need to install `.rpm` packages. See Appendix B for a list of websites in which you can find the `.rpm` packages.

LDAP Configuration

After completing the installation, you need to configure OpenLDAP or ADAM/AD LDS for it to work properly.

ADAM Configuration

The following steps walk you through ADAM configuration:

1. To start configuring ADAM, choose Create an ADAM Instance from the Windows Start Menu (see Figure 16-9).

FIGURE 16-9: Configuration shortcut.

As described earlier, AD LDS shortcuts are available from the Administrative Tools in the Control Panel. Two shortcuts are of interest to us for this example: Active Directory Lightweight Directory Services and ADSI Edit (see Figure 16-10). The first shortcut is an equivalent of the Create an ADAM Instance shortcut.

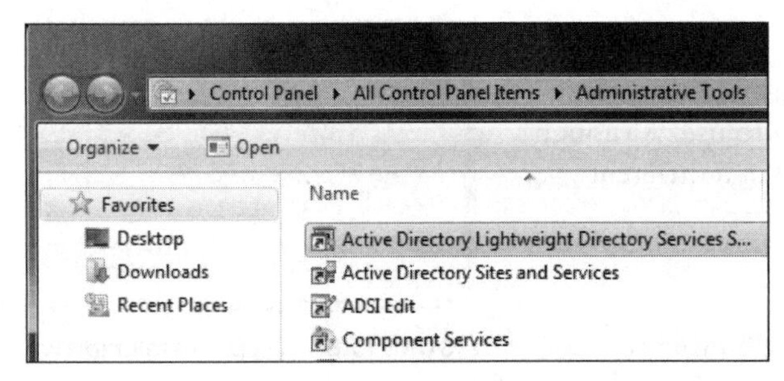

FIGURE 16-10: AD LDS Control Panel shortcuts.

2. After clicking "Create an ADAM instance," a welcome page for the ADAM/AD LDS instance creation wizard displays, as shown in Figure 16-11.

The steps are the same for ADAM and for AD LDS from this point through importing LDAP Data Interchange Format (LDIF) files.

FIGURE 16-11: ADAM configuration welcome page.

3. On the next page, you need to furnish an instance name that will be visible in Windows Services. If you want to use more than one instance, you should provide meaningful names (see Figure 16-12).

Type a name for this instance. The name should reflect the use for which this instance of ADAM is intended.

Instance name:

WroxInstance

Example: Addressbook1

FIGURE 16-12: ADAM instance name page.

4. The next screen, shown in Figure 16-13, asks about instance ports. The default ports are commonly used: 389 for a plain connection and 636 for a secure connection. These port numbers are also the default in other LDAP implementations. Note that if you try to create a second instance without deleting the previous one, you will see some other ports as the defaults. This is annoying in most cases because you cannot set 389/636 ports.

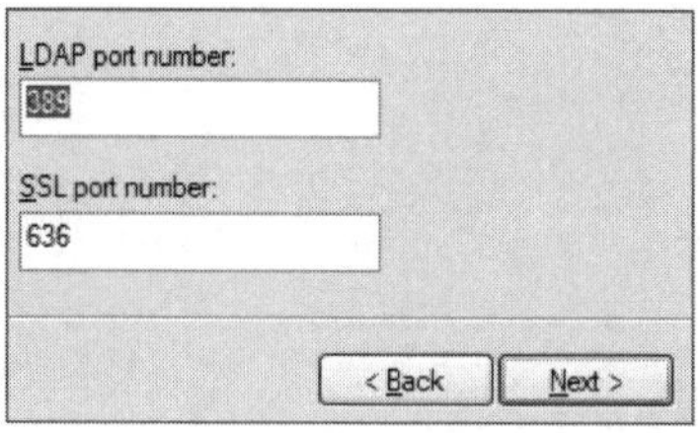

FIGURE 16-13: ADAM instance port settings.

5. Next, you should set the main distinguished name. In the example, it's `o=wrox,c=us`. The main DN should be simple, but also meaningful. Figure 16-14 shows how to set a DN.

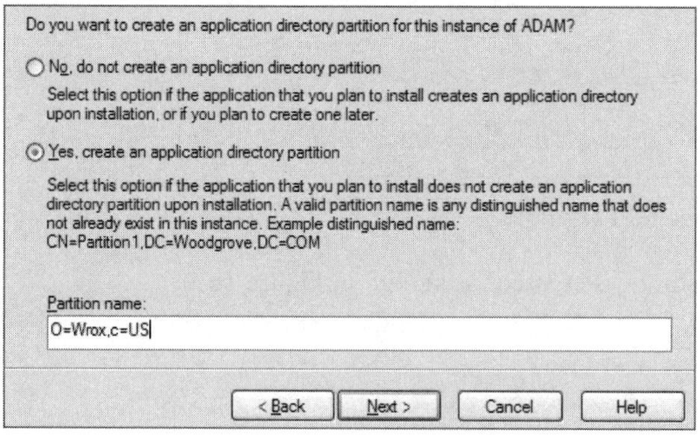

FIGURE 16-14: ADAM instance main DN setting.

6. After setting the main distinguished name, you should also specify which LDIF files should be imported into the ADAM/AD LDS instance. LDIF files are commonly used to modify any LDAP entry or setting. These files have an `.ldif` or `.ldf` extension. To make it simple, apart from modifying LDAP entries, these files are also sometimes used to define kind of a model-like structure of users that will be stored in LDAP. Generalizing, you can compare it with defining a table with structures like *id*, *username*, *password*, and so on. In this case, you need only `MS-User.LDF` because you will define only users. This LDIF adds Microsoft-specific attributes as well, which are not commonly used except by Microsoft solutions. In Figure 16-15, three LDIFs are selected to be added.

   Each instance exists as a service. These services have their associated permissions. In the case of web applications, it is easier to start an ADAM/AD LDS instance with Windows default privileges, as shown in Figure 16-16.

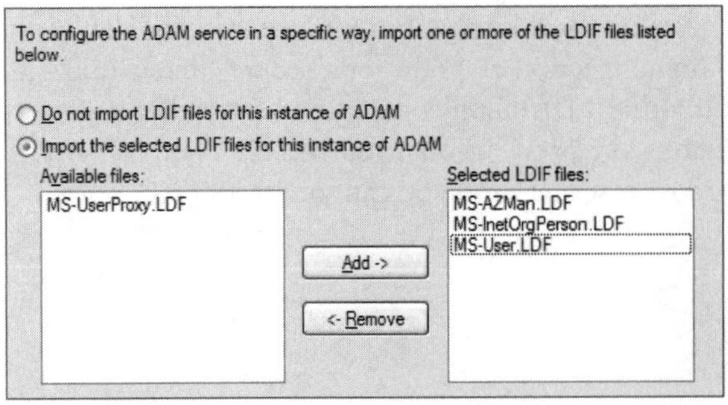

FIGURE 16-15: ADAM LDIF importing.

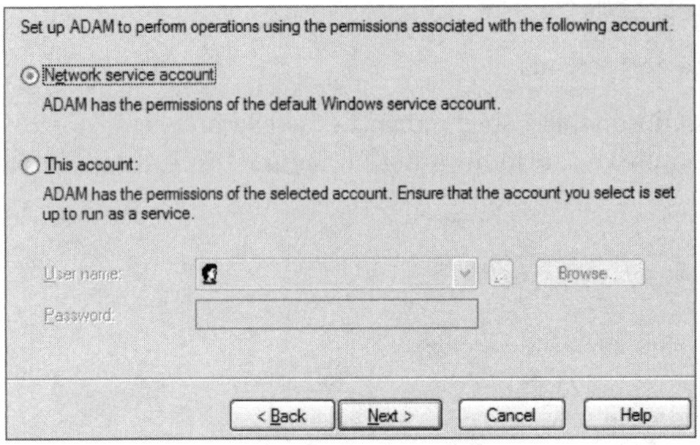

FIGURE 16-16: ADAM Instance port settings.

7. After clicking Next, an instance is created, as shown in Figure 16-17.

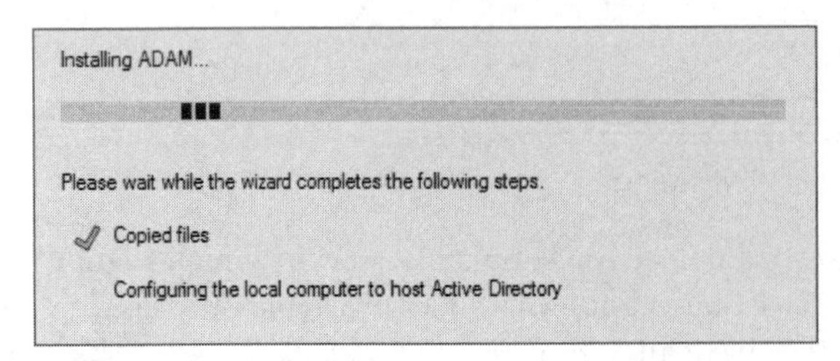

FIGURE 16-17: ADAM instance creation.

The ADAM/AD LDS instance is now visible in Services. To see it, go to Administrative Tools in the Control Panel. There should be a shortcut to Services. The instance is shown in Figure 16-18. You can start/stop and restart particular instances.

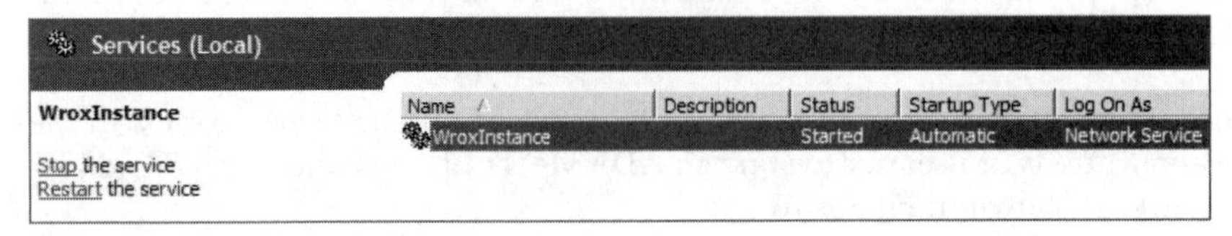

FIGURE 16-18: ADAM instance service.

The preceding steps illustrate only the beginning of ADAM/AD LDS configuration. For the example, you also need to create a few user accounts, as shown in the following steps, to make it possible to authenticate users.

1. To connect to an instance, you need to run the ADSI Edit application and right-click the ADSI Edit root node. There should be an option available called Connect To, as shown in Figure 16-19.

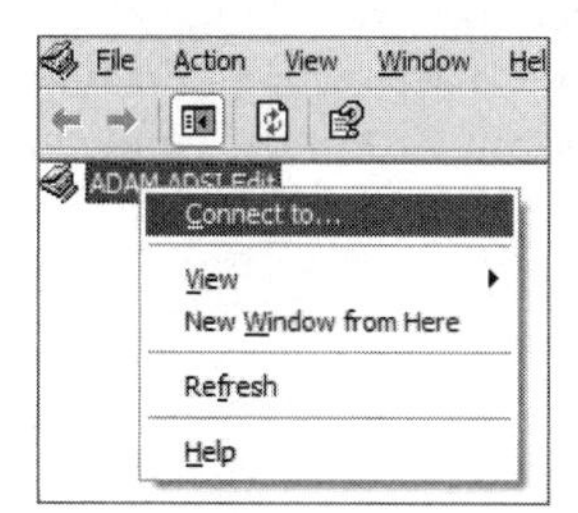

FIGURE 16-19: ADAM browser.

2. There are two main connection types that you can use to configure the instance. The first is to connect as a user, and the second is to connect as an administrator (super-user) to configure the LDAP server. The second one is named Configuration. This example uses the configuration context to connect to it, as shown in Figure 16-20.

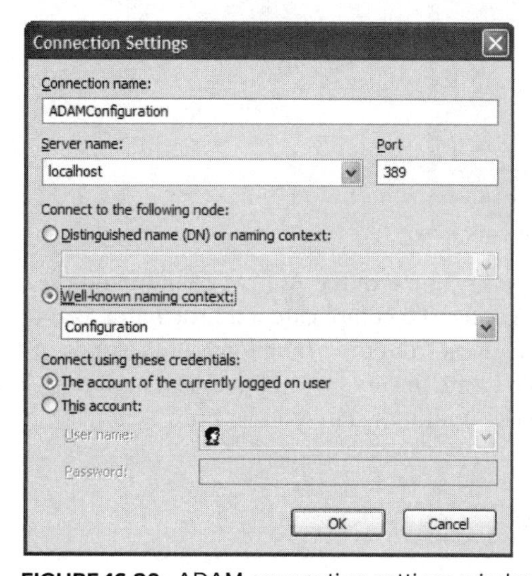

FIGURE 16-20: ADAM connection settings window.

This connection type allows you to change instance configuration.

3. After filling in the connection settings and clicking OK, you should see a new entry, as shown in Figure 16-21.

Adding New Users

To add a user, you need to use the second connection type mentioned in Step 2 and shown in Figure 16-20 in the previous section.

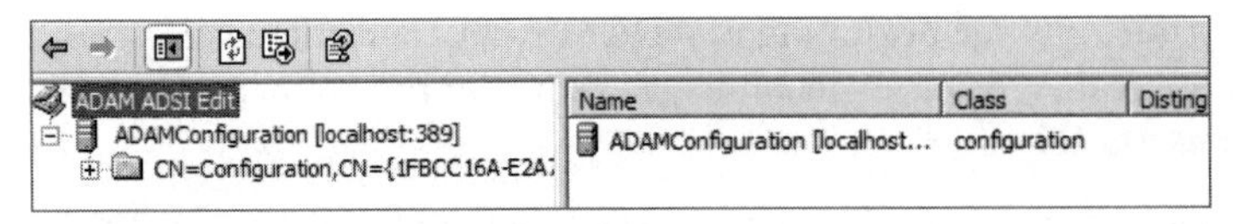

FIGURE 16-21: ADAM configuration browser.

1. A good idea is to start adding users to the root node. Therefore, you should connect to the server using as the connection point the main DN, which is `o=wrox,c=us`. In Windows 7, the server name (or server IP) and port number are in the bottom part of the window. The filled form shown in Figure 16-22 allows you to connect to LDAP.

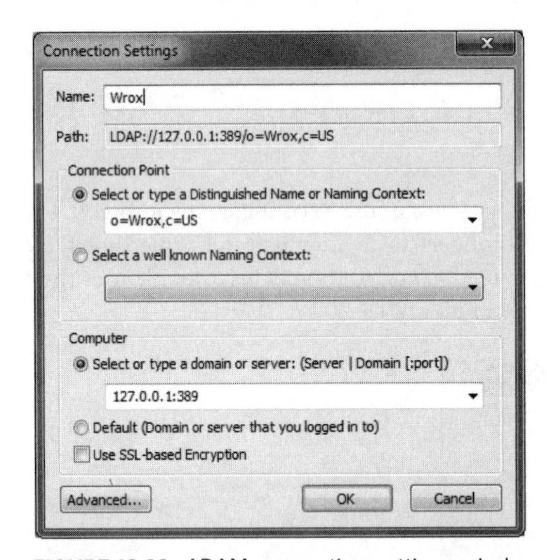

FIGURE 16-22: ADAM connection settings window.

2. Now because you added `MS-User.LDF` (in Step 6 of the ADAM configuration section), you can create users as objects in the LDAP tree. To complicate it a little more, you can add units like `authors` and `editors` to separate users from their functions. These kinds of objects are called `organizationalUnits`. To create the `authors` object, you need to right-click the main DN and invoke the New ➪ Object option as shown in Figure 16-23.

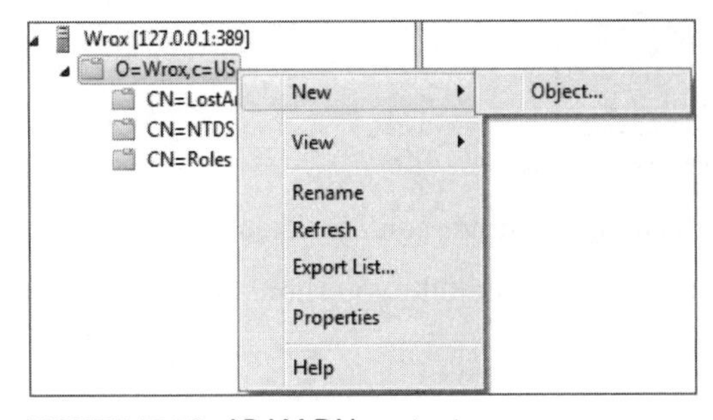

FIGURE 16-23: ADAM DN context menu.

3. Next, choose the proper object class from the list, as shown in Figure 16-24.

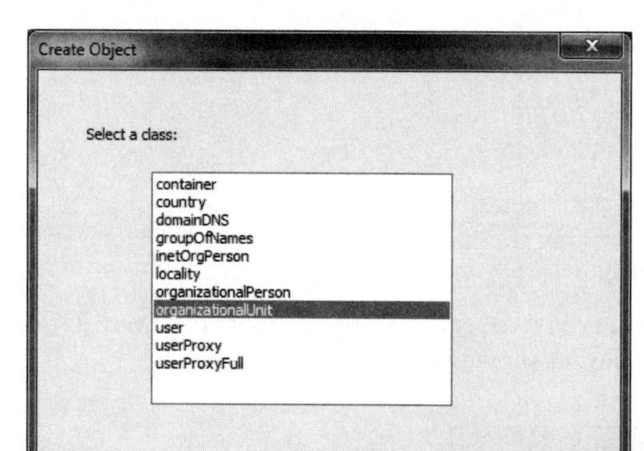

FIGURE 16-24: ADAM object class list.

4. After you press Next you can enter the unit name, as shown in Figure 16-25.

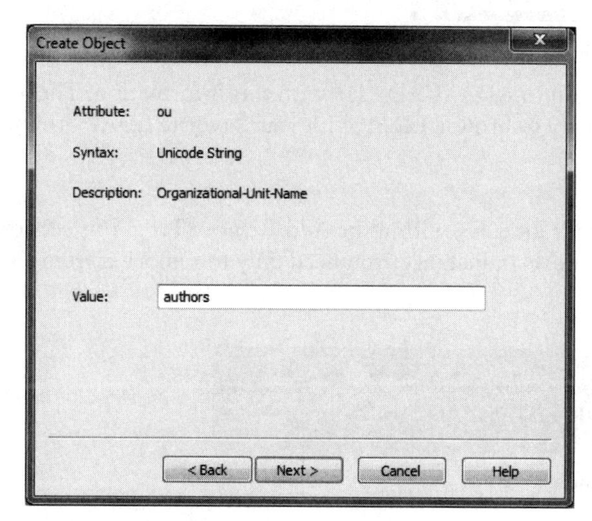

FIGURE 16-25: ADAM unit naming window.

This creates an `authors` unit. You can do the same with other units. You should see these units in the tree as new nodes.

5. Adding users should be done in the same way as units, but instead of right-clicking `o=wrox,c=us`, just add users by right-clicking the proper unit, which can be `ou=authors,o=wrox,c=us`, for example. After that, you should see a list of users as shown in Figure 16-26.

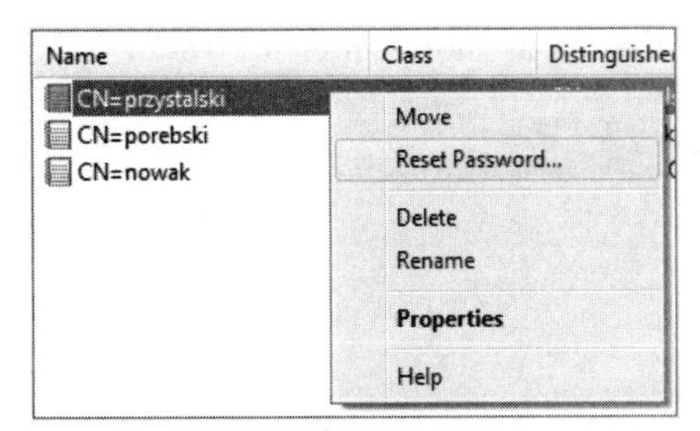

FIGURE 16-26: Password changing.

6. To finish the configuration, you need to reset passwords for users that were just created. A password dialog should display, as shown in Figure 16-27.

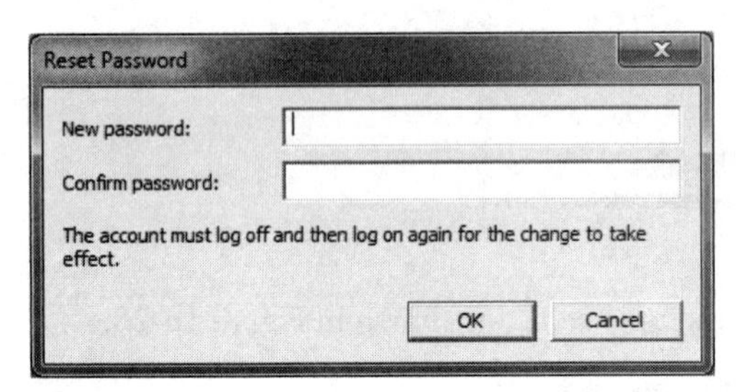

FIGURE 16-27: Password changing popup.

After password resetting, you can log in to ADAM/AD LDS with this information. The login name is the DN of each user. Now you can try to browse LDAP with your favorite LDAP browser tool.

Uninstalling ADAM

While being created, each instance adds an entry within the Add/Remove Programs section of the Control Panel in Windows XP. To remove an instance, you need only to remove it from this list (see Figure 16-28).

FIGURE 16-28: Uninstalling ADAM instance.

In Windows 7, instances are shown in Programs and Features in the Control Panel. From there, you can remove unneeded AD LDS instances.

OpenLDAP Configuration

The following steps walk you through configuration of OpenLDAP, which is not as clickable as it is with ADAM/AD LDS. Almost all steps are done from the command line. OpenLDAP configuration differs a little bit from ADAM/AD LDS because you don't need to create instances.

1. Start by importing LDIFs delivered with OpenLDAP. To import those files, you need root privileges and to go to the `/etc/ldap` directory. Then you need to execute these commands:

```
# ldapadd -Y EXTERNAL -H ldapi:/// -f /etc/ldap/schema/cosine.ldif
# ldapadd -Y EXTERNAL -H ldapi:/// -f /etc/ldap/schema/inetorgperson.ldif
# ldapadd -Y EXTERNAL -H ldapi:/// -f /etc/ldap/schema/nis.ldif
```

   These commands add some basic schemas.

2. Next you need to configure LDAP's back end. Configuring the back end is just setting the database that will be behind the LDAP. To make it possible, you need to create a LDIF file (call it `database.ldif`) and execute it. Executing this file just adds entries within LDAP. To configure the database, you need to fill in `database.ldif` with this piece of code:

```
dn: cn=module{0},cn=config
objectClass: olcModuleList
cn: module
olcModulepath: /usr/lib/ldap
olcModuleload: {0}back_hdb
```

code snippet /ldap/config/database.ldif

These entries set just the most basic information. To invoke these changes, you need to execute this command:

```
# ldapadd -Y EXTERNAL -H ldapi:/// -f database.ldif
```

3. Next, the database type needs to be set — and also the suffix, root, and some additional database configuration data. By default, OpenLDAP gives everyone privileges to write and read, so you need to create a root user that should have write permissions and give everyone else only read permissions. Define the suffix, database configuration, and root user as follows:

```
dn: olcDatabase={1}hdb,cn=config
objectClass: olcDatabaseConfig
objectClass: olcHdbConfig
olcDatabase: {1}hdb
olcDbDirectory: /var/lib/ldap
olcSuffix: o=wrox,c=us
olcRootDN: cn=admin,o=wrox,c=us
olcRootPW: secret
olcDbConfig: {0}set_cachesize 0 2097152 0
olcDbConfig: {1}set_lk_max_objects 1500
olcDbConfig: {2}set_lk_max_locks 1500
olcDbConfig: {3}set_lk_max_lockers 1500
olcLastMod: TRUE
olcDbCheckpoint: 512 30
olcDbIndex: uid pres,eq
olcDbIndex: cn,sn,mail pres,eq,approx,sub
olcDbIndex: objectClass eq
```

code snippet /ldap/config/root.ldif

Save the previous lines as `root.ldif` and execute this command:

```
# ldapadd -Y EXTERNAL -H ldapi:/// -f root.ldif
```

You should see something similar to this:

```
SASL/EXTERNAL authentication started
SASL username: gidNumber=0+uidNumber=0,cn=peercred,cn=external,cn=auth
SASL SSF: 0
adding new entry "cn=module{0},cn=config"
adding new entry "olcDatabase={1}hdb,cn=config"
```

4. If no error messages appear, you can add a user, whose distinguished name is `cn=admin,o=wrox,c=us`, and who was set as the `root` user before. This user doesn't exist now. A good approach is to set a password that is encrypted with a one-way hashing algorithm such as MD5. To set an MD5 password, you need to generate it. OpenLDAP delivers a tool that generates the proper value that can be copied directly into LDIF files. To generate a password hashed with the MD5 algorithm, execute this command:

```
# slappasswd -h {MD5}
```

For password `secret`, you get this output:

```
{MD5}Xr4ilOzQ4PCOq3aQ0qbuaQ==
```

5. This value should be set for the `userPassword` attribute, which is a part of the `user` object structure. Earlier you set only an assignation to the root node and to the root user base structures, but not real objects. Now it's time to create both as existing objects. To do that, save the following lines within `admin.ldif` file:

Available for download on Wrox.com

```
dn: o=wrox,c=us
objectClass: dcObject
objectclass: organization
o: wrox.com
dc: wrox
description: LDAP Root
dn: cn=admin,o=wrox,c=us
objectClass: simpleSecurityObject
objectClass: organizationalRole
cn: admin
userPassword: {MD5}Xr4ilOzQ4PCOq3aQ0qbuaQ==
description: LDAP administrator
```

code snippet /ldap/config/admin.ldif

7. To create a root node and LDAP administrator account using the above lines, execute the following command:

```
# ldapadd -Y EXTERNAL -H ldapi:/// -f admin.ldif
```

You should now see something similar to this:

```
SASL/EXTERNAL authentication started
SASL username: gidNumber=0+uidNumber=0,cn=peercred,cn=external,cn=auth
```

```
SASL SSF: 0
adding new entry "o=wrox,c=us"
adding new entry "cn=admin,o=wrox,c=us"
```

The output gives you information about added entries. Note that each added entry has a type. Types are called `objectClass`. Compared to relational databases such as MySQL, `objectClass` is a kind of table structure. `objectClass` says that this entry should consist of specific columns. For example, an entry with `objectClass` set to `person` should have at least `sn` and `userPassword` attributes.

Securing OpenLDAP

OpenLDAP is available for everyone by default and allows writing and reading within it. This is something you don't want to allow, so let's allow only the LDAP administrator to write to LDAP. This sounds fairly secure and still makes LDAP usable.

1. Set a hashed password for the config admin user by filling in `admin-config.ldif` with the following lines:

```
dn: olcDatabase={0}config,cn=config
changetype: modify
add: olcRootDN
olcRootDN: cn=admin,cn=config
dn: olcDatabase={0}config,cn=config
changetype: modify
add: olcRootPW
olcRootPW: {MD5}Xr4ilOzQ4PCOq3aQ0qbuaQ==
```

code snippet /ldap/config/admin-config.ldif

   To make it easier, you can use the same hashed password.

2. Now you need to modify these entries.

```
# ldapadd -Y EXTERNAL -H ldapi:/// -f admin-config.ldif
```

3. Set some kind of ACL. Because LDAP enables you to add more than one attribute within an object, you can define more than one access rule. Let's see what changes need to be made to allow only `cn=admin,o=wrox,c=us` to write while allowing everyone else to read. (All `olcAccess:` entries must be single lines even if they had to be split for print.)

Available for download on Wrox.com

```
dn: olcDatabase={1}hdb,cn=config
add: olcAccess
olcAccess: to attrs=userPassword,shadowLastChange by dn="cn=admin,o=wrox,c=us"
    write by anonymous auth by self write by * none
olcAccess: to dn.base="" by * read
olcAccess: to * by dn="cn=admin,o=ibm,c=us" write by * read
```

code snippet /ldap/config/acl.ldif

The last line makes the whole tree available for `cn=admin,o=ibm,c=us` to write and for all to read. The tree is also available for reading when the base distinguished name is set to an empty string. The middle entry allows users with a DN set to write `cn=admin,o=wrox,c=us`. This entry also allows authenticating by anonymous users and making changes within the user node; that's why write permissions need to be granted. To add these changes to LDAP, you need to execute this command:

```
# ldapmodify -x -D cn=admin,cn=config -W -f acl.ldif
```

Note that you log in with administrator permissions.

Adding New Users

Now it's time to add units and users that you will use in the framework examples to authenticate.

1. To add an `authors` unit, you need to define a LDIF file with the following lines:

```
dn: ou=authors,o=wrox,c=us
objectClass: organizationalUnit
ou: authors
```

code snippet /ldap/config/authors.ldif

As you can see, it's very simple to add the `authors` unit. It's an object of `organizationalUnit` class type, the same as in the case of ADAM.

2. To add authors you need to execute following command:

```
# ldapadd -cvx -D cn=admin,o=wrox,c=us -W -f authors.ldif
```

Note that now you need to log in as the administrator to make any changes. You will be asked for a password. It's the same one that you added as a hashed MD5 password. You can also create other units like `editors` in the same way.

3. Next you need to add a user. You can define this user as more than one object class type. Add the following lines within `users.ldif`:

```
dn: cn=nowak,ou=authors,o=wrox,c=us
userPassword: {MD5}Xr4ilOzQ4PCOq3aQ0qbuaQ==
sn: Leszek Nowak
cn: nowak
objectClass: top
objectClass: person
objectClass: organizationalPerson
objectClass: inetOrgPerson
```

code snippet /ldap/config/users.ldif

4. As you did previously, you need to execute the following command with a different LDIF file as the parameter:

```
# ldapadd -cvx -D cn=admin,o=wrox,c=us -W -f users.ldif
```

After executing this command, you should see output similar to this:

```
Enter LDAP Password:
add userPassword:
    {MD5}GJaRVPnFMt38q41QWE1CVQ==
add sn:
```

```
        Karol Przystalski
    add cn:
        przystalski
    add objectClass:
        top
        person
        organizationalPerson
        inetOrgPerson
    adding new entry "cn=przystalski,ou=authors,o=wrox,c=us"
    modify complete
```

You can do the same with other users.

LDAP Browsers

To browse OpenLDAP, you can use free applications such as Apache Directory Studio or phpLDAPadmin (which is available in most Linux distributions' package managers). You can install them just from sources or binary packages available at the phpLDAPadmin homepage (`http://phpldapadmin.sourceforge.net/`). After downloading, you need to unpack sources. If you are using Windows, use the context menu to unzip them. If you are using Linux, the best way to unpack them is to execute the following commands:

```
$ tar zxvf phpldapadmin-1.x.x.x.tgz
```

Note that you need to set your phpLDAPadmin version. Unpack it to the Apache main `/htdocs` directory. (On Linux, it's usually the `/var/www/` directory. XAMPP has it in `C:\xampp\htdocs\`.) After unpacking and copying it to a proper directory (for example, `/var/www/phpldapadmin`), create a config file, which is placed in the`/config` directory. To do that, just change the name of the `config.php.example` file to `config.php`. Now your phpLDAPadmin tool is available through `http://localhost/phpldapadmin/` if you deploy it on your desktop. Log in as `cn=admin,o=wrox,c=us` with the password chosen earlier and you should be able to see phpLDAPadmin, as shown in Figure 16-29.

You can easily browse available entries and create new ones. It's an easy-to-use tool for beginners and doesn't need additional packages except these, which are already installed when you install all applications required to deal with described frameworks (see Chapter 2).

A different approach, but in fact with almost the same functionalities, is presented in Apache Directory Studio (ADS). This is a nice, free LDAP tool that can also be used with Active Directory. It's based on Eclipse, which should be a sufficient recommendation. To use it, download it from `http://directory.apache.org/studio/`. For Linux distributions, you need to unpack it with the same commands as you use for phpLDAPadmin. For Windows, the Apache Foundation delivers an ADS installer. The installation procedure is obvious, so it will not be explained here. After unpacking under Linux, execute `ApacheDirectoryStudio`, which is within the unpacked ADS directory.

```
$ ./ApacheDirectoryStudio
```

Note that to make ADS work properly, you need to install the Java Runtime Environment before starting work. After launching LDS, you need to choose LDAP ⇨ New connection from the main menu in the top of the ADS window. A wizard window appears. In the first page, you need to fill in all needed network parameters, as shown in Figure 16-30.

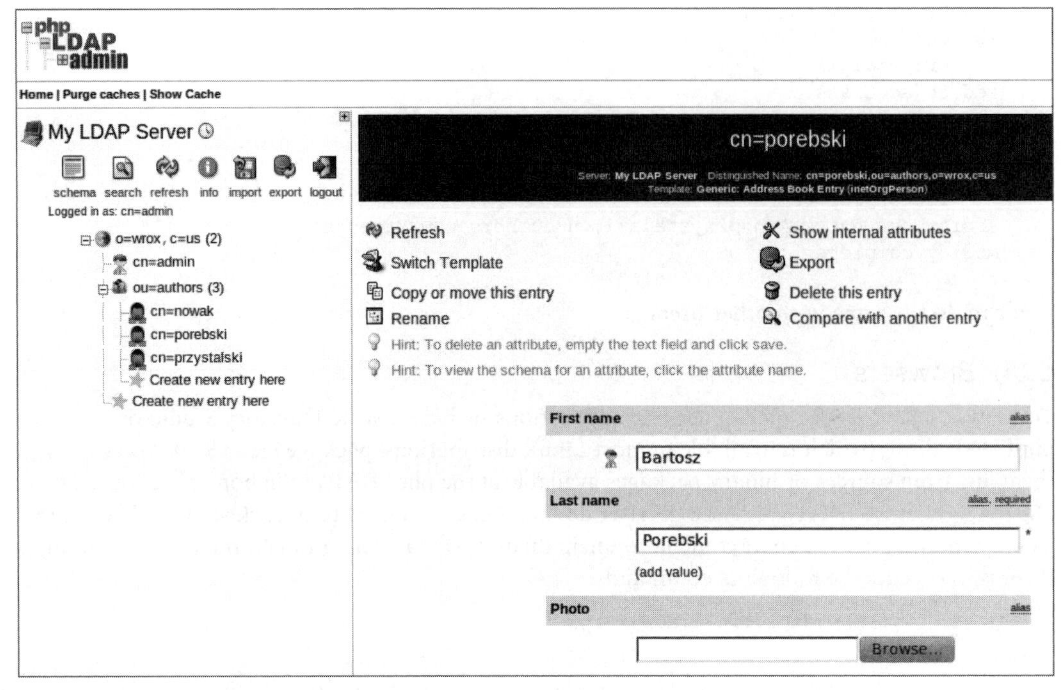

FIGURE 16-29: Browsing entries with phpLDAPadmin.

Properties for "Wrox LDAP"
type filter text
Connection
Root DSE
Schema
Connection
Network Parameter | Authentication | Browser Options | Edit Options
Connection name: Wrox LDAP
Network Parameter
Hostname: localhost
Port: 389
Encryption method: No encryption
Check Network Parameter

FIGURE 16-30: Apache Directory Studio network parameters.

Note that Figures 16-30, 16-31, and 16-32 present connection properties that use the same values that you enter in the wizard pages. After you fill in all Network Parameter fields, you need to go to the Authentication tab. In the example, the user is `cn=admin,o=ibm,c=us` (see Figure 16-31).

Finally you must set the base DN in the Browser Options tab. Base DN is, in fact, the root DN that you set earlier. You don't need to put it into the form, just click the Fetch Base DNs button to get it directly from LDAP (see Figure 16-32).

This was the last step of this wizard and you can use LDAP now. You should see something similar to Figure 16-33.

Using the context menu, you can do operations such as adding users, units, and so on.

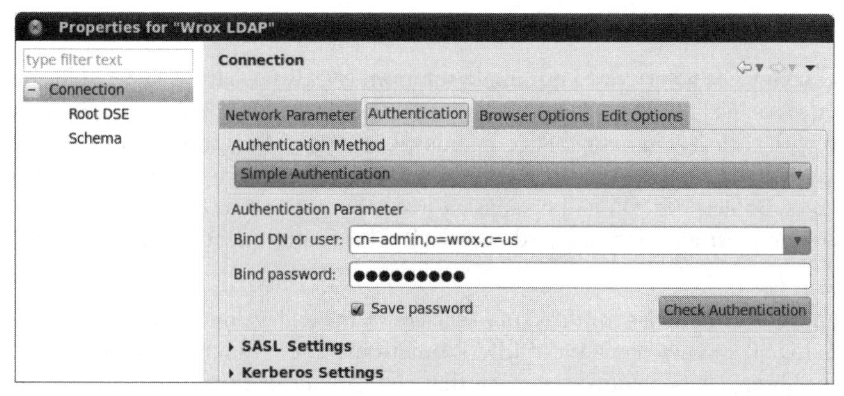

FIGURE 16-31: Apache Directory Studio authentication parameters.

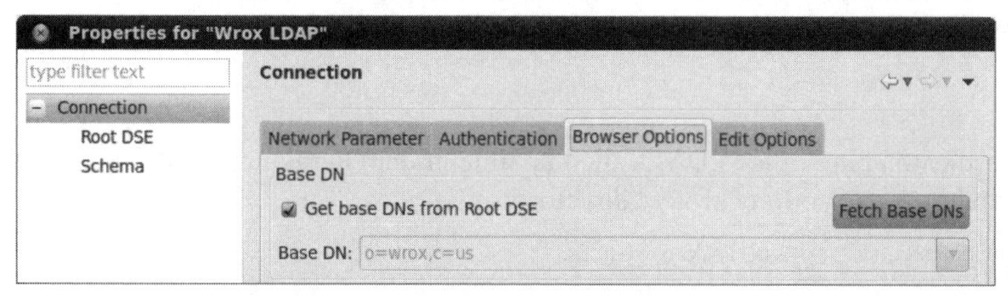

FIGURE 16-32: Apache Directory Studio browser options.

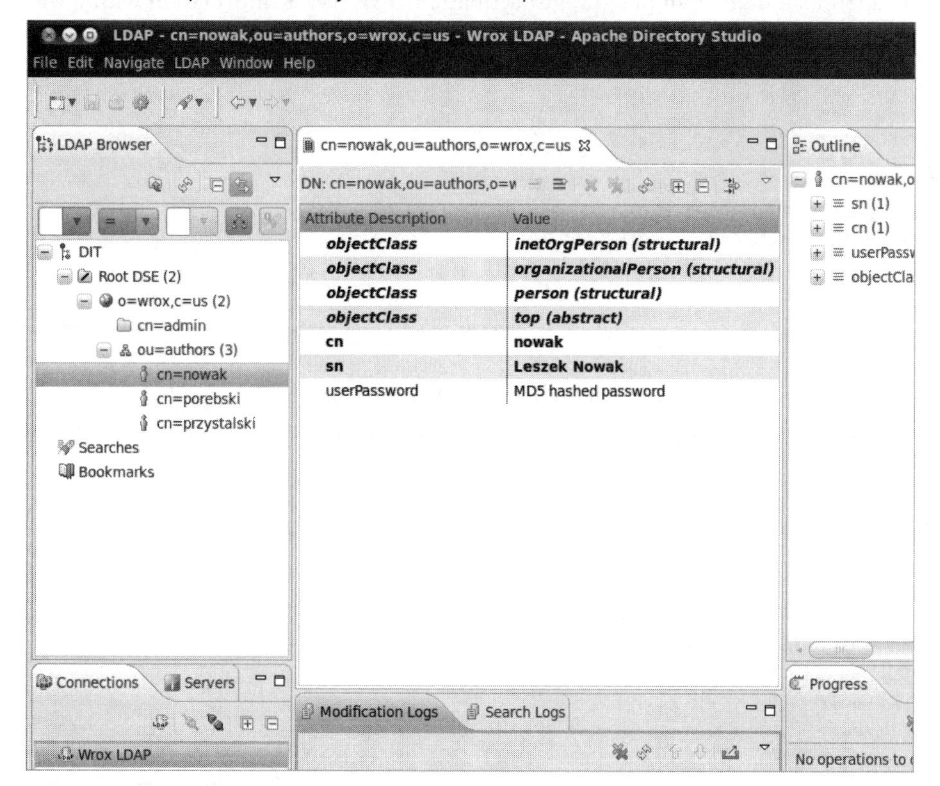

FIGURE 16-33: Apache Directory Studio.

Solution

LDAP is commonly known to be a very fast and simple solution. It's also usually a faster solution than relational databases such as MySQL, PostgreSQL, or Oracle. Probably you are wondering now what LDAP has to do with security. In many big companies, LDAP (or Microsoft's equivalent Active Directory) is used to authenticate users because it's fast and it's a great solution to represent users in companies' hierarchies. Sometimes you will be constrained to integrate a new application that you are developing with an existing solution based on LDAP. This is a frequent scenario because of LDAP's popularity.

Frameworks deliver add-ons or libraries for directory services to make developers' lives easier. By default, PHP supports LDAP and delivers a lot of LDAP functions. These functions stand behind any plug-in, add-on, or library. As a solution we mean that you can authenticate previously created users using frameworks features, plug-ins, and so on. Additional steps may include integration of described solutions with authentication modules, actions, or libraries.

Symfony

Symfony provides a dedicated plug-in for LDAP called upSimpleLdapPlugin. To install it, execute the following command in your Symfony project directory:

```
$ symfony plugin:install upSimpleLdapPlugin
```

To configure the upSimpleLdapPlugin plug-in, just set basic LDAP server information within the application's `app.yml`. In this case, it should look like the following:

Available for download on Wrox.com

```
all:
  ldap:
     host: 127.0.0.1
     port: 389
     user: cn=admin,o=wrox,c=us
     pass: secret
     baseuser: ou=authors,o=wrox,c=us
     version: 3
```

code snippet /ldap/symfony/apps/frontend/config/app.yml

Note that you need to insert the password that you set earlier. You point to `ou=authors,o=wrox,c=us` because you want only to check authors. You can expand it to include the whole tree in the future. Let's see how the upSimpleLdapPlugin plug-in works by looking at the `authenticate()` method:

```
$sr = ldap_search($this->ds, $this->base_user, "uid=$login");
if (ldap_count_entries($this->ds, $sr) <= 0)
  return false;
$entry = ldap_first_entry($this->ds, $sr);
$dn = ldap_get_dn($this->ds, $entry);
ldap_free_result($sr);
if (is_string($dn) && !empty($dn)) {
   if (!@ldap_bind($this->ds, $dn, $password)) {
```

```
            return false;
        } else {
            return true;
        }
    }
    return false;
```

As you can see in the first line, users are searched by a unique ID. All users don't have this attribute set because you didn't add it before. The easiest way to add unique IDs for every user is by using ADS. Select one of the users and on the right use the context menu to add a new attribute (see Figure 16-34).

Set the attribute's type, which in this case is `uid`. ADS delivers a list of available attributes that is very helpful for beginning developers (see Figure 16-35). Choose `uid` and press Next and Finish.

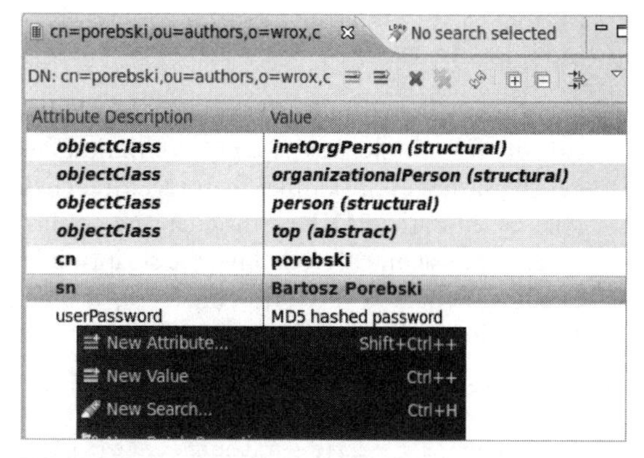

FIGURE 16-34: Apache Directory Studio's entry context menu.

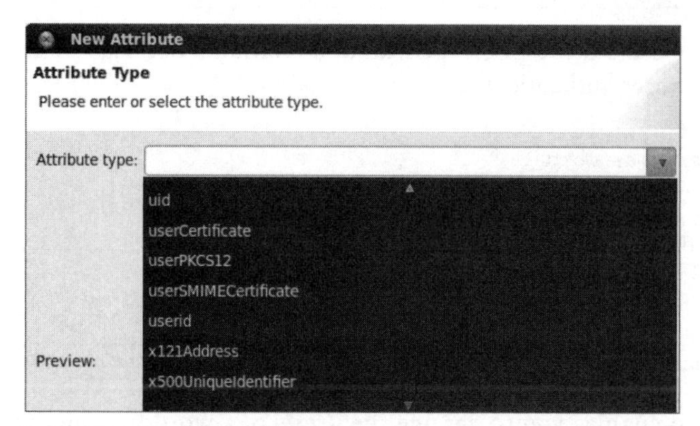

FIGURE 16-35: Apache Directory Studio: selecting the attribute type.

Now you can see the new attribute. By default, it's set to an empty string, as shown in Figure 16-36.

cn	porebski
sn	Bartosz Porebski
uid	
userPassword	MD5 hashed password

FIGURE 16-36: Apache Directory Studio: new attribute.

Note that the `uid` attribute needs to be set to a unique value. Let's assume that the user's surname is unique in the scope of this example, so you can set it as the value for `uid`. After setting the value, the user's attributes should look like Figure 16-37.

sn	Bartosz Porebski
uid	Porebski
userPassword	MD5 hashed password

FIGURE 16-37: Apache Directory Studio: setting a new attribute.

In most cases, you have to set the attribute `uid` for many users. This is not possible to do for a lot of users in the way you have done it in this example, but ADS has a great feature that generates a proper LDIF section for every change. If you scroll to the bottom, you should be able to see something similar to what is shown in Figure 16-38.

Attribute Description	Value
objectClass	***inetOrgPerson (structural)***
objectClass	***organizationalPerson (structural)***
objectClass	***person (structural)***
objectClass	***top (abstract)***
cn	**porebski**
sn	**Bartosz Porebski**
userPassword	MD5 hashed password

Modification Logs | Search Logs

```
#!RESULT OK
#!CONNECTION ldap://localhost:389
dn: cn=porebski,ou=authors,o=wrox,c=us
changetype: modify
add: uid
uid: Porebski
-
```

FIGURE 16-38: Apache Directory Studio's LDIF section.

If you copy these lines to a separate LDIF file and execute it with the `ldapmodify` command, you get the same result. Unlike the preceding clickable method, the LDIF method can be automated when you use one of your favorite scripting languages. If you add the following lines, you get a `True` value in the `$result` variable.

```
$login = "Nowak";
$pass = "secret";
$result = $ldap->authenticate($login, $pass);
```

code snippet /ldap/symfony/apps/frontend/modules/ldapexample/actions/actions.class.php

This can be used easily to authenticate users using LDAP instead of a relational database. The following code provides an example of user authentication:

```
$login = $request->getParameter('login');
$pass = $request->getParameter('password');
$user = $this->getUser();
if($ldap->authenticate($login, $pass)) {
        $user->setAuthenticated(true);
        $user->addCredential('user');
}
```

code snippet /ldap/symfony/apps/frontend/modules/ldapexample/actions/actions.class.php

The upSimpleLdapPlugin plug-in also enables you to change the user's password by using the `updatePassword()` method. This is possible because you log in as `cn=admin,o=wrox,c=us`, and this user has write permissions.

```
$ldap->updatePassword($login, $oldpass, $newpass);
```

Active Directory

Symfony also delivers an equivalent plug-in for Active Directory, which can be installed with the following command:

```
$ symfony plugin:install bhLDAPAuthPlugin
```

You can also use a modified variant of the sfGuard plug-in used for authentication with Active Directory:

```
$ symfony plugin:install vjGuardADPlugin
```

CakePHP

CakePHP doesn't deliver any additional LDAP or AD add-ons/plug-ins. But this doesn't mean that it's impossible to achieve LDAP integration in an easy manner. You need to write a little bit more code than you do in Symfony, however.

Model

There are a few ways to solve the problem of user authentication through LDAP in CakePHP. One of the solutions is to define a model that connects, disconnects, and searches LDAP and also validates users. You need to create a model within the `/model` directory. In the example, you call this model `Ldap`. The `Ldap` model should look like this:

Available for download on Wrox.com

```
<?php
class Ldap extends AppModel {
    var $name = 'Ldap';
    var $useTable = false;
?>
```

code snippet /ldap/cakephp/app/models/ldap.php

Note that you don't want to use a database. By default, any time you invoke this class, CakePHP will search for a table named `Ldap`. In this case, it is an undesirable behavior. To force a different behavior, you need to set the `$useTable` model variable to `false`. Now CakePHP will not search for any table for this model.

Next, you need to set some basic LDAP-specific data as the main variables. Note that information like hostname, base distinguished name, or administrator login and password does not change very often. Therefore, you can define the `Ldap` model as follows:

Available for download on Wrox.com

```
<?php
class Ldap extends AppModel {
    var $name = 'Ldap';
    var $useTable = false;
    var $hostname       = 'localhost';
    var $baseDn          = 'o=wrox,c=us';
    var $username       = 'cn=admin,o=wrox,c=us';
    var $password       = 'secret';
    var $ldapConn;
}
```

code snippet /ldap/cakephp/app/models/ldap.php

The `$ldapConn` variable handles the current connection to the LDAP server. This variable will often be used in the code because each time you want to get any information, you will use a handle to a LDAP server on which you want to do a search or any other actions. If you want to use the `Ldap` model very often, it's a good idea to connect to LDAP within the class constructor. Note that you inherit the `AppModel` class, so you should first invoke its class constructor and after that use the built-in PHP LDAP functions. The code should look like the following:

Available for download on Wrox.com

```
    function __construct() {
        parent::__construct();
        $this->ldapConn = ldap_connect($this->hostname, 389);
```

```
        ldap_set_option($this->ldapConn, LDAP_OPT_PROTOCOL_VERSION, 3);
        ldap_bind($this->ldapConn, $this->username, $this->password);
    }
    function __destruct() {
        ldap_close($this->ldapConn);
    }
```

code snippet /ldap/cakephp/app/models/ldap.php

An LDAP connection is defined in the third line, and the LDAP protocol is set in the following line. More options can also be set. To see all available options, go to: `http://php.net/manual/en/function.ldap-set-option.php`. Finally, before the destructor method, you need to bind the connection with a user. Then the class destructor closes the current LDAP connection. Now when you create an instance of the LDAP object type, you should be connected anytime while invoking any object methods. So let's find users so you can implement the authentication method.

```
    function findAuthor($attribute = 'uid', $value = '*') {
        $baseDn = 'ou=authors,o=wrox,c=us';
        $result = ldap_search($this->ldapConn, $baseDn, $attribute . '=' . $value);
        return ldap_get_entries($this->ldapConn, $result);
        }
    }
```

code snippet /ldap/cakephp/app/models/ldap.php

In the preceding code, you find an author by searching within the *`ou=authors,o=wrox,c=us`* subtree, as defined earlier. To make this example as compatible as possible with the other two framework examples, you use `uid` as the attribute for the search. All entries that match the search query are returned. As mentioned before, you use a unique ID, so note that the result should be only one entry.

The final method, shown in the following code, is responsible for user authentication. This method is based on the previously implemented `findAuthor()` method. If a user for given `$uid` and `$password` variables is found, try to bind with the user's distinguished name. If this method binds successfully, a `true` value is returned, which means that a user with given parameters exists and can be authenticated.

```
function authenticate($uid, $password) {
        $result = $this->findAuthor('uid', $uid);
        if($result[0]) {
            if (ldap_bind($this->ldapConn, $result[0]['dn'], $password)) {
                return true;
               } else {
               return false;
               }
       } else {
        return false;
       }
}
```

code snippet /ldap/cakephp/app/models/ldap.php

Controller

To use the model described previously, you can create a controller that will utilize it. Let's create `ldap_controller.php` in CakePHP's `/controllers` path. Note that CakePHP will automatically assign the `Ldap` model to this controller, so you don't need to define the `$uses` variable. As shown in the following code, you create an object of the `Ldap` type, which is in fact the model. Next, you need to invoke the `authenticate()` method to make sure that the user with a `uid` set to `Nowak` and a password of `secret` exists in LDAP. If it does, `authenticated` is printed. Of course, in a real application you should replace the printing action with the actions you want to be done after the user is authenticated.

```
<?php
class LdapsController extends AppController {
    var $name = "Ldaps";
    function index(){
        $a = new Ldap();
        $result=$a->authenticate("Nowak","secret");
        if($result){
           echo "authenticated";
        } else {
           echo "not authenticated";
        }
    }
}
?>
```

code snippet /ldap/cakephp/app/controllers/ldap_controller.php

To make LDAP authentication usable for production, integration with CakePHP's `Auth` component should be done as well.

View

Don't forget to create a view template for this example as `view/ldaps/index.ctp`.

Zend Framework

In Zend Framework, *adapters* are commonly used to implement database authentication easily. ZF also delivers other kinds of adapters out of the box, such as openID, LDAP, digest, or HTTP. Each of them can be used to implement a different method of user authentication.

Adapter

In this example you use the LDAP adapter to provide LDAP authentication. To make it simpler and easier to learn, use the `IndexController` as the authentication code holder. First, you need to have a `Zend_Auth` instance and define an example user that you want to authenticate.

```
$auth = Zend_Auth::getInstance();
$username= "cn=nowak,ou=authors,o=wrox,c=us";
$password= "secret";
$wrongUsername= "cn=unknown,ou=authors,o=wrox,c=us";
$wrongPassword= "wrongPass";
```

code snippet /ldap/zf/application/controllers/IndexController.php

The next step is to define LDAP connection options that are provided to `Zend_Auth_Adapter_Ldap`. As in previous examples, you connect as the administrator with the base distinguished name set to `o=wrox,c=us`.

Available for download on Wrox.com

```
$options= array(array('host'=>'localhost',
                      'username'=> 'cn=admin,o=wrox,c=us',
                      'password' =>'secret',
                      'baseDn' => 'o=wrox,c=us',
                      ,bindRequiresDn'=>1,
                      ));
```

code snippet /ldap/zf/application/controllers/IndexController.php

Now everything is ready to create an instance of the ZF LDAP authentication adapter, as shown in the following code:

```
$adapter = new Zend_Auth_Adapter_Ldap($options, $username, $password);
```

To make sure that the adapter is working properly, you previously defined the `$wrongUsername` and `$wrongPassword` variables. After you test the proper `username` and `password`, you can check how the authentication works with the `$wrongUsername` and `$wrongPassword`. The LDAP authentication process works like database authentication. You need to send to the `Zend_Auth` `authenticate()` method an `adapter` as the parameter. Because all needed information to make the authentication possible is assigned to the LDAP adapter, `$auth` returns a `Zend_Auth_Result` object.

Available for download on Wrox.com

```
$result = $auth->authenticate($adapter);
if($result->isValid()) {
    print "authenticated";
}else {
    print "not authenticated";
}
```

code snippet /ldap/zf/application/controllers/IndexController.php

The `isValid()` method owned by the `$result` returns a `true` or `false` value, depending on whether authentication succeeded or not.

Refactoring

LDAP connection information is supposed to be used more than once; that's why when refactoring the code it's a good idea to export all this information to the ZF `application.ini` configuration file. For example, the LDAP connection entries in the configuration file might look like the following:

Available for download on Wrox.com

```
 [development]
ldap.server.host = 127.0.0.1
ldap.server.username = "cn=admin,o=wrox,c=us"
ldap.server.password = secret
ldap.server.baseDn = "ou=authors,o=wrox,c=us"
ldap.server.bindRequiresDn = true
```

code snippet /ldap/zf/application/configs/application.ini

You should also set LDAP connection configuration for any other environment in which this information is used. To load LDAP information from a configuration file, you need to read it using the `Zend_Config_Ini` class:

Available for download on Wrox.com

```
$config = new Zend_Config_Ini(
                                '../application/configs/application.ini',
                                'development'
                                );
$options = $config->ldap->toArray();
```

code snippet /ldap/zf/application/controllers/IndexController.php

`Zend_Config_Ini` inherits from `Zend_Config` and is responsible for changing configuration parameters within `.ini` configuration files. Note that the configuration variables start with the `ldap` prefix. That's why you can use `$config->ldap` to get only variables that start with this prefix. The `toArray()` method returns an array that looks almost the same as defined previously without using the configuration file.

To make authentication easier, you can also define a suffix that can be concatenated with a username.

Available for download on Wrox.com

```
$suffix=",ou=authors,o=wrox,c=us";
$username = "cn=".$this->_request->getParam('username').$suffix;
$password = $this->_request->getParam('password');
```

code snippet /ldap/zf/application/controllers/IndexController.php

This way, you get only the username from the form; the rest is added automatically.

Active Directory

To connect to Active Directory, you need only to set these example variables:

Available for download on Wrox.com

```
 [development]
ldap.server.host = 127.0.0.13
ldap.server.baseDn = "CN=authors,DC=wrox,DC=com"
```

code snippet /ldap/zf/application/configs/application.ini

17

Performance

There is no such thing as innocence, only degrees of guilt.

— Warhammer 40,000: Dawn of War

WHAT'S IN THIS CHAPTER?

- Creating a performance test using JMeter.
- Benchmarks.
- Development speed comparison.

There are various benchmarks showing that some frameworks are faster than others. There are two reasons not to trust them too much. First, they depend heavily on the configuration of the server and the framework itself, so they may be biased, on purpose or not. Second, as a general rule, the more a framework is stacked with features, the slower it is. Pure PHP is always fastest in benchmarks, but that doesn't mean it is the best way to develop apps.

In this chapter we are going to introduce you to Apache JMeter, a tool designed specifically to test server performance. With JMeter, you can carry out your own benchmarks and diagnose problems with server performance. If you really can't wait for your own results, in this chapter we perform two simple benchmarks for you. Furthermore, you will see a comparison of development speed, which is in many cases more important than server throughput.

USING JMETER FOR STRESS, LOAD, AND PERFORMANCE TESTS

Apache JMeter is a great tool for stress, load, and performance tests of your application. It was developed under the banner of Apache Jakarta. It can simulate multiple user requests for server resources simultaneously. You can use it to test any of the examples introduced in this book or your own applications.

First of all, you need to download JMeter for your environment at `http://jakarta.apache.org/jmeter/`. It is a Java application, so it is OS-independent. Unpack it to a directory of your choice. Inside the `/bin` folder is `ApacheJMeter.jar`, a runnable Java archive, and shell script launchers for various operating systems.

Run JMeter as a window application. It may not look very impressive, but under this window, tremendous capabilities are hidden. JMeter can create lots of threads to simulate users, one user per thread. Suppose that you want to run a simple test, in which 10 users simultaneously request a web page, 100 times each. To do that, you need first to define threads. Adding these is possible by right-clicking Test Plan in the Apache JMeter window and choosing Add ➪ Threads (Users) ➪ Thread Group, as shown in Figure 17-1.

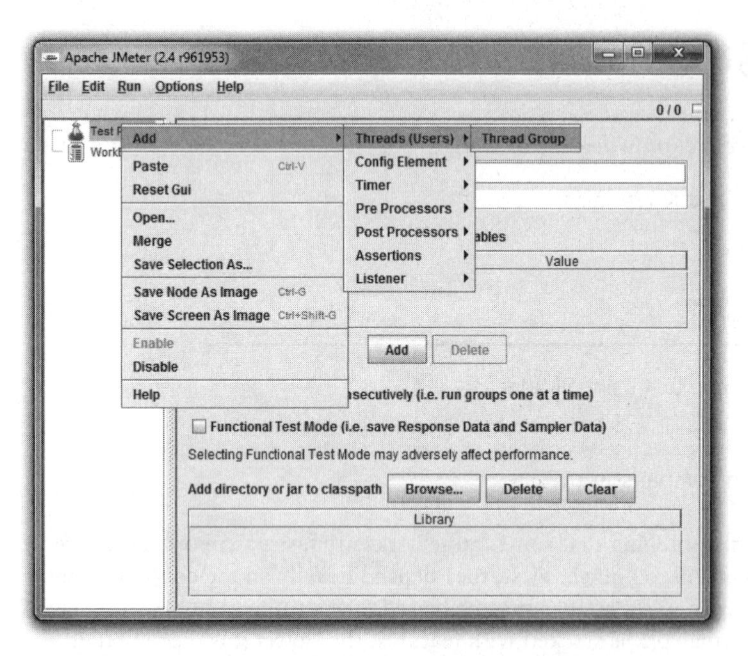

FIGURE 17-1: JMeter: Adding threads in the main window

Thread Group configuration is very important. If you put the wrong values here, you can make your desktop unresponsive until the next reboot. If you do not believe that, put **100000** into the Number of Threads and Loop Count fields. A reasonable configuration is shown in Figure 17-2. Of course, you can increase these values if you wish.

After defining a thread group, you should also specify what kind of requests should be executed. You can use JMeter's Sampler to specify this. Right-click the newly created Thread Group and choose Add ➪ Sampler ➪ HTTP Request to simulate a website visit. As you can see, JMeter allows different tests as well, such as LDAP, FTP, SOAP, or MOM (JMS). JMeter is like an all-in-one harvester.

To see your results, you need JMeter's Listeners. *Listeners* are modules used to visualize the output. Just right-click the Thread Group and choose Add ➪ Listeners to see the full list of them. In this example, we recommend adding Graph Results and View Results Tree. The first one draws the throughput and other data as a graph; the second provides page output and response information in the form of a tree.

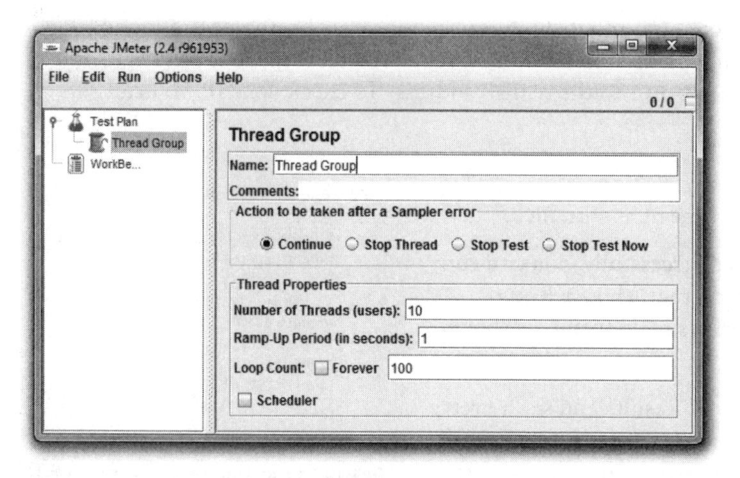

FIGURE 17-2: JMeter: Thread Group configuration

When all needed components are added, you should see in the left panel of JMeter a Test Plan structure like that shown in Figure 17-3. Now you can configure each module. Start with the Graph Results, as shown in the right panel of Figure 17-3. Here you can change the name of the item, set a log file to write into, and use display options. In this case, only Throughput is needed, but feel free to try the other options.

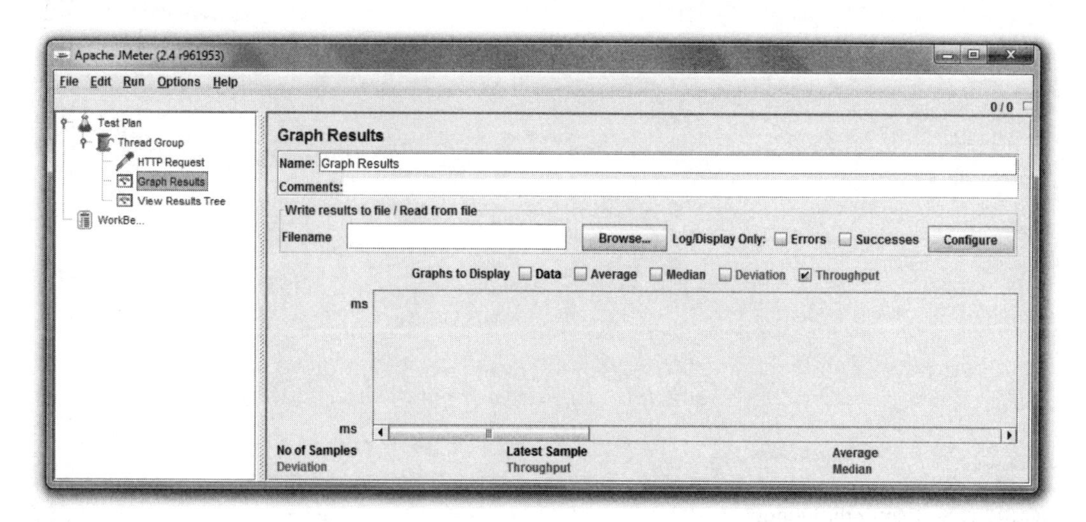

FIGURE 17-3: JMeter: Graph Results configuration

Now you are ready to start a simple test. To make it possible, you should first run the JMeter server. Under Windows, you need to click the `JMeter-server.bat` batch icon. Make sure that `java.exe` is added to the `PATH` environment variable (this process is described in Chapter 2). Under Linux, you should run `jmeter-server.sh` from the shell level as follows:

```
$ ./jmeter-server
```

In some cases, the server will not start, and it shows errors that your hostname is a loopback interface. To solve this problem, you need to edit the `/etc/hosts` file with root privileges and change your hostname from `127.0.0.1` to the real IP address. To check your IP, you can run this command:

```
$ ifconfig
```

You should set the IP address of the `eth0` interface.

After starting the JMeter server successfully, you can run the previously defined test. To do that, choose Run ➪ Remote Start ➪ 127.0.0.1 from the main menu, as shown in Figure 17-4.

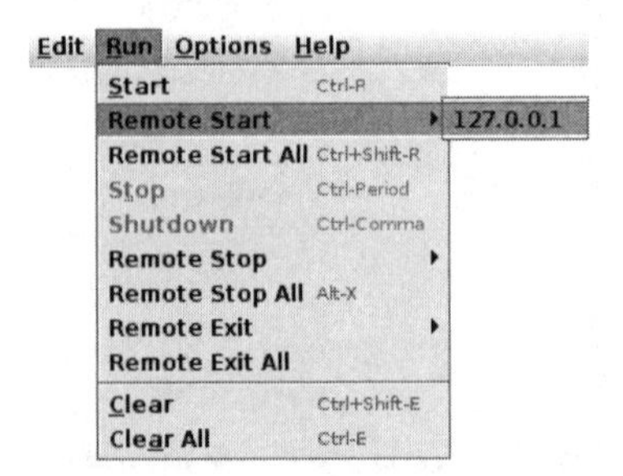

FIGURE 17-4: Running a test in JMeter

Now you can switch to the Graph Results and see a pretty chart. It's generated on the fly, so you can observe how the throughput is growing when more and more threads are running (see Figure 17-5). Results are also shown on the bottom, below the chart.

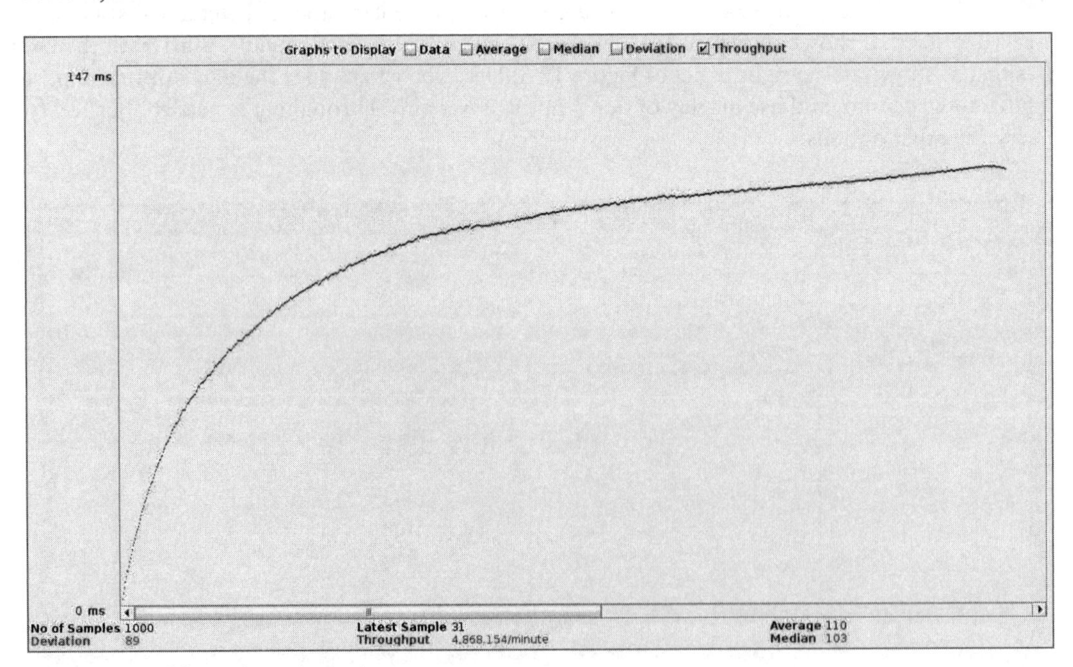

FIGURE 17-5: JMeter throughput chart

When you switch to Results Tree, you can see the details of each request (see Figure 17-6). As long as the tree is green, everything is going well. When you choose one of the items, you can see detailed information on the right.

Now you know how to run benchmarks with JMeter. You have a reliable tool to test the performance of any web application on any framework.

You can also increase thread count and loop count and try to crash your application with a stress test. When your desktop freezes for a few seconds after the test has started, you can be pleased because you have successfully crashed your web application and now you know its performance boundaries. By checking the Forever field in the Thread Group's Loop Count field, you can easily test your application in heavy load conditions. You should run these tests on the target machine because hardware and operating system configuration are decisive factors here.

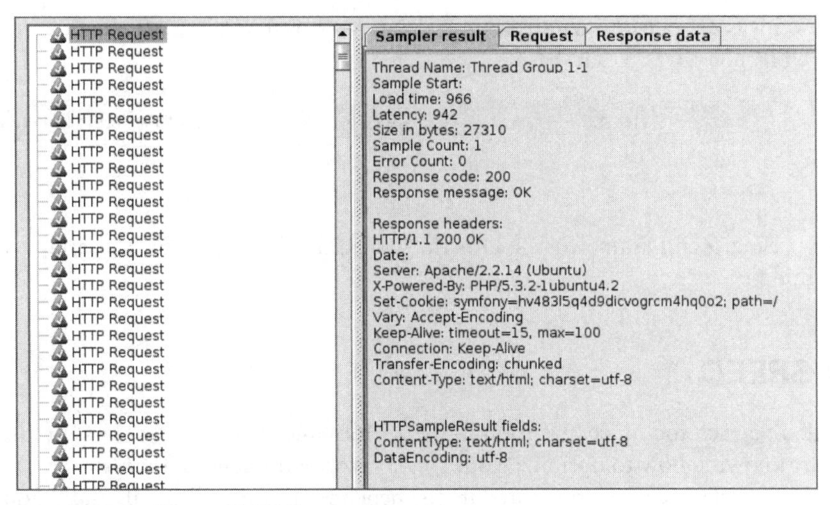

FIGURE 17-6: JMeter: HTTP Requests results

BENCHMARKING

We have done benchmarks of two simple applications: a pretty standard Hello World example and a CRUD database access app. Both were explained in Chapters 2 through 4, so you can easily copy source code from there or create your own custom set of benchmarks.

The benchmarks were carried out on Ubuntu 10.04 kernel 2.6.32-25. The hardware used was an i5-750 2.67-GHz Intel processor with 8GB RAM. JMeter was used to simulate 10 users making 1,000 requests each. The numbers are amounts of page views per second handled by the server. So the higher amount is better.

Hello World

This is the simplest application without a database connection; it just uses a controller to display a view. While these results are far from benchmarking a full-featured application, they can show the speed of the frameworks' cores. The benchmarked frameworks are Symfony 1.4, CakePHP 1.3, Zend Framework 1.11, and (as a bonus) Symfony 2.0 beta.

	SYMFONY 1.4	CAKEPHP 1.3	ZEND FRAMEWORK 1.11	SYMFONY 2.0 BETA
THROUGHPUT	221	178	348	401

As you can see, Symfony 2.0 is exceptionally good; it's almost twice as fast as Symfony 1.4. Zend Framework 1.11 is second, being the fastest stable release of these three frameworks. CakePHP 1.3 is the last one, being slightly slower than Symfony 1.4. These results are generally consistent with various other benchmarks found in the web.

Simple CRUD Application

This example application was extended to database usage. For every page request, 10 e-mail addresses were retrieved from a MySQL database.

	SYMFONY 1.4	CAKEPHP 1.3	ZEND FRAMEWORK 1.11
THROUGHPUT	139	105	187

The results are not surprising: Zend Framework 1.11 is the first, CakePHP 1.3 is the last, and Symfony 1.4 is in the middle.

DEVELOPMENT SPEED

As discussed before, don't attach too much attention to the performance benchmarks. First of all, you gain more speed by knowing how to optimize your single favorite framework than switching to another. Second, the differences demonstrated in our benchmarks are still small, and if you really need a fast framework, try a lightweight one like CodeIgniter or Yii. Or use plain PHP if you want the app to work even faster. And finally, the server costs are generally much lower than the programming costs. That's why we feel the development speed benchmark in this section is more important.

We have discussed how much work was needed to make the previous CRUD application. These results do not scale to bigger projects, in particular because the controllers and views generated by Symfony are just stubs that need to be expanded. But these numbers can give you a good idea of relative development speeds. The fewer lines, the faster you can start your project.

	SYMFONY	CAKEPHP	ZEND FRAMEWORK
COMMAND LINE	4 commands	1 command	5 commands
SCHEMA/MODEL	23 schema lines	9 schema lines	168 model lines
CONFIG	1 line	1 line	1 line
CONTROLLER	0 lines (40 generated)	38 lines	95 lines
VIEW	0 lines (83 generated)	42 lines	42 lines

As you can see, CakePHP and Symfony are far ahead of Zend Framework. Symfony needs the least hand-written code in this example because it could easily take advantage of its command-line tools that can generate simple CRUD controllers and views. CakePHP allows even more rapid development, because in general it needs the least overall code for the same effects. Its schemas also are very short: only nine lines. Zend Framework, however, doesn't look good here. This example shows the sensitive spot of ZF — the model layer — so in general, the difference should be less dramatic. But you'll see throughout this book that ZF examples were usually the most time-consuming. So the execution speed comes at the price of development speed.

18

Summary

The more you know, the more you realize you know nothing.

— SOCRATES

WHAT'S IN THIS CHAPTER?

- Pros and cons of the three frameworks.
- Table of features.
- Final comparison.

First of all, we want to say thank you for reading such a thick book and staying with us for so long! We hope you found it helpful and informative.

This is the part many of you have been waiting for: the final comparison of the three frameworks. It goes far beyond listing their unique features; we will mercilessly point out all their advantages and disadvantages here.

FEATURES

We want to start with the big picture: this section presents lists of features for each framework, both good and bad. We've listed only unique traits; if all frameworks perform similarly in an area, that area is not included here. These lists are far from complete and exhaustive, and of course they are affected by our personal experiences, including those we gained while writing this book.

Symfony

Symfony is a great tool for real professionals. It is full-featured and strictly follows all good coding practices.

Advantages

Here is our list of Symfony's advantages:

- Doctrine object-relational mapping (ORM)–integrated; easy to switch to Propel in a few steps (Chapter 3).
- Model classes can be generated based on schema or on database tables using command-line interface (CLI) tools. This accelerates the development process (Chapter 4).
- A lot of plug-ins are available in one place, most of which are well documented, divided into categories. (Used in many chapters; making a plug-in is covered in Chapter 11)
- Provides interesting plug-ins that introduce additional widgets and validators, extending form-building capabilities (Chapter 5).
- Form elements encapsulation allows for easy creation of your own widgets and validators (Chapter 5).
- Provides plug-ins for Sphinx and Lucene search engines (Chapter 7).
- CLI tools dedicated for testing (Chapter 15).
- `PHPUnit` plug-in available for Symfony 1.*x*; `PHPUnit` is integrated with Symfony 2.0 (Chapter 15).
- Symfony 2.0 is integrated with the Twig template engine that introduces its own template language and keeps high performance (Chapter 9).
- Built-in mechanism that protects against cross-site request forgery (CSRF) attacks (Chapter 8).
- Forms are filtered by the framework engine (Chapter 8).
- Some good content management systems (CMSs) are available; many others are available also as plug-ins (Chapter 13).
- Very good debugging tools (debugging in general — Chapter 15).
- Version 2.0 upcoming as the first new version among the featured frameworks.

Disadvantages

Here is our list of Symfony's disadvantages:

- The default testing framework of Symfony 1.*x* is the Lime framework, which leaves much to be desired (Chapter 15).
- Some plug-ins are dedicated for old versions of Symfony or are not documented at all, which greatly degrades their quality.

- Symfony's documentation can be described only as good, while there are many frameworks for which it is excellent.
- Symfony is great when you finally get to know it. But until you learn how to use it properly, the "500 Internal Server Error" screen (Figure 17-1) will be a common sight for you. Symfony has a great debugger tool with detailed log files, but you have to know how to use it, too. This can be very annoying for beginners.

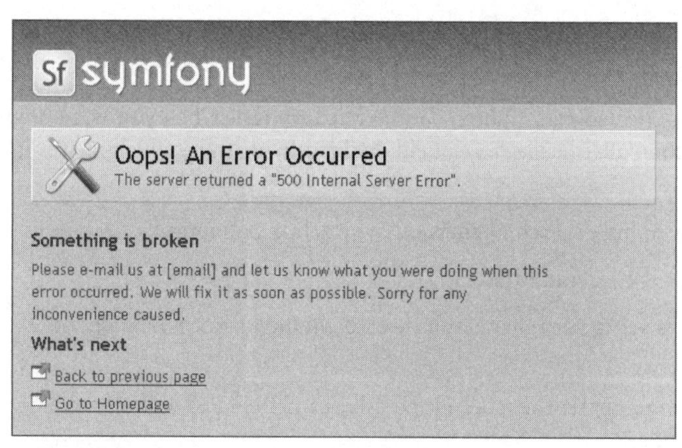

FIGURE 18-1: Symfony's 500 Internal Server Error

CakePHP

CakePHP combines very rapid development and friendliness. It is very intuitive and provides a great tutorial base, which makes using it a real pleasure and allows fast progress even for beginners.

Advantages

The advantages of CakePHP include the following:

- CakePHP offers its own ORM solution, and it is good enough (Chapter 3).
- `AppModel` provides a few basic methods to realize create, read, update, and delete (CRUD) operations, so `AppModel` is a generic model class. It allows you to very easily create your methods in models or extend inherited ones (Chapter 4).
- Great integration of models with forms without much coding (Chapter 4).
- Although there is no official support, there are a few community components and tutorials for Sphinx, Apache, Lucene, and Google Search integration (Chapter 7).
- SimpleTest testing suite integrated (Chapter 15).
- Web interface for test execution — an awesome feature (Chapter 15)!
- CLI tools for test execution (Chapter 15).
- Delivers the `Sanitize` class that allows you to filter or clean user input (Chapter 8).

- Security salt defined in a config file, which helps to secure your application against CSRF attacks (Chapter 8).
- A lot of tutorials and code snippets in the Bakery — the official CakePHP resource site at `http://bakery.cakephp.org/`.
- Some nice CMS solutions — both simple and advanced (Chapter 13).

Disadvantages

The disadvantages of CakePHP include the following:

- Controller and model are connected very tightly. This is hard to hack when you want a custom behavior. Also, every controller has a `$uses` field enabled by default, which means it expects to use a model.
- Does not support Lucene or Sphinx search engines out of the box (Chapter 7).
- No Selenium test suite support by default (Chapter 15).
- Debug level for production is set to zero by default — error hiding is not really a good practice.
- Sticks to PHP4 support for no apparent reason. Hopefully, CakePHP 2.0 will abandon it.
- Slow performance (Chapter 17).

Zend Framework

Some people argue that ZF is not a framework at all, but a library of useful classes. That makes some sense as ZF is loosely coupled and not really into the ORM thing. It means that it is flexible and easily extensible, but also quite "neutral" (the lists of advantages and disadvantages are both much shorter compared with other frameworks).

Advantages

- Encapsulates form elements as decorators (Chapter 5).
- Supports Apache Lucene out of the box (Chapter 7).
- `PHPUnit` is integrated with ZF, too (Chapter 15).
- Provides a few functions and filters to escape user input (Chapter 8).
- Supports plug-ins through `Zend_Plugin` (Chapter 11).
- A few CMSs available, all trying to keep an enterprise impression (Chapter 13).
- Great high-quality documentation.
- Good performance speed (Chapter 17).

Disadvantages

- `DbTable` is not a real ORM. You have to write three different files full of code to use one model (Chapters 3, 4, and 17).
- There is no plug-in repository for Zend Framework.
- It's heavy: 25MB and thousands of files (Chapter 2).

Table of Features

The following table summarizes and compares all the features of the three frameworks that you have observed while reading this book.

	SYMFONY	CAKEPHP	ZEND FRAMEWORK
SCAFFOLDING			
Dedicated IDE	Netbeans	None now; will be supported by Netbeans 7	Netbeans, Zend Studio (based on Eclipse)
Code generation	Great CLI tools	A few CLI tools	Poor CLI tools
VIEW			
Helpers	Core helpers available, easy to use	There are core helpers for most common tasks, easy to use	Core helpers available, easy to use
Template engine	Twig for Symfony2	A bunch of useful helpers only	Zend_view
Additional template engines	Smarty3 available as plug-in	Smarty and Dwoo can be integrated	Smarty and Dwoo can be integrated
COMMUNITY			
Plug-ins	Lots and all in one place	Some, but scattered	None
Documentation	Good documentation; some official books published	Excellent, well organized, all in one place, lots of examples	Huge, well organized, lots of examples
Video tutorials	Only a few on YouTube	Nice screencasts, a few paid videos, too	A good number of well-done videos

continues

(continued)

	SYMFONY	CAKEPHP	ZEND FRAMEWORK
I18N SUPPORT			
Localization	Helper functions, XML translation files	POT files	Zend_Locale
Internationalization	Doctrine i18n support	CLI tools, schema	Zend_Translate
Database	Supported by Doctrine, available out of the box	Supported, CLI tools available	Not available out of the box; possible to implement
ORM			
Default ORM	Doctrine	Cake's ORM	Zend's DbTable
ORM support	Very easy to switch to Propel	Possible switch to Doctrine or Propel	Possible switch to Doctrine or Propel
MAILING			
Default mailer	swiftMailer	Cake Mail component	Zend_Mail
TESTING			
Testing framework	PHPUnit	SimpleTest + web testing	PHPUnit
Selenium integration support	Through PHPUnit	Add-on needed	Through PHPUnit
SEARCHING			
Default search engine	Doctrine Search; Lucene and Sphinx as plug-ins	Doesn't support natively	Built-in Apache Lucene support

AND THE WINNER IS...

And the winner is *you*! Now you know all three frameworks with their features and weaknesses. We hope that you have paid attention to code examples in this book, and perhaps even executed most of them. So you should be familiar with all frameworks and know which one best fulfills your needs.

Well, if you really need our guidance, we can help you make the decision. Just read the following summary and decide which description fits you best. These are partially our personal opinions, so you may not agree with them, of course.

Symfony is a good all-purpose framework. It is very configurable, has great features, and provides tons of plug-ins, mostly useful. With the release of Symfony 2.0, we have a feeling that this framework is generally a half step ahead of the others, but this situation may change soon. If we wanted to point out a decisive winner, we would have said it explicitly.

The bad thing about Symfony is its very steep learning curve. When you finally get to know it, it is great, but many people spend significant time trying to learn it, only to finally switch to another framework, and they are successful at once. There are more intuitive and better-documented frameworks, which in many cases is the decisive factor in rapid web development. We have observed, however, that many people who like Linux operating systems feel good with Symfony and enjoy configuring it to their liking.

CakePHP is also full-featured, but in contrast to Symfony, it is nearly configuration-less and much simpler to use. Simpler is usually faster, and this is the main goal of web frameworks: to speed up the development process! That's why if you are new to PHP frameworks or web development in general, CakePHP may be a much better choice for you. It is also great if you want to make a relatively simple website quickly — baking with Cake is lightning fast!

The convention-over-configuration approach has its price, however. You must know this convention and follow it in your code, which makes the learning curve still rather steep and decreases the framework's flexibility. To make things worse, CakePHP cannot use object-oriented features of PHP 5.0 due to its support for PHP 4.0. This is good when your PHP hosting or PHP skills are five years obsolete and not upgradeable, but in other cases it is a drawback.

Zend Framework generally needs more coding than the previous two solutions to achieve the same effects. On the other hand, Zend Framework doesn't impose its own conventions and it doesn't need much configuration. We have also noticed that many Java programmers like ZF with its library-like approach. It is the preferred solution in these two situations:

- When you don't need a full framework, but rather a library of components to support your work without taking control over it
- If you want to buy the full Zend suite

ZF is very popular among corporate users, because with Zend Studio support it is a really great framework and we would love to see it open-sourced (or at least free for use) this way. However, without Zend Studio support ZF lacks several important features, the greatest drawback being its lack of an ORM mapper. Of course, you can install Doctrine quite easily, but it's not supported by the framework itself.

Web Resources

We have gathered a few links to websites that were useful for us, so we thought they could be useful for you as well. This list includes some essential articles, but is by no means exhaustive.

GENERAL

PHP: `http://php.net/`

IBM developerWorks: `http://www.ibm.com/developerworks/opensource/`

SYMFONY

Symfony official forum: `http://forum.symfony-project.org/`

Symfony code snippets: `http://snippets.symfony-project.org/`

Yet another Symfony community site: `http://symfonians.net/`

CAKEPHP

Unofficial forum: `http://www.cakephpforum.net/`

Cake's tutorial bakery: `http://bakery.cakephp.org/`

CakePHP questions and answers: `http://ask.cakephp.org/`

Nice CakePHP video tutorials by Andrew Perk: `http://www.youtube.com/user/andrewperk`

ZEND FRAMEWORK

Zend Framework's API: `http://framework.zend.com/apidoc/1.11/`

Zend video tutorials: http://www.zendcasts.com/

Zend Framework tutorials: http://www.zftutorials.com/

Zend developers zone — more tutorials: http://devzone.zend.com/public/view

DESIGN PATTERNS

Design patterns at SourceMaking: http://sourcemaking.com/design_patterns

IBM developerWorks design patterns in PHP: http://www.ibm.com/developerworks/library/os-php-designptrns/

Martin Fowler's articles on design patterns and software architecture: http://martinfowler.com/articles.html

ORM

Doctrine: http://www.doctrine-project.org/

Propel: http://www.propelorm.org/

Graphvis, the library used by Propel to draw database schema diagrams: http://www.graphviz.org/

DBDesigner — nice tool to export your database to a picture: http://www.fabforce.net/dbdesigner4/

DATABASES

MySQL: http://www.mysql.com/

PostgreSQL: http://www.postgresql.org/

Oracle database: http://www.oracle.com/us/products/database/index.html

IBM DB2: http://www-01.ibm.com/software/data/db2/

Microsoft SQL Server: http://www.microsoft.com/sqlserver/en/us/default.aspx

SQLite: http://www.sqlite.org/

MongoDB — NoSQL database: http://www.mongodb.org/

LDAP

OpenLDAP: http://www.openldap.org/

Active Directory: http://www.microsoft.com/windowsserver2008/en/us/ad-main.aspx

Active Directory Lightweight Directory Services: http://www.microsoft.com/downloads/en/details.aspx?familyid=A45059AF-47A8-4C96-AFE3-93DAB7B5B658&displaylang=en

IBM Tivoli Directory Server: http://www-01.ibm.com/software/tivoli/products/directory-server/

389 Directory Server — Red Hat's LDAP: http://directory.fedoraproject.org/

Equivalent for phpMyAdmin for LDAP: http://phpldapadmin.sourceforge.net/

Apache Directory Studio: http://directory.apache.org/studio/

SEARCHING

Sphinx search engine website: http://sphinxsearch.com/

Apache Lucene: http://lucene.apache.org/

Zend_Search_Lucene official documentation: http://framework.zend.com/manual/en/zend.search.lucene.html

Google Search API — REST-based: http://code.google.com/apis/customsearch/

Google Search AJAX API — deprecated: http://code.google.com/apis/loader/signup.html

TESTING

PHPUnit: http://www.phpunit.de/

SimpleTest: http://www.simpletest.org/

Selenium: http://seleniumhq.org/

Selenium integrated with Eclipse: http://cubictest.seleniumhq.org/

Jmeter — performance-testing tool: http://jakarta.apache.org/jmeter/

SECURITY

Wireshark — sniffing tool: http://www.wireshark.org/

OWASP: http://www.owasp.org/index.php/Main_Page

ReCaptcha: http://www.google.com/recaptcha

OpenCaptcha: http://www.opencaptcha.com/

Zend Captcha library: http://framework.zend.com/manual/en/zend.captcha.html

PDF

TCPDF library for PDF generation: http://www.tecnick.com/public/code/cp_dpage.php?aiocp_dp=tcpdf

FPDF — another PDF generation library: http://www.fpdf.org/

WEB SERVICES

SOAP UI — nice SOAP testing tool: http://www.soapui.org/

cURL library — command-line services tool : http://curl.haxx.se/

MAILING

Swift mailer: http://swiftmailer.org/

PHPMailer: http://phpmailer.worxware.com/

TEMPLATES

Smarty: http://www.smarty.net/

Dwoo: http://dwoo.org/

Twig: http://www.twig-project.org/

OPT template engine: http://www.invenzzia.org/en/projects/open-power-libraries/open-power-template

Tiny But Strong template engine: http://www.tinybutstrong.com/

Rain TPL: http://www.raintpl.com/

Savant3: http://phpsavant.com/

IDE

Netbeans for PHP: http://netbeans.org/features/scripting/index.html

Eclipse PHP IDE: http://www.eclipse.org/pdt/

JAVASCRIPT

JQuery: http://jquery.com/

Dojo: http://www.dojotoolkit.org/

YUI: `http://developer.yahoo.com/yui/`

Mootools: `http://mootools.net/`

Ext: `http://www.sencha.com/products/js/`

Google Web Toolkit: `http://code.google.com/webtoolkit/`

AJAX

Ten autocomplete AJAX scripts: `http://webtecker.com/2008/03/10/10-auto-complete-ajax-scripts/`

Nice library of ready-to-use AJAX solutions: `http://www.ajaxrain.com/`

CMS

Apostrophe: `http://www.apostrophenow.com/`

Diem: `http://diem-project.org/`

Sympal: `http://www.sympalphp.org/`

Croogo: `http://www.croogo.org/`

Wildflower: `http://wf.klevo.sk/`

TomatoCMS: `http://www.tomatocms.com/`

Pimcore: `http://www.pimcore.org/`

Digitalus CMS: `http://digitaluscms.com/`

CODEIGNITER

Official CodeIgniter's video tutorials: `http://codeigniter.com/tutorials/`

List of more than 40 CodeIgniter tutorials: `http://www.2expertsdesign.com/tutorials/codeigniter-framework-tutorials-for-php-application`

LITHIUM

Official Lithium blog tutorial using MongoDB: `http://rad-dev.org/lithium/wiki/drafts/blog-tutorial`

Longer Lithium tutorial using MySQL: `http://www.sanisoft.com/blog/2010/04/12/the-lithium-blog-tutorial-part-1/`

AGAVI

Agavi official documentation: http://www.agavi.org/documentation/tutorial

Agavi unofficial FAQ: http://www.mivesto.de/agavi/agavi-faq.html

A tutorial showing how to build a sophisticated web application with Agavi: http://www.ibm.com/developerworks/views/xml/libraryview.jsp?search_by=Introduction+to+MVC+Programming+with+Agavi

B

CodeIgniter, Lithium, and Agavi with Code Examples

WHAT'S IN THIS CHAPTER?

- Installing and configuring CodeIgniter, Lithium, and Agavi.
- Building a simple news app in each of these frameworks.

The PHP world does not begin, nor end, with Symfony, CakePHP, and Zend Framework. There is a multitude of other frameworks and some of them are useful, brilliant, and (most important) increasingly popular. In this appendix we will take a closer look at three of them: CodeIgniter (CI), Lithium, and Agavi.

The sample applications presented here will cover the first two of the create, read, update, and delete (CRUD) functionalities: creating and reading entries. We call them news publishing applications, but with a little modification they can be used for blogging, commenting, or as a guest book. That should give you enough sense of what each framework is up to.

We will use the two of the hosting environments presented in Chapter 2: Windows 7 64-bit with XAMPP 1.7.3; and Ubuntu Linux Desktop 10.04.1 64-bit with the standard Linux, Apache, MySQL, and PHP (LAMP) environment. If you need help with setting them up, Chapter 2 covers that in detail.

CODEIGNITER

CodeIgniter had an explosion of popularity recently and if the trend continues, it will become the leading framework in 2011. So, what's so unique about it? It's incredibly *nimble*:

- **Lightweight** — Less than 2MB.
- **Fast** — No performance tweaks needed.

- **Easy** — Single configuration file, great documentation, no need to learn a templating language.
- **Flexible** — Loosely coupled architecture that does not need much hacking to extend. Model layer is optional.
- **Adaptable** — No command-line tools. Not cool, but facilitates deployment on hosts without a command line. Runs on PHP 4 (also not cool, but makes it even more adaptable).

Many people do not need the advanced features of heavy-duty frameworks. CI has all the important things that are sufficient for most projects. It is also popular because it works in shared hosting environments, where using a minimal framework without command-line tools is often the only choice you have. Finally, CI is both simple to learn and very well documented, which gets it the approval of the community and often makes it the first choice for beginners in PHP development. Let's check it out now.

Installation

The installation couldn't be easier. The CodeIgniter version used here is 1.7.2 but we encourage you to install the newest version from this website:

```
http://codeigniter.com/downloads/
```

Uncompress the package to your web root folder. Optionally, change the name to something short for your convenience. In this example, it was changed from `/CodeIgniter_1.7.2` to `/ci`. Go with your browser to `http://localhost/ci` and you should see the welcome page shown in Figure B-1.

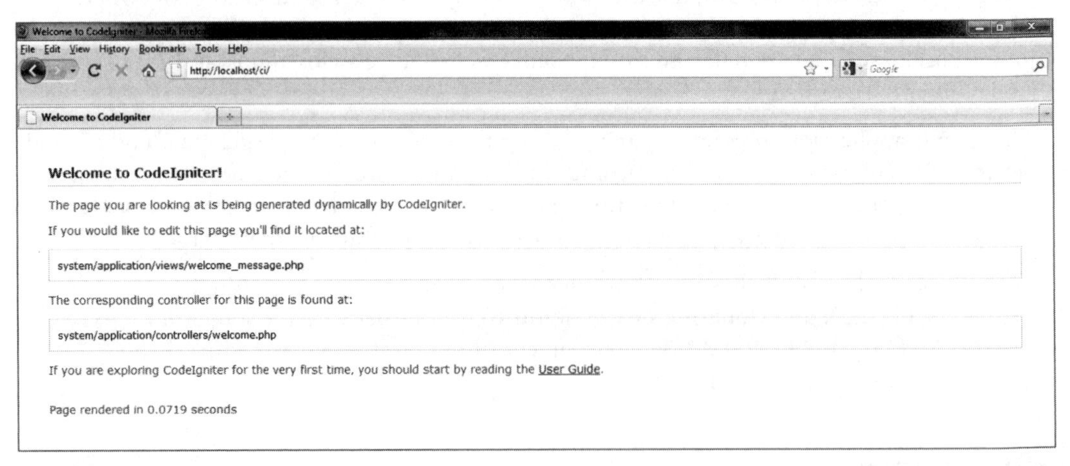

FIGURE B-1: CodeIgniter's welcome page

The welcome page is clean and informative. The paths to the default view and controller are displayed there. You can start experimenting with CodeIgniter just by editing those files. There is also a link to the included User Guide. It is both good introduction material and a full documentation of CI classes. This documentation is a big advantage of this framework. Hint: if it's late at night and you have a hard time looking for the table of contents, there is a dark tab at the top of the User Guide to help you locate it.

Setting Up the Database

In this example, you need to create the `news` database and `entries` table for the application. The single table will hold an autoincremented `id`, short `title` of the news, full `description` of it, and (optionally) the `date` when it was added. You can do it conveniently with phpMyAdmin, or just by invoking the following commands from the command line:

```
CREATE DATABASE news;
CREATE TABLE `news`.`entries` (
`id` INT NOT NULL AUTO_INCREMENT PRIMARY KEY ,
`title` VARCHAR( 50 ) NOT NULL ,
`description` VARCHAR( 1000 ) NULL DEFAULT NULL ,
`date` DATE NULL DEFAULT NULL
) ENGINE = MYISAM ;
```

Then configure the CodeIgniter to make it establish a connection to this database:

```
$db['default']['hostname'] = "localhost";
$db['default']['username'] = "root";
$db['default']['password'] = "your password";
$db['default']['database'] = "news";
$db['default']['dbdriver'] = "mysql";
```

code snippet /ci/system/application/config/database.php

Go to the `autoload.php` configuration file. Find the line responsible for autoloading libraries. Insert into the array the `'database'` string to enable automatic loading and instantiation of the database on each page load:

```
$autoload['libraries'] = array('database');
```

code snippet /ci/system/application/config/autoload.php

Unfortunately, no database connection check is made in the default module, but soon you will be able to access this database with your application.

Configuration

If you do not want to develop your app in the web root folder, but in the home folder or anywhere else on the system, you need to reconfigure Apache. This is optional because you can store the folder in the web root and still access the application with `http://localhost/ci`, but many developers prefer it that way. Just supply the CI's main folder path, and the rest is done with `.htaccess` files, which is quite convenient:

```
Alias /ci /home/username/public_html/ci
<Directory /home/username/public_html/ci>
    Options Indexes FollowSymLinks MultiViews
    AllowOverride All
    Order allow,deny
```

```
        allow from all
    </Directory>
```

code snippet /apache/httpd.conf

Change the base URL in your CI configuration file to point to the root of your application. Don't forget the trailing slash.

```
$config['base_url']    = "http://localhost/ci/";
$config['index_page'] = "index.php";
```

code snippet /ci/system/application/config/config.php

Set the routing. Find the default `welcome` controller:

```
$route['default_controller'] = "welcome";
```

code snippet /ci/system/application/config/routes.php

And change it to the name of the controller you are about to create:

```
$route['default_controller'] = "news";
```

code snippet /ci/system/application/config/routes.php

Your First Application

Now you can finally create the `News` controller. It extends the standard `Controller` class and uses its constructor. `News` provides one `index()` action that loads the single model, gets a list of the freshest news, and passes them to the view as the `$data` variable. At this point the database is empty, so it's not anything spectacular.

```
<?php
class News extends Controller {
    function News() {
        parent::Controller();
    }

    function index() {
        $this->load->model('Newsmodel');
        $data['list'] = $this->Newsmodel->getList();
        $this->load->view('newsview', $data);
    }
}
```

code snippet /ci/system/application/controllers/news.php

Please note one very important thing: the database query result must be passed as a value of the `'list'` key in the `$data` array. Then this array is passed to the view. It may seem tempting to pass just the variable like this:

```
$list = $this->Newsmodel->getList();
$this->load->view('newsview', $list);
```

But don't try it; the `$list` variable will not be visible to the view and it won't work.

Now create the model. It is not obligatory to create models in CI, but we recommend it as a good practice. Another point is that it is almost always very useful. The solution used here is a modified Active Record pattern, which means that database tables and properties are wrapped by a database object `$db` inside the model. We are using the `database` helper here. The `get()` method is a shortcut for selecting all rows from the `entries` table:

```
<?php
class Newsmodel extends Model {
    var $title   = '';
    var $description = '';
    var $date = '';
    function Newsmodel() {
        parent::Model();
    }

    function getList() {
        $query = $this->db->get('entries');
        return $query;
    }
}
```

code snippet /ci/system/application/models/newsmodel.php

The view presented here is already fully functional and does not need to be modified later.

```
<html>
<head>
<title>The news application</title>
</head>
<body>
<h1>The latest news!</h1>
<?php
foreach ($list->result() as $row):
    echo "<h3>". $row->title ."</h3>";
    echo "<p>". $row->description;
    echo "<p><small>Added on: ". $row->date ."</small>";
endforeach;
?>
<h1>Adding news:</h1>
<?php
$this->load->helper('form');
echo form_open('news/add');
    echo form_label('Title')."<br>";
```

```
        echo form_input('title')."<br>";
        echo form_label('The Contents')."<br>";
        $params = array(
                    'name'        => 'description',
                    'id'          => 'description',
                    'value'       => '',
                    'maxlength'   => '1000',
                    'rows'        => '5',
                    'style'       => 'width:50%',
                    );
        echo form_textarea($params)."<br>";
        echo form_submit('submit', 'Add News');
    echo form_close('');
    ?>
    </body>
    </html>
```

code snippet /ci/system/application/views/newsview.php

There are a few important things here. In the `foreach` loop, individual rows are extracted with the `$list->result()` method. Then the `title` and `description` fields are accessed to print out the content.

The forms are created with CodeIgniter's `form` helper, which is loaded manually in this example, unlike the `database` utility class that was included for autoloading. You can also autoload the `form`.

The input form is opened with the following function:

```
echo form_open('news/add');
```

It is shorthand for this line:

```
<form method="post" action="http://localhost/ci/index.php/news/add" />
```

Actually, it is a little more than shorthand because the full link is constructed using the `base_url` configured earlier. This adds to the portability of the application when you have multiple forms.

Also, the `form_input()` and `form_textarea()` methods are the helper's shorthand for well-known form creation tags. The first method is created using only a name string for simplicity, and the textarea is configured using an array of parameters. All form creation methods accept arrays, though. There are many other kinds of forms this helper can create, such as `form_hidden()`, `form_checkbox()` or `form_password()`.

Finally, the `form_submit()` method creates a submit button that sends the form to the `add` action of the `News` controller. That's what the argument of `form_open('news/add')` was for. There is no `add()` function in the controller yet, but it will be created in the next section.

Adding Entries

To add some entries into the database, you must go back to the `Newsmodel` and add a function that would insert the data into the database. The following function reads the submitted form, sets the corresponding variables (defined earlier in the model), gets the current time in ISO format, and finally inserts the complete entry into the database:

Available for download on Wrox.com

```
function addNews() {
    $this->title = $_POST['title'];
    $this->description = $_POST['description'];
    $this->date = date('c');
    $this->db->insert('entries', $this);
}
```

code snippet /ci/system/application/models/newsmodel.php

With this tool you can create the action to handle the form submission. It must load the model first; then it checks to be sure the form is not empty. If it's not, it adds the news item into the database. Finally, this action redirects to the `index` action to display the new content. You can see a sample of the outcome in Figure B-2.

Note that the `url` helper is loaded just before that. Helpers need to be included just once and then they are globally available, but we have loaded it in the `add` action just before the `redirect()` method where it is needed.

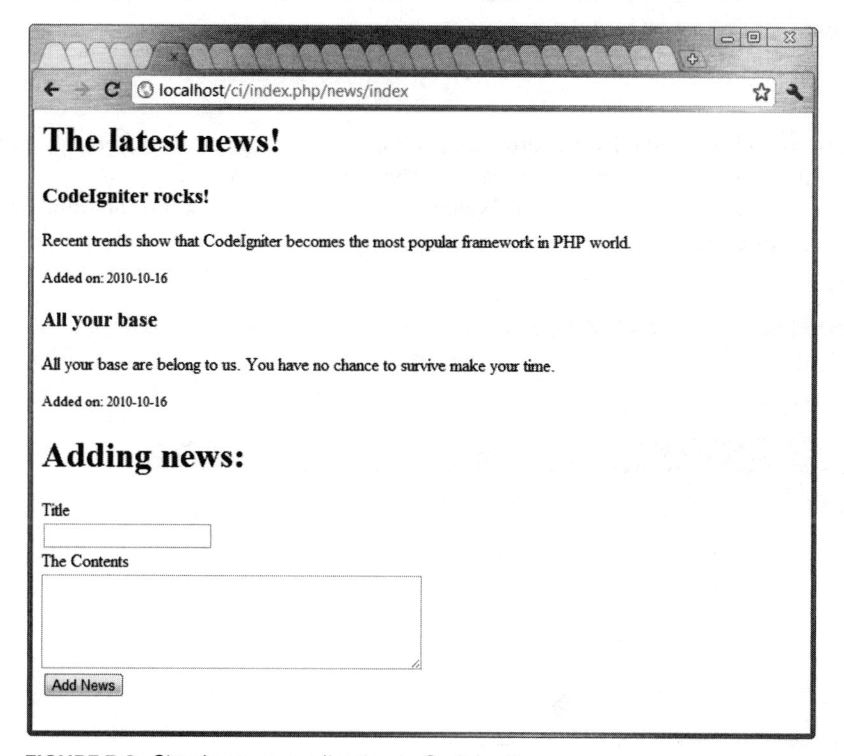

FIGURE B-2: Simple news application in CodeIgniter

Available for download on Wrox.com

```
function add() {
    $this->load->model('Newsmodel');
    if($this->input->post('submit')){
        if($_POST['title'] != NULL && $_POST['description'] != NULL)
            $this->Newsmodel->addNews();
    }
```

```
        $this->load->helper('url');
        redirect('news/index','refresh');
    }
```

code snippet /ci/system/application/controllers/news.php

Congratulations! You have created your first half-CRUD application in CodeIgniter.

LITHIUM

Lithium is a young framework that has already caused much excitement among the PHP crowd. A quick look at Lithium's website, `http://lithify.me/`, shows that they really want to be unique. Both an unusual visual style and a large concentration of daring catchwords build up quite a lot of tension and raise expectations for the upcoming stable version. The Lithium version used here is 0.9.5. By the time you read this book, the 1.x release will probably be available. Will it meet all the expectations? The current version may be a good forecast of that. We will create the same simple app as in the CodeIgniter section to compare them.

Installation

To install Lithium, go to its website and click the download() link. That opens a page where you can grab the latest release. Alternatively, you can use Git version control system (available from `http://git-scm.com/`). Unpack the folder to your web root. We have renamed it `/lith`, so do the same or adjust paths from our examples. At `http://localhost/lith`, you will see Lithium's welcome page (see Figure B-3):

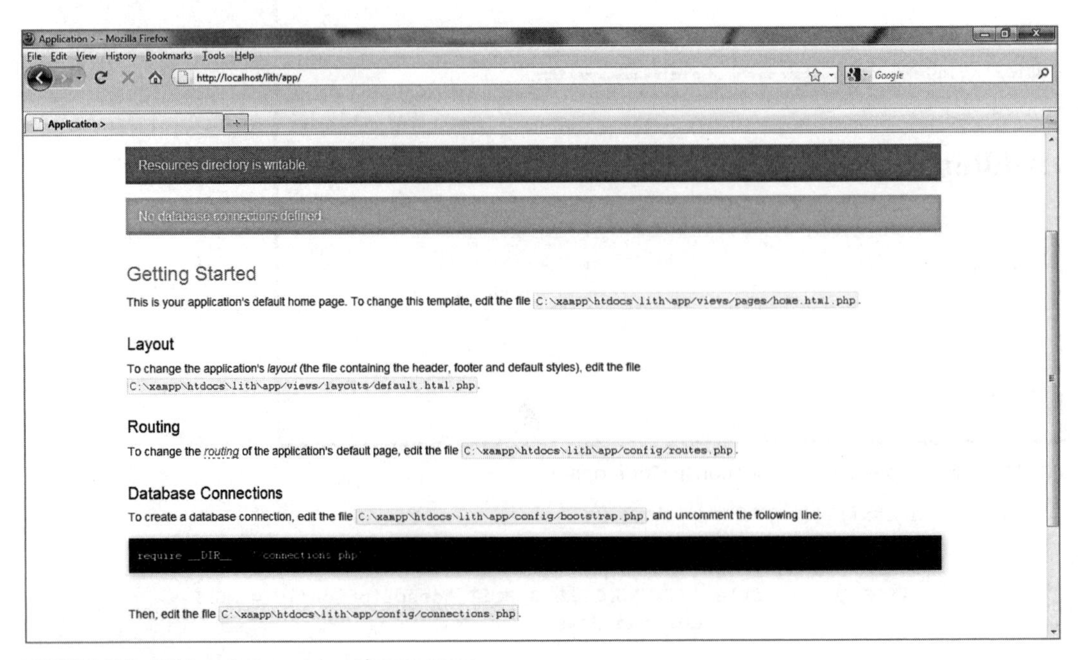

FIGURE B-3: Lithium framework welcome page

Smells like Cake, doesn't it? Well, Lithium was started by the people who previously developed CakePHP. They were not happy with it, mainly because of its conformance with PHP 4, so they first made a PHP 5.3 fork called Cake3, and then turned that into a separate framework called Lithium. Even if Lithium's core is completely rewritten, when you look at the welcome page's graphic style, the relation to CakePHP is evident.

CLI

To get direct access to the `/lith/libraries/lithium/console/li3` (or `li3.bat` for Windows) application, which is the all-in-one command-line tool of Lithium, you must add its path to the `PATH` environment variable. The process for adding this path was described in Chapter 2. For UNIX-like systems, use this:

```
$ export PATH=${PATH}:/path_to_lithium/lith/libraries/lithium/console/
```

When the path is set, you can type the following command in the console:

```
$ li3
```

You will see the following output:

```
COMMANDS
    Create
    The 'create' command allows you to rapidly develop your models, views,
    controllers, and tests by generating the minimum code necessary to test
    and run your application.

    G11n
    The 'G11n' set of commands deals with the extraction and merging of message
    templates.

    Help
    Get information about a particular class including methods, properties, and
    descriptions.

    Library
    The Library command is used to archive and extract Phar::GZ archives. Requires
    zlib extension. In addition, communicate with the a given server to add plugins
    and extensions to the current application. Push archived plugins to the server.

    Test
    Runs a given set of tests and outputs the results.

See 'li3 help COMMAND' for more information on a specific command.
```

Notice that i18n has been renamed to G11n, meaning globalization. The name is different, yet it works like all other localization tools.

Setting Up the Database

Going back to our example, the application you are working on here will be very similar to the news application for CodeIgniter shown earlier in this chapter. They can share the `news` database. If you have not created the database for the CI example, you can do it with the following command:

```
CREATE DATABASE news;
```

Now create the table for the Lithium application. Note that this table is called news, while the CI table was called entries. This is the only difference, as Lithium needs the tables to be named like the models (or rather models like tables).

```
CREATE TABLE 'news'.'news' (
'id' INT NOT NULL AUTO_INCREMENT PRIMARY KEY ,
'title' VARCHAR( 50 ) NOT NULL ,
'description' VARCHAR( 1000 ) NULL DEFAULT NULL ,
'date' DATE NULL DEFAULT NULL
) ENGINE = MYISAM ;
```

Then you need to establish a connection to your database. Just as the welcome page suggests, go to the bootstrap.php file and uncomment the following line:

```
/**
 * Include this file if your application uses a database connection.
 */
require __DIR__ . '/connections.php';
```

code snippet /lith/app/config/bootstrap.php

Uncommenting this line allows loading of the connections.php file when the application is executed.

Edit this file now. The 'default' in the following code means that models will use this connection by default. In the current version, you have to uncomment all database lines first.

```
use \lithium\data\Connections;
 Connections::add('default', array(
  'type' => 'database',
  'adapter' => 'MySql',
  'host' => 'localhost',
  'login' => 'root',
  'password' => '',
  'database' => 'news'
 ));
```

code snippet /lith/app/config/connections.php

Configuration

You need to set the routing to the news controller you are about to create, instead of the default one. Also set the default action to the index action.

```
/**
 * Here, we are connecting '/' (base path) to the controller called 'Pages',
 * its action called 'view', and we pass a param to select the view file
 * to use (in this case, /app/views/pages/home.html.php)...
 */
Router::connect('/', array('controller' => 'news', 'action' => 'index'));
```

code snippet /lith/app/config/routes.php

You may also reconfigure Apache to use a folder other than the web root. This was shown in the CodeIgniter configuration and is the same here with obvious path changes.

Your First Application

So you probably want to see how rapid the development with Lithium can be. Create a model as shown here:

Available for download on Wrox.com

```
<?php
namespace app\models;
use \lithium\data\Connections;
class News extends \lithium\data\Model {
}
?>
```

code snippet /lith/app/models/News.php

That's it. Nothing more is needed to make a working model; you can just call it in your controller and then load or save data into it. This file will not be modified in this example app any more.

Prepare the stub of the `NewsController` with two empty actions: `index` and `add`. Make it use the `News` model created earlier in this chapter. Add the line `use app\models\News;` just after the `namespace` declaration.

Available for download on Wrox.com

```
<?php
namespace app\controllers;
use app\models\News;
class NewsController extends \lithium\action\Controller {
    public function index() {
    }
    public function add() {
    }
}
?>
```

code snippet /lith/app/controllers/NewsController.php

It's time to make a basic view. Look how easy it is in Lithium to create forms: just open the form with the `create()` method, add some fields with the `field()` method, use `submit()` for the submit button, and close the form with the `end()` method. All these methods belong to the `Form` helper class. The `create()` method can be bound to a data object to analyze column types, fill in input form fields, and throw error messages. In this example, it is not used, so the first parameter is `null`. The second parameter is an array of options, of which the most important is the `action` that can be used to direct the form to a chosen action of the controller. If it is not set, the form is directed by default to the action associated with this view.

Available for download on Wrox.com

```
<html>
<head>
<title>The news application</title>
</head>
<body>
```

```
<h1>Adding news:</h1>
    <?=$this->form->create(NULL,array('action' => 'add')); ?>
        <?=$this->form->field('title');?>
        <?=$this->form->field('description', array('type' => 'textarea'));?>
        <?=$this->form->submit('Add News'); ?>
    <?=$this->form->end(); ?>
</body>
</html>
```

code snippet /lith/app/views/news/index.html.php

When you enter the link to this application in your browser, you should see the following output (shown in Figure B-4). It is nicely styled with Lithium's default layout.

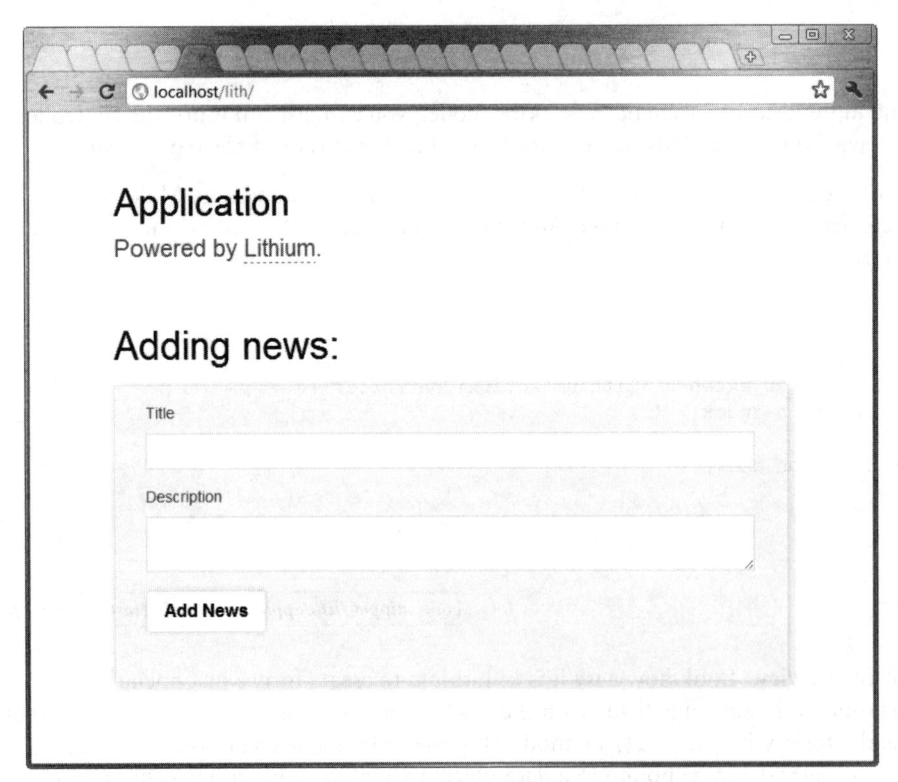

FIGURE B-4: Adding a news form with the default Lithium layout

You may have noticed that Lithium has adopted a few conventions:

- Uses auto-loading feature and namespaces introduced in PHP 5.3.
- A full path with backslashes (\) is required when extending base framework classes.
- There are strict naming conventions. Models must be named the same as the corresponding database tables, and the controllers' class names must have a suffix of `Controller`. Both must be capitalized and stored in files named exactly the same as the class names.

- Views must be named the same as the actions they are linked to and must have `.html.php` extensions. They also must be stored in additional folders named after their controllers. For example, for the `index` action of the `NewsController` controller, the full path to the index view is `/lith/app/views/news/index.html.php`.

Adding Entries

When you've got such a nice form, it would be a waste not to use it. Locate the `add()` method of your controller and fill it with following code:

```
public function add() {
    if ($this->request->data) {
        if($this->request->data['title'] != NULL &&
         $this->request->data['description'] != NULL){
            $news = News::create($this->request->data);
            $news->date = date('c');
            $news->save();
        }
    }
    $this->redirect(array('action' => 'index'));
}
```

code snippet /lith/app/controllers/NewsController.php

The form input data is accessed by `$this->request->data`. It is an array, so the array operator is used to retrieve the values. If the post passes all checks and is considered non-empty, a `$news` model object is created. The current date is added to the object. All you have to do then is to invoke the `save()` method of the object. Finally, the control flow is redirected to the `index` method to show the news list.

Showing the news list is also very simple, as presented in the following code. Prepare a `$data[]` array and write under the `list` key some entries associated with the `News` model. Use the `find('all')` method of this model class to get all entries from the database table. If you pass an integer instead of the `'all'` string, only this amount will be returned.

```
public function index() {
        $data['list'] = News::find('all');
        return $data;
}
```

code snippet /lith/app/controllers/NewsController.php

Finally, add into your view a loop that goes through all rows of the table and writes out their contents. The full file is presented here:

```
<html>
<head>
<title>The news application</title>
</head>
<body>
```

```
        <h1>The latest news!</h1>
        <?php foreach($list as $row):
            echo "<h3>". $row->title ."</h3>";
            echo "<p>". $row->description;
            echo "<p><small>Added on: ". $row->date ."</small>";
        endforeach; ?>
    <h1>Adding news:</h1>
        <?=$this->form->create(NULL,array('action' => 'add')); ?>
            <?=$this->form->field('title');?>
            <?=$this->form->field('description', array('type' => 'textarea'));?>
            <?=$this->form->submit('Add News'); ?>
        <?=$this->form->end(); ?>
    </body>
    </html>
```

code snippet /lith/app/views/news/index.html.php

Well, that's it! You've got your first app in Lithium. There is just one small thing to do.

Changing Templates

The default template provided by Lithium is nice, but you probably do not want the big *Application* header in your new application. Go to the default layout, find the `header` div, and shorten it to something modest:

Available for download on Wrox.com

```
<div id="header">
    <h2>
        Self - powered.
    </h2>
</div>
```

code snippet /lith/app/views/layouts/default.html.php

You may also want to modify the default cascading style sheet (CSS). It is stored in `/lith/app/webroot/css/lithium.css`. First, decrease the vertical padding in the `container` div from `60px` to something like `10px`:

Available for download on Wrox.com

```
#container {
    position: relative;
    padding: 10px 10%;
}
```

code snippet /lith/app/webroot/css/lithium.css

And change some colors of your headers; for example, make `<h3>` red:

Available for download on Wrox.com

```
h3, h6 { font-size: 1.7em; color: #ff0000; }
```

code snippet /lith/app/webroot/css/lithium.css

Time to see the result. The header should change to *Self-powered*, your news titles should be blood-red, and vertical distances greatly decreased, just as shown in Figure B-5.

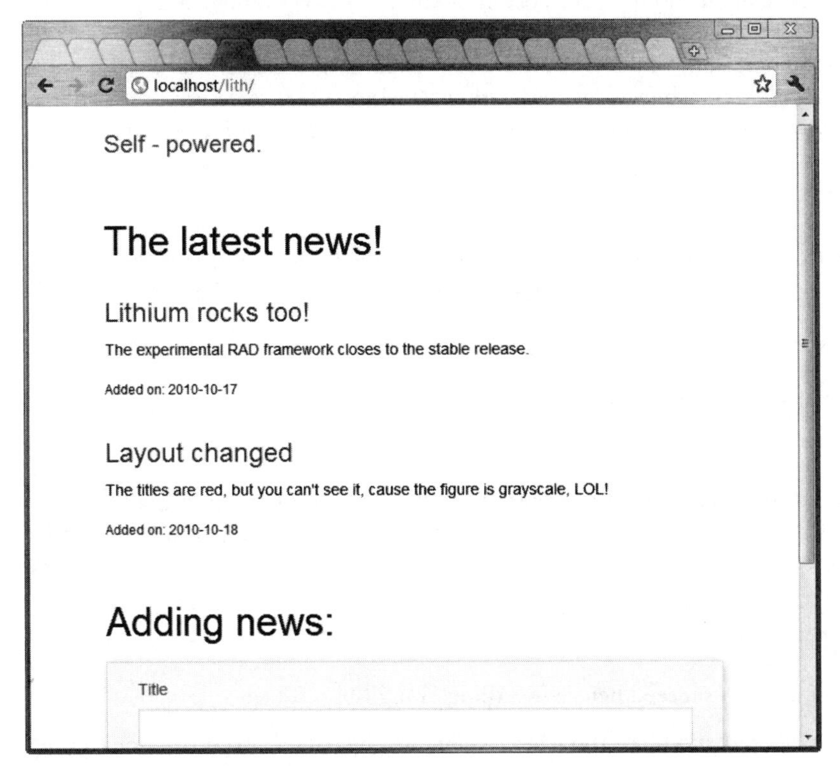

FIGURE B-5: Full Lithium application with modified layout

As you have seen, Lithium allows very rapid development indeed, and this little application is just the tip of the iceberg. Now it seems a little bit overloaded with conventions and authors' personal attitude, but these should mitigate as it gains maturity. Also, the documentation is missing now, as there are only two tutorials on the Web, so it is more a curious experiment than a maintainable solution. However, the hype is high and it seems that the authors will stand up to the task, so soon you will have a rapid, powerful, extensible, and strictly PHP 5.3 framework to use.

AGAVI

The creators of Agavi want you to think about it as a "serious framework for serious development" and not a "website building kit." This basically means two things: first, it could be viewed as an excuse for quite scarce documentation, compared with Symfony or CodeIgniter. The authors admit that and suggest that many developers feel comfortable just reading Agavi source code. By the way, it is very well commented; that's a plus. On the other hand, without a big base of working examples and friendly tutorials, this framework will not reach as many developers as it might have. And that's the second thing: the authors explicitly address this framework to advanced programmers who will be able to use and appreciate its unique traits.

So what is so unique about Agavi? Well, most frameworks strive for completeness — they provide as many features as they can, and there's no way to avoid coupling of these components. This means they enable really rapid development, but at the cost of flexibility. Agavi's uniqueness lies in the extendibility and quality of its code. This allows using it for applications that will evolve for a long time and are meant to be completely scalable from the very beginning. Agavi prides itself on not restricting developers' freedom to achieve any goal without hacking the framework itself. So if you are a gifted mastermind who wants to dominate the world, that's the tool for you!

Installation

Agavi provides a PHP Extension and Application Repository (PEAR) channel that is the recommended way of installing it. (PEAR is discussed in Chapter 2.) First, find this channel:

```
# pear channel-discover pear.agavi.org
```

And then install Agavi using this command:

```
# pear install -a agavi/agavi
```

There is a prerequirement: the Phing. What is Phing, then? ***PHing Is Not Gnu make***, yet it shares some similarities with *GNU make* because it is a tool for PHP project building. You can install it with PEAR as well:

```
# pear channel-discover pear.phing.info
# pear install phing/phing
```

Retry installing Agavi if it didn't succeed before installing Phing.

You will need the following PHP modules, too (they are enabled by default, so if you don't have them, you'll probably know why):

- libxml
- dom
- SPL
- Reflection
- pcre
- xsl
- tokenizer
- session
- xmlrpc
- soap
- iconv
- gettext

If you can't (or don't want to) use PEAR, you can use direct download from the Agavi website:

```
http://www.agavi.org/download
```

Creating the Project

When PEAR is done with installing Agavi, you should check if the installation is successful. Type the following in your console:

```
$ agavi
```

You will see output similar to this:

```
Buildfile: /usr/share/php/agavi/build/build.xml

Agavi > status:

     [echo] PHP:
     [echo]   Version: 5.3.2-1ubuntu4.5
     [echo]   Include path: .:/usr/share/php:/usr/share/pear
     [echo]
     [echo] Phing:
     [echo]   Version: Phing 2.4.2.1
     [echo]
     [echo] Agavi:
     [echo]   Installation directory: /usr/share/php/agavi
     [echo]   Version: 1.0.3
     [echo]   URL: http://www.agavi.org
     [echo]
     [echo] Project:
     [echo]   (not found)
     [echo]
     [echo] For a list of possible build targets, call this script with the -l
            argument.

BUILD FINISHED

Total time: 0.0032 seconds
```

The buildfile on Windows is located at `C:\xampp\php\PEAR\agavi\build\build.xml` by default. This file is responsible for the project build process described in the next steps.

You can get the list of all available targets with this command:

```
$ agavi -l
```

To build a project, you need to create an `/agavi` folder in your web root directory, or somewhere else, and make an Apache alias as shown in the "Configuration" section of the "CodeIgniter"section earlier in this chapter. Go to this folder with your command line and execute this:

```
$ agavi project-wizard
```

Then you will be asked for the project base directory, as shown in the following code snippet. Here the directory is the default web root directory for Windows with XAMPP, so we leave it this way.

Then provide the project name and project prefix. In this example, both will be `News`. All other options can be left at the defaults.

```
Agavi > project-wizard:

Agavi > project-create:

Project base directory [C:\xampp\htdocs\agavi]:
 [property] Loading C:\xampp\htdocs\agavi\build.properties
 [property] Unable to find property file: C:\xampp\htdocs\agavi\build.properties...
            skipped
Project name [New Agavi Project]: News
Project prefix (used, for example, in the project base action) [News]:
Default template extension [php]:
 [property] Loading C:\xampp\htdocs\agavi\build.properties
     [copy] Copying 1 file to C:\xampp\htdocs\agavi
...
```

The amount of configurable options is simply tremendous! Go through all messages of the project wizard; when it's done, you may skip to your browser and type `http://localhost/agavi/pub`. If everything went well, you will see a welcome page like the one shown in Figure B-6.

FIGURE B-6: Agavi welcome page

Configuration

The first thing you need to set is the routing scheme. Agavi provides a sophisticated routing mechanism that even includes regular expression matching. You will not need that here, so your pattern will be terminated by `^` at the left side and `$` at the right side, meaning that an exact match is needed. Go to `routing.xml`, remove the default routing, and write these two lines instead:

Available for download on Wrox.com

```
<!-- default action for "/" -->
<route name="index" pattern="^/$" module="News" action="Index" />
<route name="add" pattern="^/add$" module="News" action="Add" />
```

code snippet /agavi/app/config/routing.xml

This includes setting the root directory for the `index` action of the `News` module and the `/add` directory for the `add` action of the same module.

Next you need to enable the database support. Find `settings.xml` in application's configuration directory and set `use_database` to `true`:

Available for download on Wrox.com

```
<settings>
<setting name="app_name">News</setting>
<setting name="available">true</setting>
<setting name="debug">false</setting>
<setting name="use_database">true</setting>
<setting name="use_logging">false</setting>
<setting name="use_security">true</setting>
<setting name="use_translation">false</setting>
</settings>
```

code snippet /agavi/app/config/settings.xml

Now configure the database. The file is `databases.xml` in the same directory. Have you noticed that all Agavi configuration files are elegant XML files? You need to specify the details needed to connect to the database server as well as the database name:

Available for download on Wrox.com

```
<ae:configuration>
    <databases default="pdo_mysql_main">
        <database name="pdo_mysql_main" class="AgaviPdoDatabase">
            <ae:parameter name="dsn">mysql:host=localhost;dbname=news</ae:parameter>
            <ae:parameter name="username">root</ae:parameter>
            <ae:parameter name="password"></ae:parameter>
        </database>
    </databases>
</ae:configuration>
```

code snippet /agavi/app/config/databases.xml

In this example, we'll use the same `news` database that was used in previous examples and the `entries` table created for CodeIgniter. If you have not created that application, go to the "Setting Up the Database" section of the "CodeIgniter" section and run the SQL queries listed there.

There was a problem with the Propel database configured by default in this file. We assumed in the previous listing that this part is deleted. The exact lines are as follows (don't hesitate to delete them if they cause errors):

```
<database name="propelom" class="AgaviPropelDatabase">
    <ae:parameter name="config">%core.app_dir%/config/project-conf.php</ae:parameter>
</database>
```

First Application

The following code snippets provide complete listings of all files needed to get the sample app running. It is much easier to comprehend Agavi's principles this way, without wandering off into its intricacies. If you want a complete step-by-step tutorial, please refer to the official Agavi documentation. It is extremely detailed and will keep you amused for many hours.

Start by creating a module for your application and the two basic actions with the command-line tool. Run the following command in your console:

```
$ agavi module-wizard
```

When the command-line wizard asks for the module name, type `News`. In the next step, type `Index Add` (separated only by a space) to create these two actions. Then the wizard will ask you to provide names of views for the `Index` action. The default `Success` view is all you need, so agree by pressing Enter. Then do the same for the `Add` action.

The first file discussed is `IndexAction.class.php`. It holds the `Index` action of the `News` module. Why does `News` appear twice in the name of the `NewsNewsBaseAction` class? The first `News` comes from the project name, and the second comes from the module's name. The `executeRead()` method is invoked when this action is called by the routing system. It first calls the data model and then sets the data to be used by the view. When the method returns a `'Success'` string, it means that the `IndexSuccessView` is called.

Now fill this file with the following code:

```
<?php
class News_IndexAction extends NewsNewsBaseAction {
    public function getDefaultViewName() {
        return 'Success';
    }
public function executeRead(AgaviRequestDataHolder $rd) {
        $model = $this->getContext()->getModel('Entries', 'News');
        $this->setAttribute('posts', $model->load());
        return 'Success';
    }
}
?>
```

code snippet /agavi/app/modules/News/actions/IndexAction.class.php

The view, presented here, doesn't do anything important. It sets up the HTML document, sets the title (visible as `<h1>` header), and calls the template file:

```
<?php
class News_IndexSuccessView extends NewsNewsBaseView {
    public function executeHtml(AgaviRequestDataHolder $rd) {
        $this->setupHtml($rd);
        $this->setAttribute('_title', 'Latest News!');
    }
}
?>
```

code snippet /agavi/app/modules/News/views/IndexSuccessView.class.php

In Agavi, each view must have its template file. The IndexSuccess.php template consists of two parts. The first part uses the $posts data set to display the table contents. Note the htmlspecialchars() function that escapes the output in a smart way. The second part is a standard form for user input. See that the form action is set as "index.php/add". When you press the Add News button, two values are sent: title and description.

```
<?php foreach ($t['posts'] as $post): ?>
    <h3><?php echo htmlspecialchars($post['title']); ?></h3>
    <p> <?php echo htmlspecialchars($post['description']); ?> </p>
    <small><p> <?php echo htmlspecialchars($post['date']); ?> </small></p>
<?php endforeach; ?>
<h1>Adding news</h1>
<form action="index.php/add" method="post">
  <fieldset>
    <div class="form_row">
      <label for="title">Title:</label>
</div>
<div class="form_row">
      <input type="text" name="title" id="title" />
    </div>
    <div class="form_row">
      <label for="description">Description:</label>
</div>
<div class="form_row">
      <textarea name="description" id="description"></textarea>
    </div>
    <div class="form_row form_row_submit">
      <button type="submit" class="submit">Add News</button>
    </div>
  </fieldset>
</form>
```

code snippet /agavi/app/modules/News/templates/IndexSuccess.php

Adding Entries

Creating a form is obviously not enough; you need to have the Add action and data model as well. The source code for the Add action is presented as follows. The executeRead() method is used when somebody calls the Add action through routing. He is then directed to the Success view of the Add action immediately. The executeWrite() method is much more important here. It first calls for the data model, sets the model object's fields to corresponding form values, and finally calls the save() method of the model. It also invokes the AddSuccessView then.

```
<?php
class News_AddAction extends NewsNewsBaseAction {
    public function getDefaultViewName() {
        return 'Success';
    }
    public function executeRead(AgaviRequestDataHolder $rd) {
        return 'Success';
    }
    public function executeWrite(AgaviRequestDataHolder $rd) {
```

```
            $model = $this->getContext()->getModel('Entries', 'News');
            $model->title = $rd->getParameter('title');
            $model->description = $rd->getParameter('description');
            $model->save();
            return 'Success';
        }
    }
    ?>
```

code snippet /agavi/app/modules/News/actions/AddAction.class.php

The `Success` view of the `Add` method differs little from the `Success` view of the `Index` method. The only difference is redirection to the root of the application. The redirection uses a direct URL here. Agavi offers methods for redirecting to specific actions as well.

```
<?php
class News_AddSuccessView extends NewsNewsBaseView {
    public function executeHtml(AgaviRequestDataHolder $rd) {
        $this->setupHtml($rd);
        $this->setAttribute('_title', 'Add');
        $this->getContainer()->getResponse()->setRedirect('/agavi/pub');
        return;
    }
}
?>
```

code snippet /agavi/app/modules/News/views/AddSuccessView.class.php

There are two very important things to say here:

- The only places where redirections work are views. You cannot just redirect from one action to another.
- Each view needs its own template. Go to `/agavi/app/modules/News/templates` and create an empty file called `AddSuccess.php`.

After all actions and views are done, you can build the model. You will probably be surprised that Agavi provides no object-relational mapping (ORM) tool. Of course, you can quite easily integrate Doctrine with it, but we want to make this example as simple as possible, so SQL statements will be used here.

The full `News_EntriesModel` class is presented in the following listing. The `load()` method executes a pretty simple SQL query and returns all contents of the `Entries` table as the result. This method is invoked by the `Index` action to list all the news. The `save()` method inserts the form input into the table. Unlike the previous frameworks' examples, here the MySQL's `NOW()` function is used to determine the current time instead of the PHP equivalent. The SQL query has two question marks instead of values. They are placeholders for values and they are filled by the `bindValue()` method. After the statement has been prepared, it is executed to store the values into the database.

Copy the contents of the following listing into `EntriesModel.class.php` file in the `/agavi/app/modules/News/models` directory:

Available for download on Wrox.com

```
<?php
class News_EntriesModel extends NewsNewsBaseModel {
    var $title;
    var $description;
    function load() {
        $sql = 'SELECT * FROM entries ORDER BY date';
        $stmt = $this->getContext()->getDatabaseManager()->getDatabase()->
          getConnection()->prepare($sql);
        $stmt->execute();
        return  $result = $stmt->fetchAll();
    }
    function save() {
        $sql = 'INSERT INTO entries (title, description, date) VALUES(?, ?, NOW())';
        $stmt = $this->getContext()->getDatabaseManager()->getDatabase()->
          getConnection()->prepare($sql);
        $stmt->bindValue(1, $this->title, PDO::PARAM_STR);
        $stmt->bindValue(2, $this->description, PDO::PARAM_STR);
        $stmt->execute();
    }
}
?>
```

code snippet /agavi/app/modules/News/models/EntriesModel.class.php

You Should Be Going on a Date

But instead, you have to stay here and finish this sample app. Guess what? Agavi discards all input that is not validated. It doesn't matter that you made a nice form and politely wanted to use the values sent by POST. Agavi drops them without warning. Disgusting, isn't it?

When the CLI tool created the actions for you, it also created validation files. That's where you need to validate the two form input fields. Go to `/agavi/app/modules/News/validate` and edit the `Add.xml` file to make it look like this:

Available for download on Wrox.com

```
<?xml version="1.0" encoding="UTF-8"?>
<ae:configurations
xmlns="http://agavi.org/agavi/config/parts/validators/1.0"
xmlns:ae="http://agavi.org/agavi/config/global/envelope/1.0"
parent="%core.module_dir%/News/config/validators.xml">
    <ae:configuration>
        <validators method="write">
            <validator class="string">
                <arguments>
                    <argument>title</argument>
                    <argument>description</argument>
                </arguments>
                <errors>
```

```
                    <error for="required">ERROR: Name is missing</error>
                </errors>
                <ae:parameters>
                    <ae:parameter name="required">true</ae:parameter>
                </ae:parameters>
            </validator>
        </validators>
    </ae:configuration>
</ae:configurations>
```

code snippet /agavi/app/modules/News/validate/Add.xml

The good thing is that you don't need to manually check whether the values are not `null`, as you did in previous examples.

You think that's all? No. You must have a special view for error handling. Open up your command line and execute the following command in the project root:

```
$ agavi view-create
```

When you are asked for the module, answer `News`; for action, answer `Add`; and call the new view `Error`. Go to this new file and add redirection to the main page as shown here:

Available for download on Wrox.com

```
<?php
class News_AddErrorView extends NewsNewsBaseView {
    public function executeHtml(AgaviRequestDataHolder $rd) {
        $this->setupHtml($rd);
        $this->setAttribute('_title', 'Add');
        $this->getContainer()->getResponse()->setRedirect('/agavi/pub');
    }
}
?>
```

code snippet /agavi/app/modules/News/views/AddErrorView.class.php

No, you are not finished yet because every view needs its template. It doesn't matter that this template will be an empty 0-kB file; it must be created anyway. Go to `/agavi/app/modules/News/templates` and create an empty file called `AddError.php`. The sample app should work now, finally. The output is shown in Figure B-7.

Agavi is certainly not a framework for everyone. The development pace is sluggish, and the learning curve is incredibly steep. The sample application at the Agavi website, the only official guide to this framework, takes a few hours to follow and a few days to understand (and only slightly at best). If you do not really know exactly how you will benefit from using Agavi, we recommend trying CodeIgniter or Lithium instead.

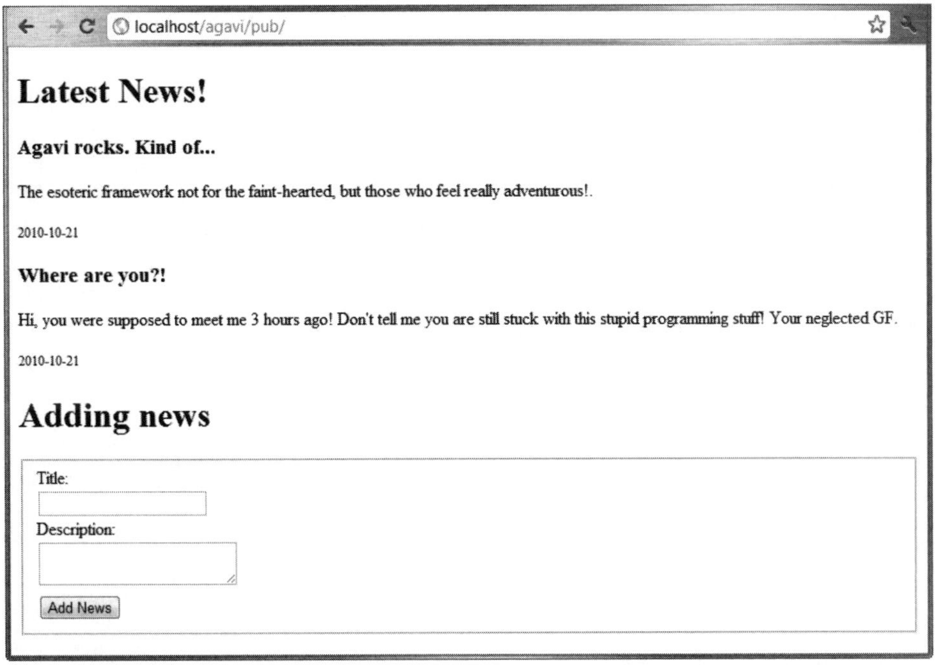

FIGURE B-7: News application made using Agavi

On the other hand, if you are able to harness Agavi's strength, you will get a strictly elegant, inherently extensible, and architecturally powerful application. The routing system is the best one among all major frameworks and the filter chain mechanism can do wonders as well. The news application presented here doesn't even come close to showing the full capabilities of this product. A dish for connoisseurs, indeed.

GLOSSARY OF ACRONYMS AND TECHNICAL TERMS

This is a quick reference for numerous acronyms and technical terms you will come across while reading this book. It is deliberately oversimplified, and if you need fuller explanations, use the index to find the corresponding pages in the book or check the appropriate Wikipedia articles. This glossary is intended to just help refresh your memory or to help you tell one acronym from another. We hope you'll find it useful in case you got a little lost among all these technologies.

access control list (ACL) A security approach that involves creating a list of users allowed to access a resource.

application programming interface (API) An interface offered by a program that allows developers to create other programs that can communicate with it.

Asynchronous JavaScript and XML (AJAX) Enables changing page content without reloading. Chapter 10 is devoted to this technology.

cascading style sheet (CSS) A markup language that defines the look of your web apps. Usually saved as `.css` files imported into your views or templates.

command-line interface (CLI) The console window used to interact with the operating system or CLI tools.

create, read, update, and delete (CRUD) Four basic database operations.

cross-site request forgery (CSRF) An attack that exploits form vulnerability to hijack a user's session after clicking a prepared link.

cross-site scripting (XSS) A web attack that injects malicious code into a targeted website.

Document Object Model (DOM) Representation of objects in web pages, used to change content dynamically.

Don't Repeat Yourself (DRY) A programming principle that forbids pasting copies of code in favor of elegant generalized solutions. Also known as: Duplication is Evil (DIE). It is related to Keep It Simple, Stupid (KISS).

Extensible HyperText Markup Language (XHTML) HTML presented using XML structure, not a successor to HTML.

Extensible Markup Language (XML) An open standard for structured document representation.

Git Distributed revision control system designed by Linus Torvalds; used by CakePHP and Lithium.

HyperText Markup Language (HTML) The markup language read by browsers to display web page contents.

Hypertext Preprocessor (PHP) Everyone can see what PHP is, but many still don't know the name is a recursive acronym. (It initially stood for *Personal Home Page*.)

HyperText Transfer Protocol (HTTP) Application layer networking protocol commonly used to exchange web content. It defines nine request methods, including `GET` and `POST`. Uses port `80`.

HyperText Transfer Protocol Secure (HTTPS) HTTP encrypted by TLS/SSL on the lower transport layer. Uses port `443`.

integrated development environment (IDE) The piece of software that makes programmers' lives easier thanks to integration of a code editor with syntax highlighting and autocomplete, a compiler (where applicable), a debugger, or even a source code generator.

internationalization (i18n) Shortened spelling made by counting the letters in this word. Closely related to l10n (localization) and g11n (globalization).

Inversion of Control (IoC) A software design principle that promotes removing dependencies between components for loose coupling.

Lightweight Directory Access Protocol (LDAP) An application layer protocol used to query directory services such as openLDAP, ADAM, or AD LDS.

Model-View-Controller (MVC) The main structural design pattern behind most frameworks.

object-relational mapping (ORM) Making object-oriented software work with relational databases.

OS (Operating System) Windows, Linux, Mac OS, FreeBSD, or any other system you are currently using.

PATH An environment variable, present in every discussed operating system, but accessed in a different manner in each one. It specifies which directories will be searched at startup for executable files. You will be able to run these executables in CLI globally with their names only instead of the full file paths.

PHP Data Object (PDO) A PHP extension that provides a unified interface for accessing databases.

PHP Extension and Application Repository (PEAR) A smart tool for PHP software installation.

relational database management system (RDBMS) There is much theory to it, but basically this is what we developers call "an SQL database."

Representational State Transfer (REST) A stateless web application architecture that is based on HTTP requests. When something implements these specifications, it is called RESTful.

Role-Based Access Control (RBAC) A security approach that defines roles and then assigns users to these roles.

search engine optimization (SEO) A set of techniques for promoting a website by increasing its rank in the search engine's results page.

Simple Mail Transfer Protocol (SMTP) Application layer protocol for sending e–mail.

Simple Object Access Protocol (SOAP) Internet protocol based on XML format; often used for web services development.

Structured Query Language (SQL) The language used for database communication.

Subversion (SVN) A revision control system, used by most community projects.

test-driven development (TDD) A programming technique that requires developers to write tests first and develop functionalities later.

Transport Layer Security/Secure Sockets Layer (TLS/SSL) TLS is the successor of SSL. They are both cryptographic protocols working on the transport layer. This means they can be used to encrypt any application layer protocol (such as HTTP or FTP).

Uniform Resource Locator (URL) An identifier that specifies where a resource can be located and how to retrieve it (for example, a web address with a protocol).

web root The main folder that is translated to `http://localhost/` by your web server. You usually develop and deploy your applications there.

What You See Is What You Get (WYSIWYG) A visual in-page editor that allows editing web content without the need to use HTML.

X Apache, MySQL, PHP, and Perl (XAMPP) The bundle of tools commonly used to develop and run web apps on Windows and Mac OS. On Linux it is referred to as LAMP.

YAML Ain't Markup Language (YAML) Data serialization language used by Symfony for configuration and schemas.

INDEX

A

B

C

D

E

K

L

M

Q

R